Teaching and Learning Mathematical Problem Solving:

Multiple Research Perspectives

Edward A. Silver, *Editor*

Teaching and Learning Mathematical Problem Solving:

Multiple Research Perspectives

LAWRENCE ERLBAUM ASSOCIATES, PUBLISHERS

1985   Hillsdale, New Jersey   London

Lawrence Erlbaum Associates, Inc., Publishers
365 Broadway
Hillsdale, New Jersey 07642

Library of Congress Cataloging in Publication Data
Main entry under title:

Teaching and learning mathematical problem solving.

Proceedings of a conference held June 1983 at San Diego State University.
Includes index.
1. Problem solving — Study and teaching — Congresses.
I. Silver, Edward A., 1941-
QA63.T43   1984   510'.7'1   84-18828
ISBN 0-89859-681-5

Printed in the United States of America
10 9 8 7 6 5 4 3 2 1

Note

Preparation of all the papers in this volume was supported by the editor's National
Science Foundation Grant No. SED 80-19328. Any opinions, conclusions or recommendations expressed are those of the authors and do not necessarily reflect the views
of the National Science Foundation.

Acknowledgments

No undertaking of this sort is ever accomplished by a single individual. Naturally, I am grateful to the authors, who generously contributed their knowledge and energy to this project. Thanks also go to Julia Hough, of The Franklin Institute Press, for her patient encouragement throughout the preparation of this volume. But, even with the authors' contributions and Julia's encouragement, the volume would never have been produced in such a timely fashion without the invaluable assistance and careful attention to detail provided by Verna Adams, who had a major hand in editing and organizing the papers for publication. Finally, I acknowledge the support of National Science Foundation Grant No. SED 80-19328, which provided both the impetus for the problem-solving research synthesis project to begin and the funds to support the conference which led to this volume.

Contributors

Nicholas A. Branca
Dept. of Mathematical Sciences
San Diego State University

Thomas P. Carpenter
University of Wisconsin
School of Education

Gerald A. Goldin
Dept. of Mathematical Sciences
Northern Illinois University

James G. Greeno
Learning Research Development Center
University of Pittsburgh

Douglas A. Grouws
University of Missouri
School of Education

Joan I. Heller
Dept. of Physics
University of California

Harriet N. Hungate
Dept. of Physics
University of California

James J. Kaput
Dept. of Mathematics
Southeastern Massachusetts University

Jeremy Kilpatrick
University of Georgia
School of Education

Richard A. Lesh
Northwestern University
School of Education

Frank K. Lester, Jr.
Indiana University
School of Education

Richard E. Mayer
Dept. of Psychology
University of California

Douglas B. McLeod
Dept. of Mathematical Sciences
San Diego State University

Nel Noddings
Stanford University
School of Education

Edwina L. Rissland
Computer and Information Sciences
University of Massachusetts

Alan H. Schoenfeld
University of Rochester
Graduate School of Education

J. Michael Shaughnessy
Dept. of Mathematical Sciences
Oregon State University

Lee S. Shulman
Stanford University
School of Education

Edward A. Silver
Dept. of Mathematical Sciences
San Diego State University

Larry K. Sowder
Dept. of Mathematical Sciences
Northern Illinois University

Alba G. Thompson
San Diego State University
College of Education

Patrick W. Thompson
Dept. of Mathematical Sciences
San Diego State University

Judith Threadgill-Sowder
Dept. of Mathematical Sciences
Northern Illinois University

Introduction

Edward A. Silver

San Diego State University

In recent years, considerable progress has been made in understanding the nature of complex human thought, with particular insights into the mechanisms of skilled problem solving. Much of the early research on human problem solving concentrated on general problem-solving skills and used puzzle problems and highly structured tasks with a dearth of semantic content, such as the ''Towers of Hanoi'' or ''Missionaries and Cannibals'' problems. More recent research, however, has focused on problem-solving behavior in semantically rich knowledge domains with direct or indirect relevance to mathematics. The participants in this research enterprise have come from many fields, but primarily from mathematics education, cognitive psychology, science education, and artificial intelligence.

Corresponding to the intense level of research attention to the mechanisms of mathematical problem solving has been a growing interest in the topic among educational practitioners. Since the publication by the National Council of Teachers of Mathematics of the *Agenda for Action,* which asserted that the acquisition of problem-solving skills should be one of the goals of school mathematics instruction in the 1980s, problem solving has been a dominant topic at virtually all professional meetings of mathematics teachers and supervisors. Rarely in the history of education has a topic simultaneously captured so much of the attention of both researchers and practitioners. Usually, the research community is busy investigating a topic long after it ceases to be of real interest to practitioners.

Another interesting trend—a focus on the processes of learning—has made the time ripe for fruitful contributions of research on human cognition to classroom practice. Although some early workers in artificial intelligence were apparently quite interested in learning, it is only in recent years that much attention has been given to creating systems that learn. Similarly, cognitive psychologists who had heretofore focused their attention on the issue of performance, perhaps as a negative reaction to the obvious interest of behaviorist psychologists in learning (e.g., operant conditioning, maze learning), have re-discovered learning as an issue of import and interest. In recent years, a great deal of enthusiasm for tackling the mechanisms of learning has appeared in the cognitive science community. Thus, the moment seems opportune for the mathematics education and cognitive science communities to benefit from one another.

Despite the fact that a considerable amount of research on the topic of mathematical problem solving has been amassed, and despite the widespread interest on the part of practitioners, there have been few attempts to synthesize that research base and even fewer attempts to synthesize the research from the perspective of educational practice. This observation led me to propose to the National Science Foundation that the time was ripe for an assessment of the state-of-the-art in research on mathematical problem solving. The proposed synthesis was to have particular emphasis on classroom practice and on increased communication across the disciplines that have been active in this research.

It was in that spirit, and as a result of that proposal, that almost 40 researchers and practitioners interested in mathematical problem solving gathered at San Diego State University in June 1983. Many of the participants at the conference were consultants to the NSF project who had prepared papers that reported on new developments in their particular fields of expertise. The conference on "Teaching Mathematical Problem Solving: Multiple Research Perspectives" had three specific aims: (1) to provide a current assessment of the state-of-the-art in research on mathematical problem solving from a mathematics education perspective; (2) to explore the potential contributions of other research and other perspectives from fields such as cognitive psychology, scientific problem solving, and artificial intelligence; and (3) to identify some productive directions for research on mathematical problem solving in the next decade. Although the conference agenda was quite broad, it succeeded in all its aims. This book contains the set of papers that were read by the participants in advance, discussed at the meeting, and subsequently revised by the authors to reflect participants' comments.

In keeping with the aims of the conference, this volume is organized into sections corresponding to the three major aims of the meeting. Part A includes four papers written by mathematics educators who survey the field broadly and provide summaries of major bodies of problem-solving research or research issues. Part B includes four pairs of papers presenting the contrasting perspectives of researchers who work in different fields — mathematics education, cognitive psychology, scientific problem solving, or artificial intelligence. Part C includes 11 papers that point the way toward potentially fruitful directions for future research on mathematical problem solving. Many of the papers in Part C especially embody the spirit of the conference, since they represent perspectives that are compatible with research in both cognitive science and mathematics education. The volume concludes, as the conference did, with a summary paper by Lee Shulman, who presents his own unique perspective concerning research on mathematical problem solving.

Part A opens with "A Retrospective Account of the Past Twenty-five Years of Research on Teaching Mathematical Problem Solving," in which Jeremy Kilpatrick reviews and summarizes many of the major issues that have occupied research attention in the field during the past two and one-half decades. In the next paper, Tom Carpenter discusses and summarizes the voluminous literature on young children's abilities to solve addition and subtraction story problems. Carpenter's paper is one of the first serious attempts to relate this area of problem-solving research to the rest of the field. Important methodological issues are the focus of Frank Lester's paper. He discusses the changes in methodology that have occurred in problem-solving research over the past several decades and gives serious attention to the problems that those changes have created as well as to the problems that still remain from previous research methodologies. In the final paper in this section, Nick Branca, fresh from his travel in Great Britain, discusses the British perspective on problem solving and draws lessons from his experience in England.

Cross-discipline perspectives are presented in Part B. This section contains four pairs of papers; one paper in each pair summarizes important research findings or perspectives from one discipline, and the second paper presents the reaction of a person representing another discipline. Edwina Rissland presents a useful summary of much of the work in artificial intelligence, and Alan Schoenfeld, a mathematician whose own research has carried him into the realm of cognitive science, provides a reaction from the perspective of mathematics education. In his paper dealing with research on cognitive psychology, Richard Mayer surveys some of the work that is relevant to standard textbook story problems; Larry Sowder, whose own recent research has dealt with story problems, provides his reaction from a mathematics education perspective. In the area of scientific problem solving, Joan Heller and Harriet Hungate provide an excellent and detailed summary of some of the interesting research dealing with problem solving in physics; Gerald Goldin, whose research interests include theoretical physics as well as mathematics education, provides the reaction. The fourth pair of papers consists of Patrick Thompson's views on reasonable research perspectives to guide curriculum design, especially in developing computer microworlds, and Jim Greeno's reaction from the perspective of a cognitive psychologist. Thompson's paper makes vivid the contrast between researchers who study only what *is* and those who also study what *ought to be* in the curriculum.

Part C is introduced with my paper, "Research on Teaching Mathematical Problem Solving: Some Underrepresented Themes and Needed Directions," in which I discuss a number of issues and themes that have emerged from review and synthesis of the mathematical problem-solving literature. Subsequent papers discuss in more detail the themes and issues developed in my paper. The fundamental importance of epistemological issues (e.g., beliefs, conceptions, misconceptions) is reflected in the papers by Jim Kaput, Richard Lesh, Alan Schoenfeld, and Mike Shaughnessy. Another common theme is the need for the careful study of classroom processes and teachers and their role in problem-solving instruction. That theme is reflected in the papers by Alba Thompson, Doug Grouws, and Nel Noddings. The importance of affective issues in the study of problem-solving performance, an oft-forgotten theme in problem-solving research, is discussed by Doug McLeod and Nel Noddings. In other papers, Judith Threadgill-Sowder addresses the role of individual cognitive differences in mathematical problem solving, and Patrick Thompson examines some of the potential impact that computers may have in research on mathematical problem solving. Taken collectively, this set of papers constitutes an ambitious research agenda for the next decade.

Those who attended the conference reported a great deal of enthusiasm about the experience. Although it is not possible to capture on paper all of what occurred at the meeting, this volume represents an accurate rendering of the substance of the conference. I hope that readers of this book will experience some of the excitement that the conference participants felt for the ideas expressed in these papers. If this volume leads to an increased understanding of the nature of past problem-solving research, or an increased appreciation of the potential benefits of cross-fertilization of ideas among workers in different fields, or a renewed enthusiasm for attacking some of the underrepresented themes and issues from previous research, then it will have served its purpose. I look forward eagerly to a future volume on this topic, in which the specific results of this next wave of research could be presented and discussed.

Contents

Part C. Problem-Solving Research: Themes and Directions

Summary

PART A.
PROBLEM-SOLVING RESEARCH: MATHEMATICS EDUCATION PERSPECTIVES

A Retrospective Account of the Past 25 Years of Research on Teaching Mathematical Problem Solving

Jeremy Kilpatrick

University of Georgia

I readily accepted the assignment posed by the title of this paper because I was interested in where it might lead. It is a little like a grown-up version of "what I did on my summer vacation"—the challenge is to discover what you can make of someone else's attempt to draw you out on a theme.

In this case, my first thoughts concerned the choice of 25 years as a time span for this retrospective account. What were you doing 25 years ago? Were you interested in problem solving in mathematics? If I can wax autobiographical for a bit, 25 years ago this month I was finishing up my first year as a junior high school teacher of mathematics and science in the Berkeley, California, public schools. I was also working part-time on a master's degree in education at the University of California. Despite my greenhorn status, I had been selected to attend an institute for mathematics teachers at Stanford University that was being offered during that summer of 1958. The institute was sponsored by General Electric and was one of the forerunners of the National Science Foundation institutes. I was about to overcome my natural aversion to crossing the San Francisco Bay to Palo Alto because I wanted to learn more about mathematics teaching from people like Harold Bacon, Ivan Niven, and Morris Kline. I also wanted to see what Stanford was like as a place for graduate study in mathematics education. I was hoping that, if I went to Stanford, I might have some opportunity to get to know George Polya and his ideas better.

I had run across Polya before—as a high school student I had purchased a copy of *How to Solve It* and, although I couldn't always see the point of Polya's remarks, it was obvious that he was on to something. As a senior in high school, I took the Stanford Mathematics Examination—which I later learned had been created and conducted by Polya and Gabor Szego—and was dismayed to discover the depth of my ignorance of mathematics; I had never encountered mathematical problems before that required more than 10 minutes' thought, and here were three problems to be solved in 3 hours.

1

Later, when I was an undergraduate mathematics major, I sat in on some lectures that Polya, who was visiting at Berkeley, was offering for liberal arts students. The lectures gave me a clearer impression of what he meant by problem solving and how that might be an important thing for mathematics teachers to know about.

In June 1958, after a year of teaching first-year algebra, I could see that the solution of word problems was posing special pedagogical difficulties. Despite my lucid explanations of how to translate from English to algebra, my firm insistence that students write out their assignment of letters to variables in the problem, my helpful suggestions that they use tables to organize the variables and diagrams to represent relationships, and my rigid requirement that the last part of the solution be an English sentence that responded to the question posed in the problem statement, my students nonetheless moaned with pain when the word-problem sections of our textbook rolled around and stared with incomprehension and chagrin when we discussed the word problems they had failed to solve on their homework or a test. Conferences with parents were all too likely to revolve around the parents' claim that Barbara or Steve, though blessed with the genius of a von Neumann when it came to solving equations or simplifying fractions, could make no sense whatsoever of those three-line epigrams about mixing peanuts and cashews. "Problem solving," in the guise of the hackneyed word problems in Mallory's *First Algebra*, had become my Tar Baby, and a quarter of a century later I am still wrestling with it.

Why am I telling you this? Partly, perhaps, because the author of a keynote paper ought to be entitled to a little self-indulgence. But primarily because I would like to trace for you some strands in the research done on the teaching of mathematical problem solving over the last 25 years, and I want to use my situation as a mathematics teacher in June 1958 as an anchoring point for these strands.

WHAT IS A PROBLEM?

One strand concerns our view of what a mathematical problem is. This view can be general—in which we look at a problem and the process of solving it from different perspectives—or it can be specifically focused on the roles that problems play in mathematics teaching. Let us consider each in turn.

Perspectives on Mathematical Problems

In what might be termed the *psychological* perspective on problems, a problem is defined generally as a situation in which a goal is to be attained and a direct route to the goal is blocked. The psychologists usually add that the situation requires the presence of a person who "has" the problem; to be a problem, it has to be a problem for someone. (The psychologists are not usually concerned with mathematical problems per se, but one could add to the formulation that for a problem to be mathematical, mathematical concepts and principles should be used in seeking the answer.) From this perspective, we see the problem as an *activity* of a motivated subject.

The subjective nature of a mathematical problem, although often overlooked in discussions of problem solving, has been understood and accepted in mathematics education for at least 40 years. In the autumn of 1957, I had taken a psychological foundations course from William Brownell, who was the Dean of the College of Education at Berkeley, and in the spring of 1958, I was taking a course from him on research in the teaching of arithmetic. I had read his classic paper on problem solving (Brownell, 1942) and was familiar with his definition:

> Problem solving refers (a) only to perceptual and conceptual tasks, (b) the nature of which the subject by reason of original nature, of previous learning, or of organization of the task, is able to understand, but (c) for which at the time he knows no direct means of satisfaction. (d) The subject experiences perplexity in the problem situation, but he does not experience utter confusion. . . . Problem solving becomes the process by which the subject extricates himself from his problem. . . . Defined thus, problems may be thought of as occupying intermediate territory in a continuum which stretches from the 'puzzle' at one extreme to the completely familiar and understandable situation at the other.(p. 416)

Researchers in mathematics education have long accepted the truth that a problem for you today may not be one for me today or for you tomorrow.

Something the last 25 years have given us, however, is a greater appreciation of the mathematical problem as *task*—a *social-anthropological* perspective. Namely, the problem is given and received in a transaction. The mathematics classroom is a social situation jointly constructed by the participants, in which teacher and students interpret each other's actions and intentions in the light of their own agendas (Mehan, 1978).

> The teacher ordinarily assigns a problem to one or more students, who are then expected to solve it. Students who are assigned a problem in class can bring to bear on the task a whole set of considerations that would not be operative if the students had formulated and posed the problems on their own: For example, they can usually assume that the problem will have a single, well-defined answer obtainable using procedures they have studied recently in class; they can assume that they will be evaluated by the teacher according to how hard they appear to try in solving the problem and how successful they appear to be; they may have some indication that the teacher knows the solution to the problem, and they may be able to get clues to the solution by asking the teacher certain questions; and they may be able to use gestural and postural cues from the teacher to tell whether or not they are on the right track in their solution. (Kilpatrick, 1982, pp. 10–11)

Researchers in mathematics education are just beginning to examine the implications of the social-anthropological point of view (Brandau, 1981).

Other views include the *mathematical* (problem as *construction*) and the *pedagogical* (problem as *vehicle*). From the mathematical, or subject-matter, point of view, one sees mathematical problems as defining the discipline of mathematics. Mathematics is not simply the famous problems that great mathematicians have worked on; "*all* mathematics is created in the process of formulating and solving problems" (Kilpatrick, 1982, p. 2). Schoolchildren seldom see much of this face of mathematics; for them, the construction scaffolding has been taken away, and all that remains is the completed edifice through which they are guided. Although the subject-matter point of view has some important implications for research, I want to consider at length instead the pedagogical, or curricular, point of view—what a mathematical problem means in teaching—as a way of accounting for some of the variety to be seen in the research on teaching mathematical problem solving.

The Roles of Mathematical Problems in Teaching

Word problems (sometimes termed verbal problems or story problems) were my own point of entry into the problem-solving domain, and they serve to define the territory for many researchers. Polya (1981, Vol. 2, p. 139) has given us a nice classification of problems from a pedagogical perspective:

1.   *One rule under your nose*—the type of problem to be solved by mechanical application of a rule that has just been presented or discussed.

2.   *Application with some choice*—a problem that can be solved by application of a rule or procedure given earlier in class so that the solver has to use some judgment.

3.   *Choice of a combination*—a problem that requires the solver to combine two or more rules or examples given in class.

4.   *Approaching research level*—a problem that also requires a novel combination of rules or examples but that has many ramifications and requires a high degree of independence and the use of plausible reasoning.

Polya argues that both the degree of difficulty and the educational value (with respect to teaching students to think) increase as one goes from type 1 to type 4. Most research over the past 25 years has concentrated on problems of types 1 and 2, but increasing attention is being given by some researchers in mathematics education to type 3 and 4 problems.

I would like to offer a somewhat different view that is meant to encompass both in-school and out-of-school mathematical problems. Consider the following six problems. They are chosen only to illustrate various meanings of "problem"; in no sense are they meant to be typical or estimable.

a. $^7/_{25} = ^{12}/_x$. What is x?

b.

c.   If a 7-oz. cup of cola costs 25¢, what is the cost of a 12-oz. cup?

d.   A group of three sixth-graders has been given the problem of planning a picnic. They have been told that 7-oz. cups of cola cost 25¢ each, and they are trying to find out what 12-oz. cups should cost.

e.   Your neighborhood association is having a picnic and is hoping to make some money selling cups of cola. One of the officers has set a price of 25¢ for the 7-oz. cups and has asked you what price would be fair for the 12-oz. cups.

f.   If a 7-oz. cup of cola costs 25¢, the proportional cost of a 12-oz. cup is not a whole number. What is the smallest whole number one could add to the cost of the 7-oz. cup to make the proportional cost of the 12-oz. cup a whole number?

Problem *a* might be termed the computational skeleton beneath the skin of the other problems, although there are, of course, many other ways to pose the computational question. Problems *b* and *c* are straightforward "word problems" of the type in which seventh- and eighth-grade textbooks abound. They are meant to give students an opportunity to apply what they might have learned—in this case, what they might have learned about proportion. Problem *b* is something of a new breed: the "wordless" word problem. Such problems can be seen in recent textbooks whose authors are attempting to cope with the difficulties students have in reading word problems or other material with understanding. Problem *c* is the word problem in its more traditional garb.

Problem *d* is meant to exemplify a class of problems sometimes termed "real problems." These are problems that students either pose for themselves or are given, in which the students are in a "realistic" situation that is meaningful to them and must come up with a solution that takes account of the problem setting as well as any mathematics that might be appropriate. The problem is meant to simulate a real problem the students might face. Problem *e*, on the other hand, is meant to exemplify the class of problems—potentially involving some mathematics—that students might encounter outside the school setting, when scores, grades, and research results are not at stake. Problem *f* represents, in a very limited fashion, the class of nonroutine mathematical problems of greater complexity and greater mathematical interest than the ordinary word problem—in this instance, Problem *f* might lead to a consideration of Diophantine equations in two unknowns.

Which of these kinds of problems would we like students to be able to solve? Some people might hold that it is problems like *e* and *f* that we are ultimately interested in—Problem *e* for everyone; Problem *f* for the more capable in mathematics, perhaps—and the other problems are the ones we should be concerned with in school. Some might say that if we teach students how to solve problems of type *a* and type *b* or *c*, everything else will take care of itself. Others might want to substitute problems of type *d* or *f* for the masses of type-*c* problems in the textbooks, arguing that the type-*c* problems are a case of bad currency driving out good. The point is that different people hold different views concerning the kinds of problems that ought to be dealt with in the mathematics curriculum and how much weight each kind of problem should be given. These different views have not always been distinguished by researchers concerned with problem solving, nor have they explored the consequences of these views in any detail.

The media have given considerable attention to the results of the Second Mathematics Assessment of the National Assessment of Educational Progress (Carpenter, Corbitt, Kepner, Lindquist, & Reys, 1981), which suggest that American schoolchildren are a lot better at solving type-*a* problems than type-*c* problems. One needs to be somewhat cautious in drawing inferences from this finding, however. First, we have no evidence to suggest that there was a time when students solved both types of problems with equal facility. Second, and more important, a failure to solve type-*c* problems does not necessarily imply that students, in their lives outside school, will not be able to give satisfactory solutions to type-*e* problems. Much has been made of the implications of the poor showing students have made on type-*c* problems. But where is it written—indeed, where has it been shown—that facility with type-*c* problems is a prerequisite for intelligent problem solving outside of school? The evidence we have suggests that children often fail to use the standard methods they have been taught when type-*c* problems are presented out of context (Hart, 1983); how much more are they likely to avoid such methods in their out-of-school life? It might also be noted that no one has shown that an increased facility with type-*d* problems—real problems—transfers out of school either, despite their apparent face validity.

I raise these issues about the kinds of problems to be used in instruction because, first, over the past 25 years they seem not to have been given much attention by researchers, and second, different assumptions about the instructional uses of problems seem to have led researchers in somewhat different directions. In particular, some researchers—many but by no means all of whom are psychologists—have accepted the type-*c* word problem as the vehicle for problem solving in the mathematics curriculum and have aimed their efforts at improving instruction so that more students will learn how to solve more such problems correctly. Such efforts are not to be disparaged. Many facets of the conventional word problem are not well understood, and it still provides fertile ground for research. However, other researchers—many but not all of whom are mathematics educators—seeking to reduce the emphasis on type-c problems in the curriculum, have concentrated on improving students' abilities to deal with problems of types d or f. If researchers are operating with different assumptions about the problems in the mathematics curriculum, it may be difficult for them to communicate about their work.

Task Variables in Mathematical Problem Solving

Back in 1958, I was interested in why certain problems gave students so much difficulty. Having taken some courses at Berkeley from Guy Buswell on research in reading, I sought, in my master's thesis, to measure the "readability" (by which I meant the ease of converting problem statement to algebraic formation) and "solvability" (by which I meant the ease of achieving a solution from the algebraic formulation) of selected word problems from the first-year algebra course I was teaching (Kilpatrick, 1960). I found, for example, that sentence length and number of prepositional phrases predicted both readability and solvability. Looking back on that modest effort, I can see the naivete of placing so much weight on naturally occurring variation in problem wording as a source of difficulty and how sterile the work was in the absence of any reasonable theoretical foundation.

Since 1958, our understanding of the contribution to problem difficulty made by various facets of a problem has grown considerably. A vast literature has grown up on what are now termed syntax variables (Barnett, 1979), and other types of task variables have also been explored. A landmark in this line of research was the publication in 1979 of a book edited by Goldin and McClintock that reviewed the literature and explored its relevance for research and teaching. A fair summary of the work on syntax variables over the last 25 years might start with the observation that about 10–15 years ago there was a flurry of dust-bowl empiricism involving linear regression models. Problem characteristics selected for no special reason other than that they were easily measured and looked like they might have something to do with making a problem tough to solve were used to predict problem difficulty. The flurry of research did not last long, primarily in my view because without a theoretical framework to guide the selection of variables the work had no place to go. Recently, researchers such as Brown (Brown & Burton, 1978), Mayer (1982), and Briars (Briars & Larkin, 1982) working from an information-processing perspective have revived interest in syntax variables—as well as other task variables—with an emphasis on modeling the processes used in solving a problem and predicting the types of errors likely to be made. In the past two decades we have clearly come to a much more sophisticated view of the interaction between task characteristics and the characteristics of the problem solver, and this new view seems likely to yield much useful research (although many of my colleagues in mathematics education appear skeptical on this point).

I recall Brownell, in our class on research in the teaching of arithmetic, pointing out the fruitlessness of the research in the 1920's that sought to discover whether $9 \times 6 = 54$ was intrinsically more or less difficult than $6 \times 9 = 54$. (According to Norem & Knight, 1930, it's much less difficult.) Brownell noted that the difficulty of such combinations clearly depended upon how they had been taught and learned. Perhaps in the past quarter century researchers have at last assimilated the message that problem difficulty is a function of the solver and that the prediction of the errors a solver will make requires careful mapping of the solver's knowledge, understanding, and motivation.

HOW ARE PROBLEMS SOLVED?

I was privileged to serve on a panel that reviewed prospective articles for the 1980 yearbook—on problem solving—of the National Council of Teachers of Mathematics (Krulik & Reys, 1980). The one thread that seemed to run through the manuscripts was some reference to Polya's work. It seems that everyone in mathematics education who works on problem solving must come to terms with Polya's view of problem solving—even if the response is to reject it.

In my own case, one of Polya's influences was to turn my attention to the study of the processes students use in solving mathematical problems. Today, when any graduate student with a tape recorder feels free to assemble a batch of case studies as a dissertation, it may be difficult to understand the difficulty I had 20 years ago persuading a committee of Stanford professors that an analysis of problem-solving behavior was a suitable dissertation topic. I had seen how the early computer simulations of problem solving had used Polya's observations on heuristic and thought it might be useful to see if and how students solving problems aloud made use of heuristic processes like those Polya had identified. To be fair to the committee that approved my prospectus, they were probably not so much restricted in their view of research as they were reluctant to let me embark into such murky territory. (And perhaps they were right.)

In any event, I emerged from the dissertation experience (Kilpatrick, 1968) with a scheme for classifying problem-solving processes and some appreciation of the complexity of problem-solving behavior. Similar schemes have been developed for various purposes by researchers such as Webb, Lucas, Blake, and Kantowski (see Lucas et al., 1979; McClintock, 1979). Such schemes have had some utility in helping researchers concerned with instruction in problem solving assess whether their instructional treatments are influencing students' approaches to problems—somewhat apart from the question of whether the students are solving more problems correctly. At present, it appears that schemes to take what might be termed a microscopic look at problem solving have fallen out of favor as researchers turn their attention to cognitive behavior such as monitoring one's progress and reflecting on one's performance. It would be unfortunate, however, if shifts in fashion caused researchers to overlook entirely the potential usefulness of a careful scheme for analyzing problem-solving behavior—a scheme chosen, of course, in harmony with one's research goals.

Attention to problem-solving processes did not originate with Polya any more than it did with Duncker (1945) or with Bloom and Broder (1950)—to name two influences on thinking about problem solving that were prominent in 1958. Such attention has been given a healthy assist among American researchers in mathematics education in the last two decades by the translation into English of some Soviet research on problem solving (e.g., Kilpatrick & Wirszup, 1972). Perhaps the most influential Soviet work has been that of Krutetskii (1976), whose identification of problem-solving processes used by schoolchildren gifted in mathematics seems to have stimulated research in this country on memory for problems and students' perceptions of relations between problems (Silver, 1979). The Soviet work has also contributed to a growing interest in case studies and "teaching experiments."

Although some mathematics educators might question the impact that computer simulation models of cognitive processes have had on our thinking about the teaching of mathematical problem solving, one of the healthy lessons these models have taught us is that people do not live by processes alone. Studies of expert problem solvers and computer simulation models have shown that the solution of a complex problem requires (*1*) a rich store of organized knowledge about the content domain, (2) a set of procedures for representing and transforming the problem, and (3) a control system to guide the selection of knowledge and procedures. It is easy to underestimate the deep knowledge of mathematics and extensive experience in solving problems that underlie proficiency in mathematical problem solving. On the other hand, it is equally easy to underestimate the sophistication of the control processes used by experts to monitor and direct their problem-solving activity.

HOW IS PROBLEM SOLVING LEARNED?

Research over the past two and a half decades suggests that ''slowly and with difficulty'' is probably the best answer to the question of how problem solving is learned. Several approaches to instruction in problem-solving techniques and attitudes have met with some success, but that success has usually required a substantial investment of instructional time. Researchers have found that the effectiveness of an instructional method depends heavily on the class of problems used in instruction. The more restricted the problems, in general, the easier and faster it is likely to be for students to learn the new techniques and attitudes. Transfer from the problems used in instruction to more diverse problems remains an elusive goal.

One can analyze problem solving from the top down or from the bottom up, and one can approach instruction in problem solving from either direction. Some researchers in mathematics education have tended to use a top-down approach, concentrating on strategies of approach and training students in heuristic techniques of wide applicability. Other researchers, usually influenced by hierarchical analyses of learning tasks, have built their instruction from the bottom up, teaching first the concepts and fundamental skills needed to work problems of a given type and only then having students tackle the problems themselves. The bottom-up approach tends to place relatively more weight on the pedagogical and cognitive advantages of making skills automatic before incorporating them into problem-solving activity (Gagné, 1983a, 1983b; Steffe & Blake, 1983; Wachsmuth, 1983).

Another way to compare approaches to teaching problem solving is by drawing a parallel to Stolurow's (1965) contrast between ''modeling the master teacher'' and ''mastering the teaching model.'' In this case, one either models the master problem solver or masters the problem-solving model. Some researchers have begun with expert problem solving and have tried to identify its characteristics so that they can be taught. Stolurow argued that the idea of modeling the master teacher does not work because teaching behavior is so complex and difficult to control, and one can certainly make the same claim about problem-solving behavior. Stolurow's argument was that the computer permits researchers to construct predictive and descriptive models that can be used to make explicit various elements of teaching and their relationships. The parallel argument with respect to problem solving might suggest that from the various computer simulations of problem-solving behavior one can get some guidance for problem-solving instruction, and that is the direction some researchers have pointed (Briars & Larkin, 1982; Resnick & Ford, 1981). Whether mastering the model is superior to modeling the master in mathematical problem solving remains a largely unexplored question.

The various perspectives on teaching mathematical problem solving that have been advocated in recent years can be put, with some oversimplification, into five categories: osmosis, memorization, imitation, cooperation, and reflection. The names are meant to reflect the primary emphasis of the approach; most programs of problem-solving instruction combine features of several categories.

Osmosis

Some instructional approaches attempt to immerse the student in an environment of problems, assuming thereby that techniques will be absorbed through a process seldom made explicit but presumably akin to osmosis. Two decades ago authorities such as Van Engen (1959) were suggesting that the best advice the research literature had to give was that problem solving should be taught by giving students lots of problems to solve. Practice in solving many problems does appear to be a necessary condition for improving one's problem-solving abilities, but its sufficiency seems unlikely.

Related to approaches that assume students will pick up appropriate problem-solving techniques through practice alone are approaches that assume students already possess a "master thinking strategy" (Covington & Crutchfield, 1965) for problem solving and that they are primarily in need of a supportive atmosphere in which to apply what they already know. This view, although it may underestimate the content-specific techniques students need for solving certain kinds of problems, reminds us that students may well be capable of solving problems that they do not solve in the classroom or on tests. A lack of interest coupled with the pressures of time, fear of failure, fear of success, anxiety about one's performance, and a host of other factors can inhibit capable students from demonstrating their capability. No instructional program can be successful that does not deal with the effects of students' negative attitudes and beliefs about themselves as problem solvers.

Memorization

Some bottom-up approaches to instruction in mathematical problem solving are built upon task analyses that decompose the solution of a problem into atomic procedures, each of which is then taught. Essentially, an algorithm is developed that will handle a class of problems, and students are "programmed" to follow the algorithm to obtain a solution (Dahmus, 1970). Such approaches can be effective within narrow limits, but they cannot be used with problems to which the algorithm does not apply, and students often have trouble recognizing when the algorithm is applicable.

Approaches that are somewhat less restrictive, although still based on memorization, treat heuristic suggestions as procedures to be followed and attempt to organize them into an algorithm. In these approaches, students are taught to recite to themselves a list of steps in problem solving. Such approaches appear to be difficult for students to manage and may even be counterproductive (Brian, 1967; Burch, 1953). Students also seem to find it difficult to learn to classify problems by type (Kilpatrick & Wirszup, 1972).

Imitation

In the belief that modeling the master problem solver can be useful advice, some investigators have had students analyze the difference between their solutions and those of a model student, an analysis that then becomes the basis for remedial instruction (Bloom & Broder, 1950). Others have relied upon the student's identification with children in a narrative who are gaining confidence in their ability to solve problems as they work with an adult on various mysteries and puzzles (Covington & Crutchfield, 1965). The effectiveness of a teacher who playacts ignorance, uncertainty, and then a growing assurance in trying various problem-solving procedures in a dialogue with the class has not been given systematic study; anecdotal evidence suggests that the approach might be effective in gaining students' rapport and creating a setting for productive inquiry.

Cooperation

Researchers are increasingly using group problem-solving sessions as a vehicle for research (Dees, 1983; Lesh & Akerstrom, 1982; Noddings, 1982; Schoenfeld, 1982) and advocating them as a vehicle for instruction. By getting tentative ideas out into the open, where they can be refined and defended, small-group discussion may help students clarify concepts and rehearse procedures in ways that are difficult to do alone. Polya (1981, Vol. 1, p. 211) has used discussion groups to give teachers practice in guiding problem-solving instruction; such groups can also be instruments for developing one's problem-solving skills.

Reflection

John Dewey is usually credited with having said that children "learn by doing," but as Papert (1975) notes, the appropriate dictum—which he credits to Dewey, Montessori, and Piaget—is that "children learn by doing and by thinking about what they do" (p. 219). Schoenfeld (1983) and Silver (1982) have emphasized the key role that metacognition (cognition of one's own cognition) plays in problem solving. As Silver notes, many of Polya's heuristic suggestions are "metacognitive prompts"—they are designed to get the problem solver to reflect on his or her progress in problem solving and to assess the effectiveness of the procedures being used. Approaches to teaching problem solving differ in how much weight they place upon having students reflect on their problem-solving performance.

This classification of instructional approaches is meant only to be heuristic. Although the research literature in mathematics education is full of studies in which methods of teaching problem solving are compared, we do not have a comprehensive scheme for classifying various features of different methods. Some priority should be given in the next quarter century of research on problem solving in mathematics to delineating instructional approaches and attempting to link their features to their effectiveness.

WHAT HAVE WE LEARNED ABOUT PROBLEM SOLVING?

If I could travel back in time to Garfield Junior High School in Berkeley, California, in June 1958, and sit down in a classroom with that fledgling mathematics teacher I once was, what would I tell him that we have learned in the last 25 years about the teaching of mathematical problem solving?

Be Clear About Your Goals

First, I would stress that a teacher needs to understand that there are various sorts of problems, that problems can be used to serve various instructional goals, and that a problem or technique that works in one instructional setting may not work in another. A teacher should be clear about what sorts of problems he or she wants students to be able to solve. If the goal is for students to learn to solve relatively complex mathematical problems that do not fall into standard categories, then the teacher should be willing to invest substantial instructional time in demonstrating and giving practice in heuristic procedures. Some of these procedures may be quite general; others are likely to be specific to the illustrative problems. If the goal is for students to learn to solve some relatively simple problems that illustrate a recently taught technique, then the time required will be much less and it can be used in a different way. If the goal is for students to learn how to decide which of a variety of techniques apply to various problems, then perhaps the instructional time can be given over to having students identify what characteristics of a problem seem to be associated with particular techniques, and they might be asked to compose problems solvable by each of several techniques.

In each case the teacher must decide what to do; no one has a foolproof recipe that will work every time, and textbooks are notoriously unable to provide practical help. Research over the last two and a half decades has not provided much explicit guidance to the teacher in matching teaching techniques to goals, but it has clearly shown that one cannot expect to accomplish one goal in problem solving by teaching for another.

Understand that Problem Solving Is Highly Complex

Of course, we knew 25 years ago that problem solving was complex, but we did not appreciate how complex it is. As Begle (1971) noted in what he calls the second law of mathematics education, "Mathematics education is much more complicated than you expected even though you expected it to be more complicated than you expected" (p. 30).

We now recognize that most of the difficulties students have in solving a mathematical problem do not stem simply from failure to know the vocabulary and understand the language of the problem statement—important as these may be. Successful problem solving in a given domain depends upon the possession of a large store of organized knowledge about that domain, techniques for representing and transforming the problem, and metacognitive processes to monitor and guide performance. We have also learned to appreciate the importance of "frames," or schemata (Silver, 1982), for understanding and recalling problems.

Be Prepared to Find Problem-Solving Performance Difficult to Improve

We also knew 25 years ago that it was not easy to improve problem-solving performance, but perhaps we now understand better some of the reasons why. Researchers have had some success in getting students to use heuristic procedures when the procedures have been explained, illustrated, and practiced. They have had much more difficulty getting an improvement in the number of problems solved correctly. Successful treatments take a long time. Success is possible, however, as the recent work of Charles and Lester (1984), Burton, Ruddock, and Hill (1981), and Good, Grouws, and Ebmeier (1983) attests. In addition to providing some sort of regular, guided practice in problem solving, successful programs appear to have two other features in common: they get the students to adopt an active stance toward problem solving, and they provide a congenial setting in which problem solving can occur.

Get Students to Shift to an Active Stance

Polya's (1981) first principle of teaching is what he terms *active learning*: "let the students *discover by themselves as much as feasible* under the given circumstances" (Vol. 2, p. 104). His view is that students should be given the responsibility for their own learning:

> What the teacher says in the classroom is not unimportant, but what the students think is a thousand times more important. The ideas should be born in the students' mind and the teacher should act only as midwife. (p. 104)

One way of involving students in problem solving is to have them formulate and solve their own problems. Another is to have them rewrite problems. Sometimes the format of a problem—whether or not it contains a diagram or superfluous data, for example, or where the question is placed—can affect its difficulty. Begle (1979) proposed the interesting hypothesis that "if certain format changes turn out to reduce problem difficulty, then it would be worth experimenting with attempts to teach students to make the format changes themselves" (p. 145). Taking Begle's proposal seriously, Stover (Cohen & Stover, 1981; Stover, 1982) taught sixth-graders to modify one of three structural format variables (adding a diagram, removing extraneous information, and reordering information) in the statement of a problem and managed to get substantial improvement in the students' ability to solve word problems of the type they had learned how to modify. Stover's work may have opened up a productive new research area.

Provide a Congenial Environment for Problem Solving

Research in the "social-anthropological" tradition (see page 3) has alerted us to the social contract negotiated in classrooms between teacher and students. It seems highly plausible that approaches that have been successful in improving students' problem-solving performance have somehow been able to change the terms of the social contract. Researchers such as Carpenter and Lester (both this volume) have noted that many children approach problems in an impulsive way, attending primarily to surface features of the problem statement in order to decide what action to take. The child's goal is to do something — anything. Much school instruction, rather than encouraging children to take a problem seriously and reflect on what the problem statement says, seems to reinforce their impulsivity. Because the children see the problem as a school task rather than as an intellectual challenge that is worth accepting, they grab at answers so as to escape from the task as fast as possible. Successful problem-solving instruction often needs to transform the terms of the school situation that previous instruction has negotiated and reinforced.

CODA

The preceding remarks represent an attempt not so much to review the research literature of the last 25 years as to examine some points of contact between that literature and the concerns of teachers and researchers today. I have enjoyed my assignment of looking back over the years I have been professionally concerned with mathematical problem solving and trying to identify some important strands of thought. It was especially challenging to return in my imagination to the student and teacher I was in 1958 by rereading my notes and papers from those days. I am struck by the enormous scholarly output on the subject of problem solving in mathematics that is available to teachers and researchers compared to what was around in 1958. As I have tried to suggest, we do not have a final vision of what problem solving is and how to teach it, but we are much more keenly aware of the complexity of both.

The most heartening developments of the past few years reside not in the tangible contributions of specific research studies but in changing approaches to research. The converging interests of cognitive scientists and mathematics educators, as represented vividly in the papers at this conference, can only strengthen future research efforts in both camps. And the emerging view of the mathematics teacher as a full partner in the research process, rather than an imperfect system for delivering instruction, can only yield research that will better mediate between theory and practice. Such developments suggest that by 2008 the harvest from research will be rich indeed.

REFERENCES

Barnett, J. The study of syntax variables. In G.A. Goldin & C.E. McClintock (Eds.), *Task variables in mathematical problem solving.* Columbus, OH: ERIC Clearinghouse for Science, Mathematics, and Environmental Education, 1979.

Begle, E.G. Research and evaluation in mathematics education. In School Mathematics Study Group, *Report on a conference on responsibilities for school mathematics in the 70's.* Stanford, CA: SMSG, 1971.

Begle, E.G. *Critical variables in mathematics education: Findings from a survey of the empirical literature.* Washington, DC: Mathematical Association of America & National Council of Teachers of Mathematics, 1979.

Bloom, B.S., & Broder, L.J. *Problem-solving processes of college students.* Chicago: University of Chicago Press, 1950.

Brandau, L. *The practices of an elementary mathematics teacher—An ethnographic approach to the study of problem solving.* Paper presented at the annual meeting of the American Educational Research Association, Los Angeles, April 1981.

Brian, R.B. Processes of mathematics: A definitional development and an experimental investigation of their relationship to mathematical problem-solving behavior. *Dissertation Abstracts,* **28,** 1202A, 1967. (University Microfilms No. 67–11,815)

Briars, D.J., & Larkin, J.H. *An integrated model of skill in solving elementary word problems* (A. C. P. No. 2). Pittsburgh: Carnegie-Mellon University, Department of Psychology, November 1982.

Brown, J.S., & Burton, R.R. Diagnostic models for procedural bugs in basic mathematical skills. *Cognitive Science* **2,** 155–92, 1978.

Brownell, W.A. Problem solving. In N.B. Henry (Ed.), *The psychology of learning* (41st Yearbook of the National Society for the Study of Education, Part 2). Chicago: University of Chicago Press, 1942.

Burch, R.L. Formal analysis as a problem-solving procedure. *Journal of Education* **136,** 44–47, 1953.

Burton, L., Ruddock, G., & Hill, C. *The skills and procedures of mathematical problem solving project* (Social Science Research Council Project Number HR5410/1). London: Polytechnic of the South Bank, 1981.

Carpenter, T.P., Corbitt, M.K., Kepner, H.S., Jr., Lindquist, M.M., & Reys, R.E. *Results from the Second Mathematics Assessment of the National Assessment of Educational Progress.* Reston, VA: National Council of Teachers of Mathematics, 1981.

Charles, R.I., & Lester, F.K., Jr. An evaluation of a process-oriented instructional program in mathematical problem solving in grades five and seven. *Journal for Research in Mathematics Education* 15, 15–34, 1984.

Cohen, S.A., & Stover, G. Effects of teaching sixth-grade students to modify format variables of math word problems. *Reading Research Quarterly* 16, 175–200, 1981.

Covington, M.V., & Crutchfield, R.S. Facilitation of creative problem solving. *Programed Instruction* 4, 3–5, 10, 1965.

Dahmus, M.E. How to teach verbal problems. *School Science and Mathematics* 70, 121–38, 1970.

Dees, R.L. *The role of co-operation in increasing mathematics problem-solving ability.* Paper presented at the annual meeting of the American Educational Research Association, Montreal, April 1983.

Duncker, K. On problem-solving. *Psychological Monographs* 58 (5, Serial No. 270), 1945.

Gagné, R.M. A reply to critiques of some issues in the psychology of mathematics instruction. *Journal for Research in Mathematics Education* 14, 214–16, 1983(a).

Gagné, R.M. Some issues in the psychology of mathematics instruction. *Journal for Research in Mathematics Education* 14, 7–18, 1983(b).

Goldin, G.A., & McClintock, C.E. (Eds.). *Task variables in mathematical problem solving.* Columbus, OH: ERIC Clearinghouse for Science, Mathematics, and Environmental Education, 1979.

Good, T.L., Grouws, D.A., & Ebmeier, H. *Active mathematics teaching.* New York: Longman, 1983.

Hart, K.M. I know what I believe; do I believe what I know? *Journal for Research in Mathematics Education* 14, 119–25, 1983.

Kilpatrick, J. *Formulas for predicting readability and solvability of verbal algebra problems.* Unpublished master's thesis, University of California, Berkeley, 1960.

Kilpatrick, J. Analyzing the solution of word problems in mathematics: An exploratory study. *Dissertation Abstracts International* 28, 4380A, 1968. (University Microfilms No. 68-6442)

Kilpatrick, J. What is a problem? *Problem Solving* 4(2), 1–2, 4–5, 1982.

Kilpatrick, J., & Wirszup, I. (Eds.). *Instruction in problem solving* (Soviet Studies in the Psychology of Learning and Teaching Mathematics, Vol. 6). Stanford, CA: School Mathematics Study Group, 1972.

Krulik, S., & Reys, R.E. (Eds.). *Problem solving in school mathematics* (1980 Yearbook of the National Council of Teachers of Mathematics). Reston, VA: NCTM, 1980.

Krutetskii, V.A. *The psychology of mathematical abilities in schoolchildren* (J. Teller, Trans.). Chicago: University of Chicago Press, 1976.

Lesh, R., & Akerstrom, M. Applied problem solving: Priorities for mathematics education research. In F.K. Lester & J. Garofalo (Eds.), *Mathematical problem solving: Issues in research.* Philadelphia: The Franklin Institute Press, 1982.

Lucas, J.F., Branca, N., Goldberg, D., Kantowski, M.G., Kellogg, H., & Smith, J.P. A process-sequence coding system for behavioral analysis of mathematical problem solving. In G.A. Goldin & C.E. McClintock (Eds.), *Task variables in mathematical problem solving.* Columbus, OH: ERIC Clearinghouse for Science, Mathematics, and Environmental Education, 1979.

Mayer, R.E. Memory for algebra story problems. *Journal of Educational Psychology* 74, 199–216, 1982.

McClintock, C.E. Heuristic processes as task variables. In G.A. Goldin & C.E. McClintock (Eds.),

Task variables in mathematical problem solving. Columbus, OH: ERIC Clearinghouse for Science, Mathematics, and Environmental Education, 1979.

Mehan, H. Structuring school structure. *Harvard Educational Review* **48**, 32–64, 1978.

Noddings, N. On the analysis of four-person problem-solving protocols. In M.J. Shaughnessy (Chair), *Investigations of children's thinking as they go about solving mathematical word problems.* Symposium presented at the annual meeting of the American Educational Research Association, New York, March 1982.

Norem, G.M., & Knight, F.B. The learning of the one hundred multiplication combinations. In G.M. Whipple (Ed.), *Report of the Society's Committee on Arithmetic* (Twenty-Ninth Yearbook of the National Society for the Study of Education). Chicago: University of Chicago Press, 1930.

Papert, S. Teaching children thinking. *Journal of Structural Learning* **4**, 219–29, 1975.

Polya, G. *Mathematical discovery: On understanding, learning, and teaching problem solving* (2 vols.; combined ed.). New York: John Wiley & Sons, 1981.

Resnick, L.B., & Ford, W.W. *The psychology of mathematics for instruction.* Hillsdale, NJ: Lawrence Erlbaum Associates, 1981.

Schoenfeld, A.H. On the analysis of two-person problem-solving protocols. In M.J. Shaughnessy (Chair), *Investigations of children's thinking as they go about solving mathematical word problems.* Symposium presented at the annual meeting of the American Educational Research Association, New York, March 1982.

Schoenfeld, A.H. Episodes and executive decisions in mathematical problem solving. In R. Lesh & M. Landau (Eds.), *Acquisition of mathematics concepts and processes.* New York: Academic Press, 1983.

Silver, E.A. Student perceptions of relatedness among mathematical verbal problems. *Journal for Research in Mathematics Education* **10**, 195–210, 1979.

Silver, E.A. Knowledge organization and mathematical problem solving. In F.K. Lester & J. Garofalo (Eds.), *Mathematical problem solving: Issues in research.* Philadelphia: The Franklin Institute Press, 1982.

Steffe, L.P., & Blake, R.N. Seeking meaning in mathematics instruction: A response to Gagné. *Journal for Research in Mathematics Education* **14**, 210–12, 1983.

Stolurow, L.M. Model the master teacher or master the teaching model. In J.D. Krumboltz (Ed.), *Learning and the educational process.* Chicago: Rand McNally, 1965.

Stover, G.B. Structural variables affecting mathematical word problem difficulty in sixth graders. *Dissertation Abstracts International* **42**, 5050A, 1982. (University Microfilms No. DA8211361)

Van Engen, H. Twentieth century mathematics for the elementary school. *Arithmetic Teacher* **6**, 71–76, 1959.

Wachsmuth, I. Skill automaticity in mathematics instruction: A response to Gagné. *Journal for Research in Mathematics Education* **14**, 204–09, 1983.

Learning to Add and Subtract:
An Exercise in Problem Solving[1]

Thomas P. Carpenter
University of Wisconsin

Consider the following problems:

James had 13 marbles. He lost 8 of them. How many marbles does he have left?

Nancy won 14 stuffed animals at the carnival. Ronald won 6 stuffed animals. Nancy won how many more animals than Ronald?

Such problems frequently are not included in discussions of problem solving because they can be solved by the routine application of a single arithmetic operation. A central premise of this paper is that the solutions of these problems, particularly the solutions of young children, do in fact involve real problem-solving behavior. A related premise is that research on children's solutions of simple arithmetic word problems can provide insights into the development of more complex problem-solving abilities.

In the last few years a substantial body of research has focused on children's solutions of simple addition and subtraction word problems (Carpenter, Blume, Hiebert, Anick, & Pimm, 1982; Carpenter & Moser, 1983; Carpenter, Moser, & Romberg, 1982; Riley, Greeno, & Heller, 1983). There are several reasons for the interest in these problems. The domain of problems is simple enough that differences between problems can be specified with a reasonable degree of clarity. On the other hand, the domain is rich enough to provide a variety of problems, solution strategies, and errors. By the same token, children's solution processes appear to be simple enough to provide some hope of understanding and modeling them but complex enough to be interesting. Furthermore, it has been suggested (Carpenter, 1981) that the transition from children's informal counting and modeling strategies developed outside of formal instruction to the use of memorized number facts and formal addition and subtraction algorithms is a critical stage in children's learning of mathematics and that some of children's later difficulty in problem solving can be traced to initial instruction in addition and subtraction.

1. The research reported in this paper was funded by the Wisconsin Center for Education Research, which is supported in part by a grant from the National Institute of Education (Grant No. NIE-G-81-0009). The opinions expressed in this paper do not necessarily reflect the position, policy, or endorsement of the National Institute of Education.

CLASSIFICATION OF PROBLEMS

Recent studies have found that young children use different strategies for solving different types of addition and subtraction word problems. In general, their solutions are based on the semantic structure of the problems (Carpenter, Hiebert, & Moser, 1983; Carpenter & Moser, 1982; Riley et al., 1983). This has led to the refinement of schemes for classifying addition and subtraction word problems based on dimensions that reflect potential differences in children's solutions. This framework is generally consistent with earlier classification schemes (Carpenter & Moser, 1982; Greeno, 1980; Nesher & Katriel, 1977) and incorporates the "take away," "joining," and "comparison" situations identified by Gibb (1956), Reckzeh (1956), and Van Engen (1949). This analysis proposes four broad classes of addition and subtraction problems: Change, Combine, Compare, and Equalize.

There are two basic types of Change problems, both of which involve action. In Change/Join problems, there is an initial quantity and a direct or implied action that causes an increase in that quantity. For Change/Separate problems, a subset is removed from a given set. In both classes of problems, the change occurs over time. There is an initial condition at T_1 which is followed by a change occurring at T_2 which results in a final state at T_3.

Within both the Join and Separate classes, there are three distinct types of problems depending upon which quantity is unknown (see Table 1). For one type, the initial quantity and the magnitude of the change are given and the resultant quantity is the unknown. For the second, the initial quantity and the result of the change are given and the object is to find the magnitude of the change. In the third case, the initial quantity is the unknown.

Both Combine and Compare problems involve static relationships for which there is no direct or implied action. Combine problems involve the relationship existing among a particular set and its two disjoint subsets. Two problem types exist: the two subsets are given and one is asked to find the size of their union, or one of the subsets and the union are given and the solver is asked to find the size of the other subset (see Table 1).

Compare problems involve the comparison of two distinct, disjoint sets. Since one set is compared to the other, it is possible to label one set the referent set and the other the compared set. The third entity in these problems is the difference, or amount by which the larger set exceeds the other. In this class of problems, any one of the three entities could be the unknown, the difference, the reference set, or the compared set. There is also the possibility of having the larger set be either the referent set or the compared set. Thus, there exist six different types of Compare problems (see Table 1).

The final class of problems, Equalize problems, is a hybrid of Compare and Change problems. There is the same sort of action as found in the Change problems, but it is based on the comparison of two disjoint sets. Equalize problems are not commonly found in the research literature or in most American mathematics programs; however, they do appear in the *Developing Mathematical Processes* (DMP) program (Romberg, Harvey, Moser, & Montgomery, 1974). These problems are also present in experimental programs developed in the Soviet Union (Davydov, 1982) and in Japan (Gimbayashi, 1980). As in the Compare problems, two disjoint sets are compared; then the question is posed, "What could be done to one of the sets to make it equal to the other?" If the action to be performed is on the smaller of the two sets, then it becomes an Equalize/Join problem. On the other hand, if the action to be performed is on the larger set, then

Table 1. Classification of Word Problems. (Reprinted from Carpenter & Moser[1984] by permission of the *Journal for Research in Mathematics Education*.)

Change

Join

1. Connie had 5 marbles. Jim gave her 8 more marbles. How many marbles does Connie have altogether?

3. Connie has 5 marbles. How many more marbles does she need to have 13 marbles altogether?

5. Connie had some marbles. Jim gave her 5 more marbles. Now she has 13 marbles. How many marbles did Connie have to start with?

Separate

2. Connie had 13 marbles. She gave 5 marbles to Jim. How many marbles does she have left?

4. Connie had 13 marbles. She gave some to Jim. Now she has 8 marbles left. How many marbles did Connie give to Jim?

6. Connie had some marbles. She gave 5 to Jim. Now she has 8 marbles left. How many marbles did Connie have to start with?

Combine

7. Connie has 5 red marbles and 8 blue marbles. How many marbles does she have?

8. Connie has 13 marbles. Five are red and the rest are blue. How many blue marbles does Connie have?

Compare

9. Connie has 13 marbles. Jim has 5 marbles. How many more marbles does Connie have than Jim?

11. Jim has 5 marbles. Connie has 8 more than Jim. How many marbles does Connie have?

13. Connie has 13 marbles. She has 5 more marbles than Jim. How many marbles does Jim have?

10. Connie has 13 marbles. Jim has 5 marbles. How many fewer marbles does Jim have than Connie?

12 Jim has 5 marbles. He has 8 fewer marbles than Connie. How many marbles does Connie have?

14. Connie has 13 marbles. Jim has 5 fewer marbles than Connie. How many marbles does Jim have?

Equalize

15. Connie has 13 marbles. Jim has 5 marbles. How many marbles does Jim have to win to have as many marbles as Connie?

17. Jim has 5 marbles. If he wins 8 marbles, he will have the same number of marbles as Connie. How many marbles does Connie have?

19. Connie has 13 marbles. If Jim wins 5 marbles he will have the same number of marbles as Connie. How many marbles does Jim have?

16. Connie has 13 marbles. Jim has 5 marbles. How many marbles does Connie have to lose to have as many marbles as Jim?

18. Jim has five marbles. If Connie loses 8 marbles, she will have the same number of marbles as Jim. How many marbles does Connie have?

20. Connie has 13 marbles. If she loses 5 marbles she will have the same number of marbles as Jim. How many marbles does Jim have?

Equalize/Separate problems result. As with comparison problems, the unknown can be varied to produce three distinct Equalize problems of each type (see Table 1).

DESCRIPTION OF SOLUTIONS

Studies of the processes used to solve addition and subtraction problems date to the early part of the century (Arnett, 1905; Browne, 1906). Since that time a number of studies have investigated children's solutions of addition and subtraction problems (e.g., Brownell, 1928, 1941; Carpenter et al., 1983; Gibb, 1956; Groen & Parkman, 1972; Groen & Poll, 1973; Ilg & Ames, 1951; Rosenthal & Resnick, 1974; Svenson, 1975; a more complete discussion of additional studies appears in Carpenter et al., 1982). Although different studies have aggregated results in slightly different ways and individual studies have sometimes used different dimensions for characterizing children's solutions, there has been remarkable consistency in the findings reported over a period of almost 50 years, and a reasonably well-defined set of strategies has emerged.

The distinctions between problems illustrated in Table 1 are generally reflected in children's solutions. Children's solution processes tend to model the action or relationships described in a problem.

Addition Strategies

Three basic levels of addition strategies have been identified and are summarized in Table 2: strategies based on direct modeling with fingers or physical objects, strategies based on the use of counting sequences, and strategies based on recalled number facts (Carpenter et al., 1982; Carpenter & Moser, 1982). In the most basic strategy, physical objects or fingers are used to represent each of the addends, and then the union of the two sets is counted starting with one.

Table 2.   Addition Strategies.

Type	Description
Direct Modeling	
Counting All	Both sets are represented using physical objects or fingers, and the union of the two sets is counted.
Counting	
Counting On From First	The counting sequence begins with the first number given in the problem and continues the number of units represented by the second number.
Counting On From Larger	The counting sequence begins with the larger of the two numbers given in the problem and continues the number of units represented by the smaller number.
Number Fact	
	The number fact is immediately retrieved from long-term memory or derived from a recalled number fact.

The two counting strategies are more efficient and imply a less mechanical application of counting. In applying these strategies, a child recognizes that it is not necessary to reconstruct the entire counting sequence. In Counting On From First, a child begins counting forward with the first addend in the problems. For example, to solve 3 + 5, the child would count "3 (pause), 4, 5, 6, 7, 8. The answer is 8." The Counting On From Larger strategy is identical except that the child begins counting forward with the larger of the two addends. To solve 3 + 5, the child would count "5 (pause), 6, 7, 8. The answer is 8."

Children's solutions to word problems are not limited to modeling and counting strategies. Children do learn number facts both in and out of school and do apply this knowledge to solve word problems, although knowledge of the appropriate number fact does not ensure that modeling or counting will not be used. Certain number combinations are learned before others; and before they have completely mastered their addition tables, some children use a small set of memorized facts to derive solutions for problems involving other number combinations.

Subtraction Strategies

Each of the three levels of abstraction described for addition strategies also exists for the solution of subtraction problems. However, a number of distinct classes of subtraction strategies have been observed at the direct modeling and counting levels, reflecting the distinctions between problems observed in Table 1. The strategies are described in Table 3. For clarity the solutions are based on the problems $a - b = ?$ and $b + ? = a$.

Table 3. Subtraction Strategies.[a]

Type	Description
Direct Modeling	
Separating From	Using objects or fingers, a set of a objects is constructed. b objects are removed. The answer is the number of remaining objects.
Separating To	A set of a elements is counted out. Elements are removed from it until the number of elements remaining is equal to b. The answer is the number of elements removed.
Adding On	A set of b elements is constructed. Elements are added to this set until there is a total of a elements. The answer is found by counting the number of elements added.
Matching	A set of a objects and a set of b objects are matched one to one until one set is the number of objects remaining in the unmatched set.
Counting	
Counting Down From	A backward counting sequence is initiated starting with a. The sequence contains b counting number words. The last number in the counting sequence is the answer.
Counting Down To	A backward counting sequence starts with a and continues until b is reached. The answer is the number of words in the counting sequence.
Counting Up From Given	A forward counting sequence starts with b and continues until a is reached. The answer is the number of counting words in the sequence.
Choice	Either Separating From or Counting Up From Given is used depending upon which is more efficient.

a. For $a - b = ?$ or $b + ? = a$.

The strategy that best models the Separate Result Unknown problem (Table 1, Problem 2) involves a subtractive or separating action. In this case, the larger quantity in the subtraction problem is initially represented and the smaller quantity is subsequently removed from it (Separating From). There is a related counting strategy (Counting Down From) in which the separating action is represented by counting backward. For example, to solve the problem 8 − 5, a child would count "8, 7, 6, 5, 4, (pause), 3. The answer is 3."

The Separate Change Unknown problem (Table 1, Problem 4) also involves a separating action. The strategy generally used to solve this problem is similar to the Separating From strategy except that objects are removed from the larger set until the number of objects remaining is equal to the smaller number given in the problem. Similarly, the backward counting sequence in the Counting Down To strategy continues until the smaller number is reached; the number of words in the counting sequence is the solution to the problem. For example, to solve 8 − 5, a child would count "8, 7, 6, (pause), 5. The answer is 3."

The strategy related to the Join Change Unknown problem (Table 1, Problem 3) involves an additive action. The child starts with the smaller quantity and constructs the larger. With concrete objects (Adding On), the child adds objects to a set until the new collection is equal to the total given in the problem. The number of objects added is the answer. For the parallel counting strategy (Counting Up From Given), the child initiates a forward counting strategy beginning with the smaller given number. The sequence ends with the larger given number. Again, by keeping track of the number of counting words uttered in the sequence, the child determines the answer. For example, to solve 3 + ? = 8, the child counts "3(pause), 4, 5, 6, 7, 8. The answer is 5."

The Compare problems (Table 1, Problems 9 and 10) describe a matching process. Matching is only feasible when concrete objects are available. The strategy involves the construction of a one-to-one correspondence between two sets until one set is exhausted. Counting the unmatched elements gives the answer.

The Choice strategy involves a combination of Counting Down From and Counting Up From Given, depending on which is the most efficient. In this case, the child decides which strategy requires the fewest number of counts and solves the problem accordingly. For example, to find 8 − 2, it would be more efficient to Count Down From whereas the Counting Up From Given strategy would be more efficient for 8 − 6.

Modeling Problem Structure

The results of a number of studies show that the strategies children use are generally consistent with the action or relationships described in the problem. This tendency is especially pronounced for children below the second grade, but for some children the structure of the problem influences the choice of strategy at least through the third grade.

The results summarized in Table 4 are from a 3-year longitudinal study of the processes that children use to solve basic addition and subtraction word problems (Carpenter & Moser, 1984). The problems involved subtraction facts with the larger number between 11 and 16. Manipulative objects were available to aid in the solution, but children were not required to use them. At the time of the Grade 1 interview, the children in the study had received no formal instruction in addition and subtraction. By the second-grade interview, they had received about 8 months of instruction in addition and subtraction. Progress toward mastery of number facts was expected, but there had been no instruction on the two-digit subtraction algorithm. By the third-grade interview,

Table 4. Relation of Strategy to Problem Structure: Longitudinal Study Results.[a]

Problem type	Grade	Percent correct	Strategy (Percent Responding)[b]					
			Subtractive		Additive			
			Separate From	Count Down From	Add On	Count Up From Given	Matching	Number Facts
Separate Result Unknown	1	61	68	1	1	3	0	3
	2	83	34	8	1	10	0	29
	3	95	9	3	1	12	0	67
Join Change Unknown	1	57	2	0	42	12	1	6
	2	93	1	2	18	31	0	41
	3	95	0	1	6	27	1	62
Compare Difference Unknown	1	41	8	0	3	9	30	2
	2	70	11	6	2	17	14	26
	3	89	3	3	2	14	2	69

a. Data from Carpenter & Moser (1984).
b. Percentages do not sum to 100 because inappropriate and infrequently used strategies are not included.

students were expected to have learned their number facts and to have learned the addition and subtraction algorithms.

In Grade 1, the vast majority of responses were based on problem structure. Almost all of the first-graders who solved the problems correctly used the Separating From strategy for the Separate problem and the Add On or Count Up From Given strategy for the Join Change Unknown problem. The results were not quite so overwhelming for the Compare problem, but the Matching strategy was used by the majority of children who solved the problem correctly. Furthermore, it was the only problem for which more than two children used a Matching strategy.

By the second grade, about a third of the responses were based on number facts and the effect of problem structure was not quite so dominant; however, the structure of the problem continued to influence the responses of a large number of second-graders. Forty-two percent of the second-graders used a subtractive strategy to solve the Separate problem; only 11% used an additive strategy. For the Join problem 49% used an additive strategy, and only 3% used a subtractive strategy. Thus, for these two problems, most of the children who used a counting or modeling strategy continued to represent the action described in the problem. The structure of the Compare problem did not continue to exert as strong an influence, and many second-graders abandoned the Matching strategy for the more efficient Separating From or Counting Up From Given strategies.

By the third grade about two thirds of the responses were based on number facts, and there was more flexibility in the use of counting strategies. For the Separate problem, the most popular strategy apart from recalled number facts was Counting Up From Given. The Matching strategy was seldom used for the Compare problem. For the Join problem, however, almost all children who did not use number facts used an additive strategy. This represented about a third of the third-grade children in the study.

Similar results have been found in other studies (Blume, 1981; Carpenter et al., 1983; Hiebert, 1982). These results indicate that when possible, young children initially solve addition and subtraction problems by directly modeling the action or relationships described in the problems. Some problems, however, cannot be readily modeled. For example, in the Change Start Unknown problems (Table 1, Problems 5 and 6) the unknown is the initial quantity given in the problem. Unless a child uses trial and error, these problems cannot be directly modeled because there is not an initial quantity to increase or decrease. The results summarized in Table 5 indicate that problems that cannot be easily modeled are significantly more difficult than problems that can be (Riley et al., 1983). Similar results have been reported in other studies (Gibb, 1956; Lindvall & Iberra, 1980; Nesher, 1982; Schell & Burns, 1962; Shores & Underhill, 1976).

THE EFFECT OF LANGUAGE

Although the semantic structure of a problem appears to be the major factor that determines how it will be solved, the wording of a problem can also significantly affect whether a child will be able to solve a given problem or not. Some wordings appear to make the semantic structure of the problem clearer than others. As a consequence, they are easier to model. For example, although traditional Compare problems (Table 1, Problem 9) are generally relatively difficult for young children, Hudson (1980) found that almost all children could solve them if the language was made more transparent. Children from nursery school through first grade were shown a picture of a group of birds and a group of worms. Two questions were asked: the standard Compare question "How

Table 5. Relative Difficulty of Word Problems.[a]

Problem type	Grade			
	K	1	2	3
Join Result Unknown (1)[b]	.87[c]	1.00	1.00	1.00
Separate Result Unknown (2)	1.00	1.00	1.00	1.00
Join Change Unknown (3)	.61	.56	1.00	1.00
Separate Change Unknown (4)	.91	.78	1.00	1.00
Join Start Unknown (5)	.09	.28	.80	.95
Separate Start Unknown (6)	.22	.39	.70	.80
Combine addition (7)	1.00	1.00	1.00	1.00
Combine subtraction (8)	.22	.39	.70	1.00
Compare Difference Unknown (9)	.17	.28	.85	1.00
Compare Difference Unknown (10)	.04	.22	.75	1.00
Compare Compared Quantity Unknown (11)	.13	.17	.80	1.00
Compare Compared Quantity Unknown (14)	.17	.28	.90	.95
Compare Referent Unknown (13)	.17	.11	.65	.75
Compare Referent Unknown (12)	.00	.06	.35	.75

a. Reprinted with permission from Riley, M.S. *Conceptual and procedural knowledge in development.* Unpublished master's thesis, University of Pittsburgh, 1981.
b. Refers to problem number in Table 1.
c. Proportion correct.

many more birds than worms are there?'' and an alternative ''Suppose the birds all race over and each one tries to get a worm. Will every bird get a worm? . . . How many birds won't get a worm?'' Most children were unable to solve the standard problem but could solve the alternative version. This suggests that much of the difficulty that children at this level experience with problems of this type is with the language of the problem, not with representing the problem structure.

Alternative wordings of the Join Change Unknown problem (Table 1, Problem 3) have also resulted in different patterns of performance. Using the following version of the problem, Riley (1981) found that Join Change Unknown problems were significantly more difficult than Join addition and Separate subtraction problems (Table 1, Problems 1 and 2):

> Connie had 5 marbles. Jim gave her some more marbles. Now she has 13 marbles. How many marbles did Jim give Connie?

Riley concluded that Join Change Unknown problems could not be solved simply by constructing external representations of the problem and that additional knowledge about the problem structure was required that was not required to solve Join addition or Separate subtraction problems.

The results from the study by Carpenter and Moser (1984) provide a different picture. They used the following version of the same problem:

> Connie has 5 marbles. How many more marbles does she have to win to have 13 marbles?

With this wording Join Change Unknown problems were not significantly more difficult than common Join addition or Separate subtraction problems.

One difference between the two versions of the problem is the time frame in which the action is performed. In the easier version, the initial quantity is described in the present tense. The question is then framed in the context of "how many marbles have to be added to get 13?" This seems to cue the child that the purpose of adding elements to the initial set is to find out how many have to be added to get 13. Therefore the elements added need to be kept track of so they can be counted. In the more difficult version the initial quantity is described in the past tense. Marbles *were* added so that now there *are* 13. The question of how many marbles were added comes later and is not as clearly connected to the process of adding elements to the initial set. Since the 13 marbles exist in the present, it may be necessary to somehow transform the problem to model it. Problems are much harder if they must be transformed and cannot be solved directly.

Other explanations for the difference in difficulty between the two problems are equally plausible. It is clear that differences in wording contribute to a problem's difficulty, but it is not at all clear exactly how. We have a reasonably clear picture of how semantic structure affects children's solution processes, but beyond knowing that certain wordings are more difficult, we have a much less precise picture of how differences in wording influence children's solutions.

THE DEVELOPMENT OF ADDITION AND SUBTRACTION PROCESSES

Counting strategies are more efficient and appear to require more sophisticated counting skills and a deeper understanding of addition and subtraction than direct modeling with physical objects. This suggests that younger children use the more concrete direct modeling strategies and that more abstract and efficient counting strategies are used by older children. Empirical support for this conjecture is provided by several cross-sectional studies involving children of different ages (Blume, 1981; Davydov & Andronov, 1981; Houlihan & Ginsburg, 1981) and by two longitudinal studies (Carpenter & Moser, 1983; Ilg & Ames, 1951).

Results for addition problems with sums between 11 and 16 are presented in Figure 1 (Carpenter & Moser, 1984). These results indicate that children initially solve these problems with a Counting All strategy and that this strategy gradually gives way to Counting On and the use of number facts. Although there was a great deal of variability in the time at which Counting On was initially observed, virtually all students used Counting On at some point during the study. The shift to Counting On was generally not initially complete and Counting All and Counting On were often used concurrently for some period of time.

Ilg and Ames (1951) suggest that Counting On From First emerges before Counting On From Larger, but Carpenter and Moser (1984) found little support for this conclusion. For 43% of the subjects in their study, both Counting On strategies were first used during the same interview, 34% used Counting On From Smaller before using Counting On From Larger, and 22% used Counting On From Larger before Counting On From Smaller.

Results for the subtraction problems (Table 4) generally parallel the findings for addition. For Join Change Unknown problems the modeling and counting strategies are closely related to the Counting All and Counting On strategies used in addition, and the transition from Adding On to Counting Up From Given occurs concurrently with the

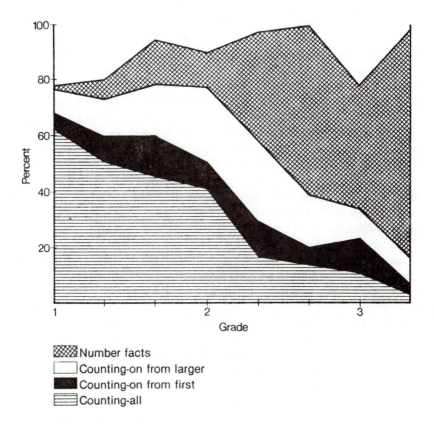

Figure 1. Strategy use over time on join addition problems with larger number facts and manipulative objects available. (Reprinted from Carpenter & Moser [1984] by permission of the *Journal for Research in Mathematics Education*.)

transition from Counting All to Counting On. The transition from modeling to counting is not as straightforward for other subtraction problems. For the Join Change Unknown problem, the direct modeling strategy is replaced by a counting strategy that continues to reflect the structure of the problem. Other direct modeling strategies are not as easily abstracted. There is no parallel counting strategy for the Matching strategy, so Compare problems are eventually transformed and solved using the Counting Up From Given strategy. The counting analogs of the Separating strategies involve counting backwards. Although there is some evidence that children eventually become as efficient in solving subtraction problems by Counting Down as by Counting Up From Given (Groen & Poll, 1973; Woods, Resnick, & Groen, 1975), other results indicate that Counting Down is not used consistently (Carpenter & Moser, 1983). Children do eventually solve Separate problems (Table 1, Problem 2) by counting, but the transition occurs later than for Change Unknown problems and both Counting Down and Counting Up are used (Table 4).

Children's ability to solve addition and subtraction problems appears to fall into four basic levels (Carpenter & Moser, 1984), as described in the following sections.

Level 1

Most of the research on addition and subtraction has involved school-children, so the initial development of the first level is not clearly documented. Starkey and Gelman (1982) have found that children as young as 3 can solve simple addition and subtraction problems, and most children can solve a number of different problems by the time they enter school (Blume, 1981; Carpenter & Moser, 1983; Riley et al., 1983).

Children in level 1 are limited to direct modeling solutions using concrete objects. They solve Combine and Join addition problems (Table 1, Problems 1 and 7) by Counting All, and Separate problems (Problem 2) by Separating From. Problems that cannot be easily modeled (e.g., Problem 6) cannot be solved by children at this level. Level 1 children are not uniformly successful in solving all problems that can be modeled. At best only about a third of the children in level 1 can solve Compare problems (Problem 9), and many studies have found lower levels of performance (Riley et al., 1983). However, if the wording of the Compare problems makes the matching structure sufficiently transparent, it appears that children at this level can solve them (Hudson, 1980).

There is some debate about whether Join Change Unknown problems can be solved at this level. Based on studies of problem difficulty, Riley et al. (1983) concluded that there is a separate level of development during which children acquire the ability to solve Join Change Unknown problems and to Count On From First to solve Join addition problems. This conclusion, however, was based on children's solutions to a version of the Join Change Unknown problem that has turned out to be more difficult than others. In fact, it is possible that the version used in Riley's study may require a transformation, which would clearly put it beyond level 1 ability.

Carpenter and Moser (1983) used an easier version of the Join Change Unknown problem and found much higher levels of performance. Children who were clearly limited to direct modeling for other problems were able to solve these Join Change Unknown problems by Adding On. About 10% of the children had difficulty with Join Change Unknown problems at the beginning of first grade, but virtually all the children in the study were able to solve Join Change Unknown problems before they exhibited any evidence of the counting strategies characteristic of more advanced levels. Since this study started when the children were in the first grade, it is possible that younger children experience greater difficulty with Join Change Unknown problems, but a study by Blume (1981) involving kindergarten children reported similar results.

In summary, children in level 1 can solve simple addition and subtraction problems by using physical objects to represent the action or relationships in the problems. They readily solve common Join and Combine addition problems and Separate subtraction problems, and they can solve Compare and Join Change Unknown problems if the structure of the problem is made sufficiently transparent. There is some evidence that early in level 1 children are unable to solve Join Change Unknown problems, but the ability to solve these problems by Adding On is fully developed while children are still in this level. Problems that cannot be modeled easily cannot be solved at this level.

Level 2

Level 2 is a transition period. At this level children use both modeling and counting strategies. Some process models for addition and subtraction assume that children use the most efficient strategies available (Groen & Parkman, 1972; Groen & Poll, 1973;

Woods et al., 1975), but the evidence from clinical studies clearly suggests this is not the case (Carpenter et al., 1983; Carpenter & Moser, 1984). During this transition phase children use all three addition strategies—Counting All, Counting On From First, and Counting On From Larger — and both Adding On and Counting Up From Given. Counting Down is not used as frequently. Only about 20% of the subjects in Carpenter and Moser's (1983) longitudinal study used Counting Down when they were in level 2.

Children in level 2 tend to continue to model the structure of the problem using either modeling or counting strategies, but some flexibility is possible. The structure of both Separate and Join Change Unknown problems generally continues to dominate children's solutions in level 2, but almost as many children at this level solve Compare problems by Counting Up as by Matching.

Some of the variability observed during this level is explainable. Some children who use the more efficient counting strategies when objects are not available tend to fall back on modeling strategies when physical objects are provided. However, there is no discernible pattern for much of the inconsistency. A child will use Counting On From Larger on one problem and Counting All on another that has all the same characteristics. One potential explanation for the variability in children's performance is that their executive procedures for monitoring their performance are not adequately developed. Thus, the distinction between level 2 in which children only sometimes use more efficient strategies and level 3 in which they consistently do may not lie in the further development or strengthening of the strategies themselves but in the refinement of the executive processes that govern the use of strategies.

Level 3

In level 3, children rely primarily on counting strategies although they may occasionally fall back to direct modeling with concrete objects. Some children consistently use Counting On From Larger, but a number of children continue to use both Counting On strategies except in extreme cases. Most children at this level can use Counting Down, but some evidence suggests that few of them use it consistently (Carpenter & Moser, 1983). In level 3 children can represent problems to solve them with counting procedures that are not consistent with the semantic structure of the problem.

Studies of children's solutions to number sentence problems ($8 - 3 = ?$ or $3 + ? = 8$) suggest that children at this level use the Choice strategy to solve subtraction problems (Groen & Poll, 1973; Resnick, 1983; Woods et al., 1975). This strategy is based on the number combinations rather than the semantic structure of the problem. Either Counting Down From or Counting Up is chosen, depending on which requires the fewest counting steps. Although there are a number of studies that point to the Choice strategy as the dominant strategy at this level, the support for the Choice strategy is based primarily on reaction time data with a limited range of number facts. The key studies generally do not provide a rigorous test of the Choice model over a wide range of number combinations. The Choice strategy appears reasonable for problems in which the differences are extreme and/or involve relatively small numbers (e.g., $11 - 2$ or $11 - 9$), but the argument is less compelling for combinations like $14 - 6$ or $14 - 8$.

Thus, children at this level have a range of strategies available. They are no longer limited to directly modeling the semantic structure of the problem. They generally use counting strategies rather than physical modeling, but there continues to be a great deal of random variability in their choice of strategy. They have a number of viable strategies available, and although they often choose the easiest or more efficient, they may choose almost any of the appropriate strategies in some cases.

Level 4

In the final level, children solve addition and subtraction problems using number facts. Facts are not learned all at once and selected number facts are used at all three levels of modeling and counting. However, the evidence suggests that most children pass through each of the levels described above. In the 3-year longitudinal study reported by Carpenter and Moser (1984), two thirds of the children were at level 1 or level 0 at the start of the first grade (Figure 2). By the end of the first grade, only about 10% were in level 1. Most children were in level 2 for less than 6 months and most children were level 3 an average of about 10 months before they started relying on recall of number facts.

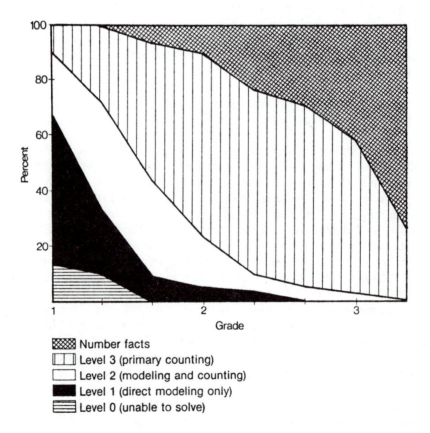

Figure 2.   Levels of performance over time for addition and Join Change Unknown problems. (Reprinted from Carpenter & Moser [1984] by permission of the *Journal for Research in Mathematics Education.*)

ANALYSES OF COGNITIVE PROCESSING

The transition from direct modeling to the use of counting strategies involves significant advances in understanding and procedural skills. In direct modeling, each of the entities in the problem is represented sequentially so that it is only necessary to keep track of one piece of the problem at a time. For the primary counting strategies, the relationship between each of the different entities in the problem is represented in a single counting sequence. As a consequence, it is necessary to have a much clearer understanding of the relation between the different parts of the problem. The counting strategies also involve much more sophisticated counting skills. In direct modeling, each of the sets is constructed individually so that it is only necessary to be able to construct or count a set of a given size. The counting strategies, on the other hand, involve some form of double counting. It is necessary to count forward or backward from a given number and to keep track of the number of steps in the counting sequence in order to know when to stop.

Fuson (1982) has analyzed the transition from Counting All to Counting On in addition in some detail. She hypothesizes that this transition depends on the development of specific concepts and counting skills. Counting On depends on understanding the following concepts:

1. The dual relation between cardinality and counting.

2. That the final word in a counting sequence is a legitimate representation of the entire counting sequence.

3. That the enumeration of the elements in the first addend can serve as the enumeration of those same elements in the sum.

The counting skills required include the ability to initiate a count at an arbitrary point and a keeping-track process to maintain the double count involved in Counting On. The results of a recent study by Secada, Fuson, and Hall (1983) support this analysis and suggest that these principles may be both necessary and sufficient for Counting On.

Steffe and his associates (Steffe, Thompson, & Richards, 1982; Steffe, Von Glasersfeld, Richards, & Cobb, 1984) have considered the problem from a somewhat different perspective. They believe that children's arithmetic concepts and skills can best be characterized in terms of their emerging counting abilities. They have developed what they call a theory of children's counting types. They argue that counting involves the construction of "units" or things to be counted, and children can be classified in terms of the units that they are capable of counting. They identify five basic levels of counting behavior ranging from "counters with perceptual unit items," who can only count physical objects or actions that can be directly perceived, to "counters of abstract unit items," who can construct abstract representations of the units to be counted in the absence of perceivable objects. The hallmark of the most advanced level is the ability to count the words in a counting sequence. The ability to "double count" is what makes Counting On possible. The ability to solve Join Change Unknown problems also emerges at this level.

Models of Problem Solving

The most explicit analyses of the knowledge and procedural skills required to solve addition and subtraction problems is provided by two computer simulation models developed by Riley et al. (1983) and Briars and Larkin (in press). The models are based on similar analyses of performance, but somewhat different characterizations of knowledge at each stage of problem solving. (In this paper, I will refer to the Riley et al. model as Model A and the Briars and Larkin model as Model B.)

Riley et al. identify three basic levels of knowledge involved in problem solving: (1) problem schemata, (2) action schemata, and (3) strategic knowledge for planning solutions to problems. There are three basic problem schemata: one corresponding to Change problems, one corresponding to Combine problems, and one corresponding to Compare problems. Problems are represented as semantic networks that specify the relations between elements in the problem.

Action schemata relate the knowledge represented in the semantic networks to the actual problem-solving procedures. Action schemata are organized into different levels. The most basic level includes schemata for making sets, adding elements to sets, removing elements from sets, counting sets, and so on. There are also global schemata which are composites of the basic schemata. These schemata essentially correspond to the solution processes described in Tables 2 and 3.

Strategic knowledge is organized to permit top-down planning. First a general approach is selected, then more specific actions that are involved in this approach are identified, and finally the details are carried out. When given a problem, a goal is set. If the initial goal cannot be satisfied, subgoals are set. This process of setting goals and subgoals continues until the problem is solved.

Riley identified three levels of skill for solving Change problems, and a computer simulation model was constructed for each level. For Change problems, children in level 1 are limited to external representations of problem situations using physical objects. They can solve simple Join and Separate problems (Table 1, Problems 1 and 2) using Counting All and Separating strategies. They cannot solve Join Change Unknown problems because they have no way to keep track of the double role played by some elements in Adding On.

The major advance of level 2 over level 1 is that it includes a schema that makes it possible to keep a mental record of the role of each piece of data in the problem. This allows children in level 2 to solve Join Change Unknown problems (Table 1, Problem 3). Level 2 children are also capable of Counting On From First, but they are still limited to direct representation of problem action and are unable to solve Start Unknown problems because the initial set cannot be represented.

Both level 1 and level 2 children are limited to direct representation of problem structure. Level 3 includes a schema for representing part-whole relations that allows children to proceed in a top-down direction in order to construct a representation of the relationships among all the pieces of information in the problem before solving it. This frees children from relying on solutions that directly represent the action of the problem. Level 3 children can solve all six Change problems. The flexibility also allows children to use Counting On From Larger to solve addition problems.

The model proposed by Briars and Larkin hypothesizes the same three levels of performance. Although the details differ, both models predict essentially the same set of cognitive mechanisms governing the first two levels. At level 3, however, there are some fundamental differences between the models. Although both models predict the same responses for all problems, they attribute the responses to different knowledge structures. Briars and Larkin hypothesize that two schemata are required to represent problems in level 3. There is a subset equivalence schema, which is similar to Riley's part-whole schema, but it is more limited in its application. It allows children to interchange subsets, which provides the basis for Counting On From Larger and for solving Join Start Unknown problems, but it does not provide a means for solving Separate Start Unknown problems. These solutions require a time reversal schema, which allows joining and separating actions to be reversed in time.

Similar models are proposed for Combine and Compare problems. However, since the Combine and Compare problems do not contain the implicit action cues inherent in Change problems, additional knowledge is required to represent the problems using the available action schemata. For Combine addition problems, level 1 knowledge is sufficient. Combine subtraction problems, however, are more difficult. Briars and Larkin hypothesize that more sophisticated language understanding is required for these problems, but they can be solved with the mathematical knowledge available in level 1. Riley et al., on the other hand, propose that a Combine schema that allows children to infer part-whole relationships is required.

For both Model A and Model B, simple Compare problems (Table 1, Problems 9 and 10) are solved by a Matching procedure. The other Compare problems appear to require more sophisticated language comprehension than has been implemented, so the models do not yet solve these problems.

Both Briars and Larkin and Riley et al. propose the same basic levels of performance; their models solve the same problems using essentially the same general strategies. They do, however, propose different knowledge structures to account for this performance, especially at the third level. There also appear to be some fundamental differences in the general design of the models.

Model A initially represents problems in semantic networks using three basic problem schemata to represent Change, Combine, and Compare problems. These representations are then matched to the available action schemata. Model B does not contain specific schemata for representing different classes of problems. Problems are mapped directly to the appropriate action schemata. There is a language processor that encodes each word in order. As each word is encoded, the model performs the cued action. Model B can theoretically solve any problem for which the appropriate action schemata are available. Model A also requires an appropriate problem schema. For example, to solve simple Compare problems, Briars and Larkin simply added a Match schema to the procedures available to solve Change problems; Riley et al. also constructed a Compare schema. To extend Model A to include multiplication and division problems would require the construction of additional problem schemata, whereas Briars and Larkin would only add appropriate action schemata along with necessary language-processing capacity. This distinction appears critical.

In so far as the models are valid models of children's abilities, Model B suggests that children at a given level may be able to solve a wide range of problem types, as long as they can directly model the semantic structure of the problem. Model A, on the other hand, suggests that children must also have available the appropriate problem schema to represent the problem; each distinct class of problems appears to require a corresponding problem schema.

Nesher, Greeno, & Riley (1982) have proposed a revised version of the Riley et al. model that appears to abandon separate problem schemata for each problem class. The revised model includes "operations for deriving class and order relations that cross the boundaries of the semantic categories" (p. 376). This model proposes four levels for solving all addition and subtraction problems. The first three levels correspond to the three levels for solving Change problems, but a child must attain the fourth level to solve the most difficult Compare problems (Table 1, Problems 12 and 13). The knowledge that is available at this level and not before is an understanding of the relation between equality and inequality (i.e., if $a > b$, then there is a number c such that $a - c = b$ or $b + c = a$). This model is less explicit than the original and has not been implemented on a computer.

The data on complex Compare problems are rather sparse, so it is difficult to evaluate the necessity of a fourth level. Riley's (1981) data do support this analysis. On the other hand, *Developing Mathematical Processes* (Romberg et al., 1974) introduced addition and subtraction using an equalizing process that was based on the knowledge of inequalities that characterizes level 4. Most first-graders successfully learned to equalize but did not exhibit problem-solving performance expected at level 3.

Currently there is no compelling evidence to support one model or the other. The problem of evaluating the relative merits of the models is compounded by the fact that they both predict essentially the same behavior on the same problems. One of the most critical differences between the two primary models is their characterization of level 3. Riley et al. hypothesize that a part-whole schema makes it possible to solve both Start Unknown problems (Table 1, Problems 5 and 6), whereas Briars and Larkin believe that a subset equivalence schema is involved in the solution to Join Start Unknown (Problem 5), and a time reversal schema is used for Separate Start Unknown (Problem 6). Since Riley et al. predict that the same schema is required for both problems, their model suggests that the same levels of performance should be found on both; inconsistent performance would be more consistent with Briars and Larkin's analysis. The data do not provide conclusive support for either analysis. Research on word problems shows only small differences in performance between the two problems. However, number sentence problems of the form $? - a = b$ are significantly more difficult than problems of the form $? + a = b$ (Grouws, 1972; Lindvall & Ibarra, 1980; Weaver, 1971).

From an educational perspective the important difference between the two models is that they suggest significantly different programs of instruction. Since it appears difficult to directly test the validity of either model, it may be more productive to take the next step and investigate the effect of instructional programs based on each model. A program has been developed based on a part-whole analysis (Kouba & Moser, 1979). Preliminary analysis indicated that children were able to use the procedure designed to identify part-whole relationships to solve basic word problems, but interviews with teachers suggest that both students and teachers have some serious misconceptions about the particular part-whole analysis in the program (Stephens, 1982). Further investigation is clearly needed; at this point the contribution of the models to instruction is not resolved.

More critical than the relative validity of the two models is the fact that neither model is entirely consistent with the results of empirical studies of children's behavior. The models are based primarily on error data from studies that used particular wordings of problems. Recent studies that analyzed children's solution processes and used slightly different wordings of problems suggest different conclusions. Whereas the primary differences between the models occurred at level 3, it is level 1 and 2 that provide the poorest match with children's behavior. Both models hypothesize as follows:

1. That the lowest stage children can solve Join addition and simple Separate problems but not Join Change Unknown problems.

2. That there is a stage at which children acquire the ability to solve Join Change Unknown problems and to solve addition problems by Counting On From First.

3. That Counting On From First and Counting On From Larger are acquired in different stages.

Data from Carpenter and Moser (1984) and a series of related studies suggest that these conclusions are not warranted. Furthermore, the models do not take into account children's knowledge of number facts, which is clearly a critical variable.

Finally, the models are completely deterministic. They imply that children at a particular level solve a given problem using a specific procedure. The results of studies of children's solution processes clearly document a great deal of variability in children's selection of strategies. Children do not consistently use the most efficient process available to them, and much of this variability cannot be easily accounted for. Moreover, the increasing ability to consistently use the most efficient strategy appears to be a significant variable in characterizing children's development. Larkin is exploring procedures for devising a stochastic model of children's performance (Sophian, Larkin, & Kadane, 1983) to capture this variability, but this project is still in the formative stage.

How Knowledge Is Acquired

Perhaps the most serious limitation of our knowledge of the development of addition and subtraction problem-solving skills is that we know very little about how more advanced concepts and skills are acquired. We have a clear picture of the strategies that children use and some reasonable models of development. But the models are snapshots of behavior at a particular point in time; they do not address the question of how change occurs.

Neches (1981) has developed a computer model that attempts to explain how Counting On is acquired. The model contains general redundancy elimination procedures, and after a number of trials using Counting All, it attempts to eliminate the extra counting steps.

A different analysis of development is provided by Case (1982, 1983). He argues that different problems and solution procedures place different demands on working memory. He suggests that the development of more advanced levels of performance in addition and subtraction correspond to increases in working memory capacity. However, although measures of information-processing capacity have been found to be positively correlated with performance on addition and subtraction problems (Hiebert, Carpenter, & Moser, 1982; Romberg & Collis, 1980), they have not been particulary useful in explaining children's behavior. A number of children identified as having limited processing capacity demonstrate advanced levels of performance.

MATHEMATICAL REPRESENTATIONS OF WORD PROBLEMS

Although young children develop quite sophisticated processes for analyzing and solving addition and subtraction word problems, they have difficulty relating this knowledge to the formal mathematical procedures they learn in school. A major objective of the mathematics curriculum is to teach children to represent problem situations mathematically. The earliest application of this skill is writing number sentences to represent simple word problems. Although children quite easily learn to write number sentences for simple Join and Separate problems (Table 1, Problems 1 and 2), they often have difficulty writing number sentences for other problems, even when they can solve them by modeling and counting (Carpenter, Hiebert, & Moser, 1983; De Corte & Verschaffel, 1983). For example, Carpenter et al. (1983) found that fewer than half of the first-graders in their study could write an appropriate number sentence for a simple Compare problem (Table 1, Problem 9) after 2 months of instruction that emphasized writing number sentences to solve word problems. However, almost all of the children solved the problem correctly even though they had written an incorrect sentence. They regarded the sentence writing and solving the problem as unrelated activities.

The difficulty that the children had with standard canonical number sentences $(3 + 5 = ?, 8 - 4 = ?)$ is that the sentences often did not correspond to their modeling or counting solutions. Carpenter and Moser (1982) found that first-grade children could readily learn to represent a variety of addition and subtraction word problems if they were taught to use noncanonical open sentences (e.g., $3 + ? = 5, ? - 7 = 4$). Children in their study faithfully represented the structure of each problem, even in cases for which they were not expressly taught the appropriate number sentence form. These representations corresponded to the way they attempted to solve the problem. In other words, children naturally represent problems using physical objects. They can learn to represent the problems mathematically as long as the mathematical representation corresponds to their semantic analysis of the problem. Children who are incapable of transforming a problem to solve it are probably also unable to represent the problem with a canonical number sentence that requires a transformation.

DISCUSSION

At the most basic level, problem solving reduces to a question of finding an appropriate representation for a problem so that it can be solved. Naive views of problem solving regarded the representation problem as one of simply translating the problem to mathematical symbolism (cf. Gagné, 1983). Although this point of view is not supported by most current research in problem solving, it is reflected in most mathematics textbooks at the elementary and secondary level. Research on addition and subtraction word problems offers additional evidence that representing the problem involves more than translating a problem into a mathematical form that can be solved by the routine manipulations of symbols.

This research suggests that the process of representing a problem and the process of deriving a solution are not isolated components of problem solving. At least with simple word problems, children do not represent a problem in one phase and then operate on this representation in a second phase to calculate the solution. The representation processes are integrally related to the solution procedures. Riley et al.'s (1983) model of problem solving suggests that children construct semantic networks that specify the relations between principal elements in the problem. A great deal of the solution process is carried out on this semantic representation, not on the mathematical or physical representation that is derived from it. In other words, children do not just represent a problem mathematically and then manipulate the mathematical representation. They use their understanding of the problem situation itself to transform the problem before they represent it mathematically.

Another naive conception of problem solving that is widely reflected in the mathematics curriculum is that problems can be represented by syntactic translations of words into mathematical symbols. This has led to techniques like the keyword approach for solving word problems. The analysis of problems in Table 1 shows that problems with similar syntax and most of the same words have very different interpretations and lead to different mathematical solutions. Approaches based strictly on syntax or key words will clearly result in many incorrect solutions. The analysis of children's solution processes indicates that successful problem solvers attend to the semantics of the problem. This finding is also consistent with other research in problem solving (cf. Paige & Simon, 1966). It is noteworthy that most young children clearly attend to the semantics of a problem in solving it, and it is not until they have been in school for several years that they begin to focus on surface features of problems.

A great deal of the research on problem solving in mathematics has focused on the use of general heuristic strategies in poorly defined content domains. This research only provides part of the picture. The research on addition and subtraction suggests that knowledge of the problem domain is critical for certain types of problem solving. Schemata for representing key relationships play a central role in problem solving. Better problem solvers have more powerful and more flexible schemata. The differences between the three levels in Riley et al.'s and Briars and Larkin's models of problem solving are attributable to the development of more powerful schemata for representing problems, not to the acquisition of more sophisticated heuristics or the mastery of computational skills.

In developing skill in solving addition and subtraction problems, children pass through several stages or levels of skill. In general terms, the less skilled or younger problem solvers are limited to directly representing the problem. Older or more skilled problem solvers conduct a more elaborate semantic analysis of the problem and often transform the problem to a form that is easier to solve before they represent it mathematically. There appear to be some clear parallels in the development of related concepts with children of approximately the same age. For example, children's solutions to multiplication and division problems follow much the same pattern (Hendrickson, 1979; Nelson, 1976). It is not clear that older, more sophisticated problem solvers necessarily pass through the same general states in learning to solve problems in a new domain, but it is plausible.

Most of the general conclusions about problem solving that can be drawn from research on addition and subtraction problems are consistent with results from the more general problem-solving literature and do not provide any startling new insights. What is unique about this research, however, is that it provides a picture of successful problem solving. Even before they have received formal instruction in arithmetic, almost all children exhibit reasonably sophisticated and appropriate problem-solving skills in solving simple word problems. They attend to the content of the problem; they model the problem; they invent more efficient procedures for computing the answer. Given the limits of their mathematical skills, this peformance is remarkable. Contrast this with performance several years later, when many children solve any problem by choosing a single arithmetic operation based on surface details of the problem (Carpenter, Corbitt, Kepner, Lindquist, & Reys, 1980). After several years of instruction in mathematics, children abandon a reasonably good general problem-solving approach for mechanical application of arithmetic skills. This is foreshadowed in children's initial use of number sentences in solving word problems. They do not see that the number sentence is in any way related to the real solution which is found by modeling and counting. From the beginning they are learning that mathematics is just an exercise in symbol manipulation and is not related to real problem solving. This suggests that initial instruction in addition and subtraction may be a critical point in developing problem-solving skills and that children's later deficiencies may be traced to this point in the curriculum.

REFERENCES

Arnett, L.D. Counting and adding. *American Journal of Psychology* 16, 327–36, 1905.

Blume, G. *Kindergarten and first-grade children's strategies for solving addition and subtraction and missing addend problems in symbolic and verbal problem contexts.* Unpublished doctoral dissertation, University of Wisconsin-Madison, 1981.

Briars, D.J., & Larkin, J.H. An integrated model of skill in solving elementary word problems. *Cognition and instruction,* in press.

Browne, C.E. The psychology of simple arithmetical processes: A study of certain habits of attention and association. *American Journal of Psychology* 17, 1–37, 1906.

Brownell, W.A. *The development of children's number ideas in the primary grades* (Supplementary Educational Monographs, No. 35). Chicago: University of Chicago Press, 1928.

Brownell, W.A. *Arithmetic in grades I and II: A critical summary of new and previously reported research* (Duke University Research Studies in Education, No. 6). Durham, NC: Duke University Press, 1941.

Carpenter, T.P. Initial instruction in addition and subtraction: A target of opportunity for curriculum development. In *Proceedings of the National Science Foundation Director's Meeting,* Washington, D.C., 1981.

Carpenter, T.P., Blume, G., Hiebert, J., Anick, C.M., & Pimm, D. *A review of research on addition and subtraction* (Working Paper No. 330). Madison: Wisconsin Center for Education Research, 1982.

Carpenter, T.P., Corbitt, M.K., Kepner, H.S., Lindquist, M.M., & Reys, R.E. Solving verbal problems: Results and implications from National Assessment. *Arithmetic Teacher* 28, 8–12, 1980.

Carpenter, T.P., Hiebert, J., & Moser, J.M. The effect of instruction on children's solutions of addition and subtraction word problems. *Educational Studies in Mathematics* 14, 56–72, 1983.

Carpenter, T.P., & Moser, J.M. The development of addition and subtraction problem-solving skills. In T.P. Carpenter, J.M. Moser, & T.A. Romberg (Eds.), *Addition and subtraction: A cognitive perspective.* Hillsdale, NJ: Lawrence Erlbaum Associates, 1982.

Carpenter, T.P., & Moser, J.M. The acquisition of addition and subtraction concepts. In R. Lesh & M. Landau (Eds.), *Acquisition of mathematics concepts and processes.* New York: Academic Press, 1983.

Carpenter, T.P., & Moser, J.M. The acquisition of addition and subtraction concepts in grades one through three. *Journal for Research in Mathematics Education* 15, 179–202, 1984.

Carpenter, T.P., Moser, J.M., & Romberg, T.A. (Eds.), *Addition and subtraction: A cognitive perspective.* Hillsdale, NJ: Lawrence Erlbaum Associates, 1982.

Case, R. General developmental influences on the acquisition of elementary concepts and algorithms in arithmetic. In T.P. Carpenter, J.M. Moser, & T.A. Romberg (Eds.), *Addition and subtraction: A cognitive perspective.* Hillsdale, NJ: Lawrence Erlbaum Associates, 1982.

Davydov, V.V. The psychological characteristics of the formation of elementary mathematical operations in children. In T.P. Carpenter, J.M. Moser, & T.A. Romberg (Eds.), *Addition and subtraction: A cognitive perspective.* Hillsdale, NJ: Lawrence Erlbaum Associates, 1982.

Davydov, V.V., & Andronov, V.P. *Psychological conditions of the origination of ideal actions* (Project Paper No. 81-2). Madison: Wisconsin Research and Development Center for Individualized Schooling, 1981.

De Corte, E., & Verschaffel, L. *Beginning first graders' initial representation of arithmetic and word problems.* Paper presented at the annual meeting of the American Educational Research Association, Montreal, April 1983.

Fuson, K. An analysis of the counting-on solution procedure in addition. In T.P. Carpenter, J.M. Moser, & T.A. Romberg (Eds.), *Addition and subtraction: A cognitive perspective.* Hillsdale, NJ: Lawrence Erlbaum Associates, 1982.

Gagné, R.M. Some issues in the psychology of mathematics instruction. *Journal for Research in Mathematics Education* 14, 7–18, 1983.

Gibb, E.G. Children's thinking in the process of subtraction. *Journal of Experimental Education* 25, 71–80, 1956.

Gimbayashi, H. Mathematics and mathematics education. In G. Hatano & H. Gimbayashi (Eds.), *Logic and psychology of school subjects: 4. Mathematics.* Tokyo: Meiji-Tosho, 1980.

Greeno, J.G. Some examples of cognitive task analysis with instructional implications. In R.E. Snow, P.A. Federico, & W.E. Montague (Eds.), *Aptitude, learning, and instruction: Cognitive process analyses.* Hillsdale, NJ: Lawrence Erlbaum Associates, 1980.

Groen, G.J., & Parkman, J.M. A chronometric analysis of simple addition. *Psychological Review* 79, 329–43, 1972.

Groen, G.J., & Poll, M. Subtraction and the solution of open sentence problems. *Journal of Experimental Child Psychology* 16, 292–302, 1973.

Grouws, D.A. Open sentences: Some instructional considerations from research. *Arithmetic Teacher* 19, 595–99, 1972.

Hendrickson, A.D. An inventory of mathematical thinking done by incoming first-grade children. *Journal for Research in Mathematics Education* 10, 7–23, 1979.

Hiebert, J. The position of the unknown set and children's solution of verbal arithmetic problems. *Journal for Research in Mathematics Education* 13, 341–49, 1982.

Hiebert, J., Carpenter, T.P., & Moser, J. Cognitive development and children's performance on addition and subtraction problems. *Journal for Research in Mathematics Education* 13, 83–98, 1982.

Houlihan, D.M., & Ginsburg, H. The addition methods of first and second grade children. *Journal for Research in Mathematics Education* 12(2), 95–106, 1981.

Hudson, T. Young children's difficulty with "How many more ... than ... are there?" questions. *Dissertation Abstracts International* 41(01), July, 1980.

Ilg, F., & Ames, L.B. Developmental trends in arithmetic. *Journal of Genetic Psychology* 79, 3–28, 1951.

Kouba, V., & Moser, J. *Development and validation of curriculum units related to initial sentence writing* (Technical Report No. 522). Madison: Wisconsin Research and Development Center for Individualized Schooling, 1979.

Lindvall, C.M., & Ibarra, C.G. *A clinical investigation of the difficulties evidenced by kindergarten children in developing "models" for the solution of arithmetic story problems.* Paper presented at the annual meeting of the American Educational Research Association, Boston, April 1980.

Moser, J.M., & Carpenter, T.P. *Using the microcomputer to teach problem solving skills: Program development and initial pilot study* (Working Paper No. 328). Madison: Wisconsin Center for Education Research, 1982.

Neches, R. *Models of heuristic procedure modification.* Unpublished doctoral dissertation, Carnegie-Mellon University, 1981.

Nelson, D. Problem solving in a model for early mathematics learning. In A.R. Osborne (Ed.), *Models for learning mathematics.* Columbus OH: ERIC Clearinghouse for Science, Mathematics, and Environmental Education, 1976.

Nesher, P.A. Levels of description in the analysis of addition and subtraction. In T.P. Carpenter, J.M. Moser, & T.A. Romberg (Eds.), *Addition and subtraction: A cognitive perspective.* Hillsdale, NJ: Lawrence Erlbaum Associates, 1982.

Nesher, P., Greeno, J.G., & Riley, M.S. The development of semantic categories for addition and subtraction. *Educational Studies in Mathematics* 13, 373–94, 1982.

Nesher, P.A., & Katriel, T. A semantic analysis of addition and subtraction word problems in arithmetic. *Educational Studies in Mathematics* 8, 251–70, 1977.

Paige, J.M., & Simon, H.A. Cognitive processes in solving algebra word problems. In B. Klein-muntz (Ed.), *Problem solving: Research, method, and theory*. New York: John Wiley & Sons, 1966.

Reckzeh, J. Addition and subtraction situations. *Arithmetic Teacher* **3**, 94–97, 1956.

Resnick, L.B. A developmental theory of number understanding. In H.P. Ginsburg (Ed.), *The development of mathematical thinking*. New York: Academic Press, 1983.

Riley, M.S. *Conceptual and procedural knowledge in development*. Unpublished master's thesis, University of Pittsburgh, 1981.

Riley, M.S., Greeno, J.G., & Heller, J.I. Development of children's problem-solving ability in arithmetic. In H.P. Ginsburg (Ed.), *The development of mathematical thinking*. New York: Academic Press, 1983.

Romberg, T.A., & Collis, K.F. Cognitive level and performance on addition and subtraction prob-lems. In *Proceedings of the Fourth International Congress for the Psychology of Mathematics Education*. Boston: Birkhauser, 1983.

Romberg, T.A., Harvey, J.G., Moser, J.M., & Montgomery, M.E. *Developing mathematical pro-cesses*. Chicago: Rand McNally, 1974.

Rosenthal, D.J.A., & Resnick, L.B. Children's solution processes in arithmetic word problems. *Journal of Educational Psychology* **66**, 817–25, 1974.

Schell, L.M., & Burns, P.C. Pupil performance with three types of subtraction situations. *School Science and Mathematics* **63**, 208–14, 1962.

Secada, W.G., Fuson, K.C., & Hall, J.W. The transition from counting-all to counting-on in addition. *Journal for Research in Mathematics Education* **14**, 47–57, 1983.

Shores, J.H., & Underhill, R.G. *An analysis of kindergarten and first grade children's addition and subtraction problem solving modeling and accuracy*. Paper presented at the annual meeting of the American Educational Research Association, San Francisco, April 1976. (ERIC Document Reproduction Service No. ED 121 626)

Sophian, C., Larkin, J.H., & Kadane, J.B. *A developmental model of search: Stochastic estimation of children's rule use*. Paper presented at the meeting of the Society for Research in Child Development, Detroit, 1983.

Starkey, P., & Gelman, R. The development of addition and subtraction abilities prior to formal schooling in arithmetic. In T.P. Carpenter, J.M. Moser, & T.A. Romberg (Eds.), *Addition and subtraction: A cognitive perspective*. Hillsdale, NJ: Lawrence Erlbaum Associates, 1982.

Steffe, L.P., Thompson, D.W., & Richards, J. Children's counting in arithmetical problem solv-ing. In T.P. Carpenter, J.M. Moser, & T.A. Romberg (Eds.), *Addition and subtraction: A cognitive perspective*. Hillsdale, NJ: Lawrence Erlbaum Associates, 1982.

Steffe, L.P., von Glasersfeld, E., Richards, J., & Cobb, P. *Children's counting types: Philosophy, theory, and application*. New York: Praeger, 1984.

Stephens, W.M. *Mathematical knowledge and school work: A case study of the teaching of developing mathematical processes* (Project Report). Madison: Wisconsin Center for Educa-tion Research, 1982.

Svenson, O. Analysis of time required by children for simple additions. *Acta Psychologica* **39**, 389–400, 1975.

Van Engen, H. An analysis of meaning in arithmetic. *Elementary School Journal* **49**, 321–29, 395–402, 1949.

Weaver, J.F. Some factors associated with pupil's performance levels on simple open addition and subtraction sentences. *Arithmetic Teacher* **18**, 513–19, 1971.

Woods, S.S., Resnick, L.B., & Groen, G.J. An experimental test of five process models for subtrac-tion. *Journal of Educational Psychology* **67**, 17–21, 1975.

Methodological Considerations In Research on Mathematical Problem-Solving Instruction

Frank K. Lester, Jr.

Indiana University

Several years ago I had the rare good fortune to hear George Polya talk about teaching problem solving at a meeting of the American Mathematical Society. I remember quite vividly his closing remarks. He said that mathematics teachers must bear in mind that their primary goal is to get their students to "use their heads." I must confess that at that time I was a bit disappointed with so "simplistic" a piece of advice. In retrospect I see his advice as both simple and profound because his message is one that seems not to be heeded in most problem-solving instruction. The message is that the ultimate goal of instruction in mathematical problem solving is to enable students to think for themselves. It is my view that most problem-solving instruction not only does not enable students to use their heads, but in fact it does more harm than good. Let me give an example from my own research with elementary schoolchildren to support this position.

The following problem is typical of a class of problems I call "process" problems that I have used in my research with third- and fifth-grade students:

> Tom and Sue visited a farm and noticed there were chickens and pigs.
> Tom said, "There are 18 animals." Sue said, "Yes, and they have 52 legs in all." How many of each kind of animal were there?

In a recently completed study I found that almost all third-graders "solved" this problem by adding 18 and 52 and most fifth-graders attempted to solve it by dividing 52 by 18 (Lester & Garofalo, 1982). When questioned about their solutions, the third-graders typically responded with something like "It asks 'how many *in all*' so you add." The fifth-graders were guided by what was for them equally as compelling a method of attack. They often said, "It says 'in all' but you don't add because that would be legs plus animals. The key words are 'how many of each,' so you divide." Another distressing aspect of the fifth-graders' methods was that many of them wrote 52 ÷ 18 and stopped because "you can't take 18 into 52." They sensed something was wrong but felt powerless to do anything but give up. For both third- and fifth-graders, even when they were made aware that their answers were incorrect, they were unable to devise an alternative procedure for attacking the problem.

Over the years I have asked quite a large number of third-, fourth-, and fifth-graders to try to solve this problem. The overwhelming majority have tried to "crunch the numbers" to get an answer. Very few (less than 1 in 20) have approached the problem by trial-and-error, estimation, or similar strategies. In general, these children have an extremely limited repertoire of skills (both tactical and strategic) at their disposal for attacking mathematical problems. Four principles guide their problem-solving behavior:

1. Problem difficulty is determined by the size of the numbers and how many numbers there are.

2. All mathematics problems can be solved by direct application of one or more arithmetic operations.

3. Which operations to use is determined by the key words in the problem (these key words usually appear in the last sentence or question).

4. Whether or not to check computations depends upon the availability of time. For story problems, only computations need to be checked.

As it happens, this approach to solving verbal mathematics problems works for nearly all the "exercises" these children are asked to solve in school. Furthermore, since it is the only approach they know, they use it to solve any problems, even when it is inefficient or inappropriate. The most troubling aspect of this example is that the problem-solving behavior exhibited by these children may be a direct result of instruction—by either the teacher or the textbook. These children have become mentally handicapped to solve problems that involve anything more than direct use of an arithmetic operation.

The problem obviously is not confined to the elementary grades. Those of us who have taught university students know that they have some of the same difficulties as younger students and some other deficiencies as well. An illustration of one particularly prevalent deficiency is related by Koplowitz (1979). He gave the following problem to a group of undergraduates in a Math Learning Skills course:

> I go to a certain place at 40 miles per hour and it takes me 20 minutes to get there. I return at 50 miles per hour. How long does the return trip take? (p. 305)

Koplowitz reported that a variety of incorrect solutions based on faulty reasoning of one sort or another were offered by his students (15, 17½, and 25 minutes were among the most common incorrect answers). Furthermore, when students discussed their solutions, they were not at all surprised that several different solutions were presented. As Koplowitz put it:

> I was able to lead the group to see the correct answer to the problem. My way of solving the problem did not, however, appear to seem more logical to the students than their own ways. I think they saw my method as one more way of coming to an answer to the problem, but a way which had the stamp of the authority's approval. (pp. 305–6).

One point Koplowitz was making was that, although his students had all the necessary skills at their disposal, they were unable to determine *when* they had solved the problem. These students stopped work on the problem when they felt they had solved it. Also, as often as not, they were just as confident in their wrong answers as Koplowitz was in his correct one. Clearly, something important was lacking in the type of instruction in problem solving they had experienced.

Of course, I could easily devote this entire paper to accounts of difficulties individuals have in solving mathematics problems. My purpose in discussing these two examples is not to point out how poor many people are at solving problems, but rather to provide perspective for the discussion of problem-solving research which will follow. There is a very real danger that the type of mathematics instruction we provide students is training them to be rigid in their thinking, not *flexible* and *adaptable*, is teaching them how to perform procedures but not *when* and under what conditions to perform them, and is showing them what to do but not *why* to do it.

Mayer (1982) has suggested that at least four types of knowledge are involved in successful problem solving in mathematics: linguistic and factual, schematic, algorithmic, and strategic. According to him, schematic and strategic knowledge have been ignored in most mathematics instruction. I agree, but the real shortcoming of instruction involves much more than this. Even if instruction did not ignore schematic and strategic knowledge, it would still fall far short of its potential. In addition to having sufficient domain-general and domain-specific knowledge of the types discussed by Mayer, successful problem solving depends also upon knowing when and how to utilize such knowledge and upon having the ability to monitor and evaluate the application of this knowledge both during and after implementation. Furthermore, the problem solver's "belief system" plays an important role as well (Schoenfeld, 1983a). When faced with a mathematics problem to be solved, competent problem solvers will assess its scope and goals and estimate their chances of success. They will consider alternate plans of attack, decide on an initial plan, choose and engage in appropriate tactics to implement the plan, and monitor and evaluate both the progress and outcome of the chosen tactics and plan. If deemed necessary, they will modify or replace the tactics, abandon and replace the initial plan, and reassess the scope of the problem. In short, quite a bit more is involved than possessing a repertoire of skills, facts, algorithms, and strategies, in much the same way that being a good tennis player involves more than knowing how to keep score and having a strong serve, a good overhead, and sound ground strokes. This repertoire is essential but not sufficent.

To date, with very few exceptions (viz., Schoenfeld, 1983b; Silver, Branca, & Adams, 1980; Stengel, LeBlanc, Jacobson, & Lester, 1977), research on mathematical problem-solving instruction has focused on the discrete skills and procedures (tactics) involved in problem solving and has ignored the managerial aspects (e.g., executive strategies) which serve as "guiding forces" (Lester, 1982; Schoenfeld 1983a; Silver, 1982). In addition, too little attention has been paid to the total environment in which problem solving takes place. Kantowski (1982) has pointed out that a student's problem-solving ability develops slowly over time and the numerous skills and procedures involved develop at different rates. The growth of problem-solving ability, then, should be studied longitudinally, the teacher should be considered a part of the environment, and attempts should be made to catch processes as they are developing rather than looking for their presence at the end of a predetermined period of time. What is being suggested is that more emphasis be placed on the design and conduct of "teaching experiments" (Kantowski, 1978). (More will be said about teaching experiments later in this paper.)

This paper offers a discussion of selected recent (within the past 10 years) problem-solving instruction research and provides suggestions as to how it should be studied in the future. The paper is not a literature review but rather is a position paper focusing on research methodology. That is, the focus is on *how to study* questions associated with mathematical problem-solving instruction.

WHAT ARE THE KEY QUESTIONS?

Questions related to problem-solving instruction are inextricably tied up with many other questions about the nature of problem solving in mathematics. At the risk of over-simplifying, I wish to suggest that three main questions constitute the core of all mathematical problem-solving research:

1. What does the individual do, both correctly and incorrectly (efficiently and inefficiently) during problem solving?

2. What should the individual be able to do?

3. How can individual problem-solving ability be improved?

The first question calls for the development of both competency and performance models of problem-solving behavior as well as developmental models. Far too little is known about the nature of the problem-solving abilities of individuals. Models of competent problem solvers can serve not only to indicate what good problem solvers do, but also to point out the deficiencies in the problem-solving behavior of novice or poor problem solvers. Performance models, on the other hand, provide information about what "typical" individuals do—the types of misconceptions they have and errors they make, as well as the types of strategies they naturally employ. Also, although we know individuals' problem-solving abilities change dramatically over time in qualitative ways, the specific character of these changes is not well understood. Before useful models of instruction can be developed we must have useful models of how individuals solve problems without instruction. Efforts in this direction are promising.

The second question should be approached from two directions. One direction involves the systematic analysis of task variables. A big first step has been taken by the researchers involved in the writing of the excellent monograph edited by Goldin and McClintock (1979), which identifies and describes several categories of task variables. As Kulm (1979) points out in his paper in the monograph, the study of task variables has direct implications for problem-solving instruction. In order to maximize the potential benefits of instruction, it is important for teachers to be fully aware of characteristics of the problems they are asking students to solve, which characteristics are likely to pose difficulties and, in general, in what ways problem characteristics affect performance. It is especially important that attention be given to the analysis of the cognitive demands a particular class of problems makes on a particular type of problem solver. Such analyses would make it possible to identify potential sources of difficulty, to match problems to students' developmental level, and otherwise to design better instruction.

The other direction from which to approach the second question has already been mentioned; that is, to investigate how competent individuals solve problems. It is important to identify those behaviors that characterize good problem solvers in order to establish benchmarks to strive for in developing instructional methods. Such knowledge might even alter the emphases of instruction. For example, the work of Larkin and her associates (Larkin, 1980; Larkin, McDermott, Simon, & Simon, 1980) has led to the creation of models of physics problem solving that serve to describe what experts do differently from novices. Among other things, her work suggests that a main difficulty in solving physics problems lies not with *applying* principles, but rather with *selecting* which principles to apply. This is a major source of the difference between expert and novice physics problem solvers. If this observation is valid for mathematics problem solvers as well, it suggests that more emphasis in instruction should be given to helping students acquire useful strategy-selection procedures. (While it is important to identify behaviors that distinguish good problem solvers from poor ones, it is far from axiomatic to assume that these behaviors can be taught.)

The third question is a natural consequent of the first two. Once we know what a class of individuals can and cannot do and what they should be able to do in order to be successful, we then ask, "How can we bring their behavior to be more like that of good problem solvers?" This, of course, is a question of instruction. The next two sections provide a look at some ways in which this question has been and should be addressed.

STUDIES OF PROBLEM-SOLVING INSTRUCTION

Until recently, most problem-solving instruction research could be classified into four categories: (1) instruction to develop master thinking strategies (e.g., originality and creativity training); (2) instruction in the use of specific "tool skills" (e.g., making a table, organizing data, writing an equation); (3) instruction in the use of specific heuristics (e.g., looking for a pattern, working backward); and (4) instruction in the use of general heuristics (e.g., means-end analysis, planning). As might be expected, none of these four approaches has been shown to be clearly superior to the others; rather, good problem-solving instruction probably involves some combination of instruction in the use of both specific and general heuristics together with training to develop tool skills. Also, experience in solving a wide variety of problems over an extended period of time seems to be essential (Lester, 1980, 1983).

But, as has been pointed out earlier in this paper, even an ideal combination of these approaches might fall far short of the mark unless attention also was given to the "guiding forces" of problem solving (i.e., the metacognitive aspects). In the final section of this paper the role of metacognition in problem solving is considered at some length, so I will not elaborate on it at this point. Instead, I will discuss what I believe are the primary stumbling blocks for mathematics students when they solve problems, and then I will describe two related studies in which I have been involved, to illustrate how problem-solving instruction can be studied in real classroom settings.

Stumbling Blocks to Successful Problem Solving

A discussion of the major stumbling blocks encountered by problem solvers (especially novices) can be organized around the four phases of problem solving specified by Polya (1957): understanding, planning, carrying out the plan, and looking back. It is my judgment that instruction that enables students to avoid or overcome these blocks would be very effective.

Understanding

Hayes and Simon (1977) have suggested that understanding involves two things.

First, he [the problem solver] must read the sentences of the text and extract information from them by grammatical and semantic analysis. Second, he must construct from the newly extracted information a representation of the problem that is adequate for its solution. This representation must include the initial conditions of the problem, its goal, and the operators for reaching the goal from the initial state. (p. 21)

A distinguishing characteristic of expert problem solvers is that they spend considerably more time than novices in developing meaningful representations of problems and in marshaling their resources before taking specific action. Novice problem solvers tend to be impulsive, seek closure prematurely, and base their problem representations on syntactic information and contextual details. Thus, the first, and biggest, stumbling block for novices is that they devote too little attention to gaining an adequate degree of understanding of problems before planning and executing their plans.

Planning and Carrying Out Plans

Results of my own research with elementary school students indicate that children in the age range of 9–12 years can be taught several rather sophisticated problem-solving strategies (Lester, 1978; Stengel et al., 1977). There is nothing surprising in this observation when one considers the instructional approach employed. My colleagues and I have found that if the teacher models the use of a strategy for students and then asks them to solve a different problem whose solution can be obtained by using the modeled strategy, the students do very well. This may make the students and teacher feel good about the accomplishment, but have they done any problem solving? Probably not! Problem solving takes place when there is uncertainty involved. The major obstacle to success at the planning and implementing stages lies with the difficulties in *recognizing the conditions* under which a strategy can be used effectively and in *selecting a particular strategy* from among two or more alternatives. What is needed in instruction are guidelines to enable the problem solver (*1*) to recognize when a strategy may be useful, (*2*) to select an appropriate strategy when more than one can be used, and (*3*) to execute the strategy correctly. Unfortunately, most instruction has been restricted to the third step. There is also the issue of metacognition at these stages, in particular the sort of managerial activities that help the problem solver decide if progress is being made.

Looking Back

In the final analysis, the success of any instruction can be judged by the extent to which what has been taught generalizes to novel situations. Greeno (1977) has suggested that a problem has been solved with "good understanding" only when the problem solver recognizes the relation of the solution to some general principle. That is, true transfer has taken place only when the problem solver recognizes that task B has certain properties in common with a previously solved task A. It is likely that little transfer will take place unless direct attention is given in instruction to having students look back at what they have done with an eye toward answering the question, "What have I learned by solving this problem?" It is not enough to train students to "check their work" and make sure the solution satisfies all conditions of the problem. It is at least as important for the problem solver to identify the key features of a solution effort which may prove to be useful in future problem solving. A step in the direction of making students better able to look back at their efforts might be for teachers to focus more attention on solution attempts and less on correct answers. Post-problem-solving sessions in which students share their attempts and discuss reasons for their actions might be one way to bring about this change in focus.

Indiana University's Mathematical Problem Solving Project

The Mathematical Problem Solving Project (MPSP) existed for 2 years (1974–76) under the cosponsorship of Indiana University and the National Council of Teachers of Mathematics, with funding from the National Science Foundation. The main goal of the MPSP was to develop instructional materials for improving the problem-solving performance of children in Grades 4, 5, and 6. In particular, the emphasis was on improving children's abilities to use certain heuristics (e.g., looking for patterns), tool skills (e.g., making a table), and other problem-solving tactics to solve a wide range of types of elementary school mathematics problems. The activities of the MPSP are detailed fully in the final report to the National Science Foundation by LeBlanc and Kerr (1977).

Although the MPSP was primarily a curriculum development effort, several small-scale research studies sprang from questions which arose as work progressed. A great deal of attention was given to observing individual and small-group problem solving. In addition, many children were interviewed both during and after problem-solving sessions and their written work was closely scrutinized in order to gain insights into the problem-solving behavior of children in this age range.

Three members of the MPSP staff devoted the entire second year of the project's operation to an investigation of the hypothesis that children become better problem solvers simply by solving problems with relatively little direct instruction by the teacher. More specifically, the goals of this investigation were to:

1. Reduce impulsivity on the part of the children (i.e., the tendency to "crunch numbers" and generally to fail to gain "good" understanding of the problem statement before beginning to try to solve the problem).

2. Make the children aware that most problems can be solved in more than one way.

3. Decrease the children's tendency toward premature closure (e.g., make them aware that many interesting problems take more than 1 or 2 minutes to solve).

4. Make the children aware that some problems may have more than one correct answer while others may have no answer due to insufficient information.

5. Help the children realize the importance of—and gain skill in—organizing information.

6. Increase the children's willingness to engage in problem solving.

This list of goals indicates that the overall aims of the study were affective and metacognitive in spirit. It was felt that students must bring appropriate willingness and motivation to a problem-solving situation, but positive attitudes toward problem solving are not sufficient for developing good problem-solving behaviors. At the same time, making students more aware of and knowledgeable about their cognitive processes helps them manage and monitor their own problem-solving activities.

The investigation proceeded in three stages. The first stage involved work with two groups of six fifth-graders once or twice per week for 8 weeks. One group of six children worked individually or in pairs as they chose. Children in the other group were asked to work together, to share ideas, and to ask questions of one another. Students were asked to write down as much detail of their work as possible, and each session was either audio- or video-taped. During each session a problem was read to the group and questions concerning the problem statement were answered by the teacher. As the children worked on the problem, the teacher (an MPSP staff member) was available to answer questions of a general nature only. In a few sessions the teacher experimented with giving hints, initiating group discussion, and posing questions to refocus students' attention on relevant information in the problem. Two observers were present at each session, and immediately following a session the observers and teacher discussed what took place and analyzed the students' papers. The purpose of this stage was to develop a scheme for engaging an entire classroom of children in problem solving that would involve relatively little teacher direction. Secondary purposes were to determine what sort of teacher input would be most appropriate given the goals of the study and to select a set of suitable problems. Details of the instructional scheme, the role of the teacher, and the problems chosen are given in the report by Stengel et al. (1977).

The format that was used in the next two stages contained three phases: (*1*) Problem Presentation, (*2*) Solution Effort, and (*3*) Problem and Solution Discussion. Desirable teacher and student behaviors at each phase plus the intended outcomes are listed in Table 1.

Table 1. Desirable Teacher and Student Behaviors and Intended Outcomes for Three Phases of Instruction.

Phase	Intended outcome	Teacher behavior	Student behavior
Problem Presentation	Students develop appropriate understanding of the problem.	• Presents problem to class. • Answers questions about problem comprehension. • Organizes students to begin work on the problem.	• Reads and/or listens to problem statement. • Asks questions for clarification. • Records pertinent information.
Solution Effort	Students develop and implement a plan for solving the problem.	• Encourages students to share ideas with others. • Poses questions to refocus students' attention on relevant information. • Provides hints to help students make progress (only as a last resort).	• Works alone or with peers on problem.
Problem and Solution Discussion	Students gain new "insights" into the problem and "good" problem-solving behavior.	• Allows students (3–5) to demonstrate their solution. • Points out the importance of checking work. • Aids in bringing to light any possible generalizations.	• Offers to discuss his or her solution. • Listens/discusses others' solutions. • Attempts to identify generalizations. • Attempts to analyze what worked and why.

Stages 2 and 3 of the investigation consisted of two short-term experiments. The first experiment involved one third-grade, four fourth-grade, and three fifth-grade classes ranging from 22 to 28 students in each class. Teachers of these classes were the students' regular teachers and represented a wide range of experience and styles. Over a 5-week period the students in these classes worked on ten problems using the instructional procedure outlined in the preceding paragraph. The purposes of this experiment were to gather data regarding the effectiveness of various teacher behaviors as well as to observe student behavior in large group settings. Conclusions drawn from observations of problem-solving sessions were that the children were eager to work on the problems and they had little difficulty adjusting to a classroom environment which was less teacher-directed than usual. However, teachers experienced a great deal of uneasiness. Several found it difficult initially to keep from telling students what to do. For example, these teachers were uncomfortable at first in responding to questions like "Does this mean to add?" or "Is this right?" with "I can't tell you; try to decide for yourself" or "Compare your solution with Billy's." The final phase, Problem and Solution Discussion, was the least successful phase of the three for teachers. Often they were unsure of how directive they should be in modeling good strategies or in accepting student efforts no matter how naive. Frequently they were unable to identify any possible generalizations.

Despite the lack of success with phase 3 of the instructional scheme, students' problem-solving behavior improved dramatically. In order to measure behavior changes, a post-test consisting of two "process" problems was administered to samples of experimental and control students. Members of the MPSP staff who were not involved in the study were asked to analyze the students' work in terms of (1) use of an appropriate strategy, (2) use of relevant information in the problem, and (3) evidence of planning and evaluating. These evaluators were asked to sort the papers into three piles: papers of experimental students, papers of control students, and indeterminate papers. Sixty-four percent of the experimental students' papers were placed in the correct pile, whereas only 27% of the papers of control students were placed in the experimental group pile. Though this sort of evaluation was informal and fraught with shortcomings, it did suggest that solving problems does improve problem-solving ability.

After making some modifications in the instructional procedures, a second teaching experiment was conducted using one sixth-grade, three fifth-grade, and two fourth-grade classes (all different from classes involved previously). Class sizes were about the same as in the first experiment with the exception of the sixth-grade class, which had 16 students. Teachers had the same general characteristics as those in the earlier study. During a 4-week period the six classes worked on 15 problems as time permitted. An added feature of this study was that 14 of the problems were chosen as seven pairs, with each pair being equivalent with respect to one or more factors. These factors were context, mathematical structure, type of information provided, and size of numbers in the problem statements. Pairing of problems was done to facilitate an unobtrusive examination of student growth.

As in the first experiment, the Discussion phase remained problematic for teachers. Perhaps this is to be expected, since it is difficult to teach students to analyze and generalize, and teachers are rarely required by the mathematics (or other) textbooks they use to engage students in these types of activities. Consequently, it was unreasonable to expect much success without providing teachers with in-service training.

Notwithstanding the difficulties inherent in the instructional scheme, the results of the second experiment, like the first, were very encouraging. Students were enthusiastic, and evidence was found of changes in their manner of attacking problems. Also, from an analysis of students' work, there was a discernible change from the first to the second problem of the paired problems. Interviews with both teachers and students supported this observation. It was common to hear remarks from students like "We've done this one before except the days are different." In some cases as much as 4 weeks had elapsed between the first and second problems, yet memory for both contextual details and appropriate solution strategies was high. In most cases the second problem had become a routine exercise.

In general, each of the six goals was achieved to some extent. At the same time evidence was found that problem-solving ability is facilitated significantly by solving problems. The fact that student growth was widespread for both studies in spite of the failure of the Problem and Solution Discussion phase adds additional weight to this claim. Formal instruction in the sense of teacher modeling appropriate solution behaviors was never consciously employed, yet virtually every child improved in either or both of the cognitive and affective domains.

The West Virginia Study: A Refinement of the MPSP Model

During the 1980–81 school year an evaluation was conducted of an instructional program based on the MPSP model. This program included the following features not found in the MPSP: complete sets of instructional materials for problem solving; guidelines concerning how to create a classroom atmosphere conducive to problem solving, how to group students for instruction, and how to evaluate student performance; and a teaching strategy. The primary purposes of the evaluation were to compare the problem-solving performance of students who had participated in the program to the performance of students whose only exposure to problem solving was that provided by the regular textbook, and to examine the nature of the changes in students' problem-solving performance during the course of a school year (actually 23 weeks). The program was funded by the West Virginia Department of Education through the E.S.E.A. Title IV-C office and involved over 900 students and 44 teachers in Grades 5 and 7 in schools in four West Virginia counties. A detailed description of the program is found in a report by Charles (1982). A discussion of the instructional model is provided by Charles and Lester (1982), and an extensive report of the results of the evaluation of the program is provided by Charles and Lester (1984).

Results from the comparisons of treatment and control groups, trend analyses, and interviews with teachers indicated that the program did promote the improvement of students' problem-solving performance. More particularly, improvement was noted on three measures of problem-solving performance — understanding, planning, and result — for two types of problems — complex translation and process. (Complex translation problems necessitate translating real-world situations into mathematical expressions with more than one translation involved. Process problems lend themselves to exemplifying the processes inherent in thinking through and solving a problem. They cannot be solved by a given group of students simply by translating situations to mathematical expressions.) Five additional conclusions were drawn:

1. The program was more effective with process problems than with complex translation problems, particularly with respect to *understanding* and *planning*.

2. Treatment and control classes did not differ significantly in performance on the result measure on complex translation problems for either Grade 5 or Grade 7. This

may be due to the fact that only one complex translation problem was solved per week by treatment classes. It is reasonable to expect that since both groups had had several years of exposure to complex translation problems, 23 weeks of one complex translation problem per week would not be enough to cause a significant improvement in performance.

3. Performance on understanding and planning measures improved faster than did performance on the result measure for both types of problems and at both grade levels. The slower rate of growth in obtaining correct results suggests that the ability to coordinate successfully newly learned problem-solving skills and processes is a complex task in itself. Learning to perform a skill is one thing; knowing when to use it and how to use it in conjunction with other procedures is quite another.

4. A significant factor in forming teachers' attitudes toward a problem-solving program is the program's structure. In this case, the fact that the program provided a set of guidelines that was specific with respect to teachers' actions had a very positive influence on their attitudes.

5. Among the most important benefits of the program were that the program improved students' willingness to engage in problem solving; students gained confidence in their ability to succeed in problem solving; and in the estimation of the teachers, students were beginning to learn "how to think."

This evaluation distinguished itself from many of the other studies of problem-solving instruction in four ways:

1. It investigated long-term (23 weeks) changes in performance.

2. Performance changes were examined on three measures—understanding, planning, and results.

3. Differences in the nature of performance changes from Grade 5 to Grade 7 were considered.

4. In addition to quantitative measures of performance, teachers' perceptions and opinions about the program were solicited and served as an integral part of the evaluation data.

The findings across grade levels were very consistent; that is, findings at Grade 5 generally held for Grade 7 as well. This observation suggested that the effectiveness of the program may not be unique to a single grade level.

Summary

The MPSP study and the evaluation of the West Virginia program were similar in several ways, as has been pointed out in the preceding discussion. There is another similarity, a similarity in research methodology, which makes a discussion of these two studies particularly appropriate for this paper. Both of them were approximations of "teaching experiments" in the sense characterized by the Soviet Study series of Kilpatrick and Wirszup (1969–75) and Kantowski (1978). Briefly, a teaching experiment has at least the following five traits:

1. It is nonexperimental in design.

2. It takes place over an extended period of time.

3. It attempts to catch processes as they develop.

4. The teacher is not a controlled variable but is a vital part of the classroom environment.

5. Subjective analysis of qualitative data is often of more interest than quantitative analysis (these data involve affective and metacognitive behaviors in addition to cognitive behavior).

If progress is to be made toward establishing sound principles to guide instruction in mathematical problem solving, it will come most likely from research employing methodologies of the teaching experiment variety. The next section is concerned with research methodologies and other related issues.

ISSUES FOR THE FUTURE

Among the trends in the research on problem-solving instruction, four stand out as being especially in need of attention:

1. Shift away from experimental and toward naturalistic methodologies.

2. Increased interest in problem-solving processes in addition to various product variables.

3. Increased interest in the development of problem-solving instructional programs that are "classroom ready."

4. Growing interest in the role of metacognition in problem solving.

These four trends clearly indicate my bias regarding the manner in which problem-solving instruction should be studied.

Adopting a Naturalistic Perspective

Since problem solving is an extremely complex activity involving a wide range of interacting behaviors, and since it is so heavily influenced by a large number of factors, it should be studied *holistically* (as opposed to atomistically). Furthermore, adopting a holistic view of problem solving and problem-solving instruction necessitates the use of naturalistic rather than traditional scientific research paradigms. What I mean by "naturalistic" inquiry deserves some attention. At the risk of oversimplifying a much-discussed issue, a research paradigm is more or less naturalistic depending on the extent to which constraints are imposed on independent, mediating, and dependent variables; or to use the language of naturalistic inquiry, the extent to which constraints are imposed on antecedent conditions and possible outcomes (Willems & Rausch, 1969). An "ideal" naturalistic study would impose a very low degree of constraints on these conditions and outcomes, whereas an "ideal" experimental (scientific) study would impose a high degree of constraints on them. It is probably fair to say that most, if not all, educational research falls somewhere between these two extremes (see Lester & Kerr, 1979, for a somewhat more extensive discussion of research methodology). I do not intend to argue for the merits of naturalistic inquiry; this has been done elsewhere by several individuals (e.g., Bronfenbrenner, 1976; Guba & Lincoln, 1981; Willems & Rausch, 1969; Wolf, 1979). Instead, I wish to point out some of the characteristics of naturalistic research which have come to be associated with, but are not essential parts of, this type of inquiry.

Characteristics of Naturalistic Inquiry

It is my opinion that the typical educational researcher characterizes naturalistic inquiry as follows:

- It relies on *qualitative* methods.

- It eschews rigor for the sake of *relevance*.

- It relies on *tacit* knowledge in the formulation of theory.

- It adopts an *expansionist* (as contrasted with a reductionist) stance toward research.

- Its purpose is to *discover theory* and ground it in real-world data rather than verify theory.

Reliance Upon Qualitative Methods. Perhaps the most pervasive view of naturalistic inquiry is that it uses qualitative techniques exclusively. There is nothing inherent in the nature of naturalistic inquiry to preclude quantitative methods; rather, the state of our understanding of the phenomena that typically are investigated naturalistically has necessitated the use of qualitative methods. That is, it is the nature of what is being studied, not how it is being studied, that determines the type of data that should be collected. Problem solving is a complex form of behavior; as a result, the degree of our understanding of problem solving has been considerably less than that of simpler forms of behavior. A consequence of this lack of understanding has been a corresponding lack of valid and reliable instruments for measuring any but the most routine aspects of performance. Since the use of quantitative methods assumes the existence of satisfactory measurement instruments, present-day problem-solving researchers have seen a need to abandon quantitative methods in favor of qualitative ones. In most studies of problem-solving instruction it is likely to be the case that both qualitative and quantitative methods can be employed. However, we must be careful when we assign numbers to measure problem-solving behaviors that the instruments being used actually measure what we want them to measure.

Relevance Versus Rigor. Scientific (or experimental) research relies heavily on rigor (i.e., internal and external validity, reliability, and objectivity) as a primary criterion of quality. It does not follow, however, that naturalistic research is not equally as concerned about rigor. On the contrary, rigor is important for both domains of inquiry. It does seem fair to say that naturalistic inquiry is more concerned with relevance than scientific inquiry is.

Tacit Knowledge as a Basis of Theory Development. Intuitions, hunches, apprehensions, and other types of knowledge that cannot be stated in words are acceptable for the purpose of theory development in naturalistic research. By contrast, until quite recently, most scientific behavioral research has steadfastly avoided tacit knowledge and other subjective data. It is due largely to the acceptance of tacit knowledge as data that naturalistic inquiry has gained a reputation as being "soft" research. The use of tacit knowledge and other subjective information is vital to naturalistic research. Indeed, it can be argued that hunches stemming from thoughtful reflection have been the primary sources in the discovery of new knowledge throughout history. Nevertheless, it behooves all researchers to attempt to formulate explicit, unambiguous statements about the phenomena they are studying. The use of naturalistic methods does not obviate the value of clarity and precision of expression.

Expansionist Versus Reductionist Stance. Scientific researchers tend to reduce their inquiry to a relatively small focus by imposing constraints on the variables involved for the sake of control. Consequently, these researchers start with preformulated questions and they search for information that will answer those questions. This may be a desirable approach if it is clear which variables should be controlled, which questions should be asked, and how answers can be obtained. However, naturalistic inquirers tend to view phenomena holistically and try to avoid placing constraints on variables whenever possible. Instead of restricting their focus they believe that for complex phenomena, the whole may be quite different from the sum of its parts. Thus, the naturalistic researcher can be considered as having an expansionist view.

Discovery Versus Verification. It is a widely held belief that naturalistic research is appropriate *only* when the field of inquiry is "sloppy" and ill-defined (as much has been said about the field of problem solving). This view suggests that naturalistic inquiry should be conducted only at the early stages of research in a field; that is, at the stages when good ideas are difficult to come by and the body of knowledge is weak. Furthermore, when the rudiments of a theory begin to emerge it is believed to be best to shift to scientific methods in order to begin testing the theory. Glaser and Strauss (1967) argue that a more sensible approach is to derive theory by grounding it in real-world data from the start and to continue this approach thoughout the development of the theory. It is their position that "grounded" theory not only has the desirable attribute of relevance but, like a priori theories, it provides a basis for predictions, explanations, and applications. Thus naturalistic inquiry is not "preresearch" that serves only to help the researcher cope with a muddled field of inquiry; rather, it is a legitimate, in many cases preferred, research mode in its own right.

Naturalistic Inquiry and Mathematical Problem-Solving Research

The foregoing discussion of naturalistic inquiry is meant to provide perspective about the manner in which research in mathematical problem-solving instruction should be conducted. In the past 5 or so years much has been written about the need to get away from our reliance on quantitative measures of problem-solving performance. As is often true in education, we are in danger of throwing out the baby with the bathwater. Yes, let us adopt a process-oriented focus and employ qualitative techniques of data analysis, but we must realize that much can be gained from also using the quantitative methods that have been useful in our pursuit of knowledge in other areas.

The issue of relevance versus rigor was raised because it is vital that, as more and more researchers begin to employ naturalistic methods, there be a realization that good naturalistic research is much more difficult to conduct than experimental research. Consequently, it might be argued that rigor and attention to detail are even more important for the naturalistic inquirer than the experimentalist. Most of us who are currently engaged in mathematical problem-solving research were trained in our graduate studies in the use of various quantitative techniques and in the design of experimental research. But how many of us have ever taken a course in interviewing techniques or the design and conduct of naturalistic research? Rigor is a necessary ingredient of any type of scholarly inquiry; let us be sure to keep this in mind as we continue our investigations of problem solving.

A respected colleague once told me that "the reason we do educational research is that most of us don't have the intuition of a good teacher and good teachers don't know how to tell us what they know." In my view an ultimate goal of research on teaching mathematical problem solving is to develop instructional theories that contain the essence of what it is that a good teacher does. Most of us presently engaged in research in this area are experienced mathematics teachers, many of us were (are) even good ones. It would be wrong not to take advantage of the collective tacit knowledge (intuition and "common sense") that has accrued from our teaching experiences. In this regard, at least, we have a big advantage over those cognitive psychologists who are trying to derive theories of mathematics learning.

Attempts to create models of problem-solving behavior have become extremely popular in recent years among cognitive psychologists and mathematics educators. This development may be well and good, but we must keep in mind that model-building must take place within the structure of a theory. If the theory is ambiguous, the resulting model will be at least as ambiguous. Adopting a global, expansionist stance toward problem solving may make theory development, and hence model-building, a much slower process than might be the case with a more focused, reductionist stance. To put it another way, it is easier to create a theory about or to model a small portion of a complex phenomenon than to develop a theory or model of the entire phenomenon. Thus, we must be aware that the development of sound and relevant models of mathematical problem solving is likely to be extremely slow going.

Finally, there is the issue of theory. Should we be in the business of theory development or theory verification? In my mind, there is no question but that theory development should take precedence. This is not to suggest that extant theories should not be verified, but rather that current theories of problem solving are tied to particular perspectives about cognition and hence are limited in their potential for studying the whole spectrum of processes involved in solving problems. Lin (1979) provides a nice illustration of this point:

> Consider a student and a teacher in a room, talking about physics, being observed by a behaviorist, a Piagetian, and a psychoanalyst. When they record a signficant event in the interaction, they ring a bell. Under these circumstances, they probably will not ring their bells in synchronization; each person has his own view of what constitutes a significant interaction and what is irrelevant. (p. 15)

Furthermore, existing theories of problem solving developed by cognitive psychologists provide little help when it comes to questions related to instruction. A big question for many cognitive psychologists interested in problem-solving instruction revolves around the teachability of *general* problem-solving skills. The dichotomy regarding the domain-independence versus the domain-specificity of problem solving is central to most of their research. Unfortunately, not only has cognitive psychology not provided any prescriptions for instruction that have broad application to mathematics classrooms, it has yet to come up with a reasonable (let alone relevant) theory of problem-solving instruction.

A top priority in developing a theory of instruction must be placed on the articulation of the tacit components of what "experts" know and do. (I refer to "experts" in the sense preferred by Schoenfeld [1982]. He makes an interesting distinction between expertise and "mere" proficiency.) This focus involves more than pursuing an answer to the second of the three key questions I raised earlier, the question of what the individual should be able to do. It does indeed mean that models of competent problem solving are needed, but it also means that models of competent *teaching* of problem solving are needed. We will make no progress toward developing practical guidelines for mathematics teachers to follow until we are able to make explicit that knowledge about teaching that good teachers have internalized and made "second nature." This articulation will require us to spell out in detail what good teachers mean when they say students learned "how to think" or when they say, "I know good problem solving when I see it." It should be obvious that a theory of instruction capable of this level of articulation would have great relevance for mathematics instruction at every level. This type of theory development would have to be grounded in data gathered from extensive observations of "real" teachers teaching "real" students "real" mathematics in "real" classrooms. That is, what we should be after is grounded theories of instruction created from empirical data coming from observations of problem-solving instruction in natural classroom settings.

Categories of Factors Related to Problem-Solving Instruction

The decision to employ a naturalistic paradigm to study problem-solving instruction does not preclude the need to give thoughtful consideration to the factors involved. In fact, if we are interested in studying the influence of instruction on certain student behaviors it seems appropriate to identify, however tentatively, categories of possible antecedents of those behaviors.[1] The best analysis of the factors involved in mathematical problem-solving instruction has been done by Kilpatrick (1978). Although his categories are specifically restricted to research on teaching heuristics in mathematics, they are applicable to a large extent to problem-solving instruction in general. A much broader view of the important categories of factors is provided by Dunkin and Biddle (1974) in their

---

1. My colleague at Indiana University, Professor Egon Guba, is a leading proponent of naturalistic inquiry. He has persuaded me that the use of terms like "dependent variable" and "independent variable" represents a built-in bias on the researcher's part. He insists that these terms tend to suggest a cause-effect relationship among variables; a suggestion that is not made when "antecedents" and "outcomes" are used. The idea is at least provocative and is offered in that spirit.

survey of research on teaching. Borrowing liberally from both Kilpatrick and Dunkin and Biddle, I offer my own analysis of the factors relevant to the study of mathematical problem-solving instruction. This analysis is presented schematically in Figure 1. There is nothing particularly new in this analysis, but it is somewhat different from both Kilpatrick's and Dunkin and Biddle's efforts. As shown in Figure 1, there are three broad categories of factors— *Antecedents, Classroom Processes,* and *Outcomes* —with each category having two or more subcategories.

Figure 1. Categories of factors in mathematical problem-solving instruction.

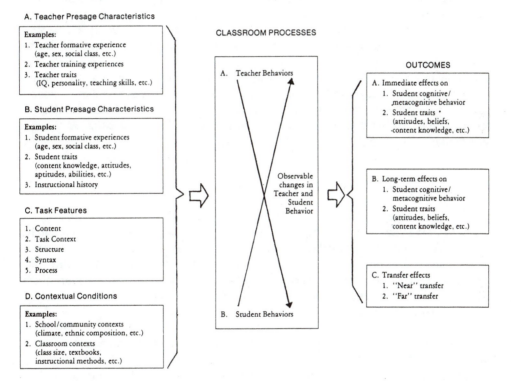

Antecedent Factors

Antecedent factors are of four types: teacher presage characteristics, student presage characteristics, task features, and contextual conditions. *Teacher and student presage characteristics* are the characteristics of teachers and students that may be examined for their effects on the instructional process. As a rule, in experimental research these characteristics have potential for control by the researcher. In naturalistic research they help describe the individuals involved in the study. *Task features* serve to characterize the problems used in both instruction and evaluation. The five types of task features included in this analysis—mathematical content, task context, structure, syntax, and process— are the same as those identified in Goldin and McClintock's (1984) volume on mathematical task variables.

Contextual conditions concern the conditions to which the teacher and students must adapt. A special feature of this type of antecedent is that instructional methods are considered contextual conditions instead of classroom processes. In an experimental study, instructional method typically would be considered an independent variable and the teacher would have to be trained to use the method (or the teacher might be regarded as a part of the instructional method). In both experimental and naturalistic inquiry the instructional method would provide a context within which both teacher and student behavior would take place.

Classroom Processes

Classroom processes have been largely ignored in problem-solving research. This is particularly worrisome since without conscious attention to them no reasonable theory of problem-solving instruction can evolve. These processes are of two types, *teacher behaviors* and *student behaviors,* and refer to what the teacher and students do during instruction and how their actions interact (the crossing arrows in Figure 1 are intended to depict the interaction of teacher and student behaviors). Furthermore, as a result of this interaction various changes in behavior may occur. Referring to the criteria of a "good" problem-solving instruction study I specified earlier, it is by looking for behavior changes resulting from teacher and student interaction that one *observes processes as they are developing.*

Outcomes

The third category consists of three types: *immediate effects on student behavior and traits, long-term effects on behavior and traits,* and *transfer effects*. Unfortunately, most instruction-related research has been focused on short-term effects only. Furthermore, transfer has only rarely been investigated in the problem-solving instruction research conducted by mathematics educators. It would be valuable to know more about *how much* transfer takes place as a result of instruction and, perhaps more importantly, *what* transfer takes place.

Whether or not this analysis represents the best way to identify and classify factors is unimportant. What is important is that the systematic pursuit of a better understanding of how to teach students how to solve problems must include concern about the kinds of factors involved, how these factors are related to each other, and how they may influence instruction. This survey is a "first approximation" of the categories involved and how they interact.

Considerations for Designing Problem-Solving Instruction

The importance of developing students' abilities to solve problems has been unchallenged within the mathematics education community. In recent years mathematics educators have begun to realize that, with few exceptions, the mathematics instruction offered to students does very little to enhance the development of these abilities. As a result, several mathematical problem-solving programs have evolved; some have even been quite good. (To avoid the risk of omitting some of these programs, I will not name any of the ones with which I am familiar. Suffice it to say that I am aware of at least six programs that have come into existence since 1975.) It is probably safe to say that none of these programs has had a strong research basis. That is, none of them has been guided by the results of problem-solving research. This can be attributed either to ignorance on the part of the directors of these programs or to the perception that research has nothing to offer. Whatever the reason, the fact remains that the instructional prescriptions proposed by these programs were derived not from research, but from the folklore of mathematics teaching and learning, which in turn evolved from the common sense and intuition of master teachers such as George Polya (this is the *tacit knowledge* referred to in an earlier section of this paper). In my opinion, this approach has been both inevitable and sensible because it has the advantage of building on contemporary "wisdom" about the nature of mathematical problem solving. However, if a sound body of knowledge about how to teach problem solving is to develop, it will be necessary to abandon this approach in favor of conceptualizations based clearly on empirically verified theory. Furthermore, research involving the evaluation of instructional programs should more closely heed psychological and sociological theories of problem solving in the design and implementation of the evaluation plans.

Sternberg (1983) suggests that the development of "intellectual skills training" programs should be based on a set of eight criteria:

1. The program should be based on a theory of intellectual performance specifying mental processes that has received experimental verification outside the context of the training program.

2. The underlying theory of intellectual performance should be socioculturally relevant to the individuals who are exposed to the training program based on the theory.

3. The program should provide explicit training in both executive and nonexecutive information processing, as well as interactions between the two kinds of information processing.

4. The program should be responsive to motivational as well as to intellectual needs of the students it trains.

5. The program should be sensitive to individual differences.

6. The program should furnish links between the training it provides and real-world behavior.

7. The program should receive careful empirical evaluation that assesses both durability and transferability of training, and the evaluation should assess facets of the training program as well as the training program as a whole.

8. The claims made for the training program should be modest, at least at this point in time. (pp. 6–12)

Sternberg cites several reasons why programs need a set of criteria to guide their development. First, a common set of prerequisites makes possible some degree of uniformity of standards for development, implementation, and evaluation. Also, as I mentioned above, several programs have been developed in the recent past and there are good reasons to believe that more will be created in the future. The time is ripe for establishing some guidelines. Finally, and in my mind most importantly, it is not difficult to imagine that at least some of these programs have the potential for doing considerable harm as well as good. It would be a great service to education if something could be done to help us avoid mistakes before they are committed.

Sternberg, a cognitive-developmental psychologist with particular interests in intelligence and intellectual development, argues the merits of his set of criteria from the perspective of an experimental psychologist who is very much interested in the creation of useful theories of intellectual activity but, at the same time, is also concerned that the knowledge about intellectual performance that has accrued from research has not been heeded in instructional development. These criteria and his discussion of them are provocative and should be considered seriously by anyone planning to develop a mathematical problem-solving instructional program, be it for research purposes or otherwise. I endorse these criteria, but with a few reservations.

Various remarks throughout this paper are evidence of my support for the first criterion, but current theories of intellectual performance that have "received experimental verification outside the context of the program" hold little promise for mathematical problem-solving instruction. The theories to which Sternberg refers are information-processing ones. I am prepared to be dissuaded from my belief but, as far as I can judge, information-processing theories do not incorporate such important components of success in solving problems as beliefs, motivation, and metacognitive activity. That is, there is a great deal involved in mathematical problem solving that presently cannot be modeled using information-processing conceptualizations. Furthermore, to my knowledge, no extant information-processing theory of intellectual performance is grounded in data collected from observations of individuals solving "real" problems in natural contexts.

The sixth criterion raises another caution. The "real-world behavior" referred to is not necessarily the real world of everyday life, but rather the real world to which the instructional program seeks to generalize. Thus, an instructional program aimed at problem solving in elementary algebra may have as its real world the universe of elementary algebra problems. An instructional program that attempts to generalize beyond a rather restricted domain probably is doomed to failure.

Metacognition and Mathematical Problem Solving[2]

The view that metacognitive decisions play a vital role in problem solving is becoming increasingly popular within the mathematics education community (Lesh, 1982; Lester, 1982; Schoenfeld, 1983a; Silver, 1982). To be brief, metacognition refers to an individual's awareness of his or her own cognitive processes and "to the active monitoring and consequent regulation and orchestration of these processes" (Flavell, 1976, p. 232). Thus, metacognition consists of a cognitive self-awareness component and a behavior regulation component. Of particular interest to several researchers outside of mathematics education has been metamemory; that is, the individual's awareness of and ability to regulate information storage and retrieval processes. Flavell and Wellman (1977) have identified three metamemory-relevant classes of variables as influencing performance on memory tasks: person, task, and strategy variables. Person variables include both knowledge of enduring properties such as the capacities and limitations of human

---

2. This section is a modification of an excerpt from a paper by Garofalo and Lester (1983).

memory, as well as the more transient processes involved in the monitoring and inter-preting of one's immediate mnemonic states. Task variables include knowledge about the factors and conditions that make some retrieval tasks more difficult than others—why some information is harder to store and also why some information is harder to retrieve. Strategy variables refer to the knowledge of storage and retrieval strategies — both strategies to prepare for future retrieval as well as strategies to facilitate present retrieval.

The metamemory-relevant knowledge and behaviors listed above seem to corres-pond to the more general functions attributed to the executive components in many information-processing models (e.g., Atkinson & Shiffrin, 1968; Butterfield & Belmont, 1975; Case, 1974; Hayes-Roth, 1980; Sternberg, 1980). Indeed, Brown (1978) believes that the metacognitive skills involved in the intelligent control of one's actions while engaging in a memory task are not necessarily different from those involved in success-fully performing other problem-solving tasks. In particular, such knowledge and skills seem not unlike many of those needed to be successful in solving mathematical tasks. Consequently, the three classes of metamemory variables identified by Flavell and Wellman also seem to be relevant to the study of the more general notion of metacognition.

One reasonable way to begin to study the role metacognition plays in mathematical problem solving is to identify a model of problem solving into which a metacognitive component can be incorporated. Several models of problem solving have been created but, unfortunately, most of them are only grossly descriptive of the process of solving problems (Lester, 1978). The prototypic model upon which most recent mathematical problem-solving research has been based is Polya's (1957) four-phase model. A brief overview of Polya's model is provided and its limitations for purposes of studying metacognition are discussed. Following the discussion of Polya's model a ''cognitive-metacognitive model'' of mathematical problem solving will be presented.

Polya's Model

It is unnecessary to describe Polya's model in detail since it is familiar to every researcher who has undertaken the study of mathematical problem solving in a serious way. The four phases of his model (understanding, planning, carrying out the plan, and looking back) serve as a framework for identifying a multitude of heuristic processes that may foster successful problem solving. However, his model does not consider metacogni-tive processes, at least not explicitly. More specifically, while his model allows for the identification of strategy-relevant classes of variables that affect performance, it does not incorporate either person or task variables in the sense specified by Flavell and Wellman. Furthermore, his model does not consider the interaction between metacognition and cognition, clearly an unsatisfactory condition if one accepts the position that metacogni-tive actions are guiding forces in problem solving.

An unfortunate consequence of this shortcoming of Polya's model is that research generated by it has largely ignored metacognition. Instead, this research has focused on instruction in heuristics (Lester, 1980). Hatfield (1978) pointed out that ''a number of studies have used various treatments of task-specific and general 'heuristics' in attempt-ing to improve subjects' problem-solving competence through instruction'' (p. 25). An implied assumption underlying this type of research is that equipping students with the ability to use a variety of heuristics and skills is sufficient to make them good problem solvers. However, anyone who has taught mathematics or has studied mathematics seriously is aware that there is much mental activity underlying the application of algorithms and heuristics; metacognition may account for a significant part of that activity. Indeed, the failure of most efforts to improve students' problem-solving performance may be due in large part to the fact that instruction has overemphasized the development of heuristic skills and has virtually ignored the managerial skills necessary to regulate one's activity. A reformulation of Polya's model to include metacognition might have the effect of influencing researchers to address this important aspect of problem-solving behavior. An attempt at such a reformulation is described in the next section.

A Cognitive-Metacognitive Model of Mathematical Problem Solving

The modification of Polya's model considered here has two distinct but interconnected components: a cognitive component based on Polya's model and a metacognitive component based on Flavell and Wellman's classes of variables.

The Cognitive Component. Four categories of activity comprise this component: orientation, organization, execution, and verification. Table 2 provides a description of each category together with sample metacognitive decisions that might be associated with each.

While these categories correspond closely to Polya's four phases, the categories are labeled differently in order to highlight the interactive, interdependent nature of the various categories of problem-solving behaviors. Also, Polya (1957) was interested in identifying questions and suggestions which teachers could use to help their students develop the ''mental operations typically useful for the solution of problems'' (p. 2). On the other hand, this model purports to describe the categories of the cognitive component in terms of points during problem solving where metacognitive actions might occur.

The Metacognitive Component. Flavell and Wellman's consideration of person, task, and strategy variables was restricted to metamemory. It seems appropriate to consider these same three classes of variables in discussing metacognition in general, and in particular, metacognition related to solving mathematical tasks.

- Person Variables—This class encompasses the individual's belief system as well as affective characteristics that may influence performance (e.g., motivation, anxiety, perseverance). It also includes the individual's assessment of his or her capabilities and limitations both in general and with respect to a particular mathematical task.

- Task Variables—The individual's awareness of features of a task that may influence performance on the task involves five subcategories: content, context, structure, syntax, and process (cf. Kulm, 1979). *Content* variables are those associated with the mathematical content of a task. *Context* variables involve the nonmathematical meanings in the statement or presentation of a task as well as the extent of the individual's familiarity with the setting of a task. *Structure* variables describe the mathematical (logical) relationships among the elements of a task. *Syntax* variables are those involving the relationship among, as well as the arrangement of, words and symbols in the statement of a task. Finally, *process* variables, when viewed as task

Table 2. Cognitive Categories of the Cognitive-Metacognitive Model.

Category	Sample metacognitive decisions
Orientation: strategic behavior to assess and understand a problem A. Comprehension strategies B. Analysis of information C. Initial and subsequent representation D. Assessment of level of difficulty and chances of success	I'll just look for the key words; they will tell me what to do. The numbers in this problem are too big for me. This looks like a [type] problem. I don't know what to do to solve this problem. There are too many numbers, it's not like problems I've done before.
Organization: planning of behavior and choice of actions A. Identification of goals B. Global planning C. Local planning (to implement global plans)	I think the problem is asking for [result]. I can solve this problem by finding [quantity]. I think I should first [operation] these numbers. I'm not sure, but I think [algorithm, method] might work for this type of problem. I'm not sure what to do. I'll try guessing first. This is a [type] problem. I'll solve it like the others.
Execution: regulation of behavior to conform to plans A. Performance of local actions B. Monitoring both progress and consistency of local plans C. Trade-off decisions (e.g., speed vs. accuracy, degree of elegance)	I'm sloppy at doing [algorithm]; I'd better go slow. This is complicated. I should go through the steps carefully. This method isn't working. I'll try something else. I need to vocalize what I'm doing to help me keep on track. I need to write these steps out.

Verification: evaluation of decisions made and of outcomes of executed plans
A. Evaluation of *orientation* and *organization*
  1. Adequacy of problem representation
  2. Adequacy of organizational decision
  3. Consistency of local plans with global plans
  4. Consistency of global plans with goals
B. Evaluation of *execution*
  1. Checking results of local actions
  2. Consistency of intermediate results with existing plans and problem conditions
  3. Consistency of final results with problem conditions
	I wasn't careful. I'd better check my steps. I'm not sure this plan is appropriate. I'd better look it over again. I'm not sure I've understood the problem. I'll reread it again. This answer seems too big. I should check my work. I thought it was a [type] problem, but I don't think it is.

variables, describe the interaction between the mental operations of the problem solver and the problem to be solved. That is, a particular problem may evoke, or even necessitate, the use of certain mental processes. In the latter case the processes are considered to be inherent in the problem.

- Strategy Variables—Variables included in this category are those associated with the individual's awareness of strategies that aid in comprehending, organizing, planning, executing plans, and checking and evaluating. For example, being aware of the value of skimming a problem statement to identify key features or to get a better feel for a problem falls in this category. Recognizing the usefulness of drawing a picture to represent the salient information in a problem is another example. Some other strategies include awareness of "coping" strategies (i.e., strategies that aid in resolving comprehension failures or in overcoming obstacles), knowing when to use certain heuristics (e.g., working backward, solving an analogous problem, identifying subgoals), and knowing how and when to monitor progress (e.g., knowing when to abandon unproductive plans).

Of course, interactions between pairs of classes and among all three classes are also a part of this component. For example, sample person–task interactions include the individual's estimate of a task's difficulty and preference for a particular type of task. Person–strategy interactions include, among others, the individual's familiarity with and confidence in using potentially useful strategies. Awareness that a particular class of problems can all be solved using a certain heuristic or that long "story" problems typically require more than one reading are examples of task–strategy interactions. It is safe to say that all three classes of variables interact to some degree during any problem-solving situation, but in many situations the interaction between two classes is particularly apparent. The point is that the three classes of variables in the metacognitive component have a direct impact on cognitive behavior.

Interaction Between Components. How, when, and to what extent metacognition serves to guide, direct, and otherwise regulate problem solving, are, of course, the questions of primary interest. That is, what is of concern is the nature of the interaction that takes place between the two components. Figure 2 points out the interrelatedness among the four categories of cognitive activity and suggests an interactive relationship among the three classes of metacognitive variables. The bold arrow from the metacognitive component to the cognitive component is meant to imply that metacognitive decisions serve to guide cognitive actions.

Some specific examples of how and when person, task, and strategy variables might interact with the four cognitive categories are illustrated by the metacognitive decisions listed in Table 2.

How the Model Can Be Used. As is typically true of any inchoate model of a complex phenomenon, the cognitive-metacognitive model offers no direct insights about possible answers to questions associated with the role of metacognition in mathematical problem solving. However, it can serve to provide direction and focus to research efforts. For example, it indicates that metacognitive behaviors are a function of three classes of variables—person, task, and strategy—and that these three classes interact with each other. The nature of this interaction could be the focal point of a considerable amount of important research. Also, the model suggests that metacognitive actions can influence cognitive behavior at all phases of problem solving, and that these actions may act as guiding forces throughout the problem-solving process. (Both Schoenfeld, 1982, and Silver, 1982, refer to metacognitive actions as "driving" forces. I prefer the milder phrasing.) It would be interesting to investigate the hypothesis that metacognitions are guiding forces by contrasting the metacognitive behaviors of expert and novice problem

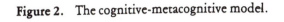

Figure 2.   The cognitive-metacognitive model.

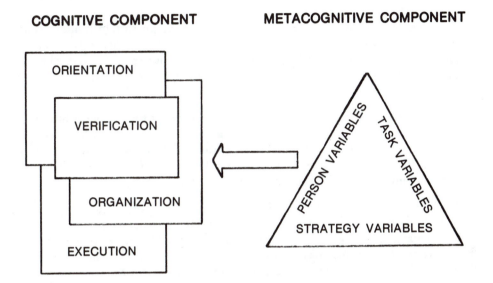

COGNITIVE COMPONENT   **METACOGNITIVE COMPONENT**

solvers. Furthermore, if one accepts the ''guiding forces'' hypothesis, it would be natural to wonder about the extent to which students' cognitive awareness and ability to regulate their actions can be improved through training. My colleague, Joe Garofalo, and I currently are designing a study that will explore the effectiveness of ''metacognition'' instruction with sixth-grade children.

Perhaps an even more important implication that can be drawn from the model is that the tasks used in metacognition research must be chosen with great care. Intertask variability with respect to metacognition is high. That is, an individual may exhibit quite a lot of metacognitive behavior on one problem and very little on another. Since the influence of metacognition on problem-solving performance may often be subtle and difficult to describe, one must be sure to select carefully designed tasks and administer them under appropriate conditions. This was a particularly troublesome issue in a study of certain metacognitive behaviors of third- and fifth-graders I completed recently (Lester & Garofalo, 1982). Several of the tasks we used did not elicit metacognitive behaviors associated with the execution or verification stages.

FINAL COMMENTS

The original task I set for myself as I began to think about this paper was to offer some prescriptions about how research on problem-solving instruction should be conducted. The more I thought, the less sanguine I became about the prospects of such an undertaking. Instead of prescriptions, we need a clearer perspective regarding the purposes of problem-solving instruction and the variables involved. Furthermore, in the design of our research studies we need to put into sharper focus what we know about how individuals solve problems. Once these matters are resolved, issues of research methodology may be taken care of as well.

In this paper I have considered several issues related to problem-solving instruction. By way of summary, let me recapitulate the key features of my discussion of these issues.

1. The primary purpose of mathematical problem-solving instruction is not to equip students with a collection of skills and processes, but rather to enable them to think for themselves. The value of skills and processes instruction should be judged by the extent to which the skills and processes actually enhance flexible, independent thinking.

2. Mathematical problem-solving performance is dependent upon a nexus of person, task, and instructional variables. Research aimed at determining the interrelationship among these variables can be organized around three questions: What does the individual do during problem solving? What should the individual be able to do? How can individual problem-solving ability be improved?

3. Teaching experiments offer a sensible approach to studying problem-solving instruction. A good teaching experiment has the following characteristics: it is nonexperimental in design; it focuses on observing processes as they develop; the teacher is not a controlled variable but is a part of the instructional environment; instructional treatments last at least several weeks; and a range of student behaviors—affective, cognitive, and metacognitive—are considered.

4. The trend toward the use of naturalistic methodologies raises a concern about what this type of inquiry involves. Five traits should characterize naturalistic inquiry: it makes use of qualitative methods, but quantitative methods can be employed as well; it is concerned with both relevance and rigor; it makes use of tacit knowledge; it adopts an expansionist stance toward research; and it is concerned with both theory generation and theory verification.

5. There are three categories of factors that influence problem-solving instruction: antecedents, classroom processes, and outcomes. Each of these categories is comprised of two or more subcategories.

6. Sternberg has suggested that the design of programs in intellectual skills training be guided by a set of eight criteria. In particular, he suggests that such programs be based on an experimentally verified theory, more specifically an information-processing theory.

7. Metacognition may play a vital part in successful problem solving. The extent to which metacognitive actions are "guiding forces" in problem solving or are otherwise related to cognitive behaviors is an important question for problem-solving research.

REFERENCES

Atkinson, R.C., & Shiffrin, R.M. Human memory: A proposed system and its control processes. In K.W. Spence & J.T. Spence (Eds.), *The psychology of learning and motivation* (Vol. 2). New York: Academic Press, 1968.

Bronfenbrenner, U. The experimental ecology of education. *Educational Researcher* 5(9), 5–15, 1976.

Brown, A. Knowing, when, where, and how to remember: A problem of metacognition. In R. Glaser (Ed.), *Advances in instructional psychology*. Hillsdale, NJ: Lawrence Erlbaum Associates, 1978.

Butterfield, E.C., & Belmont, J.M. Assessing and improving the executive cognitive functions of mentally retarded people. In I. Bailer & M. Sternlicht (Eds.), *Psychological issues in mentally retarded people*. Chicago: Aldine, 1975.

Case, R. Structures and strictures: Some functional limitations on the course of cognitive growth. *Cognitive Psychology* 6, 544–74, 1974.

Charles, R.I. An instructional system for mathematical problem solving. In S.L. Rachlin (Ed.), *MCATA monograph on problem solving*. Calgary, Canada: University of Calgary, 1982.

Charles, R.I., & Lester, F.K. *Teaching problem solving: What, why and how.* Palo Alto, CA: Dale Seymour, 1982.

Charles, R.I., & Lester, F.K. An evaluation of a process-oriented mathematical problem-solving instructional program in grades five and seven. *Journal for Research in Mathematics Education* 15, 15–34, 1984.

Dunkin, M.J., & Biddle, B.J. *The study of teaching*. New York: Holt, Rinehart & Winston, 1974.

Flavell, J.H. Metacognitive aspects of problem solving. In L.B. Resnick (Ed.), *The nature of intelligence*. Hillsdale, NJ: Lawrence Erlbaum Associates, 1976.

Flavell, J.H., & Wellman, H. Metamemory. In R. Kail & J. Hagen (Eds.), *Perspectives on the development of memory and cognition*. Hillsdale, NJ: Lawrence Erlbaum Associates, 1977.

Garofalo, J., & Lester, F.K. *Adopting a metacognitive perspective on mathematical problem solving.* Unpublished manuscript, 1983. (Available from the authors, School of Education, Indiana University)

Glaser, B.G., & Strauss, A.L. *The discovery of grounded theory*. Chicago, IL: Aldine, 1967.

Goldin, G.A., & McClintock, C.E. (Eds.). *Task variables in mathematical problem solving*. Philadelphia: The Franklin Institute Press, 1984.

Greeno, J.G. Process of understanding in problem solving. In N.J. Castellan, D.B. Pisoni, & G.R. Potts (Eds.), *Cognitive theory* (Vol. 2). Hillsdale, NJ: Lawrence Erlbaum Associates, 1977.

Guba, E.G., & Lincoln, Y.S. *Effective evaluation*. San Francisco: Jossey-Bass, 1981.

Hatfield, L.L. Heuristic emphases in the instruction of mathematical problem solving: Rationales and research. In L.L. Hatfield & D.A. Bradbard (Eds.), *Mathematical problem solving: Papers from a research workshop*. Columbus, OH: ERIC Clearinghouse for Science, Mathematics, and Environmental Education, 1978.

Hayes, J.R., & Simon, H.A. Psychological differences among problem isomorphs. In N.J. Castellan, D.B. Pisoni, & G.R. Potts (Eds.), *Cognitive theory* (Vol. 2). Hillsdale, NJ: Lawrence Erlbaum Associates, 1977.

Hayes-Roth, B. *Flexibility in executive strategies*. Rand Corporation (Research Report #N-1170-ONR). Santa Monica, CA, September 1980.

Kantowski, M.G. The teaching experiment and Soviet studies of problem solving. In L.L. Hatfield & D.A. Bradbard (Eds.), *Mathematical problem solving: Papers from a research workshop*. Columbus, OH: ERIC Clearinghouse for Science, Mathematics, and Environmental Education, 1978.

Kantowski, M.G. Problem solving. In E. Fennema (Ed.), *Mathematics education research: Implications for the 80's*. Alexandria, VA: American Society for Curriculum Development, 1981.

Kilpatrick, J. Variables and methodologies in research on problem solving. In L.L. Hatfield & D.A. Bradbard (Eds.), *Mathematical problem solving: Papers from a research workshop*. Columbus, OH: ERIC Clearinghouse for Science, Mathematics, and Environmental Education, 1978.

Kilpatrick, J., & Wirszup, I. (Eds.). *Soviet studies in the psychology of learning and teaching mathematics* (14 vols.). Stanford, CA: School Mathematics Study Group, 1969–75.

Koplowitz, H. The feeling of knowing when one has solved a problem. In J. Lochhead & J. Clement (Eds.), *Cognitive process instruction: Research in teaching thinking skills*. Philadelphia: The Franklin Institute Press, 1979.

Kulm, G. The classification of problem-solving research variables. In G.A. Goldin & C.E. McClintock (Eds.), *Task variables in mathematical problem solving*. Columbus, OH: ERIC Clearinghouse for Science, Mathematics, and Environmental Education, 1979.

Larkin, J.H. Skilled problem solving in physics: A hierarchical planning model. *Journal of Structural Learning* **6**, 271–97, 1980.

Larkin, J., McDermott, L., Simon, D.P., & Simon, H.A. Expert and novice performance in solving physics problems. *Science* **208**, 1335–1542, 1980.

LeBlanc, J.F., & Kerr, D.R. *The Mathematical Problem Solving Project: Problem-solving strategies and applications of mathematics in the elementary school* (Final Report). Bloomington, IN: Indiana University Mathematics Education Development Center, 1977.

Lesh, R. *Metacognition in mathematical problem solving*. Unpublished manuscript, 1982. (Available from the author, School of Education, Northwestern University)

Lester, F.K. Mathematical problem solving in the elementary school: Some educational and psychological considerations. In L.L. Hatfield & D.A. Bradbard (Eds.), *Mathematical problem solving: Papers from a research workshop*. Columbus, OH: ERIC Clearinghouse for Science, Mathematics, and Environmental Education, 1978.

Lester, F.K. Research in mathematical problem solving: In R.J. Shumway (Ed.), *Research in mathematics education*. Reston, VA: National Council of Teachers of Mathematics, 1980.

Lester, F.K. Building bridges between psychological and mathematics education research on problem solving. In F.K. Lester & J. Garofalo (Eds.), *Mathematical problem solving: Issues in research*. Philadelphia: The Franklin Institute Press, 1982.

Lester, F.K. Trends and issues in mathematical problem-solving research. In R. Lesh & M. Landau (Eds.), *Acquisition of mathematics concepts and processes*. New York: Academic Press, 1983.

Lester, F.K., & Garofalo, J. *Metacognitive aspects of elementary school students' performance on arithmetic tasks*. Paper presented at the annual meeting of the American Educational Research Association, New York, March 1982.

Lester, F.K., & Kerr, D.R. Some ideas about research methodologies in mathematics education. *Journal for Research in Mathematics Education* **10**, 228–32, 1979.

Lin, H. Approaches to clinical research in cognitive process instruction. In J. Lochhead & J. Clement (Eds.), *Cognitive process instruction: Research on teaching thinking skills*. Philadelphia: The Franklin Institute Press, 1979.

Mayer, R.E. The psychology of mathematical problem solving. In F.K. Lester & J. Garofalo (Eds.), *Mathematical problem solving: Issues in research*. Philadelphia: The Franklin Institute Press, 1982.

Polya, G. *How to solve it* (2nd ed.). New York: Doubleday, 1957.

Schoenfeld, A.H. Some thoughts on problem solving research and mathematics education. In F.K. Lester & J. Garofalo (Eds.), *Mathematical problem solving: Issues in research*. Philadelphia: The Franklin Institute Press, 1982.

Schoenfeld, A.H. Beyond the purely cognitive: Belief systems, social cognitions, and metacognitions as driving forces in intellectual performance. *Cognitive Science* **1**, 329–63, 1983(a).

Schoenfeld, A.H. Episodes and executive decisions in mathematical problem solving. In R.Lesh & M. Landau (Eds.), *Acquisition of mathematics concepts and processes*. New York: Academic Press, 1983(b).

Silver, E.A. *Thinking about problem solving: Toward an understanding of metacognitive aspects of mathematical problem solving*. Paper prepared for the Conference on Thinking, Suva, Fiji, January 1982.

Silver, E.A., Branca, N.A., & Adams, V.M. Metacognition: The missing link in problem solving? In R. Karplus (Ed.), *Proceedings of the Fourth International Conference for the Psychology of Mathematics Education*. Berkeley: University of California, 1980.

Stengel, A., LeBlanc, J.F., Jacobson, M., & Lester, F.K. *Learning to solve problems by solving problems: A report of a preliminary investigation* (Technical Report II.D. of the Mathematical Problem Solving Project). Bloomington, IN: Mathematics Education Development Center, 1977.

Sternberg, R. Sketch of a componential subtheory of human intelligence. *Behavioral and Brain Sciences* 3, 573–83, 1980.

Sternberg, R.J. Criteria for intellectual skills training. *Educational Researcher* 12(2) 6–12, 26, 1983.

Willems, E.P., & Rausch, H.L. *Naturalistic viewpoints in psychological research.* New York: Holt, Rinehard & Winston, 1969.

Wolf, R.L. *Strategies for conducting naturalistic evaluation in socioeducational settings: The naturalistic interview.* Paper prepared for the Occasional Paper Series, Western Michigan University, May 1979.

Mathematical Problem Solving: Lessons from the British Experience

Nicholas A. Branca[1]

San Diego State University

I spent a large part of the 1982–83 academic year at the Mathematics Education Centre at Chelsea College, University of London. During the time I was in England, I spoke with many educators at various academic levels and visited institutions and teachers' centers that are involved in the preservice and in-service education of teachers and in the preparation of curriculum materials. In this paper, I present some of my observations regarding the nature of mathematical problem solving in the British experience as evidenced by official reports, research studies, the development of curriculum materials, and theoretical models. In contrast to this evidence are my observations of a large number of classroom situations, including some highly recommended as places to send my own children. In most classrooms, I found a general lack of instruction in problem solving and in many cases an ignorance on the part of classroom teachers of the concepts of problem solving that were being advocated at the teachers' centers and by teacher educators.

OFFICIAL REPORTS

In 1978, a committee was established by the English government to consider the teaching of mathematics in primary and secondary schools in England and Wales. The committee was charged to make recommendations concerning the teaching of mathematics after first investigating the mathematics required in further and higher education, in employment, and in adult life. During the next few years, the committee met as a

1. I would like to express my sincere appreciation to David C. Johnson, Shell Professor of Mathematics Education at the Centre for Science and Mathematics Education, Chelsea College, University of London, and to Kathleen Hart, Director of Strategies and Errors in Secondary Mathematics Project, for allowing me the opportunity to work with them during my sabbatical. I would also like to thank Leone Burton of Avery Hill College for her assistance during my stay in England.

whole and in smaller working groups, visited schools and companies of various kinds, and met with teachers, departments of education, and institutes. Individual members also attended conferences and meetings of a number of professional bodies, including the Fourth International Congress on Mathematics Education held at Berkeley in August 1980. In addition to the data collected at these various meetings, the committee requested the Department of Education and Science to commission two complementary studies into the mathematical needs of employment and also a small study into the mathematical needs of adult life. A review of existing research on the teaching and learning of mathematics was carried out by Alan Bell of the University of Nottingham and by Alan Bishop of the University of Cambridge. The committee's report is commonly known as the Cockcroft Report (Cockcroft, 1982).

Mathematical problem solving plays an important role in the report of the committee. Drawing on the research review prepared for the inquiry, the committee distinguished different elements in the teaching of mathematics: facts, skills, conceptual structures, general strategies, and appreciation. Each of these is defined in the report, and a call is made for attention to each for effective teaching. General strategies and appreciation are related directly to mathematical problem solving and the process of carrying out an investigation. Although the committee does not indicate a specific style for the teaching of mathematics and, in fact, declares that to do so would be both impossible and undesirable, it does specify elements that are needed in successful mathematics teaching for students of all ages. Two of these elements are "problem solving, including the application of mathematics to everyday situation" and "investigational work" (paragraph 243).[2]

According to the report, each of the elements had been listed in earlier reports and/or recommendations about teaching. However, the report also claims that a major weakness of the previous reports was the lack of specificity in describing them. The report, therefore, expands on each of the elements.

The first discussion is about problem solving:

> The ability to solve problems is at the heart of mathematics. Mathematics is only "useful" to the extent to which it can be applied to a particular situation and it is the ability to apply mathematics to a variety of situations to which we give the name "problem solving." However, the solution of a mathematical problem cannot begin until the problem has been translated into the appropriate mathematical terms. This first and essential step presents very great difficulties to many pupils—a fact which is often too little appreciated. At each stage of the mathematics course the teacher needs to help pupils to understand how to apply the concepts and skills which are being learned and how to make use of them to solve problems. These problems should relate both to the application of mathematics to everyday situations within the pupils' experience, and also to situations which are unfamiliar. For many pupils this will require a great deal of discussion and oral work before even very simple problems can be tackled in written form. (paragraph 249)

The concept of investigation, not yet popular in this country, is treated in the same way. The report stresses that teachers should encourage students to think in an investigative way.

> The idea of investigation is fundamental both to the study of mathematics itself and also to an understanding of the ways in which mathematics can be used to extend knowledge and to solve problems in very many fields. We suspect that there are many teachers who think of

---

2. The committee used a system of numbering paragraphs for reference purposes.

"mathematical investigations" as being in some way similar to the "projects" which in recent years have become common as a way of working in many areas of the curriculum; in other words, that a mathematical investigation is an extensive piece of work which will take quite a long time to complete and will probably be undertaken individually or as a member of a small group. But although this is one of the forms which mathematical investigation can take, it is by no means the only form nor need be the most common. Investigations need be neither lengthy nor difficult. At the most fundamental level, and perhaps most frequently, they should start in response to pupils' questions, perhaps during exposition by the teacher or as a result of a piece of work which is in progress or has just been completed. (paragraph 250)

Specific examples of problem solving and investigation, covering different age and grade levels, are given, and a call is made for more study on the teaching of problem-solving strategies and processes. The report indicates that the teacher must be willing to pursue questions raised by students and to follow some false trails. It suggests that the teacher resolve questions raised by students either individually, with groups of pupils, or with the whole class. Sometimes students may be asked to pursue the question by themselves or discussion may be delayed to another occasion. The report emphasizes the need to discuss the outcome of an investigation evaluating not only the method used and the results but also false trails and mistakes.

To investigate further the origins of the committee's remarks and recommendations concerning problem solving and investigations, I consulted the research report prepared for the committee. The research evidence supported the notion of different components of mathematics. It drew heavily on previous work of one of the authors, Alan Bell, whose thesis (Bell, 1976) described a number of studies of generalizing and proof activity of students. The research report discussed the notion of general mathematical strategies and related mathematical investigation to investigation as means of acquiring knowledge. Figure 1 illustrates some of the relations among these notions.

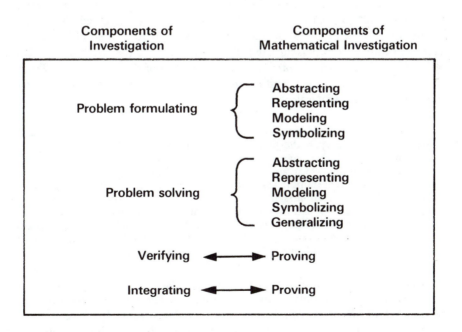

Figure 1. Relations between investigation and mathematical investigation.

In my opinion, the theoretical model of the ability for mathematical activity placing emphasis on process was an important contribution of the research report and provided Cockcroft's committee with a strong foundation on which it could make recommendations.

The report gave an extensive review of research on teaching methods beginning with Brownell's (1942) work on meaningful teaching, but failed to report on any of the studies that were done or were then being done in the area of teaching problem solving per se. This absence of research that dealt specifically with teaching problem solving led me to interview one of the committee members directly. On this occasion, the notion of the relatively small amount of problem solving and investigation that goes on in the schools was underscored. I was informed that problem solving and investigations are not in the experience of prospective teachers and that it was difficult to change the attitudes of teachers regarding their views of mathematics and their roles in schools. We discussed the importance of the belief systems of teachers and the need to involve teachers in the development of problem solving and investigational materials.

These last points are among the most important lessons to be learned from the British experience. It is crucial to make teachers aware of the nature of mathematical problem solving (and I include here the notion of investigation) and also to actively involve teachers in activities related to mathematical problem solving, which can range over a wide variety of experiences. Included among these activities are providing opportunities for students to attempt problems, providing instruction in problem solving, and creating problem-solving situations and materials.

RESEARCH PROJECTS

At about the same time as the Cockcroft committee began preparing its report, the Social Science Research Council funded a research project designed to establish the feasibility of using a problem-solving approach with 9- to 13-year-olds. The project, directed by Leone Burton, was initiated at the Polytechnic of the South Bank in London. Its origins lay with a research interest group of the National Association of Teachers in Higher and Further Education, and it combined two distinct areas of concern, namely, mathematical and pedagogical:

> The mathematical concern was to address the relationship between content and process and to attempt to improve upon the precision of definition of mathematics as a process based discipline. It was felt that those who describe mathematics as a process would benefit if the skills and procedures which are used to solve problems were identified, classified and presented in a coherent form. It was clear that the presentation of mathematics in schools was dominated by an information/skills approach. The consequent mismatch between the view of mathematics as a process and the content emphasis in schools could, it was thought, be one explanation for the poor quality of teaching and learning in the subject. The pedagogical concern, therefore, was to find a means whereby teachers and pupils could experience problem solving as part of their mathematics curriculum. (Burton, 1980, p. 4)

The objectives of the project were to develop a reference of skills and procedures and to develop a program of problem-solving assignments. The first objective was met by the production of an inventory for mathematical problem solving. The inventory was produced after many hours of observation of individuals solving problems, comparison of observations with appropriate problem-solving behavior, and collaborated introspection by the research staff. It was based on a four-phase model of problem solving consisting of entry, attack, review, and extension. For each of these phases, there were organizers and procedures. The organizers were introduced to provide a structure for inexperienced problem solvers to use. They were stated in the form of a question the student could ask himself or herself. The procedures were suggestions independent of the content which might help to obtain a solution (they corresponded to heuristics). A restricted list of skills that could be taught to students aged 9–13 was also part of the inventory. They were not specific to any particular phase and consisted of ways of handling information, representing the problem, and so forth.

The second objective of the project, the development of a structured program of problem-solving assignments, was accomplished by collecting suitable problems; analyzing them by mathematical knowledge and skills, problem-solving skills and procedures, and Piagetian developmental level; and by providing teachers with suitable backup material to introduce the assignments for 1 hour per week over a term. A pilot study was conducted to assess the feasibility of the approach, to assess the reactions of pupils and volunteer teachers, and to examine difficulties associated with the induction of the teachers and the classroom administration.

After revising the program based on the results of the pilot study, a main study was conducted with approximately 800 students in 27 schools covering five areas in England. The program finally used consisted of eight components:

1. Thirty laminated cards each containing one problem.

2. Teacher's version of each problem.

3. A problem-solving starter book for pupils.

4. A teacher's version of the problem-solving starter book.

5. An introductory booklet for teachers.

6. Comment sheets and cards for keeping records.

7. Wall posters, one on the problem-solving process and one on getting materials.

8. A classroom frieze on communicating mathematics.

The main study was composed of seven phases, beginning with teacher induction at the end of the term. Pretests were given to experimental and control classes, then introductory work using the problem-solving starter book with the experimental classes was completed. Problem-solving sessions were followed by post-testing and interviewing of 10% of each experimental class. Teachers completed questionnaires and were interviewed.

The study established the feasibility of teaching problem solving to students aged 9–13. However, the 1-hour problem-solving session held each week for one term was judged to be insufficient to teach specific skills and procedures. The attitudes of pupils and teachers were positive, and the teachers were enthusiastic about the program. Teachers were able to adjust to the roles required. The study concluded that support for teachers and carefully prepared material were essential. The inventory of skills was regarded by the teachers as theoretical background not important to the practice of problem solving. The study concluded that this impeded the acquistion of skills and procedures and recommended that teachers and pupils be introduced to a simpler structure of the inventory initially.

A much smaller-scale study was reported by Billings (1975). She examined how children's mathematical reasoning could be developed in problem-solving situations. A small group of 8-year-olds were taught in a variety of situations, each of which contained more than one problem. The children first had to find a problem and then produce a solution. Children worked individually and in small groups and were asked to do tasks such as creating polynomials from unit squares and subsequently classifying them. They constructed trains to fit exactly into a given station and classified the resultant trains.

Billinge observed student responses at the beginning of the study and noted that they tended to be "answers" to be evaluated as correct or incorrect without any explanations for the derivation of the answers. After participation in the study, students produced hypotheses, looked for evidence to support hypotheses, and learned to use counterexamples to refute them. The encouragement to look for reasons seemed to produce a more logical and systematic approach to the situation.

As a result of the study, Billings concluded that the one factor that outweighed all others in effect was the expectation of the teacher. She claimed that the development in reasoning of the children in her study could be best explained through their reactions to her attitude to problem-solving situations; one child said, "You're mad on reasons," thereby reflecting precisely what she considered mathematics to be about.

A current project investigating the introduction of microcomputers into the United Kingdom is being conducted in the Chiltern region (Noss, 1984). The project is concentrating on the ways in which the mathematical and heuristic ideas of primary school children (ages 8–10) develop as they learn to program using LOGO. An unstructured approach has been developed as a teaching strategy. The teacher's intervention is restricted primarily to informal advice and suggestions, and this role is also the subject of research. Initial results indicate the development of a number of problem-solving strategies, including generalization and particularization. Children have learned to program using LOGO without difficulty and have been enthusiastic throughout the year. Experimentation and exploration have been facilitated by the use of LOGO, and the report claims that a sense of the existence of underlying rules and theorems has gradually emerged. The project presents a unique model for conducting research and when completed should provide us with insight into both the development of mathematical problem solving in young children and their facility with LOGO.

Although there are large differences in size and scope among these research projects, a commonality is seen in their emphasis on the role of process in the learning of problem-solving skills and strategies. Each presents a model of the teacher quite different from the traditional role and in that way each adds to the lessons to be learned from the British experience.

MATERIAL DEVELOPMENT

In addition to the projects that are mainly concerned with researching the nature of problem solving, there exists a number of projects that have a primary objective of developing materials for the teaching of problem solving and investigations. A project that was aimed at preparing investigational materials suitable for mixed-ability students was carried out at two South Nottinghamshire comprehensive schools (Bell, Wigley, & Rooke, 1978). Strategies for generalizations were focused on, with an emphasis on making the students aware of the process aspects of mathematics through reflexive activity. The development of the pupils' ability to experiment, record, draw conclusions, and write up results was considered a valid and attainable objective. The students recognized and named strategies for generalizations such as generating examples to test a given conjecture or to lead to the formulation of a conjecture and the systematic organization of examples.

A different approach, aimed at encouraging teachers of mathematics to include opportunities for primary school children to explore and investigate potentially mathematical situations, has been undertaken by the Association of Teachers of Mathematics. This organization has produced a series of publications (Hardy et al., 1977a and 1977b) containing examples of suitable starting points for such investigations. These examples cover a wide range of types and levels of difficulty and have been used in connection with in-service courses designed to develop mathematical expertise in teachers. A similar publication (Lingard, 1980) is also intended for those teachers with little or no experience in using mathematical investigations in the classroom. It includes a discussion of the solutions, problems likely to be encountered, and examples of student solutions.

The Spode Group is a small group of mathematics teachers from schools, colleges, and higher education who have come together to develop practical material for the secondary mathematics classroom. The group, meeting for weekend sessions at Spode, Straffordshire, England, began with the premise that using mathematics to solve practical problems is in no way the same activity as solving mathematical problems and, therefore, developed case studies that would be of help in providing practical problems which really show that mathematics is a useful discipline. The Spode Group has produced two volumes containing problems that require advanced mathematics (Spode Group, 1981) as well as one volume for those who are taking courses in vocational training (Spode Group, 1983). In these materials a problem is presented and then is followed by teaching notes, possible solutions, and related problems.

Each of these projects presents nonstandard examples of tested materials. The layout, form, and techniques of these examples and the experiences of the developers in their preparation can provide us with valuable lessons for curriculum development in this country.

THEORETICAL MODELS

A number of British authors have written papers presenting models of learning or teaching problem solving. Burton (1982) puts forth a model of mathematical thinking which she used as the basis of her study. It comprises a "mathinking" helix containing an unspecified number of loops which build upon understandings and awareness achieved in transversing previous loops. The cognitive processes involved are labeled manipulating, getting a sense of pattern, and articulating that pattern symbolically. The helix permits the thinker to transverse backward as well as forward. The cognitive level is charted by three phases that she describes as affective responses: entry, attack, and review. Four processes considered to be the substance of mathematical activity complete the model: specializing, conjecturing, generalizing, and convincing. Burton believes that "the operations and processes of mathematical thinking are essential to learning [and that] an expanding field for learning depends upon continuously improving and deepening awareness" (p. 14). Evidence is presented to show that mathematical thinking can be taught, and practical considerations are given regarding the implications of the model.

Biggs (1973) emphasizes that investigation can play a vital part in the learning of mathematical concepts and in problem solving and indicates that the teacher has an essential part to play. In offering guidelines for introducing investigation into the classroom, she describes three different stages in learning by investigation, all of which she sees as important for sound learning: (*1*) free exploration, (*2*) directed discovery led by teacher questions focused upon a particular concept, and (*3*) varied experience and practice to fix the concept. Biggs claims that those learning through investigations are accustomed to problem situations and do not find problems difficult, and they can be expected to use far more imagination as they grow older.

In a similar vein, Jeffrey (1978) attempts to provide a model for teachers to use in developing lessons in doing mathematics rather than lessons in absorbing a relatively restricted number of skills. He advocates trying imaginative ideas and then sharing experiences with other teachers. He provides a model for investigative lessons: (*1*) experimentation, (*2*) formulation and testing of conjectures about relationships, and (*3*) formulation of explanations for observed rules.

Each of the models separates and refines various stages of the problem-solving process. Although the models are not identical and in fact vary considerably in their degree of specificity, they do share common elements. Each provides us with a particular viewpoint, and each of the authors presents us with examples from his or her experience to substantiate the model.

DISCUSSION

I have tried to present an overview of what is going on in England with respect to problem solving in mathematics. It by no means represents all that is happening, nor does it reflect the degree to which these concerns affect the different segments of the educational community. Certainly the view from the top is that problem solving and investigations should be a part of all teachers' repertoires. However, this is not the case for the majority of teachers. In my visits to teachers' centers and institutes, I was most impressed with the level of commitment of the teachers I met. The teachers who voluntarily take part in the various offerings of workshops and courses, however, represent less than 10% of all teachers. An important question is, How does one go about increasing the level of participation? The attitudes and belief systems of teachers, as mentioned earlier, are considered important with respect to their teaching. How these are developed and/or changed is an important area for research.

There has been relatively little support for research on problem solving, but this may change with the recognition of the need for more study that was indicated by the Cockcroft Report. Some individuals and groups are now developing problem solving and investigational materials. The developments are based on their conceptions of mathematics and mathematics teaching, and these are not always made explicit. The range of available material is extensive, but most material gives little or no direction for teachers. The project directed by Burton is an exception. It provided detailed backup material for teachers, including a theoretical framework and more recently a theoretical model. The theoretical background material was not used by the teachers and was not considered by them to be important. How valuable theoretical materials are for teachers and what kinds of materials are most useful are questions that need to be investigated.

My overall reaction regarding mathematical problem solving in the British experience is that it is on the verge of becoming a dominant force in mathematics education. The British and American systems of education share many of the same concerns, and there is much that we can learn from their experiences. Professional societies and organizations and mathematics education leaders advocate a strong commitment to making mathematical problem solving an integral part of mathematics curriculum and pedagogy. The British notions of mathematical investigations can help us to clarify the many variations we currently have when we refer to problem solving.

The Cockcroft Report presents ambitious recommendations regarding the teaching of problem solving. The report recognized the need to indicate in detail what is meant by problem solving and investigation. It is not enough to simply state that the curriculum should include instruction in problem solving or be taught in a problem-solving spirit. Rather, it is crucial that teachers be given explicit definitions, examples, suggestions, materials, and models to aid in their teaching. This lesson should not be lost on the many individuals and groups who are currently in the process of reporting on the status and role of education in our country.

The British experience places a heavy emphasis on the teacher's role as leader or facilitator of discussion about strategies and processes. There is an emphasis on the teacher encouraging students' questions and being willing and able to answer questions that are of an investigatory nature. Many examples of curriculum development at the local level exist in England. The network of teacher centers is having an immediate effect on developing materials both by and for teachers and more importantly on giving teachers experiences in problem solving that can then be transferred to their teaching. Teachers need these experiences because the pedagogical principles employed are markedly different from the current situation. Although the number of teachers actively involved is relatively small at present, the quality of, and commitment to, the experiences is generating a ripple effect which in time will involve more and more teachers. Lessons to be learned from these experiences include the importance of involving teachers at all stages of curriculum development and implementation and the importance of setting up a networking system to communicate to others and to provide support when necessary.

A more general lesson that we can learn from the British experience is the importance of communication among the various groups concerned with the educational system. The Cockcroft committee drew heavily on the reports of subgroups. Teachers of mathematics at all levels were consulted, as were users of mathematics and those involved in research in mathematics and mathematics education. Each of these groups has a role to play in the educational system, and communication among the groups enhances these roles.

There are many positive things happening but there is much to be done to transform the schools to places where children learn to think about mathematics and become involved in mathematical processes. We in this country can profit from the British experience, and the integration of mathematical problem solving into our curriculum can be facilitated by relating what has been accomplished there to our particular situation, and by heeding the lessons mentioned above.

REFERENCES

Bell, A.W. *The learning of general mathematical strategies.* Unpublished doctoral dissertation, University of Nottingham (England), 1976.

Bell, A.W. The learning of process aspects of mathematics. *Educational Studies in Maths* **10**, 361–87, 1979.

Bell, A.W., Wigley, A., & Rooke, D. *Journey into maths: The South Nottinghamshire project.* London: Blackie, 1978.

Biggs, E. Investigation and problem solving in mathematical education. In Howson (Ed.), *Mathematical Education: Proceedings of the Second International Congress on Mathematical Education.* Cambridge: Cambridge University Press, 1973.

Billinge, C.L. Problem solving in the primary school. *Mathematics Teaching* **70**, 8–13, 1975.

Brownell, W.A. Problem solving. In Henry (Ed.), *Forty-first yearbook of the National Society for the Study of Education.* Chicago: University of Chicago Press, 1942.

Burton, L. *The skills and procedures of mathematical problem solving project* (SSRC HR5410/1). London: Polytechnic of the South Bank, 1980.

Burton, L. *Mathematical thinking: The struggle for meaning.* Paper presented at the Conference on Thinking, University of the South Pacific, Suva, Fiji, January 1982.

Cockcroft, W.H. *Mathematics counts: Report of the Committee of Inquiry Into the Teaching of Mathematics under the Chairmanship of Dr. W. H. Cockcroft.* London: Her Majesty's Stationery Office, 1982.

Jeffrey, B. Making and testing conjectures. *Mathematics Teaching* **82**, 15–17, Spring 1978.

Hardy, T., Howarth, A., Love, E., & McIntosh, A. *Points of departure 1.* Derby, England: Association of Teachers of Mathematics, 1977a.

Hardy, T., Howarth, A., Love, E. *Points of departure 2.* Derby, England: Association of Teachers of Mathematics, 1977b.

Lingard, D. *Mathematical investigations in the classroom.* Derby, England: Association of Teachers of Mathematics, 1980.

Mason, J., Burton, L., & Stacey, K. *Thinking mathematically.* Longon: Addison-Wesley, 1982.

Noss, R. *Children learning LOGO programming* (Interim Report No. 2 of the Chiltern Logo Project). Hatfield, England: Advisory Unit for Computer Based Education, January 1984.

Spode Group. *Solving real problem with mathematics* (2 vols.). Cranfield, England: Cranfield Press, 1981.

Spode Group. *Solving real probelm with C. S. E. mathematics.* Cranfield, England: Cranfield Press, 1983.

PART B.
PROBLEM-SOLVING RESEARCH: CROSS-DISCIPLINE PERSPECTIVES

Implications for Mathematics Instruction of Research on Scientific Problem Solving[1]

Joan I. Heller
Harriet N. Hungate
University of California, Berkeley

A major goal of instruction is to improve students' abilities to perform tasks they were not able to perform well prior to instruction. Of course, such improvement can only come about if students learn something as a result of their exposure to instruction; that is, if the students' knowledge undergoes some changes during the instructional process. The primary task facing educators, then, is to set up the instructional conditions under which desired changes in students' knowledge will occur. Ideally, the design of instruction should be guided by general theoretical principles about the relationship between instructional conditions and changes in student knowledge. Without such general principles, the development of effective instruction remains heavily dependent on the skills, experience, and frequently the personality of the particular educator designing or delivering the instruction.

There are a great many variables that affect the relationship between instructional conditions and learning, and a number of them need to be understood for principled or theory-based instruction to become possible. These variables include cognitive, affective, and social aspects of the educational process; structure and content of instructional materials; medium of delivery of the instruction; the nature and structure of the subject matter being taught; and a myriad of student variables, such as aptitudes, prior knowledge, and personality. A comprehensive instructional theory would explain the ways in which all of these factors interact during instruction. Progress toward that end is being made through the gradual accumulation of insights into each factor, insights that need to be synthesized eventually into a complete account.

In this chapter, we review selected findings in the area of cognition during problem solving and explore the instructional implications of that piece of the complex puzzle we

1. Preparation of this paper was supported in part by National Science Foundation Grant SED 79-20592. Any opinions, conclusions, or recommendations expressed are those of the authors and do not necessarily reflect the views of the National Science Foundation.

confront. The work we will discuss has evolved from several decades of interest in the psychology of problem solving. Early psychological analyses of problem solving considered fairly general aspects of problem-solving activities. Gestalt theorists such as Duncker (1945), Köhler (1927), and Wertheimer (1959) saw as most important for problem solution the achievement of understanding of the problem as a whole. They were interested in sudden "insights" during problem solving and saw problem solving as requiring the integration of previously learned responses in novel ways. Beginning around 1950, theorists taking a behaviorist approach (such as Maltzman, 1955) concerned themselves primarily with general connections between actions performed by the problem solver and conditions under which actions are performed. More recent information-processing analyses incorporate both the Gestalt psychologists' interest in internal mental states involved in understanding problems, and the behaviorists' emphasis on actions that are performed in response to specific stimuli. The aim of these more recent analyses has been to characterize the knowledge required for solving problems in considerably greater detail than was attempted in earlier work.

Central to the information-processing approach is an interest in the ways people store and process information to perform complex intellectual tasks. The aim is to build theoretical models of the conceptual knowledge structures, procedures, and general strategies required for understanding and solving problems. These theories are implemented in the form of programs, which are often run on a computer because they tend to be quite complex. The models are intended to be hypotheses about limited aspects of cognition. They are tested by assessing the match between a "trace" of the processes performed by the model as it solves a problem and the data from subjects performing the same task. The claim is that the existence of such programs and their ability to simulate human behavior demonstrate that the theories "are operational and do not depend on vague, mentalistic concepts" (Larkin et al., 1980a).

While early information-processing studies focused on the study of puzzle-like problems in areas such as cryptarithmetic, chess, and symbolic logic (Newell & Simon, 1972), interest has turned toward analyzing solutions of problems in complex subject-matter domains such as physics (Simon & Simon, 1978; Larkin et al., 1980a), geometry (Greeno, 1978), and arithmetic word problems (Riley et al., 1983). The problems looked at in this body of work have been fairly standard textbook problems of the kind students typically encounter in school.

These problems are well-structured—they provide a clearly specified problem situation containing a small amount of given information and a specific goal that can be determined from the given information. Such problems are used throughout mathematics and science curricula both to teach content material and to assess students' abilities to apply the concepts and principles taught in courses. Despite their high degree of structure, these problems generally require very complex knowledge for their solution, and most students find them quite difficult. Effective methods for teaching students how to solve such problems continue to elude educators. They remain, therefore, a serious educational challenge.

As we mentioned earlier, it is useful to think about instruction as a process that involves modification of students' knowledge for performing tasks. This process can be viewed as a series of transitions from one knowledge state to another. A theory of instruction would specify how to bring about these transitions between knowledge states. To date, information-processing analyses have focused primarily on individual knowledge states, but some progress has been made in specifying the nature of transitions between states (Anderson, 1981).

Our contribution to this volume is to identify some of the implications these cognitive analyses have for the design of instruction in mathematical problem solving. In particular, we focus on analyses of problem solving in scientific domains and the instructional implications of this work. In order to make the implications concrete, we consider how some of these ideas might be applied to instruction in a sample mathematical domain, integration problems in calculus.

DESCRIPTIVE ANALYSES OF PROBLEM-SOLVING PERFORMANCE

Studies of Problem-Solving Performance

One method for discovering the kinds of knowledge required for solving scientific problems is to compare solutions by highly skilled, "expert" problem solvers with those by "novices." Such analyses can provide theoretical insights into the nature of skilled performance as well as into the kinds of difficulties beginning problem solvers experience. Once the components of skilled performance have been identified, it becomes possible to consider teaching this knowledge to novices (Greeno, 1976; 1980). Furthermore, explication of the prior knowledge of students could guide the design of instruction specifically intended to address their difficulties. In this section, we review the major findings of research exploring differences between the scientific problem-solving performance of individuals at different levels of expertise.

Simon and Simon (1978) analyzed the differences between expert and novice solutions of 19 kinematics problems. Their expert had extensive experience solving mechanics problems; their novice had only recently studied the kinematics chapter of an elementary physics textbook and had never solved problems of this kind before. The problems involved situations in which objects moved with uniform acceleration. The following is an example:

> A bullet leaves the muzzle of a gun at a speed of 400 m/sec. The length of the gun barrel is 0.5 m. Assuming that the bullet is uniformly accelerated, what is the average speed within the barrel? (p. 329)

There were major differences in the overall solution strategies used by the two problem solvers. Not surprisingly, the expert solved the problems in less than one quarter of the time needed by the novice and made fewer errors. But of more interest was the fact that he seemed to solve the problems almost automatically. Immediately upon reading the problem statement, the expert generated equations into which known values had already been substituted. That is, he spontaneously and almost effortlessly combined information given in the problem statement with his knowledge of physical laws, to produce already instantiated equations. He then easily solved these equations.

The novice's solution was in sharp contrast to the expert's smoothly executed sequences of identifying, instantiating, and solving equations. The novice had to ask herself at each step what to do next, and frequently expressed little confidence in her abilities. She had to search through pages of the textbook for formulas that might apply, and would explicitly mention which formulas she was considering.

Simon and Simon found some evidence that the expert used what they referred to as "physical intuition." They defined physical intuition in information-processing terms as the construction of a mental representation of the physical situation, and the use of that representation to guide the generation and application of equations.[2] The expert's thorough qualitative understanding of the problem situation, in the form of such a representation, allowed him to solve the problems efficiently and quickly. Simon and Simon contrasted this "physical" approach of the expert (moving from the problem statement to a representation of the physical situation, and from that representation to equations) with the novice's "algebraic" approach (going directly from the problem statements to the equations). They asserted that knowledge of the physical laws or equations needed for solving these problems comprises only the "algebra of kinematics." To "know physics," an individual must be able to understand complex problem situations in terms of the laws of physics.

There were also differences observed in the sequence in which equations were generated by the expert and novice. The expert seemed to use a "working-forward" strategy, operating from the givens of the problem by successively applying equations until the desired values were found. The novice's strategy was nearly opposite to the expert's—she used a "working-backward" approach, going from the unknowns to the givens. She would look for formulas that contained variables that were wanted in the problem, and apply those formulas. If those formulas contained other variables for which the values were unknown, she would apply the same procedure to find values for these new variables.

Simon and Simon hypothesized that these two strategies accounted for the differences between the orders in which equations were generated by the expert and novice. To test this hypothesis, Simon and Simon created two very simple production systems to try to model the observed performances. Productions are condition-action pairs, which are more sophisticated versions of the stimulus-response pairs of classical behaviorist psychology. Whenever the conditions in one of the productions are satisfied, the action associated with that condition is performed. (One can think of these as a type of if-then statement.) Production systems are lists of these condition-action pairs that constitute a theory about the contents and organization of some portion of memory. Many of the recent information-processing theories are in the form of production systems.

Simon and Simon created one production system representing the working-forward strategy of the expert, and one representing the working-backward strategy of the novice. In both cases, the action part of each production was one of the kinematic equations and the condition part was a list of variables in that equation. The systems differed in only one respect. In the expert system the rule was: If the equation contains known variables (condition), then try to solve that equation (action). In the novice system the rule was: If the equation contains one or more desired variables (condition), then try to solve that equation (action).

Simon and Simon compared the sequences of equations that each of these systems generated with the sequences produced by their two subjects. They found that their simple models matched the equation-generating behaviors of the expert and novice very

---

2. This notion of understanding as the construction of a mental representation of the elements and relations in a situation is central to recent cognitive theories of language understanding (Anderson, 1976; Norman & Rumelhart, 1975; Schank & Abelson, 1977).

well, thus confirming that the working-forward and working-backward strategies constituted reasonable explanations of some differences between the observed solutions.

Substantially expanded, computer-implemented versions of the models were developed to account for the performance of a larger group of subjects solving kinematics and dynamics problems (Larkin et al., 1980b). One model simulated naive performance; the other, competent performance. The naive system (ME) used "means-ends analysis," and the other (KD) used "knowledge development"—strategies that correspond, respectively, to Simon and Simon's working-backward and working-forward procedures. The KD model also had knowledge of problem-solving "methods" (such as an "energy method" or "force method") consisting of clusters of physics principles.

The models were run on Simon and Simon's 19 kinematics problems plus 2 new problems requiring different principles. The resulting traces were compared with the performance of 8 novices (undergraduate students taking their first physics course) and 11 experts (physics professors and advanced graduate students) solving the 2 new problems, plus the data from Simon and Simon's expert and novice solving the other 19 problems. The models predicted well the order in which the human subjects applied principles during their solutions. They also reflected the greater automaticity with which experts used physics principles—in the ME model, the selection and instantiation of equations are done in separate steps; in the KD model, they are performed in a single step.

Larkin (1981a, b) also explored the question of how a less-skilled problem solver might improve through practice. She created a production system, ABLE, that "learns" from experience in solving problems. This model, which initially uses an algebraic, means-ends strategy in its "barely ABLE" state, acquires new knowledge each time it solves a problem, until it becomes "more ABLE." The process by which it learns is to notice, whenever it successfully applies a principle, how and under what problem conditions that principle was applied, and to create a new production based on that information. In its final state, the program uses the KD strategy to generate equations automatically.

In the studies thus far discussed, the experts were solving what were for them very easy problems. To obtain more information about experts' capabilities, Larkin (1977, 1980) observed physicists solving more complex problems in mechanics. These studies revealed a rich sequence of problem representations, which the experts used at different points in their solutions.

The experts' solutions included an initial period of "qualitative analysis," which was performed before any equations were generated. In this preliminary phase, the experts first drew sketches representing the physical situation described in the problem, then drew more abstract diagrams representing the problem in terms of concepts from their knowledge of physics (such as force and energy). The information in these abstract representations was not mentioned in the problem statement, yet this information apparently was required for understanding the problem.

During the qualitative phase, the experts also explored alternative ways to solve the problem. This planning was done at a very general level. The experts referred to a small set of candidate solution methods, which consisted of clusters or "chunks" of physics principles to be applied as a group. The experts considered these alternatives, exploring the utility of one or more before selecting an approach to use. After this exploratory stage was completed, as signaled by their writing of an equation, none of the experts subsequently changed his or her approach to a problem.

Novices, in contrast, generated equations shortly after reading the problem, without this intervening step of checking the usefulness of coherent solution methods. Frequently, the novices did sketch physical situations described in the problems, and sometimes they drew abstract representations, especially force diagrams. However, they then went directly to, and stayed at, a single detailed level during the rest of their solutions, always writing and manipulating equations.

Larkin (1980) modeled some of the experts' planning processes in a production system, and McDermott and Larkin (1978) developed a model, known as PH632 (for the number of the most advanced mechanics course at Carnegie-Mellon University), that simulates experts' reliance upon a sequence of problem representations. Four types of representations are used by these systems: the verbal statement of the problem, a sketch of the physical situation in the problem, a more abstract representation including conceptual entities in physics, and a quantitative representation in the form of equations (referred to as verbal, naive, scientific, and mathematical representations by Larkin [1982a]). Larkin (1982b) has also modeled the important role of spatial knowledge in construction of the naive and scientific representations.

Problem Perception

Knowledge for constructing problem representations has also received attention in studies of subjects performing tasks other than solving problems. Chi and her colleagues (Chi, Feltovich, & Glaser, 1981; Chi, Glaser, & Rees, 1981) asked expert physicists and novice physics students to sort mechanics problems and analyzed the categories they constructed and their justifications for those categories. Novices were found to sort problems on the basis of physical objects (such as pulleys and inclined planes) and concepts of physics (such as friction) mentioned in the problem statements. Experts sorted problems on the basis of more abstract physics principles (such as conservation of energy) that were applicable to the problems but were not mentioned in the problem statements. (Very similar results have been found in mathematics by Silver [1979] and Schoenfeld and Herrmann [1982].) Chi et al.'s data are quite consistent with the findings that experts represent and plan solutions for problems in terms of underlying physics principles, whereas novices' solutions are not guided by this kind of understanding, since they do not "see" the physics principles underlying the problem statements.

Knowledge of Basic Concepts

Not only do novices lack the ability to understand problems in terms of scientific principles, they also have been found to misinterpret individual concepts. A catalog of students' nonscientific conceptions is being accumulated by researchers around the world. For example, a number of studies document students' inability to predict or explain correctly the motion of objects (Champagne et al., 1980; Clement, 1982; diSessa, 1982; McCloskey, 1983; McCloskey et al., 1980; McCloskey & Kohl, 1983; Minstrell, 1982a; Shanon, 1976; Trowbridge & McDermott, 1980; Trowbridge & McDermott, 1981; Viennot, 1979), or to explain basic concepts like gravity and heat (Albert, 1978; Gunstone & White, 1981; Mali & Howe, 1979). It has been shown that students' naive conceptions are extremely widespread and are very resistant to change, persisting after considerable exposure to scientifically correct explanations in traditional instruction and in experimental laboratory settings.

Artificial-Intelligence Programs

Processes for building and using problem representations have also been explored in artificial-intelligence programs. (Although the programs were not intended to model human cognition, they can identify processes for which functionally equivalent mechanisms might exist in human performance.) Novak (1977), for example, has demonstrated the process of translating verbal problem statements (for statics problems) into representations of the objects and relations in the problems. His program, ISAAC, can read, understand, draw pictures of, and solve a set of problems stated in English. A program called NEWTON, by de Kleer (1975, 1977), models qualitative analysis involving "envisionment" of how objects will move in problem situations. For some simple problems, this analysis is sufficent for reaching a solution. When it is not, NEWTON uses means-ends analysis to select formulas to apply. Another program, MECHO (Bundy, 1978; Bundy et al., 1979; Byrd & Borning, 1980), models several levels of representation in the solution of statics and dynamics problems. All of the programs cited model the critical role of problem understanding and representation in achieving solutions to complex problems.

Summary

We have briefly reviewed several empirical and theoretical analyses related to scientific problem solving. These include detailed studies of individuals at different levels of expertise; computer models simulating some aspects of human information processing during problem solving; and artificial-intelligence models of problem solving. A good deal has been learned from these analyses about the nature of the knowledge required for solving problems in complex subject-matter domains.

Knowledge for understanding and representing problems frequently is critical for reaching correct, or even reasonable, problem solutions. Understanding is viewed as a process of creating a representation of the problem. This representation mediates between the problem text and its solution, guiding expert human and computer systems in the selection of methods for solving problems. Novices tend to be quite deficient with respect to understanding or perceiving problems in terms of fundamental principles or concepts. They cannot or do not construct problem representations that are helpful in achieving solutions.

Strategic knowledge governs the approach problem solvers take to the task. Experts solve problems using a process of successive refinements—unless they are faced with a simple problem for which they can immediately recall a specific solution method. The strategy used by experts is to perform high-level planning and qualitative analysis before beginning to generate equations. Novices do not have the knowledge required to approach problems in this way, and tend to go directly from the problem text to equations.

Problem solving also requires extensive *knowledge of basic concepts and principles.* Experts have a great amount of domain-specific factual knowledge that is both technically correct and well organized. Experts also have knowledge about when concepts and principles are applicable and useful, and procedures for interpreting and applying their factual knowledge. Novices are lacking much of this knowledge, do not have their knowledge well organized, and frequently exhibit naive preconceptions rather than scientifically correct ideas.

Finally, *repertoires of familiar patterns and known procedures* are necessary for reliable performance. Experts have such repertoires, including knowledge of problem types and solution methods, which novices have not yet developed.

THE PRESCRIPTIVE APPROACH

The psychological analyses discussed thus far have provided detailed descriptions of the performance of problem solvers at different levels of expertise. These analyses have revealed that the knowledge required for solving problems is much richer, more extensive, and more complex than we had realized. This complexity was not recognized earlier because so much knowledge is implicit in skilled performance and remains "tacit" (Polyani, 1967) for the person who has the knowledge. Since the expert problem solvers themselves are unaware of this tacit knowledge, those who teach problem solving have not been able to make explicit for students the knowledge needed to achieve good performance. Since this tacit knowledge has rarely been taught explicitly, it is not surprising that novices differ so much from experts, even after the novices have completed courses that cover the problem-solving material.

It might appear that we should now begin to remedy the problem by directly teaching students the knowledge possessed by experts. Although this approach has merit, we believe it is not always the one to follow. First, we may not always want to teach beginning students this expert knowledge. For one thing, not all students need to reach the very advanced level of performance exhibited by the experts in the studies. Students vary widely in their professional goals, and it is not reasonable to expect extensive expertise in a scientific domain of every student enrolled in each course in that domain. Also, there is no reason to assume that individuals we somewhat arbitrarily dub "experts" on the basis of their positions or titles always perform optimally. We want students to achieve at least minimally competent levels of performance, and competent performance is not necessarily synonymous with expert performance.

Even if we wanted to teach novices to be experts, it is not clear that we could. Experts acquire their knowledge through years of experience. Their large repertoires of familiar patterns and highly automatized procedures develop gradually through repeated exposure to problems and may be extremely difficult to teach directly. We are also well aware that novices do not begin instruction as "blank slates." Their prior knowledge includes strong preconceptions that are frequently incompatible with the ideas and language of the science to be learned. That existing knowledge must be reorganized and restructured to accommodate and assimilate the new knowledge, and some of the prior ideas must be relinquished and replaced. As demonstrated by Minstrell (1982b, 1983), it may be necessary to engage students in extended periods of intense discussion before they accept "expert" scientific explanations and definitions that differ from their earlier intuitions.

Instead of teaching novices to be experts, then, a more realistic goal might be what we could call "expert novice" performance. An individual at this level would be able to solve problems competently, but not necessarily by the same processes as experts. In order to design instruction for this purpose, we need to generate theories of the knowledge novices could rely on to achieve good performance. This approach, which has been referred to as "prescriptive" (Bruner, 1964; Reif, 1979), involves identification of effective problem-solving methods that we might wish to prescribe for students to learn. Purely descriptive analyses, in contrast, are intended to document and explain naturally occurring performance whether or not that performance is effective.

A prescriptive theory of problem-solving performance could incorporate components of descriptive theories of expert performance, but it would differ from the latter in important ways. For the highly automatized procedures of the expert, it would substitute alternative procedures that draw on the knowledge available to novices. For example, experts recognize types of problems and rapidly retrieve and apply solution methods that are associated with problem types, but novices have neither knowledge of problem types nor stores of known methods. A prescriptive theory would explicate procedures novices could use to recognize features of problems and decide which solution method to use for which problem. Such a theory would also take into consideration the preconceptions and knowledge deficiencies of novices that lead to common errors, and would include preventive or compensatory procedures to block or catch these errors. For example, a variety of powerful checks not necessarily evident in experts' solutions could be included throughout the solution procedure.

It should be noted that the "expert novice" level of performance is not necessarily a level where individuals would remain for long periods of time after instruction. It encompasses a set of minimal, reliably effective procedures intended for conscious and deliberate use by individuals who have not yet acquired years of experience. For those individuals who continue in the field, problem-solving procedures would be expected to evolve naturally, becoming less explicit, and more automatized and efficient. As Resnick (1976) has suggested, efficient instruction is not necessarily direct instruction in skilled performance. Rather, the aim can be to teach routines "that put learners in a good position to discover or invent efficient strategies for themselves" (p. 72).

As described by Heller and Reif (1984), the formulation and testing of a prescriptive model involves five major steps:

- Specify the characteristics of the tasks to be performed and of the persons who are to perform these tasks.

- Formulate a model of the procedures and associated factual knowledge required by such persons to perform those tasks.

- Translate the model into a detailed "program" consisting of a sequence of specific steps and associated facts.

- Pilot test and modify the program until all steps can be easily interpreted and reliably executed.

- Carry out studies in which individuals act in accordance with the program for the model, and observe in detail the resulting performance.

Experiments can also compare the performance that results when different subjects work in accordance with different models. By comparing models that differ in specific ways, one can ascertain which particular features of the models are necessary or sufficient for good performance.

The approach is analogous to that used in artificial intelligence for building and evaluating models of effective performance by computers. In both cases, one develops a program that embodies a theory of how a task can be performed, and tests that program by running it. If the task is performed well, the model is judged to be sufficient; if not, the model is inadequate and needs modification.

The use of this approach with human problem solvers is, however, motivated by very different goals from those generally pursued by artificial-intelligence theorists. In general, an effective artificial-intelligence program is an end in itself. In contrast, development of a sound model of human performance is a means for identifying potentially teachable problem-solving methods. Once a prescriptive model is shown to lead to good problem-solving performance by human subjects, there still remains the question of whether to teach people to use that model. The answer to this question depends on factors such as how easily learnable the knowledge in the model is. Teaching experiments would be required to evaluate these aspects of a validated model of performance.

An Example from Physics Problem Solving

Heller and Reif (1984) applied the prescriptive approach to one aspect of scientific problem solving, namely the initial qualitative description of problems. Because their methods may be very useful as a bridge between descriptive studies and the design of instruction, we present here some of the details of their work.

Prescriptive Model of Problem Description

Reif and Heller (1982) formulated a prescriptive model of effective human problem solving in the domain of physics and studied one component of the model, the process for generating a useful initial description (or "representation") of any problem. According to their model, the generation of the initial description can conveniently be decomposed into two stages. In the first of these, a person generates a "basic description" of the problem, which summarizes explicitly the information specified and wanted in the problem, introduces useful symbols, and expresses the relevant information in convenient symbolic representations (in pictorial as well as verbal forms). Although generation of the basic description is nontrivial, Heller and Reif restricted their attention to the second, more complex and interesting stage of the description process, the generation of a "theoretical description" of a problem.

A theoretical description of a problem is a description deliberately expressed in terms of special concepts and properties in the knowledge base for the problem domain (corresponding to the "abstract" or "scientific" problem representations in descriptive analyses). The prescriptive model specifies the *exact* steps by which the declarative knowledge should be applied to generate a theoretical description. That is, it specifies how to decide which particular objects to describe, how to apply concepts to describe these objects, how to exploit properties of these concepts, and how to apply principles in the knowledge base to check that the description is internally consistent and correct.

The procedure for generating theoretical descriptions of any problem in mechanics is summarized in Table 1. For each system, two diagrams are drawn: one describing its motion; the other, its interaction with other systems. An algorithm is provided for identifying all short- and long-range forces on a system. This algorithm stresses identification of systems responsible for exerting those forces. An example will help to make clear how this procedure is used to describe a problem.

Consider the problem in Figure 1. The description procedure would be applied to both block *A* and block *B*, yielding motion and interaction diagrams of each. For example, for block *B*, first a motion diagram is drawn to describe its velocity and acceleration. We have been told that block *B* is pulled to the left at constant speed—hence a labeled arrow is drawn on a simple sketch of block *B* to indicate that the velocity is to the left,

Table 1. Procedure for generating a theoretical problem description in mechanics.

---

1. *Descriptions of relevant systems.* At each relevant time, describe in the following way each relevant system (if simple enough to be considered a single particle), introducing convenient symbols and expressing simply related quantities in terms of the same symbol:

   • *Description of motion:* Draw a "motion diagram" indicating available information about the position, velocity, and acceleration of the system.

   • *Description of forces:* Draw a "force diagram" indicating available information about all external forces on the system. Identify the forces as follows:

      • *Short-range forces.* Identify every object that touches the given system and thus interacts with it by short-range interaction. For each such interaction, indicate on the diagram the corresponding force and all available information about it.

      • *Long-range forces.* Identify all objects interacting with the given system by long-range interactions. (Ordinarily this is just the earth interacting by gravitational interaction.) For each such interaction, indicate on the diagram the corresponding force and all available information about it.

2. *Checks of descriptions.* Check that the descriptions of motion and interaction are qualitatively consistent with known motion principles (e.g., that the acceleration of each particle has the same direction as the total force on it, as required by Newton's motion principle, ma = F).

---

and a note is made that the acceleration of the block is zero (it moves at constant speed). Then the interaction diagram is drawn to describe all forces on block B. First all objects that touch the block are identified, and all of the corresponding short-range forces exerted on B by those objects are indicated. As shown in Figure 1, the objects are the system pulling block B to the left, which exerts an applied force $\mathbf{F_0}$; the string, which exerts a tension force $\mathbf{T}$; the floor, which exerts normal and friction forces $\mathbf{N}$ and $\mathbf{f}$; and block A, which exerts normal and friction forces $\mathbf{N}'$ and $\mathbf{f}'$. Then the procedure identifies the long-range force $\mathbf{F_g}$ exerted on block B by the earth.

Despite its seeming simplicity, this procedure is far from trivial. Application of the procedure ensures that highly important declarative knowledge is systematically and correctly incorporated in the initial description of any problem, and that common errors are prevented. For example, the procedure exploits motion principles in mechanics to check the correctness of problem descriptions. One such check requires that the descriptions of the motion and interaction of each system be qualitatively consistent with the motion principle ma=F; that is, that the acceleration of a particle have the same direction as the total force on it. In order for this check to be performed, both the motion and interaction of each system must have been described explicitly, as required by the model.

The power of this checking procedure can be seen in the case of the problem in Figure 2. It is quite easy for subjects to determine that the acceleration of block C is directed to the right. However, subjects very frequently claim that the friction force on this block is directed to the left, because "friction opposes the motion" of an object and block C moves to the right. (In fact, friction opposes the relative motion of objects,

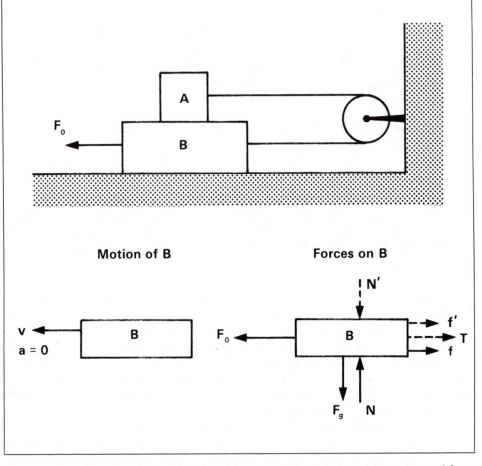

Figure 1. Sample mechanics problem involving two sliding blocks, with motion and force descriptions of block B. (Forces frequently omitted by subjects are indicated by dashed arrows.)

and block C would move to the left relative to block A, in the absence of friction.) The checking procedure would immediately reveal that the direction of this force is inconsistent with that of the acceleration and must therefore be incorrect. Thus this check provides a reliable method for detecting and correcting the common error of ascribing the wrong direction to the friction force in this problem.

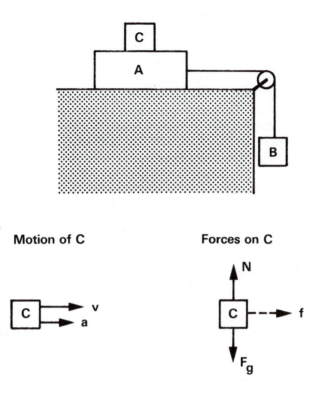

Figure 2. Problem involving three blocks, with motion and force descriptions of block *C*. (The friction force f, indicated by a dashed arrow, is frequently ascribed the wrong direction, i.e., to the left.)

Testing the Model of Problem Description

The basic paradigm for testing a prescriptive model of human performance is to induce subjects to act in accordance with the model, and to observe whether the resulting performance is effective in the predicted ways. In the experimental procedure used by Heller and Reif (1984), subjects were asked to carry out the description and subsequent solution of various problems by executing "external-control" directions that were read to them successively according to the program specified by the model. For purposes of comparison, a modified model was formulated omitting selected features of the proposed model of good performance. The experiment could then reveal whether the particular features omitted from the original model were actually necessary for good performance.

It should be emphasized that the aim of such external-control experiments is to evaluate the merits of a proposed model of good performance, not to teach. Subjects may, of course, learn incidentally while working under conditions of external control. However, such learning need not occur, because no effort is made to have the subjects internalize the directions. A subject, performing very well while working under external control, might revert to poor performance if that control were removed.

Heller and Reif's experiment compared the performance of three groups of subjects: a group *M*, guided by external-control directions based on the full model M; a group

M^*, guided by similar directions based on the modified model M^*; and a comparison group C, working without any external guidance. The procedures in model M were elaborated into detailed external-control directions (see Heller & Reif, 1984). The relevant factual knowledge was summarized in written form so that subjects could refer to it during problem-solving sessions. The external-control directions for generating problem descriptions were supplemented with some additional directions to provide minimal guidance for generating and combining equations.

The modified model was designed to approximate the descriptive advice commonly found in physics textbooks, and is considerably less complete and explicit than the proposed model M. The differences between the two versions are the following: (*a*) M includes descriptions of both motion and interaction for every system, while M^* includes only a description of interactions. (*b*) M includes a detailed procedure specifying how to enumerate all forces on a system, while M^* includes only a direction to enumerate all forces on the system by other objects. (*c*) M contains some explicit references to elements in the knowledge base (particular properties of motion and interaction), while such explicit references are omitted in M^*. (*d*) M includes some powerful checks based on general physics principles, while M^* does not include such checks. Refer to Heller & Reif (1984) for detailed differences between the elaborated versions of model M and model M^*.

To ensure that the directions could be implemented, we pretested them extensively with pilot subjects, and designed practice activities to familiarize experimental subjects with the directions.

Experimental Method

Two approximately matching sets of mechanics problems, three in each set, were selected from commonly used introductory physics texts (French, 1971; Resnick & Halliday, 1977; Symon, 1971). All of the problems could be solved by application of one fundamental motion principle, Newton's second law (ma = F).

The subjects in the experiment were 24 undergraduate students enrolled in the second course of an introductory physics sequence at the University of California, Berkeley. First one set of problems was individually administered to all subjects as a pretest. Then, subjects in groups M and M^* solved a second set of problems working under external control, while subjects in group C did the problems without such guidance. Subjects were asked to talk aloud about what they were thinking while solving the problems, and their verbalized statements were recorded. All subjects, during all sessions, had access to the printed summary of mechanics principles.

Subjects working with external guidance were read the standard directions from a script, one step at a time. Each direction had to be performed by the subject before the next one was read. As long as the subject implemented the direction, the experimenter considered that direction executed, regardless of whether it had been done correctly. However, if instead of answering the question or performing the step, a subject prematurely skipped to a later step, he or she was stopped and the direction was repeated until an appropriate response was made.

Once some initial resistance to surrendering control to the experimenter had been overcome, many subjects became overtly positive in their response to the directions. Several remarked with notable surprise that the steps "really work" and that the problems suddenly seemed "easy" to solve. These reactions contrasted sharply with comments made during the pretests, when subjects complained that the problems were very hard and that they did not know how to begin, what to do next, or whether they were doing anything correctly.

Results

The adequacy of every solution was assessed with respect to four performance criteria: the adequacy of subjects' analyses of motion, the adequacy of subjects' analyses of interaction, the adequacy of the set of equations generated, and the correctness of the final answer obtained. The data summarized in Figure 3 show the mean number of correct responses for each of these measures on problems solved during the pretest and the treatment sessions.

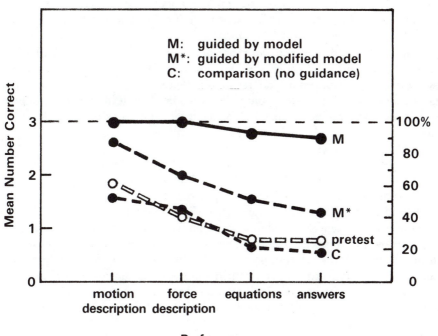

Figure 3. Graph of the mean number of solutions (out of three) with correct performance on specified measures.

The data show that (*a*) the procedures proposed by the model are sufficient for producing successful solutions (subjects in group *M*, working under external control, performed nearly perfectly), (*b*) the subjects' prior knowledge was definitely not sufficient to adequately solve the kinds of problems given (performance on the pretest and by subjects in the comparison group was quite poor), and (*c*) at least some of the components deleted from model *M* to create model *M** are indeed necessary for achieving good problem solutions (the performance of subjects in group *M** was significantly worse than that of subjects in group *M*).

Relevance of the Prescriptive Approach

In this work, Heller and Reif formulated and validated a prescriptive model of some of the knowledge and procedures needed for generating initial descriptions of mechanics problems. The model was tested by a method of inducing human subjects to solve problems using the prescribed procedures. Results indicated that the model does lead to explicit and correct problem descriptions, and that these descriptions markedly facilitate the construction of correct problem solutions.

Descriptive analyses have shown that novices typically lack the kinds of strategic knowledge that were included in Heller and Reif's model—that is, the meta-knowledge that it is important to describe a problem with care before attempting to solve it, explicit knowledge about what types of information should be included in an effective description, and knowledge of explicit procedures for generating such descriptions. Experts usually possess such knowledge, but it is predominantly in tacit form, and the knowledge is rarely taught explicitly in physics courses. The work discussed here shows that *such knowledge can be made more explicit, and that, if used by students, it can strikingly improve their problem-solving performance.*

What is the relevance of this work for problem-solving instruction? A prescriptive model can be thought of as a specification of the target knowledge students should acquire as a result of instruction or, in Greeno's (1976) terminology, the "cognitive objectives" of instruction. Such a model, once it has been shown to lead to good performance, provides a concrete set of procedures and factual information for students to learn in the classroom.

INSTRUCTIONAL IMPLICATIONS

The studies of novice performance in scientific domains have shown that, even after instruction, many students lack real qualitative understanding of the concepts and problems they encounter in science courses. They also do not know how to approach problems, or when to apply which formulas, and why. We have every reason to believe that this situation holds for mathematics. At the risk of stating the obvious, we would say that a first, very general instructional implication of these findings is simply that there is a strong need for more effective instruction, particularly to prepare students to solve problems with understanding.

Such instruction should be specifically tailored to prepare students to solve the kinds of problems they will encounter. For the design of such instruction, an understanding of the *knowledge* required for solving problems is of paramount importance. Greeno (1980) summarized this point well:

> To teach students how to solve a class of problems, first analyze the knowledge that they need in order to solve that class of problems, and then carry out instruction that will result in their acquisition of the required knowledge. (p. 13)

At this point, both descriptive and prescriptive efforts have contributed powerful methods for identifying that knowledge. In order to design effective instruction in mathematical problem solving, then, we should continue to apply those methods in different problem domains to identify the specific knowledge that would need to be taught in each of those domains.

The literature also demonstrates the impressive *quantity*, level of *detail*, and *complexity* of the knowledge we must transmit to our students—it begins to seem amazing that some people do learn to solve even fairly standard problems in technical domains. The studies and theoretical models consistently show that one cannot solve problems correctly without a large amount of domain-specific knowledge. When even a small amount of this knowledge is missing or removed from descriptive or prescriptive models, performance deteriorates dramatically. Instruction must somehow supply students with the extensive body of knowledge needed to solve problems and must do so at a very fine level of detail.

Further, the scientific problem-solving literature has underscored the importance of particular kinds of knowledge that are needed for solving problems and that must be considered in the design of problem-solving instruction. We have learned that qualitative understanding of problems and concepts is extremely important in problem solving, yet is not acquired by students in science classes. This has also been shown in studies of mathematical problem solving (Paige & Simon, 1966; Hinsley et al., 1978). Students are not learning the importance of qualitative processes in problem solving. They seem instead to hold the serious misconception that mathematics and science are entirely quantitative fields, hence only quantitative reasoning is respectable. We need to communicate the greater value of seemingly vague qualitative exploration, including construction of sketches and general solution plans prior to generation of equations.

In addition, very specific procedures are needed for accomplishing these aspects of problem solving, as well as for constructing solutions by selecting and applying formulas. These procedures can and should be made explicit in instruction. Along with knowledge about *how* to perform the procedures, knowledge about *when* to perform them has been shown to be critical; the conditions under which to use knowledge must be made explicit to students.

By examining a given problem domain in mathematics, we can illustrate in more detail the implications of the scientific problem-solving literature. In the following discussion, we focus first on the question of *what* should be taught, by considering the kinds of knowledge required for solving the chosen class of problems. (This discussion is intended to exemplify the analysis that would be required prior to designing any actual instruction.) We then turn to some more speculative remarks about *how* this knowledge might be taught.

Instruction in Integration Problem Solving

Students in their first calculus course are typically required to solve the kind of problem illustrated in Figure 4. Such a problem involves the graphing of relatively elementary functions, with which students are expected to have had some experience in earlier mathematics courses. Theoretically, the student can now focus on the new notion of finding the area bounded by curves.

We observed an experienced mathematician solving this problem. She began by sketching the two curves, pausing briefly to determine their relative positions between their intersection points at $x = 0$ and $x = 1$ and including on the graph an indication of the interval to be considered. She then generated a fully instantiated expression for the integral (shown in Figure 4) without making explicit comments about the processes she was using. At that point, she stopped with a wave of her hand, stating that the rest was uninteresting, that the expression constituted the essence of the problem solution.

Problem statement

Find the area bounded by the curves $y = x^2$ and $y = x^3$ between $x = -1$ and $x = 2$.

Problem description

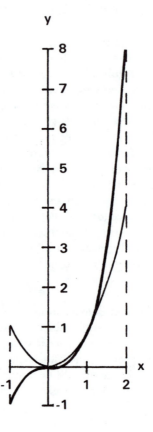

Solution

$$\int_{-1}^{0} (x^2 - x^3)\,dx + \int_{0}^{1} (x^2 - x^3)\,dx + \int_{1}^{2} (x^3 - x^2)\,dx$$

or

$$\int_{-1}^{1} (x^2 - x^3)\,dx + \int_{1}^{2} (x^3 - x^2)\,dx$$

Figure 4. Integration problem involving finding the area bounded by curves.

This performance conforms precisely with what would be expected of an expert. Her solution was guided by her understanding of the problem posed. Before generating an equation, she constructed a qualitative description of the problem situation, in this case a graph. She relied upon a smoothly executed procedure for selecting and applying the appropriate form for the integral. Much tacit knowledge was required for the performance of these activities, including familiarity with common patterns (in particular, the behavior of functions of the form $y = x^n$), knowledge of how to draw a sufficiently precise graph for this kind of problem, and knowledge of how to instantiate the expression for an integral representing the area between the curves on a given interval.

The importance of this tacit knowledge is made more evident when the performance of novices is examined. In a study by Patterson (1983), 34 students in second- and third-term undergraduate calculus courses were asked to solve the problem in Figure 4. Only a small portion (9%) of the students succeeded in generating a correct expression for the integral. Although many of the students (82%) did draw a graph for the problem, only a quarter of those graphs were accurate and complete enough to allow a correct solution to be determined.

The importance of knowledge of how to generate an expression for the integral is demonstrated by two findings in Patterson's study. First, only three of the seven students who had drawn accurate graphs went on to solve the problem correctly. Furthermore, even when Patterson subsequently provided the students with a correct graph for the problem, only a quarter of the sample could write a correct integral.

Clearly, traditional instruction is failing to provide students with the knowledge they need to solve such problems. Let us examine in more detail what that knowledge consists of.

Construction of an Initial Qualitative Description

First, the problem solver must know that a qualitative description of the problem should be constructed. In Patterson's study, 18% of the sample did not draw a graph, and another 12% drew incomplete sketches that contained only one of the two graphs required. It appears that instruction must become more effective in communicating to students that a graphic problem description is often useful, even critical, for achieving a solution to problems of this kind.

Second, the problem solver must know how to draw graphs. Although presumably these students have taken analytical geometry courses at some time during their mathematics education, apparently the experience was not sufficient to leave them with the skills required here. This may in part be related to the fact that problems of different kinds require somewhat different graphing skills, and analytic geometry courses do not stress the particular knowledge needed for describing calculus problems. Calculus instructors and teaching assistants tend to be aware of this difference, but their attempted remedies may be aggravating the students' difficulties instead of helping. Students report, for example, that their instructors stress that graphs for calculus problems do not need to be as precise as those the students were required to draw in high school. The instructors urge that the students not plot points, suggesting that they draw rough sketches of the curves instead. (In fact, students report that some teaching assistants take off grade points when points are plotted.)

What is not emphasized enough, however, is that some very specific knowledge is needed for sketching curves, and the students cannot simply abandon their earlier methods without some new procedures to take their place. Since the students have not had enough experience to be able to draw curves quickly on the basis of known patterns, some explicit instruction is needed to teach the students how to generate curves of approximately the right shape, in approximately the right position. Methods for doing so frequently do include plotting points—but these are critical points, such as intercepts, maxima, minima, or turning points. Intensive practice might be provided in sketching curves for various common functions.

In addition to the special knowledge that sketching curves requires, the particular demands of integration problems require some other, more specific, knowledge. It is critical that a graph of two curves in an integration problem depict all intersection points of the two curves and the relative positions of the curves on the interval of interest. This was not accomplished in over 60% of the graphs in Patterson's study. Her subjects overlooked points of intersection, reversed the positions of the curves, or represented them as equal over an entire interval. Examples of these common errors are shown in Figure 5.

To reiterate, students must know both that the intersection points and relative positions must be determined and how to determine them. Our expert "just knew" that the functions $y = x^2$ and $y = x^3$ intersect at exactly two points, $x = 0$ and $x = 1$. Novices lacking this fact may instead need to learn, for example, that they should find the roots of the equation $x^2 = x^3$. They must then know to determine the relative positions of the curves between these points, and must have a technique for doing so.

The major point here is that the nature of the problem dictates the particular activities required for constructing problem representations. That is, the use to which a graph is to be put determines the kinds of features that are critical in that graph. For problems involving the area between curves, the intersection points and relative positions are critical, but the precise shape of the graphs on that interval is not relevant to the problem solution. If the graph were to be used to determine the number of real solutions of an equation (such as $x^2 = x^3$), only the intersection points would be critical — the relative positions of the curves would be irrelevant. If the graph were to be used to provide specific values for the dependent variable over an interval, the curve would have to be drawn with far greater precision than that required for the first two purposes. Students need to gain an awareness of the relationship between the nature of the problem and the features needed in the description of that problem, and they must implement procedures that are appropriate for the current problem context.

Experts describe and solve problems on the basis of their understanding of the problems. Further evidence of experts' knowledge about the general nature of problems is their ability to classify problems in terms of their "deep structure," that is, the concepts or principles underlying the problem statement. Novices lack this knowledge and instead see only the surface features of the problems they encounter. This creates a serious educational challenge. With respect to integration problems, knowledge about critical features of the graph is intricately tied to the person's basic understanding of the notion of integration. That is, a concern for the relative positions of two curves grows out of the knowledge that a definite integral defines a region with specified boundaries, every one of which must be identified in order to generate a meaningful expression for the integral. Without this general notion of integration, a novice would have little reason to examine carefully the relative positions of curves in these problems. And if the relative positions are not correctly determined, any resulting expression for the integral is likely to be incorrect.

It may seem obvious that once a graph has been generated, it is important to make

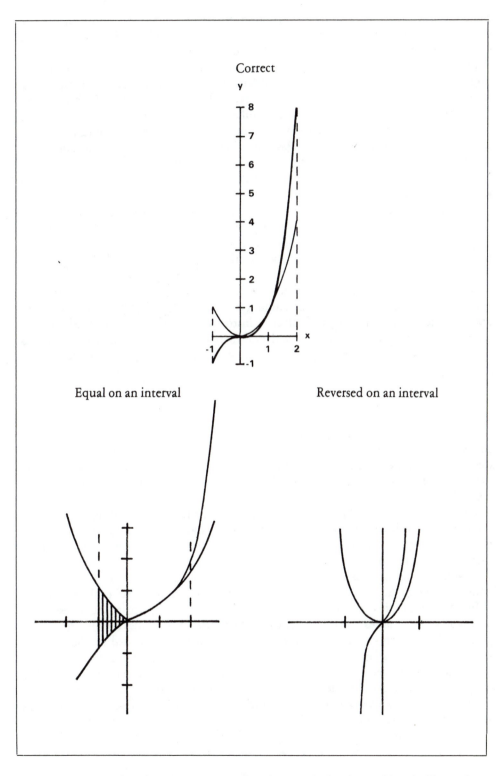

Correct

Equal on an interval

Reversed on an interval

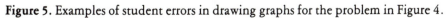

Figure 5. Examples of student errors in drawing graphs for the problem in Figure 4.

some use of it, but novices do not always do so. Patterson found that approximately one third of the students in her sample who drew graphs did not refer to them when writing an expression for the integral. The students' failure to use the graphs is just another symptom of the larger problem we have alluded to. On a very general level, the students do not really understand the concept of integration and the nature of the problem they have been asked to solve, hence they do not realize that a graph can contain information that is critical for the solution. One reasonable conclusion is that teaching novices ''to think to use'' the specific procedures we have been mentioning should not be attempted in isolation from instruction that stresses qualitative understanding of the concept of integration. Once this essential meaning has been understood, there will be some motivation for performing the specific graphing procedures and, in turn, a felt need to know how to perform those procedures.

Effective instruction would make clear to the students why the information in the graph is of great importance in solving the problem. If students were to learn that they should construct descriptions, how to do so, and how to generate equations to solve the problems, then we would expect that they would in turn naturally use the graphs they constructed.

Note that our account of the knowledge required for drawing and using graphs includes what may seem an excruciating amount of detail. We claim that this is the level of analysis required for the design of effective instruction. It is necessary to teach, and to have students practice, activities of such detail; there is no reason to assume that students will avoid the kinds of errors observed by Patterson without such explicit instruction.

Generation of Equations

The solution to the integration problem (Figure 4) requires the formulation of a symbolic expression for the area specified in the problem. A graphic representation that contains all of the elements in the problem and the relationships among these elements should already exist. The task then is to translate some of this information into mathematical notation.

Our expert accomplished that process easily—she drew an integral sign, glanced at the graph and filled in the limits of the integral and an expression for the integrand, glanced at the graph again and repeated the process for a second portion of the interval, then indicated that she was done.

None of the students in Patterson's study displayed such a reliable and easily executed procedure. Several did not even try to write an integral, instead evoking a variety of formulas from other topics in calculus. These gross errors underscore the necessity for instruction that includes criteria for deciding when different formulas or concepts are applicable. The students who did not even know that integration is used to find the area under curves are missing very basic knowledge about the meaning of integration.

Most of the students did generate expressions for integrals, but the errors they made reveal major deficiencies in their procedures for doing so. Close to 40% of the sample simply integrated across the entire interval mentioned in the problem statement, thus generating the expression

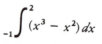

$$\int_{-1}^{2} (x^3 - x^2)\, dx$$

(presumably x^3 is everywhere greater than x^2 because 3 is greater than 2!). Others left out part of the total area or neglected an intersection point, even when such information was represented in their graphs. Several of the students who drew the curves as equal over part of the interval stated that there was no area there and so omitted an expression for the integral over that interval—a disturbing case involving correct interpretation of an incorrect graph. In general, whether or not a correct graph had been drawn, the students were unable to represent the requested area correctly as an integral.

Why is this activity so difficult for students? An analysis of the knowledge required for generating an integral shows that it involves a nontrivial set of actions for which the students are apparently lacking a complete procedure.

First, the problem solver must be clear about the goal of the enterprise. To understand the goal, it is necessary to know what is meant by "the area bounded by curves." Some students seem to take the words literally, and include only those areas completely enclosed by the curves (in our problem, the area between $x = 0$ and $x = 1$), while disregarding the rest of the interval specified in the problem. An area "bounded by curves" does not, in fact, need to be totally enclosed by those curves; the boundaries can, and frequently do, include vertical line segments.

The goal of the problem is to find this area, and the procedure for generating an integral can be thought of as a method for making explicit, in a particular way, the boundaries of the area of interest. In some cases, such as the problem we are examining, the total area has more than one part, where the "parts" are formed by changes in the relative positions of the two curves. Separate integrals are sometimes required to represent the areas in the different parts. The features of the graph that the problem solver must notice to distinguish such parts are not self-evident to novices—students must learn how to tell that the graph changes in an important way, and what the implications of the changes are.

A simple way to distinguish parts of the graph, and hence to determine how many integrals are needed, is on the basis of intersection points within the interval of interest, together with the endpoints. Sometimes this method yields more integrals than are needed (as in our problem), but it always identifies regions that differ in important ways. In any event, an explicit procedure is needed for determining subintervals for integration.

The problem solver then needs a set of rules specifying how to express the integrand for each segment of an interval. Generally, the integrand is formed by subtracting the "lower" function from the "higher," but in some cases this method does not apply and another expression for the area must be generated. Also, when problems ask for the "area under a curve," the integrand is not formed by taking a difference. Thus, students need specific knowledge of how to formulate the integrand under a variety of different conditions.

Finally, students need a procedure for evaluating the integral. We will not discuss this procedure here except to say that such "routine" activities are known to involve quite complex knowledge (see, for example, analyses of subtraction [Brown & Burton, 1978]).

What Should Be Taught?

We have focused in this section on identifying some of the knowledge that students need in order to be able to describe and solve problems involving the area between curves. Our analysis is far from exhaustive—it was primarily intended to demonstrate what can be revealed by such a focus. Yet, it is already evident that there is a tremendous amount to know, hence a great deal to teach. In our discussion, we have stressed knowledge for understanding problems, for constructing useful problem descriptions, and for selecting and applying principles or concepts to solve the problem. The knowledge for performing these activities includes meta-knowledge about the activities, and knowledge about when and how to perform them.

A simple answer to the question of what should be taught (or at least learned) is, as Greeno (1980) indicated, *the knowledge required for solving the problem.* This knowledge can, as we have shown, be explicated through descriptive and prescriptive analyses.

How Should Problem-Solving Knowledge Be Taught?

Research has told us much less about how to teach problem solving than about what to teach and about how to determine what to teach. But these questions are not unrelated.

Students need to become better able to reason qualitatively about problems, and to know when and how to perform the many component procedures required for solving problems. In order to encourage this learning, the students' attention should be turned to these particular activities. The following are some ways in which this might be accomplished.

Make Tacit Processes Explicit

Traditionally, class lectures have been ineffective means for developing problem-solving skills. This is in part because problem solving is heavily procedural, thus is probably best learned by doing (Anzai & Simon, 1979). However, we know that under certain conditions learning can occur through observation of a model performing the activity (Bandura, 1977). Instructors should be able to communicate some aspects of problem-solving knowledge in a large group setting, but only if they model in sufficient detail the process of building a solution. Too often, instructors jump from reading a problem statement to writing on the board an already completed solution, skipping the qualitative analyses, strategic decisions, and explanations of how and why each step was done. Missing too are the mistakes, tentativeness, and exploration that are all parts of problem solving. If these aspects of problem solving were modeled by instructors in greater detail, students would have at least a chance of learning some of these processes by observation.

Get Students Talking About Processes

Although observing an instructor modeling solution processes should be beneficial, more active involvement on the part of the student is very important. Students should be encouraged to generate those processes themselves and to think about their own thought processes. One technique that has been found useful is to have students solve a problem aloud, examine or observe a model solving the same problem using desired processes, and then discuss differences between their own and the model's procedures (Bloom &

Broder, 1950). Repeated activities of this type should help develop in students explicit awareness of the processes involved in describing and solving problems.

Provide Guided Practice

Students typically have an opportunity to practice solving problems, usually through homework. But these experiences are rarely structured in a way that ensures that the *right* activities are being practiced. We suggest that students need guided practice provided by intelligent coaches (human or computer). A coach would oversee the student's performance, interject comments when the student is performing in less than optimal ways, and provide suggestions for alternative methods. We use coaching to teach activities involving motor skills, such as athletics and playing musical instruments. It is ridiculous to think of someone learning to shoot baskets or play the violin only by watching a skilled performer, and the close scrutiny and feedback of a knowledgeable observer is known to be extremely useful for improving performance. It seems very likely that students would benefit from this kind of guidance when learning complex intellectual procedures as well.

Ensure That Component Procedures Are Well Learned

Carefully structured exercises could be used to help students develop the component procedures required for solving problems. What might such exercises look like? A promising approach is to provide students with problems that are partially solved, and have them practice performing selected subsets of the entire solution procedure (cf. Vygotsky, 1978). For example, with respect to generating equations for the type of integration problem we discussed, we could provide students with graphs and have them practice writing integrals for the area bounded by various curves on different intervals. By designing these graphs carefully, we could ensure that the students are exposed to the main kinds of situations that they should be able to handle. And by providing explicit guidance and prompt feedback on the basis of prescriptive analyses of knowledge, we could ensure that they were indeed practicing effective procedures.

Similarly, we could pose a variety of problems and ask only that the students draw graphs that are sketched appropriately for problems of this type. Again, with guidance and feedback, such exercises could develop specific components of the problem-solving knowledge students need to acquire.

Emphasize Both Qualitative Understanding and Specific Procedures

We have stressed that instruction in problem solving should differ from traditional educational efforts in two main ways: Much more attention should be paid to qualitative reasoning, and the component procedures and knowledge structures that are required for competent performance should be taught directly and explicitly. There are various ways in which those kinds of knowledge might be taught. For example, we could try to develop qualitative understanding of problems and concepts prior to attempting instruction in specific problem-solving procedures; or we could first provide practice using such procedures in the hope that experience would naturally bring about understanding of the problems. As Resnick (1983) explains:

> Research has not yet told us whether it is better to first become skillful at a procedure and then analyze it, or to allow procedures to grow out of understanding a situation. But research has made it clear that procedures must take on meaning and make sense or they are unlikely to be used in any situation that is at all different from the exact ones in which they were taught. (p. 478)

Careful instructional research is needed to inform us about how to teach in a way that communicates the meanings of procedures to our students. However, we can reasonably conclude that both understanding and procedures need to be emphasized, and we therefore recommend an iterative instructional strategy in which attention would shift frequently between practice of specific procedures and qualitative analysis of underlying concepts. Neither can be very meaningful or useful in the absence of the other, hence both must be stressed. We might first introduce the notion of integration for finding the area between curves in general, qualitative terms. We could then turn to specific problem-solving procedures, but intersperse frequent discussions about why the particular procedures are useful, and how they relate to earlier and later procedures. By performing detailed procedures for interpreting and applying principles and concepts, students may begin to understand better the general concepts involved in the problems. If they understand the general nature of the problems, students will have more reason to perform the procedures and may in fact be better at remembering how to perform them.

This combination of attention to qualitative reasoning and to performance of procedures is also needed to help students resolve conflicts between their conceptions and technically correct definitions and explanations. Specific feedback on details of their performances could flag such contradictions (recall our example of students' misinterpretation of "area bounded by curves"). Extended discussions may be needed to force students to confront the contradictions between their notions and scientific or mathematically correct conceptions (see Minstrell, 1982b, 1983).

Test for Understanding and Reasoning Processes

Unfortunately, students are very resistant to giving attention to anything that is not "going to be on the test." While we may be convinced that the kinds of knowledge we have been discussing are crucial to performing well on tests involving problem solving, it is difficult to convince students that that is the case. An alternative would be to accept students' preoccupation with exams, as distasteful as it may be, and use that concern to motivate attention to the problem-solving skills we know are important. Test items could ask for qualitative problem descriptions only, or for identification and justification of a solution method, rather than an answer to the problem. We would stress, in effect, that the problem *solution* is not synonymous with the *answer*, and it is the solution with which we are most concerned.

Some Pragmatic Comments

We have suggested a variety of general techniques and approaches for effective instruction. Some of them are currently practiced on a limited basis—for example, some instructors place strong emphasis upon both qualitative and quantitative aspects of subject matter, and some examinations are designed and graded for solutions, not just correct answers. However, even these occasional efforts have probably been based on insufficiently detailed analyses of underlying knowledge.

The basic approach of analyzing knowledge and tailoring instruction to teach that knowledge would be extremely time-consuming and seems overwhelming indeed. It requires expertise and energy on the part of teachers and instructional designers, considerable effort by students, and perhaps even serious restructuring of curricula and courses. Such restructuring may be necessary for educational systems to place the goal of teaching for mastery over that of screening out all but the most able students. Less material would be taught, in greater depth, and the focus would be on students' progress, not on the quantity of material covered.

As an alternative to restructuring current courses, another option would be to introduce special problem-solving courses or labs, or to design supplementary materials for individual use (such as computer-based tutors). Such measures might allow students continued exposure to the large amount of basic factual information traditionally considered important in each discipline, while they also learn how to solve problems that involve application of those facts and concepts.

Achieving a balance between traditionally stressed domain-specific facts and the large body of procedures, strategic knowledge, and qualitative understanding called for by recent research may indeed be a major pragmatic problem for the field of education. We know now that these kinds of knowledge are all critically important for competent technical problem solving.

REFERENCES

Albert, E. Development of the concept of heat in children. *Science Education* **62**, 389–99, 1978.

Anderson, J.R. *Language, memory, and thought*. Hillsdale, NJ: Lawrence Erlbaum Associates, 1976.

Anderson, J.R. *Acquisition of cognitive skill* (Technical Report 81-1). Pittsburgh: Carnegie-Mellon University, 1981.

Anzai, Y., & Simon, H.A. The theory of learning by doing. *Psychological Review* **86**, 124–40, 1979.

Bandura, A. *Social learning theory*. Englewood Cliffs, NJ: Prentice-Hall, 1977.

Bloom, B.S., & Broder, L.J. *Problem-solving processes of college students*. Chicago: University of Chicago Press, 1950.

Brown, J.S., & Burton, R. Diagnostic models for procedural bugs in basic mathematical skills. *Cognitive Science* **2**, 155–92, 1978.

Bruner, J.S. Some theorems on instruction illustrated with reference to mathematics. In E.R. Hilgard (Ed.), *Theories of learning and instruction: The 63rd yearbook of the National Society for the Study of Education* (Part 1). Chicago: University of Chicago Press, 1964.

Bundy, A. Will it reach the top? Prediction in the mechanics world. *Artificial Intelligence* **10**, 129–46, 1978.

Bundy, A., Byrd, L., Luger, G., Mellish, C., & Palmer, M. Solving mechanics problems using meta-level inference. In *Proceedings of the Sixth International Joint Conference on Artificial Intelligence*. Pittsburgh: International Joint Conferences, Inc., 1979.

Byrd, L., & Borning, A. *Extending MECHO to solve statics problems* (Technical Report DAI 137). Edinburgh: University of Edinburgh, Department of Artificial Intelligence, 1980.

Champagne, A.B., Klopfer, L.E., & Anderson, J.H. Factors influencing the learning of classical mechanics. *American Journal of Physics* **8**, 1074–75, 1980.

Chi, M.T.H., Feltovich, P., & Glaser, R. Categorization and representation of physics problems by experts and novices. *Cognitive Science* 5, 121–52, 1981.

Chi, M.T.H., Glaser, R., & Rees, E. Expertise in problem solving. In R. Sternberg (Ed.), *Advances in the psychology of human intelligence* (Vol. 1). Hillsdale, NJ: Lawrence Erlbaum Associates, 1981.

Clement, J. Students' preconceptions in introductory mechanics. *American Journal of Physics* 50, 66–71, 1982.

de Kleer, J. *Qualitative and quantitative knowledge in classical mechanics* (Technical Report AI-TR-352). Cambridge: Massachusetts Institute of Technology, Artificial Intelligence Laboratory, 1975.

de Kleer, J. Multiple representations of knowledge in a mechanics problem solver. In *Proceedings of the 5th International Joint Conference on Artificial Intelligence*. Cambridge, MA: The MIT Press, 1977.

diSessa, A. Unlearning Aristotelian physics: A study of knowledge-based learning. *Cognitive Science* 6, 37–76, 1982.

Duncker, K. On problem solving. *Psychological Monographs* 58, 1–112, 1945.

French, A.P. *Newtonian mechanics*. New York: W.W. Norton, 1971.

Greeno, J.G. Cognitive objectives of instruction: Theory of knowledge for solving problems and answering questions. In D. Klahr (Ed.), *Cognition and instruction*. Hillsdale, NJ: Lawrence Erlbaum Associates, 1976.

Greeno, J.G. A study of problem solving. In R. Glaser (Ed.), *Advances in instructional psychology* (Vol. 1). Hillsdale, NJ: Lawrence Erlbaum Associates, 1978.

Greeno, J.G. Trends in the theory of knowledge for problem solving. In D.T. Tuma & F. Reif (Eds.), *Problem solving and education: Issues in teaching and research*. Hillsdale, NJ: Lawrence Erlbaum Associates, 1980.

Gunstone, R.F., & White, R.T. Understanding of gravity. *Science Education* 65, 291–99, 1981.

Heller, I., & Reif, F. Prescribing effective human problem-solving processes: Problem description in physics. *Cognition and Instruction* 1, 177–216, 1984.

Hinsley, D.A., Hayes, J.R., & Simon, H.A. From words to equations: Meaning and representation in algebra word problems. In P.A. Carpenter & M.A. Just (Eds.), *Cognitive processes in comprehension*. Hillsdale, NJ: Lawrence Erlbaum Associates, 1978.

Kohler, W. *The mentality of apes*. New York: Harcourt Brace, 1927.

Larkin, J.H. *Problem solving in physics* (Technical Report). Berkeley: University of California, Group in Science and Mathematics Education, 1977.

Larkin, J.H. Skilled problem solving in physics: A hierarchical planning approach. *Journal of Structural Learning* 6, 121–30, 1980.

Larkin, J.H. Cognition of learning physics. *American Journal of Physics* 49, 534–41, 1981(a).

Larkin, J.H. Enriching formal knowledge: A model for learning to solve textbook physics problems. In J. Anderson (Ed.), *Cognitive skills and their acquisition*. Hillsdale, NJ: Lawrence Erlbaum Associates, 1981(b).

Larkin, J.H. The role of problem representation in physics. In D. Gentner & A. Stevens (Eds.), *Mental models*. Hillsdale, NJ: Lawrence Erlbaum Associates, 1982(a).

Larkin, J.H. *Spatial reasoning in solving physics problems* (Technical Report C.I.P. No. 434). Pittsburgh: Carnegie-Mellon University, 1982(b).

Larkin, J.H., McDermott, J., Simon, D.P., & Simon, H.A. Expert and novice performance in solving physics problems. *Science* 208, 1335–42, 1980(a).

Larkin, J.H., McDermott, J., Simon, D.P., & Simon, H.A. Models of competence in solving physics problems. *Cognitive Science* 4, 317–45, 1980(b).

Mali, G.B., & Howe, A. The development of earth and gravity concepts among Nepali children. *Science Education* 63, 685–91, 1979.

Maltzman, I. Thinking: From a behavioristic point of view. *Psychological Review* 62, 275–86, 1955.

McCloskey, M. Intuitive physics. *Scientific American* **248**, 122–30, 1983.

McCloskey, M., Caramazza, A., & Green, B. Curvilinear motion in the absence of external forces: Naive beliefs about the motion of objects. *Science* **210**(5), 1139–41, 1980.

McCloskey, M., & Kohl, D. Naive physics: The curvilinear impetus principle and its role in interactions with moving objects. *Journal of Experimental Psychology* **9**, 146–56, 1983.

McDermott, J., & Larkin, J.H. Re-representing textbook physics problems. In *Proceedings of the 2nd National Conference, the Canadian Society for Computational Studies of Intelligence*. Toronto: University of Toronto Press, 1978.

Minstrell, J. Conceptual development research in the natural setting of a secondary school science classroom. In M.B. Rowe (Ed.), *Education in the 80's—Science*. Washington, DC: National Education Association, 1982(a).

Minstrell, J. Explaining the ''at rest'' condition of an object. *Physics Teacher* **20**, 10–14, 1982(b).

Minstrell, J. Getting the facts straight. *Science Teacher* **50**, 52–54, 1983.

Newell, A., & Simon, H.A. *Human problem solving*. Englewood Cliffs, NJ: Prentice-Hall, 1972.

Norman, D.A., & Rumelhart, D.E. *Explorations in cognition*. San Francisco: W.H. Freeman, 1975.

Novak, G.S., Jr. Representations of knowledge in a program for solving physics problems. *Proceedings of the Fifth International Joint Conference on Artificial Intelligence*. Cambridge, MA: MIT Press, 1977.

Paige, J.M., & Simon, H.A. Cognitive processes in solving algebra word problems. In B. Kleinmuntz (Ed.), *Problem solving:Research, method, and theory*. New York: John Wiley & Sons, 1966.

Patterson, D. *Calculus students' utilization of graphs as visual representations*. Unpublished doctoral dissertation, University of California, Berkeley, 1983.

Polyani, M. *The tacit dimension*. Garden City, NY: Anchor Books, 1967.

Reif, F. Theoretical and educational concerns with problem solving: Bridging the gaps with human cognitive engineering. In D.T. Tuma & F. Reif (Eds.), *Problem solving and education: Issues in teaching and research*. Hillsdale, NJ: Lawrence Erlbaum Associates, 1980.

Reif, F., & Heller, J.I. Knowledge structure and problem solving in physics. *Educational Psychologist* **17**, 102–27, 1982.

Resnick, L.B. Task analysis in instructional design: Some cases from mathematics. In D. Klahr (Ed.), *Cognition and instruction*. Hillsdale, NJ: Lawrence Erlbaum Associates, 1976.

Resnick, L.B. Mathematics and science learning: A new conception. *Science* **220**, 477–78, 1983.

Resnick, R., & Halliday, D. *Physics* (3rd ed.). New York: John Wiley & Sons, 1977.

Riley, M.S., Greeno, J.G., & Heller, J.I. Development of children's problem-solving ability in arithmetic. In H.P. Ginsburg (Ed.), *The development of mathematical thinking*. New York: Academic Press, 1983.

Schank, R.C., & Abelson, R.P. *Scripts, plans, goals, and understanding: An inquiry into human knowledge structures*. Hillsdale, NJ: Lawrence Erlbaum Associates, 1977.

Schoenfeld, A.H., & Herrmann, D.J. Problem perception and knowledge structure in expert and novice mathematical problem solvers. *Journal of Experimental Psychology* **8**, 484–94, 1982.

Shanon, B. Aristotelianism, Newtonianism and the physics of the layman. *Perception* **5**, 241–43, 1976.

Silver, E.A. Student perceptions of relatedness among mathematical verbal problems. *Journal for Research in Mathematics Education* **10**, 195–210, 1979.

Simon, D.P., & Simon, H.A. Individual differences in solving physics problems. In R. Siegler (Ed.), *Children's thinking: What develops?* Hillsdale, NJ: Lawrence Erlbaum Associates, 1978.

Symon, K.R. *Mechanics* (3rd ed.). Reading, MA: Addison-Wesley, 1971.

Trowbridge, D.E., & McDermott, L.C. Investigations of student understanding of the concept of velocity in one dimension. *American Journal of Physics* **48**, 1020–28, 1980.

Trowbridge, D.E., & McDermott, L.C. Investigations of student understanding of the concept of acceleration in one dimension. *American Journal of Physics* 49, 242–53, 1981.

Viennot, L. Spontaneous reasoning in elementary dynamics. *European Journal of Science Education* 1, 205–21, 1979.

Vygotsky, L.S. *Mind in society*. Cambridge, MA: Harvard University Press, 1978.

Wertheimer, M. *Productive thinking* (enlarged ed.). New York: Harper & Row, 1959.

Thinking Scientifically and Thinking Mathematically: A Discussion of the Paper by Heller and Hungate

Gerald A. Goldin[1]

Northern Illinois University

It is a pleasure to respond to the interesting remarks by Joan Heller and Harriet Hungate. I would like to begin by very briefly summarizing the main points from their paper to be addressed here.

The research described by Heller and Hungate is principally based on detailed cognitive analyses of textbook problem solving by means of expert-novice comparisons. Thus the main question being asked is, "What knowledge (in physics, for example) do expert problem solvers possess that novices do not possess, and what consequent differences are there in their respective cognitive processes?" Among the most prominent differences found is the presence of a phase called *qualitative analysis* in expert problem solving, which is largely absent from the problem solving of the novice. During this phase, the expert apparently constructs and manipulates a coherent nonverbal "internal representation" of the problem situation. Another important finding is the essential role played by complex domain-specific knowledge in the problem solving of the expert, much of which is tacit knowledge. Experts tend to incorporate this knowledge into "working forward" strategies, while novices make use of a far richer class of heuristic processes; these processes, however, cannot compensate for the novices' lack of domain-specific procedures.

Having gathered information by comparing experts and novices, the next step for Heller and Hungate is to develop prescriptive theories, explicating procedures which are accessible to novices and of assistance to them in solving the problems under consideration. They stress that such procedures may differ from those actually employed by experts, due either to the condition that they be available to the novice at the novice's level

---

1. The author acknowledges hospitality from Teachers College, Columbia University, and from the Department of Physics, Princeton University, where he was privileged to spend his 1982–83 sabbatical leave.

of knowledge, or to choices of long-range educational objectives more appropriate for the novice. Perhaps the most innovative idea in the Heller and Hungate paper is that of "external-control" experimentation, where the investigator directs to some degree the methods used by novice problem solvers. Thus the prescriptive theory is implemented in a very concrete way, and its consequences are observed. The authors' success in facilitating successful problem solving by this means speaks in favor of the accuracy of the cognitive analyses that they have carried out.

Finally, there are the instructional implications drawn by Heller and Hungate, which can be summarized as follows:

1. Teach "the knowledge needed to solve the problem."

2. In order to do this, develop the component procedures in detail.

3. Develop qualitative understandings of procedures.

4. Incorporate guided practice, testing for reasoning processes as well as qualitative understandings.

With these "lessons from scientific problem solving" in mind, I shall begin my response by trying to place this paper in a wider "scientific problem-solving" context. Then I shall comment from two vantage points in mathematical problem-solving research: first, from the perspective of the study of task variables; and, second, from the standpoint of a model for mathematical problem-solving competency. Finally, I shall discuss the value and limitations of Heller and Hungate's recommendations for mathematics education.

THE SCOPE OF SCIENTIFIC PROBLEM SOLVING

Let us consider what might come under the heading of "scientific problem solving," broadly construed, and ask how it differs from problem solving in mathematics. Perhaps the most important distinctions between the two follow from the special place in science held by experimental observation. In mathematics, the ultimate test of "correctness" in problem solving is whether the solution is logically consistent with a set of axioms; in science, the ultimate test is whether the solution is consistent with empirical data. Thus, there are fundamentally important classes of problems in science having to do with interpretation of experimental findings, development of new theory, and relationships between the two, which are not ordinarily encountered in mathematics.

Such problems are of many kinds. Problems in the interpretation of data include reconciliation of a set of data with existing theory, determination of the most important questions raised by the data, and determination of what bearing a given set of observations has on deciding open questions in a theory or on making the best choice between alternate theories. Related problems in theory development include constructing mathematical models that are consistent with given data; making choices among alternate models; modifying and improving a particular model to fit new data more closely, to achieve greater generality, or to maximize parsimony; generating testable hypotheses from theories; and designing experiments whose outcomes will help test the predictions of a particular theory or decide between competing theories.

From an epistemological standpoint, these considerations of "scientific method" suggest the importance of studying the origin and development of children's conceptions of physical reality and causation (Piaget, 1969). They also motivate the well-known roles played by balance beam tasks, pendulum tasks, and related activities in research on concrete operational and formal operational stages of thought. Such tasks assist in understanding how children form "scientific" theories; that is, how they go about predicting what will happen in structured environmental situations which are subject to physical law and can be experimentally manipulated.

The interplay between theory and experiment in science also implies that there is a fundamental place for heuristic processes such as "guess and check" or "search for a pattern" in scientific problem solving. Of course, these processes are of great psychological importance in mathematical problem solving as well. In science, however, it is immediately evident that without them empirical information cannot even be gathered, and hypothesis formation and testing cannot occur. The processes used in reconciling scientific theory with experiment are very similar to the "discovery learning" processes advocated so strenuously by a generation of mathematics educators and psychologists, represented at this meeting by Robert Davis and Lee Shulman (Shulman & Keislar, 1966). What better means could there be, perhaps, to learn about "mathematical discovery" than to study its occurrence in the domain of scientific problem solving, where our dependence on information from the empirical world denies to us a strictly deductive methodology?

In addition to scientific problems having to do with theory development and the reconciliation of experiment with theory, there is the class of narrower problems posed strictly within a given theory, which might be called problems in "applied science." Here a single, well-defined scientific model, such as Newtonian mechanics, is used to answer questions from given information without further experimental input. Such problems occur frequently as subproblems within the broader problems of theory development and experimental interpretation, and of course they predominate in standard textbook presentations. It should not be surprising that, in studying problems of this kind, it is found that the discovery processes tend to take a back seat to more technical, domain-specific procedures.

My first observation then, in response to Heller and Hungate, is to note the severe limitation that they have imposed upon themselves in selecting for discussion problems of the "textbook" variety. It would be more accurate to describe their conclusions as coming from "research on problem solving in the applied science domain," rather than from "research on scientific problem solving" generally. Of course, it is unquestionably important for classroom teachers of science to understand the cognitive processes involved in solving "standard" problems, and I certainly do not want to suggest that this constitutes an unworthy topic. However, we must be aware at the outset that implications drawn for mathematics education may tend to underemphasize greatly the importance of exploratory activities, observation and discovery, trial and error, and related heuristic processes, in favor of conventional "working forward" strategies based on domain-specific knowledge.

Next it may be instructive to look more closely at the nature of the tasks on which Heller and Hungate report, and ask in more detail which characteristics of the tasks most influence the conclusions reached.

PERSPECTIVES FROM THE STUDY OF TASK VARIABLES

Considerable research has been devoted to understanding how the properties of problem tasks affect mathematical problem solving (Goldin & McClintock, 1979). This work stems from the view that problems function as measuring instruments used to obtain information about the competencies of problem solvers, and that it is therefore essential to understand how task characteristics affect problem-solving outcomes. It is well established that different tasks elicit widely different processes, and that small changes in a problem's syntax, content, or structure can result in large changes in problem difficulty and observed behaviors. It therefore seems valuable to try to understand the discussion by Heller and Hungate from this viewpoint.

Researchers have classified the task variables that affect problem-solving outcomes under the headings of syntax variables, content and context variables, structure variables, and heuristic behavior variables (Goldin, 1983a; Kulm, 1979). *Syntax* variables describe the arrangement of and grammatical relationships among the words and symbols in the problem statement. *Content* variables describe the mathematical information in the problem statement, with reference to the meanings (semantics) of terms and phrases, but without further mathematical processing of this information. *Context* variables similarly describe nonmathematical information, including features of the problem embodiment, the verbal context or setting, and the information format. *Structure* variables describe the mathematical properties of one or more formal representations of the problem. A major tool for their definition is analysis of the "state-space," which results from specifying a problem representation as an initial configuration of symbols together with a set of well-defined procedures for moving from one symbol-configuration to another. Finally, *heuristic behavior* variables describe characteristics of the task that elicit particular heuristic processes from solvers, including processes for understanding the problem, selecting and exploiting a representation, and utilizing alternate representations.

Now let us consider a scientific problem of the kind that Heller and Hungate discuss (Simon & Simon, 1978):

> A bullet leaves the muzzle of a gun at a speed of 400 m/sec. The length of the gun barrel is 0.5 m. Assuming that the bullet is uniformly accelerated, what is the average speed within the barrel?

Study of this problem reveals that its syntax poses no special complications. Its mathematical structure is rather elementary; for example, in an algebraic representation, if s denotes the length of the barrel, t the time spent in the barrel, a the (uniform) acceleration, v the final velocity and u the desired average velocity, one has the equations "$u = s/t$," "$s = (½)at^2$," and "$v = at$," from which the short steps "$u = (½)at = v/2$" provide the solution "$u = 200$ m/sec" (independent of the length s). The heuristic processes involved in solving this problem by algebraic means might include "drawing a diagram," "assigning letters to unknown quantities," and "recalling equations." But the real reason why the problem is interesting lies not in any sophisticated use of heuristics to which it finally yields, but in its specialized and complicated content domain. The solver must be able to interpret the semantics of a term such as "average velocity," relating it to the total distance traveled and the total time. The solver must also understand that the assumption of constant acceleration means that the velocity varies linearly with time, and supply the "default" information that the initial velocity of the bullet is zero. Thus the decision must be made that the previously learned formulas "$v = at$" and "$s = (½)at^2$" are appropriate here, while the "constant velocity" formula "$s = vt$" is not.

The rich semantic relationships which characterize the content of this problem are typical of the "scientific problems" that Heller and Hungate discuss. It seems fair to say that scientific problem solving generally involves greater complexity of content than does mathematical problem solving, because of the nontrivial "real-world" relationships which characterize the scientific enterprise. Thus, its study can convey vividly to mathematics teachers the importance of stressing "mathematical meanings" as well as formal manipulations. On the other hand, scientific problem solving need not be restricted to tasks that are structurally elementary or that make no use of more sophisticated, "discovery-oriented" heuristic processes. Both the reported use of "working forward" strategies by experts and their heavy reliance on "tacit" knowledge seem to me to be direct consequences of *complexity* of task content combined with *simplicity* of syntactic, structural, and heuristic attributes.

The examples from Newtonian mechanics discussed by Heller and Hungate, as well as the problem they discuss of finding the area bounded by two curves, illustrate very convincingly how detailed cognitive analyses can be carried out in a complex "content" domain. Aided by subjects' protocols, one is able to describe in detail "the knowledge needed to solve the problem," and to conclude that this knowledge is indeed more complex than most experts probably realize. I think it is important not to limit this kind of cognitive analysis to problems whose main claim to nontriviality lies in their semantic content. There is the need for a similar elaboration of the knowledge base for problems with complicated syntax, structure, and heuristic behavior characteristics, before we can claim to understand in a general way the knowledge structures needed for scientific or mathematical problem solving.

PERSPECTIVES FROM A MODEL FOR MATHEMATICAL PROBLEM SOLVING

In trying to understand how each family of task variables produces its observed effects, I have constructed the framework of a model for competency in mathematical problem solving (Goldin, 1982, 1983b). Proceeding on the assumption that meaningful simulation of the human being as a problem solver should be based on higher-level language systems, the model attempts the preliminary description of the languages that are needed, and the relationships among them. (The term "language" is understood here in its information-processing sense, not in its more restrictive everyday meaning of a system for verbal intercourse.) Many of the observations described by Heller and Hungate seem to fit rather well with the resulting description.

Four higher-level language systems are entailed by the model:

- A system for verbal and syntactic processing of "natural" language, accounting for effects of task syntax variables.

- A system for imagistic (nonverbal) processing, accounting for effects of task content and context variables.

- A system for generating moves within formal notational languages, accounting for effects of task structure variables.

- A system for planning and executive control, accounting for effects of task heuristic behavior variables.

Appropriately transformed, output from any one of these systems can serve as input for any of the others. Furthermore, planning language has a self-referential capability, so that heuristic processes can act on the domain of heuristic processes, as well as on domains from the other language systems. Some of the relationships among the language systems in this model are summarized in Figure 1.

Now let us consider the correspondence between the model and the cognitive analysis of physics problems discussed by Heller and Hungate. Particular attention is due

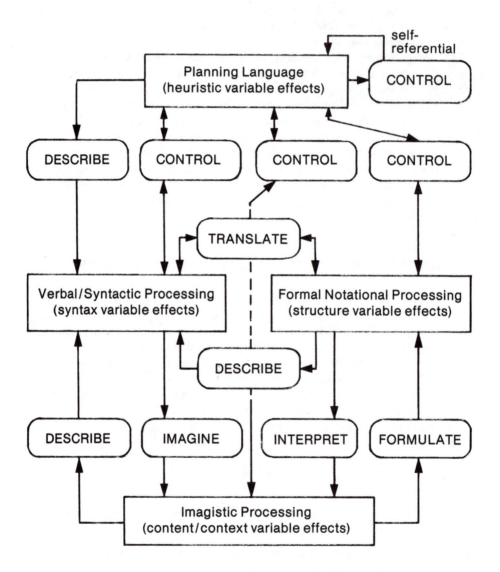

Figure 1. A model for competency in mathematical problem solving. [Reprinted with permission from Goldin, G.A. Levels of language in mathematical problem solving. *Proceedings of the Fifth Annual Meeting of the International Group for the Psychology of Mathematics Education, North American Chapter* (Vol. 2). Montreal: Concordia Univ. Dept. of Mathematics, September 1983.]

the "imagistic" level of processing, since we have already noted the content complexity of these problems, and it is the imagistic language system which is posited to account for task content effects.

The word "imagistic" has been selected to refer to the encoding and processing of nonverbal configurations. It is not intended to suggest only spatial and visual images, but to have the connotations of the word "imagine," including auditory, tactile, and kinesthetic representations as well. One reason that imagistic language may be difficult to comprehend from the perspective of information processing is that we do not know even approximately how imagistic configurations are encoded. Pattern recognition, for example, is largely unexplained on the level of understanding how essential features from one configuration are extracted and identified as "the same" as essential features from another.

In solving mathematics "textbook" problems, students sometimes try to translate directly from the problem statement (natural language) to an arithmetic or algebraic sentence (formal notational language), without constructing a representation of the nonverbal situation that the problem statement describes (imagistic language). Sometimes "key words" are used to facilitate this "direct translation" process according to rules such as " 'altogether' means to add" and " 'each' means to multiply." We rightly consider this to be noninsightful problem solving. Similarly, novice problem solvers in physics tend to try to translate directly from the problem statement to a formal notational representation, and thus obtain equations without imagistic processing. However, while direct translation is often possible for routine "textbook" mathematics problems, physics problems have sufficiently complex content domains to render it virtually impossible. The qualitative analysis phase of the expert appears to include the construction and processing of an imagistic representation of the problem. Referring to Figure 1, novices try to move from left to right across the diagram, from verbal to formal representations, while experts move first from verbal to imagistic and then to formal representations.

In the experiment described by Heller and Hungate, in which external control is exercised by the investigator, it seems that direction occurs at the "planning language" level. "Uncontrolled" novices who find themselves without the capability of imagistic processing for these problems (because of their lack of domain-specific knowledge) resort unsuccessfully to using the more powerful heuristic processes of planning language. By assuming control at this level, the investigator is able to avoid this, and to *compel* imagistic processing—in mechanics problems, for instance, by directing subjects to indicate all forces exerted on a system by other objects, or by directing subjects to determine whether any object other than those already named touch the system of interest.

Thus, the model of Figure 1 helps us here in two ways. It allows us to understand the differences between expert and novice as following from the novice's inability to construct an imagistic representation of the problem situation and to process information in that representation. Consequently some novices write equations which do not apply, or use complicated heuristic processes which for these problems are not helpful. It also allows us to understand the assumption of control by the investigator as a replacement of the subject's executive planning level by that of the investigator's script, which can *command* the processing of information imagistically by specifying the necessary steps. Subjects then often express surprise that the resulting procedures lead to problem solutions.

Now let us turn to consideration of the education implications drawn by Heller and Hungate.

THE VALUE AND LIMITATIONS OF THE LESSONS DRAWN

What are the cognitive objectives of instruction in problem solving? My model suggests that problem-solving competency can be achieved by developing students' abilities to work within each of the four indicated language systems, and to exchange information among them. From this point of view, let us consider the recommendation of Greeno (1980) paraphrased by Heller and Hungate, that we "teach the knowledge needed to solve the problem." Though this recommendation may seem almost like a truism, I find it to be the one "lesson" with which I fundamentally disagree. It is often the case in mathematical problem solving that the knowledge needed to solve the problem does not include the capacity for insightful, imagistic processing, though the latter may have been the main reason for introducing the problem in the first place. *Teachers and students are exasperatingly ingenious at substituting formal algorithmic procedures for insightful methods.* Thus, paradoxically, the knowledge needed to solve the problem may not be the most desirable educational objective.

Nor does this "lesson" follow from the research described by Heller and Hungate. No evidence is presented that defining the knowledge needed to solve the problem as the teaching objective will maximize learning through problem-solving instruction, if learning is construed to include generalizability (the capability of transferring knowledge to new domains). What has occurred, I think, is that as cognitive researchers have become better able to identify the knowledge needed to solve the problem, and have observed experts using this knowledge and novices unable to use it, they have made a tacit assumption: that because the knowledge can now be described, it is just what we should teach.

To me this reverses the direction in which we should be thinking. We should not develop the mathematics curriculum by first selecting problems and then defining the objectives of instruction through cognitive analyses of those problems. On the contrary, we should first define our cognitive objectives with reference to the entire field of study, and then try to provide experiences with problems selected in order that the desired cognitive processes can be fruitfully applied to them. Often, such problems can be solved in alternate, noninsightful ways which do not employ the desired cognitions. Teachers who, in such cases, teach only the knowledge needed to solve the problem may not even understand the cognitive objectives which were the purpose for including such problems in the mathematics curriculum.

For example, the decision to teach number bases other than ten in some of the "new mathematics" materials developed in the 1950's and 1960's had several rationales. One was to foster a better understanding of the arbitrary, conventional nature of our base ten system of numeration; another was to provide opportunities for discovery in mathematics. Teachers and authors who substituted computational algorithms for these cognitive objectives may have taught the knowledge the children needed to solve textbook problems, but in so doing sacrificed the very objectives the topic was intended to achieve.

Next let me turn to the other instructional implications drawn by Heller and Hungate. To develop the component procedures of problem solving in detail is a worthwhile recommendation for mathematics educators as well as science educators, but not in order to teach the knowledge required to solve the problem. Rather it is a procedure to follow in order to best utilize a problem to achieve desired cognitive objectives. In Newtonian mechanics, for example, the main cognitive objective should be for students to be able to construct and process valid, efficient internal representations of problems involving forces. If this objective is achieved, it will not only enable the student to solve a whole class of textbook physics problems, but also give them a "physical intuition" about how the Newtonian world works, laying the groundwork for the meaningful understanding of other systems (such as special relativity or quantum mechanics). Thus the purpose of analyzing component procedures in problem solving should be to foster students' use of those procedures that are most helpful in achieving the cognitive objectives.

The recommendation by Heller and Hungate that we should develop qualitative understandings of procedures is one with which mathematics educators should heartily agree. I interpret this recommendation in two ways: first, we should develop in students the capability to represent problem situations nonverbally, and to obtain information from such representations; second, we should develop on the planning level their understanding of the reasons for the steps they take, and their ability to describe those reasons. This recommendation follows logically from the observed importance of "qualitative analysis" in expert problem solving.

Finally, there is the recommendation that we incorporate guided practice, testing for reasoning processes and qualitative understandings. This is also a recommendation with which mathematics educators should agree. Indeed, it is the reasoning processes (planning level) and qualitative understandings (imagistic level) which form the major cognitive components of "insightful problem solving." Nevertheless, one all too rarely sees objectives formulated explicitly at these levels, and still more rarely sees the achievement of such objectives actually evaluated through testing.

To sum up, we need first to formulate the cognitive objectives of teaching problem solving, including the heuristic processes we want students to use and the nonverbal representations we want them to construct. Then we should choose problems to which those processes can be applied. This can be done effectively through the kind of cognitive task analysis described by Heller and Hungate. Next, we should use problem examples to guide students in constructing the desired representations and using the desired heuristics. Finally, we should write examinations to evaluate as directly as possible whether our objectives have been achieved. This modified version of Heller and Hungate's program, it seems to me, not only suggests how best to use mathematical and scientific "textbook" problems, but also reminds us of the importance of incorporating into the curriculum "nonroutine" problems which require richer heuristic processes for their solution.

REFERENCES

Goldin, G.A. Mathematical language and problem solving. *Visible Language* 16, 221–38, 1982.

Goldin, G.A. Characteristics of problem tasks in the study of mathematical problem solving. In M. Zweng, T. Green, J. Kilpatrick, H. Pollak, & M. Suydam (Eds.), *Proceedings of the Fourth International Congress on Mathematical Education.* Boston: Birkhauser, 1983(a).

Goldin, G.A. Levels of language in mathematical problem solving. In J.C. Bergeron & N. Herscovics (Eds.), *Proceedings of the Fifth Annual Meeting of the International Group for the Psychology of Mathematics Education, North American Chapter.* (Vol. 2). Montreal: Concordia Univ. Dept. of Mathematics, September 1983(b), pp. 112–120.

Goldin, G.A., & McClintock, C.E. (Eds.). *Task variables in mathematical problem solving.* Philadelphia: The Franklin Institute Press, 1984.

Greeno, J.G. Trends in the theory of knowledge for problem solving. In D.T. Tuma & F. Reif (Eds.), *Problem solving and education: Issues in teaching and research.* Hillsdale, NJ: Lawrence Erlbaum Associates, 1980.

Kulm, G. The classification of problem-solving research variables. In G.A. Goldin & C.E. McClintock (Eds.), *Task variables in mathematical problem solving*. Philadelphia: The Franklin
Institute Press, 1984.

Piaget, J. *The child's conception of physical causality*. Totowa, NJ: Littlefield, Adams, 1969.

Shulman, L.S., & Keislar, E.R. (Eds.). *Learning by discovery: A critical appraisal*. Chicago: Rand
McNally, 1966.

Simon, D.P., & Simon, H.A. Individual differences in solving physics problems. In R.S. Siegler
(Ed.), *Children's thinking: What develops?* Hillsdale, NJ: Lawrence Erlbaum Associates,
1978.

Implications of Cognitive Psychology for Instruction in Mathematical Problem Solving

Richard E. Mayer

University of California

The learning of school mathematics has been widely recognized as an opportunity for students to learn about problem solving. In their policy statement, the first recommendation of the National Council of Teachers of Mathematics (1980) is "that problem solving be the focus of school mathematics in the 1980's" (p. 1). Similar policy recommendations have been made at the state level. For example, in California, a recent committee report on the California Assessment Program (1980) "recommended that time and effort be redirected from drill and practice on computation to the development of problem solving strategies. . . .[and] that problem solving analysis and modeling should be used as an umbrella in the general math curriculum" (p. 210).

In his book *Mathematical Discovery,* Polya (1965) makes a similar plea:

> In mathematics, know-how is much more important than mere possession of information. . . . What is know-how in mathematics? The ability to solve problems—not merely routine problems but problems requiring some degree of independence, judgement, originality, creativity. Therefore, the first and foremost duty of the high school in teaching mathematics is to emphasize *methodological work in problem solving.* (p. xii)

DEFINITION OF PROBLEM SOLVING

While there appears to be a growing consensus for the importance of teaching problem solving in school mathematics, there may be a lack of agreement on what problem solving means. In order to define problem solving, it is useful to first define what is meant by "problems." A problem occurs when you are confronted with a given situation—let's call that the *given state*—and you want another situation—let's call that the *goal state*—but there is no obvious way of accomplishing your goal. For example, suppose I asked you to find the volume of a frustrum of a right pyramid and gave you values for the sides of the two bases and the height. If you did not know a formula for volumes of frustrums, this would be a problem for you (Polya, 1965). As another example, sup-

123

pose that you were given two intersecting sets of parallel lines along with the value of one of the angles and asked to find the value of another angle (Greeno, 1978). If you did not have a memorized algorithm, this would constitute a problem for you. Lastly, suppose you were asked to find the sum of 6 + 8 = ____ but you did not have that fact memorized (Carpenter, 1980). Each of these predicaments corresponds to the definition of a problem—wanting to get from the given state to the goal state but lacking a direct route to the goal.

Problem solving refers to the process of moving from the given state to the goal state of a problem. I summarized thinking or problem solving as a series of mental operations that are directed toward some goal (Mayer, 1983). Similarly, Hayes (1981) described problem solving as "finding an appropriate way to cross a gap." Two major parts of problem solving are (1) representing the problem and (2) searching for a means to solve the problem. For example, in solving algebra word problems, you must translate the problem into an internal representation such as an equation, and you must be able to apply the rules of algebra and arithmetic to solve the equation (Mayer, 1983). As will be discussed in the next section, this paper focuses on techniques aimed at improving the "representing" phase of problem solving (e.g., translation training and schema training), and techniques aimed at improving the "searching" phase of problem solving (e.g., strategy training and algorithm automaticity).

INTERACTION BETWEEN COGNITIVE RESEARCH
AND MATHEMATICS INSTRUCTION

During the past decade there has been increasing interaction among those interested in cognitive research and those interested in mathematics instruction (Lester, 1982). Psychologists have become interested in the problem solving within real-world domains such as mathematics. Resnick and Ford (1981) summarize this approach as follows:

> As psychologists concerned specifically with mathematics, our goal is to ask the same questions that experimental and developmental psychologists ask about learning, thinking, and intelligences but to focus these questions with respect to a particular subject matter. What this means is that instead of asking ourselves, "How is it that people think?" we ask ourselves, "How is it that people think about mathematics?" (p. 3)

Similarly, mathematics educators have become increasingly interested in the techniques and theories of cognitive psychology. Schoenfeld (1982) summarizes this approach as follows:

> The mathematics education community cannot afford to ignore the psychological research on problem solving. But it cannot afford to swallow it whole, either. Mathematics educators, I think, have had their hearts in the right place but have lacked the methodological tools that allowed for substantive and rigorous inquiries into problem solving. (p.35)

Schoenfeld's comments are particularly relevant in light of the relatively minor emphasis cognitive psychologists have placed on learning and instruction.

The study of problem solving can only benefit from the bridges between cognitive psychology and mathematics education. Cognitive psychologists can contribute tools for analyzing problem-solving procedures and knowledge; mathematics educators can contribute a rich domain of problem-solving tasks and observations from the mathematics curriculum. Cognitive psychologists can attempt to refine general theories of problem solving to learning and instruction for specific tasks in mathematics; mathematics educators can attempt to extend specific information about learning of mathematical tasks to broader frameworks of problem solving.

This paper is concerned with the implications of recent cognitive psychology research for the teaching of mathematical problem solving. In particular, this paper examines four major issues in the cognitive literature that are relevant to instruction for mathematical problem solving:

- *Translation training*—The first issue concerns the role of linguistic comprehension in problem solving. In order to represent a problem, a student must be able to translate each sentence of the problem into an internal representation. Recent research has suggested that the process of linguistic comprehension is the source of many difficulties in problem solving.

- *Schema training*—The second issue concerns the role of what the Gestalt psychologists called structural understanding (Wertheimer, 1959) of problem statements. In order to represent a problem, a student must be able to put the elements of the problem together into a coherent whole. Recent research has suggested that lack of knowledge of problem types is a critical source of difficulty in problem solving.

- *Strategy training*—The third issue concerns the role of direct instruction in how to solve problems. Recent research has suggested that it may be possible to train students on ''how to'' solve problems.

- *Algorithm automaticity* —The fourth issue concerns the role of algorithms in problem solving. Recent research has suggested that errors in problem solving can often be traced to systematic errors in the students' computational algorithms; furthermore, recent developmental research suggests that the development of sophisticated problem-solving strategies requires that simpler algorithms have become automatic in the student.

Table 1 summarizes these issues and their implications for instruction in mathematical problem solving. The rest of this paper will discuss these issues in detail.

TRANSLATION TRAINING: COMPREHENSION VERSUS SOLUTION

Issue

In order to solve a problem, a problem solver must first translate the problem into an internal representation. One aspect of this comprehension process is that each sentence or proposition must be encoded into memory. Instruction often emphasizes solution of problems but less often deals with how to comprehend or represent problems.

Table 1. Some Issues and Implications for Instruction in Mathematical Problem Solving.

Issues	Implications
Translation training: comprehension versus solution	Let students draw pictures or move blocks to represent propositions. Ask students to rephrase propositions. Ask students to reword propositions into another context. Ask students to derive equations or number sentences for problem sentences.
Schema training: understanding versus executing	Mix problem types in exercises. Ask students to recognize problem types. Ask students to select relevant and irrelevant information. Ask students to draw or state problems.
Strategy training: process versus product	Let students describe their solution strategies. Let students compare their solution process to that of "experts" such as in worked-out examples. Provide direct instruction in strategies for specific problems.
Algorithm automaticity: procedures versus response	Provide practice in basic algorithms before moving to complex algorithms. Evaluate and remediate performance in algorithms in terms of bugs in subprocesses.

This section of the paper addresses the problem of how to teach students to become effective comprehenders of sentences from mathematics problems.

Research

The important role of linguistic comprehension in problem solving is exemplified by students' difficulty with relational propositions. A relational proposition is a statement that expresses a quantitative relation between two variables. For example, "Mary is twice as old as Betty" is a relational proposition of the type often found in "age" problems.

Recent work by Greeno and his colleagues (Greeno, 1980; Riley, Greeno, & Heller, 1982) points to difficulties that children have in comprehending relational sentences in word problems. For example, children in primary grades were asked to listen to a problem involving a relational sentence, and then to repeat the problem. A problem such as "Joe has three marbles. Tom has five more marbles than Joe. How many marbles does Tom have?" was sometimes repeated as "Joe has three marbles. Tom has five marbles. How many marbles does Tom have?"

Soloway, Lochhead and Clement (1982) asked college students to write equations to represent relational propositions such as "There are six times as many students as professors at this university." Approximately one third of the students produced the wrong equation, such as $6S = P$. In a follow-up study, Soloway et al. found that the error rate in translation of relational propositions fell nearly in half when students were asked to write BASIC programs to express the problem. One conclusion is that algebraic equations offer a static notation that is ambiguous, whereas the procedural language of computer programming allows for more accurate translations of relational statements.

In another series of experiments, I asked college students to read a series of eight algebra story problems and then to recall them (Mayer, 1982b). The problems contained both relational propositions, such as "the rate in still water is 12 mph more than the rate of the current," and assignment propositions, such as "the cost of the candy is $1.70 per pound." The recall results indicated a much higher error rate for relational propositions (29%) as compared to assignment propositions (9%). Subsequent analyses revealed a tendency for students to change relational propositions into assignments; for example, some subjects recalled "the rate in still water is 12 mph more than the rate of the current" as "the speed of the boat in still water is 12 mph." These results support the idea that some subjects lack the appropriate linguistic skill for translating relational sentences into internal representations.

There is some evidence that the ability to comprehend propositions such as those given above increases with age. For example, Riley et al. (1982) asked children to use wooden blocks to represent propositions such as "Joe has five more marbles than Pete." The incidence of correct translations increased steadily from Grades K to 3. In addition, Trabasso (1977) found that correct encoding of relational facts such as "the red stick is longer than the blue stick" increases from age 6 to adulthood. In summary, there seems to be a developmental progression in which comprehension of relational statements increases with age.

Implications

The foregoing review suggests that one difficulty that students may have is a lack of skill in translating sentences of the problem. In order to develop this skill, the following proposal is offered as a tentative research idea:

1. Students who are given practice in representing propositions (either in equations, pictures, programs, words, or concrete objects) will show improved performance in problem solving.

SCHEMA TRAINING: UNDERSTANDING VERSUS EXECUTING

Issue

The previous section addressed the idea that representing the problem is a crucial step in problem solving, specifically sentence-by-sentence translation of the problem. This section addresses the representation idea from another perspective: that parts of the problem derived from a line-by-line translation must be put together into a meaningful problem statement.

In particular, the Gestalt psychologists (Wertheimer, 1959) made a distinction between understanding a problem and rote execution of a solution for a problem. For example, a student could learn to find the area of a parallelogram by memorizing the formula, Area = Height × Base, or by seeing that the triangle on one end of the parallelogram could be cut off and attached to another end to form a rectangle. The former approach involves "rote" or "senseless" actions; the latter approach involves "structural insight" and "understanding." While the distinction between understanding and rote behavior was not clearly defined by the Gestaltists, the issue is still one of importance to current research in mathematical problem solving. In particular, the issue can be stated as, "What does it mean to understand a problem?" The research reviewed in this section suggests that understanding involves being able to build a schema for problem types (Mayer, 1982b).

Research

Building an internal representation of a problem requires more than a sentence-by-sentence translation. For example, Paige and Simon (1966) presented impossible problems such as

> The number of quarters a man has is seven times the number of dimes he has. The value of the dimes exceeds the value of the quarters by two dollars and fifty cents. How many has he of each coin?

A student who does not understand this problem could translate each sentence into an equation, such as $Q = 7D$ and $D(.10) = 2.50 + Q(.25)$. However, a student who integrates this problem into a coherent structure will be able to recognize that the problem is self-contradictory. Paige and Simon found both types of students.

More evidence concerning the process of understanding a problem comes from the work of Hinsley, Hayes, and Simon (1977). Subjects were given a series of algebra problems like those in standard textbooks. The task was to organize the problems into categories. Hinsley et al. found that students were readily able to perform this task, with high levels of agreement among the subjects. The categorization process yielded 18 categories such as river current, work, interest, triangle, and so on.

In addition, Hinsley et al. noted that students tended to make their categorization decisions after reading only the first few words of a problem. In follow-up studies, Hayes, Waterman, and Robinson (1977) and Robinson and Hayes (1978) found that students use their category decisions to make accurate judgments concerning what information is relevant in a problem and what is not. Apparently, students try to find the appropriate "schema" for a problem after reading only a few words; once a schema has been identified, it is used to guide the student's selective attention toward relevant information.

When a person uses the wrong schema, errors in understanding the problem can result. For example, Hinsley et al. (1977) presented a problem that could be interpreted as either a triangle problem or a distance-rate-time (DRT) problem. Subjects who interpreted the problem as a triangle problem attended to irrelevant information about triangles and one subject even misread "4 minutes" to be "4 miles." Similarly, students who interpreted it as a DRT problem paid attention to different information, and made assumptions about the direction of travel of vehicles in the problem. These results suggest that subjects use either a triangle schema or a DRT schema as a template for understanding the problem, and that these schemas influence what the students look for in the problem. In another study, Silver (1979) has shown that many students use superficial aspects of the problem in order to categorize problems into groups.

A recent analysis of the types of problems found in standard algebra textbooks yielded a taxonomy with over 100 basic problem types (Mayer, 1981). Each general category of problem, such as "motion problem," was represented by several different types, such as "overtake," "closure," "round trip," and "speed change." Some versions were fairly common (occurring with a frequency of 25 or more per 1,000 problems), and others were rare (occurring with a frequency of less than 4 per 1,000).

In a recent study (Mayer, 1982b), I asked students to read and then recall a series of eight story problems. Students tended to recall high-frequency versions of problems more easily than low-frequency versions; in addition, there was a pattern of errors in which subjects changed low-frequency versions of problems to higher-frequency versions. Apparently, when students lack a schema for a problem—as would be expected for low-frequency problems—representation of the problem is more prone to error.

Several researchers have also identified problem types for algebra word problems. For example, Greeno (1980) and Riley et al. (1982) have identified three types of word problems: cause/change problems (Joe has 3 marbles. Tom gives him 5 more marbles. How many marbles does Joe have now?); combination problems (Joe has 3 marbles. Tom has 5 marbles. How many marbles do they have altogether?); and comparison problems (Joe has 3 marbles. Tom has 5 more marbles than Joe. How many marbles does Tom have?). Although each of these examples requires the same computation (3 + 5), these researchers found substantial differences in children's performance on different problem types. Children in Grades K and 1 performed well on cause/change problems but poorly on comparison problems; in contrast, children in Grades 2 and 3 performed well on all types. This pattern suggests a developmental trend in which children begin with the idea that all problems are cause/change problems, and later begin to differentiate among different types of schemas. Thus, errors in comparison problems may be due to students' lack of appropriate schemata.

Weaver (1982) has distinguished between a "unary operation" view of computation and a "binary operation" view. The unary operation approach is based on the idea that a problem like 5 + 3 means "add 3 to 5"; the binary operation approach to this problem is "combine 3 and 5." The unary operation view is similar to Greeno's cause/change problem, whereas the binary operation view is more like Greeno's combine problems. Fuson (1982) has observed that the unary operation view tends to be the first to develop in children, even before formal instruction.

Implications

The implications of research on problem types includes the following proposals, each of which merits additional research study:

1. Problem-solving performance will increase if students are given practice in recognizing problem types, for example, naming or categorizing problems.

2. "Recognition" training is enhanced when exercises contain a mixture of problem types rather than having all problems solvable by the same procedure.

3. Problem-solving performance will increase if students are given practice in representing problems—whether concretely, in pictures, in symbols, or in words.

4. Problem-solving performance will increase if students are given practice in selecting relevant and irrelevant information in a problem.

While each of the preceding ideas follows from current research, much more study is needed before implementing them.

STRATEGY TRAINING: PROCESS VERSUS PRODUCT

Issue

Another major issue concerns the distinction between the products of problem solving and the process of problem solving. The product of problem solving refers to whether the student arrives at the correct final answer or not. The process of problem solving refers to the strategy that is used in order to derive an answer. Whereas much instructional effort emphasizes the products of problem solving, there is also a need to emphasize the process of problem solving.

Research

As an example of the distinction between process and product, let's consider a classic study on teaching of problem-solving skills to college students that was carried out by Bloom and Broder (1950). Subjects in this study were University of Chicago students who were required to pass a series of comprehensive examinations in various subjects. Students could take the examinations whenever they felt they were ready, and each examination consisted of a wide variety of problems covering the subject. As might be expected, some students performed quite well while others were unable to pass in spite of their high scholastic ability and conscientious study.

Bloom and Broder recruited a group of students who were having trouble passing the comprehensive examinations, but who also scored high in scholastic aptitude, claimed to study hard, and asserted that the examinations did not reflect what they knew. These students, called the "remedial group," seemed to have the ability, the knowledge, and the motivation needed for success but somehow failed to adequately answer the problems on the examinations. Other students, called the "model group," had the same general scholastic ability as the remedial students but scored high in solving examination problems.

How could Bloom and Broder boost the problem-solving performance of the remedial students so that they would behave like the model students on the examinations? In order to answer this question, they determined that previous research had placed too much emphasis on the products of problem solving—i.e., on getting the right answer—instead of emphasizing the processes involved in creative problem solving. They pointed to several examples in which two people might come up with the same answer for a problem by using entirely different approaches. Differences in the problem-solving process were determined by asking students to describe their thought processes. Based on these observations, Bloom and Broder decided that instruction for the remedial students should not focus on reinforcing the right final answers but rather on teaching problem-solving strategies that are useful in generating answers. They asserted that the "habits of problem solving, like other habits, could be altered by appropriate training and practice" (p. 67).

In order to teach problem-solving strategies to the remedial students, Bloom and Broder relied on the strategies used by the model students. Model students were asked to describe what was going on in their minds as they approached a problem and worked through it. Remedial students were taught to imitate and make use of the processes used by model students.

In a typical experiment, remedial students were asked to solve problems like those on the examinations. Students were asked to "think aloud"—i.e., describe their problem-solving processes as they worked through the problem. Then the students were given a transcript of the procedure that a model student used for the same problem. Each remedial student was asked to list in his or her own words all of the differences between the model's strategy and the remedial student's own strategy. The experimenter helped to stimulate discussion. Then remedial students were given another problem so that the new techniques could be practiced. Over the course of 10–12 training sessions remedial students learned how to compare their problem-solving strategies to those of model students on specific problems.

The results of the study are encouraging. Students who participated in the training tended to score .49 to .68 grade points higher on the examination than matched groups who did not take the training. In addition, the trained students expressed high levels of confidence and optimism concerning their newly learned problem-solving abilities. In spite of their success, Bloom and Broder caution that it would be incorrect to conclude that general problem-solving skill can be taught:

> It became clear that some specific information was necessary for the solution of examination problems and that a certain amount of background in the subject was indispensable. It became apparent that methods of problem solving, by themselves, could not serve as a substitute for basic knowledge of the subject matter. (pp. 76–77)

Thus, Bloom and Broder's major contributions are the emphasis on process rather than product, the use of "worked-out problems" by model problem solvers, and the finding that both specific knowledge and general strategies are needed to be a successful problem solver in a given domain.

More recently, there have been numerous attempts to teach problem-solving strategies within quantitative domains such as mathematics, engineering, and the physical sciences. One of the best known problem-solving sources is Rubinstein's *Patterns of Problem Solving* course. This course has been taught at UCLA since 1969, and has attracted yearly enrollments of over 1,000 students. The course is based on Rubinstein's textbook, *Patterns of Problem Solving* (1975), which emphasizes both how to represent problems and how to generate solution plans. Students meet in groups to discuss their problem-solving strategies for various problems. Thus, like Bloom and Broder who focus on problem-solving process, Rubinstein seems to believe that certain basic problem-solving strategies can be taught. Unfortunately, it is not possible to assess students' learning, because as Reif (1980) points out, there has not been an attempt to objectively evaluate the course. Rubinstein (1980) offers student testimonials, but such data are notoriously unreliable.

Schoenfeld (1979) has reported a study in which students were taught problem-solving heuristics that are directly related to mathematics. All subjects took a five-problem pretest and a five-problem posttest, consisting of algebra story problems, series sum problems, proofs, and the like. All subjects received written and tape-recorded instructions on how to solve 20 problems, during several sessions. In addition, the experimental group was given a list and description of five useful strategies, such as "draw a diagram" or "try to establish subgoals" or "consider a similar problem with fewer variables." For the experimental subjects, all problems in a given session were solvable by the same strategy, and subjects were explicitly told to use a particular strategy. The control group received the same 20 practice problems, but there was no list of heuristics, no mention of which strategy to use, and a mixture of problem types in each session.

Even though only a few subjects were used in this study, the results were quite strong. The experimental subjects showed a strong pretest-to-posttest gain whereas the control group did not. These preliminary results encourage the idea that it might be effective to teach heuristics within the domain of mathematics.

Problem-solving strategies have also been successfully taught in elementary school mathematics. Carpenter (1980) observed the strategies used in early grades for solving addition and subtraction problems. For example, students in this study had not yet memorized all the "addition facts," but instead used strategies such as "decomposition" or "compensation." In solving the problem $4 + 7 = $ ____, a child described a decomposition strategy, as follows: "7 and 3 is 10, so I put 1 more on there and got 11." In solving the problem of $6 + 8 = $ ____, a child displayed a compensation strategy, as follows: "I took one from 8 and gave it to 6. $7 + 7 = 14$."

Thornton (1978) conducted a series of experiments in order to determine whether strategies such as these could actually be taught to second- and fourth-graders. The experimental group received training in strategies like these for 20 minutes a day, 3 days a week, for 8 weeks. The control group learned their arithmetic facts in the traditional way using the same amount of class time. The results indicated that the experimental group performed better on a delayed test of arithmetic problems as compared to the control group. Such results complement those of Schoenfeld and suggest that young children can learn to make use of problem-solving heuristics for specific types of problems.

More recently, cognitive psychologists have provided detailed analyses of mathematics and reasoning tasks. For example, Greeno (1978) developed a computer model, PERDIX, for solving geometry proofs. One of the major aspects of the program includes knowledge of "propositions of inference" such as "vertical angles are congruent"; these kinds of rules are a major component in instruction. Similarly, "concepts" such as recognizing that two angles are vertical angles constitute another major aspect of the program; training in recognition of concepts is also a part of instruction. However, another major aspect of the program is "strategic knowledge" for setting goals and forming solution plans; training in how to approach a problem is not generally a part of formal instruction. Greeno (1978) notes that "principles used in setting goals and forming place are not mentioned in any text that I have examined" (p. 60). Yet, he also presents evidence that "the strategic knowledge needed for problem solving can be learned" (p. 62).

As another example of task analysis of mathematical problem solving (Mayer, 1982a; Mayer, Larkin, & Kadane, 1983), I have investigated algebraic problem solving. Some subjects were given equations such as the following:

$(8 + 3x)/2 = 3x - 11$

Other subjects were given the same problem expressed in words:

Find a number such that if 8 more than 3 times the number is divided by 2, the result is the same as 11 less than 3 times the number.

These problems were analyzed as a problem space (Newell & Simon, 1972) containing all possible states that the problem could be in. An analysis of the pattern of response time performance revealed that the equation group tended to use an "isolate strategy" while the word group tended to use a "reduce strategy" for solving the problem. In an isolate strategy, the problem solver attempts to get all of the unknowns on one side of the equality and all of the numbers on the other side. In a reduce strategy, the problem solver attempts to reduce the size of the problem by carrying out all possible arithmetic operations. This result is interesting because it shows that different contexts for presenting a problem encourage problem solvers to use qualitatively different solution strategies.

There has also been some encouraging evidence that complex tasks can be analyzed into components, and that individual components can be explicitly taught. For example, researchers have been successful in teaching component processes for solving series completion problems (Holtzman, Glazer, & Pellegrino, 1976), analogy problems (Sternberg & Ketron, 1982), and GRE-Analytic problem solving (Swinton & Powers, 1983). These results encourage the idea that successful analyses of mathematical problem solving will lead to implications for direct instruction of component processes.

Implications

Based on the current state of research, the following proposals seem worthy of continued study:

1. Worked-out examples can be used to teach problem-solving strategies to students.

2. Direct instruction and practice in using specific strategies can be used to enhance performance.

3. Having students systematically describe and compare their solution procedures can improve problem-solving performance.

These implications follow from the general theme that instruction should focus on process as well as product.

ALGORITHM AUTOMATICITY: STRENGTHENING RESPONSES VERSUS AUTOMATING PROCEDURES

Issues

Another issue concerns the nature of the component skills in mathematical problem solving. For example, computational skill is a major component in many problems. The student must be able to generate computational answers promptly and correctly. The traditional view of skill learning, offered by Thorndike (1922), is that arithmetic skill involves the acquisition of stimulus-response bonds. For example, the stimulus of the problem "6 + 7 = ____" is "6 + 7" and the response is "13." A shortcoming of this view is that it would require an enormous memory load to deal with more complex computations. An alternative view is that skill learning involves the acquisition of algorithms that grow in complexity.

Research

Computational algorithms depend on the availability of well-practiced subskills in the problem solver. In particular, early computational algorithms tend to build on the child's experience with counting. For example, Groen and Parkman (1972) have suggested several counting models of how children might solve single-digit addition problems of the form $m + n =$ ____. Three of the models are the following:

- *Counting-all*—Set a counter to 0. Increment it by m and then by n. For $3 + 4$, the child recites, "1, 2, 3, 4, 5, 6, 7."

- *Counting-on*—Set a counter for the first number (m); increment it by the second number (n). For $3 + 4$, the child recites, "4, 5, 6, 7."

- *Choice (for counting-on)*—Set a counter to the larger of m or n; increment the counter by the smaller of m or n. For $3 + 4$, the child recites, "5, 6, 7."

In order to determine whether children actually use models such as these, Groen and Parkman asked first-graders to solve all single-column addition problems (i.e., all problems yielding sums less than 10). Each of the three models makes different predictions concerning the pattern of response times for the problems. The predictions may be summarized as follows:

- *Counting-all*—Response time should be a function of the sum of $m + n$. For example, $3 + 4$ requires 8 increments and $4 + 3$ requires 8 increments, so both should require about the same response time.

- *Counting-on*—Response time should be a function of n (i.e., the second number on the problem). For example, $3 + 4$ requires 4 increments but $4 + 3$ requires 3 increments, so the second problem should be faster.

- *Choice*—Response time is a function of the lesser of m or n. For example, $3 + 4$ requires 3 increments and $4 + 3$ requires 3 increments.

Groen and Parkman found that most first-graders tended to behave as predicted by the choice model, while the other models did not predict first-graders' performance as well. Apparently, by the first grade, the dominant algorithm for simple addition is a sophisticated version of a counting-on procedure (i.e., the choice model). However, Fuson (1982) has observed that preschool children often use counting-all procedures; more sophisticated strategies (such as counting-on) tend to develop as children gain more experience in addition problems.

As children acquire even more experience with simple addition problems, a new procedure develops—what Fuson (1982) calls *known facts*. The new procedure is to memorize answers for simple addition problems. Groen and Parkman (1972) found some evidence that first-graders were beginning to rely on known facts for certain problems; for example, first-graders were very fast on "doubles" such as "2 + 2" or "3 + 3." Apparently, they have memorized answers for some but not all of the simple addition facts. Thus, a known facts procedure is used for some problems, but a counting-on procedure is used for others. By adulthood, of course, the basic number facts are well memorized and counting algorithms may no longer be needed. As students are progressing to a known facts procedure, they may use the facts they know to derive answers for related problems. Fuson (1982) calls this *derived facts*. For example, if a student already has memorized answers for doubles (such as "6 + 6"), then a problem like "5 + 7" can be converted by taking one from the 7 and giving it to the 5. Thus, Fuson (1982) suggests that there is a developmental progression in which students move from counting-all to counting-on (including the more sophisticated choice model) to known facts and then to derived facts.

Woods, Resnick, and Groen (1975) have provided similar examples of counting models for simple subtraction. Three simple models for simple subtraction problems of the form $m - n =$ _____ are as follows:

- *Incrementing*—Set a counter to n and count up until you reach m. For the problem $6 - 4$, you would start with 4, and then recite "5, 6"; as you recite you might extend 1 and then 2 fingers.

- *Decrementing*—Set a counter to m and count down n times. For the problem $6 - 4$, you would start with 6 and recite, "5, 4, 3, 2," as you extend 1, 2, 3, and then 4 fingers.

- *Choice*—Use either the incrementing or decrementing model depending on which requires the lesser amount of counting. For $6 - 4$, the incrementing model requires 2 increments whereas the decrementing model requires 4 decrements. For $6 - 2$, the incrementing model requires 4 increments but the decrementing model requires 2 decrements.

Woods et al. presented all single-column subtraction problems to second- and fourth-graders. The three models make different predictions concerning the pattern of response times:

- *Incrementing*—Response time depends on the difference of $m - n$. For example, $6 - 4$ requires 2 steps while $6 - 2$ requires 4 steps.

- *Decrementing*—Response time depends on the value of the smaller number. For example, $6 - 4$ requires 4 steps while $6 - 2$ requires 2 steps.

- *Choice* —Response time depends on the lesser of n or $m - n$.

The results of the Woods et al. study indicate that most second-graders and all fourth-graders behaved as predicted by the choice model. For about 20% of the second-graders, less sophisticated algorithms were observed, such as the decrementing model. Thus, there is some evidence that children move from less sophisticated to more sophisticated counting models for simple arithmetic.

Once a child has acquired proficiency in single-digit addition and subtraction—i.e., once the answers to single-column addition and subtraction become automatic—the student may be able to learn more complex algorithms such as three-column addition and subtraction. In order to carry out three-column arithmetic, the child must have efficient access to answers for single-column problems. Thus, once simple algorithms become automatic, they may be incorporated into more complex algorithms.

Brown and Burton (1978) have analyzed error patterns in children's performance in three-column subtraction. Consider the answers given for each of the following problems:

522	819	714	481	655
−418	−305	−602	−382	−160
116	514	112	101	515

As can be seen, the answers are correct for two out of the five problems, or 40% accuracy. Another way of characterizing students' performance is to say that there is a "bug" in the students' algorithm—they tend to subtract the smaller number from the larger number in each column. Brown and Burton have argued that students' computational performance can be described by saying that they are using a computational algorithm that may have one or more bugs. Thus, many errors can be attributed to systemic bugs in procedures rather than to random guessing.

In order to test this idea, Brown and Burton gave a set of 15 subtraction problems to 1,325 primary school children. Using a computer program called BUGGY, the researchers attempted to locate the algorithm that each child was using. If the child was 100% correct, the BUGGY program would categorize the child as using the correct algorithm. If there were some errors, BUGGY tried to change the algorithm by adding one bug that would account for the errors. If no single bug could account for all the errors, then combinations of bugs were tried. Although BUGGY was based on hundreds of bugs or bug combinations, it was able to find algorithms for only about half of the subjects. The other students may have been making random responses, may have been inconsistent, or may have been using bugs that BUGGY didn't know about. Some of the most common bugs were "smaller from larger" (as exemplified above) and "borrow from zero." Expertise in computation involves being able to use algorithms—even complex ones such as required in three-column subtraction—automatically and without error.

Recently, several developmental psychologists have provided evidence that learning a skill involves building increasingly more sophisticated algorithms. For example, both Case (1978) and Siegler (1978) have shown that children progress through a series of stages in which a simple algorithm is used, then incorporated into a more complex one, and so on. Case (1978) argues that the development of sophisticated algorithms requires that the simple ones become automatic. Since the simpler procedures are components in more sophisticated procedures, their automaticity frees up limited processing capacity for monitoring the complex procedure.

Implications

The instructional implications of the research on algorithm development include the following proposals for further study:

1. Students should achieve high levels of automaticity on component skills before extensive training on more sophisticated algorithms. For example, proficiency in counting is required in order to make use of counting models, and automatic knowledge of number facts is required for efficient use of algorithms for three-column arithmetic.

2. Students' performance on simple computation should be analyzed in terms of the algorithm that is being used, including possible bugs; instruction should be directed specifically at remediating the identified bugs.

CONCLUSION

This paper has suggested four types of training that could be used in order to increase students' mathematical problem solving performance: training in how to comprehend difficult linguistic propositions, training in how to recognize problem types, training in how to use appropriate strategies, training in efficient algorithms. Table 1 summarizes some suggestions for implementing each type of training. These suggestions follow from current psychological research, but require extensive study. As can be seen, cognitive research often involves analysis of mathematical problem-solving performance but generally does not deal directly with learning and instruction. My hope is that this paper will help to stimulate additional research on these issues.

REFERENCES

Bloom, B.S., & Broder, L.J. *Problem-solving processes of college students.* Chicago: University of Chicago Press, 1950.

Brown, J.S., & Burton, R.R. Diagnostic models for procedural bugs in basic mathematical skills. *Cognitive Science* **2**, 155–92, 1978.

California Assessment Program. *Student achievement in California school: 1979–80 annual report.* Sacramento: California State Department of Education, 1980.

Carpenter, T.P. Hueristic strategies used to solve addition and subtraction problems. In R. Karplus (Ed.), *Proceedings of the Fourth International Conference for the Psychology of Mathematics Education.* Berkeley: University of California, 1980.

Case, R. Intellectual development from birth to adulthood: A neo-Piagetian interpretation. In R.S. Siegler (Ed.), *Children's thinking: What develops?* Hillsdale, NJ: Lawrence Erlbaum Associates, 1978.

Fuson, K.C. An analysis of the counting-on solution procedure in addition. In T.P. Carpenter, J.M. Moser, & T.A. Romberg (Eds.), *Addition and subtraction: A cognitive perspective.* Hillsdale, NJ: Lawrence Erlbaum Associates, 1982.

Greeno, J.G. A study of problem solving. In R. Glaser (Ed.), *Advances in instructional psychology* (Vol. 1). Hillsdale, NJ: Lawrence Erlbaum Associates, 1978.

Greeno, J.G. Some examples of cognitive task analysis with instructional implications. In R.E. Snow, P. Federico, & W.E. Montague (Eds.), *Aptitude, learning, and instruction* (Vol. 2). Hillsdale, NJ: Lawrence Erlbaum Associates, 1980.

Groen, G.J., & Parkman, J.M. A chronometric analysis of simple addition. *Psychological Review* **97**, 329–43, 1972.

Hayes, J.R. *The complete problem solver.* Philadelphia: The Franklin Institute Press, 1981.

Hayes, J.R., Waterman, D.A., & Robinson, C.S. Identifying relevant aspects of a problem text. *Cognitive Science* **1**, 297–313, 1977.

Hinsley, D., Hayes, J.R., & Simon, H.A. From words to equations. In P. Carpenter & M. Just (Eds.), *Cognitive processes in comprehensions.* Hillsdale, NJ: Lawrence Erlbaum Associates, 1977.

Holtzman, T.G., Glaser, R., & Pellegrino, J.W. Process training derived from a computer simulation theory. *Memory and Cognition* **4**, 349–56, 1976.

Lester, F.K. Building bridges between psychological and mathematics education research on problem solving. In F.K. Lester & J. Garofalo (Eds.), *Mathematical problem solving: Issues in research.* Philadelphia: The Franklin Institute Press, 1982.

Mayer, R.E. Frequency norms and structural analysis of algebraic story problems into families, categories, and templates. *Instructional Science* **10**, 135–75, 1981.

Mayer, R.E. Different problem solving strategies for algebra word and equation problems. *Journal of Experimental Psychology: Learning, Memory and Cognition* **8**, 448–62, 1982(a).

Mayer, R.E. Memory for algebra story problems. *Journal of Educational Psychology* **74**, 199–216, 1982(b).

Mayer, R.E. *Thinking, problem solving, and cognition.* San Francisco: W.H. Freeman & Co., 1983.

Mayer, R.E., Larkin, J.H., & Kadane, J. A cognitive analysis of mathematical problem solving ability. In R. Sternberg (Ed.), *Advances in the psychology of human intelligence.* Hillsdale, NJ: Lawrence Erlbaum Associates, 1983.

National Council of Teachers of Mathematics. *An agenda for action: Recommendations for school mathematics of the 1980's.* Reston, VA: Author, 1980.

Newell, E., & Simon, H.A. *Human problem solving.* Englewood Cliffs, NJ: Prentice-Hall, 1972.

Paige, J.M., & Simon, H.A. Cognitive processes in solving algebra word problems. In B. Kleinmentz (Ed.), *Problem solving: Research, method, and theory.* New York: John Wiley & Sons, 1966.

Polya, G. *Mathematical discovery: On understanding, learning, and teaching problem solving* (Vol. 2). New York: John Wiley & Sons, 1965.

Reif, F. Theoretical and educational concepts with problem solving: Bridging the gaps with human cognitive engineering. In D.T. Tuma & F. Reif (Eds.), *Problem solving and education: Issues in teaching and research.* Hillsdale, NJ: Lawrence Erlbaum Associates, 1980.

Resnick, L. B., & Ford, W. *The psychology of mathematics for instruction.* Hillsdale, NJ: Lawrence Erlbaum Associates, 1981.

Riley, M., Greeno, J.G., & Heller, J. The development of children's problem solving ability in arithmetic. In H.P. Ginsburg (Ed.), *The development of mathematical thinking.* New York: Academic Press, 1982.

Robinson, C.S., & Hayes, J.R. Making inferences about relevance in understanding problems. In R. Revlin & R.E. Mayer (Eds.), *Human reasoning.* Washington, DC: Winston, 1978.

Rubinstein, M.F. *Patterns of problem solving.* Englewood Cliffs, NJ: Prentice-Hall, 1975.

Rubinstein, M.F. A decade of experience in teaching an interdisciplinary problem-solving course. In D.T. Tuma & F. Reif (Eds.), *Problem solving and education: Issues in teaching and research.* Hillsdale, NJ: Lawrence Erlbaum Associates, 1980.

Schoenfeld, A.H. Explicitly heuristic training as a variable in problem solving performance. *Journal for Research in Mathematics Education* 10, 173–87, 1979.

Schoenfeld, A.H. Some thoughts on problem solving research and mathematics education. In F.K. Lester & J. Garofalo (Eds.), *Mathematical problem solving: Issues in research.* Philadelphia: The Franklin Institute Press, 1982.

Siegler, R.S. The origins of scientific reasoning. In R.S. Siegler (Ed.), *Children's thinking: What develops?* Hillsdale, NJ: Lawrence Erlbaum Associates, 1978.

Silver, E. Students' perceptions of relatedness among mathematical verbal problems. *Journal for Research in Mathematics Education* 10, 195–210, 1979.

Soloway, E., Lochhead, J., & Clement, J. Does computer programming enhance problem solving ability? Some positive evidence on algebra word problems. In R.J. Sediel, R.E. Anderson, & B. Hunter (Eds.), *Computer literacy.* New York: Academic Press, 1982.

Sternberg, R.J., & Ketron, J.L. Selection and implementation of strategies in reasoning by analogy. *Journal of Educational Psychology* 74, 399–413, 1982.

Swinton, S.S., & Powers, D.E. A study of the effects of special preparation on GRE analytical scores and item types. *Journal of Educational Psychology* 75, 104–15, 1983.

Thorndike, E.L. *The psychology of arithmetic.* New York: Macmillan, 1922.

Thornton, C.A. Emphasizing thinking strategies in basic fact instruction. *Journal for Research in Mathematics Education* 9, 214–27, 1978.

Trabasso, T. The role of memory as a system in making transitive inference. In R.V. Kail & J.W. Hagen (Eds.), *Perspectives on the development of memory and cognition.* Hillsdale, NJ: Lawrence Erlbaum Associates, 1977.

Weaver, J.F. Interpretations of number operations and symbolic representations of addition and subtraction. In T.P. Carpenter, J.M. Moser, & T.A. Romberg (Eds.), *Addition and subtraction: A cognitive perspective.* Hillsdale, NJ: Lawrence Erlbaum Associates, 1982.

Wertheimer, M. *Productive thinking.* New York: Harper & Row, 1959.

Woods, S.S., Resnick, L.B., & Groen, G.J. An experimental test of five process models for subtraction. *Journal of Educational Psychology* 67, 17–21, 1975.

Cognitive Psychology and Mathematical Problem Solving: A Discussion of Mayer's Paper[1]

Larry Sowder

Northern Illinois University

It is always a pleasure to read Mayer's writings. His experiments invariably involve some clever aspect, and his interpretations and extrapolations are creative. The paper at hand meets those standards. In reacting, I shall roughly follow his outline—encoding a problem, schema training, strategy training, and component skills—after an obligatory opening section on what a problem *really* is.

ALL "PROBLEMS" ARE NOT EQUAL

Mayer adopts a standard definition of problem (given state, desired goal state, but no obvious route from the former to the latter). Several of the examples in the studies he cited, however, fail to meet that definition, at least in some mathematics educators' worlds. For example, tasks such as, for first-graders, finishing basic addition facts and, for college students, writing the students-professor equation or solving linear equations in one unknown would be considered exercises. Their goal states are not blocked by the lack of obvious routes; some sort of algorithm is a part of the conventional curriculum for each task. To many, even the typical algebra story "problem" should be an exercise for college students. (Goldin, 1982, discusses the various nuances of "problem.")

In the production systems camp (Simon, 1980), the approach has been to turn small classes of tasks, which might otherwise be problems, into easy tasks. Insofar as this approach has had satisfactory results (as in a computer simulation), parsimony alone would suggest that other tasks (including other problems) could be equally managed. Thus, the colloquial "problem" is an adequate title for these tasks. The drawback is that once an algorithm for a task has been learned, the task is no longer a problem, but an exercise.

---

1. Occasional first person plural references are to work under a National Science Foundation grant (SED 81-08134) with M. Moyer, J. Threadgill, and J. Moyer. Any opinions in this paper about that work do not necessarily reflect those of the Foundation (or of my collaborators).

(Becoming proficient at an algorithm is not always an instantaneous process, of course, but then the task is no longer the original one but has become the task of remembering the algorithm.)

Even allowing for an "in-between" category like the usual algebra word problem, for which the algorithm calls on a higher-order skill like translate-into-an-equation, there must be psychological differences, perhaps not cognitive, in solving the varieties of mathematical tasks.

Reaction 1: Is it merely word games to distinguish among exercises, routine problems, and genuine problems?

ENCODING A PROBLEM

Arriving at an internal representation of a problem is, as Mayer points out, a first step. I shall use "encoding" for this step since it is not always clear whether "representation" means internal or external representation. The distinction is made explicit in Figure 1, a diagram of a possible solution sequence for a typical story problem.

Mayer's examples are typical word problems, for which translation to equation form makes sense and is part of the standard curricular treatment (at least from algebra on). Consequently, his points about more work on translations are well taken. Goldin and McClintock's monograph on variables in mathematical tasks (1984) shows the immense number of considerations in devising mathematical tasks. For example, our work with elementary school children indicates that a routine problem presented pictorially may be easier than the "same" problem presented verbally (Threadgill-Sowder & Sowder, 1983; Moyer & Moyer, 1983). I suspect that the problem "Find all integral m, n ($m \neq n$) such that $m^n = n^m$" would be approached differently than would the problem "Find all integral x, y ($x \neq y$) such that $x^y = y^x$." (The first version looks like a number theory problem whereas the second looks like a graphing problem.) Mayer (1978) notes that "different presentation formats can result in different encodings of the same information" (p. 238).

Reaction 2: What does psychology offer with respect to encoding tasks presented in algebraic, pictorial, or geometric form?

Word problems *are* an important class of tasks (to most of us), so Mayer's focus does have considerable merit. Teachers would readily agree that the translation of relations needs much explicit attention. The usual treatments of translation, coupled with the similarity of "...6 times as many (period)" and "...6 times as many as ...," give a predictable mess. The in-depth looks at the students-professor problem (Clement, 1982; Wollman, 1983) suggest that learning to translate is not hopeless—Wollman says that instruction can give at least *pro tem* correct translations—but that some students' grasp of the equality relation is faulty. To an outsider, the relative difficulty of relational proposition vis-à-vis assignment propositions should be easy to explain (e.g., on the basis of coordinating two variables, or on the relative demands on memory).

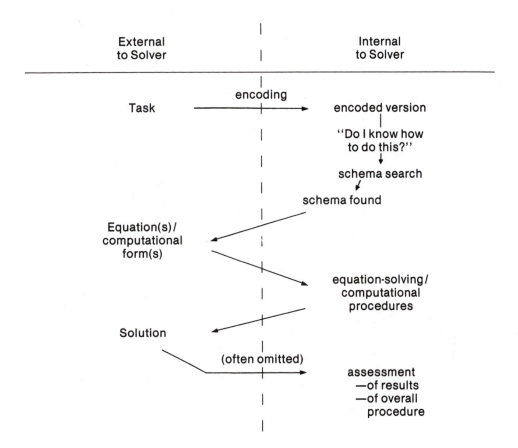

Figure 1.   Simplified sequence for many routine problems or exercises.

Reaction 3: Why, cognitively, are relational propositions more difficult to translate?

SCHEMA TRAINING

Teaching problems by type is the antithesis of teaching problem solving. How many times have students said "But we don't know how to do that kind," as though already knowing how to do a particular type were the *only* way to solve a problem? It is clear that Mayer's focus on the usual word problems, and on studies in which the subjects have had significant training in algebra, have led him in this direction. The heart of problem solving to most mathematics educators is "What do I do when I don't know what to do?" Teaching problems by type results in knowing exactly what to do, for problems of that type. Hence, to repeat the argument, that type of problem would then be an exercise (or "routine problem" to some of us), calling as it does on an already-learned algorithm. This is emphasized in Figure 2.

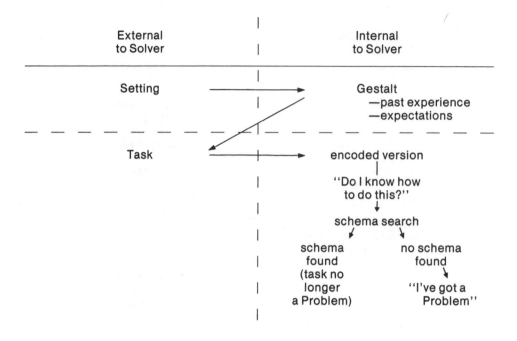

Figure 2. Sequence illustrating the distinction between a routine problem and a genuine problem.

Figure 2 reminds us that prior instruction is an important consideration when experimenting with schooled tasks. It *is* disappointing but understandable when, for $215/216 + 0/189 = m$, a student starts looking for a common denominator, or when students start writing equations for impossible problems (see Mayer's reference to Paige & Simon). The curriculum does not teach one to reflect about exercises. And, unless we teach students about *problems,* they will go on expecting exercises.

Reaction 4: A curriculum must include attention to problems, so that students' overall executive views of appropriate actions and solution time frames will not be narrowly defined.

There are positive aspects to learning problem schemas. Schemas are certainly better than pseudostructures, based on similar contextual features in the problem statements (Silver, 1979). Also, an extremely useful heuristic is to think of a similar problem. Obviously, that heuristic is valueless unless one already knows how to solve some problems!

A key issue is, *which* schemata should be taught? Reliance on contextual cues like "boats in a river" has been impugned above. But such schemata as "part + part = whole" or "whole − part = part" for many primary school story problems, or "try writing equations based on relationships in the problem" for most high school algebra story problems, appear rich enough to warrant instruction.

Reaction 5: Which problem schemata should be taught?

A couple of Mayer's implications about schemata have received attention. Sumagaysay (1972) found that a gradual mix of the three types of percentage problems gave a better performance on such problems than did one type at a time or all types at all times, with seventh-graders. Thus, her study supports Mayer's proposal that a mix of problem types helps students discriminate among problems. On the other hand, Zimmerman (1979) found that contextual cues carry an inordinate influence on sixth-graders' solutions, even when the problems used in instruction involved a variety in the underlying mathematics. Finally, our work with third- through seventh-graders, some of whom are labeled learning disabled, suggests that they already do a fair job of picking out relevant data and ignoring irrelevant data for many routine problems. Another of Mayer's implications leads to this reaction:

Reaction 6: What is the rationale for proposing that problem-solving performance will increase if students practice representing problems concretely, pictorially, symbolically, or verbally?

STRATEGY TRAINING

Mayer will be delighted that recent work on teaching heuristics to fifth- and seventh-graders has been somewhat successful (Charles & Lester, 1984), and that other efforts like those reported by Branca (1983) have been promising. It is encouraging to learn of successes, since some earlier studies with young children (e.g., Post, 1968, with seventh-graders) had given unclear signals on the feasibility of teaching general heuristics before high school. (I am not counting the basic facts strategies noted by Mayer.) Experienced problem solvers seem able to draw on exactly the heuristic(s) needed for a problem, as though some subliminal guidance system is pointing the way. Are there features of problems which generate heuristic-specific schema?

Reaction 7: Can a herd of heuristics be corralled into a production system by instruction?

In watching children solve routine problems, we have been struck by the rapid but incorrect responses of some learners. The impulsivity-reflectivity construct has been around for some time, and studies on slowing impetuous behavior still pop up. Items on Bloom and Broder's (1950) "Check List on Problem Solving," derived in part from a contrast of successful and unsuccessful students' performances, remind the student to slow down, to consider the problem, not to jump to conclusions, and so on. Rowe's (1969) provocative work with "wait-times" after classroom questions and responses also suggests that even young children can profit from time for thought. Can we teach a strategy of reflection for both before and after the solution of a problem?

Reaction 8: Can children trained to be less impulsive also be taught to use the new time profitably when problem solving?

COMPONENT SKILLS

In trying to relate Mayer's remarks on automatizing component skills to problem solving, I almost immediately falter. Certainly translation skill would be a gross component, as would skills with particular heuristics. But we already know about these, and teaching those skills is, to my knowledge, part of everyone's instruction about problem solving. What else? Examination of a study cited by Mayer, on solving letter series (Holtzman, Glaser, & Pellegrino, 1976), showed that the component skills were very task-specific: detection of interletter relations and discovery of periodicity, for example.

Reaction 9: Is the number of components of mathematical problem solving relatively small? What are they? Are they teachable? Some answers are obliquely suggested by noting that Holtzman et al. found that practice alone enabled fifth-graders to improve about as much as learners given instruction in component skills.

CONCLUSION

Thanks to Mayer's wide-ranging interests and talents, we have an idea of what cognitive psychology currently says to us about problem solving. He would no doubt agree that there are many gaps left to fill. But there is promise. For example, metacognition, a currently attractive construct, apparently has nothing specific to offer yet, but may in the near future. And many of the gaps may be addressed by other branches of psychology: practice schedules, learner characteristics, the important role of affect, and so forth. We are grateful to Mayer and his counterparts for their contributions to an understanding of problem solving.

REFERENCES

Bloom, B.S., & Broder, L.J. *Problem-solving processes of college students.* Chicago: University of Chicago Press, 1950.

Branca, N.A. *Problem solving processes of upper elementary school children.* Final report of NSF grant FED-79-19617, August 1983.

Clement, J. Algebra word problem solutions: Thought processes underlying a common misconception. *Journal for Research in Mathematics Education* 13, 16–30, 1982.

Charles, R.I., & Lester, F.K., Jr. An evaluation of a process-oriented instructional program in mathematical problem solving in grades 5 and 7. *Journal for Research in Mathematics Education* 15, 15–34, 1984.

Goldin, G.A. The measure of problem-solving outcomes. In F.K. Lester & J. Garofalo (Eds.), *Mathematical problem solving: Issues in research.* Philadelphia: The Franklin Institute Press, 1982.

Goldin, G.A., & McClintock, C.E. (Eds.) *Task variables in mathematical problem solving.* Philadelphia: The Franklin Institute Press, 1984.

Holtzman, T.G., Glaser, R., & Pellegrino, J.W. Process training derived from a computer simulation theory. *Memory and Cognition* 4, 349–56, 1976.

Kilpatrick, J. *Research on problem solving — as seen from the mathematics classroom.* Paper presented at the annual meeting of the National Council of Teachers, Detroit, April 1983.

Mayer, R.E. Effects of meaningfulness on the representation of knowledge and the process of inference for mathematical problem solving. In R. Revlin & R.E. Mayer (Eds.), *Human reasoning*. Washington, DC: Winston, 1978.

Moyer, J.C., & Moyer, M.B. *The relationship between the performance of learning-disabled students on story problems of differing format, and selected trait variables.* Paper presented at the annual meeting of the National Council of Teachers of Mathematics, Detroit, April 1983.

Post, T.R. The effects of the presentation of a structure of the problem-solving process upon problem-solving ability in seventh grade mathematics. *Dissertation Abstracts* **28**, 4545A, 1968. (University Microfilms No. 68-4746)

Rowe, M.B. Science, silence, and sanctions. *Science and Children* **6**, 11–13, 1969.

Silver, E.A. Student perceptions of relatedness among mathematical verbal problems. *Journal for Research in Mathematics Education* **10**, 195–210, 1979.

Simon, H.A. Problem solving and education. In D.T. Tuma & F. Reif (Eds.), *Problem solving and education: Issues in teaching and research.* Hillsdale, NJ: Lawrence Erlbaum Associates, 1980.

Sumagaysay, L.A. The effects of varying practice exercises and relating methods of solution in mathematics problem solving. *Dissertation Abstracts International,* **32**, 6751A, 1972.

Threadgill-Sowder, J., & Sowder, L. *Story problem formats and individual differences.* Paper presented at the annual meeting of the National Council of Teachers of Mathematics, Detroit, April 1983.

Wollman, W. Determining the sources of error in a translation from sentence to equation. *Journal for Research in Mathematics Education* **14**, 169–81, 1983.

Zimmerman, C.W. Contextual details and mathematical problem difficulty. *Dissertation Abstracts International* **40**, 143A–44A, 1979.

Artificial Intelligence and the Learning of Mathematics: A Tutorial Sampling[1]

Edwina L. Rissland

University of Massachusetts, Amherst

In this paper, I discuss studies of mathematics made from an artificial intelligence (AI) point of view. There is a spectrum of work in this area that ranges from studies whose purpose is solely to understand better the learning of mathematics to studies whose purpose is to perform a mathematical task ·without human involvement or consideration. Such a spectrum reflects the purposes of AI researchers themselves: from those who use AI as an approach to study cognition and understand it better to those who use AI to build systems to do tasks without making claims that the manner in which the programs perform says anything about the way in which humans perform the task (Samuel 1983; Schank, 1983).

In reviewing the literature, the relevant work can be divided into the following categories:

1. AI conceptual analyses of mathematical tasks.

2. AI process models for mathematical tasks.

3. AI programs to do mathematics somewhat like a mathematician.

4. AI programs to do mathematics without claims of similarity to mathematicians.

This paper by no means covers all the papers of relevance in AI, cognitive science, and mathematics education. Rather, it is a sampling of work that I consider interesting and indicative of what can be done in each of the first three categories. The purpose is to give the reader an idea of what has been done already and to help a researcher outside of AI find entry points into the literature.

1. Preparation of this paper was supported in part by grant IST-8017343 of the National Science Foundation. Any opinions, conclusions, or recommendations expressed are those of the author and do not necessarily reflect the views of the National Science Foundation.

Some of the programs discussed are not new; they have been selected because they are "classics." Some of the work discussed is not really AI; it is included because it is the sort of study necessary before one can build an AI program—what I call one's "epistemological homework."

I have not tackled the vast literature on problem solving per se; it is too extensive to review well in a paper of this scope and it is not necessarily directed at the concerns of this workshop, namely, mathematics and education. I also have not ventured into areas related to mathematics such as physics and computer programming; but one would be well-advised to take a look at the work done in these areas. Throughout this paper the reader will find various terms from AI. A discussion of these terms is found in *The Handbook of Artificial Intelligence* (Barr & Feigenbaum, 1981, 1982; Cohen & Feigenbaum, 1982).

AI CONCEPTUAL ANALYSES OF MATHEMATICAL TASKS

Davis's Work on Mathematical Understanding

Davis and his co-workers at the Curriculum Laboratory at the University of Illinois have amassed an extraordinary body of material on children learning mathematics ranging from arithmetic to calculus (Davis, 1984; Davis, Jockusch, & McKnight, 1978; Davis & McKnight, 1980). Their studies over the past 10 years have involved extensive, thorough, and sensitive protocol analyses of students working problems. They have elucidated mathematical skills by paying attention to student mistakes and misconceptions. In their explanations, Davis et al. concentrate on discussing the mathematics involved rather than specifying or building a detailed computational model. In their discussions of the processes and knowledge, they have used ideas, like "frames" and "subgoals," from AI.

These researchers have not pushed their work in the direction of developing a conceptual framework for mathematics; rather, they have probed deeply into the mathematical tasks themselves and used AI ideas when appropriate. Their work offers an extensive base on which others can build; see, for example, the following section on Matz's work.

I present here an example typical of Davis's project taken from his recent final report (Davis, Young & McLoughlin, 1982). The subtraction example is part of a discussion arguing for the need for careful analysis of skills and not just superficial consideration of right and wrong answers à la "drill and practice."

> One of our studies (Davis & McKnight, 1980) dealt with a third-grade girl, Marcia, who subtracted
>
> $$\begin{array}{r} 7{,}002 \\ -25 \\ \hline \end{array}$$
>
> by writing
>
> $$\begin{array}{r} 5 \\ \cancel{6} \\ \cancel{7}{,}002 \\ -25 \\ \hline 5{,}087 \end{array}$$

Marcia was convinced that she had performed the subtraction correctly.... What does this have to do with *understanding*?... What has made the remediation so difficult ... is that she believes

1. She has learned the subtraction algorithm carefully and well (and she has, provided there are no zeroes in "inside" columns in the minuend);

2. She always gets correct answers by using this algorithm (and she does—again, provided there are no zeroes in the "inside" columns in the minuend);

3. She is using the *same* algorithm for

$$7,002$$
$$\underline{-25}$$

that she uses for, say,

$$1,985$$
$$\underline{-296}$$

It is, of course, this third belief that causes the trouble. But, unfortunately, one cannot really say whether Marcia is correct, or not, in this belief. There are two possible rules that she *might* be using:

a) When necessary, "borrow" from the next digit on the left (in the minuend);

or else

b) When necessary, "borrow" from the nearest non-zero digit on left (in the minuend).

No case had previously arisen that would distinguish between these two rules. (Indeed, the theory of "knowledge" which underlies our work suggests that probably Marcia had not formulated her "rule" so precisely that such a distinction could be described.) (pp. 5–9)[2]

Davis places great emphasis on the problem of retrieval and matching in understanding, and his project has gathered the kind of evidence that can be capitalized on in AI work. For instance, he discusses the valid and invalid retrieval of the axiom ("the zero product principle") "$A \times B = 0 \implies [A = 0 \vee B = 0]$" and its mis-generalization as "$A \times B = k \implies [A = k \vee B = k]$" (Davis et al., 1982, pp. 94–95). This is exactly the sort of mathematical behavior that Matz (1980, 1982) describes in terms closer to those of AI. Davis suggests that the problem Marcia has is related to an incorrect, or rather an incomplete, retrieval of relevant knowledge.

Davis is making links with AI by using AI conceptual constructs to describe what he sees in his work; for instance, he uses the notions of "slots" and "frames" to address the retrieval problem. He uses "procedures" and "sub-procedures" to describe the hierarchical nature of plans and skills like those involved in synthetic division. I chose the excerpts on subtraction and the zero product principle because they are related to the work of Matz and vanLehn described in other sections of this paper.

Davis also uses the ideas of "planning" and "critics," which are central in AI, to describe what he sees in students like Marcia. In particular, Marcia lacks, or is not using, the "size" critic for numbers, which says that if one has about \$7,000 and spends \$25, one should *not* end up with about \$5,000. (An AI critic or "demon" is a process that is always watching what is going on and when it sees something of interest, it "shouts.")

---

2. Reprinted by permission of the *Journal of Mathematical Behavior*.

Matz's Work on High School Algebra

Matz's work is an example of research on the cognitive aspects of mathematics, which seeks explanations in terms of AI concepts such as rules and procedures. Matz discusses how systematic errors in high-school algebra problem solving are the result of reasonable, although unsuccessful, attempts to adapt known procedures to a new situation by applying what she calls "extrapolation" techniques (Matz, 1980, 1982). She suggests that many common errors arise from one of two processes: (*1*) inappropriate use of an old rule in a new situation, or (*2*) incorrect adaptation of a known rule to solve a new problem.

In particular, with regard to the second class of error, she is interested in (*1*) errors generated by an incorrect choice of an extrapolation technique, (*2*) errors reflecting an inadequate base knowledge, and (*3*) errors made during a procedure.

Particularly interesting is her discussion of extrapolation technique errors of generalization and linear decomposition. In the class of linearity errors are those errors resulting from the overgeneralization of a distribution rule. These are typified by SQRT(*A* + *B*) = SQRT(*A*) + SQRT(*B*). In such errors, a composite algebraic expression is decomposed linearly by distributing its topmost operator. The following incorrect generalizations are described by Matz (1982).

$$\sqrt{A + B} \quad \Rightarrow \quad \sqrt{A} + \sqrt{B}$$

$$(A + B)^2 \quad \Rightarrow \quad A^2 + B^2$$

$$A(BC) \quad \Rightarrow \quad AB \cdot AC$$

$$\frac{A}{B + C} \quad \Rightarrow \quad \frac{A}{B} + \frac{A}{C}$$

$$2^{a+b} \quad \Rightarrow \quad 2^a + 2^b$$

$$2^{ab} \quad \Rightarrow \quad 2^a 2^b$$

Matz organizes these errors into three schemas, one of which is $\Box(X \mathbin{\triangle} Y) \Rightarrow \Box X \mathbin{\triangle} \Box Y$. Its use is based on the past experience that the distributive law worked successfully in past problems. Incorrect retrieval and application of this schema results in mistakes typically involving square roots and powers. This is exactly the sort of retrieval problem that Davis discussed.

Another common way to generalize a schema is to replace specific constants by variables, as in the zero product principle. This type of generalization is based on the typically valid assumption that the numbers involved in a procedure are incidental. Unfortunately, zero is the well-known counterexample to this heuristic. For example, the problem

$$(X - 3)(X - 4) = 0$$
$$(X - 3) = 0 \text{ or } (X - 4) = 0$$
$$X = 3 \text{ or } X = 4$$

generalized to the following is an excellent example of a good strategy going awry:

$$(X-3)(X-4) = 7$$
$$(X-3) = 7 \text{ or } (X-4) = 7$$
$$X = 10 \text{ or } X = 11$$

It is exactly the kind of strategy one would build into an AI learning program; however, such a program would need a means to prune away false generalizations (for instance, through "critics" or "generate and test" methodologies). Nevertheless, it would be the right kind of strategy to try.

Schoenfeld's Work on Heuristics

Schoenfeld has devoted much of his research to discussing heuristics and their role in problem solving (Schoenfeld, 1978). He has been particularly interested in whether high-level strategies can be taught to college undergraduates (Schoenfeld, 1980). His work, while not pushed to the level of description favored by AI researchers nor explicitly couched in AI terms, is an example of the kind of in-depth discussion needed to explicate the topic of heuristics, which AI researchers often assume to be explained by its mere mention. Heuristics are used heavily in AI work (for instance, in expert systems like MYCIN) and play a key role in the work of Slagle (1962) and Lenat (1982), described later in this paper.

Schoenfeld (1980) asks (1) if we can accurately describe the strategies used by "expert" mathematicians to solve problems and (2) if we can teach students to use those strategies. He answers in the affirmative, as I and others like Davis would. He discusses the complexity of using a heuristic strategy like the often-cited "find an analogous problem" heuristic and the inherent difficulties of carrying it out: which analogous problem, by what analogy, in what representation? Even the heuristic "If there is an integer parameter, look for an inductive argument" can be difficult to implement, especially for students, who often operate at the "syntactic" and not "semantic" level of understanding. Such heuristic strategies are really labels for a collection of more detailed procedural and descriptive knowledge and further (sub)strategies. Recognition of this complexity is often missing in problem-solving discussions, even those of that great master Polya (1973).

A problem-solving strategy outlined by Schoenfeld (1980) uses modules to perform problem analysis, argument design, problem exploration, solution implementation, and solution verification. He presents a flowchart-like schematic outline of his problem-solving strategy (Schoenfeld, 1980, Figure 2, p. 800) and describes aspects of each of these components. Some of the modules in his schema could be forced to a descriptive level which would be implementable in AI-style programs; some need much more specification.

More recently Schoenfeld (1983a, 1983b) has been interested in exploring issues in the analysis of protocols and describing problem-solving behavior, especially its "control" component. He distinguishes three types of knowledge needed in problem solving:

- *Resources*—typically, domain-specific knowledge such as facts and algorithms, routine procedures and heuristics, representations, and other knowledge possessed by the individual which can be brought to bear on the problem at hand.

- *Control*—planning, monitoring, assessment, "metacognitive" acts and other ingredients related to the selection and implementation of tactical resources.

- *Belief systems*—about self, the environment, the topic, and mathematics that influence an individual's behavior.

Schoenfeld elaborates on these types of knowledge in a paper that he presented to the American Educational Research Association in 1983. The paper contains a nice example of problem solving which not only illustrates his points but also shows how specific examples (like "reference" examples) enter into the problem-solving process (see Schoenfeld, 1983b, p. 8).

A laudatory aspect of Schoenfeld's work is the inquiry into the nature of strategies and control-level knowledge. Too often such high-level knowledge is glossed over in favor of tactical or algorithmic knowledge because the latter is easier to grapple with, in the sense of being more describable or implementable because of its step-by-step focus. Yet it is strategic-level knowledge—or control—that is critical to learning; this theme will be apparent in my discussion of Category III programs.

Rissland's Work on Understanding Understanding Mathematics

In my 1977 Ph.D. thesis, I sought to elucidate how one understands a mathematical theory like eigenvalues or continuity. I posed the question, "What is it that I know when I understand an area of mathematics well?" The answer is couched in terms of a mapping out of the knowledge in a scheme of "spaces," which are semantic networks of framelike items linked together through various sorts of relations (Rissland, 1978a, 1978b, 1980). The description of the conceptual framework relies heavily on notions from computer science like data-base items and pointer structures.

I had planned (though never implemented) an interactive environment for the professional mathematician to explore and retrieve information in a theory, such as real analysis, and an environment built on it to help a neophyte learn *how* to explore and understand.

My elucidation of understanding contains the following main ingredients:

- Spaces of items and relations, such as Examples-space, Results-space and Concepts-space.

    Items are strongly bound clusters of information: for instance, the statement of a theorem, its name, its proof, a diagram, an evaluation of its importance, and remarks on its limitations and generality.

    Spaces are sets of similar types of items related in similar ways: for instance, proved results and their logical dependencies constitute *Results-space*.

- A taxonomy of epistemological classes of items based on their role in teaching, learning, and understanding, and *worth ratings* of items based on importance.

- Detailed laying out of *item-frames* for each of the principal types of item (example, result, concept).

- Detailed discussion of links between items: *in-space* links between items within a space (like constructional derivation between example items) and *across-space* ("dual") links.

"Understanding" involves enriching one's store of knowledge, particularly inter-frame and interspace connections. The following questions "prompt and probe" under-standing (Rissland, 1978b):

1. What is the statement of this item. The setting?

2. Do I understand the statement? Should I review or examine the ingredient concepts, especially the important ones and those to which I have previously not done justice?

3. What is a picture or diagram for this item?

4. Am I reasonably comfortable with this item's immediate predecessors? Are there any predeccesors on which I should bone up? Or remember to come back to?

5. Do I know any dual items for this item, such as counter-examples, model examples, reference examples, culminating results, basic results, etc.? Am I aware of the important ones? Should I peruse some of the others?

6. Can I say what is the gist of this item? Of its statement? Of its demonstration?

7. What is it good for? Why should I bother with it? What is its significance to the theory as a whole?

8. What is the main idea of its proof, construction or procedure? Are the details important? If so, can I summarize them?

9. Is there some way I can fiddle with this item? Perhaps check out a few test cases?

10. What happens if I perturb its statement? Does it generalize? Is it true in other settings? Can it be strengthened by dropping some hypotheses or adding some conclusions. If not, why not: can I cite a counter-example and can I pinpoint what goes wrong? If so, is the new demonstration similar or different from the original? Is it much harder? Should I just be aware that it exists, and forget about the details until I need them?

11. Can I see how this item fits in with the development of the theory as developed in the ap-proach I am taking? What about other approaches? Is this item important or critical or is it simply a stepping-stone or a peripheral embellishment?

12. Can I close my eyes and visualize or describe this item's connections to other items in the theory, to the theory as a whole, to other theories? Have I seen anything like it before? (p. 375) [3]

One should try to answer as many questions as possible initially, and one should fre-quently return to the list if the item is important enough. Eventually most of the ques-tions will be answered through work directly with the item and indirectly with other items. "The last question is a keystone to understanding in a deep way and should be given a try during the very first exposure to an item and repeatedly thereafter" (p. 375).

In essence the idea is that items, which include results, concepts, examples, goals, and strategies, are cohesive clusters of information and that there are important relations between them. Each space of items plus relations describes a different aspect of knowl-edge. Another important point is that one can taxonomize items on the basis of how they are used in learning, doing, teaching, and understanding mathematics. The following describes these ideas as they relate to the aspects of mathematics having to do with ex-amples.

An example, by which is meant a specific situation, case, or experience, is comprised of many aspects or pieces of information: a name, taggings and annotations as to epistemological class and importance, lists of pointers to other examples from which it is constructed and to whose construction it contributes, the process of how it is constructed,

---

3. Reprinted by permission of *Cognitive Science,* Ablex Publishing Corporation.

a schematic or diagram, pointers to items like definitions and theorems in other spaces, statements of what the example is good for or how it can be misleading, and sources of further information about the example. Examples are linked through the relation of *constructional derivation* of how one example is built from others. Examples plus this relation constitute an "examples-space."

When one considers the different effects and uses examples can have with respect to teaching and learning, one can distinguish different epistemological classes. (There are similar analyses for results and concepts.) It is important to recognize that not all examples serve the same function. One can develop a taxonomy:

- Start-up examples—perspicuous, easily understood and easily presented cases.

- Reference examples—standard, ubiquitous cases.

- Counter examples—limiting, falsifying cases.

- Model examples—general, paradigmatic cases.

- Anomalous examples—exceptions and pathologies.

Start-up examples are simple cases that are easy-to-understand and to explain. They are particularly useful when one is learning or explaining a domain for the first time. Such examples can be generated with minimal reference to other examples; thus one can say that they are structurally uncomplicated. A good start-up example is often "projective" in the sense that it is indicative of the general case and that what one learns about it can be "lifted" to more complex examples.

Reference examples are examples that one refers to over and over again. They are "textbook cases" which are widely applicable throughout a domain and thus provide a common point of reference through which many concepts, results, and other items in the domain are (indirectly) linked together.

Counter examples are examples that refute or limit. They are typically used to sharpen distinctions between concepts and to refine theorems or conjectures. They are essential to the process of "proofs and refutations," described beautifully by Lakatos (1976).

Model examples are examples that are paradigmatic and generic. They suggest and summarize expectations and default assumptions about the general case. Thus, they are like "templates" or Minsky's "frames."

Anomalous examples are examples that do not seem to fit into one's knowledge of the domain, and yet they seem important. They are "funny" cases that nag at one's understanding. Sometimes resolving where they fit leads to a new level of understanding.

Applying this taxonomy to an introductory study of continuity from the domain of real function theory one might classify the function $f(x) = x$ as a start-up example; $f(x) = x^2$ and $f(x) = e^x$ as reference examples; $f(x) = 1/x$ as a counterexample; "$f(x)$ with no gaps or breaks'' as a model example; and $f(x) = \sin(1/x)$ as an anomalous example. The first example, $f(x) = x$, is also a reference example (the ''identity'' function). Thus, such a classification need not be exclusive. The anomaly $\sin(1/x)$ will most likely become a favorite counterexample as one understands that a function can fail to be continuous in at least two ways: by having gaps and breaks and by failing to settle down to a limit. Thus, such a classification is not static. Increased understanding will, of course, lead to qualifications on this model of a continuous function, although it will still serve to summarize one's expectations.

PROCESS MODELS FOR MATHEMATICAL TASKS

Bundy's Work on Equation Solving

In connection with his work on automatic theorem proving, Bundy looked at the processes involved in solving algebraic equations. He described high-level processes that account for the line-to-line transitions in solving equations for an unknown (Borning & Bundy, 1981; Bundy, 1975; Bundy & Silver, 1981). He called these processes *strategies*; they are isolation, collection, attraction, cancellation, and removing nasty function symbols. The first three constitute what he calls the ''basic method.''

Bundy's analysis of automatic theorem proving is an example of research pursued for AI purposes which turns out to be very relevant to the study and explication of mathematical expertise in humans. It provides a detailed description in ''hard'' computational terms of a skill and provides an opportunity for its use in mathematics education since his descriptors and procedures are readily understandable. One could easily talk to a class working on equation solving using his ideas of strategies and basic methods. In fact, I would recommend exactly that.

The following example illustrates his analysis:

1. $\ln(x + 1) + \ln(x - 1) = 3$ . . . . (i)

2. $\ln[(x + 1)(x - 1)] = 3$ . . . . (ii)

3. $\ln(x^2 - 1) = 3$ . . . . (iii)

4. $x^2 - 1 = e^3$ . . . . (iv)

5. $x^2 = e^3 + 1$ . . . . (v)

6. $x = \sqrt{e^3 + 1}$ or $x = -\sqrt{e^3 + 1}$

(Bundy, 1975, p. 12)

In his analysis of this sequence of equations, Bundy is interested in explicating what happens in between the lines, that is, the transitions and transformations used. He points out that many of the solution steps are not shown and that one is using more than the usual axioms of the real numbers (this last observation stems from his concern about automatic theorem proving in which the prover must have access to such knowledge). For instance, any prover must have a wealth of knowledge on how to perform *simplification*. (As Bundy discusses, there is no universal standard of simplification: what is simpler in one context is not necessarily so in another). In considering step ii, the transition from line 2 to line 3, he speculates that the axiom $(u + v)(u - v) = u^2 - v^2$ was used, producing $\ln(x^2 - 1^2) = 3$, and that the simplification step, from this equation to line 3, was omitted.

Bundy's (1975) analysis goes as follows:

> We look first at the end of the solution, lines 3 to 6. In line 3, for the first time the equation contains only a single occurrence of the unknown, x. From here on the solution is straight-forward. The next three steps consist of stripping away the functions surrounding this single occurrence of x until it is left isolated on the left hand side of the equation. Each step consists of identifying the outermost (or dominant) function symbol on the left-hand-side, recovering the axiom which will remove it from the left-hand-side and insert its inverse on the right-hand-side, and then applying this axiom. We will call the strategy which guides these three steps *isolation*. . . . It can be regarded as the basis of nearly all work in equation solving.
>
> As with simplification, mathematicians often omit isolation steps from their written pro-tocols, crowding as many as three or four into the transition from one line to another.
>
> We next look at line 2:
>
> 2. $\ln[(x + 1)(x - 1)] = 3$
>
> This contains 2 occurrences of x, so isolation is not applicable. However, we can see step (ii) as *preparing for isolation* (our emphasis), by achieving a reduction in the number of oc-currences of x from 2 to 1. This is done by applying the identity:
>
> $$(u + v)(u - v) = u^2 - v^2.$$
>
> This is an example of our second strategy, which we call *collection*, namely, when there is more than one occurrence of the unknown, try to find an axiom which will collect occurrences together.
>
> Finally we look at line 1 and step (i).
>
> 1. $\ln(x + 1) + \ln(x - 1) = 3$
>
> The two occurrences of x cannot be immediately collected, presumably because a suitable ax-iom was not stored. We can however *prepare* . . . *for collection* (our emphasis) by moving them closer together, so that more identities will match the term containing them both. This is what happens in step (i). . . . The strategies of moving occurrences closer together to increase their chances of collection, we call attraction.
>
> When the above three strategies are combined in this way we call the resulting equation solv-ing strategy, the basic method. (p. 17)[4]

Bundy describes his three strategies in computational terms. This involved, for in-stance, providing "harder" definitions of "term" and the notion of "closer," as seen in his discussion on collection:

> If the two occurrences are on the same side of the equation this will be a term called the *containing term*, otherwise it will be the whole equation. We deal with the former case first. The containing term must now be replaced by another term containing one occurrence of the unknown, say x, so we must look for an axiom, say A, which will do this. We can easily build up a description, which A must obey.
>
> (i)   A must be an identity, i.e., an expression of the form: s1 = s2 or B $\Longrightarrow$ s1 = s2, where B is called its precondition.
>
> (ii) One of the variables, say u, must occur either
>   (a) twice in s1 and once in s2 or
>   (b) twice in s2 and once in s1; without loss of generality we will assume case (a).
>
> (iii) s1 must match the containing term, with u being instantiated to x.
>
> . . . .

---

4. Reprinted by permission of Alan Bundy.

If A obeys parts (i) and (iia) of the above description we will say that it is *useful to collection, left to right, relative to u.* If A obeys parts (i) and (iib) we will say that it is *useful to collection, right to left, relative to u.* . . . .E.g.,

$$\sin 2u = 2 \cdot \sin u \cdot \cos u$$

is useful to collection, right to left, relative to u.

$$(u + v)(u - v) = u^2 - v^2$$

is useful to collection, left to right, relative to u. (p. 21)[5]

Bundy forces all three strategies—isolation, collection, and attraction—to this degree of specificity in computational terms. He then gives two more examples of equation solving, one involving trigonometric functions, the other a general quadratic, to illustrate his strategies.

Bundy's last major point concerns the removal of nasty function symbols in equation solving. Examples of nasty symbols in this context are radicals and inverse trigonometric functions like arcsin. Bundy provides a hierarchy of niceness/nastiness. In removing nasty symbols, he identifies and describes three major strategies: cancellation, collection, and inversion. The end result of such an analysis in the case of a rationalization goes as follows (Bundy, 1975):

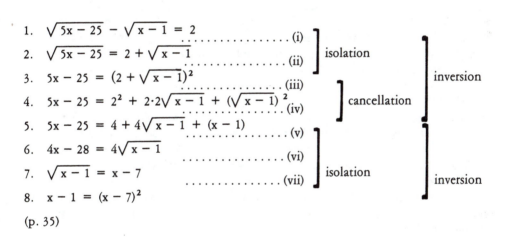

1. $\sqrt{5x - 25} - \sqrt{x - 1} = 2$ . . . . (i) ⎤
2. $\sqrt{5x - 25} = 2 + \sqrt{x - 1}$ . . . . (ii) ⎦ isolation
3. $5x - 25 = (2 + \sqrt{x - 1})^2$ . . . . (iii) ⎤ inversion
4. $5x - 25 = 2^2 + 2 \cdot 2\sqrt{x - 1} + (\sqrt{x - 1})^2$ . . . . (iv) ⎥ cancellation
5. $5x - 25 = 4 + 4\sqrt{x - 1} + (x - 1)$ . . . . (v) ⎦
6. $4x - 28 = 4\sqrt{x - 1}$ . . . . (vi) ⎤
7. $\sqrt{x - 1} = x - 7$ . . . . (vii) ⎦ isolation   inversion
8. $x - 1 = (x - 7)^2$

(p. 35)

Eliminating radicals, the process of "rationalization," is a paradigmatic example of removing a nasty function symbol. Reproducing Bundy's analysis here would take too much space. One comment on these processes is that they now apply to function symbols rather than unknowns. For instance, one tries to get occurrences of a function and its inverse, like sin and arcsin, closer together.

Brown and Burton's Work on BUGGY

To account for student errors in simple procedural skills like subtraction, Brown and Burton (1978; Burton, 1982) proposed the Buggy model. In that model, student errors are seen as symptoms of a "bug," that is, a discrete modification of a correct procedural

---

5. Reprinted by permission of Alan Bundy.

skill. For example, the bug "$0 - n = n$" accounts for the errors in both of the following subtraction problems:

```
  500        312
 -  65       -243
  565        149
```

The bug dictates that one write the bottom digit as the answer when the top digit in a column is zero.

BUGGY is a computerized game based on the diagnostic interactions between a student and a teacher. The computer plays the part of a student who has a bug. The challenge to the user is to find the bug; BUGGY presents examples of the "student's" incorrectly done homework problems. The user/diagnostician describes the bug. The conjectured diagnosis is then tested with more examples of problems done by the student.

The main thrust of the BUGGY work is thus the diagnosis of bugs with the assistance of a computer program (which can be seen as a gaming environment). This leads (it is hoped) to an improvement in the skill of the diagnostician, for example, a student teacher. BUGGY thus can be used to explore such high-level skills as hypothesis formation, strategic knowledge, debugging, and theory testing through examples. Brown and Burton feel that their BUGGY work provides a common language for teachers and students that enables them to talk about their work. This principle also underlies my work and that of Bundy, described in the previous section of this paper, and Papert (1980) has often addressed the same issue.

The BUGGY work was motivated in part by the often incorrect assumption that student errors are "random" or that students do not follow procedures very well. The BUGGY work suggests quite the opposite: students are often too faithful to procedures. Such conclusions have also been reached by Davis and his colleagues (Davis, Jockusch, & McKnight, 1978; Davis & McKnight, 1980; Davis, Young, & McLoughlin, 1982).

Often the manifestations of a "buggy" procedure do not permit easy diagnosis; it is easy to see something is awry but much harder to say exactly what. For instance, Brown and Burton (1978) challenge their readers to diagnose the bug in the following series of addition problems:

```
   7        9        8        6        8        9       17       19
  +8       +5       +3       +7       +8       +9       +8       +4
  15       14       11       13       16       18       25       23


   87      365      679      923    27,493              797
  +93     +574     +794     +481   +1,509          +48,632
   11      819      111      114    28,991           48,119
```

(pp. 157–158)[5b]

The bug here is that every time there is a carry, the student is simply writing down the carry and forgetting about the units digit. This student also had the same bug in his multiplication method. Thus, bugs can piggyback on subprocedures into higher-level

---

5b. Reprinted by permission of *Cognitive Science*, Ablex Publishing Corporation.

procedures and cause bugs in these as well. Remediation of the higher-level skill would require remediation of the lower-level skill much like the fact that debugging procedures in computer programming often requires debugging subprocedures.

The theme here is the breakdown of skills into simpler and more primitive subskills. For instance, in ordinary addition, primitives might be recognizing a digit, writing a digit, and so forth. The analysis of a skill in terms of such primitives is a standard AI approach; it is seen in the work of Selfridge discussed later in this paper.

BUGGY makes its diagnosis by picking a bug from approximately 100 known bugs by comparing the student's answers with the output of each bug run on the test problems. The initial hypothesis set contains any bug that explains at least one of the student's bugs on the problem as a whole (as compared to an error in a single column). This initial hypothesis set is reduced by finding and removing primitive bugs that are completely subsumed by other primitive bugs.

The information BUGGY uses is summarized in "bug comparison" tables, an excerpt of which is given by Brown and Burton (1978):

8	99	353	633	81	4769	257	6523	103	7315	1039	705	10038	10060	7001
3	79	342	221	17	0	161	1280	64	6536	44	9	4319	98	94
5	20	11	412	64	4769	96	5243	39	779	995	696	5719	9962	6907

Student answers:

—	—	—	—	98	—	418	—	169	738	1095	706	14319	10078	7097

•DIFF/0 − N = N:

*	*	*	*	!	*	!	*	!	839	!	!	***	9978	!

•ADD/INSTEADOF/SUB:

11	178	695	854	***	*	***	7803	167	13851	1083	714	14357	10158	7095

(p. 175)[5b]

The problems with the correct answers appear at the top of the table. Student answers appear on the next line with "−" indicating a student correct answer. Each of the remaining lines contains the name of a bug and information regarding the running of the subtraction procedure with that bug. For these lines, "***" indicates that the bug predicts the student's incorrect answer; "*" indicates that both the student and the bugged procedure got the problem right; "!" indicates that the bugged procedure gave the correct answer but the student did not; and a number entry is the answer the bugged procedure would get when it is different from both the student and the correct answer. Thus, "*" and "***" are confirming evidence for the student having a bug—both are producing the same results—and "!" is disconfirming evidence. Using such evidence, BUGGY then rates each bug according to how well it explains the student bug. The system does this by means of a "symptom" vector that contains information such as the number of "***"s.

In their work, Brown and Burton discuss many of the subtleties that may occur: (1) some bugs are caused by performance lapses (e.g., the student copies a number wrong); (2) some bugs are due to errors in subskills (e.g., errors in standard subtraction fact table); (3) bugs can act in concert and thus one bug can hide the existence of another (e.g., the "smaller-from-larger" bug will hide any bug in the borrowing procedure).

Brown and VanLehn's Repair Theory

Given that bugs do occur in procedural skills, a natural question to ask is "How do they arise?" Matz (1980, 1982) has given some answers with her analysis of overgeneralization. Brown and VanLehn (1980) offer another explanation by generating "bug stories" that describe how particular bugs could arise. Their work, which deals with subtraction errors, is a natural extension of Brown and Burton's work.

Brown and VanLehn (1980) offer the following "Repair Theory" explanation for the origin of bugs:

> When one has unsuccessfully applied a procedure to a given problem, one attempts a *repair*. The need to make a repair is often triggered by a procedure (or sub-procedure) reaching an *impasse* by which is meant a state in which it cannot execute. One tries to remedy the impasses by applying repair heuristics, of which the following are considered:
>
> 1.   skip
> 2.   quit (the procedure)
> 3.   swap vertically (the subtrahend and minuend entries)
> 4.   dememorize. (p. 391)

Brown and VanLehn experiment with the principles of their theory by taking a production-rule representation of a standard school subtraction algorithm, performing deletions on it to create buggy procedures, and then running the repair theory. They are in no way claiming that the incorrect procedures are generated by one forgetting or deleting lines from correct procedures; these incorrect procedures are just a means to study the repairs.

An example of Repair Theory is given in Figure 1 and in the following discussion from Brown and VanLehn (1980).

> When a rule is deleted, its sister rules will often be executed in its place, which frequently leads to an impasse. For example, when L4 of Figure 1 has been deleted, and the procedure is run on the problem
>
> $$\begin{array}{r} 27 \\ -4 \\ \hline \end{array}$$
>
> an impasse is reached in the tens column because the interpreter chose L6, the only rule that applies given that L4 is gone. Running L6 results in calling the primitive action Diff. Diff takes a column difference by taking the difference of its first two arguments' contents and writing the result in the cell pointed to by the third argument. But Diff has a precondition that neither of its arguments be blank. Since this precondition is violated when Diff is called on the tens column, the procedure is at an impasse. This impasse can be repaired in a variety of ways. For example, the procedure could simply do nothing instead of take the column difference (the "no-op" repair heuristic). Control would return from Diff, and ultimately the

---

REPAIR THEORY

The syntax is:

Goal (goal's argument) Satisfaction Condition: *goal's satisfaction condition*
    label: {rule's conditions} →   *rule's action*
    other rules for achieving the goal . . .

The rules for the version of subtraction used in this paper are:

Sub() Satisfaction Condition: TRUE
    L1:   {} →   (ColSequence RightmostTopCell
                                              RightmostBottomCell RightmostAnswerCell)

ColSequence (TC BC AC) Satisfaction Condition:(Blank? (Next TC))
    L2:   {} →   (SubCol TC BC AC)
    L3:   {} →   (ColSequence (Next TC)(Next BC)(Next AC))

SubCol (TC BC AC) Satisfaction Condition: (NOT (Blank? AC))
    L4:   {(Blank? BC)} →   (WriteAns TC AC)
    L5:   {(Less? TC BC)} →   (Borrow TC)
    L6:   {} →   (Diff TC BC AC)

Borrow (TC) Satisfaction Condition: FALSE
    L7:   {} →   (BorrowFrom (Next TC))
    L8:   {} →   (Add10 TC)

BorrowFrom (TC) Satisfaction Condition: TRUE
    L9:   {(Zero? TC)} →   (BorrowFromZero TC)
    L10:   {} →   (Decr TC)

BorrowFromZero (TC) Satisfaction Condition: FALSE
    L11:   {} →   (Write9 TC)
    L12:   {} →   (BorrowFrom (Next TC))

TC, BC, and AC are variables. Their names are mnemonic for their contents, which happen to be the top, bottom and answer cells of a column.

The primitive actions and their associated preconditions are listed below. All of their arguments are cells. The actions expecting digits in certain arguments have a precondition that those cells not be blank.

Diff — Subtracts the digit contained in its second argument from the digit contained in its first argument and writes the result in the third argument. The second argument can not be larger than the first argument.

Decr — Subtracts one from the digit contained in its argument and writes the result back in the same cell. The input digit must be larger than zero.

WriteAns — Writes the digit contained in its first argument in its second argument.

Add10 — Adds ten to the digit contained in its argument and writes the result back in the same cell.

Write9 — Writes a nine in its argument. The cell can not be blank originally.

Figure 1. A GAO graph for a standard version of subtraction. [Brown and VanLehn, 1980, p.387][6]

---

6. Reprinted from *Cognitive Science* by permission of Ablex Publishing Corporation.

procedure would terminate normally leaving 3 as the answer. This way of repairing the impasse generates the bug Quit-When-Bottom-Blank. (p. 388)[7]

Brown and VanLehn (1980) describe several bugs generated by repairs to procedures with incorrectly deleted lines. For instance, if L5 (from Figure 1) is deleted, the following is executed:

> [Rule L5] says to borrow when the top digit is too small. If L5 is deleted, then L6, the rule for processing ordinary columns, will be executed on every column, including larger from smaller (LFS) columns where one ought to borrow. LFS columns violate a precondition of the Diff (the action called by L6), namely that the first input number be larger than the second input number. This precondition violation is an impasse, and the problem solver is called to repair it. (p. 390)[8]

Several bugs can be generated by repairing the impasse:

- The "no-op" repair heuristic (which says to skip the operation whose precondition is violated) leads to the bug "Blank-Instead-of-Borrow," which simply does not write an answer in the LFS column.

- The "quit" repair causes the subtraction process to halt at the first LFS column.

- The "swap vertically" repair generates the interesting "Smaller-From-Larger" bug, which results in the absolute difference entered as the answer in LFS columns.

- The "dememorize" bug of answering 0 in all LFS columns (i.e., $m - n = 0$ when $n > m$) is so called because it involves the inverse of "memorizing," which involves learning the fact table and semantics of subtraction.

Brown and VanLehn point out that some repairs generate bugs which have never been observed in student subjects; and a repair to one impasse can lead to a second impasse. These are issues involving control. For instance, the second means that the repair proposed must be constrained. They also discuss the role of "critics" in a generate-and-test architecture of the repair generator to filter down the proposed repairs.

Repair Theory is a good example of "principled" modeling of human mathematical behavior. Once Brown and VanLehn select their approach for repairs, they stick to it (and do not introduce *ad hoc* repairs to it) to see how far it can be pushed and how it squares with the observed data. It provides a detailed account of mathematics in a narrow area which is most likely transferable to other tasks. Of course, using their approach in other tasks would involve background work on, for instance, the domain-specific procedures, impasses, and repairs in the new area.

Rissland's Work on Constrained Example Generation

Almost all episodes of learning—whether by person or machine—depend on having a rich store of examples (worked and posed problems, specific cases, etc.); see for instance the discussions of Lenat's, Selfridge's, and Mitchell's work in the next section of this

---

7, 8.   Reprinted from *Cognitive Science* by permission of Ablex Publishing Corporation.

paper. Without the experience gained by consideration of examples, skill acquisition, proving theorems, debugging programs, and so forth all come to a halt (or cannot even begin). Despite the central role played by examples, they are often overlooked or taken for granted. Yet, any expert teacher knows not only the value of examples but also that not all examples serve equally well to make a point or provide a test case and that what often distinguishes one example from another is the properties it possesses.

Thus, with regard to learning and teaching, one does not pick examples at random: they are generated for a purpose—like giving evidence for or against a conjecture—and are usually (carefully) chosen to possess certain desired properties or *constraints*. I call this process of generating examples that meet prescribed constraints Constrained Example Generation or CEG (Rissland, 1980, 1981; Rissland & Soloway, 1980). The CEG model is based upon observations of people working problems in which they are asked to generate examples satisfying certain constraints. It incorporates three major phases: *retrieval, modification,* and *construction*.

When an example is sought, one can search through one's storehouse of examples for one that matches the properties desired. If one is found, the example generation problem has been solved through *retrieval*. In retrieval, there are many semantic and contextual factors—like the last generated example—and therefore one is not merely plunging one's hand into an unorganized knowledge base. Thus, even though retrieval sounds simple, it can be very complex.

However, when a match is not found, how does one proceed? In many cases, one tries to *modify* an existing example that is judged to be close to the desired example, or to have the potential for being modified to meet the constraints. Often the order of examples selected for modification is based on judgments of closeness between properties of known examples and the desiderata, that is, how "near" the examples are to what is sought.

If attempts at generation through modification fail, experienced example generators, like teachers or researchers, do not give up; rather they switch to another mode of example generation, which we call *construction*. Construction processes include combining two simple examples to form a more complex one and instantiation of general model examples or templates to create an instance. Construction is usually more difficult than either retrieval or modification.

In the general skeleton of the CEG model there are subprocesses for retrieval, modification, construction, judgment, and control. Presented with a task of generating an example that meets specified constraints, the generator

- searches for and (possibly) retrieves examples judged to satisfy the constraints from an examples knowledge base (EKB); or

- modifies existing examples judged to be close to, or having the potential for, fulfilling the constraints with domain-specific modification operators; or

- constructs an example from domain-specific knowledge, such as definitions, general model examples, principles, and more elementary examples.

In human protocols, two types of generation have been observed: (*1*) retrieval plus modification and (*2*) construction. That is, retrieval is not necessarily tried first, followed by modification and then construction; sometimes construction is attempted straightaway. Clearly, this model needs many other features to describe the CEG process in its entirety; more details can be found in my 1981 report.

The richness and complexity of the CEG process can be seen here in a synopsis of a CEG problem taken from the domain of elementary function theory:

> Give an example of a continuous, nonnegative function, defined on all the real numbers such that it has the value 1,000 at the point $x = 1$ and that the area under its curve is less than $1/_{1000}$.

Most protocols for this question begin with the subject selecting a function (usually, a familiar reference example function) and then modifying it to bring it into agreement with the specifications of the problem. There are several clusters of responses according to the initial function selected and the stream of the modifications pursued. A typical protocol goes as follows (Rissland, 1980):

> Start with the function for a "normal distribution." Move it to the right so that it is centered over $x = 1$. Now make it "skinny" by squeezing in the sides and stretching the top so that it hits the point (1, 1000).
>
> I can make the area as small as I please by squeezing in the sides and feathering off the sides. But to demonstrate that the area is indeed less than $1/_{1000}$, I'll have to do an integration, which is going to be a bother.
>
> Hmmm. My candidate function is smoother than it need be: the problem asked only for continuity and not differentiability. So let me relax my example to be a "hat" function because I know how to find the areas of triangles. That is, make my function be a function with apex at (1, 1000) and with steeply sloping sides down to the x-axis a little bit on either side of $x = 1$, and 0 outside to the right and left. (This is OK, because you only asked for non-negative.) Again by squeezing, I can make the area under the function (i.e., the triangle's area) be as small as I please, and I'm done. (p. 281)[9]

Notice the important use of such modification operations as "squeezing," "stretching," and "feathering," which are usually not included in the mathematical kit bag since they lack formality, and the use of descriptors such as "hat" and "apex."

Another thing observed in *all* the protocols is that subjects make implicit assumptions—e.g., they impose additional constraints—about the symmetry of the function (about the line $x = 1$) and its maximum (occurring at $x = 1$ and being equal to 1,000). There are no specifications about either of these properties in the problem statement. These are the sort of tacit assumptions that Lakatos (1976) talks about; teasing them out is important to studying both mathematics and cognition.

AI PROGRAMS TO DO MATHEMATICS
SOMEWHAT LIKE A MATHEMATICIAN

Slagle's Symbolic Automatic Integrator (SAINT)

One of the classic programs in AI is Slagle's program written in 1961 as a doctoral dissertation to perform indefinite integration. SAINT (*S*ymbolic *A*utomatic *INT*egrator) performed at about the level of a good freshman calculus student (Slagle, 1962). A successor to SAINT was Joel Moses's SIN program which has evolved into the

---

9. Reprinted by permission of the author.

highly successful MACSYMA system, which can perform exceedingly complicated symbolic mathematics and is used by the professional mathematics community.

The integration problems that SAINT can handle involve a class of elementary functions defined by Slagle as follows:

1. any constant is an elementary function;
2. the variable is an elementary function;
3. the sum of elementary functions is elementary;
4. any elementary function raised to an elementary function as a power;
5. a trigonometric function of an elementary function;
6. a logarithmic or inverse trigonometric function of an elementary function.[10]

SAINT works as follows when given a problem:

1. It determines whether the integrand is one of 26 standard forms; that is, when it is a substitution instance of a standard form, like $\int 2^x dx$ is an instance of $\int c^x dx$. If so, the answer can be given immediately.

2. If not of standard form, it is tested to see if it is amenable to a well-defined transformation which, when applicable, is usually appropriate, such as factoring the constant outside the integral, interchanging finite summation and integration, or making a linear substitution. There are eight transformation rules.

3. If not of standard form, the integral is tested to see if it is amenable to a heuristic transformation, which usually helps with the solution. There are ten heuristic transformations, the most useful of which is the "derivative-divide" rule described below.

To give the reader an idea of how SAINT works, here is an example from Slagle (1962, pp. 192-193)[10]:

As a concrete example we sketch how SAINT solved

$$\int \frac{x^4}{(1 - x^2)^{5/2}} \, dx$$

in eleven minutes. SAINT's only guess at a first step is to try substitution: $y = \arcsin x$, which transforms the original problem into

$$\int \frac{\sin^4 y}{\cos^4 y} \, dy$$

For the second step SAINT makes three alternative guesses:

A. By trigonometric identities $\qquad \int \frac{\sin^4 y}{\cos^4 y} \, dy \; = \; \int \tan^4 y \, dy$

---

10.   Reprinted by permission of McGraw Hill Book Co.

B. By trigonometric identities $\qquad \displaystyle\int \frac{\sin^4 y}{\cos^4 y}\, dy = \int \cot^{-4} y\, dy$

C. By substituting $z = \tan (y/z)$ $\qquad \displaystyle\int \frac{\sin^4 y}{\cos^4 y}\, dy = \int 32\, \frac{z^4}{(1 + z^2)\,(1 - z^2)^4}\, dz$

SAINT immediately brings the 32 outside of the integral.
After judging that (A) is the easiest of these three problems SAINT guesses the substitution $z = \tan y$, which yields

$$\int \tan^4 y\, dy = \int \frac{z^4}{1 + z^2}\, dz$$

SAINT immediately transforms this into

$$\int \left(-1 + z^2 + \frac{1}{1 + z^2}\right) dz = -z + \frac{z^3}{3} + \int \frac{dz}{1 + z^2}$$

Judging incorrectly that (B) is easier than

$$\int \frac{dz}{1 + z^2}$$

SAINT temporarily abandons the latter and goes off on the following tangent. By substituting $z = \cot y$,

$$\int \cot^{-4} y\, dy = \int - \frac{dz}{z^4(1 + z^2)} = -\int \frac{dz}{z^4(1 + z^2)}$$

Now SAINT judges that

$$\int \frac{dz}{1 + z^2}$$

is easy and guesses the substitution, $w = \arctan z$ which yields $\int dw$. Immediately SAINT integrates this, substitutes back and solves the original problem.

$$\int \frac{x^4}{(1 - x^2)^{5/2}}\, dx = \arcsin x + \tfrac{1}{3} \tan^3 \arcsin x - \tan \arcsin x$$

One of the noteworthy mechanisms in SAINT is the use of an "and-or" goal tree. Each integration problem can be treated as a goal which involves the solution of other integration (i.e., subgoal) problems. When there are alternatives to achieving a goal, each of which would suffice, this represents an "or" branch in the tree. When there are necessary subgoals, each of which is needed, this represents an "and" branch.

By use of a "goal stack," Slagle maintains the "focus of attention" in his problem solver. Each time there is a new task to be done, it is added to the goal stack. For instance, an "algorithmlike" or heuristic transformation usually adds goals to the goal stack. Satisfying goals allows the stack to be reduced. Slagle maintains two goal stacks, one of which is the "heuristic goal list" of goals which are neither of standard form nor amenable to standard algorithmlike transformations. This is like keeping a list of things to do. Part of the determination of the amenability of a goal to a transformation is a list of characteristics which include function type (rational, algebraic, etc.) and a measure of the depth of the deepest functional composition in the integrand.

The most successful heuristic in Slagle's program is "derivative-divide" which searches for a subexpression $s(x)$ in the integrand $g(x)$ such that $s'(x)$ divides $g(x)$ and results in an expression with fewer factors and then makes the substitution $u = s(x)$ in the integration. For instance, in $\int x \exp(x^2)\, dx$ substitute x^2. SAINT actually discovered the substitution $u - \exp(x^2)$.

There are three points to be made about SAINT which are relevant to the mathematics education community. First, the skill involved in a task like integration can be explicated in procedural terms. Second, much skill knowledge can be described in terms of rules of an if-then nature. Third, Slagle's program illustrates the use of goals, heuristics, and knowledge representation.

SAINT was tested on a total of 86 problems (54 of them chosen from final examinations in freshman calculus at MIT) and correctly solved all but 2.

The most difficult were

$$\int \frac{\sec^2 t}{1 + \sec^2 t - 3\tan t}\, dt \quad \text{and} \quad \int \frac{x^4}{(1 - x^2)^{5/2}}\, dx$$

Lenat's AM Program

Lenat's doctoral dissertation program Automated Mathematician (AM) is a knowledge-based program which discovered mathematical concepts (Lenat, 1977; Lenat & Davis, 1982). Provided with a rich arsenal of heuristics (especially those to measure discovery and "interestingness"), and a basis of concepts in set theory, it developed concepts in set and elementary number theory such as "prime." Lenat's program has the themes of strong knowledge-based programming, heuristics encoded as if-then rules, and an agenda mechanism to control the focus of attention on things to do.

AM is a program that expands a knowledge base of mathematical concepts. Each concept is stored as a frame data structure. Creating a new concept frame is the principal task for AM; this activity involves setting up a new data structure for the concept and filling in the slots. Filling in a slot is accomplished by executing a collection of relevant heuristic rules. The possible things for AM to do—like setting up a new concept and filling in a concept slot—are kept track of by the AI mechanism known as an "agenda." AM looks at the agenda of things to do and selects the next task on the basis of considerations such as its importance and "interestingness." Filling in a slot, like "Fill-in examples of primes," is a typical task. A heuristic rule is relevant if executing it brings AM closer to satisfying the task. Relevance is determined a priori by predetermined connections between the heuristic and the slot it effects.

Once a task is chosen from the agenda, AM gathers relevant heuristic rules and executes them. Then AM picks a new task. There are three kinds of effects from such execution:

1. Slots of concepts get filled in. A heuristic relevant to filling in an example slot is as follows:

> To fill in examples of X, where X is a kind of Y, check examples of Y; some of them might be examples of X as well. For instance, to fill in an example for the "prime number" concept, AM would consider examples of the "number" concept.

2. New concepts are created. A heuristic relevant to this task is the following:

> If some (but not most) examples of X are also examples of Y, then create a new concept defined as the intersection of the concepts X and Y.

3. New tasks are added to the agenda, for instance by execution of the following heuristic:

> If very few examples of X are found, then add the following task to the agenda: "Generalize the concept X."

The knowledge of mathematical concepts is encoded in a network of about 115 frames; each frame has several slots describing different aspects of the concept like its NAME, DEFINITION, EXAMPLES, GENERALIZATIONS, SPECIALIZATIONS, and WORTH. AM uses about 250 heuristics. A heuristic (which turned out to be quite powerful) is the one dictating the examination of extreme cases.

AM has roughly 40 heuristics that deal with the creation of new concepts. Some are general and apply to any concept; others apply only to functions and relations. The general heuristics include (1) generalization through such mechanisms as dropping a condition or changing a constant to variable, (2) specialization, (3) exception handling (e.g., if a concept has negative examples, AM might create a new concept whose instances are the negative examples).

To give the reader an idea of how AM works, the following excerpt from Lenat and Davis (1982) describes the run in which AM discovered the concept of "prime." (Note that AM does not have any natural language fluency; what follows is a transcript that was edited by Lenat to improve its readability.)

Task 65:
Filling in examples of the following concept: "Divisors-of".

       3 Reasons: (1) No known examples for Divisors-of so far.
                         (2) Times, which is related to Divisors-of, is now very interesting.
                         (3) Focus of attention: AM recently defined Divisors-of.

26 examples found, in 9.2 seconds, e.g.: Divisors-of(6) = {1 2 3 6}

Task 66:
Considering numbers which have very small set of Divisors-of (i.e., very few divisors).

       2 Reasons: (1) Worthwhile to look for extreme cases.
                         (2) Focus of attention: AM recently worked on Divisors-of.

Filling in examples of numbers with 0 divisors.
  0 examples found, in 4.0 seconds.
  Conjecture: no numbers have 0 divisors.

Filling in examples of numbers with 1 divisors.
  1 example found, in 4.0 seconds, e.g.: Divisors-of (1)={1}
  Conjecture: 1 is the only number with 1 divisor.

Filling in examples of numbers with 2 divisors.
  24 examples found, in 4.0 seconds, e.g.: Divisors-of (13) = {1 13}
  No obvious conjecture. This kind of number merits more study.
  Creating a new concept: "Numbers-with-2-divisors."

Filling in examples of numbers with 3 divisors.
  11 examples found, in 4.0 seconds, e.g.: Divisors-of (49) = {1 7 49}
  All numbers with 3 divisors are also Squares. This kind of number merits more study.
  Creating a new concept: "Numbers-with-3-divisors."

Task 67:

. . .

Considering the square-root of Numbers-with-3-divisors. (p. 21)[11]

This session was preceded by AM's discovery of multiplication and division; this led to the concept of "divisors of a number." AM found examples of this concept; in particular, AM investigated *extreme cases*, that is, numbers with very few or very many divisors. AM then was ready to discover "primes":

> AM thus discovers Primes in a curious way. Numbers with 0 or 1 divisor are essentially nonexistent, so they're not found to be interesting. AM notices that numbers with 3 divisors always seem to be squares of numbers with 2 divisors (primes). This raises the interestingness of several concepts, including primes. (Lenat & Davis, p. 25)

AM then goes on to use the concept of prime in generating various conjectures like "unique factorization" which arise out of the heuristic to ask if the relation between a number and its divisors is a function.

Lenat's AM is an example of a strongly knowledge-based AI program which can do quite interesting tasks—the sort of tasks that if a person did them, one would say that there was intelligence involved. It is a good example of an AI program which starts with knowledge and power and is able to generate new knowledge. Thus, AM has strength as an AI program; Lenat's remarks about its psychological validity are not that compelling. However, his program is a very good demonstration of the power of heuristics, knowledge representation, and agenda mechanisms.

Selfridge's COUNT Program

Selfridge's (1979) COUNT program was designed to explore the issue of learning through a teacher challenging a student to solve problems. This work is at the opposite end of the spectrum from Lenat's: whereas Lenat uses a strong knowledge-based approach rich with control and search heuristics, Selfridge's program starts with minimal knowledge and has a very simple control structure.

---

11. Reprinted from *Knowledge-based Systems in Artificial Intelligence*, by permission of McGraw-Hill Book Company.

The task of the COUNT program is to learn to count the number of characters in a string. The program initially possesses a few "primitive capabilities" from which it is to derive a new capability, for example, learn how to count, or reverse the order of characters in the string.

It has available to it a register (N), the position of a pointer (PTR), and the length of the string (LENGTH). Its primitive capabilities affect those three data. The capabilities are INCREMENT, DECREMENT, EXCHANGE, LEFT, RIGHT, REPEAT, and N TIMES. INCREMENT and DECREMENT affect the register N; EXCHANGE interchanges two letters in the string; LEFT and RIGHT affect the pointer; REPEAT causes a capability to be repeated until it cannot be performed; and N TIMES causes a capability to be repeated N times, where N is the value in the register.

The teacher starts out by being shown a "world state" which consists of a string of letters, a pointer position, and a value in N. The teacher then describes a new world state which it wishes COUNT to achieve (this is the "posed problem"). For instance, the teacher might ask COUNT to get the register N to be zero. By a sequence of posed problems and COUNT's discovering how to do them, COUNT can build up new capabilities (which are sequences of prior capabilities) and can eventually, if taught, count the number of letters in the string. Actually, the counting problem is just a preproblem to learning how to reverse the letter string—a much harder problem.

One important point of COUNT is that the teacher gets COUNT to do more not by programming it but by challenging it to discover new capabilities. This is much the situation with children and other learners: one cannot "make" the learner do the skill, but rather must challenge the learner to develop the needed skills. (Think of getting a child to pitch—first, the child must learn to throw; or think of getting a horse and rider to jump a 4-foot fence...)

The sequence of posed problems must challenge but not overwhelm the program (the same would be true of children and horses). Overwhelming in the case of COUNT means exceeding its search resources. The program uses "blind breadth-first" search to discover a sequence of actions that solve a posed problem: first search all the capabilities on the current menu; then search all pairs; then all triplets; etc. The current menu consists of the primitive capabilities plus any new ones that the teacher has caused the program to add. This is done by asking the program to save what it has done in the successful solution of a posed problem (the solution is given a name of the teacher's choosing). Thus, new capabilities only get added in response to success on a posed task. COUNT provides a demonstration that a program can learn without highly sophisticated control techniques, but the subtlety comes in the selection of problems to pose.

The following is an excerpt of a session to teach COUNT how to count. COUNT presents a tableau of its world state and the teacher responds by posing a new world state:

```
A  B  C  D  E                 N = 16
                              (PTR = 4    LENGTH = 5)

TYPE PROBLEM:
     *
     0
     *
```

The order of specifying the posed world state is (1) the new string, (2) the new value in N, and (3) the new pointer position. An asterisk indicates that the teacher does not care about the value. In this first problem, the teacher is solely interested in getting the register to be zero and does not care about the actual letters in the string or the position of the pointer.

COUNT responds to this first challenge:

> I think I've got it.
> Yes, it works. Shall I try it again? Y or N: N.
> Here's new status. Pose problem again. If you don't like status, Type S (and return).
> A   B   C   D   E   F   G   H   I   N = 6
>   (PTR = 3   LENGTH = 10)

The most streamlined way to teach COUNT to count is as follows:

1. Zero out the register N (call it NZERO).

2. Move the pointer all the way to the left and zero out the register (INIT).

3. Move the pointer one letter right and add one to N (MOVE-RIGHT-AND-ADD).

4. Count the number of letters in the string.

Thus, at the end of teaching COUNT to count, four new capabilities (NZERO, INIT, MRAA, COUNT) have been added to COUNT's repertoire of capabilities. Most people end up with more capabilities on the menu simply because they too are performing a "search" of problems to pose and solutions for COUNT to remember. It is possible to impede COUNT by asking it to remember too many capabilities, because this causes an increase in the size of the space COUNT must search for answers to new problems.

Selfridge's program provides a laboratory in which to study issues in learning like the role of the teacher, posed problems, and search. He does not claim that humans necessarily learn like COUNT with its emphasis on search. He does claim that humans need exercise and evaluation of their capabilities to learn. One could claim that early learning, when one is like an infant with regard to a task, might very well be something like COUNT, for what else can one do but try with the capabilities one possesses. The other end of the learning spectrum is a program like Lenat's, where the learner has a vast, rich, well-structured body of knowledge to bring to bear on new problems. Note that regardless of the kind of learning, the examples, data, and experiences involved are critical. I would claim that without a rich body of examples there can be no learning.

Mitchell's LEX Program

Mitchell (1983) has built the LEX (*L*earn by *EX*perimentation) program in the domain of symbolic integration, the same domain as Slagle's much earlier work. Where Slagle's SAINT was endowed with certain heuristics, like derivative-divide, which it used in its task of doing integration problems, the task of Mitchell's LEX is to *learn* such heuristics. In other words, LEX's task is to learn the kind of knowledge that made SAINT powerful.

Mitchell's work on LEX is an application of his idea of "version spaces" which he developed in his doctoral thesis (Mitchell, 1978). Version spaces are a mechanism to represent the range of incompletely learned heuristics in terms of the possibilities spanned by the most specific case and the most general case of successful application of the heuristic.

Mitchell is attacking a central and classic problem in AI, namely "learning." It is relevant to the concerns of this paper because some of its methods can be transferred to the teaching of mathematics; in particular, the notion of refining one's notion of a heuristic on the basis of "positive" and "negative" examples. LEX thus forms a bridge between the concerns of Schoenfeld and those of Slagle, Lenat, and the AI learning community. It also is another case in point on the ubiquitous role of examples.

LEX acquires and modifies heuristics by iteratively cycling through the processes of (1) generating a practice problem, (2) using available heuristics and other knowledge to solve this problem, (3) analyzing and criticizing the search steps in obtaining the solution, and (4) proposing and refining new domain-specific heuristics. LEX, like other AI programs, starts out with some initial store of domain-specific knowledge as well as an architecture embodying general knowledge about learning, representation, control, and so forth. Its initial domain-specific knowledge consists primarily of two sorts, much like SAINT:

1. *Operators*—These include heuristic algorithmlike (to use Slagle's term) transformations as well as "book knowledge" like common antiderivatives and standard transformations. The operators are stored in "If-Then" format, where the "If" clause contains the conditions necessary for application of the operator, and the "Then" contains the result of the application. For example:

   1. OP1: $\int r \cdot f(x)\,dx \implies r \cdot \int f(x)\,dx$

   2. OP2 (Integration By Parts):
      $\int u\,dv \implies uv - \int v\,du$
      (This is represented as $\int f1(x)f2(x)\,dx$, where $f1(x)$ corresponds to u and $f2(x)\,dx$ corresponds to dv.)

   3. OP3: $1 \cdot f(x) \implies f(x)$

   4. OP4: $\int [f1(x) + f2(x)]\,dx \implies \int f1(x)\,dx + \int f2(x)\,dx$

   5. OP5: $\int \sin(x)\,dx \implies -\cos(x) + C$

   6. OP6: $\int \cos(x)\,dx \implies \sin(x) + C$

2. *A type hierarchy*—This lays out the relationships between major types of domain items, like functions, which LEX must manipulate. LEX derives much of its power to learn from this hierarchy, which essentially captures the notion of generality in LEX's domain. For instance, the specific functions sin, cos, and tan are *trig* functions and ln and exp are *expln* functions; *trig* and *expln* functions are *transcendental* functions. The identity function, constant function, and integer exponent are *monomials* which in turn are *polynomials*.

LEX's task is to learn when a heuristic should be applied and how. For instance, in the case of Integration by Parts (IBP), LEX is to learn how to "bind" the u and the dv. As anyone who has learned or taught calculus knows, there is some art in choosing the u and the dv; LEX is trying to discover and express that art.

The LEX program contains four modules: Problem Solver, Critic, Generalizer, and Problem Generator. Their functions are as follows:

- *Problem Solver* tries to solve the problem at hand with its available store of operators, including the current status of its heuristics.

- *Critic* analyzes the trace of a successful solution to glean positive and negative instances. A positive instance is a problem state on the way to a successful solution; a negative instance is on a path that led away from the solution.

- *Generalizer* rewrites its knowlege of heuristics on the basis of what the Critic tells it: it squeezes in from the most general statement of the heuristic on the basis of negative instances and pushes out from the most specific on the basis of positive instances.

- *Problem Generator* poses new problems to solve which will help to further refine knowledge of the heuristics.

For instance, suppose LEX is trying to learn IBP—that is, refine OP2 to narrower classes for $f1(x)$ and $f2(x)$—and has been posed the problem:

$$\int 3x \sin x \, dx$$

At the completion of one cycle, IBP has been refined and is narrowed to a range of possibilities from most specific — apply IBP with $u = 3x$ and dv –$\sin(x) dx$ — to most general—original form of OP2 with $f1(x)$ and $f2(x)$. This range is represented by a version space that captures all the intermediate possibilities like the following:

Apply IBP to $\int 3x \, \mathrm{trig}(x) \, dx$ with $u = 3x$ and $dv = \mathrm{trig}(x) \, dx$
Apply IBP to $\int \mathrm{poly}(x) \cos(x) \, dx$ with $u = \mathrm{poly}(x)$ and $dv = \cos(x) \, dx$
Apply IBP to $\int kx \, \mathrm{trig}(x) \, dx$ with $u = kx$ and $dv = \mathrm{trig}(x) \, dx$ (k an integer)

Eventually LEX homes in on an intermediate case.

One lesson for mathematics education from this work is to mimic the learning cycle of LEX. That is, make it an explicit task for students to learn what should be the u and what should be the dv, and discover this by trying wisely chosen problems of positive and negative force to narrow down on the answer. Another less obvious message is that domain knowledge such as LEX's hierarchy of types is exceedingly powerful and should be made explicit to students; this is a point I have made (Rissland, 1984).

Note that LEX still is not clever enough to know to *group* $\int (\sin x)^2 dx + \int f(x) dx + \int (\cos x)^2 dx$ to take advantage of the obvious identity and arrive at $x + \int f(x) dx$. Because it does not have concepts like "even integer" and "odd integer," it cannot learn some of the usual tricks involving integrals of powers of sin and cos (which involve one trick when there exists an odd power and a different one for both even powers).

An example of one cycle of LEX starting with the problem $\int 3x \cos(x) \, dx$ results in the flow of information and a version space summarized in Figure 2.[12]

CONCLUSIONS

My purpose in presenting the preceding samples of research was not only to give the reader an idea of what AI-style research is and pointers into the relevant literature but

---

12. Reprinted by permission of Tioga Publishing Company.

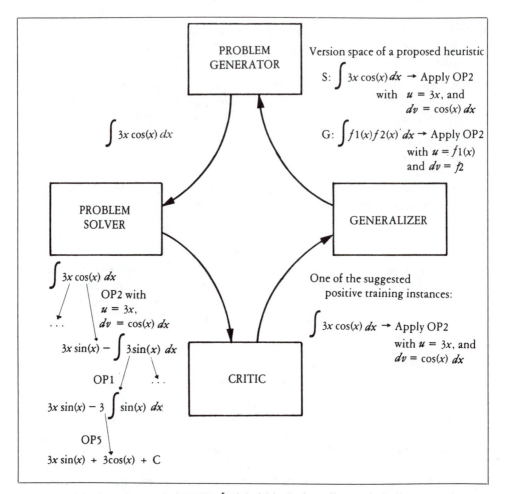

Figure 2. The learning cycle in LEX. [Michalski, Carbonell, & Mitchell, 1983, Figure 6-5, p. 170]

also to show, by example, that many questions central to AI research are also central to mathematics education. In particular, both fields are interested in questions such as

- How do we learn?

- What is understanding?

- What is the knowledge involved in mathematical expertise?

- How can we describe and represent such knowledge?

- How can we impart such knowledge to students?

I believe that the tools of AI, in particular those of knowledge representation, process description, and planning/control, provide a useful kit bag for the mathematics educator in grappling with such questions. AI concepts make it easier to describe what we know and intuit about learning and, if we want, to experiment and test out our ideas by implementing them as programs. This expressive power makes it possible to demystify and describe our knowledge: how it is structured, stored, acquired, and refined. Applying this approach to expert mathematical problem solving is especially relevant to mathematics education, because by better understanding and describing such knowledge, we will be better able to transfer it to our students and thereby help them improve.

Another epistemological lesson AI teaches is that it is very important to attend to "meta" and "tacit" knowledge: for example, strategies for understanding and non-formal aspects of mathematical knowledge. AI programs have demonstrated that such knowledge is central to machine intelligence. This can be taken as a strong hint that it might also be vital to human intelligence.

As mathematicians and educators, we may not be satisfied with the descriptions and programs of AI but they do give us a place to begin, even if only in reaction and criticism. AI offers existence proofs that important mathematical skills can be understood and detailed. AI programs, although they might not prove the necessity of certain ingredients of knowledge, can demonstrate sufficiency. AI programs do not prove psychological validity for such detailed models, but they can be used to empirically evaluate and test the sensitivity of models. They also provide a rigorous medium for testing out ideas.

AI thus offers the mathematics education researcher a body of concepts with high expressive power, demonstrations of the value of meta and tacit knowledge, a rigorous medium for testing out ideas about learning, and some strong hints about what is important for learning in humans. AI has taught us not to be afraid to tackle hard questions such as what constitutes expertise. We should take courage from this. In such research, the important point is not to be exactly right the first time, but rather to begin and then to evolve. AI offers us a way to begin.

REFERENCES

Barr, A., & Feigenbaum, E.A. (Eds.). *The handbook of artificial intelligence* (Vol. 1). Los Altos, CA: William Kaufmann, 1981.

Barr, A., & Feigenbaum, E.A. (Eds.). *The handbook of artificial intelligence* (Vol. 2). Los Altos, CA: William Kaufmann, 1982.

Borning, A., & Bundy, A. Using matching in algebraic equation solving. In *Proceedings International Joint Conference on Artificial Intelligence (IJCAI-81)*. Los Altos, CA: William Kaufmann, 1981.

Brown, J.S., & Burton, R. Diagnostic models for procedural bugs in basic mathematical skills. *Cognitive Science* **2**, 155–92, 1978.

Brown, J.S., & VanLehn, K. Repair theory: A generative theory of bugs in procedural skills. *Cognitive Science* **4**, 379–426, 1980.

Bundy, A. *Analyzing mathematical proofs (or reading between the lines)* (Research Report DAI No. 2). University of Edinburgh, Department of Artificial Intelligence, Edinburgh: 1975.

Bundy, A., & Silver, B. Homogenization: Preparing equations for change of unknown. In *Proceedings International Joint Conference on Artificial Intelligence (IJCAI-81)*. Los Altos, CA: William Kaufmann, 1981.

Burton, R.R. Diagnosing bugs in simple procedural skills. In D. Sleeman & J. Brown (Eds.), *Intelligent tutoring systems*. New York: Academic Press, 1982.

Cohen, P.C., & Feigenbaum, E.A. (Eds.). *The handbook of artificial intelligence* (Vol. 3). Los Altos, CA: William Kaufmann, 1982.

Davis, R.B. *Learning mathematics: The cognitive science approach to mathematics education*. Norwood, NJ: Ablex, 1984.

Davis, R.B., Jockusch, E., & McKnight, C. Cognitive processes in learning algebra. *Journal of Children's Mathematical Behavior* **2**(1), 10–320, Spring 1978.

Davis, R.B., & McKnight, C. The influence of semantic content on algorithmic behavior. *Journal of Mathematical Behavior* **3**(1), 39–87, Autumn 1980.

Davis, R.B., Young, S., & McLoughlin, P. *The roles of understanding in the learning of mathematics.* Urbana: University of Illinois, Curriculum Laboratory, April 1982.

Lakatos, I. *Proofs and refutations.* Cambridge: Cambridge University Press, 1976.

Lenat, D.B. Automated theory formation in mathematics. In *Proceedings International Joint Conference on Artificial Intelligence.* Los Altos, CA: William Kaufmann, 1977.

Lenat, D.B., & Davis, R. *Knowledge-based systems in artificial intelligence.* New York: McGraw-Hill, 1982.

Matz, M. Towards a computational theory of algebraic competence. *Journal of Mathematical Behavior* **3**(1), 93–166, Autumn 1980.

Matz, M. Towards a process model for high school algebra errors. In D. Sleeman & J. Brown (Eds.), *Intelligent tutoring systems.* New York: Academic Press, 1982.

Michalski, R.S., Carbonell, J., & Mitchell, T. (Eds.). *Machine learning.* Palo Alto, CA: Tioga, 1983.

Mitchell, T.M. *Version spaces: An approach to concept learning* (STAN-CS-78-711). Stanford, CA: Stanford University, 1978.

Mitchell, T.M. Learning and problem solving. In *Proceedings International Joint Conference on Artificial Intelligence (IJCAI-83).* Los Altos, CA: William Kaufmann, 1983.

Papert, S. *Mindstorms: Children, computers, and powerful ideas.* New York: Basic Books, 1980.

Polya, G. *How to solve it* (2nd ed.). Princeton, NJ: Princeton University Press, 1973.

Rissland, E.L. *The structure of mathematical knowledge* (Technical Report No. 472). Cambridge: Massachusetts Institute of Technology, Artificial Intelligence Laboratory, August 1978(a).

Rissland, E.L. Understanding understanding mathematics. *Cognitive Science* **2**(4), 361–83, 1978(b).

Rissland, E.L. Example generation. In *Proceedings Third National Conference of the Canadian Society for Computational Studies of Intelligence.* Victoria, BC, May 1980.

Rissland, E.L. *Constrained example generation* (Technical Report 81-24). Amherst: University of Massachusetts, 1981.

Rissland, E.L. The structure of knowledge in complex domains. In Chipman, Segal, & Glaser (Eds.), *Thinking and learning skills: Research and open questions.* Hillsdale, NJ: Lawrence Erlbaum Associates, 1984.

Rissland, E.L., & Soloway, E.M. Overview of an example generation system. In *Proceedings First National Conference on Artificial Intelligence.* Stanford, CA, August 1980.

Samuel, A.L. AI, where it has been and where it is going. In *Proceedings International Joint Conference on Artificial Intelligence (IJCAI-83).* Los Altos, CA: William Kaufmann, 1983.

Schank, R.C. The current state of AI: One man's opinion. *AI Magazine* **4**(1), 3–8, 1983.

Schoenfeld, A.H. Presenting a strategy for indefinite integration. *American Mathematical Monthly* **85**, 671–78, 1978.

Schoenfeld, A.H. Teaching problem solving skills. *American Mathematical Monthly* **87**, 794–804, 1980.

Schoenfeld, A.H. Beyond the purely cognitive: Belief systems, social cognitions, and metacognitions as driving forces in intellectual performance. *Cognitive Science* **7**, 329–63, 1983(a).

Schoenfeld, A.H. *Theoretical and pragmatic issues in the design of mathematical problem solving instruction.* Paper delivered at the annual meeting of the American Educational Association, Montreal, April 1983(b).

Selfridge, O.G. *Learning to count: How a computer might do it.* Unpublished manuscript, 1979.

Slagle, J.R. A heuristic program that solves symbolic integration problems in freshman calculus. In E.A. Feigenbaum & J. Feldman (Eds.), *Computers and thought.* New York: McGraw-Hill, 1962.

Artificial Intelligence and Mathematics Education: A Discussion of Rissland's Paper

Alan H. Schoenfeld

The University of Rochester

Writing a tutorial summary of "Artificial Intelligence (AI) and the Learning of Mathematics" is a nontrivial task. AI resists easy entry, as anyone who has tried to read "elementary" introductory texts like Winston (1977) or Nilsson (1980) soon discovers. It is a broad and diverse field with its own concerns, jargon, and paradigms, few of which overlap in clear ways with mathematics education. How can one convey a sense of what AI has to offer to mathematics education (ME)?

The questions that framed Rissland's tutorial were (*1*) What are the exemplary AI studies with clear mathematical content and straightforward applications/implications for mathematics education? (*2*) What is the mathematics-education content of relevance in them? (*3*) Can that content be presented in such a way that the usefulness of AI is clear, that the reader is induced to go on, and has access through the appropriate entry points? A fourth question, (*4*) And then what?, was to be my responsibility.

Rissland has met the challenge of the first three questions head on, using the methods her research would suggest: the judicious choice of examples. The reader is introduced to the AI/ME interface by means of a collection of studies that fall primarily into the first of Rissland's four categories, "*start-up* examples: perspicuous, easily understood, and easily presented cases" (p. 154). Others serve as "*reference* examples: standard, ubiquitous cases, and ... *model* examples: general, paradigmatic cases" (p. 154). There is a depressingly small collection of studies in AI with clear and obvious relevance for the reader from mathematics education. Many of the exemplary studies are discussed here. With the inclusion of a few more basis vectors,[1] we come close to

---

1. There are three additional vectors in the AI literature. First, "coaching" for the development of strategic skills has been a persistent theme. For a very readable general discussion, and the detailed description of a computer-based coach built around the competitive game "How the West Was Won," see Burton and Brown (1979). Second, there is an extensive literature on geometry, ranging from early attempts at theorem proving (Gelernter, 1963) to recent models of students' problem-solving performance with emphases on the students' cognitive representations (Greeno, 1982). Reader be warned, however; these are by no means easy papers to make one's way through. Finally, Papert's work (1980) deserves mention on at least two grounds: his elaboration of an epistemological framework, and the potential impact of LOGO in the "real world." (The whole question of micros is important, but that would take us too far afield.) *Mindstorms* is a beautifully written description of LOGO and its epistemological foundations. Whether or not one accepts Papert's arguments, one should read them.

spanning the ''clearly useful example space.'' Those suggestions are appended to round out the list of recommended readings. They are *strongly* recommended: my biased feeling is that researchers in mathematics learning who ignore the contents of AI do so at their own peril, and that the direct classroom implications of some of the findings are of vital importance.

Rissland's examples indicate how useful AI can be to the mathematics-education community. The ME reader may at first wonder about the time and energy that went into creating Slagle's (1963) SAINT program or the other studies in Categories III and IV; more about these later. But there can be no doubt about the usefulness of the types of studies in Categories I and II.

All of the conceptual analyses in Category I address, in one way or another, different aspects of the same question: What does it mean to *understand* a particular piece of mathematics? All of them demonstrate that learning and understanding are far more complex phenomena than they appear to be and than they have been taken to be for purposes of instruction. ''Simple'' arithmetic procedures are based on representation systems that are anything but simple to understand, and are fraught with dangers for naive learners: no wonder that drill-and-practice instruction at the procedural level yields marginal success! And ''straightforward'' heuristics are anything but straightforward: no surprise, then, that problem-solving instruction based on the mechanistic instantiation of those procedures fails to produce results. The discovery of such complexity can be disheartening, of course. It would be nice if learning and understanding were as simple as has been thought, and if (for example) addition and subtraction were as simple as they seem to be. But they are not. And with recognition of increased complexity comes increased ability to deal with it. The more that we understand the nature of understanding, the better prepared we are to teach for it.

The process models in Category II carry the precision of Category I to extremes, and indicate the benefits of doing so. Brown and Burton's (1978) BUGGY work is an archetypal example. At the epistemological level, that research clearly lays to rest the positivist notion of learning and its associated model of instruction. That model is based on assumptions similar to the ones that people make when training children to ride a bicycle. Component skills may be learned in simpler environments, for example, riding a tricycle. Then the child tries and tries (sometimes with the help of intermediaries like training wheels) until the skill is ''mastered.'' This instructional model has the learners repeat the procedure until they get it ''right.'' It is simple and straightforward—and wrong. A better physiological comparison for learning complex skills might be with self-taught musicians or tennis players, who often attain a certain level of skill, only to find that they cannot go further; then they must ''unlearn'' counterproductive techniques that they have developed. It's not that they haven't ''gotten it right yet,'' but that they've ''gotten something else'' instead. The BUGGY work substantiates this constructivist epistemological view. Based on the results of a diagnostic test, Brown and Burton are often able to predict the incorrect answers that students will obtain on arithmetic problems. This is compelling evidence that the students are not simply making random errors on the road to mastery, but that they have instead ''mastered'' incorrect procedures. There are strong classroom implications for this research: the task of teaching now includes diagnosing and remediating bugs, not simply presenting material.

In sum, Rissland's tutorial shows the usefulness of AI to mathematics education. It also makes AI seem accessible, perhaps even appealing. That's an important first step. But watch out for the second step: it's a lulu. As has been mentioned, there is a fairly small collection of AI studies that meet the strong criteria of direct relevance to mathematics education that are reflected in Rissland's four categories of analysis. Most of the basis vectors in that example space have been indicated, and the discussion of those has been filtered through the lens of mathematics-education perspective for purposes of presentation. The reader may be in for a surprise when the original sources are examined, for even the AI material aimed for mathematics-education consumption has other concerns close to heart and is difficult reading for those not comfortable with AI language and paradigms (e.g., VanLehn & Brown, 1980; VanLehn, 1983). Some of the other studies, especially those in the broader AI literature, may seem impenetrable. They may appear to be concerned with issues that, prima facie, are only tangentially connected to mathematics education (as reflected, say, in the NCTM's [Shumway, 1980] *Research in Mathematics Education*), if at all. What's there for a mathematics educator? How does one find the useful material, and make sense of the rest? Is it worth it? These, of course, are personal questions. The answer must be based on one's goals, interests, and values.

ONE ROSE-COLORED AND BIASED VIEW OF HISTORY: AI DOES US A FAVOR

To get some perspective on what AI (or cognitive science) has to offer, it may be worth taking a brief look at the evolution of psychological theories during this century, some mathematics-education research paradigms, and mathematical curricular ideas. (The latter two have often been affected by the first.) At the turn of the century the Associationists held sway in psychology, and the implementation of their ideas, drill-and-practice, held sway in the classroom. Mathematics education was not yet a discipline. In 1913 Poincaré wrote of his discovery of the nature of Fuchsian functions. Wallas (1926) codified Poincaré's experience in the four-step Gestalt model: Saturation, Incubation, Inspiration ("Eureka!"), Verification. Gestaltism gained momentum, especially among mathematicians. In the 1940's and 1950's Hadamard (1954) devoted a monograph to the exegesis of Poincaré's bus trip, Duncker (1945) wrote *On Problem Solving*, Wertheimer (1945/1959) wrote *Productive Thinking*, and Polya (1945) wrote *How to Solve It*. The Gestaltist's perspective is appealing: One is certainly sympathetic to (for example) Wertheimer's passionate pleas that we teach for understanding. But the Gestaltists offered little in the way of useful suggestions. "Avoid getting in a rut" from Maier (1933) was about as specific as any of the suggestions got, with the exception of Polya; yet his heuristics, in the classroom, yielded few results. That, unfortunately, is a consequence of the Gestaltists' theoretical reliance on the notion that most of the "action" takes place in the subconscious, during the inspiration phase of problem solving. The action of the subconscious is inaccessible to observation or manipulation, so issues of *how* productive thinking takes place become moot.[2] The curriculum remained largely unchanged.

---

2. In many ways I am a neo-Gestaltist, and have great sympathy with the Gestaltists' wish to look at the "whole picture." But their literature has produced some of my greatest disappointments. For example, Duncker (1945) discusses one of my favorites, the "Thirteen Problem": show that if any three-digit number is written down twice (e.g., 246 becomes 246,246) the resulting six-digit number is divisible by 13. According to Duncker, the real difficulty with the problem is overcome when the factor 1001 "emerges"; that is, $abc,abc = (1001)(abc) = (7)(11)(13)(abc)$, so there must be a factor of 13 in the twice-repeated three-digit number. I think Duncker's reliance on the emergence of 1001 finesses the *real* questions: where does 1001 "come from," and how might one be trained to "think" so that the emergence of 1001 is more likely?

So psychological theory was fairly well mired in the subconscious during the reign of the Gestaltists. One attempt to extricate psychology from the mire came from Skinner and the behaviorists, who denied the existence of mind altogether! Skinner did have curricular impact, as those of us who received gold stars in school or wrote behavioral objectives for instruction are fully aware. One should not be too harsh, for—properly used—behavioral objectives force a level of specificity and thoughtfulness about goals that is healthy. But the results of a ''mind''-less theory, and curricula derived from it, are (at least in hindsight) less than we might have asked for. We were stuck in a different mire.

In the light of this background, consider the impact of research in AI as captured early in Feigenbaum and Feldman (1963), later in Newell and Simon's classic *Human Problem Solving* (1972). Instead of focusing on behaviors and stimulus-response chains, the folks in AI focus on patterns and strategies of useful (productive?) thinking. Roughly, the ideas behind ''problem-solving'' programs in AI were as follows:

1.   Make detailed observations of people as they solve problems ''out loud.''

2.   Pick out the uniformities in their ''productive'' thinking, and abstract them as useful strategies.

3.   Write computer programs to capture the essence of those strategies.

In AI, the standards are high: the proof is in the empirical pudding, a program that does what it is supposed to. When a computer manages to play chess, solve cryptarithmetic problems, solve integrals, prove many of the theorems in Russel and Whitehead's *Principia Mathematica*—then there must be something to the underlying methodology. ''Mind'' and ''thinking'' are legitimated; detailed observations of thought processes are demonstrated to be useful sources of information about thinking; and the barriers of the subconscious that constrained the Gestaltists are broken down. (Interestingly, some recent studies, e.g., Greeno, 1982, describe more detailed ''computational'' versions of Gestaltists' ''conceptual entities.'' The push away from the subconscious may have helped, in the long run, to elaborate its workings.)

Where was mathematics education during this period of early cognitive investigation? Along with many of the social sciences aspiring to be sciences (including much of contemporary psychology) it was investing its energies in ostensibly objective, scientific, and statistical experiments. The results are too dismal, and too well known, to dwell on. In 1975, Kilpatrick suggested that we might do well to abandon such studies in favor of ''case studies'' that might suggest useful ideas and hypotheses. AI researchers could claim that they had laid the foundation for such investigations. And as the studies in Rissland's paper indicate, they can also claim that their research has useful curricular implications.

WHAT GOOD IS A SAINT FOR MATHEMATICS EDUCATION? (OR AI?)

One of the studies discussed in Rissland's AI tutorial was Slagle's SAINT program. Written in the early days of AI, SAINT (Symbolic Automatic INTegrator) solved indefinite integrals with the proficiency of a better-than-average MIT freshman. SAINT worked ''somewhat'' like a mathematician. It was not, for example, a ''mechanized table of integrals''; SAINT had roughly two dozen ''basic forms'' in memory, and had to derive answers to integrands not on that short list. A calculus student facing a final exam has memorized at least that many, probably twice as many. The eight basic transformation rules known to SAINT were neither more powerful nor numerous (actually, less) than those a student would know. SAINT did not rely on "brute force" computations for its solutions. That is, it did not "play out" all possible results of its integration "moves" and then pick the right sequence from among them, as a "brute force" tick-tack-toe program could play out all games to their conclusion and determine its strategy accordingly. So in many ways SAINT was handicapped — limited to performance on a human scale. (It did not, however, make algebra mistakes.)

While SAINT was thus "limited" to certain human performance levels, it did not really go about solving integrals the way a mathematician does. For example, well-practiced humans frequently appear to select approaches to integrals by means of pattern recognition. Having solved many problems of the form $\int P(x) \sin x \, dx$ by integration by parts, for example, it soon becomes "natural" ("intuitive?") for humans to select that technique for a similar problem. SAINT had no such mechanisms. Humans often use rather "fuzzy" criteria for deciding if they are making progress, or for choosing which of two possible paths is more likely to lead to progress. SAINT, of course, could not be fuzzy about such things. It had a reasonable way to measure the complexity of an integrand, based on the degree of composition of functions in it. Expressions of the form $f(g(h(x)))$ are more complex than ones of the form $F(G(x))$, and hypothetically more difficult; hence SAINT decided in favor of the latter for exploration. This is clearly an artificial decision criterion, though not necessarily a bad one. Also, SAINT lacked the cleverness and flexibility to take advantage of serendipitous circumstances; its approach was, well, mechanistic. For example, SAINT worked rather hard on $\int (\sin x + \cos x)^2 \, dx$. After multiplying out to obtain $\int (\sin^2 x + 2 \sin x \cos x + \cos^2 x) \, dx$, it followed a "decomposition rule" to obtain $\int \sin^2 x \, dx + \int 2 \sin x \cos x \, dx + \int \cos^2 x \, dx$. SAINT then solved each of these three integrals, with the first and third of these requiring no small amount of work. The perspicacious human problem solver, of course, "sees" that $(\sin^2 x + \cos^2 x) = 1$, which makes short work of the integral.

So SAINT is handicapped in more than being limited to a small memory and constrained set of strategies; SAINT works mechanically, does not learn from success or failure, and does not rely on any knowledge or "understanding" to solve problems. Beyond the fact that SAINT represents an interesting technical exercise, does it have any interest for mathematics educators?

The work with SAINT, now more than two decades old and undeniably primitive, still has much to offer mathematics education. The insights into cognitive processes available from current work in AI, and the methodologies it employs, have a great deal more to offer. Some of the implications of such studies are discussed in the following subsections.

AI Offers "Existence Proofs" for The Usefulness of Ideas and Strategies

SAINT solved 84 of the 86 problems it worked, 54 of which were chosen from MIT final exams in freshman calculus. There is no doubt that the strategies used in SAINT "work," or that the strategies in other AI programs do; the question, of course, is what the machine implementation of these strategies says about human problem solving. In the case of SAINT, they said a great deal: Using a small number of powerful strategies, a problem solver with fewer "basic facts" committed to memory than most students, fewer techniques than they might use, and none of the other skills that they bring to problem solving, managed to do far better than most students. The "moral" is *not* that students should be trained to do integrals like SAINT, but that a few powerful strategies—chosen for human implementation rather than machine implementation—might yield comparable results for humans.

The Human As "Information Processor" Is A Powerful Idea

By making careful observations of humans solving problems — but in carefully chosen domains with machine implementation in mind—researchers in AI were able to find "patterns of productive thinking" that would be useful for machine implementation (e.g., Newell & Simon, 1972). The idea was that one had an "information processor" with certain capacities: in the case of early computers an extensive and reliable memory, spectacular computational ability, and unfailing accuracy, but poor semantic capacity, poor pattern recognition, and little flexibility. Research in AI consisted in part of finding useful strategies for that kind of information processor. Consider a different type of information processor. This one is mediocre and not terribly reliable in long-term memory, is able to keep and manipulate only 7 ± 2 chunks in its short-term memory buffers, and has poor computational ability, but has spectacular semantic capacity and excellent inductive capacity through pattern recognition. Following the techniques of AI, it might be possible to find useful strategies ("programs" is too harsh) for this particular processor—a human.

This kind of approach, motivated in large part by the success of Slagle's SAINT program, was my first project in educational research. I believed that students were often unsuccessful at problem solving because they were inefficient in using the knowledge they were capable of applying: by trying difficult techniques where easy ones would suffice, going off on "wild goose chases," etc., they were performing at much lower levels of competence than their capabilities. If this were the case, having a good "selection strategy" for problem-solving techniques should improve their problem-solving performance. SAINT showed that a few powerful techniques could indeed produce success. It did not suggest the techniques, for the ones it used were chosen for machine rather than human use. However, AI methodologies suggested the ways to find them. By making systematic observations of successful problem solvers' choices of method when doing integrals, one might create a "decision strategy" that would guide students to the "right" techniques and allow them to be more successful. The idea was, by today's standards, crude and naive; but it worked. It produced instructional materials (Schoenfeld, 1977) that are still in use, and yield clear results (Schoenfeld, 1978). Today's "information-processing" view of cognition is far more sophisticated, and of much greater potential utility (e.g., Simon, 1979, 1981).

Research Methodologies in AI Suggest Research Methodologies for ME

Kilpatrick (1978) wrote about the state of mathematics-education methodology on problem solving in the mid-1970's:

> Experimental studies in which all the variables are under tight control are not likely to be of much value in the present state of our ignorance as to how people solve complex mathematical problems .... Too much developmental work is needed before experimentation could be effective.... A broader conception of research is needed, and an openness to new techniques, if

studies of problem-solving processes and the teaching of heuristics are to have an impact. (p.18)

The particular need was for rigorous methodologies for investigations of cognitive processes, rather than of outcomes. This, of course, is one of the foci of AI research. There are a number of available methodologies for adaptation to mathematics education, and there has been a fair amount of research on the validity of such methodologies.

"Protocol analysis," the detailed analysis of transcripts of recordings made by people solving problems "out loud," is one major source of data for AI simulations of problem solving. Again, the classic volume on detailed analyses is Newell and Simon (1972); comparisons of the kinds of information reflected in individual protocols are given in Simon and Simon (1978); one of a number of extensive reviews of the literature on "verbal data" is given in Ericsson and Simon (1980). Examples in mathematics are given in Davis (1983).

Many of the studies in Rissland's tutorial reflect methodologies, or perspectives, that can be of use to mathematics education. For example, Bundy's (1975) work on equation solving demonstrates the utility of looking at what people *do* rather than looking at task analyses of the subject matter alone. There are a variety of techniques for solving algebraic equations, which are usually low level and taught as specific subject matter. Linear equations in one unknown are solved one way, quadratics another, trig identities yet another, and so on. Only when observing competent problem solvers working a variety of problems does one see the use of higher-level strategies that are both broader and more powerful: collecting like symbols together, removing nasty terms, etc.

The work on BUGGY encompasses a variety of methodologies. In early work, bugs were identified from large collections of empirical data. Brown and Burton (1978) examined huge numbers of problems worked by students, looking for consistent patterns of errors across students. Matz (1982) did similar work in algebra. The point is that students' written work was used as a source of information, not as tests of final performance to be graded. Once error patterns were discovered, individual bugs could be modeled; then diagnostic tests could be developed for use with individual students.

The work by Briars and Larkin (1982) also provides a nice example of how AI can say a good deal about human cognitive performance. The CHIPS model is not, like the programs in Rissland's Category III, an attempt to have a machine do mathematics (perhaps somewhat like a mathematician). Rather, it represents an attempt to explain what students do when they try to do certain kinds of mathematics; it carries out what Briars and Larkin hypothesize children are doing when they work word problems. CHIPS is a model of the children's actions. "*If* kids are approaching these problems in precisely this way, and with precisely this kind of information, then CHIPS should be getting the answers they are." CHIPS can be given problems and generate its answers, which can be compared with empirical data. The program thus stands for the embodiment of a theory, which can be refined and tested. This notion of empirical testing goes far beyond earlier work whose primary purpose was to succeed at solving problems: for example, compare CHIPS with Bobrow's (1968) STUDENT.

Central Issues in AI Are Central to ME

One of the basic issues in cognitive science, of which AI is a major component, is "how is knowledge presented, stored, and accessed for competent intellectual performance?'' This issue is central to our understanding of how students understand mathematics. It includes discussions of schematic representations of problem situations (schemata, scripts, frames, etc.); the importance of specific kinds of knowledge versus the power of "general" strategies; metacognition; and more. For general discussions of the issue, see Simon (1979, 1981); for specific applications to mathematics education, see Silver (1982), Briars and Larkin (1982), and other papers from this conference.

SOME WORDS OF WARNING

Up to this point this paper has stressed the aspect of AI that can be useful to mathematics educators—and there are many. But there are also some things to watch out for.

From its inception, AI has been an engineering discipline. The goal has most often been to get certain machines to perform certain (intellectual) tasks. Clearly AI says a great deal about what machines can do. How much can we trust what it says about humans? The harsh view says that AI's perspective is severely distorted by the engineering perspective, and that extrapolations to human performance can be dangerous.

As already shown, the history of early AI (at least the problem-solving part) substantiates this view. Consider the methodologies used for developing early programs to solve problems in symbolic logic. Ultimately, a machine that knew nothing of the "meanings" of the symbols

$$\wedge, \vee, \neg, \supset,$$

which are used in symbolic logic, was to prove results of this ilk:

IF:	1. $Q \supset R$
	2. $P \vee Q$
	3. $\neg (R \wedge S)$
	4. S
THEN:	5. P

The form of the programs for making such derivations was to be modeled on successful human attempts at solving such probems. The programs were derived from the analyses of protocols of people solving such problems out loud. For good methodological reasons, anyone who knew anything about the meanings of the symbols (e.g., that "A $\supset$ B" means "A implies B" or "If A then B") was *excluded* from the sample: The machine would manipulate symbols without understanding, so its performance must be based on the (successful) performance of those humans who were able to manipulate symbols without understanding. The resulting program was good AI, but it said very little about meaningful human problem solving.

As the tools of AI were refined through the early 1970's, problem-solving programs could do more things and do them better. But the emphasis was on developing tools and techniques; "meaning" and "understanding" were issues to be dealt with later. Machines played games and worked on puzzles, with programs spending endless hours meandering through the search spaces of the Tower of Hanoi. This, of course, is perfectly reasonable and not the least bit dangerous, so long as interpretation of the results is kept within its own domain, machine "intelligence." But it is quite dangerous when the paradigms, perspectives, and results of machine intelligence studies are casually applied to discussions of human intelligence. For two exemplary studies of this type, see Simon (1976) and Klahr (1976). For a devastating criticism of both studies, see Neisser (1976).

AI has gotten a good deal more sophisticated since then, but some serious problems remain. There are great difficulties when human cognitive performance is viewed through the lens of machine-implementability. Some aspects of the "human intelligence as a reflection of machine intelligence" perspective are discussed in the following paragraphs.

One aspect of this perspective is the "if it's a good idea it can be programmed and, conversely, if we're not successful in programming it, it's probably not a good idea" view of cognition. For example: "We produced problem-solving programs without Polya-type heuristics, and when we tried to base programs on those heuristics, it didn't work. So they can't be very important." Or: "Our problem-solving system works like a successful human problem solver, and we didn't need to invoke 'control' strategies; so we don't need to worry about those kinds of things." Now it may be that heuristics, or control strategies, or whatever, are not important. This is not the argument that shows it.

Another aspect is the confusion of routinized competent performance with expertise. I believe that there are at least two major components of expertise: (1) the mastery of facts and procedures that allows the expert to dispatch routine problems quickly and accurately, and (2) the ability to use the knowledge at one's disposal to solve difficult, nonstandard problems when others with at least as much specific knowledge fail to do so. For example (see my "episodes" paper, 1983), a professional mathematician worked a plane geometry problem. He had not done any geometry for 10 years or so, and his knowledge of "basics" was rusty. From scratch, he found what he needed (after looking at a dozen possibilities that might have led him on wild goose chases, curtailing all of them, and pursuing the approaches that seemed useful) and in doing so solved a problem that none of 24 college freshmen, who knew more of the facts and procedures from geometry, even came close to solving. This, from my perspective, is an essential component of his expertise.

By and large, AI definitions of expertise are limited exclusively to the first component of expertise: the expert must have the domain down "cold" and, in machinelike fashion, perform unerringly. According to this definition, the mathematician in my example is not an expert, and the skills he used to solve that problem are not expert skills. Admittedly, he is not a *geometry* expert—but if you only look at his performance when he knows exactly what he is doing, you never get to see what makes him a good problem solver! The definition is far too narrow. There are dangerous instructional consequences to this view as well. It is very "local"; competence is defined in small chunks. As a result, there is no room for general skills in training students to think! (For an elaboration of this argument see Schoenfeld, 1982, 1983.)

A third aspect of the "human intelligence as a reflection of machine intelligence" perspective is the assumption that important strategies for AI problem solving are important strategies for human problem solving, and that things not necessary in AI are not necessary for humans. In the days of GPS (General Problem Solver; Newell & Simon, 1972), "powerful" techniques were the ones that enabled one to navigate efficiently through large search spaces: "means-ends analysis" was a (if not *the*) powerful heuristic strategy, the essence of expertise. As AI expanded to "semantically rich domains" in which one's knowledge and understanding began to play a critical role in problem-solving performance, means-ends analysis diminished in importance. The view in the late 1970's and into this decade, substantiated in part by research on schema-based performance of experts, is that novices rely on means-ends analysis, and that experts don't use it (see Simon & Simon, 1978, and the discussion of it in Larkin, 1980). With all due respect, both views are wrong. The first is a result of programming dictating perspective, the second a result of the limited definition of expertise discussed above and the fact that means-ends analysis is not needed much for schema-based solutions. Both perspectives are caricatures.

As it happens, the "novice" who used means-ends analysis in the Simon and Simon (1978) study was an expert problem solver. She happened to be new to kinematics, the domain in which the study took place. What does an expert problem solver do in such circumstances? She lists all the clearly relevant formulas, locates ones that include the variable representing the information given and the desired quantities, and manipulates the equations until the desired quantity is expressed in terms of the given ones. Far from raw novice behavior, this is highly competent. What real novices do is something else entirely!

I could give other examples, but my purpose here is not to belabor AI. It is simply to suggest that statements about human problem solving that are based on research in, or influenced by, machine problem solving, should be checked against reality. Of course, that's healthy advice for any statements about problem solving. AI has provided a pretty good share of interesting ones.

REFERENCES

Bobrow, D. Natural language input for a computer problem solving system. In M. Minsky (Ed.), *Semantic information processing*. Cambridge, MA: The MIT Press, 1968.

Briars, D.J., & Larkin, J.H. *An integrated model of skill in solving elementary word problems* (Technical Report A.C.P. No. 2). Pittsburgh: Carnegie-Mellon University, Department of Psychology, November 1982.

Brown, J.S., & Burton, R.R. Diagnostic models for procedural bugs in basic mathematical skills. *Cognitive Science* 2, 155–92, 1978.

Bundy, A. *Analyzing mathematical proofs (or reading between the lines)* (Research Report DAI No. 2). Edinburgh: University of Edinburgh, 1975.

Burton, R.R., & Brown, J.S. An investigation of computer coaching for formal learning activities. *International Journal Man-Machine Studies* 11, 5–24, 1979.

Davis, R. Complex mathematical cognition. In H.P. Ginsburg (Ed.), *The development of mathematical thinking*. New York: Academic Press, 1983.

Duncker, K. On problem solving. *Psychological Monographs* 58 (5, Whole No. 270). Washington, D.C.: American Psychological Association, 1945.

Ericsson, K.A., & Simon, H.A. Verbal reports as data. *Psychological Review* 87, 215–51, 1980.

Feigenbaum, E., & Feldman, J. (Eds.). *Computers and thought*. New York: McGraw-Hill, 1963.

Gelernter, H. Realization of a geometry theorem proving machine. In E. Feigenbaum & J. Feldman (Eds.), *Computers and thought*. New York: McGraw-Hill, 1963.

Greeno, J.G. *Forms of understanding in mathematical problem solving* (Technical Report UPITT/LRDC/ONR/APS-10). Pittsburgh: University of Pittsburgh, August 1982.

Hadamard, J. *Essay on the psychology of invention in the mathematical field*. New York: Dover Publications, 1954.

Kilpatrick, J. Variables and methodologies in research on problem solving. In L.L. Hatfield & D.A. Bradbard (Eds.), *Mathematical problem solving: Papers from a research workshop*. Columbus, OH: ERIC Clearinghouse for Science, Mathematics, and Environmental Education, 1978. (Paper revised from 1975 version.)

Klahr, D. Steps toward the simulation of intellectual development. In Lauren B. Resnick (Ed.), *The Nature of Intelligence*. Hillsdale, NJ: Lawrence Erlbaum Associates, 1976.

Larkin, J. Teaching problem solving in physics: The psychological laboratory and the practical classroom. In D.T. Tuma & F. Reif (Eds.), *Problem solving and education: Issues in teaching and research.* Hillsdale, NJ: Lawrence Erlbaum Associates, 1980.

Maier, N.R.F. An aspect of human reasoning. *British Journal of Psychology* 14, 144–55, 1933.

Matz, M. Towards a process model for high school algebra errors. In D. Sleeman & J.S. Brown (Eds.), *Intelligent tutoring systems.* London: Academic Press, 1982.

Neisser, U. General, academic, and artificial intelligence. In L.B. Resnick (Ed.), *The nature of intelligence.* Hillsdale, NJ: Lawrence Erlbaum Associates, 1976.

Newell, A., & Simon, H.A. *Human problem solving.* Englewood Cliffs, NJ: Prentice-Hall, 1972.

Nilsson, N.J. *Principles of artificial intelligence.* Palo Alto, CA: Tioga, 1980.

Papert, S. *Mindstorms.* New York: Basic Books, 1980.

Poincaré, H. *The foundations of science.* (G.H. Halstead, Trans.) New York: Science Press, 1913.

Polya, G. *How to solve it.* Princeton, NJ: Princeton University Press, 1945.

Resnick, L.B. (Ed.). *The nature of intelligence.* Hillsdale, NJ: Lawrence Erlbaum Associates, 1976.

Schoenfeld, A.H. *Integration: Getting it all together.* Newton, MA: UMAP, 1977.

Schoenfeld, A.H. Presenting a strategy for indefinite integration. *American Mathematical Monthly* 85, 673–78, 1978.

Schoenfeld, A.H. Some thoughts on problem solving research and mathematics education. In F.K. Lester & J. Garofalo (Eds.), *Mathematical problem solving: Issues in research.* Philadelphia: The Franklin Institute Press, 1982.

Schoenfeld, A.H. Episodes and executive decisions in mathematical problem solving. In R. Lesh & M. Landau (Eds.), *Acquisition of mathematics concepts and processes.* New York: Academic Press, 1983.

Shumway, R.J. (Ed.). *Research in mathematics education.* Reston, VA: National Council of Teachers of Mathematics, 1980.

Silver, E.A. Knowledge organization and mathematical problem solving. In F.K. Lester & J. Garofalo (Eds.), *Mathematical problem solving: Issues in research.* Philadelphia: The Franklin Institute Press, 1982.

Simon, D.P., & Simon, H.A. Individual differences in solving physics problems. In R.S. Siegler (Ed.), *Children's thinking: What develops?* Hillsdale, NJ: Lawrence Erlbaum Associates, 1978.

Simon, H.A. Identifying basic abilities underlying intelligent performance of complex tasks. In L.B. Resnick (Ed.), *The nature of intelligence.* Hillsdale, NJ: Lawrence Erlbaum Associates, 1976.

Simon, H.A. Information processing models of cognition. *Annual Review of Psychology* 30, 363–96, 1979.

Simon, H.A. Studying human intelligence by creating artificial intelligence. *American Scientist* 69, 300–309, 1981.

Slagle, J.R. A heuristic program that solves symbolic integration problems in freshman calculus. In E. Feigenbaum & J. Feldman (Eds.), *Computers and thought.* New York: McGraw-Hill, 1963.

VanLehn, K., & Brown, J.S. Planning nets: A representation for formalizing analogies and semantic models of procedural skills. In R.E. Snow, P.A. Federico, & W.E. Montague (Eds.), *Aptitude, learning and instruction: Cognitive process analyses.* Hillsdale, NJ: Lawrence Erlbaum Associates, 1980.

VanLehn, K. On the representation of procedures in repair theory. In H.P. Ginsburg (Ed.), *The development of mathematical thinking.* New York: Academic Press, 1983.

Wallas, G. *The art of thought.* New York: Harcourt, 1926.

Wertheimer, M. *Productive thinking* (enlarged ed.). New York: Harper & Row, 1959.

Winston, P.H. *Artificial intelligence.* Menlo Park, CA: Addison-Wesley, 1977.

Experience, Problem Solving, and Learning Mathematics: Considerations in Developing Mathematics Curricula

Patrick W. Thompson[1]

San Diego State University

Recent research in cognitive psychology and artificial intelligence (collectively called cognitive science) has made impressive progress in revealing the varieties and intricacies of mathematical problem solving. However, the connections between studies of mathematical problem solving and the practice of teaching mathematics are not always clear. That is to be expected. Due to the very nature of scientific inquiry, studies of problem solving must focus on questions of limited scope with simplified hypotheses, if only to provide a filter with which to separate signal from noise.

Also, cognitive scientists tend to focus on what *is* in the world of mathematical problem solving, which is essential. But mathematics educators have an equal charge to consider what *ought to be* and how it might be achieved. With this in mind, it is clear that research in cognitive science on mathematical problem solving can inform mathematics educators of the current state of affairs and can even suggest constructs that promise powerful ways of thinking about teaching problem solving, but it cannot dictate mathematics curricula or methods of teaching. To improve mathematics teaching and learning, mathematics educators must consider the students' passage through an entire curriculum. Thus, those involved in curriculum development will of necessity always be traveling untrodden terrain, always working beyond established data bases.

My purpose in this paper is to discuss an attempt at developing mathematics curricula that draws from research on problem solving and mathematical cognition, but goes beyond it in addressing issues unique to mathematics education—primary among them, mathematics education's concern with the learner throughout a mathematical program. By itself, a collection of models of problem solving on relatively restricted problem sets is

---

1. The author wishes to express his gratitude to the Department of Mathematical Sciences, San Diego State University, for its support in preparing the materials reported in this paper.

insufficient as a basis for designing a mathematics curriculum. A curriculum developer must augment it with some sort of model of a learner passing through the curriculum.

As I have noted, cognitive science has developed a wealth of constructs that have powerful implications for mathematics curriculum development. I wish to make clear from the start, however, that I am writing from the perspective of a practicing mathematics educator. The examples that will be given come largely from my experience as a teacher of mathematics, albeit one who is fairly well informed of the methods and constructs of cognitive science.

Perhaps another caveat is necessary. Ideas are significant only within the context of an overriding universe of discourse. The significance for mathematics education of much of recent research on mathematical problem solving can be appreciated only when we consider the aims of mathematics education. If one thinks of learning mathematics as tantamount to memorizing mathematical "facts," or an accretionary building of elaborate sets of behaviors, then much of what follows will be irrelevant. If, however, one accepts that the aim of mathematics education is to promote mathematical thinking, then this paper will be of interest.

A predominant theme of this paper, as one would guess from the title, is that learning mathematics is a constructive process. This is an idea on which Dewey and Piaget each based over 50 years of work. I make no pretense here of extending their ideas. Rather, I will show that much of current research on mathematical problem solving is consistent with Dewey's and Piaget's ideas, and will suggest ways that the three might be joined in mathematics curricula.

Another theme of the paper is that learning mathematics (and solving mathematical problems) is by and large a reflective activity. I will discuss the theoretical side of this claim later. For now, let me give an example. A student in my content course for prospective elementary school teachers was having difficulty understanding the idea of the composition of two "flips" in the coordinate plane. I had constructed several examples, drawing diagrams with specific values for the parameters of the problem, and was at the point where I was hoping that the student would generalize to arbitrary values. After much discussion about method, the student paused and then remarked, "Oh, I see! You don't care what the numbers are; you only care about where you get them and what you do to them!" Though I must have said essentially the same thing (though not as lucidly) at least five times in class, that was not sufficient for this student; she had to do her own reflecting.

A third theme is that to learn mathematics is to learn mathematical problem solving. This is in contrast to the common view that one learns a set of mathematical skills and then learns to apply them to solve problems (e.g., Gagné, 1983). However, the essential feature of constructing mathematical knowledge is the creation of relationships, and creating relationships is the hallmark of mathematical problem solving. I will return to this point in the next section and later in case studies.

The remainder of the paper is divided into three major sections. The first addresses issues that are preliminary to developing problem-based mathematics curricula. The second shows two curricula constructed according to the principles developed in the first section. The third gives a summary and concluding remarks.

PRELIMINARIES

This section is in four parts. The first addresses the issue of what a mathematics curriculum can be. This is especially important when we take the position that the development of mathematical knowledge is based on problem solving. The second part discusses the idea of cognitive objectives of instruction as a basis for curriculum development. The third investigates the role of problem solving in learning mathematics, and its place in mathematics curricula. The fourth part examines the influence of environments in learning mathematics.

Mathematics Curricula

It is common to find references in the literature to the notion that "problem structure" is a determinant factor of students' problem-solving activities (Carpenter et al., 1981; Newell & Simon, 1972). There are two ways to view this idea, depending upon one's ontology of problems. The first is to think of problems existing independently of any solver. Looked at this way, it would be possible to design a problem-based curriculum independently of the cognitive characteristics of the intended audience. It would be the teacher's (pedagogical) problem to "connect" his or her students with the problems. What it means to "connect" students with problems is not clear (Thompson, 1982a).

The second way to think of problems as determinant factors in students' problem-solving activities is to locate the problems inside the students' heads. But if we locate problems inside students' heads, then it becomes uncertain what the problem is that a student is solving at any given time. As a result, it would appear that we have no control over what we have taken to be the foundation of the curriculum—the problems.

The issue I am raising is the conflict between realism and constructivism (Lakatos, 1962, 1976; Thompson, 1982a; von Glasersfeld, 1978). The reason for speaking of epistemologies here is that I will be characterizing a curriculum as a collection of activities from which students may construct the mathematical knowledge that we want them to have. There are issues central to curriculum development that must be addressed when "curriculum" is used this way, but if the reader is not first made aware of the special sense given here to curriculum, and if the underlying constructivist epistemology is not made explicit, he or she may wonder about the points of the discussions.

Let me say it again in a slightly different way. By a mathematics curriculum I mean a selected sequence of activities, situations, contexts, and so on, from which students will, it is hoped, construct a particular way of thinking. This characterization differs considerably from most that I have seen. Notice that there are no concepts in a curriculum, nor are there topics. Concepts are the structures of thought that a curriculum is aimed at promoting. Topics are our constructions—resulting either from differentiating among concepts or classifying types of activities. Also note that a curriculum never exists in its entirety. There are the planned curriculum, the past curriculum, and the current activities of the students.

To characterize mathematics curricula as I have in the preceding discussion would seem to open any suggestions that I might give about curriculum development to the same criticism made of Dewey's progressive education—that one loses the subject matter when grounding a curriculum in students' experiences. At the time, that criticism was valid (Eisner, 1982). (However, as Dewey later noted, poor implementations of sound ideas do not affect the quality of the ideas.) Subject matter *had* been neglected.

One consideration stands out clearly when education is conceived in terms of experience. Anything which can be called a study, whether arithmetic, history, geography, or one of the natural sciences, must be derived from materials which at the outset fall within the scope of ordinary life-experience. ... But finding the material for learning within experience is only the first step. The next step is the progressive development of what is already experienced into a fuller and richer and also more organized form, a form that gradually approximates that in which subject-matter is presented to the skilled, mature adult. (Dewey, 1945, pp. 73ff)

Dewey (1945) also noted that not just any set of experiences would suffice as a curriculum. Special care had to be taken in the selection of experiences for their educative potential—what could be made of them later in the curriculum.

It is also essential that the new objects and events be related intellectually to those of earlier experiences, and this means that there be some advance made in conscious articulation of facts and ideas. It thus becomes the office of the educator to select those things within the range of existing experience that have promise and potentiality of presenting new problems which by stimulating new ways of observation and judgment will expand the area of further experience. He must constantly regard what is already won not as a fixed possession but as an agency and instrumentality for opening new fields which make new demands upon existing powers of observation and of intelligent use of memory. (p.75)

The principal difficulty that Dewey had in implementing his theory, as he admitted, was that he lacked a philosophy of experience (p. 91). By this I mean that he had neither a metaphor nor a technology through which to make specific his ideas about how people can create something like mathematical knowledge from experience. He did not have a genetic epistemology. Dewey was confident that problem solving was the key to the growth of knowledge, as evidenced by his repeated references to it, but he never explained how problem solving provided the key to intellectual growth, nor how one might actively promote it.

By characterizing a mathematics curriculum as a sequence of activities that (it is hoped) leads to students constructing mathematical knowledge of a particular kind, we are forced to face the same difficulty as Dewey. We must make explicit the nature of the knowledge that we hope is constructed and make a case that the chosen activities will promote its construction. How one characterizes the knowledge to be constructed, and how the selected activities might lead to its construction, will greatly influence the choice of activities.

The general stance taken here is that anything we might wish to call mathematical knowledge is a structure of thinking—the structure is a structure of processes. Also, it is assumed that mathematical structures arise from abstracting the invariant features of one's thinking in problematic situations. From a constructivist perspective, any curriculum aimed at promoting mathematical thinking *must*, by the very nature of the phenomenon, be problem based. The task of the curriculum developer is to select problematic situations that provide occasions for students to think in ways that have a generative power in regard to the objectives of instruction. These points will become clear from the examples given in the case studies.

The advantage that we have today over progressive educationists of midcentury in regard to developing problem-based curricula is one of both theory and technique. Cognitive science has developed a technique (and a metaphor) for explicating processes of which concepts are made. Piaget's genetic epistemology gives us a theory of structure in cognitive processes and its development. The two are supportive of one another in many areas, and there is tension between them in others. Yet, overall they both speak to difficulties in designing problem-based mathematics curricula.

Cognitive Objectives of Instruction

The objectives of a curriculum are the concepts that the curriculum is aimed at promoting. One might ask, what of skills? If one takes a schematic view of concepts, where a schema is one of mental processes, and if one also supposes that skilled behavior is merely an expression of highly structured thinking, then skills as they are colloquially thought of are subsumed by concepts. That is to say, the assessment of concept formation is made by examining the degree of skill shown in problematic situations. From this perspective, students cannot fail to be skilled if, by the above criterion, they demonstrate that they have formed the aimed-for concepts.

The objectives of a curriculum must be expressed in cognitive terms if we are to take them as goals of instruction. This idea did not originate with me. Resnick (1975, 1981) and Greeno (1980) have made a strong enough case that I need not cover that ground here. What I will argue is that cognitive objectives of instruction must have a developmental side as well. Resnick (1981) lamented that there is no cognitive theory of learning upon which to base instruction. I disagree. Piaget, though not normally thought of as a learning theorist, provided a strong framework for addressing knowledge development. His equilibration theory, which says that the epigenesis of knowledge comes from a tension between accommodation and assimilation, says essentially that one learns by solving problems.

Problem solving as a basis for learning mathematics was explicitly promoted by Gestalt psychologists (Duncker, 1945; Wertheimer, 1945). Wertheimer focused more on the idea of mathematical structure than Duncker, who concentrated along the lines of Polya (1973), stressing general strategies for solving problems. Neither Duncker, Wertheimer, nor Polya suggested how a curriculum could be based on problem solving. That is, they did not address the issue of how major mathematical concepts, such as whole number, rational number, and integer, might result from a problem-solving program. To do this they would have had to explicate the composition of the aimed-for concepts and how the problem situations they might set could lead to them.

Piaget and Wertheimer shared the view that equilibrium was a natural state toward which cognition tended, but their views of what constituted cognitive equilibrium, and of avenues to it, differed significantly. Wertheimer (1945), and Gestalt psychologists of his time, saw an isomorphism between the formation of perceptual and conceptual constancies. Piaget (Inhelder & Piaget, 1969) rejected this position on the ground that it could not account for a special character of mathematical concepts—that whatever is thought of as being done can be thought of as being undone.

> Gestaltism, as we know, interprets all intelligence as an extension, to wider and wider areas, of the "forms" initially governing the world of perceptions. What we have just said in the preceding pages, however, contradicts such an interpretation. Moreover, as far as the operations [of thought] are concerned, there are the following considerations. The perceptual structures are essentially irreversible. . . . But the operations, although they constitute integrated structures, are essentially reversible: $+n$ is completely cancelled out by $-n$. . . . It seems obvious, therefore, that operations, or intelligence in general, do not derive from perceptual structures. (pp. 49–50)

In all his work, Piaget clearly distinguished between two modes of thought, which he alluded to in the preceding quotation. The distinction is between figurative and operative thought. In one of Piaget's (1970) more classic characterizations, he described the distinction between figurative and operative thought as one between actions of thought directed towards objects and actions of thought directed towards transformations of objects.

> I shall begin by making a distinction between two aspects of thinking that are different, although complementary. One is the figurative aspect, and the other I call the operative aspect. The figurative aspect is an imitation of states taken as momentary and static. In the cognitive area the figurative functions are, above all, perception, imitation, and mental imagery, which is in fact intereorized imitation. The operative aspect of thought deals not with states but transformations from one state to another. For instance, it includes actions themselves, which transform objects or states, and it also includes the intellectual operations, which are essentially systems of transformation. They are actions that are comparable to other actions but are reversible, that is they can be carried out in both directions... and are capable of being intereorized: they can be carried out through representation and not through actually being acted out. (p. 14)

Piaget's distinction between figurative and operative thought is the most significant that I know of for mathematics education, and especially for the development of problem-based mathematics curricula. A modern translation of Piaget might substitute "control structures" for "systems of transformation" (Lawler, 1981; Thompson, 1982b, 1982c). That is to say, operative thought in a particular domain allows students to make propitious decisions about what to do next, and allows them to see what they might do next in relation to what has already taken place.

Recent developments in research on problem solving suggest a parallel with Piaget's ideas regarding levels of thought, lending a specificity that was otherwise lacking. Prominent among them are recent studies in artificial intelligence on planning and understanding. Sacerdoti (1977) implemented a program, called NOAH, that operated at a number of levels in the process of comprehending a problem statement and devising a plan of action. NOAH understood problems by assimilating them to a network of high-level actions, each of which served as a controlling mechanism for conglomerates of lower-level, context-specific actions. A solution to a problem in NOAH took the form of an arrangement of high-level actions with associated constraints that, were they implemented in lower-level actions, would (in NOAH's anticipation) produce a solution to the problem. In other words, the bulk of NOAH's high-level processing was devoted to making decisions about what to do, as opposed to actually doing it.

Hayes-Roth (1980) extended Sacerdoti's ideas by introducing the notion of "opportunities"—situations that, in their model's evaluation, hold some promise for achieving the current goal. The difference between Hayes-Roth's and Sacerdoti's models of planning is that Sacerdoti's emphasizes top-down analysis, while Hayes-Roth's allows both top-down and bottom-up processing. That is, Hayes-Roth's model allows information generated at the more data-specific levels of processing to have both proactive and retroactive implications for assumptions made at higher levels of processing. Also, Hayes-Roth's model is more easily extended so that it learns from experience. It does this by looking back to lower-level actions as a source of unexpected outcomes (Hayes-Roth et al., 1981).

Other artificial intelligence programs that reflect Piaget's division between levels of thought are DEDALUS, a program to construct computer programs to solve problems (Manna & Waldinger, 1977, 1978), Lenat's (1981) program to create heuristics, and Schank's (Schank & Abelson, 1977; Schank & Riesbeck, 1981) programs for comprehending natural discourse.

Recent studies of problem solving using expert/novice comparisons give another perspective on the idea of levels of thinking in problem solving. Larkin (1980) found that the better problem solvers in her physics study tended to operate at both highly structured/low detailed and highly structured/highly detailed levels of thinking. The thinking of poorer problem solvers tended to have little structure and tended to be bound to highly detailed levels.

Several studies in cognitive psychology and mathematics education have also shown the importance of structure in one's thinking in mathematical problem solving. Krutetskii (1976) found in over 12 years of research that students who were able to grasp the structure of a problem showed the greatest flexibility in problem solving. Resnick (1983) and Thompson (1982b) both found that children whose thinking attained a structural character in regard to whole-number numeration showed the best understanding of the subject, as manifested in the flexibility of their problem-solving behavior. Riley et al. (1983) and Briars and Larkin (1982) showed the importance of structure in children's thinking for solving addition and subtraction word problems.

In summary, concepts are not only natural goals of a mathematics curriculum, they are natural goals of problem-solving instruction. What needs to be made clear is the connection between concepts and curriculum, and between problem solving and concepts.

Problem Solving and Learning Mathematics

The aim of a constructivist mathematics curriculum is that students going through it develop operative structures of thought in relation to the domain of problems constituting the subject matter of the curriculum. The questions to be addressed in this section are, (1) How does operative thought develop? and (2) How does problem solving fit into our attempts to promote its development?

Before taking up those questions, I believe that it will be profitable to return to Piaget's distinction between figurative and operative thought. Piaget apparently offered his distinction in order to contrast sensorimotor and concrete-operational intelligence. I have found it quite useful to generalize it to any level of thought.

When a person's actions of thought remain predominantly within schemata associated with a given level (of control), his or her thinking can be said to be figurative in relation to that level. When the actions of thought move to the level of controlling schemata, then the thinking can be said to be operative in relation to the level of the figurative schemata. That is to say, the relationship between figurative and operative thought is one of figure to ground. Any set of schemata can be characterized as figurative or operative, depending upon whether one is portraying it as background for its controlling schemata or as foreground for the schemata that it controls. For instance, the thinking of a college mathematics major in an advanced calculus course, which certainly would be classified as being formal operational in Piaget's fixed sequence of cognitive development, could nevertheless be classified as figurative in regard to the kind of thinking required in a graduate course in real analysis. Of course we would have to make apparent to ourselves the possibility that the "objects" of such a student's thinking are things like functions, classes of functions, and associated operations.

By generalizing Piaget's distinction between figurative and operative thought we have a way to capture a phenomenon that I call figuration-boundness. This is the inability of a student to go beyond the elements of a problem to a network of relationships and potential transformations in which the elements exist—a phenomenon that I have seen in students ranging from first-graders studying elementary arithmetic to college mathematics majors studying point-set topology.

Development of Operative Thought

In Piaget's genetic epistemology, the key to the development of operative thought is what he calls reflective abstraction. Piaget characterized two complementary forms of reflective abstraction. The first was the attainment of more systematic control over one's mental actions through the construction of schemata composed of higher-level operations. The second was the reflection of a state of affairs in schemata at a figurative level to a representation of that state in schemata at an operative level. The first might be said to address learning, while the second addresses operative comprehension.

To understand what Piaget meant by reflective abstraction, it is worthwhile to examine its counterpart at the figurative level, empirical abstraction. Empirical abstraction is abstraction from objects (recalling that objects are mental constructs). It is the separating of the object or object's composition into similarities and differences—what Piaget (1951) also called (schematic) differentiation. Piaget (1970) gave the following example:

> A child, for instance, can heft objects in his hands and realize that they have different weights—that usually big things weigh more than little ones, but that sometimes little things weigh more than big ones. All this he finds out experientially, and his knowledge is abstracted from the objects themselves. (p. 16)

Reflective abstraction, on the other hand, is knowledge abstracted from coordinated actions. The emphasis is on the transformations these actions bring about and on that which remains constant when they are performed. To extend the preceding example, it is through reflective abstraction that the child comes to know that whatever the weight of an object, it remains the same under transformations of elongation (if it is malleable) or other deformation (as long as nothing is added or taken away). That is, the child's conservation of weight can only be abstracted as an invariant of his or her actions on objects, and not as a property of objects per se.

As the child establishes systems of operations and coordinates them relationally in terms of inversions, reciprocities, or compositions, he or she comes ever closer to a stable state within that system—a form of equilibrium. Equilibrium in this sense means that the operations, through their system of relationships, are capable of compensating perturbations of the system. This was Piaget's definition of conservation. The system of *relationships* is conserved—any state of the system is attainable from any other state (Inhelder & Piaget, 1969). The closure of any system is only relative, however, in that the child may construct operations *from* the system that result in perturbations that the system itself cannot handle (e.g., a concrete operational child trying to coordinate operations on composite units, such as combining torques).

One might think that Piaget's idea of reflective abstraction is similar to abstraction as operationalized in information-processing models (Newell & Simon, 1972), in which the "thing" abstracted is a condensed version of the original. Piaget (1976) made it clear that that is not the case:

> Indeed, it should be well understood that an operation is not the [semantic] representation of a transformation; it is, in itself, an object transformation, but one that can be done symbolically, which is by no means the same thing. (pp. 76ff)

The point to be drawn from the quotation is that an operation is not a datum that represents (in a linguistic sense) a transformation: it is itself a transformation that can be executed in place of, but with the significance of, its figurative correspondent. For example, abstracting the operative structure of constructing an equilateral triangle with ruler and compass results in operations that can be carried out in thought, in place of the figurative transformations that result in a specific triangle. The difference between the two is that logical deductions can be made from the operative structure (e.g., deducing equiangularity of an equilateral triangle), whereas only figurative analogies can be made from the transformations from which the operative structure was abstracted.

As was noted earlier, once a student has created a structure of operations, he or she may reflect the current state of affairs into that structure, and think in terms of possibilities: What would happen *if* I did (or did not) do this? By working within an operative structure, the student may then consider consequences of actions, since then one is not bound by the present situation. That is, the student may begin to generate plans.

Problem Solving and Operative Thought

The complementary forms of reflective abstraction in Piaget's genetic epistemology highlight the reciprocal relationship between problem solving and the development of operative thinking within the content domain of the problems. As students create mathematical objects, they may relate them through the construction of transformations of one to the other. As they relate them, they may reflect those relationships into subsequent problems, in turn enriching their understanding of the objects.

As an example, consider a student's creation of functions as mathematical objects (cf. Piaget et al., 1977). At first, a function is at most a rule for assigning objects (usually numbers) in a domain to objects in a range. The rule of assignment together with its domain and range is the function, but it is often not an object to students in the same sense as the objects being assigned to one another. There are ''too many parts'' to a function for it to be one thing, as one student said to me.

As students solve problems relative to properties of functions, such as injectivity, surjectivity, and bijectivity (e.g., What could you do to this function so that it is injective?), the objectivity of functions develops. Functions, as mathematical objects in a student's thinking, culminate at two levels. The first is the level of thinking of functions as objects to be composed and decomposed. The second is the level of thinking of functions as objects in a domain and range of a function. Examples of the latter are problems of morphisms between structures, derivatives as mappings between function spaces, and functions defined as limits of sequences of functions (for example, functions as elements in a metric space).

Hidden behind these examples are systems of transformation that allow students to move from aspect to aspect of their concept of function, and systems of transformation that allow them to move between levels of detail. For example, if F is thought of as a set of differentiable functions, then $D_x: F \rightarrow F'$ can be thought of in a number of ways, among which are: (1) D_x is a linear function that associates functions with functions (leaving it at that); (2) pick an element f in F and apply D_x to it (getting a function as a result); (3) pick an element f in F, apply the definition of D_x to f (getting a derived rule of assignment), and then evaluate $D_x(f)$ at an element a in the domain of f; and (4) pick an element f in F, pick an element a in the domain of f, and then apply the definition of D_x to $f(a)$.

Each way of understanding $D_x: F \rightarrow F'$ has its advantages under some circumstances, and disadvantages under others. The ideal situation is for students to be
able to jump from one form of understanding to another according to the conditions of
the problem at hand. The way to promote this ability, as proposed here, is for students to
solve problems in which they must construct, and reconstruct, functions as objects, and
to solve problems in which they must establish relationships among their various ways of
thinking of functions.

Another example of the relationship between problem solving and the development
of operative thought can be found in whole-number numeration. Children learn to construct sequences of number-names both forward and backward in increments of one and
ten; they learn how to count-on and count-back; they learn how to construct units of ten;
they learn how to (conceptually) add and subtract. To have a full concept of ten as a base
of a numeration system, they need to relate these schemata in a systematic, highly structured way—knowing each in isolation is insufficient for solving complex problems involving whole-number numeration (Thompson, 1982b). To establish relationships, they
must construct transformations among schemata so that they may adjust to the conditions of a problem—for example, by transforming the adding of ten to a quantity into
the linguistic transformation of the number-name signifying that quantity by a rule
system for "next-ten." Again, the pedagogical avenue to establishing such relationships
is by posing questions of such a nature that students must create relationships to answer
them.

A related view of the development of structures in problem solving is set forth by
Anderson and colleagues (Anderson et al., 1981; Neves & Anderson, 1981). They do not
have a direct counterpart of Piaget's notion of reflective abstraction. The closest construct
to reflective abstraction in their accounts is what they call generalization (Anderson et
al., 1981). Generalization is the abstraction of similarities in solutions to problems (in
this case, geometry proofs). In effect, they posit that students create data structures of
steps in solutions to problems, and abstract common steps taken in problems with similar
conditions and goals. The resulting "rule" is a generalization from previous problem
solutions in that, since its conditions for application are less specific than the conditions
of any of the problems from which it was abstracted, it may be applied to a larger class of
problems than that from which it was abstracted.

Although Anderson et al.'s notion of generalization and Piaget's notion of reflective abstraction would appear to lead to parallel accounts of the development of proof-
generation abilities (the subject of Anderson et al.'s article), it becomes less apparent
when we look at geometric thinking in a larger context. To Anderson and colleagues, the
objects operated upon in geometric proofs are lines, line segments, angles, and so on,
which in turn are nodes in a declarative semantic network (Anderson, 1976; Greeno,
1976; Neves & Anderson, 1981). That is, it appears that they view the items of knowledge toward which proofs are aimed as syntactic structures that are generated by
manipulating and relating letters, words, and, possibly, visual images. Theirs seems to
be a linguistic theory of geometric thinking.[2]

Piaget (1951), on the other hand, put his emphasis on the operational structure of

---

2. This statement is not completely accurate. There was some controversy among the authors as to
   the nature of the objects of geometric thinking. The discussion of learning by subsumption
   given by Greeno is less linguistically oriented than the other sections. However, subsumption
   and reflective abstraction address different issues.

the objects of reasoning, and stressed that operations upon those objects had to be consistent with their nature. In his account, the word (mental sound-image) "triangle" would be associated with certain operations of thought; for example, the operations of moving, turning, moving again, turning towards the starting position, and then going to it. If we take this view of a triangle as a geometric object, then properties of triangles in an individual's thinking must be theoretically characterized in terms of properties of their operational structure. They may well be characterized in terms of a "semantic" structure, but we would have to expand our meaning of "semantic" to that usually given to "semiotic." That is, we would have to allow operations as representations of actions (Piaget, 1968). In terms of Piaget's theory, the highest form of abstraction allowed in Anderson et al.'s theory is pseudoempirical (Piaget, 1977; von Glasersfeld, in preparation)—abstraction from (linguistically encoded) objects. In Piaget's theory, there is empirical abstraction, but there is also abstraction that has its roots in the operational structure of both the objects and the subject's actions upon them. If by "declarative" Anderson et al. mean "figurative" in Piaget's sense, then there could be a great deal of similarity between the two. I find it difficult, however, to read figurative thought into Anderson et al.'s discussions of semantic networks.

Influence of the Environment

Radical constructivist that I am, I feel a bit awkward about having a section with a title like the above. But there is a pressing problem in math education that has become ever more apparent to me: Why, even under what might appear to be the most ideal circumstances, do people in general find it difficult to construct relationships? Raising this issue here is especially important. Not every calculus student of mine creates the different ways of understanding differentiation that I have outlined; not every child that I have worked with has constructed concepts of base-ten numeration. Why? I am sure there are relatively simple explanations for why any given student does not grasp a relationship for which I have set the stage, but I believe that there is a deeper principle in operation as well.

Papert (1980) raised a similar question. He asked: If the vast majority of people construct concrete operations at a relatively early age, then why is it that it takes so long for them to construct formal operations, if they construct them at all? His answer is that the common environment of humans is impoverished of objects amenable to formal thinking. Though Papert's answer seems to conflict with his constructivist epistemology, that appearance can be avoided. To understand Papert's observation in a constructivist framework, and its significance for developing mathematics curricula, we need to return to Piaget's account of the development of concrete operations.

In interacting with a physical environment, a child isolates certain features and disregards others, but always acts on it. In cybernetic terms, the child attempts to control sensory and motor inputs by affecting the environment through actions (MacKay, 1969; Piaget, 1964; Powers, 1973, 1978; Skemp, 1979; von Glasersfeld, 1978). As a cybernetic system, the child is constantly receiving feedback from which the efficacy of actions relative to goals may be judged, and which can thus serve as a basis to refine actions into systems for achieving goals. The key feature here is the continual feedback that the child generates. The child knows when he or she is right or wrong by evaluating achievement of goals. The biological nature of humans is such that concrete operations are an inevitable outcome, within normal constraints, of interaction with the physical environment.

When we examine the development of formal operations, or mathematical thinking, the situation is quite different. The salient actions are entirely mental, and the objects acted upon are ideas. The environment of ideas *is* impoverished, in the sense that there need be nothing intrinsic to an idea that tells the person holding it that what he or she just did (with that idea) will lead to conflict if the line of thought is continued. That is, feedback need not be an intrinsic part of an action upon an idea, beyond the feedback that the action was carried out.

From this perspective it is entirely understandable why students so frequently rely solely on an answer key to tell them whether or not their answers are right. They apparently do not have the mental means to judge the efficacy of their thinking; so they employ a primitive working-backward heuristic. Similarly, it is understandable why children are quite happy to count, say, 12 Dienes' ten-blocks as "10, 20, . . . 90, 100, 101, 102." There is nothing in their thinking at that moment that signals to them that their method is faulty. Without an operative structure, they have no means to expect other than that with which they end.

Feedback analogous in its richness to that at the sensorimotor level becomes intrinsic to mental actions only when the outcome of the actions is compared with an expectation. But an expectation of an action upon an idea is an idea, and ideas can only be compared within systems of transformation (Hayes-Roth et al., 1981; Lunzer, 1969). The implication is that we must design mathematics curricula so that students can generate feedback for themselves as to the efficacy of their mental actions (methods of thinking) vis-à-vis the "environment" provided them by mathematical problems. An ideal curriculum would have the potential of being manipulable by students to the extent that they may generate feedback of whatever degree of subtlety they feel is necessary.

CASE STUDIES

Two examples of mathematics curricula developed in accord with the considerations we have discussed are outlined in this section. They are based on five guiding principles: A mathematics curriculum should

1. Be problem based.

2. Promote reflective abstraction.

3. Contain (but not necessarily be limited to) questions that focus on relationships.

4. Have as its objective a cognitive structure that allows one to think with the structure of the subject matter.

5. Allow students to generate feedback from which they can judge the efficacy of their methods of thinking.

The curricula were designed for use in a middle school mathematics program; I have used them in a mathematics course for prospective elementary school teachers. The first example is drawn from a curriculum for developing a concept of the ring of integers; only that part of the curriculum dealing with the group of integers will be discussed. The second example is a curriculum for developing a concept of Euclidean transformations in a coordinate plane. Each focuses first on developing the mathematical objects of the subject matter, and then on developing operations upon objects, relationships between objects, and relationships between operations. Both curricula are in their formative stages and are being refined as I use them. They are stable enough in their structure and spirit, however, that I feel comfortable in sharing them.

The cognitive objectives of the curricula with respect to the mathematical objects are that the students first construct them as transformations between states, and then reconstruct them as elements themselves to be transformed. This is shown in schematic form in Figure 1. Put another way, the objectives are to have students first construct transformations as "things to act with," and then to reconstruct them as "things to act on."

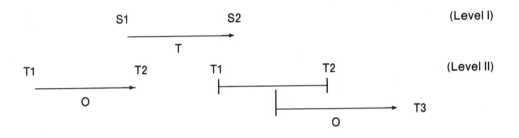

Figure 1. Schematic for levels of cognitive objectives, where "S" stands for a state, "T" for a transformation, and "O" for an operation.

In order to satisfy the principle regarding feedback (5), I have taken an approach consonant with Papert (1980), and Abelson and diSessa (1981), in that I ask my students to use the computer as a medium for exploring mathematics. The implementations that serve as the focus of the curricula are examples of what I call mathematical microworlds. A colleague has characterized them as computerized axiom systems, but I would not put it that way. I prefer to think of them as environments in which students explore their underst anding of the subject matter in the same way that scientists test their conjectures about the way the world works.

It is the rare explorer, however, who can begin the journey without a map. The curricula that surround the microworlds are intended, first, to get the students started by enticing them to begin and, second, to refine their knowledge of the terrain by throwing ever more difficult obstacles in their paths. I have yet to answer the question of how, in principle, to handle the interesting side trips that students so often find on their own. That is an issue likely to remain with the classroom teacher.

The two case studies are presented in the following format: a general description of the objectives of the curriculum, then a description of the microworld, and finally examples of activities and problems aimed at achieving the objectives. The activities and problems will be annotated wherever a discussion of their purposes seems warranted.

Case Study One: Integers

The following discussion of a curriculum for integers owes much to the spirit of Steffe (1976) and Weaver (1982) in taking transformations as a basis for instruction. The work of Vergnaud (1982) was particularly suggestive of the form that the curriculum for integers has taken.

Objects

An integer as a mathematical object is to be, in the student's thinking, a composite of a direction and a whole-number magnitude. A direction is not to be universally fixed, such as left/right, but is to be understood as being relative to the currently assumed direction. The genesis of integers is supposed to be (*1*) double counting-on and counting-back as mental operations, (*2*) transformations of quantity, (*3*) directed whole-number magnitudes (Thompson, 1982b).

Operations

The basic operations upon integers are negation and affirmation. Negation is the operation of deciding to take an integer oppositely from its statement. Affirmation is the operation of deciding to take an integer as it is stated. Negation and affirmation as operations are similar to the ideas of "crossing" and "crossing again" in Brown's (1972) theory of indication.

Milieu

The objects and operations are supposed to exist within the general environment of the student's developing ability to compose transformations, construct operations, and to apply operations recursively. This supposition is based on the further assumption that the student's experiences include solving problems in which, to the student, these abilities are demanded.

The epigenesis of addition and subtraction of integers is supposed to be of two sources. The first is compositions of transformations—composing two transformations gives *one* transformation—which have as their source consecutive execution of transformations. The second is an analogy with addition and subtraction of whole numbers.

Microworld

The integers microworld, called INTEGERS, has a graphics display of a "turtle" (a triangular graphics object) on a number line (Figure 2)[3]. At any time, the turtle is facing either left or right; when doing nothing it is, by convention, facing to the right. The turtle thus has a two-property state—a list containing its position on the number line and its current direction.

The number line is divided into three parts: zero, positions to the right of zero, and positions to the left of zero. Positions are named by numbers indicating their distance from zero. Numbers for positions to the right of zero are prefixed by a " + "; numbers for positions to the left of zero are prefixed by a "−". Note that + 5, −70, and so on, are

---

3. The INTEGERS program, and the MOTIONS program described later, are available from Cosine, Inc., Box 2017, N. Lafayette, IN 47906.

nominal numbers; they are not integers. They merely name positions on a number line by a given convention, no more and no less.

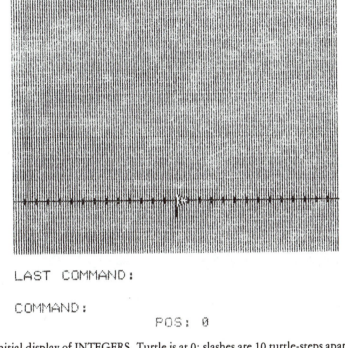

LAST COMMAND:

COMMAND:

POS: 0

Figure 2. Initial display of INTEGERS. Turtle is at 0; slashes are 10 turtle-steps apart.

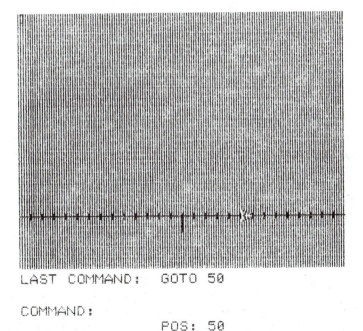

LAST COMMAND: GOTO 50

COMMAND:

POS: 50

Figure 3. Effect of entering GOTO 50 vs. entering 50 (see next page); GOTO 50 puts the turtle at the position 50; 50 moves the turtle 50 turtle-steps.

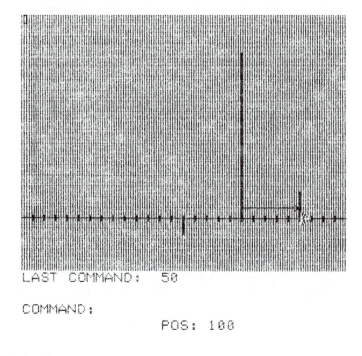

Figure 3. Continued.

Curriculum

The curriculum has two levels, corresponding to the levels of cognitive objectives discussed earlier, and illustrated in Figure 1.

Level I. Students are introduced to the curriculum with a discussion of points relative to an origin, such as temperature scales on a thermometer, numbering floors in a building that extends above and below ground, and so on. Then they are introduced to the naming conventions of "+" and "−" to indicate on which side of the origin the position lies. The students are given a sheet with a cursory description of the microworld, its conventions, an explanation of the display, and a discussion of the idea of entering commands on the keyboard to make the turtle move. The sheet also contains a description of some of the primitive commands that the students have available to them. The commands are given in Table 1.

The students are introduced to INTEGERS by having them locate points on the number line and set the turtle at them by using the GOTO x command, where x is a nominal number for a point on the line. Then they are allowed to play with the microworld so that they may begin to develop schemata at an intuitive level for its operations. Finally, they are told that they are going to be asked, eventually, to think of numbers in a new way.

Table 1. Subset of commands in INTEGERS.

Command	Action
<number>	The turtle moves <number> steps in its current direction.
N <number>[a]	The turtle turns around, does <number>, and then turns back around.
GOTO <position>	Places the turtle at <position>.

a. The use of "N" to designate negation is found in the version of INTEGERS for college students. The version for middle school uses "−".

If a student enters, say, 50 as a command, the turtle will move 50 turtle steps (approximately 5 centimeters) in its current direction (Figure 3). Fifty, and whole numbers in general, are no longer measures of sets, they are transformations of quantities (Vergnaud, 1982). To highlight this new way of thinking of numbers, the students are asked to solve problems like the following:

1 a. Enter GOTO 30. What number takes the turtle to 70?

  b. Someone entered GOTO 25. Then they entered a number. The turtle ended up at 60. What number was entered?

  c. Develop rules by which you can always predict the answers to questions like these:

  (1) The turtle is at ♦ . What number would you enter to make it end up at # ?

  (2) The turtle began at #. Someone entered a number. The turtle ended up at ♦. What number was entered?

At this point in the curriculum, the students are being asked to reflect on connections between successive states of the turtle. That is to say, they are at the entry level of creating integers (transformations) as mathematical objects. The first of the above situations focuses on an integer as a transformation from one state of the turtle to another; the second focuses, reciprocally, on two states of the turtle being related by a transformation. To this point we have involved only what we see as positive integers.

Note that variations on the above situations could be used to promote the idea that two states uniquely determine a transformation, but a transformation determines at most an equivalence class of pairs of states. The idea of transformations as equivalence relations gives a psychological basis for the classical definition of integers as equivalence classes of pairs of whole numbers that are related by a common difference (Herstein, 1975). A pair of states, on the other hand, may be identified with the integer that relates them, but we must be careful not to equate the two. A pair of states is only representative of those pairs that can be so related.

Students tend to be confused at first when applying the double meaning of numerals in the microworld. There is 50 as the nominal number naming a particular position to the right of zero, and there is 50 as a command that tells the turtle to go 50 steps in its current direction—which doesn't necessarily have anything to do with the position 50. They do, however, quickly separate the two by differentiating the meanings by the conditions of their context. To *enter* "50" is to move; to *name* as "50" is to identify. This situation is not new to the students, and they tend to realize it when it is pointed out that they overcame essentially the same confusion when they were in first and second grade. Then, they double-counted—five (is one), six (is two), seven (is three), and so forth—keeping the two meanings quite separate. However, the students must yet reconstruct this distinction several times over, as we shall see.

There is no reason at this time in the curriculum for students to give any significance to "in its current direction" as a qualifier of the turtle's movement in response to a number being entered. They typically think "to the right" in its place. This thinking will lead them astray in later problems.

The next set of questions and activities brings out the difference between the students' old ways of thinking of numbers and the new ways required of them.

2 *a.* Enter GOTO 70. What number will take the turtle to 50?

  b. Someone entered GOTO −20. Then they entered a number. The turtle ended up at −55. What number did they enter?

  c. When Mary tested her answer to 2a, she intended to enter N 30, but entered 30 instead. Tell Mary what she could enter now to make the turtle end up at 50.

Problems 2a and b are stated as they are purposely. The wording in either could have indicated "something," rather than "number," to be entered. This would have made it easier for students to conclude in b, for example, that N 35 made the turtle move from −20 to −55, because they would not have had to classify "N 35" as representing a number. But the objective of these problems is precisely that the students begin to rethink their idea of number so that N 35 falls under it. By making the problems initially easier to solve, we would merely postpone the time when the students must come to grips with the idea that N x is a number just as much as x is. In fact, by making the problems easier, we might make it more difficult for the students to rethink their idea of number when they must.

There are two ways of thinking of N x that are explicitly addressed within the curriculum. The first is the idea of N as a unary operator upon x; the second is N x as a number. The closest parallel to this distinction that I know of is found in Logo. In Logo, a procedure that takes one or more inputs and produces an output is called an operator. At one level, you can think of an operator as a relationship between three objects: input, procedure, and output. At another level, you can identify the object-output with the procedure and its input. Thus, to think of N x as a number, one must identify the action resulting from N x with the composite object made of the procedure N and its input x. To create N x as a composite object is an extremely difficult task for students. To get somewhat ahead of the discussion, they may do so only when they come to look at x formally, in the sense that it can take on any INTEGERS expression as a value. To appreciate the difficulty of creating integers as composite objects, recall that any INTEGER expression is a procedure. That is, the input to N, N itself, and the output of N are all procedures. The realization that a composition of integer expressions is an integer is similar to students' creation of derived units, such as specific gravity (Lunzer, 1969).

Problems from non-INTEGERS settings that parallel the structure of those in INTEGERS are also given to the students.

3 *a.* Mr. Quimby had 50 dollars in his pocket. He went into a bank. He came out with 20 dollars.

  (1) Rewrite the statement as if it were given about the turtle in INTEGERS.

(2)   What happened in the bank?

b. Gary played a game of marbles. He started with 30 marbles. He ended with 16 marbles.

(1)   Rewrite the statement as if it were given about the turtle in INTEGERS.

(2)   What happened during the game?

The students have already formed a generalization for 1c, which was given in the context of the turtle always moving to its right. After solving a number of problems in which the turtle ends up moving to the left, the students are asked to form a generalization paralleling, and including, 1c, if they haven't done so already.

3 c.   Develop rules so that you can predict the answers to questions like these:

(1)   The turtle is at ◆. What number would you enter to make it end up at #? (Remember, # can be either to the right or left of ◆.)

(2)   The turtle began at #. Someone entered a number. The turtle ended up at ◆. What number was entered? (Remember, ◆ can be either to the right or left of #.)

To this point in the curriculum, students still have not been explicitly asked to think of an integer (transformation) as an object. To do so, they need to abstract the transformation from any particular starting and ending position, and any particular direction, so that it represents a class of possibilities. To draw their attention to this, the students are asked questions such as the following:

4 a. Someone entered N 60. What happened?

b. List as many possible starting and ending positions of the turtle as you can. List them as pairs in the form (start,end). Can you list them all? Why?

c. What do the pairs of starting and ending positions in b have in common?

d. Is moving the turtle from 100 to 40 *exactly* the same as entering N 60? That is, will doing one always have the effect of doing the other?

e. Will <number> always move the turtle to the right? Why?

f. Will N <number> always move the turtle to the left? Why?

To further push the students to thinking of an integer as a formal entity, they are asked to predict the turtle's actions upon their entering such commands as N [N 30], N [N 60], and then to generalize their predictions to N [N x]. Their generalization, that N [N x] = x, is explictly formalized in INTEGERS by the instructor's offering to adopt their generalization as a new convention. That is done by having the students enter the command DEF ''P [N [N :X]].

The DEF command is INTEGERS's way of allowing the students to define their own constructs as new operations in INTEGERS. Once P is defined, entering P 50 produces the same effect as entering N [N 50]. With P defined, N has a counterpart in IN- TEGERS—the operation of affirmation. To paraphrase one student, using N means that you want to reverse what you had planned to do; using P means that you *really* want to do what you had planned.

Level II. The second level of the curriculum, namely, having students think about integers as objects to operate upon, begins with problems like the following:

1 *a.* *Predict* how much and in what direction the turtle will end up moving after you enter N 80 P 70.

  b. Test your prediction.

  c. What is the net effect of N 80 P 70?

2.   John entered GOTO −60 on his computer and Fred entered GOTO 40 on his. They then (independently) predicted what would happen if they entered N 60 P 90, and found that they made the same prediction. Can they both be right? Why?

3 *a.* Helen entered P 80 N 90. What is the net effect of Helen's command? What could she enter to make the turtle return to its starting position?

  b. Bruce entered P 70, and then he entered N 70. Where did the turtle end up?

  c. Rebecca entered three separate commands. The first two commands disappeared under the turtle's screen after she entered the third, so she couldn't see them anymore. She noticed that the net effect of all three was P 30. She remembered that the second command was N 60; she could see that the third was P 100. Tell Rebecca what her first command was.

  d. James entered P 60 N 30 P 40. Then he entered N [P 60 N 30 P 40]. Where did the turtle end up?

4.*a.* Paul played two games of marbles. At the first game he won 6 marbles. At the second game he lost 4 marbles. What has happened altogether? (Vergnaud, 1982)

  b. Mary made two transactions at a bank. The second transaction was a deposit of $40. She left the bank with $25 less than when she entered. What was the first transaction?

Problems 1 and 3 leave the turtle's initial and ending positions unspecified. The students must think, either initially or in retrospect, in terms of an arbitrary starting position, if they think of one at all. Some students will pick a starting position—usually 0. If they do, and if they answer in terms of a specific ending position (e.g., the turtle ended at 0), they are immediately asked if their answers would be correct were the turtle to start at, say, 10? 20? −40? That is, they are encouraged to rethink their method of answering, as distinct from rethinking their answer. Questions in problem 4 move out of the INTEGERS microworld, but ask students to think with the same structure as within it.

Questions in Level II are also an entrance into compositions of transformations as consecutive execution of two or more integers. The term "net effect" (1c) is used to refer to the elementary integer that could be entered in place of the more complex expression. As an aside, students frequently have trouble deciding the net effect of something like N 60 P 60. It seems that it is not until they think of entering 0 as a way to tell the turtle to stay put that they see 0 as an integer.

Question 3d stresses the formal relationship between x and N x. Often students can say that expressions like 30 and N 30 cancel each other, yet cannot see the same relationship in 3d, instead acting out each of the steps in the turtle's itinerary.

Consecutive execution is the first time that it is important for students to understand that the turtle resets its heading after performing a command. If they don't recall this, the students will predict that N *x* P *y* results in N (*x* + *y*). I should point out that, in line with much of the work surrounding Logo (Papert, 1980), the students are encouraged to act out their commands with the turtle whenever they either get an unexpected result or cannot predict the effect of a command.

One formalization of composition of integers that the students are asked to make is that of consecutive execution as addition of integers. The context of the activity is that they are asked to generalize from addition of whole numbers in order to define addition of integers. The only guidance that they are given is that they should make *some* definition, named ADD, and test it to see if it is satisfactory—that it adds "whole numbers" in the way we think it should. The definition that is usually given is, in form,

DEF "ADD [P :X P :Y]

or DEF "ADD [:X :Y].

Either way of defining addition of integers results in the turtle doing the first argument and then doing the second. The second definition may appear strange to the programming-wise reader, since there are no commands within the defining part of it, only variables. However, the values of the variables are integers or integer expressions, which are in fact "commands" to move the turtle—they are procedures. That is, declarative knowledge in INTEGERS is no more than represented procedural knowledge (see Figures 4 and 5).

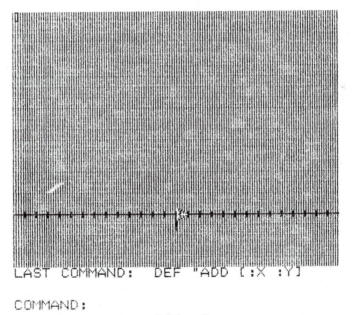

LAST COMMAND: DEF "ADD [:X :Y]

COMMAND:

POS: 0

Figure 4. DEF "ADD [:X :Y]. Commands INTEGERS to add ADD to its set of defined commands. The colon stipulates that *X* and *Y* are variables whose values will be given by the user at the time of ADD's execution. If the value entered for either *X* or *Y* is not an integer, INTEGERS will complain.

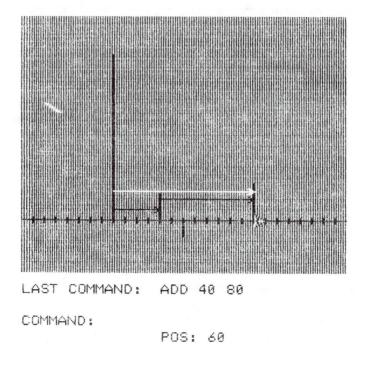

LAST COMMAND: ADD 40 80

COMMAND:

                 POS: 60

Figure 5. ADD 40 80. Commands the turtle to do 40 and then to do 80. (See Figure 4.)

A goal of the curriculum for integers is that the students develop a method of thinking in regard to definitions. They are encouraged to explore the consequences of a definition. For example, once they define addition of integers in a way that conforms to their intuitions of addition of whole numbers, they are asked to predict the results of the addition of non-whole-number integers, such as ADD 80 [N 70] and ADD [N 40] [N 60].

By defining addition and subtraction of integers, the students begin to solidify integers as mathematical objects—as something to be acted upon. They are asked to further generalize their notion of an integer as an object so that it includes integer expressions. Questions that focus on integer expressions as integers are

5 a. Predict the net effect of N [ADD 50 [N 70]].

b. Translate problem 4a into an INTEGERS expression that uses ADD.

c. ADD [N 60] [__] = P 30. What integer goes in the blank space?

d. N 60 = ADD [__] [P 70]. What integer goes in the blank space?

With regard to 5a, note that in the list of commands for INTEGERS (Table 1) N is said to operate only on numbers. When this is pointed out to students, it is a real problem for them to reconcile that requirement with their picture of ADD :X :Y as a procedure that itself operates on numbers.

Just as students are asked to construct the binary operation of addition of integers, they are asked to construct the binary operation of subtraction. Several definitions (called SUB for uniformity) have been given:

DEF ''SUB [:X [N :Y]],

DEF ''SUB [P :X N :Y],

DEF ''SUB [[:X] [N :Y]],

DEF ''SUB [ADD [:X] [N :Y]].

I will not say anything about the variations in the use of braces in the above definitions, except that the only constraint placed by INTEGERS upon the definer is that an expression that is to be taken as a unit must be enclosed in braces. Braces must also be used to avoid ambiguity, as in N 30 50, for example. N [30 50] is unambiguous, being the negation of [30 50], but in N 30 50 it is unclear whether [N 30] 50 or N [30 50] is intended.

Students who define subtraction as ADD [:X] [N :Y] have already formed a generalization that others will be asked to make, namely that SUB :X :Y is equivalent to ADD :X [N :Y]. Further generalizations that they are asked to explore are

SUB :X [N :Y] = ADD [__] [__],

N [ADD :X :Y] = SUB [__] [__],

ADD :X :Y = N [ADD [__] [__]],

N [SUB :X :Y] = ADD [__] [__],

SUB :X :Y = N [SUB [__] [__]], and so on.

Structural properties of addition and subtraction of integers are emphasized by having the students develop ''convincing arguments'' (i.e., arguments that will convince their doubting neighbors) that their generalizations will always work. Structure is also emphasized by having them examine questions such as

6 *a.* Does the net effect of ADD depend upon the order in which you supply its inputs?

   b. Does the net effect of SUB depend upon the order in which you supply its inputs?

   c. John played three games of marbles. In one game he won 8 marbles, in another he lost 5, and in another he lost 9. (The actual order in which he played the three games is not the order in which they are listed.)

   (1) Write an INTEGERS expression for John's marble account.

   (2) Compare your expression with your neighbors'. Are they exactly the same? Does it matter? Why?

So that students may ''reify'' relationships established among operations and structural properties of operations, they are given expressions to simplify and new definitions to create, as in

7 *a.* Predict the net effect of SUB [SUB 50 [N 30]] [N [ADD 40 [N 80]].

   (Figure 6 shows what would be displayed if this expression was entered.)

   b. Predict the net effect of N [ADD [N [SUB 70 20]] 90].

c. Define a new operation, called "CANCEL, using a combination of ADD, SUB, and N so that CANCEL 50 30, CANCEL 70 [N 40], and CANCEL [N 20] [N 80] each end up doing nothing. That is, define it so that no matter what two integers you put into CANCEL, the net effect is 0.

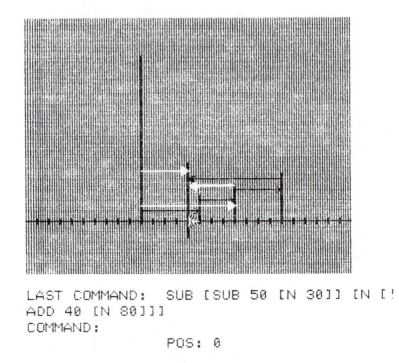

```
LAST COMMAND:    SUB [SUB 50 [N 30]] [N [!
ADD 40 [N 80]]]
COMMAND:
                        POS: 0
```

Figure 6. Effect of entering SUB [SUB 50 [N 30]] [N [ADD 40 [N 80]]]. Black arrows correspond to "simple" integers; white arrows correspond to "structured" integers.

Another type of question focuses on the layers of structure that can be put on complex expressions. Students are asked to describe pictures like those in Figure 7 in terms of integer expressions, at three levels of description.

To summarize, the curriculum for integers comprises a collection of activities and questions that are aimed at promoting the students' construction of integers as mathematical objects, and their construction of transformations and operations upon those objects. All of this takes place within the context of exploring the behavior of a turtle on a number line when it is given commands to perform various activities. The theoretical basis of the curriculum is the position that meaningful, formal mathematical reasoning develops semiotically—a transformation at one level of thought comes to stand for multitudes of possibilities at a lower level. The significance of this curriculum for solving problems involving integers is, as Lawler (1981) put it, that "the control structures of mind embody the genetic path of learning." As students formalize their actions of thought in regard to integers, the figurations (operations of mentally moving an object) then become models they can drop back to in overcoming obstacles during formal reasoning.

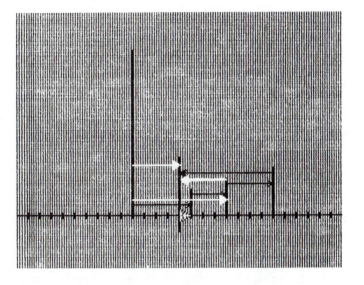

Figure 7. Picture of the effect of entering an integer. Students are to describe this integer (upper-most white arrow) at three different levels of structure. Lowest level would be [P 50 P 30 P 40 N 80]. Highest level would be ADD [ADD [P 50] [P 30]] [ADD [P 40] [N 80]] or its equivalent (cf. Figure 6).

Case Study Two: Transformation Geometry

The curriculum for transformation geometry is similar in spirit to that for integers. The students are asked to create the objects of the subject matter, to relate them, and to construct operations upon them. However, the structure of the subject matter in transformation geometry differs qualitatively from that in integers. The objects are more numerous, and their composition is more complex. Therefore, the relationships among the objects and the operations upon them are more difficult for students to construct than is the case with integers. The curriculum reflects this.

Objects

The objects within transformation geometry are rotations, translations, and reflections ("flips"). Each is to be, in the students' thinking, a mapping of the plane onto itself by the criterion that the images of points remain the same distance apart as were their preimages. Rotations, translations, and flips are special cases of this definition.

- A rotation is a mapping of the plane that leaves all points equidistant from a given point.

- A translation is a mapping of the plane that makes all segments joining images and preimages parallel.

- A flip is a mapping of the plane that leaves images and preimages equidistant from a given line.

I have found that as characterizations of the intended objects in students' thinking, the preceding are too facile and too powerful. They are too powerful in that most of transformation geometry can be constructed from them; they have far-reaching implications that are uncovered only after a great deal of elaboration. They are too facile in that students can "record" them as verbalizations, and yet fail to understand them in terms of anything resembling an operational structure.

The cognitive objectives of the curriculum are transformations of figures in a coordinate plane. In terms of the schematic in Figure 1, transformations of a figure are at Level I. The transformations serve to connect "states" of a figure, where a state is determined by some well-defined criterion. A state can be at, or between, two levels in a student's understanding: it can be a perceptual image, on par with any object in the student's field of vision, or it can be a list of property values. The properties used in the curriculum are (1) the figure's position in a rectangular coordinate plane, (2) its heading within a polar coordinate system, and (3) its orientation (each determined by an appropriately well-defined method).

As a connection between visual states of a figure, a transformation is nothing more than the students' estimate of the effects upon the figure of performing a physical relocation. As a connection between property values of a figure, a transformation is a multivariate mapping. The latter is clearly the more formal of the two, in that once students have the means to predict the effects of a transformation upon a figure's properties, they have in essence developed a system in which they can consider possibilities regardless of whether or not the figure is in their field of vision, and regardless of whether a figure has even been specified. That is, it is only in the case of the latter that a transformation in the students' thinking approximates the idea of a transformation being an isometric map of the plane onto itself. The mapping formally preserves perceptual structure.

I should point out that the creation of a system in which my students may predict the effect of a motion upon a figure's properties has been extremely difficult for them. One reason for this, I believe, is that they have difficulty equating a particular figure in the plane with an instantiation of the variable list [figure (position heading orientation)].

Put another way, students appear to consider a transformation at first as being applied to, and only to, that figure that is currently in their attention, and not to the class of congruent figures of which the current one is only representative. They do not look at a figure as a variable. Thus, for the curriculum for transformation geometry to emphasize transformations as objects, it must first emphasize the states upon which transformations operate as variables. This was not apparent in the curriculum for integers, as the college students in my courses thought naturally of position as a variable value. It is quite possible that middle school students will not.

One could make a case that the ontogeneses of variables and functions are inextricably linked, as did Piaget et al. (1977). If that were the case, the implication would seem to be that instructionally the two are inseparable. From another perspective, however, they are separable—to an extent. To bring the students to a level where, to them, the states upon which a transformation operates are objects in and of themselves, one might ask them to build concrete-operational action schemata for the transformations, indirectly placing the states into the realm of possibilities. At least then it would make sense to them to speak of a transformation independently of any particular state of the figure being transformed.

The genesis of transformations in the plane as mathematical objects can now be supposed to be (1) action schemata of physical displacement, (2) formalization of variable figures (both within and across equivalence classes of figures, (3) transformations as functions between lists of property values of a class of figures, and (4) transformations as isometric mappings of the plane.

Operations

The essential operation upon transformations in the plane is composition. The genesis of composition is supposed to be (1) coexecution—doing one transformation (of any state), doing another (of any state), and differentiating between the two; (2) consecutive execution—doing one transformation and then doing another upon the state resulting from the first; and (3) composition—the result of consecutively executing two transformations being taken as a transformation in and of itself. Note that the genesis of transformations as characterized here assumes the complexity of the genesis of transformations as mathematical objects.

Milieu

As with the integers curriculum, the objects and operations of transformation geometry are supposed to exist within the students' emerging abilities to compose transformations, construct operations, and apply operations recursively. As always, this supposition is made with the assumption that the students' experiences include solving problems in which, to them, these abilities are demanded.

Microworld

The transformation geometry microworld, called MOTIONS, has as its initial display a picture of a Cartesian coordinate system and a flag standing upright on the origin (Figure 8). The flag lies within two frames of reference, the Cartesian coordinate system and the polar coordinate system. It thus has several properties that serve to uniquely identify it—its heading (the direction that the turtle is pointing as it sits waiting for a command from the keyboard), its position (the position occupied by the turtle), and its orientation (the direction that the turtle turns when constructing the flag).

Other properties for which the program maintains values, but which are redundant with the above three, are the flag's distance from the origin (measured from the turtle); the measure of the angle formed by the turtle, the origin, and the positive x-axis; and the turtle's x- and y-coordinates. Even though these are redundant, it is pedagogically useful to have them maintained.

As a note, the students are not limited to operating upon the figure initially supplied by the program; they may define new figures at will. The pedagogical utility of the capability to define new figures will be discussed in the section Symmetries of Plane Figures.

The transformations initially supplied to the students are translations, rotations about the origin, and flips through lines that pass through the origin. The microworld works as follows: The student enters a command, or sequence of commands, and then the program executes it. For each command, a flag is drawn according to the command's effect upon the flag's properties.

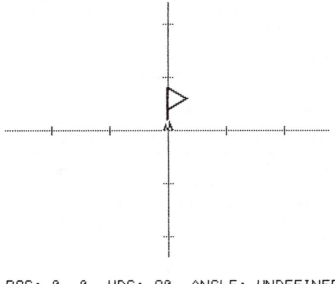

```
POS: 0. 0. HDG: 90. ANGLE: UNDEFINED
COMMAND:
```

Figure 8. Initial display of MOTIONS. Slashes on axes are in increments of 50 turtle-steps. Information given in information line: the flag's (turtle's) position, heading, and the measure of the angle formed by the turtle, the origin, and the positive x-axis.

To rotate the flag about the origin, the student enters R <number>, where <number> is the measure of the angle through which to rotate it (Figure 9). To translate the flag, the student enters T <number1> <number2>, where <number1> is a distance to move and <number2> is the heading in which to move it (Figure 10). To flip the flag, the student enters F <number>, where <number> is the heading of the line passing through the origin through which the flip is to be made (Figure 11).

A number of other commands are available to the students for "housekeeping" (e.g., clearing the screen) or for pedagogical purposes. The full glossary of commands, operations, and maintained variables for MOTIONS is given in the Appendix of this chapter.

Curriculum

Each student is given a copy of the MOTIONS program and a copy of a module that contains activities for them to do and questions for them to consider. In its current form, the module is separated into five sections: Getting Acquainted, Investigations, Symmetries of Plane Figures, Systematic Investigations, and General Motions. In the discussion of each section, I will refer to translations, rotations, and flips as motions, since that is the generic term used in the module.

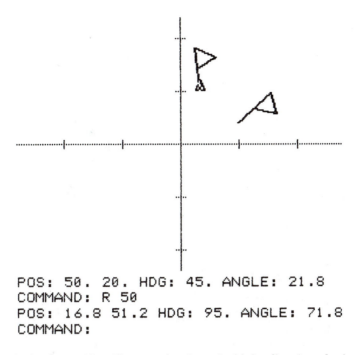

```
POS: 50. 20. HDG: 45. ANGLE: 21.8
COMMAND: R 50
POS: 16.8 51.2 HDG: 95. ANGLE: 71.8
COMMAND:
```

Figure 9. Example of a rotation. Flag started at [50 20] with heading 45 and orientation ''RT. Student entered R 50; the flag ended at [16.8 51.2] with heading 95 and orientation ''RT.

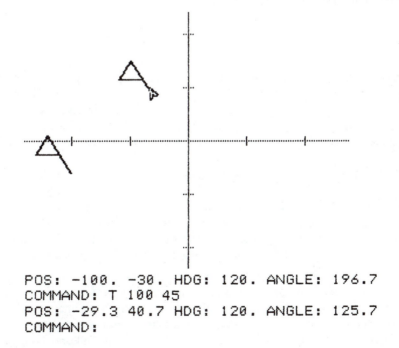

```
POS: -100. -30. HDG: 120. ANGLE: 196.7
COMMAND: T 100 45
POS: -29.3 40.7 HDG: 120. ANGLE: 125.7
COMMAND:
```

Figure 10. Example of a translation. Flag started at [-100 -30] with heading 120 and orientation ''RT. Student entered T 100 45 (100 turtle-steps in a heading of 45 degrees); the flag ended at [-29.3 40.7] with heading 120 and orientation ''RT.

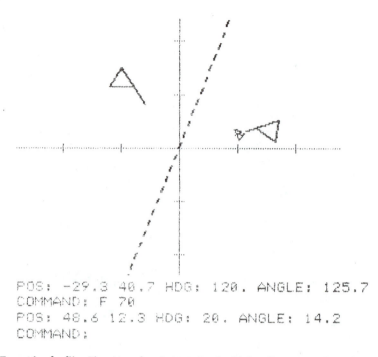

```
POS: -29.3 40.7 HDG: 120. ANGLE: 125.7
COMMAND: F 70
POS: 48.6 12.3 HDG: 20. ANGLE: 14.2
COMMAND:
```

Figure 11. Example of a flip. Flag started at [−29.3 40.7] with heading 120 and orientation ''LT. Student entered F 70 (flip through the line passing through the origin with a heading of 70). Flag ended at [48.6 12.3] with heading 20 and orientation ''RT.

Getting Acquainted. In this section, the students are informed of the screen, the information line, and how they should read the screen. They are introduced to the conventions of polar and rectangular coordinate systems, and to the idea of heading (equivalence class of rays). There is usually quite a lot of discussion about heading, as students typically fix upon the origin as the endpoint of any ray. Their fixation upon the origin leads to inordinate difficulties when they come to heading as a parameter of a translation.

The activities in the Getting Acquainted section are designed with two aims in mind—that we have occasions to discuss the idea of any flag being only one of an infinite number of possibilities, and that the students internalize the motions, that is, construct schemata whereby they can give visual estimates of the effect of a motion upon any particular flag. By "estimate" I mean that the students predict what they will see on the screen as a consequence of commanding the flag to move by a particular motion.

The activities that focus on the idea of the flag as a variable have the students use the GOTO command to make the flag appear on the screen as it does in a diagram in the module. The parameters of GOTO are the flag's *x*- and *y*-coordinates, its heading, and its orientation. The assumption is that in their examination of the pictures, the students differentiate their "flag" schema so that position, heading, and orientation are variable values in it. That is, the aim is that they see any particular flag as an instantiation of its formal properties. I must point out that these activities by themselves are not sufficient to accomplish that aim, nor are they expected to. It has been my experience that most students do not formalize the flag until they develop schemata for transformations of it. More than a few never formalize it.

The activities directed toward having the students internalize each of the motions are similar to those for formalizing the flag. Students are presented with pictures to create (Figure 12), where the means of creation is restricted to using the three motions. The kind of thinking aimed for is: The flag is here and I want to get it there. Which motion should I use? What values shall I put into it? It is hoped that in deciding upon what needs to be done to a flag in order to generate a picture, the students will separate the motions from one another by the effects they have upon the flag's properties.

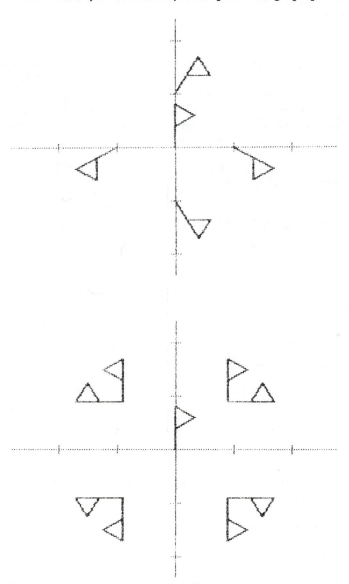

Figure 12.   Pictures for the student to create using rotations, translations, and/or flips.

As an aside, I have found that in class discussions my use of the definite article with "flag" often has a very different meaning for me than it has for my students. When I speak of "the" flag, I normally mean the equivalence class of "particular" flags. Through the beginning of the curriculum, when students use the definite article, they are normally referring to a specific visual image. Our differences in significance became most apparent when we were discussing the general effects of a motion upon the properties of the flag. I was speaking of "the" flag, when from their perspective, sometimes there were many flags and sometimes none. It took some time before we sorted this difficulty out. Afterward, I revised the module so that it directly addressed the notion of the flag as a variable.

Investigations. This section contains two distinct sets of activities and questions. The first focuses on motions as mappings between properties of the flag—that is, at this point in the curriculum the emphasis is on the initial development of motions in the plane as transformations of states. The second set of activities and questions focuses on composition as an operation upon motions. It is in the second set that the students are asked to create a motion as an object in and of itself.

The following are examples of activities and questions that focus on a motion as a mapping between states of the flag.

1.   Do each of the following and fill in the table.

  a.   (GOTO 80 0 90 "LT) CL

  b.   R 40
       R 70
       R −180
       R 60
       R −50

Old heading	New heading
90	130
130	—
—	—
—	—
—	—

(Figure 13 shows the displays that a student would see.)

2.   Complete this statement: If the flag's heading is x, its heading after doing R y will be __.

3.   Do CLS R 670. Does the flag's new heading agree with your generalization in 2?

4.   Do CLS F 45. The result looks like a rotation by −90 degrees. Is it?

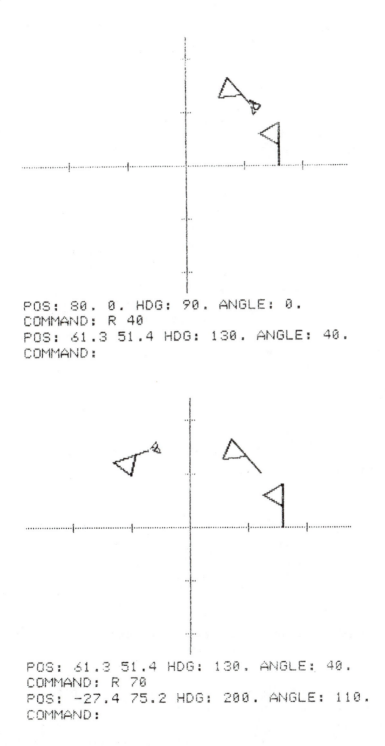

POS: 80. 0. HDG: 90. ANGLE: 0.
COMMAND: R 40
POS: 61.3 51.4 HDG: 130. ANGLE: 40.
COMMAND:

POS: 61.3 51.4 HDG: 130. ANGLE: 40.
COMMAND: R 70
POS: -27.4 75.2 HDG: 200. ANGLE: 110.
COMMAND:

Figure 13. The display as a student does successive rotations. First rotation is R 40; second is R 70; third is R –180. Students are to abstract (*1*) the effect of R *x* upon the heading of the flag, and (*2*) that the flag remains the same distance from the origin. (Continued on next page.)

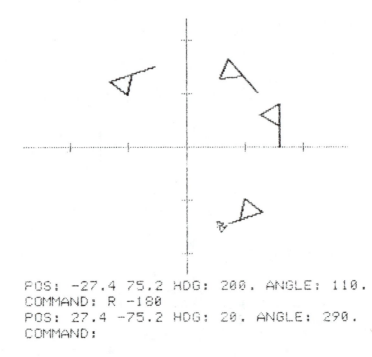

```
POS: -27.4 75.2 HDG: 200. ANGLE: 110.
COMMAND: R -180
POS: 27.4 -75.2 HDG: 20. ANGLE: 290.
COMMAND:
```

Figure 13. Continued.

5. Do (GOTO 80 20 90 "RT) CL RP. Now fill in the following table. Precede each flip with GRP.[4]

Old heading		New heading
90	F 40	—
90	F 70	—
90	F 100	—

(Figure 14 shows the displays that a student would see.)

6. The initial heading of the flag was 40. Someone entered F __. The flag's heading ended up being 110. What was the flip's heading?

---

4. RP tells MOTIONS to record the current figure's position, heading, and orientation. GRP tells MOTIONS to return to the last state recorded by RP.

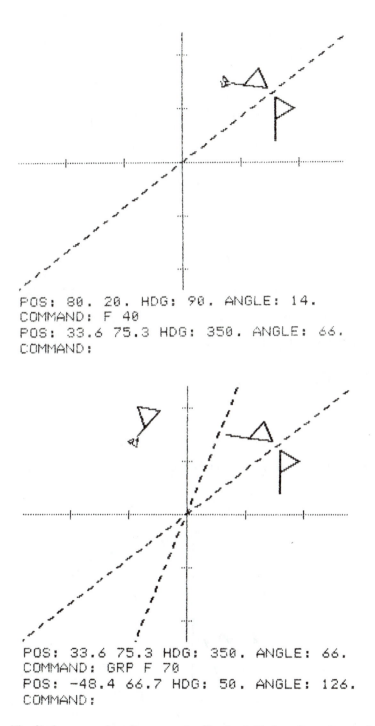

```
POS: 80. 20. HDG: 90. ANGLE: 14.
COMMAND: F 40
POS: 33.6 75.3 HDG: 350. ANGLE: 66.
COMMAND:
```

```
POS: 33.6 75.3 HDG: 350. ANGLE: 66.
COMMAND: GRP F 70
POS: -48.4 66.7 HDG: 50. ANGLE: 126.
COMMAND:
```

Figure 14. The display as a student does successive flips (each flip is performed upon the flag with properties [[80 20] 90 ''RT]. The first flip is F 40; the second is F 70; the third is F 100. Students are to abstract (1) the effect of a flip upon the flag's heading and orientation, and (2) that the segment formed by any point and its image is bisected perpendicularly by the line of the flip.

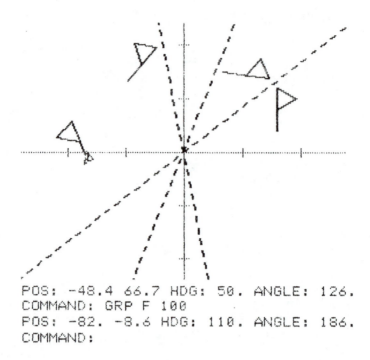

```
POS: -48.4 66.7 HDG: 50. ANGLE: 126.
COMMAND: GRP F 100
POS: -82. -8.6 HDG: 110. ANGLE: 186.
COMMAND:
```

Figure 14. Continued.

7. Give a sequence of motions that will take the flag from position *A* to position *B*.

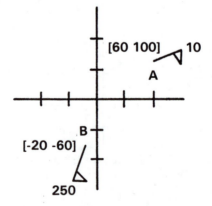

Predictions of the effect of a motion on the flag's position are not stressed, except in very simple situations. To make predictions in general would require a background in trigonometry, which these students typically do not have.

The following problems aim at having the students separate a motion from its operand, and at having them abstract the properties of a motion per se. These problems usually prove difficult for students. This appears to be because they must consolidate the details of a motion into one unit, which requires a great deal of reflection. That is, they must separate the action of mentally carrying out a motion from the experience of applying those actions to a particular flag. Apparently, the schema formed from such abstractions is at a pseudooperative level, as it is not bound to any particular image (visual or mental) or to a flag. However, they must still understand that a figure is being transformed and that it has a position, a heading, and an orientation.

8. Clear the screen.

   a. Do R 30 R 60. Now do R 90.

   b. Compare the two results of a. How are they different? How are they the same?

   c. Do (GOTO −50 −70 120 ''LT) CL. Do R 40 R 35. Now do R 75.

   d. Compare the two results of b. How are they different? How are they the same?

9. What motion is [R 20 R 80]? How is it related to R 20 followed by R 80?

10. Complete this statement: [R x R y] = __.

11. What translation is

   a. [T 60 270 T 80 0]?

   b. [T 30 80 T 40 170]?

   c. [T 50 0 T 80 90]?

12. Predict the effect of [T 80 45 T 60 0]. Test your prediction. Does the result of your test agree with your expectation? Why?

13a. Do CLS. Now do T 60 160 T 40 −50. (See Figure 15.) What translation will take the flag back to its starting position?

   b. Do (GOTO 80 −50 45 ''LT) CL. Now do T 60 160 T 40 −50. (See Figure 16.) What translation will take the flag back to its starting position? [*Hint*: Refer to a.]

14. Do DEF ''TWO.FLIPS [[X Y] F :X F :Y]. (See Appendix for a description of the DEF command.)

   a. What does TWO.FLIPS do?

   b. Test TWO.FLIPS with various inputs. What kind of motion is TWO.FLIPS?

   c. Complete this statement: TWO.FLIPS x y = ____.

   d. What is the effect of [F x TWO.FLIPS y z]?

15. The flag was taken from state A to state B by [F 40 T −100 120 F 30 R 70]. Write a sequence of motions that will take the flag from state B to state A.

The reader should note the use of brackets in the above questions. Whenever you enter a sequence of commands on a single line, MOTIONS carries them out one at a

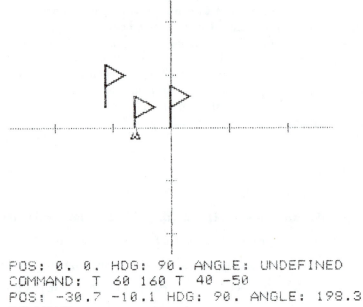

```
POS: 0. 0. HDG: 90. ANGLE: UNDEFINED
COMMAND: T 60 160 T 40 -50
POS: -30.7 -10.1 HDG: 90. ANGLE: 198.3
COMMAND:
```

Figure 15. CLS followed by T 60 160 T 40 −50. What translation will take the flag back to its starting position (in this case, home)?

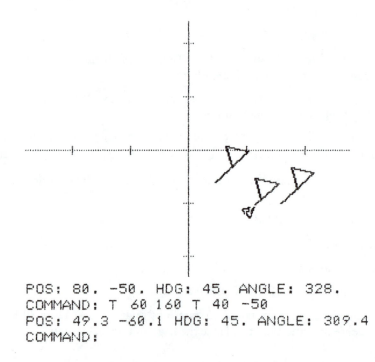

```
POS: 80. -50. HDG: 45. ANGLE: 328.
COMMAND: T 60 160 T 40 -50
POS: 49.3 -60.1 HDG: 45. ANGLE: 309.4
COMMAND:
```

Figure 16. GOTO 80 −50 45 ''LT followed by T 60 160 T 40 −50. What translation will take the flag back to its starting position? (Compare with Figure 15.)

time, just as it would were they entered separately. In other words, MOTIONS shows the effect of each motion upon the flag that is current at the time of its execution. If the sequence is enclosed in brackets, however, MOTIONS shows only the result of the composition of the sequence. In other words, enclosing a sequence of motions within brackets signifies the composition of the sequence.

Each of the activities and questions in the preceding group of problems fits with the general aim of promoting students' reflection of the actions of carrying out a motion to a level of operativity. Perhaps an anecdote will be illustrative.

I was working in my office one evening when two students literally banged on my door. They wanted to share a discovery. They had been working problem 14d and quickly decided that since they knew that the net effect of TWO.FLIPS is a rotation, they would focus upon the net effect of F x. After they entered a flip on the computer, and stared at the screen for a number of minutes, it dawned on them that the net effect of a flip is a flip. This is the discovery that they wanted to share. That a flip is a flip.

I take their discovery (and to them it was a discovery) to mean that up to that point they had looked at finding net effects much in the same way that young children look at finding sums. There was the first motion, the second motion, and the result—three separate and distinct entities. What these students discovered, I believe, is that the net effect (composition) of two motions *is* those two motions, but in combination. That is, I believe that what they discovered had nothing to do with flips. Rather, they created (at least for a time) a composition as an object in and of itself, but one that has an interior.

Symmetries of Plane Figures. There are two reasons for including a study of symmetry in the curriculum. The first is that the investigation of symmetries of plane figures provides a natural occasion to discuss sets of motions that are closed under composition. The second is that it provides an opportunity to pose questions that aim at having the students generalize their concept of a motion in the plane.

16. Enter FIG [PU FD 80 LT 54 PD REPEAT 5 [LT 72 FD 94.02]].

   This defines a regular pentagon centered at the turtle. (See Figure 17.)

   a. Enter CLS.

   (1)   List the inputs to R that will result in the figure coinciding with itself.

   (2)   List the inputs to F that will result in the figure coinciding with itself.

   b. Enter (GOTO 0 0 100 ''RT) CL.

   (1)   Answer 16a(1).

   (2)   Answer 16a(2).

Students typically answer question 16a without considering that their answers assume the figure to be in its home position, and are surprised when their answers no longer work for the figure in a non-home position. They are equally resurprised when they find that in 16b they end up giving the same answer for rotations as before, but different answers for flips.

17 *a.* Define a motion, called F.SYM, for which the inputs that you listed in 16a(2) will make the figure coincide with itself (assuming that the turtle is on the origin).

b. Define a motion, called R.SYM, for which the inputs that you listed in 16a(1) will make the figure coincide with itself, regardless of the figure's position and heading.

Most typically, question 17a is answered

DEF ''F.SYM [[X] F :HDG + :X].

The most typical answers to 17b are

DEF ''R.SYM [[X] (T −:DIST :ANGLE) (R :X) (T :DIST :ANGLE)],

and DEF ''R.SYM [[X] (T −:XCOR 0)   (T −:YCOR 90)   (R :X)   (T :XCOR 0) (T :YCOR 90)].

The following questions focus upon aspects of symmetries in a more general context than did Problem 16.

18 a. The motions M1, M2, M3, and M4 each make a figure coincide with itself. Will [M1 M2 M3 M4] make the figure coincide with itself? Why?

   b. A figure is coincident with itself under each of F 40, F 80, and F 120. What might the figure look like? What is the minimum number of sides in such a figure?

   c. Suppose that someone tells you of finding a figure for which R 180, F 45, F 90, and F 135 are the only motions under which the figure is symmetric (assuming it is at the origin). Do you believe it? Why?

The questions in 18 are the first in the curriculum that begin to focus on the formal properties of motions in the plane. In 18a the students are asked to think strictly in terms of possibilities. Typically, those who have not objectified motions in the plane (as indicated by their performances in other contexts) either will not know how to approach the question, or will answer it in terms of a specific example. For 18b they will try to construct various figures, and then test them against the requirements stated in the question. As far as I can tell, question 18c is accessible only to those who have built an operational structure, for it requires a determination of impossibility. For instance, if F 45 and F 90 are symmetries of the figure, then [F 45 F 90] = R 90 *must* be a symmetry of the figure. Therefore no figure can be symmetric under just those motions.

Systematic Investigations. The previous sections aimed at having the students create motions as objects in and of themselves, and at having them create composition as a binary operation upon motions. The Systematic Investigations section aims at their coalescence of motions in the plane into sets that have intrinsic algebraic structures. Again, the focus is on reasoning formally about sets of motions—reasoning about possibilities. Problem 19 is an example of questions in this section.

19. Find two sets of motions, each with four elements, that form closed addition tables.

Invariably, some students come up with R 0, R 90, R 180, and R 270 as one set, while others come up with R 0, F 0, F 90, and R 180 as another. I count on someone

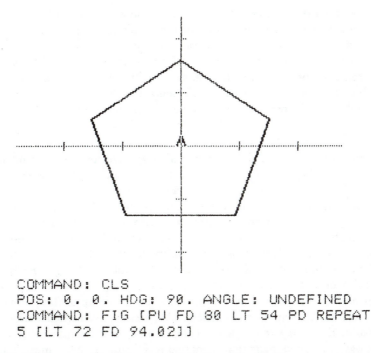

```
COMMAND: CLS
POS: 0. 0. HDG: 90. ANGLE: UNDEFINED
COMMAND: FIG [PU FD 80 LT 54 PD REPEAT
5 [LT 72 FD 94.02]]
```

Figure 17. New figure created by FIG command. T, R, and F will still operate as before.

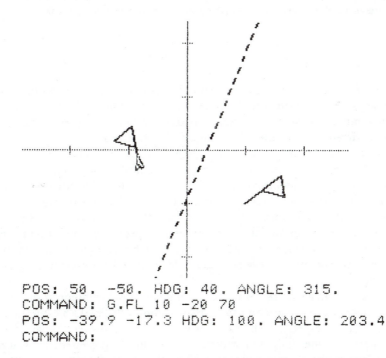

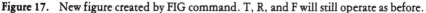

```
POS: 50. -50. HDG: 40. ANGLE: 315.
COMMAND: G.FL 10 -20 70
POS: -39.9 -17.3 HDG: 100. ANGLE: 203.4
COMMAND:
```

Figure 18. Example of a student-defined command, called G.FL (glide-flip), that will allow the student to flip through any line in the plane. In this example, G.FL is defined so that its line is represented by a heading and a point that the line passes through. This example commanded MO-TIONS to flip the plane through the line passing through [10 −20] with a heading of 70.

coming up with something like R 0, F 45, F 135, and R 180 so that I can ask if this set is different enough from the second to count it as a different set of motions. Essentially, the subject of the discussions is isomorphism. To emphasize the point, I ask the students to characterize all sets of motions that have four elements, two of which are flips, that form a closed addition table. As an additional challenge, I ask them to try to find two different sets of motions, each with five elements, that form a closed table. There is, in actuality, only one. The real aim of the question is for them to find this out.

Generalized Motions. This last section aims at a synthesis of the students' various ways of thinking about motions in the plane—as mappings between properties of a figure, as objects to operate upon, and as elements in algebraic structures. The context of the questions and activities in this section is the problem of how to generalize the motions supplied by the microworld so that it will perform rotations about any point in the plane, and perform flips through any line in the plane (Figure 18). I will not discuss this section or the students' difficulties with it at any length. I will just note that it is only after solving the problems of defining a general rotation and a general flip that they come to think of motions in the plane as point mappings, and that they are truly surprised when all of the generalizations that they have made up to this point continue to hold as special cases for motions in general. Apparently, even when working abstractly with motions, they imagined *a figure* being moved, and not the entire plane—even though it was mentioned many times over that it is the plane that is moved, and not just a figure. This suggests to me that there is much to be uncovered before a complete characterization of operativity in transformation geometry can be made.

CONCLUSION

I have taken the position that skilled behavior in mathematical problem solving is a manifestation of highly structured thinking at a number of levels of thought. With that position in mind, I outlined a theoretical basis for design principles of mathematics curricula and offered two examples of curricula designed accordingly.

The examples of curricula that were designed according to these five principles were drawn from integers and transformation geometry. Each was structured so that its aim was first to have the students construct the objects of the subject matter as transformations between states, and then to reconstruct them as objects themselves to be transformed. The case of transformation geometry was the more intricate of the two, as both the states and the transformations are more complex than is the case with integers.

The preservice elementary school teachers in my courses found the curriculum for transformation geometry to be very difficult. Many found the one for integers to be difficult as well.

The case of integers deserves a special comment. It was common at the outset for the students in my courses to attempt to translate complex INTEGERS expressions into x's, y's, $+$'s, and $-$'s, especially when all they wanted was an answer. Apparently they tried to assimilate the questions into structures they already possessed, as would anyone. However, one must not assume too much about the nature of those structures. As part of the introductory lecture to integers, I asked the students why it is *reasonable* (as opposed to correct) to rewrite $-(x - -y)$ as $-x - y$. There was not a single response that suggested other than an instrumental understanding (Skemp, 1978) of signed expressions.

Nor could I elicit a response that referred to quantities. Approximately three weeks after they had been through the INTEGERS curriculum, I gave them the expression $-(-x + y) = x + -y$, and asked them *why* removing the parentheses and changing the signs is a reasonable thing to do. They resorted, without my encouragement, to an INTEGERS interpretation, or they said nothing at all. This suggests to me that prior to working with the INTEGERS microworld they had a weak semantic base, if they had one at all, for the rules by which they transformed algebraic expressions. This further suggests that those who do develop mental operations in regard to algebra do so as reflections of transformations of quantities.

The Missing Link

I hope the reader has not developed the impression that the curricula discussed in the case studies are teacher-independent. On the contrary, they are actually more dependent upon the teacher than are conventional curricula. Moreover, I can easily imagine that in the hands of some teachers we would see very little difference, in terms of what students learn, between them and non-problem-based curricula. All it would take is a teacher whose approach is to demonstrate "the way" to solve problems "like this."

Underlying the case studies was an assumption that instruction would be in the hands of teachers who are thoroughly intimate with the subject matter, and intimate in two ways. Ideally, teachers should not only possess the cognitive structures that the curriculum aims for in the students, but possess them at a reflected level. They should understand the subject matter both intuitively and formally.

Second, teachers must be—for want of a better word—choreographers. They must have a structure that they can "dance" through as they confront the obstacles that are inevitable in the flow of classroom interactions. To my way of thinking, the only structure that can provide a basis for such flexibility is a personal model of the genesis of the cognitive objectives.

Another issue in the case studies was student affect. In my experience, it was not uncommon, at the outset of a course, for students to go through an activity, record the information that they generated, and then say, "I don't understand what the answer is supposed to be." Many students never stopped being "answer" oriented, and they became extremely frustrated. If getting right answers wasn't the name of the game, then they didn't know what the game was. They did not understand that "the answer" was most typically a method, or a generalization of a method, and not a number. It was extremely frustrating to me not to be able to influence those students' perspective on mathematics.

The Role of Cognitive Science

My concluding remarks are on the role that cognitive science can play as an inspiration for problem-based mathematics curriculum development. Reif (1980) and Larkin (1980) each commented that the nature of skilled problem solving and cognition is well enough understood that educators should look to cognitive science for guidance in how to bring them about. My assessment, however, is that at this moment the role of cognitive science in mathematics curriculum development should be minor and indirect.

I have three reasons for such an assessment. The first is that the models of mathematical problem solving one finds in cognitive science tend to do their jobs all too single-mindedly—and all too knowledgeably, in the sense that a model knows what it means to solve a problem. I have yet to see a problem-solving program daydream about an upcoming fishing trip while working a problem, or be distracted by a stray, but related, thought. Nor have I seen a program play a guessing game with the questioner as to what type of answer, among all the worldly categories it possesses, the questioner wants (Thompson, 1982b). Does the questioner want an answer, an historical account of the answer, or an explanation of why an answer has to be correct? The decision is usually made by the programmer.

The second reason is that, as far as I can tell, little attention has been given to the issue of the development of mathematical objects in people's thinking. Numbers become things to most children, while for quite awhile they were not; operations become things to some high school students; functions, groups, classes, categories, and functors become things to mathematicians. Until cognitive science deals with the nature and development of mathematical objects, I see little that it can offer as guidance for developing problem-based mathematics curricula.

The third, and most important reason for believing that cognitive science is of limited help in developing mathematics curricula is that most models of mathematical cognition fail to take into account the conceptual bases from which cognitions arise. For example, Silver (in press) found that young adults' thinking about operations on rational numbers is tremendously influenced by the specific models of rational numbers that they bring to mind (e.g., pie charts and measuring cups). Admittedly, mental representations have been of interest in cognitive science for some time now, but the issue that seems to be left aside is that of a mental re-presentation of an action upon a representation. As pointed out in the discussion of integers as mathematical objects, a transformation is not identifiable with the states upon which it acts. It can only be identified with a class of states, and in fact genetically predetermines that class. In my way of thinking, until the notion of action is brought into investigations of mathematical cognition, we will get little guidance from cognitive science regarding the promotion of operative thought in a subject matter area.

I do not mean to give the impression that cognitive science is irrelevant to mathematics education. I find the work of Lawler (1981) and diSessa (1982) to be fascinating and very much in line with the aims I have expressed here, but theirs seems to be a minority view in cognitive science.

The recent focus in cognitive science on investigations of structures in problem solving has been highly illuminating about the ways we *don't* want students to understand mathematics—for example, understanding mathematics as consisting largely of collections of routine algorithms and associated stereotypical problems (Hinsley et al., 1977). Also, the computer metaphor of cognitive science provides a powerful way to think about mathematical cognition. But we should not reify the central processing unit; we should not forget that the computer metaphor is only a metaphor (cf. Simon, 1972).

Where, then, can mathematics education find guidance for developing problem-based curricula? I find Piaget's genetic epistemology to be most helpful, but only in that it frames the task of influencing others' thinking. It sets design principles for the theory of cognition that will underly the specifications of the cognitive objectives (recalling that cognitive objectives must include a developmental side).

The details of a curriculum must come from an interaction between conceptual analyses of the subject matter (knowledge as held by competent knowers) and investigations of the genesis of that knowledge vis-à-vis instruction. That is, mathematics education must look more to itself than to any other source for guidance in developing problem-based mathematics curricula.

REFERENCES

Abelson, H., & diSessa, A. *Turtle geometry: The computer as a medium for exploring mathematics.* Cambridge, MA: The MIT Press, 1981.

Anderson, J. *Language, memory, and thought.* Hillsdale, NJ: Lawrence Erlbaum Associates, 1976.

Anderson, J., Greeno, J., Kline, P., & Neves, D. Acquisition of problem-solving skill. In J. Anderson (Ed.), *Cognitive skills and their acquisition.* Hillsdale, NJ: Lawrence Erlbaum Associates, 1981.

Briars, D.J., & Larkin, J.H. *An integrated model of skill in solving elementary word problems* (Technical Report A.C.P. No. 2). Pittsburgh: Carnegie-Mellon University, Department of Psychology, November 1982.

Brown, G. *Laws of form.* New York: Julian Press, 1972.

Carpenter, T.P., Hiebert, J., & Moser, J.M. Problem structure and first-grade children's initial solution processes for simple addition and subtraction problems. *Journal for Research in Mathematics Education* 12, 27–39, 1981.

Dewey, J. *Experience and education.* New York: Collier Books, 1963. (Originally published in 1945.)

diSessa, A. Unlearning Aristotelian physics: A study of knowledge-based learning. *Cognitive Science* 6, 37–76, 1982.

Duncker, K. On problem solving. *Psychological Monographs* 58(270), 1–112, 1945.

Eisner, E. *Cognition and curriculum: On deciding what to teach.* London: Longman, 1982.

Gagné, R. Some issues in the psychology of mathematics instruction. *Journal for Research in Mathematics Education* 14, 7–8, 1983.

Greeno, J. Indefinite goals in well-structured problems. *Psychological Review* 83, 479–91, 1976.

Greeno, J. Some examples of cognitive task analysis with instructional applications. In R.E. Snow, P.A. Federico, & W.E. Montague (Eds.), *Aptitude, learning, and instruction. Volume 2: Cognitive process analysis of learning and problem solving.* Hillsdale, NJ: Lawrence Erlbaum Associates, 1980.

Hayes-Roth, B. *Human planning processes* (Rand Report R-2670-ONR). Santa Monica, CA: Rand Corporation, 1980.

Hayes-Roth, F., Klahr, P., & Mostow, D. Advice taking and knowledge refinement: An iterative view of skill acquisition. In J. Anderson (Ed.), *Cognitive skills and their acquisition.* Hillsdale, NJ: Lawrence Erlbaum Associates, 1981.

Herstein, I. *Topics in algebra* (2nd ed.). Lexington, MA: Xerox College Publishing, 1975.

Hinsely, D., Hayes, J., & Simon, H. From words to equations: Meaning and representation in algebra word problems. In M. Just & P. Carpenter (Eds.), *Cognitive processes in comprehension.* Hillsdale, NJ: Lawrence Erlbaum Associates, 1977.

Inhelder, B., & Piaget, J. *The early growth of logic in the child.* New York: W.W. Norton, 1969.

Krutetskii, V. *The psychology of mathematical abilities in schoolchildren.* (J. Teller, Trans., J. Kilpatrick & I. Wirszup, Eds.) Chicago: University of Chicago Press, 1976.

Lakatos, I. Infinite regress and the foundations of mathematics. *Aristotelian Society Supplementary Volume* 36, 156–84, 1962.

Lakatos, I. *Proofs and refutations: The logic of mathematical discovery.* London: Cambridge University Press, 1976.

Larkin, J. Teaching problem solving in physics: The psychological laboratory and the practical classroom. In D.T. Tuma & F. Reif (Eds.), *Problem solving and education: Issues in teaching and research.* Hillsdale, NJ: Lawrence Erlbaum Associates, 1980.

Lawler, R. The progressive construction of mind. *Cognitive Science* 5, 1–30, 1981.

Lenat, D. *The nature of heuristics* (Cognitive and Instructional Science Series CIS-12 [SSL-81-1]). Palo Alto, CA: Xerox PARC, 1981.

Lunzer, E. Introduction. In B. Inhelder & J. Piaget, *The early growth of logic in the child.* New York: W.W. Norton, 1969.

MacKay, D. *Information, mechanism, and meaning.* Cambridge, MA: The MIT Press, 1969.

Manna, Z., & Waldinger, R. *Synthesis: Dreams → Programs* (Report No. STAN-CS-77-630). Stanford, CA: Stanford University, Computer Science Department, 1977.

Manna, Z., & Waldinger, R. DEDALUS — The Deductive Algorithm Ur-Synthesizer. In *Proceedings of the National Computing Conference,* Anaheim, CA, 1978.

Neves, D., & Anderson, J. Knowledge compilation: Mechanisms for the automatization of cognitive skills. In J. Anderson (Ed.), *Cognitive skills and their acquisition.* Hillsdale, NJ: Lawrence Erlbaum Associates, 1981.

Newell, A., & Simon, H.A. *Human problem solving.* Englewood Cliffs, NJ: Prentice-Hall, 1972.

Papert, S. *Mindstorms: Children, computers, and powerful ideas.* New York: Basic Books, 1980.

Piaget, J. *Psychology of intelligence.* London: Routledge & Kegan Paul, 1951.

Piaget, J. Development and learning. In R. Ripple & U. Rockcastle (Eds.), *Piaget rediscovered.* Ithaca, NY: Cornell University, School of Education, 1964.

Piaget, J. *Six psychological studies.* New York: Basic Books, 1968.

Piaget, J. *Genetic epistemology.* New York: W.W. Norton, 1970.

Piaget, J. *The child and reality.* New York: Penguin Books, 1976.

Piaget, J. *Recherches sur l'abstraction réflechissante* (Vol. I). Paris: Presses Universitaires de France, 1977. (Translation provided by E. von Glasersfeld.)

Piaget, J., Grize, T., Szeminska, A., & Bangh, V. *Epistemology and psychology of functions.* Dordrecht, The Netherlands: D. Reidel, 1977.

Piaget, J., & Inhelder, B. *The psychology of the child.* New York: Basic Books, 1969.

Polya, G. *How to solve it* (2nd ed.). Princeton, NJ: Princeton University Press, 1973.

Powers, W. *Behavior: The control of perception.* Chicago: Aldine, 1973.

Powers, W. Quantitative analysis of purposive systems: Some spadework at the foundation of scientific psychology. *Psychological Review* 85, 417–35, 1978.

Reif, F. Theoretical and educational concerns with problem solving: Bridging the gaps with human cognitive engineering. In D.T. Tuma & F. Reif (Eds.), *Problem solving and education: Issues in teaching and research.* Hillsdale, NJ: Lawrence Erlbaum Associates, 1980.

Resnick, L. Task analysis in instructional design: Some cases from mathematics. In D. Klahr (Ed.), *Cognition and instruction.* Hillsdale, NJ: Lawrence Erlbaum Associates, 1975.

Resnick, L. *The psychology of mathematics for instruction.* Hillsdale, NJ: Lawrence Erlbaum Associates, 1981.

Resnick, L. A developmental theory of number understanding. In H.P. Ginsburg (Ed.), *The development of mathematical thinking.* New York: Academic Press, 1983.

Riley, M., Greeno, J., & Heller, J. The development of children's problem-solving ability in arithmetic. In H.P. Ginsburg (Ed.), *The development of mathematical thinking.* New York: Academic Press, 1983.

Sacerdoti, E. *A structure for plans and behavior.* New York: Elsevier, 1977.

Schank, R., & Abelson, R. *Scripts, goals, plans, and understanding.* Hillsdale, NJ: Lawrence Erlbaum Associates, 1977.

Schank, R., & Riesbeck, C. *Inside computer understanding.* Hillsdale, NJ: Lawrence Erlbaum Associates, 1981.

Silver, E. Probing young adults' thinking about rational numbers. In *Focus on Learning Problems in Mathematics.* In press.

Simon, H. On the development of the processor. In S. Farnham-Diggory (Ed.), *Information processing in children*. New York: Academic Press, 1972.

Skemp, R. Relational and instrumental understanding. *Arithmetic Teacher* 26, 9–15, 1978.

Skemp, R. *Intelligence, learning, and action*. London: John Wiley & Sons, 1979.

Steffe, L. On a model for teaching young children mathematics. In A. Osborne (Ed.), *Models for learning mathematics*. Columbus, OH: ERIC Clearinghouse for Science, Mathematics, and Environmental Education, 1976.

Thompson, P. *Children's schemata in solving problems involving whole-number numeration*. Paper presented at the annual meeting of the American Educational Research Association, New York, March 1982(a).

Thompson, P. *A theoretical framework for understanding children's concepts of whole number numeration*. Unpublished doctoral dissertation, University of Georgia, 1982(b).

Thompson, P. Were lions to speak, we wouldn't understand. *Journal of Mathematical Behavior* 3(2), 147–65, 1982(c).

Vergnaud, G. A classification of cognitive tasks and operations of thought involved in addition and subtraction problems. In T.P. Carpenter, J.M. Moser, & T.A. Romberg (Eds.), *Addition and subtraction: A cognitive perspective*. Hillsdale, NJ: Lawrence Erlbaum Associates, 1982.

von Glasersfeld, E. Cybernetics, experience, and the concept of self. In M. Ozer (Ed.), *Toward the more human use of human beings*. Boulder, CO: Westview Press, 1978.

von Glasersfeld, E. On reflection and abstraction. In preparation.

Weaver, F. Interpretations of number operations and symbolic representations of addition and subtraction. In T.P. Carpenter, J.M. Moser, & T.A. Romberg (Eds.), *Addition and subtraction: A cognitive perspective*. Hillsdale, NJ: Lawrence Erlbaum Associates, 1982.

Wertheimer, M. *Productive thinking*. New York: Harper & Row, 1959. (Originally published in 1945.)

APPENDIX: SUBSET OF COMMANDS
AVAILABLE IN MOTIONS

Command	*Action*
CL	Cleans the screen; erases all but the current figure.
CLS	Clears the screen; places the figure at home position (HDG 90, POS 0 0, and orientation right).
DEF ''name [list of commands]	Defines ''name as the name of *[list of commands]*, where the commands in the list are among those allowed by MOTIONS. MOTIONS will respond *''name DEFINED''* if it accepts the definition.
	If the commands in *[list of commands]* take variable input, then the list must begin with a list of the variable names. A variable name must be preceded by a colon within the definition itself. The colon means ''value of the following name.''

Example: DEF ''TWO.FLIPS [[X Y] F :X F :Y] defines a motion named *TWO.FLIPS* that takes two inputs, and performs two
flips. The first flip is performed about the line defined by the
first input; the second flip is performed about the line defined by the second input.

F <degrees>   Flips the plane through the line that passes through the
origin at an angle of measure *<degrees>*.

GRP   Places the current figure at the position, heading, and
orientation last recorded by RP.

ID   Identity motion—leaves plane as it is.

R <degrees>   Rotates the plane about the origin through an angle of
measure *<degrees>*.

RP   Records the current figure's position, heading, and orientation. (See *GRP*.)

T <distance> <heading>   Translates the plane *<distance>* turtle steps in a heading of
<heading>.

MOTIONS maintains several variable values to which reference may be made within a
definition. These are:

Variable	*Value*
:XCOR	The current figure's x-coordinate.
:YCOR	The current figure's y-coordinate.
:HDG	The current figure's heading.
:ANGLE	The measure of the angle formed by the current figure's posi-tion, the origin, and the positive x-axis.

For example, T:XCOR 180 translates the plane so that the current figure has an
x-coordinate of 0.

Cognitive Theory and Curriculum Design: A Discussion of Thompson's Paper

James G. Greeno

University of Pittsburgh

Thompson's paper is an admirable contribution to this book. It includes a serious discussion of some important theoretical principles along with examples of implemented curriculum materials that were designed with those principles in mind. The combination of theoretical discussion and concrete instructional proposals is less common than it might be, and is a strong positive feature.

I begin my comments with a brief discussion of the relation between theoretical principles and the practical problem of designing curriculum materials. Theories can be viewed as a source of heuristic principles for curriculum design, rather than implying specific requirements for curriculum that can be deduced.

Second, I comment on Thompson's view of mathematical knowledge and its influence on the curriculum materials that he described. Thompson's conception of mathematical knowledge is one that I endorse strongly, and it is consistent with important recent developments in cognitive science, as it is with the Piagetian ideas that Thompson discussed. As his examples of curriculum indicate, the theoretical ideas are useful in the design of instruction. Even so, more detailed studies of learning processes could give a stronger evidential base for the ideas, and they would contribute additional clarifying information for cognitive theory.

My third comment is concerned with some recent developments in cognitive psychology. I consider these to be compatible with and complementary to the principles that Thompson presented. One of these developments, computational models that simulate performance in problem solving and reasoning, involves the use of more specific theoretical analyses of knowledge that students acquire when they learn successfully. Development of these more specific analyses of cognitive structures and processes would add significant information relevant to the kinds of principles that Thompson discussed. A second development involves analyses of the acquisition of cognitive skill. These analyses provide understanding of important processes of learning that are left implicit in Thompson's analysis. The third development involves analyses in which understanding of general mathematical principles is considered along with knowledge of procedures for computation and solving problems. These analyses provide a promising beginning for the task of understanding the integration of conceptual understanding and cognitive skills; I think they also can help us avoid the radical subjectivism of the constructivist epistemology that Thompson endorsed.

INTERACTIONS OF THEORY AND PRACTICE

Theories of cognitive processes can provide heuristic principles for use in the design of curriculum. Heuristic principles can suggest components and features of a curriculum, but they are weaker than axioms, which have deductive consequences.

Consider the task of designing a curriculum, or even a small part of a curriculum. It is a problem-solving task with the goal of constructing a sequence of activities that will give students new knowledge and skill in a domain. It is an ill-defined problem, as are many problems of design (cf. Greeno & Simon, 1984). The designer has a great many alternatives available, and the various possible curricula differ in a great many ways. Heuristic principles for an ill-defined problem can serve as guides in the selection of activities for inclusion in the curriculum, and they can provide criteria for judging whether certain desirable features of the curriculum have been included in materials that have been constructed.

The view that theories should provide heuristic principles for curriculum design is different, I believe, than the idea of a theory-based curriculum that is implicit in many discussions. In many discussions, we seem to consider theoretical principles as axioms, which would allow the contents of curricula to be derived. This is misleading in several ways. One is that it leads to an expectation that a theory should provide guidance for all the questions that arise in curriculum design. If we consider theories as potential resources for curriculum design, we could expect to get considerable help from a theory even if it did not address all of the questions that we recognize as important in the instructional setting. Indeed, we might expect to find heuristic principles in different theories that could be used productively in combination to address different issues of significance.

A second point about the relation of cognitive theory and curriculum design is that it is a two-way street. There are potential contributions to cognitive theory to be obtained in the design and evaluation of curriculum, just as there are important contributions to curriculum design from cognitive theory. Information about the kinds of instructional activities that lead to successful learning can be important sources of information about the nature of learning and the characteristics of knowledge and skill that are required for successful performance of significant tasks that students learn to perform.

CONCEPTUALIZATION OF MATHEMATICAL KNOWLEDGE

Thompson presents a view of mathematical knowledge that plays an important heuristic role in the curriculum materials that he developed. Thompson considers mathematical knowledge to be a structure of thinking processes, consisting of schemata for performing cognitive activities. The relation between concepts and skill is different in Thompson's conceptualization than in a view that we often encounter. Conceptual understanding and cognitive skill often are considered as alternatives that have to compete for instructional time. But in this newer view, which Thompson uses, skills and concepts are considered as different aspects of the same knowledge. Then the instructional problem is to design experiences in which skill and understanding will both be acquired in an integrated fashion. This is a more challenging task than simply choosing between skills and concepts, but it also seems to be a more valid objective for instruction.

A second component of Thompson's view of knowledge involves the importance of operative thinking and the idea that knowledge is transformed through reflective abstraction. Early forms of knowledge include properties and relations of objects and operators that change those properties and relations. In a more advanced form of knowledge the representation is changed so those properties, relations, and operators function as objects of thought, enabling more powerful understanding and organization of cognitive procedures.

A third idea in Thompson's conceptualization involves the nature of a curriculum. Thompson views learning as activity in which the learner constructs new knowledge. With this conceptualization, the curriculum is considered as a set of activities in which the desired structure of thinking processes can be constructed by the students.

I find Thompson's conceptualization of knowledge quite agreeable, partly because there has been a growing convergence toward these views involving theoretical and empirical research in several traditions. Thompson's discussion emphasized the source of his ideas in Piagetian theory, although, as he implied, it involves a significant extension of the Piagetian notion to get to it in its present form. I will mention briefly a few recent discussions in cognitive science that contribute similar insights.

First, the conceptualization of knowledge as a multilevel structure of thinking processes has been worked out in some detail. The idea was developed initially by Sacerdoti (1977) in the form of a model called NOAH, for Networks of Action Hierarchies. NOAH has a knowledge base of action schemata that it uses to reason about tasks. It uses the schemata in forming structured plans for achieving goals. The idea has proved to be very useful for psychological models of skilled performance in arithmetic (Brown & Burton, 1978), in geometry proof exercises (Greeno, Magone, & Chaiklin, 1979), and in computer software design (Polson, Atwood, Jeffries, & Turner, 1981).

The second idea in Thompson's conceptualization, concerning the growth of objects of thought, involves the question of representation. This question has been central in the theory of problem solving and reasoning. The issue arises in concrete form in models of specific problem-solving processes, where the kinds of objects available in the representation determine the reasoning processes that can be used. This has been studied in detail for representations of puzzles based on alternative instructions (Hayes & Simon, 1974), and for representations of text problems in physics (Larkin, 1983; McDermott & Larkin, 1978). Discussions of the general question have been given by McCarthy and Hayes (1969) and by Greeno (1983a).

The third idea, that knowledge is constructed by the learner's activity, is one of the main insights contributed by behaviorists such as Skinner (1938) and Hull (1943), who viewed responding by the learner as a necessary condition for learning. More recent cognitive analyses of learning have shared this feature, but have been specific about the cognitive processes and concepts that are acquired and the conditions for their acquisition. These include analyses of learning from instructional examples to solve geometry proof exercises (Anderson, 1982) and algebra equations (Neves, 1981), as well as spontaneous modifications of cognitive procedures that occur during problem solving in arithmetic (Neches, 1981) and in puzzles such as the Tower of Hanoi (Anzai & Simon, 1979).

A major strength of Thompson's paper is his use of these ideas about knowledge and learning as guiding principles for design of the curriculum materials that he described. The ideas of mathematical knowledge as a structure of thinking processes and of learning as a set of activities intended to produce transitions from properties and relations to operative thought are applied in a consistent and clear way. This provides support for the utility of the ideas as heuristic principles in the design of curriculum.

The development of curriculum materials guided by theoretical principles is an excellent step. The agenda for future activity should include some more detailed analysis of learning and performance of the tasks used in the instruction. Methods for detailed study of cognitive processes involved in learning, problem solving, and reasoning are now quite familiar in the form of teaching experiments. Empirical studies of the learning processes involved when students are working with Thompson's curriculum materials could provide stronger evidence about relations between the theoretical principles underlying the materials and the ways in which the materials work to produce learning. Such studies would also provide valuable information to extend or modify our theoretical accounts of learning and the nature of mathematical knowledge.

SOME RECENT DEVELOPMENTS IN COGNITIVE PSYCHOLOGY

In the preceding section, I discussed the main points of Thompson's characterization of mathematical knowledge, and indicated that those ideas are consistent with significant recent developments in cognitive science. In this section, I discuss some additional developments in cognitive psychology that are complementary to the ideas that Thompson used, and that also could provide useful heuristic principles for design of curriculum materials in mathematics instruction.

Detailed Characterizations of Learning Outcomes

A major achievement of cognitive psychology in the past 15 years has been the development of tools for analyzing knowledge that is required for performance in complex tasks, including tasks used in instruction. Examples include Brown and Burton's (1978) analysis of cognitive procedures in subtraction, analyses by Briars and Larkin (1982) and by Riley, Greeno, and Heller (1983) of knowledge for solving word problems in arithmetic, and my own analyses (Greeno, 1978, 1983b) of knowledge for solving proof exercises in high school geometry. These analyses all have been developed in the form of computer programs that simulate the performance of students. Different versions of the programs simulate students who perform correctly and students who make errors; thus, the analysis characterizes knowledge both in a correct form and in one or more partial or incorrect forms, all of which are based on performance of students.

Use of computer programming to formulate these characterizations is only a means to a scientific end, of course. To write a computer program that solves instructional problems, we are required to make our hypotheses more specific than the characterizations of knowledge that we usually have. For example, a model of students' geometry problem solving includes hypotheses about specific problem-solving strategies that are not evident in the text materials or, I believe, in most classroom instruction. This domain-specific strategic knowledge adds a significant idea in the theory of problem solving, since it contrasts with general problem-solving strategies such as means-ends analysis characterized in earlier theoretical discussions (e.g., Newell & Simon, 1972). It also provides a more specific characterization of the knowledge that students must acquire in order to succeed in the course.

Another example of knowledge that is made more explicit when definite process models are formulated involves knowledge for representing problems. In most discussions of solving word problems in arithmetic and algebra, it is recognized that students have to understand the problems, but no specific description of that process is provided. To form a model that simulates successful performance, we are required to make definite hypotheses about that process and the knowledge that makes it possible (Briars & Larkin, 1982; Riley et al., 1983).

In both of these cases, and in others, the theoretical and instructional advances that result from developing simulation models involve a better understanding of knowledge that usually is implicit. The examples that I have mentioned involve implicit strategic knowledge and implicit knowledge for representing problems. A model of the problem-solving process includes explicit hypotheses about implicit knowledge, and therefore provides a basis for developing more effective instruction for training. An example is discussed by Heller and Hungate (this volume), involving a definite instructional method for training physics students to represent the information in physics problems.

The capability of formulating definite computational models that simulate the knowledge that students acquire in instruction could make a significant contribution to the understanding and evaluation of curriculum materials such as those discussed by Thompson. Development of such models for the tasks that Thompson discussed would clarify some of the concepts involved, such as the differences in cognitive structure brought about by reflective abstraction. We could also expect to identify ways in which the instructional materials are particularly effective as well as sources of difficulty in achieving the cognitive objectives of the instruction.

Acquisition of Skills and Concepts

Some guidance for instructional design comes from understanding the prospective outcome of instruction, and the kinds of models that I discussed in "Detailed Characterizations of Learning Outcomes" can contribute to that. Additional help can come from analyses of the processes of acquiring knowledge, and some substantial progress has been made in the development of models that simulate acquisition of new skills and concepts. Neves (1981) developed a model of acquiring procedures for solving algebra equations from experience with example problems. Neches (1981) formulated a model that modifies its procedures, and simulates changes that occur in the counting methods that preschool children use to solve addition problems (Groen & Resnick, 1977). Anderson (1982) developed a model that simulates acquisition of procedures for solving geometry proof exercises, including acquisition of some of the strategic knowledge that is required.

In addition to these models that are concerned mainly with acquiring new cognitive procedures, there also have been some analyses that include acquisition of significant conceptual understanding. Anzai and Simon (1979) studied learning from practice with the Tower of Hanoi puzzle and concluded that a significant new strategic concept was acquired; they simulated this acquisition in a computational model. Resnick (1983) described a model that simulates children's understanding of quantitative concepts in subtraction, acquired from instruction using place-value blocks. I (Greeno, 1983b) observed geometry students who had learned to solve proof problems involving segments, and were given problems about angles that had the same structure of part-whole relations among the objects. A model was developed that simulates acquisition of knowledge from the segment problems, with the problem-solving procedures integrated in a part-whole schema, providing a basis for transfer to the novel problems involving angles.

These models of learning provide a further potential resource for the design of curriculum materials. The models of skill acquisition provide useful guidance regarding an aspect of Thompson's instruction that he did not emphasize, namely, the requirement of acquiring low-level skills involved in performing the basic tasks that make up the instructional activities. Even though Thompson's main focus was on more general conceptual structures, the students must also learn to perform the basic tasks, and models of learning at that level could provide helpful principles for presentation of the tasks to reduce the likelihood of interference from lack of low-level knowledge. The more conceptual concerns of Thompson's instruction are addressed in the models that have begun to characterize acquisition of cognitive procedures in ways that are integrated with conceptual structures.

Integration of Understanding and Skill

The third set of recent developments that I will mention involves analyses of understanding of general mathematical principles. Understanding of the principle of deductive proof has been simulated in a model that discriminates between valid proofs and arguments that are not deductively valid (Greeno, 1983b). Preschool children's implicit understanding of principles of number and counting, such as cardinality and one-to-one correspondence, has been characterized in a hypothesis of conceptual competence that underlies procedures of counting (Greeno, Riley, & Gelman, 1984).

These developments have implications regarding a point that Thompson made about epistemology. The version of constructivism that Thompson endorsed is quite radically subjective, involving the view that mathematical principles are the constructions that individuals form in their mental activities. I would prefer a more moderate view, one that allows for correct knowledge of concepts and principles as well as an analysis of cognitive variations such as incomplete knowledge and misconceptions. The issue is complex and subtle, and we have only begun to make significant headway on it, but the analyses now available seem promising for the possibility of characterizing cognitive structures and their relation to correct principles in a coherent way.

REFERENCES

Anderson, J.R. Acquisition of cognitive skill. *Psychological Review* 89, 396–406, 1982.

Anzai, Y., & Simon, H.A. The theory of learning by doing. *Psychological Review* 86, 124–40, 1979.

Briars, D.J., & Larkin, J.H. *An integrated model of skill in solving elementary word problems* (Technical Report A.C.P. No. 2). Pittsburgh: Carnegie-Mellon University, Department of Psychology, November 1982.

Brown, J.S., & Burton, R.R. Diagnostic models for procedural bugs in basic mathematical skills. *Cognitive Science* 2, 155–92, 1978.

Greeno, J.G. A study of problem solving. In R. Glaser (Ed.), *Advances in instructional psychology* (Vol. 1). Hillsdale, NJ: Lawrence Erlbaum Associates, 1978.

Greeno, J.G. Conceptual entities. In D. Gentner and A.L. Stevens (Eds.), *Mental models.* Hillsdale, NJ: Lawrence Erlbaum Associates, 1983(a).

Greeno, J.G. Forms of understanding in mathematical problem solving. In S.G. Paris, G.M. Olson, & H.W. Stevenson (Eds.), *Learning and motivation in the classroom.* Hillsdale, NJ: Lawrence Erlbaum Associates, 1983(b).

Greeno, J.G., Magone, M.E., & Chaiklin, S. Theory of constructions and set in problem solving. *Memory and Cognition* 7, 445–61, 1979.

Greeno, J.G., Riley, M.S., & Gelman, R. Conceptual competence and children's counting. *Cognitive Psychology* 16(1), 94–143, 1984.

Greeno, J.G., & Simon, H.A. *Problem solving and reasoning* (Technical Report No. UOITT/LRDC/ONR/APS-14). Pittsburgh: University of Pittsburgh, Learning Research and Development Center, 1984.

Groen, G.J., & Resnick, L.B. Can preschool children invent addition algorithms? *Journal of Educational Psychology* 69, 645–52, 1977.

Hayes, J.R., & Simon, H.A. Understanding problem instructions. In L.W. Gregg (Ed.), *Knowledge and cognition.* Hillsdale, NJ: Lawrence Erlbaum Associates, 1974.

Hull, C.L. *Principles of behavior: An introduction to behavior theory.* New York: Appleton-Century-Crofts, 1943.

Larkin, J.H. The role of problem representation in physics. In D. Gentner & A.L. Stevens (Eds.), *Mental models.* Hillsdale, NJ: Lawrence Erlbaum Associates, 1983.

McCarthy, J., & Hayes, P.J. Some philosophical problems from the standpoint of artificial intelligence. *Machine Intelligence* 4, 463–502, 1969.

McDermott, J., & Larkin, J.H. Representing textbook physics problems. In *Proceedings of the Second National Conference, Canadian Society for Computational Studies of Intelligence.* Toronto: University of Toronto, 1978.

Neches, R. *Models of heuristic procedure modification.* Unpublished doctoral dissertation, Carnegie-Mellon University, 1981.

Neves, P.M. *Learning procedures from examples.* Unpublished doctoral dissertation, Carnegie-Mellon University, 1981.

Newell, A., & Simon, H.A. *Human problem solving.* Englewood Cliffs, NJ: Prentice-Hall, 1972.

Polson, P., Atwood, M.E., Jeffries, R., & Turner, A. The processes involved in designing software. In J.R. Anderson (Ed.), *Cognitive skills and their acquisition.* Hillsdale, NJ: Lawrence Erlbaum Associates, 1981.

Resnick, L.B. A developmental theory of number understanding. In H.P. Ginsburg (Ed.), *The development of mathematical thinking.* New York: Academic Press, 1983.

Riley, M.S., Greeno, J.G., & Heller, J.I. Development of children's problem-solving ability in arithmetic. In H.P. Ginsburg (Ed.), *The development of mathematical thinking.* New York: Academic Press, 1983.

Sacerdoti, E.D. *A structure for plans and behavior.* New York: Elsevier-North Holland, 1977.

Skinner, B.F. *The behavior of organisms: An experimental analysis.* New York: Appleton-Century-Crofts, 1938.

PART C.
PROBLEM-SOLVING RESEARCH: THEMES AND DIRECTIONS

Research on Teaching Mathematical Problem Solving: Some Underrepresented Themes and Needed Directions

Edward A. Silver

San Diego State University

During the past few years, I have been struck by certain issues or themes that seemed very important for those of us interested in the teaching of mathematical problem solving but which were not seriously addressed in the literature. Closely connected to these fundamental issues is my assessment of some important directions in which research on problem solving should move in order to make substantial progress in the next decade. In some cases, these directions represent an attempt to connect research on mathematical problem solving with other active and potentially related fields of research. In other cases, these directions simply represent questions or issues which are fundamental and for which the time seems ripe for investigation. These observations led me not only to write this paper but also to ask a number of scholars in the field of mathematics education to write papers that are related to the directions in which I am suggesting we move. Thus, this paper serves not only as my personal view of some currently important issues to be addressed in research on mathematical problem solving but also as an introduction to the other papers in this section of the book.

LOOKING BACK: UNDERREPRESENTED THEMES

This section of the paper discusses some central themes which have received far less attention in the research literature than they deserve. In particular, the following three themes are discussed: (*1*) the role of the teacher in problem-solving instruction, (*2*) sensitivity to individual differences, and (*3*) acquisition of problem-solving expertise.

The Role of the Teacher in Problem-Solving Instruction

As I surveyed the problem-solving research literature to examine the role of the teacher in problem-solving instruction, I was struck by four general characteristics of the research reports that prevented me from making substantial progress in understanding the role of the teacher. The first of these was the lack of good description of *what actually happened* in the classroom when problem solving was taught. I read a number of studies which gave detailed statistical analyses of the significance of miniscule differences between experimental and control classes. In these studies, the authors tended to be philosophical about the implications of their research for the future of mathematics education, giving only brief and insufficient descriptions of what really transpired in the classroom when the instruction was being given to the experimental classes, and what transpired during the same period in the control classes. One of the early ideas in my project for NSF was to identify the characteristics that distinguished successful problem-solving instructional strategies from less successful ones. It soon became clear that the research reports rarely contained enough information on which to base a reasonable assessment of instructional characteristics. One exception to this general complaint was the large body of research studies in which the delivery system for instruction was a set of programmed instructional booklets, but these studies generally suffered from other deficiencies that are discussed below.

The second vexing general characteristic of the instructional studies was the systematic control of the so-called "teacher variable." Researchers, seemingly obsessed with concerns for statistical independence of observations and control of sources of variability, often used an unnatural instructional delivery system—programmed instructional booklets—that deviated substantially from normal classroom behavior. One benefit of the use of programmed instructional booklets was that they allowed for a clear description of the treatment for the experimental group (since booklets were often included in the report or were available from some other source), but that benefit was offset by the lack of a realistic classroom situation in which to test the instructional methodology. Other techniques were also used to "control" the "teacher variable," such as randomly assigning teachers to treatments or having teachers teach two classes, each with a different treatment. These approaches ignored completely the fact that teachers might prefer or might be more experienced using one or the other of the methods being compared.

A third disturbing characteristic of the instructional studies was the almost uniform failure to assess the direct effectiveness of the instruction. It was true that the studies included measures of problem-solving performance, usually using a test consisting of story problems, or sometimes even non-routine problems, but they rarely included tests of the direct effectiveness of the instruction. For example, a study that examined the relative effectiveness of two different methods of teaching children to solve arithmetic story problems would usually measure the effectiveness of the instruction solely on the basis of the number of problems solved correctly on a posttest by children in the experimental and control groups. Rarely did a study investigate whether or not the instruction resulted in students who exhibited the behaviors being modeled in the instruction. Surely, it is logically impossible to argue that an instructional treatment has or has not been effective solely on the basis of a problem-solving test, without specific attention to the behaviors that the instruction intended to elicit. Studies of heuristic processes have been as guilty of this flaw as any set of instructional studies. It was not at all uncommon for an author to have reached the conclusion that heuristic process instruction was or was not effective solely on the basis of counting correct answers to problems on a posttest, without regard for the students' usage of the heuristic processes being modeled in the instruction.

The fourth and final serious flaw of these instructional studies was the lack of a sound theoretical base. Many of the studies seemed to have been based on pedagogical folklore or intuition. Naturally, the studies of heuristic processes were largely based on the work of Polya (1957, 1962). It is striking that, until the past few years, there was virtually no critical evaluation of Polya's ideas as a possible theory of problem-solving instruction. Under reasonably close scrutiny, it is clear that Polya's writings suggest useful heuristic principles for teaching problem solving in much the same way that they suggest such principles for doing problem solving, but Polya does not present a theory of instruction. Given the atheoretical nature of the research on problem-solving instruction, it is not surprising that no systematic knowledge base accrued and that it became so difficult to generalize from the results of a study or even a set of related studies.

As the above description of the state of the research literature on teaching mathematical problem solving indicates, it does little to illuminate exemplary teaching practices. Thus, teachers are faced with a popular pedagogical literature replete with suggestions for the teaching of problem solving (e.g., Socratic dialogue, idiosyncratic methods to teach solution of story problems) and virtually no research base on which to support or refute the suggestions. Moreover, we can point to very few instructional studies that have any direct relevance to the classroom mathematics teacher. In fact, one of the major conclusions that I drew from my review of this literature was that the implications for instruction that could be gleaned from problem-solving research were not drawn from the instructional studies but rather the non-instructional studies of problem solving. However, it is also clear that these recommendations are weakened because they have not been validated in instructional research.

Thus, it is important that a new wave of instructional studies be undertaken that seriously addresses important classroom-based issues in the teaching of mathematical problem solving and which is based on the substantial body of knowledge that has been accumulated in the non-instructional studies of the past two decades. Furthermore, it is important that this next wave of instructional research relate to the substantial bodies of research that have developed using the teacher decision making, teacher belief, or classroom process-product paradigms. Thus far, these bodies of research have remained largely unconnected to problem-solving research. In order to make substantial progress in the near future, it seems prudent to utilize the available theoretical paradigms and build from the extant research results.

Sensitivity to Individual Differences

In Robert Sternberg's (1983) recent article, "Criteria for Intellectual Skills Training," he argues that any program that aims at improving students' general thinking and reasoning skills should be sensitive to individual differences. Although Sternberg was referring primarily to programs that seek to improve the performance of underachievers and low ability students, his criterion seems equally valid for any program seeking to improve higher level thinking skills in mathematics for all ability levels. As we look back at the research that has investigated the teaching of mathematical problem solving, we find very little evidence of this sort of concern for individual differences. Where are the programs that help students become aware of their cognitive strengths and weaknesses and that teach students to capitalize on their strengths and compensate for their weaknesses?

Nick Branca and I (in connection with his National Science Foundation project), interviewed a large number of fifth- and sixth-grade students and asked them to solve a wide range of mathematical problems. One striking observation that I made about their performance was that many students exhibited what I called "raw" heuristic tendencies.

These "raw" heuristics were exhibited in a student's tendency, prior to any overt instruction, to draw a diagram, to examine special cases, to generalize from test cases, and so on. It was clear that individual students showed differences in their tendency to use certain heuristic processes "au natural" (i.e., without specific instruction) and that some students had no evident "raw" heuristic tendencies. It was also clear for students who did exhibit such tendencies that their usage of these heuristic processes was primitive and in need of improvement before they were likely to be consistently useful. This observation leads me to speculate about the feasibility of studying the influence of instruction on these "raw" heuristic tendencies. Should we devise individually tailored courses that teach students to capitalize on and further develop their "raw" heuristic tendencies? Might these "raw" heuristics be a determining factor in the success or lack of success of instructional research that has aimed at the teaching of heuristic processes? How should these "raw" heuristics be measured and accommodated in subsequent research that aims at studying the teaching and learning of heuristic processes?

As noted above, problem-solving research would benefit from concern for issues of individual differences. There are a few exceptions to the general tendency to ignore individual differences. When individual differences have been considered, two approaches have dominated: the "cognitive correlates" approach, in which a general ability or cognitive style is examined with respect to its correlation with performance on some measure of problem-solving ability; and the "expert-novice" approach, in which the performance of a highly capable and experienced problem solver in a task domain is contrasted with that of a far less capable problem solver. Each approach has made some contributions to understanding some aspects of individual differences, but each also has serious limitations.

The "cognitive correlates" approach is chiefly associated with the ATI (aptitude-treatment-interaction) research paradigm. An unkind critic of the ATI approach to cognitive research might point out that the amount of time needed to read the typical ATI research report is usually longer than the time needed to conduct the treatment in the study. Thus, many are skeptical about the value of this approach in the study of problem-solving instruction. We usually expect problem-solving treatments to be lengthy, and we often feel that more longitudinal measures and approaches would be appropriate. Up to now, ATI research has not produced many generally useful results for mathematical problem-solving instruction, although the evidence that some individual difference characteristics that had been treated as stable characteristics of individuals may be modifiable might lead to some interesting studies related to problem solving. Moreover, the current approach to studying individual differences within an information-processing model of task performance on measures of aptitudes has considerable promise for providing teachers and researchers with useful information to guide problem-solving instruction. This is discussed in more detail in the second part of this paper.

Another type of problem-solving research that has used the "cognitive correlates" approach has examined the relationship of attitudes and interests on problem-solving performance. These studies have not been instructional in nature but have examined either the correlation between one's attitude toward mathematics and one's problem-solving performance or the relative problem-solving performance of students in solving problems that have contexts that do or do not match their interests. In general, these studies have not found a consistent pattern of positive relationship that one might expect. We shall discuss further the link between cognition and affect in a later part of this paper.

The other general approach to the study of individual differences in problem solving— the "expert-novice" paradigm—has become very popular in recent years, and it has led to some important observations about the nature of problem-solving expertise. For example, a consistent observation across a wide range of "expert-novice" studies in different domains, such as physics, chemistry, and mathematics, is that, when faced with a reasonably complex problem, expert problem solvers tend to perform a qualitative analysis of the problem's conditions and relationships among the problem's elements before attempting a quantitative solution. This observation, and others like it that can be gleaned from these studies contrasting the problem-solving behavior of experts and novices, is a valuable contribution to our understanding of problem-solving expertise, but the instructional implications are far less clear. Some have suggested that the "clear" implication of these "expert-novice" studies is that one should teach the novices to behave in the same way that the experts behave. This is specious reasoning and such advice may be counterproductive to learning. Surely the behavior of experts is highly efficient and often elegant, but the polished, mature problem-solving behaviors of experts fail to reveal the successive approximations that preceded these mature procedures. Moreover, this naive instructional recommendation assumes that there is a continuous path between "novice" and "expert"—an assumption that is far more likely to be false than it is to be true.

One deficiency of the "expert-novice" approach that relates to individual differences is that, while it has sharpened the distinctions between highly skilled and relatively unskilled performance, it has blurred or ignored distinctions among "experts" and among "novices." In most fields, isn't it true that there are "experts" and then there are EXPERTS? Although there are many mathematicians whose area of research expertise is number theory, there are only a handful who will ever win a Fields Medal for their research. And only a few nuclear physicists will ever be recognized as outstanding experts in that field. It seems that, among the set of persons considered to be "experts" in many of the "expert-novice" studies, we may really have EXPERTS, "experts," the "highly competent," the "competent," and so on. Are there fundamental differences in the ways that these different categories of "experts" approach and solve challenging problems in their field? If there aren't such differences, then what is it that distinguishes these classes? Moreover, being an "expert" in one field of mathematics does not make one an "expert" in other fields. Thus, we should be very careful in assigning labels like "expert" mathematical problem solver.

When we turn our attention to "novices," we realize that there are "novices" who will someday become "experts" (or even EXPERTS), those who will become reasonably competent and skillful in the task domain, and those who will never become more than "highly experienced novices." In summary, I would argue that it is quite reasonable and theoretically useful to study the beginning and ending points of a presumed continuum of expertise in a knowledge domain, but we would be wise to remember the following points: (1) there may be discontinuities along the path from novice to expert, (2) we must not act as if "novice" and "expert" were terms denoting equivalence classes of interchangeable elements, and (3) we need to characterize carefully the domain of expertise that we are studying and avoid extrapolating too far beyond the boundaries of the domain.

Acquisition of Problem-Solving Expertise

In the last section, careful study of the path from noviciate to expert status in a task domain was proposed as an important research activity. The lack of serious research attention to the acquisition of problem-solving expertise is an unfortunate characteristic of much of the research in problem solving. For whether one is primarily interested in issues of learning or teaching, this is a truly fundamental issue.

In the past 15 years or so, we have made considerable progress in creating models of problem-solving performance. These models have led to a deeper understanding of the complexities of problem-solving processes in a wide variety of task domains. In mathematics education, some researchers have created detailed descriptions of the behavior of individual problem solvers engaged in a problem-solving episode. These researchers have used process-sequence coding, largely based on the seminal work of Kilpatrick (1968), to analyze individual subject protocols and provide a process trace of the subject's solution. In cognitive science, a number of interesting computer models of problem-solving performance have been developed, but relatively little attention has been given to the acquisition of problem-solving expertise. The lack of attention to issues of learning may be due in part to the modern rejection of traditional behaviorist psychology, which had been very interested in fundamental issues of learning (e.g., operant conditioning, maze learning by rats).

Although some early workers in the field of Artificial Intelligence were apparently very interested in issues connected with learning, it is only recently that much attention has been given to creating computer systems that improve their own ability to solve problems. One example of a contemporary program that *learns* is ABLE, developed by Jill Larkin. ABLE learns to solve increasingly complex (though fairly elementary) physics problems by augmenting its store of knowledge through experience in solving problems. ABLE's knowledge consists of "productions" (condition-action pairs) and it utilizes this knowledge to solve problems by matching the condition part of a production with the contents of its working memory. From a very limited knowledge base, in the version of the program called "Barely ABLE," the program learns to improve its performance by acquiring new productions derived from its problem-solving experience. Since Larkin's simulations of novices (Barely ABLE) and experts (ABLE) are quite similar to the behaviors of human problem solvers, her accomplishments are quite substantial and suggest that this methodology could be used to study the acquisition of problem-solving expertise. At the moment, however, the knowledge that is accounted for in this model, or others like it, is quite specific and essentially algebraic. There is no account of abstraction, generalization, or the cognitive reorganization that seems to occur when individual learners develop more powerful problem-solving processes.

A currently popular view among many of those engaged in computer modeling is that learning is simply an accretion of productions, but I believe that view will prove inadequate for providing a useful understanding of the acquisition of problem-solving expertise in complex domains. (For an alternate view, see the discussion of LEX in Rissland's paper in this volume.) If we are to make substantial progress in understanding the processes involved in acquisition of problem-solving expertise, I suspect that we are going to have to take into account both the essential conservatism of human learning (i.e., the nearly ubiquitous tendency of human beings to try to "get by" with available knowledge) and the apparent discontinuities that one often observes as human learners transform themselves from novices to experts in a task domain. Moreover, we are going to need to provide more complicated models that allow for simultaneous knowledge-sharing across several task domains, for it is clear that in many task situations one often obtains useful problem-solving information from sources outside the primary knowledge domain. It is encouraging that there have been signs of recent interest in issues of learning and acquisition of problem-solving expertise. I hope that this issue will be well represented in the research of the next decade.

One locus for the study of the acquisition of problem-solving expertise is the mathematics classroom, for formal schooling must surely have an important influence on this growth process. It is striking that so few studies have focused on the longitudinal study of growth in problem-solving ability. Methodologies that are currently available (e.g., computer simulation, detailed case study) are adequate for such longitudinal studies, and the potential dividends to be accrued from such studies appear to be great.

LOOKING AHEAD: NEEDED DIRECTIONS

I would like to suggest some issues that need to be addressed seriously in the next wave of research on mathematical problem solving. These issues for future research grow out of the concerns expressed in the previous part of this paper, especially the need for longitudinal studies of development of problem-solving ability. I propose ten issues that I believe are fundamental in the search for knowledge that will be useful to us in understanding the processes of teaching and learning mathematical problem solving. I do not claim that this list is complete, but I do believe that we will make substantial progress if we address these issues. Since it is impossible to assign priorities to these issues, they are discussed in alphabetical order.

Affect

The first issue may appear to be out of place in the current climate of cognitive research on human problem solving, relying as heavily as it does on machine models of human performance. However, it is precisely because of the current climate that the issue is so important. In his paper, "Twelve Issues for Cognitive Science," Donald Norman (1981) suggested the fundamental importance of emotion as an issue that had been neglected by cognitive science. Borrowing heavily from George Mandler's (1975) thesis proposed in *Mind and Emotion*, Norman argued that an individual's emotional system was an important mediating force between one's cognitive and regulatory systems.

There is apparently some neurological basis for asserting a link between affective and cognitive aspects of human functioning. In his paper, "Neurological Knowledge and Complex Behaviors," Geschwind (1981) points out that "the portions of the brain involved in memory functions, e.g., the hippocampus, amygdala, mamillary bodies, etc., are all portions of the limbic system which is clearly involved in emotional activities." According to Geschwind's argument, affective stimulation may increase receptiveness to certain inputs and thereby affect cognitive functioning.

In proposing affect as one of our fundamental issues, I want to echo Norman's call for a careful consideration of the non-cognitive aspects of human performance. When students approach mathematical tasks, and especially those that are problematic, they do not enter the arena as purely cognitive beings. Students' behaviors may be influenced by their feelings of self-esteem, their perceived control—or lack of control—over the situation with which they are faced, or their sense of satisfaction in engaging in mathematical tasks. Similarly, one's attitude toward mathematics in general, to problem solving in general, or to a host of other factors (e.g., school, teacher, textbook, classroom social structure, the task or some aspect of it) may have a powerful influence on the nature and quality of one's engagement with the mathematical problem.

One important aspect of the affective domain is motivation. Although it is not clear that motivation resides entirely within the affective domain, it is reasonable to assert that a substantial component of one's motivation is non-cognitive in nature. The research of Zigler (1971) and Feuerstein (1979) suggests that motivation may be an important mediating factor in the intellectual performance of retarded individuals and those who are ''culturally deprived.'' More recently, Sternberg (1983) has suggested that ''for student samples restricted in range with respect to ability, differences in motivation may account for large shares of the observed differences in performances'' (p. 10). Although a high degree of motivation is not a sufficient condition for adequate intellectual performance, it may be a necessary condition.

Attempts have been made to study some affective aspects of mathematical problem-solving performance, either by examining the effects on performance of presenting problems in different contexts that might be more or less ''interesting'' to groups of students or by correlating performance with one or more measures of attitude toward mathematics. In general, the research has not shown a clear relationship between affective factors and problem-solving performance, and these considerations have generally been ignored in problem-solving research over the past ten years. The movement away from considering affective aspects of problem-solving performance has been fueled both by a general dissatisfaction with the type of research that has been done in this area and the tendency among psychologists to describe problem-solving performance in purely cognitive terms. The latter has also been accompanied by an emphasis on computer models as the standard for rigorous research on human problem solving. Since one rarely associates affective issues with a computer's problem-solving performance, it has been common to ignore or overlook affective aspects of human performance in these models.

Anyone who has worked with students in mathematics classes knows that affective considerations have a substantial influence on student performance. Any relationship that has such substantial face validity and such weak research support deserves to be studied in more detail. The time has come to renew our efforts to uncover the affective/cognitive links in problem-solving performance and in the learning of problem-solving procedures in school settings. The notion of metacognition, which will be discussed later in this paper, may be a useful way of bridging the affective/cognitive chasm. It might also be productive to study the affective aspects of some problem-solving research studies that were not explicitly designed to have an affective focus. For example, the improvements in students' problem-solving performance reported by Keil (1964), who had students write their own story problems for other students to solve, may have a significant affective component. Also, the startling improvements in students' performance reported by Stover (1982) and Cohen and Stover (1982), and discussed earlier in Kilpatrick's paper, merit a closer look from an affective perspective. In particular, it is likely that the students in Stover's study increased their sense of control over the problem-solving situation as a result of her direct instruction in manipulating problem text characteristics.

These last two examples should serve to remind us that, as researchers in this domain of human problem solving, we need to remember that our perceptions of problem solving as a largely cognitive domain of human activity are influenced by our largely cognitive approach to the phenomenon that we are studying. We are highly cognitive beings who spend much of our time in thoughtful reflection about the intellectual nature of the activity. If we were to ask psychotherapists, artists, or novelists to examine the same questions that we attempt to answer, we might well get answers that were less cognitive and more affective in their essence.

Beliefs

Fairly closely connected to the affective considerations discussed above is the notion of one's belief system. Recent work in cognitive anthropology and sociology (e.g., D'Andrade, 1981) has demonstrated that cultural belief systems can profoundly influence memory, perception, and cognition.

The influence of one's beliefs on problem-solving performance has recently gained some attention. Lester and Garofalo (1982) reported that third and fifth graders believed that mathematical problems could always be solved by using basic operations and could always be solved in only a few minutes. Students' responses to attitude items on the Third National Assessment of Educational Progress in Mathematics (Carpenter et al., 1983) indicated the general belief among junior high and high school students that there was always one correct way to solve any mathematical problem, that there was always a rule that could be followed to solve any mathematical problem, and that mathematics is mostly memorization. Research reported by Lesh (1983) suggests that many students do not believe that mathematics is applicable to solving real-world problems. And Schoenfeld (1983) has suggested that students' failures to solve mathematical problems can often be directly attributed to their erroneous beliefs about the nature of mathematics and mathematical problem solving. (See Schoenfeld, this volume, for further discussion of this issue.)

Carbonell (1981) has constructed a mechanism that incorporates knowledge contained in belief systems (in this case, political ideologies) into the process of formulating plans for action. This might serve as a useful analogy for someone to use in creating a model of mathematical problem solving that incorporated belief systems as an important and influential factor in planning and performance.

Perhaps the most insidious components of a person's belief system are the misconceptions and erroneous beliefs that one holds. An extensive list of scientific misconceptions has been compiled for physics, including misconceptions about velocity (Lochhead, 1983), motion (McCloskey, 1983), and force (Nickerson, 1982). In mathematics, important misconceptions have been documented in areas of probability, geometry, and algebra. Naive probabilistic reasoning has been studied extensively (see Shaughnessy's paper in this volume) and a number of resilient misconceptions have been identified, such as the so-called "law of small numbers" (Tversky & Kahneman, 1971) that leads people to believe that a coin is not a fair coin if it is tossed four times and lands "heads" each time; people tend to believe that the "fairness" (i.e., the equiprobable possible outcomes) of the coin should guarantee the same number of "heads" and "tails" in any string of tosses. In algebra, Wagner (1981, 1983) has provided evidence of students' misconceptions about the nature of variables and Kieran (1981, 1983) has documented students' misconceptions and missing conceptions about the nature of equations.

The literature on misconceptions, which has grown considerably in the past few years, tends to suggest a reformulation of the famous quote attributed to Jerome Bruner; the modern version would be: "Any topic can be misunderstood by anyone at any age in some intellectually honest way." Beyond its humorous value, that reformulation points out both that these misconceptions are widespread and that they are reasonable. In general, these popular misconceptions are beliefs about the world that originate from a person's experience and work fairly well in restricted contexts (e.g., an Aristotelean view of physics works well for the situations encountered daily by most people). Thus, it is not surprising that the literature also suggests that these misconceptions are very resilient and quite resistant to instruction.

For those of us interested in mathematical problem solving, several important questions immediately suggest themselves: (*1*) What is the geneology of these misconceptions? Can we uncover the ancestral roots? (*2*) For what classes of problems are these beliefs likely to be debilitating, and in what ways are they likely to affect performance? (*3*) Are there reasonable instructional approaches that might allow learners to correct these misconceptions or erroneous beliefs? In what ways would these approaches differ from "typical" instructional practices?, and (*4*) Since these misconceptions are so widespread and resilient, how is it that anyone ever achieves expertise in these domains? Could we study individuals on their path to expertise, as they shed their misconceptions and naive beliefs?

It is important to study not only the beliefs about mathematics that are held by students but also those held by their teachers. A. Thompson (1982) and Shirk (1972) have demonstrated that teachers' beliefs about the nature of mathematics and the teaching of mathematics can have a tremendous influence on teaching behavior, on the outcomes they teach for, and on the way that they evaluate their success. One would suspect that the influence of teachers' beliefs would be evident in the area of problem solving, and this would appear to be a fertile field for further investigation. (See Alba Thompson's paper in this volume for a discussion of this issue.)

The serious study of belief systems may yield substantial dividends in the near future. However, before "belief systems" becomes the next research "bandwagon" upon which we jump, we need to tackle some fundamental issues that are intertwined with the notion of belief system. For example, some researchers have proposed (as I also did above) using data from attitude surveys as an indicator of beliefs. This seems quite reasonable, but we need to investigate the relationship between beliefs and attitudes. Are all attitudes also beliefs; if not, then how do we distinguish those that are from those that are not? Similarly, beliefs about mathematics or about problem solving can be viewed as items of personal knowledge. In what ways are these items of knowledge called "beliefs" the same as or different from other items of knowledge that we might readily call "facts" (e.g., knowing that $2 + 2 = 4$ or knowing your name, address, and telephone number)? Beliefs appear to lie at the junction of propositional knowledge and affect. As such, they are fundamental elements of mathematical thinking and deserve careful analysis.

Classroom Ecology

What is it that happens in classrooms where mathematical problem solving is taught well? Are there common features that can be identified across successful classrooms? How can a "problem-solving atmosphere" be created in a mathematics classroom? What is the nature of the social, general educational, and mathematical contracts that are formed between teacher and student and among students in such classrooms?

We all know teachers who have excellent reputations as mathematics teachers or as teachers of problem solving. Where are the in-depth studies of those teachers and their classrooms? Some interesting studies have been done recently in mathematics classrooms (e.g., Brandau, 1981), using techniques borrowed from cultural anthropology, but we need more of these investigations to focus on the critical interactions that characterize successful teaching of problem solving in the classroom.

The picture of mathematics classrooms painted by the NSF Case Studies (Stake & Easley, 1978) a few years ago suggests that successful teachers of problem solving might need to alter drastically the environment of the mathematics classroom. According to the NSF Case Studies, the student in a typical mathematics classroom has few opportunities to challenge ideas, propose and solve interesting problems, or simply spend time *thinking* before answering a question. This picture of mathematics classrooms suggests that it might also be productive to document those aspects of classroom ecology that inhibit growth in problem-solving ability.

One aspect of classroom ecology that bears special attention with respect to problem solving is evaluation. It has become fashionable in mathematics education to "teach for problem solving." But what does that mean? How do we measure growth and success? What are the available measures that can be used to assess problem-solving performance? Can we simply count correct responses to word problems as our only measure? Can we define more appropriate measures of problem-solving ability and growth, such as willingness to attempt difficult problems or perseverance in attempting problem solutions? What aspects of problem solving can be appropriately measured using standardized tests and multiple-choice questions and which cannot be so measured? To what extent do innovative tests of problem solving, such as the Iowa Problem-Solving Test (Oehmke, 1979; Schoen & Oehmke, 1980) or the California Assessment Program (Pandey, 1984) overly fragment the problem-solving process? Do we have sufficient evidence for the construct validity of such process-oriented tests of problem-solving ability? These and other questions deserve serious attention from the problem-solving research community.

Conceptual Analyses

During the past twenty years, considerable progress has been made in developing procedural analyses of problem-solving performance. These procedural analyses are often implemented as computer programs, and they often provide very good descriptions of the observable behavior of a subject. The best of these analyses are consistent across a variety of tasks within a domain or across a variety of learners on the same task, and they have some predictive capability.

Without abandoning the well-developed techniques for procedural analyses, researchers need to widen the scope of the task. In particular, we need to develop rigorous conceptual analyses of knowledge and performance, and to relate those models to problem solving. There have been extensive investigations into the development of mathematical concepts in a few areas: rational numbers (Behr, Lesh, Post, & Silver, 1983), whole numbers and numeration (Steffe & von Glasersfeld, 1983; P. Thompson, 1981), and elementary geometric notions (Hoffer, 1983). This work has not been concerned with mathematical problem solving per se, but rather with the development and cognitive organization of mathematical ideas. Yet this work has important implications for those of us interested in problem solving.

In my own research with young adults who were unable to add common fractions despite many years of well-intentioned mathematics teaching that emphasized the correct procedures, I (Silver, 1983) found that some of their problem-solving deficiencies could be traced directly to their conceptions of a fraction and of addition. In his work with middle-school students trying to solve "real world" problems, Lesh (1983) has described problem-solving episodes not in terms of concatenated procedures, but rather as a sequence of "unstable conceptual systems." This work reminds us that mathematical problem-solving performance needs to be studied not only with respect to the observed and inferred procedures utilized but also with respect to the system of mathematical ideas that influences the performance.

In order to give richer characterizations of mathematical problem solving, we must go beyond process-sequence strings and coded protocols. And we need also to go beyond simple procedure-based computer models of performance. We need to develop new techniques for describing problem-solving behavior not only in terms of the procedures utilized but also in terms of the conceptual systems that influence the performance. The successful implementation of rigorous modeling techniques of this type would give us more powerful models of problem-solving performance and might provide more suitable models for learning, since they could account for the phenomena of cognitive restructuring and conceptual reorganization that are observed as people learn in complex domains.

The notion of "conceptual field" proposed by Vergnaud (1982, 1983) may be a useful vehicle for those of us interested in problem solving. Vergnaud has argued for the situational analysis of mathematical knowledge, since mathematical concepts grow out of situations and must be studied with respect to the situations to which they apply. He suggests a close epistemological link between conceptual knowledge and problem solving. In heeding Vergnaud's call that we address the basic question, "To which problem or problems does a new property of a concept, a new procedure, or a new representation, bring a solution or eventually a more powerful one?" (1983, p. 3), we might begin to make substantial progress toward establishing the links between conceptual knowledge networks (or conceptual fields) and problem-solving performance.

Group Process

The literature on group processes suggests that learning is usually enhanced by the use of small groups (Slavin, 1980). Furthermore, there is evidence that some types of problem solving are positively influenced by cooperative small groups (Johnson & Johnson, 1982). Nel Noddings and her students (Noddings, 1982; Noddings, Gilbert-Macmillan, & Leitz, 1983) have begun to study seriously the use of small groups in mathematical problem solving. They have studied the differential effectiveness of group learning for different kinds of students. In general, their results have been promising and suggest that this may be a productive direction for further research.(See Noddings' paper in this volume for more discussion of some important issues.)

The rigorous study of small groups as they relate to mathematical problem solving would appear to be important for at least two important reasons. The first reason is basically pragmatic. It is not at all uncommon to see the use of small groups advocated in the popular pedagogical literature, yet we know little about the effects of small group experiences on individual learners. Elementary school teachers often use small groups, but secondary school mathematics teachers rarely do. If the use of small groups were found to be an effective tool for secondary school students, then small groups might be used as a vehicle for altering the stultifying atmosphere of most secondary school mathematics classrooms. Before this can happen, however, we need to understand a great deal more about the conditions under which small groups are likely to promote learning. The research of Nel Noddings and that of Noreen Webb (1982; Webb & Cullian, 1983) suggest some dimensions along which to study the effects of small groups on the learning of mathematical problem solving.

The second major reason for calling for the serious study of small groups is more theoretical. Small group settings provide an opportunity to study the *externalized* internal dialogue in which a problem solver might engage. The difficulties with the use of introspection in the study of problem solving are well documented (e.g., Ericsson & Simon, 1980). Small group settings may allow the problem solver to verbalize more readily because of the need to communicate with fellow group members. This external verbalization then becomes a trace of the student's thinking processes and part of the objective data that can be studied. Cooperative small group settings may promote this externalized "think aloud" protocol more readily than individual interviews, and they may provide a useful vehicle for studying such processes (often covert in individual protocols) as planning, monitoring, and evaluating. Moreover, there is a reverse process that is also worthy of serious study: the *internalization* of the external dialogue of the group. What is it that an individual learner takes away from a cooperative small group problem-solving episode? To what extent can the benefits of such episodes be measured by studying the verbalizations of problem solvers in subsequent episodes, either in small groups or individually? The work of Vygotsky (1978) may provide us with some guiding principles for the study of the social transmission of problem-solving knowledge and skill in small group settings.

Individual Cognitive Differences

In the first part of this paper, I argued for the importance of a heightened sensitivity to individual differences. Some researchers interested in problem solving have deliberately avoided the issue of individual differences because it has been associated with the limitations of ATI research or because cognitive styles have often been described as stable characteristics of individuals (Bloom, 1976). Recent research, however, has indicated that individual cognitive styles are modifiable (e.g., Akerstrom, 1983). For example, Feuerstein (1980) has reported considerable success in modifying the impulsive behavior of unsuccessful problem solvers. Many people suspect that impulsivity is a serious deterrent to successful problem solving in school settings. If that cognitive characteristic is modifiable, then it becomes an important characteristic to study in detail as it relates to problem-solving performance.

In the traditional view of an individual difference variable, a score on a test was taken as an indicator of a stable characteristic of the individual. Not only was the assumption of stability open to question, as we noted above, but also the information that one obtained from such a score was unclear. For example, we received little or no information about the reasons why a student might have scored high or low on a particular test. In recent years, there has been an attempt to integrate information-processing models within the individual-differences paradigm (e.g., Carroll, 1976; Egan, 1979; Hunt, 1982). In this approach, the researcher analyzes the underlying cognitive processes that are associated with the tasks on the test. Thus, one obtains information about student performance on the test and infers certain information-processing characteristics of the student that can, in turn, guide instruction. (See Threadgill-Sowder's paper for a further discussion of this approach to individual differences.)

Sternberg (1980a, 1980b) has used an approach based on information-processing models to study the relationship of individual differences to problem-solving performance. Some of his research has dealt with the detailed specification of the ways in which task characteristics influence cognitive functioning, particularly problem-solving strategy selection. Sternberg has not studied in mathematical domains, but we might find his techniques and perspective useful to us in the study of mathematical problem solving.

Metacognition

For many years, mathematicians, educators, and psychologists have tried to understand the complex processes involved in mathematical problem solving. In general, their analyses of problem solving in mathematical or quasimathematical domains have focused on cognitive actions and processes (e.g., algorithm choice and utilization, heuristic approaches employed) or on cognitive products (e.g., correct or incorrect answers). In recent years some researchers (e.g., Silver, 1982b; Schoenfeld, 1983) have argued that purely cognitive explanations of complex problem-solving behavior are logically and psychologically unsound. Careful observations of many persons solving complex mathematical problems suggest that many of the important influences on the success or failure of a problem-solving episode may be metacognitive in nature.

According to Flavell (1979), metacognition refers to one's knowledge concerning one's own cognitive processes and products, and the cognition of others. It refers not only to one's awareness of cognitive processes but also to the self-monitoring, regulation, and evaluation of cognitive activity. Thus, we can see that the processes of planning, monitoring, and evaluating discussed in the previous section on small groups are all metacognitive in nature.

Mention of metacognition is not new; provision for metacognitive functioning has been provided for in most information-processing models of cognition. Atkinson and Shiffrin (1968) used the term "control processes" to identify certain voluntary and strategic behaviors that one carries out to remember something, such as rehearsing a telephone number or tying a string around one's finger. Butterfield and Belmont (1975) posited the existence of an "executive function" that selects appropriate "control processes" on the basis of task and environmental constraints. One of the earliest models of limited metacognitive functioning and regulation was provided in the TOTE (Test/Operate/Test/Exit) units proposed by Miller, Galanter, and Pribam (1960). In Skemp's (1979) model of intelligence, one finds that metacognitive activity is one aspect of "reflective intelligence" in the domain of delta-two. And Case (1974), in his description of neo-Piagetian approaches to information processing, has included an "executive scheme" that is primarily concerned with plans and regulation. The terms "control processes," "executive function," "reflective intelligence," and "executive scheme" are not synonymous with metacognition but they all cover, to a great extent, the area in which metacognition is operative.

Although many models of human information processing include metacognitive processes, there has been relatively little empirical investigation of these phenomena. If we accept the importance of metacognitive processes, then several important questions immediately suggest themselves. For example, questions regarding the accessibility of metacognitive processes for systematic study, the role of "awareness" as a factor in the acquisition or utilization of metacognitive behaviors, the locus of observation points from which to view metacognitive aspects of problem solving, and the nature of the relationship between metacognitive skills and problem-solving performance need carefully developed answers. In addition, questions regarding the nature of the processes of monitoring and evaluating need to be carefully formulated and investigated. It is clear that these processes make important contributions to human problem solving; it is far more difficult, however, to develop a formal descriptive model that accounts for the role that these processes might play. Yet, it is equally clear that no process model of problem solving will be complete unless it makes explicit provision for the metacognitive aspects of problem solving.

In the past few years, there has been a growing interest in investigating metacognitive behaviors, and there are indications that this trend will continue. In the next set of research studies, I hope that we will see rigorous investigations that focus on at least these seven areas: (1) awareness of the active nature of processing during problem solving, (2) awareness and availability of strategies, (3) the influence of differing task demands on metacognitive functioning, (4) mechanisms of strategy selection and utilization, (5) monitoring of problem-solving activity, (6) the processes of evaluating and modifying problem-solving behavior, and (7) the influence of beliefs and misconceptions about mathematics or mathematical processes on problem-solving performance.

Representation

This may seem like the most surprising entry on the list, for surely we know a great deal about representation. Or do we? Although the notion of representation plays a prominent role in most current models of problem-solving performance, the careful reader of the literature on problem solving may be struck by the variety of ways that the term is used. Since mental representations are not overt and observable, they are spoken of as "being there" or a person is described as "having one," without clearly defining what is meant by the term. As the word "representation" is currently used in the problem-solving literature, it is insufficiently constrained to be useful for theory construction or powerful explanations of human behavior. Much like the common cold, we think that we know when we have one, but we cannot describe specifically and accurately what it is. To pursue the analogy with the common cold a bit further, what we need at this time is not chicken soup. We need a fairly complete exegesis of the term *representation* and the various meanings that have been ascribed to it.

Serious attention to this task will almost certainly involve deep forays into epistemology. (See Kaput's paper in this volume for more on the epistemological roots of representation.) There also needs to be careful consideration of the differences and similarities between one's relatively permanent representation of a previously learned mathematical concept or principle and one's relatively temporary representation of a current mathematical problem. Moreover, the distinctions between physical representations (such as diagrams or equations) and mental representations need to be identified and explored.

Constructivist theories of learning are currently quite popular. Such theories attribute to the learner a central role in shaping his or her own learning on the basis of a personal construction of the material to be learned. A careful characterization of mental representations should therefore be central to any constructivist theory of learning. Moreover, if we posit the notion that a person learns to solve problems, to a large extent, by incorporating the lessons learned from solving similar problems, then the centrality of the notion of representation becomes obvious. What does it mean for two problems to appear to be similar to an individual learner (Silver, 1979, 1981)? Since many problems permit multiple representations, is there such a thing as a pair of isomorphic problems, or are there only pairs that permit isomorphic representations? Answers to these questions will probably bring us in close contact with schema-based theories of memory and knowledge organization (Silver, 1982a).

Many current theories of problem solving in complex domains assert that successful problem solving is a process of building successively richer and more refined problem representations—the solver begins with an initial representation, then gradually elaborates and refines that initial representation until a final problem representation, adequate for the solution, is obtained. Lesh proposes an alternative view of this process, in which the problem solver builds and then abandons unstable representational models of the problem until a stable model is finally reached (See Lesh, this volume, for more details). In either view, the centrality of problem representations is clear. For those of us interested in problem-solving instruction, we need to examine how to teach students better representation skills. There have been some efforts to teach diagraming, table-making, and other representational skills, but these have been treated as relatively isolated skills and the instruction has largely been devoid of any theoretical basis. The time may be ripe for us to study seriously the development of problem-representation skills, using the available theoretical bases.

Another fundamental question for instruction is how to teach students to elaborate and refine their initial problem representations. In fact, much of the current attention to metacognitive aspects of problem solving, such as monitoring and evaluating progress, has been stimulated by observations of problem solvers who did not elaborate, or who elaborated poorly, initially constructed problem representations. At this time, careful study of the processes of refinement and elaboration of problem representations is needed.

Teachers

As we noted in the first section of this paper, the teacher is truly the ''forgotten soul'' in research on the teaching and learning of mathematical problem solving. In general, the teacher and teacher-related variables have been systematically controlled (for statistical reasons) or unconsciously ignored by researchers. Earlier in this section of the paper, I argued for the careful study of the classroom ecology associated with exceptional mathematics teachers. Naturally, we should also be studying the teachers themselves.

Several studies (e.g., Shirk, 1972; A. Thompson, 1982) have demonstrated that a teacher's beliefs about mathematics, learning, and teaching can have a profound influence on the teacher's behavior. These studies have not focused primarily on the teaching of problem solving, but the methodology could be adapted to focus attention on the effect of a teacher's attitudes and beliefs about mathematics and problem solving on that particular aspect of mathematics teaching. (See Alba Thompson's paper in this volume for some insights into the ways in which the methodology could be used.) Moreover, it would be interesting to know if there were differential impact of beliefs on teaching for teachers at different levels (e.g., elementary, secondary, post-secondary) or for teachers of different ability groups (e.g., gifted, average, remedial).

Technology

It is fitting that the final issue on my list should be the one that leads us naturally into the future—technology. I have two reasons for suggesting technology as an issue for our consideration. First, the widespread availability of microcomputers now makes possible the gathering of data that were heretofore difficult to obtain. For example, if someone were to take seriously my earlier suggestion that we utilize Sternberg's techniques in studying mathematical techniques, then we would certainly need an easy way to obtain the necessary response latency data. These data would be fairly easy to obtain using a microcomputer. Moreover, some of the powerful microcomputers currently available already have the capacity to permit cognitive modeling.

The second reason for suggesting technology as an issue is that the computer can be used as a tool to create environments in which people can be given the opportunity to think mathematically and solve challenging problems. Of particular interest to researchers in problem solving should be the creation of microworlds (Papert, 1980), in which an individual learner is free to explore the environment, subject to certain constraints imposed by the programmer. The use of microworlds in mathematical settings provides students with opportunities to create mathematical entities, propose and solve problems, generate and test hypotheses, and to think mathematically. (See Pat Thompson's two papers in this volume for further details on the potential for the uses of microworlds in mathematical education.)

Even the more traditional educational uses of the computer, such as CAI (computer-aided instruction), could be beneficial in the teaching and learning of problem solving. For example, CAI interactions could be designed to provide useful feedback or help sequences that focus not simply on the calculation of an answer but also on processes or heuristics generally useful in problem solving. Traditional CAI modes could also be exploited to create "Problem Variers" which could generate sets of problems that instantiate certain programmed problem templates. As the techniques for doing this get more sophisticated, one would not have to be limited to stereotyped and generally uninteresting problems. When the interface with artificial intelligence becomes more complete, the potential for such "Problem Variers" to become "Problem Creators" can be realized.

As Herbert Simon recently noted, "Nobody really needs convincing these days that the computer is an innovation of more than ordinary magnitude, a one-in-several-centuries innovation.... It is an event of major magnitude" (Simon 1983, p. 37). The challenge to those of us interested in the teaching and learning of mathematical problem solving is to develop ways to use this powerful tool for the benefit of mathematics education.

REFERENCES

Akerstrom, M. *Reflection-impulsivity: A function or a constant.* Paper presented at the meeting of the American Educational Research Association, Montreal, Canada, April 1983.

Atkinson, R.C., & Shiffrin, R.M. Human memory: A proposed system and its control processes. In K.W. Spence & J.T. Spence (Eds.), *The psychology of learning and motivation* (Vol. 2). New York: Academic Press, 1968.

Behr, M.J., Lesh, R., Post, T.R., & Silver, E.A. Rational number concepts. In R. Lesh & M. Landau (Eds.), *Acquisition of mathematics concepts and processes.* New York: Academic Press, 1983.

Bloom, B.S. *Human characteristics and school learning.* New York: McGraw-Hill Inc., 1976.

Brandau, L. *The practices of an elementary mathematics teacher—an ethnographic approach to the study of problem solving.* Paper presented at the meeting of the American Educational Research Association, Los Angeles, April 1981.

Butterfield, E.C., & Belmont, J.M. Assessing and improving the executive cognitive functions of mentally retarded people. In I. Bailer & M. Sternlicht (Eds.), *Psychological issues in mentally retarded people.* Chicago: Aldine, 1975.

Carbonell, J. Politics. In R.C. Schank & C.K. Riesbeck (Eds.), *Inside computer understanding: Five programs plus miniatures.* Hillsdale, NJ: Lawrence Erlbaum Associates, 1981.

Carpenter, T.P., Lindquist, M.M., Silver, E.A., & Matthews, W. Results of the Third NAEP Mathematics Assessment: Secondary school. *The Mathematics Teacher* **76**, 1983.

Carroll, J.B. Psychometric tests as cognitive tasks: A new "structure of intellect." In L. B. Resnick (Ed.), *The nature of intelligence.* Hillsdale, NJ: Lawrence Erlbaum Associates, 1976.

Case, R. Structures and strictures: Some functional limitations on the course of cognitive growth. *Cognitive Psychology* **6**, 544–74, 1974.

Cohen, S.A., & Stover, G. Effects of teaching sixth-grade students to modify format variables of math word problems. *Reading Research Quarterly* **16**, 175–200, 1982.

D'Andrade, R.G. The cultural part of cognition. *Cognitive Science* **5**, 179–195, 1981.

Egan, E.E. Testing based on understanding: Implications from studies of spatial ability. *Intelligence* **3**, 1–15, 1979.

Ericsson, K.A., & Simon, H.A. Verbal reports as data. *Psychological Review* **87**(3), 215–51, 1980.

Feuerstein, R. *The dynamic assessment of retarded performers: The learning potential assessment device, theory, instruments, and techniques.* Baltimore, MD: University Park Press, 1979.

Feuerstein, R. *Instrumental enrichment: An intervention program for cognitive modifiability.* Baltimore, MD: University Park Press, 1980.

Flavell, J.H. Metacognition and cognitive monitoring: A new area of cognitive-developmental inquire. *American Psychologist* **34**, 906–11, 1979.

Geschwind, N. Neurological knowledge and complex behaviors. In D.A. Norman (Ed.), *Perspective on cognitive science.* Norwood, NJ: Ablex, 1981.

Hoffer, A. Van Hiele-based research. In R. Lesh & M. Landau (Eds.), *Acquisition of mathematics concepts and processes.* New York: Academic Press, 1983.

Hunt, E. Towards new ways of assessing intelligence. *Intelligence* **6**, 231–40, 1982.

Johnson, D., & Johnson, R. *The internal dynamics of cooperative learning groups.* Paper presented at meeting of the American Educational Research Association, New York, March 1982.

Keil, G.C. *Writing and solving original problems as a means of improving verbal problem-solving ability.* Unpublished doctoral dissertation, Indiana University, 1964.

Kieran, C. Concepts associated with the equality symbol. *Educational Studies in Mathematics* **12**, 317–26, 1981.

Kieran, C. Relationships between novices' views of algebraic letters and their use of symmetric and asymmetric equation-solving procedures. In J.C. Bergerson & N. Herscovics (Eds.), *Proceedings of the Fifth Annual Meeting of the North American Chapter of the International Group for the Psychology of Mathematics Education* (Vol. 1), Montreal, September 1983.

Kilpatrick, J. Analyzing the solution of word problems in mathematics: An exploratory study. (Doctoral dissertation, Stanford University, 1967). *Dissertation Abstracts International* **28**, 1968, 4380A. (University Microfilms No. 68-6442)

Lesh, R. *Modeling middle school students' modeling behaviors in applied mathematical problem solving.* Paper presented at the meeting of the American Educational Research Association, Montreal, April 1983.

Lester, F., & Garofalo, J. *Metacognitive aspects of elementary school students' performance on arithmetic tasks.* Paper presented at the meeting of the American Educational Research Association, New York, March 1982.

Lochhead, J. *Research on students' scientific misconceptions: Some implications for teaching.* Paper presented at the meeting of the American Educational Research Association, Montreal, April 1983.

Mandler, G. *Mind and emotion.* New York: John Wiley & Sons, 1975.

McCloskey, M. Intuitive Physics. *Scientific American*, 122–30, April 1983.

Miller, G.A., Galanter, E., & Pribram, K. *Plans and the structure of behavior*. New York: Holt, Rinehart, and Winston, 1960.

Nickerson, R. *Understanding understanding*. Cambridge, MA: Bolt Beranek & Newman, 1982. (Draft manuscript).

Noddings, N. *The use of small group protocols in analysis of children's arithmetical problem solving*. Paper presented at the meeting of the American Educational Research Association, New York, March 1982.

Noddings, N., Gilbert-Macmillan, K., & Leitz, S. *What do individuals gain in small group mathematical problem solving?* Paper presented at the meeting of the American Educational Research Association, Montreal, April 1983.

Norman, D.A. Twelve issues for cognitive science. In D.A. Norman (Ed.), *Perspective on cognitive science*. Norwood, NJ: Ablex, 1981.

Oehmke, T. *Development and validation of a testing instrument for problem-solving strategies of children in grades five through eight*. Unpublished doctoral dissertation, University of Iowa, 1979.

Pandey, T. *The structure of problem-solving assessment in the California Assessment Program*. Paper presented at the meeting of the American Educational Research Association, New Orleans, LA, April 1984.

Papert, S. *Mindstorms: Children, computers, and powerful ideas*. New York: Basic Books, 1980.

Polya, G. *How to solve it*. Princeton: Princeton University Press, 1957.

Polya, G. *Mathematical Discovery*. New York: John Wiley & Sons, 1962.

Schoen, H.L., & Oehmke, T. A new approach to the measurement of problem-solving skills. In S. Krulik & R. Reys (Eds.), *Problem solving in school mathematics*. Reston, VA: National Council of Teachers of Mathematics, 1980.

Schoenfeld, A.H. Episodes and executive decisions in mathematical problem-solving. In R. Lesh & M. Landau (Eds.), *Acquisition of mathematics concepts and processes*. New York: Academic Press, 1983.

Shirk, G.B. *An examination of conceptual frameworks of beginning mathematics teachers*. Unpublished doctoral dissertation, University of Illinois, Urbana-Champaign, 1972.

Silver, E.A. Student perceptions of relatedness among mathematical verbal problems. *Journal for Research in Mathematics Education* **10**, 195–210, 1979.

Silver, E.A. Recall of mathematical problem information: Solving related problems. *Journal for Research in Mathematics Education* **12**, 54–64, 1981.

Silver, E.A. Problem perception, problem schemata, and problem solving. *Journal of Mathematical Behavior* **3**, 169–181, 1982a.

Silver, E.A. *Thinking about problem solving: Toward an understanding of metacognitive aspects of mathematical problem solving*. Paper prepared for the Conference on Thinking, Suva, Fiji, January 1982b.

Silver, E.A. Probing young adults' thinking about rational numbers. *Focus on Learning Problems in Mathematics* **5**, 105–117, 1983.

Simon, H.A. The computer age. In A.M. Lesgold & F. Reif (Chairmen), *Computers in education: Realizing the potential* (Report of a Research Conference, Pittsburgh, November 1982). U.S. Department of Education, Office of Educational Research and Improvement, 1983.

Skemp, R.R. *Intelligence, learning, and action*. New York: John Wiley & Sons, 1979.

Slavin, R. Cooperative learning. *Review of Educational Research* **50**, 315–42, 1980.

Stake, R.E., & Easley, J.A. (Eds.). *Case studies in science education* (Vols. 1 & 2). Urbana-Champaign: University of Illinois, 1978.

Steffe, L.P., & von Glasersfeld, E. *Children's counting types: Philosophy, theory & application*. New York: Praeger Publishers, 1983.

Sternberg, R.J. Criteria for intellectual skills training. *Educational Researcher* **12**(2), 6–12 and 26, 1983.

Sternberg, R.J. Representation and process in linear syllogistic reasoning. *Journal of Experimental Psychology: General* **109**, 119–59, 1980a.

Sternberg, R.J. Sketch of a componential subtheory of human intelligence. *Behavioral and Brain Sciences* **3**, 573–83, 1980b.

Stover, G.B. Structural variables affecting mathematical word problem difficulty in sixth graders. (Doctoral dissertation, University of San Francisco, 1979). *Dissertation Abstracts International* **42**, 1982, 5050A. (University Microfilms No. DA8211361)

Thompson, A.G. *Teacher's conceptions of mathematics and mathematics teaching: Three case studies.* Unpublished doctoral dissertation, University of Georgia, 1982.

Thompson, P. *A theoretical framework for understanding children's concepts of whole number numeration.* Unpublished doctoral dissertation, University of Georgia, 1982.

Tversky, A., & Kahneman, D. Belief in the law of small numbers. *Psychological Bulletin* **76**, 105–10, 1971.

Vergnaud, G. Cognitive and developmental psychology and research in mathematics education: Some theoretical and methodological issues. *For the Learning of Mathematics* **3**, 31–41, 1982.

Vergnaud, G. Why is an epistemological perspective a necessity for research in mathematics education? In J.C. Bergeron & N. Herscovics (Eds.), *Proceedings of the Fifth Annual Meeting of the North American Chapter of the International Group for the Psychology of Mathematics Education* (PME-NA), Montreal, 1983.

Vygotsky, L. *Mind in society.* Cambridge, MA: Harvard University Press, 1978.

Wagner, S. Conservation of equation and function under transformations of variable. *Journal for Research in Mathematics Education* **12**, 107–18, 1981.

Wagner, S. What are these things called variables? *Mathematics Teacher* **76**, 474–79, 1983.

Webb, N.M. Student interaction and learning in small groups. *Review of Educational Research* **52**, 421–45, 1982.

Webb, N.M., & Cullian, L.K. Group interaction and achievement in small groups: Stability over time. *American Education Research Journal* **20**, 411–23, 1983.

Zigler, E. The retarded child as a whole person. In H.E. Adams & W.K. Boardman (Eds.), *Advances in experimental clinical psychology* (Vol. 1). New York: Pergamon Press, 1971.

Affective Issues in Research on Teaching Mathematical Problem Solving

Douglas B. McLeod

San Diego State University

Research on mathematical problem solving has concentrated on cognitive, rather than affective, issues. Generally, the same can be said for research on the *teaching* of mathematical problem solving. This concentration on cognitive variables is natural and not to be deplored. However, whenever research on teaching problem solving looks seriously at students in mathematics classes, affective issues inevitably arise and demand our attention. The purpose of this paper is to focus our attention on the affective side of problem solving and to see how affective issues might be addressed in research on problem solving.

The manner in which affective concerns come to the surface in various research programs is frequently enlightening. This paper will first outline how some of these noncognitive concerns have come up in research on cognitive performance, and then discuss how theoretical models of problem-solving behavior might be modified to take into account the affective domain. A number of the more important affective variables—that is, more important to mathematics education—will then be examined. Finally, the paper will consider some general strategies for including affective concerns in research on teaching mathematical problem solving.

For the purposes of this paper, problem solving in mathematics will refer to student performance (grades K–16) on mathematical tasks where the solution or goal is not immediately attainable, and there is no obvious algorithm for the student to use. The kinds of problems and problem-solving strategies that we have in mind are those popularized by Polya (1945). The affective domain will include the feelings, emotions, and beliefs that have some relationship to student performance in problem-solving activities. For example, we will be concerned with such topics as students' anxiety in problem-solving tasks, their enjoyment of solving problems, and their willingness to engage in problem-solving activities.

The relationship of the affective domain to problem solving is a wide-ranging research area. It can, of course, only be sampled in a paper such as this; no claim of completeness is intended. Also, the paper will not focus on the methodological difficulties that come up in research on the affective domain.

Going Beyond the Purely Cognitive

A main stimulus for this paper is the current interest among some problem-solving researchers in factors that are not purely cognitive. This concern for noncognitive issues comes up in a natural way when researchers think about teaching problem solving in mathematics classrooms. As a result, researchers who may not intend to address the affective domain find it useful to do so.

Silver (1979, 1982), for example, started out his research on problem solving by looking at the "think of a related problem" heuristic and has recently moved on to writing about metacognitive aspects of problem solving. Discussion of metacognition and its influence on problem solving produced a concern for student belief systems about mathematics and how these belief systems enhance or (usually) inhibit problem-solving performance. These belief systems remain to be specified in detail, but Silver gives examples of relevant factors, including willingness to persevere in a problem-solving task and perceived personal competence. Willingness to persist and perceptions of competence in problem solving seem to have a substantial affective component.

In a similar manner, Schoenfeld (1980) began his research program on how to teach problem solving by concentrating on the use of heuristics. More recently, Schoenfeld (1983) has become concerned with not only the cognitive resources of the problem solver, but also the metacognitive control systems that the problem solver may or may not use in managing those cognitive resources. In addition, Schoenfeld emphasizes the role that belief systems play in determining the kinds of solutions that the problem solver may attempt. The belief systems may be applied to the mathematical content, for example, or to the individual's view of the chance of success in solving the problem. Again, beliefs about mathematics or about success in solving problems are closely related to attitude and confidence, two important aspects of the affective domain.

Silver and Schoenfeld, of course, are mainly interested in cognition, but they have certainly noted the importance of the affective domain in problem solving. Many other researchers, however, show little interest in the affective domain. Norman (1981) noted that most cognitive theorists would probably prefer it if affective issues just disappeared. Zajonc (1980) observed that contemporary cognitive psychology pays little attention to affective issues; he cited a number of major works on cognition that essentially ignore affect entirely. Greeno (1980), in the same volume of the same journal where the Zajonc paper appeared, reviewed two decades of research on learning and found no need to address affective issues.

Cognitive theorists in general have concentrated their energy on explaining what Norman (1981) calls the "Pure Cognitive System" (p. 274). This concentration is a natural outgrowth of the use of information-processing terminology and metaphors, and of the recent collaborative efforts between psychologists and experts in artificial intelligence. Limiting one's research perspective to the purely cognitive seems acceptable for those interested mainly in the performance of machines; however, researchers who are interested in human performance need to go beyond the purely cognitive if their theories and investigations are to be important for problem solving in mathematics classrooms.

Norman (1981) clearly recognizes the importance of going beyond the purely cognitive. In trying to set a research agenda for the emerging discipline of cognitive science, he identifies emotions and belief systems as 2 of the 12 major issues that need to be addressed. If cognitive science can address these issues and others that fall outside of the purely cognitive, then its research may begin to have more useful implications for mathematics teaching. Norman's ideas should be particularly helpful in legitimizing research on affective issues.

In summary, researchers from scientific disciplines generally seem uncomfortable dealing with affective issues. However, affective issues inevitably arise when we consider human performance on nonroutine mathematical tasks. Leading researchers in mathematics education and cognitive science now seem more willing to address these issues than in the past. By addressing affective issues, researchers should be able to produce findings that are more applicable to the teaching of mathematical problem solving than was formerly possible.

THEORETICAL ISSUES

If the renewed interest in affective issues is to develop into a productive research area, an appropriate theoretical framework needs to be developed. This framework should take into account recent research on human information processing, since that point of view is the dominant mode for conceptualizing research on problem solving. Also, the current interest in metacognition suggests that the role of consciousness should be an important aspect of the theory.

Human Information Processing and the Affective Domain

As noted earlier, information-processing psychologists, like the behaviorists before them, have generally not been very interested in affective issues. Their focus on the purely cognitive aspects of learning has reduced the value of their work to research on learning in general and on mathematical problem solving in particular. In Norman's (1981) view, even the progress made in some areas of information-processing psychology (e.g., memory) has been marred by the overall sterility of the purely cognitive approach. As a result, he has proposed a more inclusive model of a human information-processing system that includes cognitive, emotional, and regulatory (biological) systems. The relationships among these systems, and the question of whether one system is dominant, are still to be resolved.

One of the major influences on Norman's reconceptualization of human information processing has been Mandler's (1975) work on emotion. Mandler emphasizes the physiological aspects of emotion, referred to as arousal, which would occur in the biological regulatory system outlined by Norman (1981). In educational settings, arousal can be related to either positive or negative feelings, depending on the cognitive interpretation that we give it. For example, giving a student a difficult problem to solve could result in physiological arousal (rapid heartbeat, muscle tension) that one student might interpret in terms of fear or anxiety, while another student would express feelings of excitement and anticipation. The way the student interprets the arousal determines whether the emotion is positive or negative. The interpretation will, of course, be influenced by a host of factors, including the student's previous experience with problem solving.

In Mandler's view (1975, p. 153), a major source of arousal (and hence emotion) is the interruption of an individual's plans or planned behavior. Such interruptions could come from surprising events or frustrating ones, including solving a problem that has some unexpected result, or not solving a problem that looks like it should be solvable.

Either kind of interruption can cause the physiological changes leading to arousal and emotion.

By making interruptions a focal point of his theory of emotion and arousal, Mandler is seeking to avoid some of the traditional psychological constructs (drives, needs) that he believes are unnecessary for information-processing theory. Assigning such a central theoretical role to interruptions sounds a bit implausible at first, but Mandler develops his position quite carefully. Later we will discuss in more detail how interruptions in problem solving might be related quite directly to affective consequences.

Although Mandler (1975) seems to view emotion as a complex interaction of cognitive and biological systems, other psychologists do not necessarily agree. Zajonc (1980) and Kunst-Wilson and Zajonc (1980) argue that there is evidence of independent (and at least partially separate) affective and cognitive systems. Their data suggest that reaction times and retrieval processes may be different for the affective and cognitive domains, leading them to hypothesize more independent systems. They also believe that some degree of affect is present in any task, even tasks where there is no time for conscious cognitive processing. The tasks they use are exceptionally simple ones that deal with recognition of objects (such as octagons) and identification of facial features; there is little similarity to problem-solving tasks. However, their insistence on the primacy of affect—that affect is always involved in storage and retrieval processes—makes their point of view particularly interesting.

In contrast, other psychologists seem to view affect as just more grist for the cognitive mill. Simon (1976) argues that social psychology and cognitive psychology are essentially similar and should be unified. For him, the same processes that explain cognitive performance can be used to explain the affective domain.

Abelson (1976) takes a similar view. He applies the concept of scripts to discuss the development of attitude. Scripts, which are sequences of events that involve the individual, are stored in memory either singly, in categories, or in a more abstract way according to their attributes or characteristics. In this scheme for organizing memory, the scripts include both the cognitive and affective information, and all scripts, regardless of content, are subject to the same kind of cognitive processing.

According to Abelson (1976), then, one's affective reaction to an object or situation is based on the collection of scripts that are related to that object or situation. If, for example, students are given a geometric construction problem (as reported by Schoenfeld, [1983]), their performance will be influenced by the collection of scripts that record what happened to them in similar situations in the past. If the geometric construction script has negative feelings stored with it, then these are retrieved along with the related scripts.

When a script is retrieved and activated, it may bring with it related scripts that could influence behavior. For example, our geometric construction script could be connected to a more general "tool" script that also has certain affective components. Accordingly one might expect a person who doesn't like using tools to bring that attitude to the use of ruler and compass in geometric construction problems. Thus the affective component of a script in a given situation may be obtained from the script itself or from related scripts that lie above it in a hierarchical memory structure. See Mandler (1975, p. 231) for a related discussion of how access to a particular node in a memory structure may activate more abstract nodes that lie further up in the hierarchy.

In summary, information-processing psychology has not found it easy to deal with affective issues, and progress has been slow. Models of affect are quite primitive, and Zajonc (1980) believes that it is not yet time to try to construct an affective model; in his view, the affective components of even simple tasks (e.g., recognition) are still not understood well enough. It seems most reasonable to hypothesize the existence of both affective and cognitive systems, as Norman (1981) does, but the relationships among the various systems of his model are not well understood.

The Role of Consciousness

Consciousness, like affect, is another concept that has received little attention in recent years. Mandler (1975) discusses in some detail the revival of the study of conscious (as well as unconscious) mental processes, and notes how the earlier dominance of behaviorism made the study of consciousness both unfashionable and unnecessary. But Mandler argues that such study is useful, because it helps pull together important ideas about human information processing. For example, when we talk about limitations on short-term memory, we are discussing the limited number of schemas that can be held in consciousness at the same time. When we discuss retrieval from long-term memory, we refer to the notion of focusing our attention on information that was previously in our unconscious. And part of what we can bring to consciousness, or leave in our unconscious, is emotion—the feelings and beliefs that are the focus of this paper.

Rigney (1980) presents some interesting ideas about human information processing and consciousness that I believe have relevance for affective variables. He talks about the duality between conscious and unconscious processing in problem solving. He suggests that conscious processing "is relatively slow, serial, and of limited capacity," and that unconscious processes are "relatively fast, generally thought to be parallel," and probably make up "the bulk of processing resources" (p. 326). Although Rigney is mostly concerned with cognitive learning strategies, his ideas seem to apply very nicely in the affective domain. His discussion of unconscious processes is particularly appealing in mathematics, where it echoes in contemporary terms the writing of Hadamard (1945) on the unconscious and mathematical discovery.

Student feelings about their chances of success in problem solving are frequently found in the unconscious. They may not be aware of how their feelings about problem solving are limiting the kinds of cognitive processes or problem-solving strategies that they use. Their beliefs about mathematics may cause them to use only "guess and test" strategies rather than a more systematic search for pattern. Teaching students about heuristics helps them become more aware of the cognitive strategies that they may want to use in solving problems. Teaching students about the affective variables that may be influencing them can make them more aware of limitations that they have imposed (usually unconsciously) on their choice of problem-solving strategies.

Students need to be conscious of the metacognitive decisions that they make in solving problems. Bringing these decisions out of the unconscious into the realm of conscious planning seems to be an important part of problem-solving instruction. In Rigney's terms, strategy selection must move to the conscious level, for only through consciousness can one access the human processor and its limited working space (Rigney & Munro, 1981).

Within the realm of conscious processing, Rigney (1980) finds another duality, the "duality of the self" (p. 323). He divides the functioning of the problem solver into two parts, the "doer" and the "watcher." The first carries out the demands of the second: The doer follows orders and the watcher provides rewards or punishments, depending on how well things turn out. This division of labor, which reflects similar thinking regarding metacognitive processes, has been used by Rigney and his colleagues in training students, and that experience may help to inform related research on metacognition and problem solving.

The dualities between conscious and unconscious processing and between the doer and the watcher do not appear to be part of any detailed information-processing model, according to Rigney (1980). And Mandler (1975) cautions against trying to be very specific and precise about notions like consciousness at too early a stage in the activity of theory building. In Mandler's view, such notions should be allowed to grow and evolve in a natural way, rather than being operationalized, and hence fixed, at an immature stage.

The role of consciousness has become an important concern in cognitive science, where Norman (1981) lists it as one of his 12 essential issues. The analysis of conscious and unconscious processing seems essential to a full understanding of problem-solving performance and, especially, the role of the affective domain in problem solving.

AFFECTIVE DIMENSIONS OF PROBLEM-SOLVING PERFORMANCE

A variety of affective dimensions have been considered in research on problem solving. Lester (1980), for example, lists "interests, motivation, confidence, perseverence, and a willingness to take risks" (p. 299). In some studies, these dimensions have been generated out of a broad range of observations of student performance with very little attention to theoretical considerations. Other studies have been based on specific theoretical positions, and have gathered data related to particular affective concerns. Given the limited state of our knowledge about the affective domain, both data-driven and theory-driven approaches seem reasonable, and both kinds of studies will be discussed.

Tension and Relaxation in Problem Solving

For an example of data-driven research on problem solving, consider the classic volume by Bloom and Broder (1950) on the problem-solving processes of college students. This early study clearly put its emphasis on the cognitive processes of students, but also paid considerable attention to the affective domain. Problems were chosen from a variety of disciplines, including mathematics. Although the problems that were investigated were not particularly good from a mathematical point of view (they were similar to those found in standard aptitude tests), the research procedures were relatively similar to today's use of clinical methods, and the study's comments on affective issues are fascinating.

In the study, the researchers interviewed the students extensively and asked them to think aloud as they solved the problems. The rich protocols that resulted are full of evidence on affective issues, including some that are rarely discussed in more recent research. For example, Bloom and Broder (1950) discuss at some length the way that tension and relaxation accompany problem solving (p. 95). In contrast, more recent research on problem solving rarely comments on any physiological phenomena that are related to the affective side.

Bloom and Broder note how muscular tension is evident in the bodies of students who engage in problem-solving activities. Increasing the complexity of the problem increased the amount of tension, with the greatest evidence of tension appearing in the muscles of the back, neck, and abdomen. Once the students perceived that they had solved the problem, the tension was immediately reduced. Muscles relaxed and students reported feelings of enjoyment and satisfaction.

The development of tension and discomfort, followed by relaxation and feelings of pleasure, was characteristic of successful problem solvers. Students who did not develop tension were generally unwilling to attack the problem in a serious way. Also, students who were very relaxed were said to have difficulty concentrating on the problem; apparently they were not investing enough energy in the problem to be able to focus on it clearly. Of course, too much tension could also be debilitating, leading to what students referred to as mental blocks to their thinking. However, a moderate amount of tension seemed to improve problem-solving performance for most students, and the release from tension that followed the solution of a problem appeared to be a major source of the pleasure that students received from solving problems.

The existence of tension, followed by relaxation, provides a nice example of a positive form of arousal as discussed in Mandler's (1975) analysis of emotion. The development and release of tension is an important aspect of many kinds of human behavior, and appears to be a fundamental source of positive feelings. In Mandler's terms, the tension results from the interruption of plans and behavior—that is, from the attempts to solve the problem that are not met with immediate success. If there was no interruption as the student completed the task, then the task was too simple to be a real problem for that student; in that case, no tension or subsequent relaxation would be observed, and also the feelings of satisfaction would be very slight.

The central role of tension and relaxation in problem-solving behavior helps to explain why students seldom look back to see if they could improve their problem solution. The infrequency of "looking-back" behavior by students is well documented (Kantowski, 1977). But as Bloom and Broder (1950) observed in their study, once the student perceives that the problem solution (adequate or inadequate) is complete, relaxation occurs and there is no more energy available to address the problem.

Attending to physiological aspects of problem-solving behavior seems to be a useful line of attack in research on problem solving. The interaction of cognitive, emotional, and biological systems is now present in at least one model of the human information-processing system (Norman, 1981); researchers need to pay attention to all three systems in their investigative efforts.

Causal Attributions and Problem Solving

Once students solve a problem, to what do they attribute their success? Or if they fail to find a solution, how do they explain their lack of success? The notions of causal attribution and locus of control are at the center of some of the most interesting current research related to the affective domain and problem solving.

Causal attribution has roots going back to earlier theories of motivation and personality (Heider, 1958), but two of its main proponents have been Rotter (1966) and Weiner (1979). Rotter's social-learning theory originally referred to this variable in terms of locus of control. According to Rotter, individuals with an internal locus of control perceive the outcomes of their actions as being due to their own behavior; on the other hand, those who have an external locus of control attribute the consequences of their actions to chance or fate. One's locus of control, then, is a system of beliefs about whether the rewards and successes of life (or its punishments and failures) can be attributed to causes that are internal or external (with respect to oneself).

Weiner (1979), in a recent revision of his theoretical position, presents a somewhat more elaborate version of the attributions of causes for either success or failure (see Table 1). Weiner considers not only the locus of the cause (whether it was internal or external to the individual), but also whether the cause is stable or unstable, and whether the cause is controllable or not. For Weiner, student ability is a stable, internal cause (of success or failure) that is basically uncontrollable, at least in the short run. A student's typical effort, like ability, is relatively stable and internal, but it is controllable. For examples of external causes of success or failure, consider task difficulty (stable, external, and uncontrollable by the student) or luck (unstable, external, and also uncontrollable).

Table 1. Some causes of success and failure. [Adapted from Weiner, 1979, p. 7.]

	Internal		External	
	Stable	Unstable	Stable	Unstable
Uncontrollable	Ability	Mood	Task difficulty	Luck
Controllable	Typical effort	Immediate effort	Teacher bias	Unusual help from others

A number of researchers have tried to apply these ideas in educational settings. The theory implies that students who attribute their success to internal causes should be able to solve problems independently, with relatively little help from the teacher. Such students will be more willing to rely on their own internal resources. On the other hand, students who attribute their success to external causes may be more likely to rely on external sources, like the teacher, in order to solve problems. There are some studies of mathematics learning in the literature that support this view (Janicki & Peterson, 1981; McLeod & Adams, 1981). For a more comprehensive review of research on attributions, see Stipek and Weisz (1981); for a discussion of attributions from an information-processing perspective, see Frieze (1976); for a more detailed analysis of the relationship of attribution research to mathematics, see Kloosterman (1983).

Ideas related to attribution theory seem to play a prominent role in the study of affective influences on learning and problem solving in science and mathematics. For example, in her investigations of problem solving in science education, Rowe (1983) identified two classes of students. In one group she puts students who feel that their success or failure is mainly due to chance. These students are characterized by a relatively passive approach to problem solving and low persistence at problem-solving tasks. In Rowe's terms, they have a low fate-control orientation. Another group of students has a high fate-control orientation, and they feel that they can influence the odds of success. These students are more willing to persist in addressing a problem-solving task, and to attack problems more aggressively. The differences between students with high and low fate-control views seem relevant to problem-solving performance in both mathematics and science, as well as to research on causal attributions.

Recent work on attitude toward mathematics also incorporates fate. Haladyna et al. (1983) identify fatalism as an important variable in their model of attitudinal factors.

Fatalism, "the tendency to accept the fates as determining some outcome related to the subject matter" (p. 21), seems to be another aspect of locus of control.

Fennema and her colleagues have also investigated causal attributions of performance in mathematics (Wolleat et al., 1982) with a special emphasis on sex differences. They found that males are more likely than females to attribute their success in mathematics to ability, and that females are more likely than males to attribute their failure to lack of ability. In addition, females tend to attribute success to effort, but males attribute failure to lack of effort. These results contribute to our understanding of why females are less confident than males about their ability to learn mathematics and why males are more likely than females to persist in the study of mathematics. Further, the attribution of failure to a lack of ability (a stable, internal, uncontrollable cause) seems to contribute to the development of "learned helplessness," a phenomenon that appears to be more prevalent among females than males.

The relationship between student attributions and their performance in problem-solving tasks seems to be important. If students attribute their failures in problem solving to their lack of ability, they are likely to be unwilling to persist in problem-solving tasks very long. If students attribute their success in mathematical performance to help from the teacher, an external cause, they may be more likely to see problem solving as an activity that they cannot participate in unless the teacher helps.

Fortunately, there is evidence that causal attributions can be modified through appropriate educational experiences (Lefcourt, 1976). Attributional patterns appear to be learned, and need not be thought of as personality traits that are impossible to change. For example, Johnson and Croft (1975) found that college students' attributions of success in an individualized instruction format changed substantially over a period of one semester.

Causal attributions are part of the student's belief system and, as such, seem to be related to Silver and Schoenfeld's interests in metacognition and control processes. If students attribute failure to solve a problem to their lack of ability (an internal cause) and attribute success in solving a problem to having a teacher who gives them the right algorithm (an external cause), then the students' metacognitive choices may be severely limited. Such students will rarely use the wide range of heuristics that are available to them.

Independence and Problem Solving

A variety of other affective variables also appear to influence problem-solving performance. One of the most interesting is the notion of independence. Cattell (1971) lists independence as one of his personality factors and describes it in terms of temperament considerations like criticalness, lack of rigidity, and self-control. Witkin and Goodenough's (1981) notion of field independence is related to Cattell's independence, but also includes an important cognitive component, cognitive restructuring. The difficulties in measuring field independence and in distinguishing it from general or fluid ability (Cattell's terms) make it a challenging but frustrating variable for problem-solving researchers.

Other notions of independence are also prevalent in the literature. Good et al. (1983) classified students into several different categories, including dependent and independent. Dependent students were those who performed at or near the norm on most variables (achievement, conscientiousness, and the like), but who depended heavily on the teacher for direction and guidance. Independent students, by contrast, relied less on teacher direction, preferred a wide range of choices, and showed little response to external motivation. Independent students, although somewhat stronger in mathematics than dependent students, were not in the high achievement group and were relatively frequent behavior problems. Good et al. speculate on the teaching strategies that are most effective for these categories of students, and their data indicate interesting relationships. Further investigation in the teaching of problem solving seems appropriate.

Independence is a very appealing variable, since it is so important to creative mathematical problem solving. When Pat Thompson (this volume) describes his phenomenon of figuration-boundness, he is dealing in part with the lack of independence shown by many students. Figuration-boundness, which Thompson describes as "the inability of a student to go beyond the elements of a problem to a network of relationships and potential transformations in which the elements exist," is a characteristic of dependent students and their inability (or unwillingness) to go anywhere that the teacher hasn't taken them. Of course, figuration-boundness is not just the result of affective variables; it can be defined in purely cognitive terms. But affective factors certainly must play an important role. Purely cognitive considerations are inadequate to explain student performance.

Additional variables of interest include confidence, anxiety, curiosity, persistence, and many others. Occasionally these variables are closely related; Fennema (1982), for example, found that her measures of confidence and anxiety were essentially the same. Also, many of these variables are discussed in the literature under the general title of motivation. See, for example, Malone's (1981) ideas on intrinsic motivation, or any of several more general discussions (Atkinson & Raynor, 1974).

HOW SHOULD WE PROCEED?

If we agree that mathematical problem-solving performance is influenced by affective variables, how should we proceed? First, it is important to recognize the role of the affective domain, and to include it in the theoretical frameworks that guide problem-solving research. The identification and measurement of affective variables is difficult and frustrating, but they still should be included. Eventually, taking into account affective variables should be worth the effort.

The selection of variables constitutes one difficulty. There is a tendency among researchers to analyze behavior into ever smaller components, cleverly identifying all of the possible explanations of why students' affective characteristics keep them from solving problems in the way that they should be able to, given their cognitive capabilities. However, refining affective variables into a variety of narrow subdimensions quickly becomes counter-productive. In general, affective variables can't be measured that accurately, and even if they could, such narrowly defined variables would be unlikely to have any major influence, taken individually. As a result, it seems more profitable to define constellations of variables and to look at their combined effect on problem-solving performance.

As an example of this process, consider Fennema and Peterson's (1983) recent work on autonomous learning behaviors. Autonomy is made up of a number of related factors, including independence (e.g., willingness to work on a problem without asking for help), persistence at problem-solving tasks, and confidence in one's ability to solve problems that are set at an appropriate level of difficulty. These factors are all influenced by the attributional style of the student, as well as other factors (student view of the usefulness of mathematics, previous success in problem solving, etc.). Attempts to influence a range of affective variables should have a reasonably powerful effect on problem-solving ability. It seems likely that helping students develop autonomous learning behaviors should have a positive influence on their problem-solving performance.

The development of instructional ideas related to the affective domain and problem solving is particularly interesting because this research area has great potential for both explaining and minimizing the differences that exist between the sexes and between different ethnic groups in problem-solving performance. It seems unlikely to me that differences in problem-solving performance between the sexes can be explained any other way. Research on spatial ability, for example, does not seem very illuminating (Fennema, 1982; Linn & Pulos, 1983). The attempt to attribute sex differences in problem solving to differences in course taking has also proved unfruitful (Armstrong, 1981). Other attempts to attribute differences in performance to biological factors also seem to be doomed to failure (Beckwith, 1983). Differences between ethnic groups in problem-solving performance seem to be primarily due to economic and other social factors that may be difficult for any educational program to change. However, I suspect that those differences could also be reduced substantially if appropriate programs could be devised to improve the influence of affective variables on problem-solving performance.

SUMMARY

The recent surge in interest in noncognitive aspects of mathematical problem solving is a good sign, for it reflects the fact that researchers want their efforts to result in implications for school mathematics. Information-processing models of human problem solving have generally avoided affective considerations, probably because restricting oneself to the purely cognitive domain is a simplification of the task. But since the affective domain is important, it is desirable to try to include affective dimensions in theoretical models of human problem solving. The particular affective variables that seem most useful at the moment include aspects of causal attribution and of independence, but many other variables are also appropriate for research. Whatever variable is chosen for investigation should probably be addressed as a constellation of more specific factors, each of which can be measured individually. Once the relationship between such a constellation of factors and success in problem solving has been determined, then efforts to change student characteristics with respect to that constellation of affective factors may be appropriate. Through such efforts, the research community may be able to improve problem-solving performance in mathematics for all students and especially for those groups that are currently underrepresented in mathematical careers.

REFERENCES

Abelson, R.P. Script processing in attitude formation and decision making. In J.S. Carroll, & J.W. Payne (Eds.), *Cognition and social behavior*. Hillsdale, NJ: Lawrence Erlbaum Associates, 1976.

Armstrong, J.M. Achievement and participation of women in mathematics: Results of two national surveys. *Journal for Research in Mathematics Education* 12, 356–72, 1981.

Atkinson, J.W., & Raynor, J.O. (Eds.), *Motivation and achievement*. Washington, DC: Winston, 1974.

Beckwith, J. Gender and math performance: Does biology have implications for educational policy? *Journal of Education* 165, 158–74, 1983.

Bloom, B.S., & Broder, L.J. *Problem-solving processes of college students.* Chicago: University of Chicago Press, 1950.

Cattell, R.B. *Abilities: Their structure, growth, and action.* Boston: Houghton Mifflin, 1971.

Fennema, E. *The development of variables associated with sex differences in mathematics.* Symposium conducted at the annual meeting of the American Educational Research Association, New York, March 1982.

Fennema, E., & Peterson, P.L. *Autonomous learning behavior: A possible explanation.* Paper presented at the annual meeting of the American Educational Research Association, Montreal, April 1983.

Frieze, I.H. The role of information processing in making causal attributions for success and failure. In J.S. Carroll & J.W. Payne (Eds.), *Cognition and social behavior.* Hillsdale, NJ: Lawrence Erlbaum Associates, 1976.

Good, T.L., Grouws, D.A., & Ebmeier, H. *Active mathematics teaching.* New York: Longman, 1983.

Greeno, J.G. Psychology of learning, 1960-1980: One participant's observations. *American Psychologist* 35, 713–28, 1980.

Hadamard, J. *The psychology of invention in the mathematical field.* Princeton, NJ: Princeton University Press, 1945.

Haladyna, T., Shaughnessy, J., & Shaughnessy, J.M. A causal analysis of attitude toward mathematics. *Journal for Research in Mathematics Education* 14, 19–29, 1983.

Heider, F. *The psychology of interpersonal relations.* New York: John Wiley & Sons, 1958.

Janicki, T.C., & Peterson, P.L. Aptitude-treatment interaction effects of variations in direct instruction. *American Educational Research Journal* 18, 63–82, 1981.

Johnson, W.G., & Croft, R. Locus of control and participation in a Personalized System of Instruction course. *Journal of Educational Psychology* 67, 416–21, 1975.

Kantowski, M.G. Processes involved in mathematical problem solving. *Journal for Research in Mathematics Education* 8, 163–80, 1977.

Kloosterman, P. *Attribution theory and achievement in mathematics.* Unpublished manuscript, University of Wisconsin-Madison, 1983. (Available from Peter Kloosterman, School of Education, Indiana University, Bloomington, IN 47405.)

Kunst-Wilson, W.R., & Zajonc, R.B. Affective discrimination of stimuli that cannot be recognized. *Science* 207, 557–58, 1980.

Lefcourt, H.M. *Locus of control: Current trends in theory and research.* Hillsdale, NJ: Lawrence Erlbaum Associates, 1976.

Lester, F.K., Jr. Research on mathematical problem solving. In R.J. Shumway (Ed.), *Research in mathematics education.* Reston, VA: National Council of Teachers of Mathematics, 1980.

Linn, M.C., & Pulos, S. Aptitude and experience influences on proportional reasoning during adolescence: Focus on male-female differences. *Journal for Research in Mathematics Education* 14, 30–46, 1983.

Malone, T.W. Toward a theory of intrinsically motivating instruction. *Cognitive Science* 5, 333–69, 1981.

Mandler, G. *Mind and emotion.* New York: John Wiley & Sons, 1975.

McLeod, D.B., & Adams, V.M. Locus of control and mathematics instruction: Three exploratory studies. *Journal of Experimental Education* 49, 94–99, 1981.

Norman, D.A. Twelve issues for cognitive science. In D.A. Norman (Ed.), *Perspectives on cognitive science.* Norwood, NJ: Ablex, 1981.

Polya, G. *How to solve it.* Princeton, NJ: Princeton University Press, 1945.

Rigney, J.W. Cognitive learning strategies and dualities in information processing. In R.E. Snow, P.A. Federico, & W.E. Montague (Eds.), *Aptitude, learning, and instruction* (Vol. 1). Hillsdale, NJ: Lawrence Erlbaum Associates, 1980.

Rigney, J.W., & Munro, A. Learning stategies. In H.F. O'Neil, Jr. (Ed.), *Computer-based instruction: A state-of-the-art assessment.* New York: Academic Press, 1981.

Rotter, J.B. Generalized expectancies for internal versus external control of reinforcement. *Psychological Monographs* **80**, 1966, (1, Whole No. 609).

Rowe, M.B. Science education: A framework for decision makers. *Daedalus* **112**, 123–42, 1983.

Schoenfeld, A.H. Teaching problem-solving skills. *American Mathematical Monthly* **87**, 794–805, 1980.

Schoenfeld, A.H. Beyond the purely cognitive: Belief systems, social cognitions, and metacognitions as driving forces in intellectual performance. *Cognitive Science* **7**, 329–63, 1983.

Silver, E.A. Student perceptions of relatedness among mathematical verbal problems. *Journal for Research in Mathematics Education* **10**, 195–210, 1979.

Silver, E.A. *Thinking about problem solving: Toward an understanding of metacognitive aspects of mathematical problem solving.* Paper prepared for the Conference on Thinking, Fiji, January 1982.

Simon, H.A. Cognition and social behavior. In J.S. Carroll & J.W. Payne (Eds.), *Cognition and social behavior.* Hillsdale, NJ: Lawrence Erlbaum Associates, 1976.

Stipek, D.J., & Weisz, J. Perceived personal control and academic achievement. *Review of Educational Research* **51**, 101–37, 1981.

Weiner, B. A theory of motivation for some classroom experiences. *Journal of Educational Psychology* **71**, 3–25, 1979.

Witkin, H.A., & Goodenough, D.R. *Cognitive styles: Essence and origins.* New York: International Universities Press, 1981.

Wolleat, P., Pedro, J.D., Becker, A.D., & Fennema, E. Sex differences in high school students' causal attributions of performance in mathematics. *Journal for Research in Mathematics Education* **11**, 356–66, 1980.

Zajonc, R.B. Feeling and thinking: Preferences need no inferences. *American Psychologist* **35**, 151–75, 1980.

Teachers' Conceptions of Mathematics and the Teaching of Problem Solving[1]

Alba G. Thompson

San Diego State University

The ultimate goal of mathematics educators' efforts in investigating problem solving is to find ways in which to improve students' abilities to solve problems. To this end, researchers have sought a better understanding of the nature of problem solving and of the roles that various factors play in problem-solving performance. In an attempt to identify the characteristic qualities and mental processes that lead to successful performance, some researchers have focused on the problem solver. Others have focused on characteristics of the problem tasks.

Based largely on the writings of Polya (1957, 1962, 1965), research related to instruction in problem solving has centered on the effectiveness of instructional methods designed to develop global thinking and reasoning processes, specific skills, and general and task-specific heuristics (Lester, 1980). Because the purpose of most of these studies has been to compare the effectiveness of instructional methods, there has been a tendency to control for the effect of the teacher. There are few signs of efforts to consider the classroom teacher as a vital factor in research on the teaching of problem solving.

The disproportionately small amount of attention that researchers have given to the role of the teacher is disturbing. Based on the findings of current research, we may design new curricula that are responsive to the charge of making problem solving their focus. Yet, we know from experience that the "intended" and the "implemented" curricula often differ dramatically. A tendency to regard the classroom teacher as a passive implementer of dictated curricula is likely to result, as it has in the past, in only partially successful curriculum reform (NACOME, 1975). At a time when the proverbial educational pendulum swings from an emphasis on computational facility to an emphasis on problem solving and critical thinking, it is particularly important that we view the teacher as someone who behaves rationally in making pedagogical decisions about the content and how to present it to the learners.

---

1. The research reported in this paper was supported in part by a Faculty Development Grant from San Diego State University.

In this paper I examine teachers' conceptions of mathematics and mathematics teaching in relation to their instructional behavior. First, I describe what I mean by conceptual or belief systems. Second, some of the research on teachers' conceptions of the subject matter and their relation to instructional practice is summarized. Following this I present examples of case studies that focused on the relationship between teachers' conceptions of mathematics and their teaching behavior. Finally, the discussion focuses on how this research perspective enables us to examine some important questions about the teaching of mathematical problem solving and to suggest some foci for future deliberations.

DEFINITION OF CONCEPTUAL SYSTEMS

Structurally, conceptions, or conceptual systems, may be described as complex organizations of beliefs, disbeliefs, and concepts in a given domain. Because of the philosophic and psychological considerations involved, the description of what constitutes a belief or a concept is more difficult. Several viewpoints have been offered. Scheffler (1965), for example, noted the following about beliefs:

> With independent knowledge of the social context, we may judge belief as revealed in word or deed. Where these latter two diverge, we may need to decide whether to postulate weaknesses of will, or irrationality, or deviant purpose, or ignorance, or bizarre belief, or insincerity, and the choice may often be difficult. . . . It will, in any case, never be reasonable to take belief simply as a matter of verbal response: belief is rather a "theoretical" state characterizing, in subtle ways, the orientation of the person in the world. (pp. 89–90)

Rokeach (1960) was moved to add: "Any expectancy or implicit set is also a belief, which is also to say that it is a predisposition to action. . . . We have to infer what a person really believes from all the things he says and does" (p.32). Rokeach defined a belief system as representing "all the beliefs, sets, expectancies, or hypotheses, conscious and unconscious, that a person at a given time accepts as true of the world he lives in" (p. 33).

With respect to concepts, Harvey, Hunt, and Schroder (1961) noted:

> A concept in the most general sense is a schema for evaluating impinging stimulus objects or events. . . . Once a concept has evolved, it serves as a psychological yardstick in terms of which stimuli are compared and gauged, a kind of experiential filter through which objects are screened and evaluated. (pp. 10–11)

Functionally, conceptual systems act as filters through which information is processed and interpreted. As such, they will influence a person's perception and interpretation of a given situation and the range of actions the person considers. Thus, conceptual systems may be described as "anticipatory schemata" (Neisser, 1976). A person's perception of an event or situation, created through the filter of his or her conceptions, will lead to fairly well-formed, albeit perhaps unconscious, expectations about situations that will follow from it.

Conceptual systems may change over time. Subjective beliefs may become objective in the presence of supportive evidence, or may be discarded in the presence of contradictory evidence. Thus, when a person is faced with a situation that conflicts with his or her conceptions, a modification may occur in both the person's perception of the situation and in the conceptions.

TEACHERS' CONCEPTIONS

Individual teachers often act, when faced with similar instructional situations, in stereotypical ways that constitute a pattern or set of patterns characteristic of their teaching practice (Joyce, 1978–1979; MacKay & Marland, 1978; Peterson & Clark, 1978). In some cases, these patterns may be a manifestation of consciously held notions and deliberately chosen methods. In other cases, these patterns may be a manifestation of unconsciously held beliefs or intuitions that may have evolved out of the teacher's experience. The result is a repertoire of characteristic practices or approaches to instruction in the various aspects of the subject matter.

We have little knowledge of why individual teachers behave the way they do. For example, very little is known about the role that teachers' conceptions of the subject matter and its teaching might play in the genesis and evolution of instructional practices characteristic of their teaching. Inquiry into this issue calls for an examination of teachers' cognitive and metacognitive processes during instruction. Yet, as Shulman and Elstein (1975) noted: "Research typically slights the problem of how teachers think about their pupils and instructional problems; it concentrates, instead, on how teachers act or perform in the classroom" (p. 3).

Recently, the need to study the mental processes of teachers has begun to receive increased attention from researchers (see Shavelson & Stern, 1981, for a review of recent studies on teachers' thoughts, judgments, decisions, and behavior before and during instruction). Still, however, very few studies have examined the influence that teachers' conceptions of the subject matter and its teaching have on their instructional judgments, decisions, and behavior. Two of these studies have focused on the subject matter of reading.

Bawden, Burke, and Duffy (1979) conducted surveys and naturalistic field studies to examine the existence and nature of teachers' conceptions about reading and the relation of those conceptions to their instructional practice. The teachers' conceptions were reflected in their behavior, but these conceptions alone did not guide their instructional decisions. In the majority of the teachers studied, other conceptions that did not concern reading played a part in affecting their behavior. For 7 of the 23 teachers studied, the other conceptions seemed to dominate their decisions and influence their actions more than the reading conceptions they professed. Bawden and his colleagues observed qualitative differences among the teachers' conceptions of reading. The older, more experienced teachers held skills-oriented conceptions, whereas the younger, less experienced teachers held student-oriented conceptions. The teachers of younger children professed skill-oriented conceptions, and the teachers of older children held student-oriented conceptions. Some teachers were more consistent in their professed conceptions than others, and the conceptions of some teachers were more differentiated than those of others.

In another study of teachers' conceptions of reading, Methany (1980) obtained information that was consistent with Bawden and his colleagues' findings of the relation of conceptions to grade level. He also reported that teachers had differentiated conceptions of low-ability students of low socioeconomic status. The teachers advocated different teaching strategies, teacher roles, and instructional materials for the two groups of students.

The findings of these studies show that the relationship of teachers' conceptions of the subject matter to their instructional practices is complex. They provide evidence that a variety of factors interact with the teachers' conceptions in affecting their classroom behavior. Because of this interaction, teachers with similar conceptions may be expected to act in different ways.

However, what determines the strength and consistency of the relationship between teachers' conceptions and their instructional practices is not clear from these studies. Given the scant information available, one can do little more than speculate. Perhaps the key factor is the teachers' conviction in their professed conceptions—that is, the absence of ambivalent or competing beliefs. Perhaps it is the teachers' ability to commit themselves to one of several competing beliefs. Perhaps it is the degree to which the teachers are able to exercise their professional autonomy in the classroom or the amount of administrative support that they have. In any case, for a given teacher, the key factor may be one or any combination of these.

An incongruity between teachers' conceptions and their actions may be due to the frequency with which they have to face unexpected events in the classroom. As research has indicated, the immediacy of the responses required in such cases may not allow time to reflect on alternative ways of dealing with a specific event and to make a choice that is consistent with their conceptions. Instead, the teachers have time only to react (MacKay & Marland, 1978).

As plausible as this may seem, it fails to be convincing. Experienced teachers are likely to have developed a repertoire of ways to handle the different events that, albeit unexpected, typically arise in the classroom. It seems reasonable to expect that through their years of experience in the classroom, these teachers have reflected on the relative merits of alternative actions and have developed patterned ways of handling different types of events.

Evidence in support of this hypothesis comes from a study conducted by Shroyer (1978). She examined teachers' decision making when confronted with "critical moments" in teaching mathematics and found that the teachers handled such situations in ways that reflected their beliefs about teaching. For example, she observed that one teacher showed a tendency to take a student error or suggestion and turn it back to the class for their response. This the teacher usually did without commenting on the correctness of the idea. Shroyer noted that this typical behavior reflected the teacher's "belief that students learn more by being involved, by responding rather than listening" (p. 19). Another behavior the teacher frequently displayed was to continue intentionally to present examples rather than stopping to provide explanations when confronted with expressions of confusion from her students. The teacher explained that "based on her own frustrating experiences learning mathematics, the best strategy was not to 'back-off' and offer explanations but to provide more examples" (p. 19).

In a study of the conceptual frameworks of four preservice teachers enrolled in a mathematics methods course, and the relation of their conceptions to their behavior when teaching mathematics to small groups of junior high school students, Shirk (1972) observed that the teachers' conceptions appeared to be "activated" in teaching situations, "causing" the teachers to behave in ways that were consistent with their conceptions of mathematics teaching and of their own role as teachers. Shirk conducted an in-depth case study of each preservice teacher. He obtained information about the teachers' conceptions from various sources: written essays and lesson plans, the record of the teaching sessions and interviews (audiotapes and protocols), and the students' evaluations of the lessons. Shirk found no discernible change in the teachers' conceptions as they went through the methods course.

In a similar study involving preservice secondary school mathematics teachers, Bush (1982) reported the teachers' behavior during student teaching to be not only consistent with, but also influenced by, their conceptions of mathematics teaching. He noted that the teachers' views were largely based on their own schooling experience as students of mathematics and that few apparent changes in their conceptions were effected as a result of their participation in the professional training program.

Thompson (1982) conducted case studies of three experienced junior high school mathematics teachers. The purpose of the study was to examine each teacher's conceptions of mathematics and mathematics teaching and their relation to the teacher's instructional practice. The findings indicated that the teachers' views, beliefs, and preferences about mathematics and its teaching played a significant, albeit subtle, role in shaping the teachers' characteristic patterns of instructional behavior. Thompson observed that the teachers' professed conceptions of mathematics were consistent with the manner in which they typically presented the content. With respect to the teachers' conceptions of mathematics teaching, the findings indicated that these consisted of views and beliefs that were specific to the teaching of mathematics as well as views about teaching in general—the prevalence of each type varying among the teachers. Specific examples of the case studies will be discussed in the next section of this paper.

The studies summarized in this section bring out the complexity of the relationship between teachers' conceptions of the subject matter and instructional practices. In investigating teachers' conceptions, the questions of what to look for and where to look are nontrivial. Once one decides on answers to these questions, what is found will be determined by the lens through which one looks and by how close to or far away from the object the lens is focused. Different lenses may also be used. Several studies have used an empirical lens (Bawden et al., 1979; Bush, 1982; Shirk, 1972; Thompson, 1982), others a psychological lens (Harvey et al., 1961; Rokeach, 1960), and yet others a philosophic lens (Copes, 1979; Meyerson, 1977). Moreover, the analysis may focus on the structural properties of conceptions or, instead, on their content. The lens used in the study from which the examples in the next section came was an empirical one, and the analysis focused on the content of the teachers' conceptions of mathematics and mathematics teaching.

CASE STUDIES

The case studies summarized here each lasted 4 weeks. A brief characterization of each teacher's conceptions of mathematics and mathematics teaching is presented; however, most of the anecdotal evidence that led to this characterization has been left out.

Jeanne

At the time of the case study, Jeanne had been teaching junior high school mathematics for 10 consecutive years and was the mathematics coordinator for her school, a rural school in northeast Georgia. Her undergraduate major was in education and she had a master's degree in mathematics education. She was observed teaching an eighth-grade general mathematics class, which she described as fairly homogeneous, consisting of average and slightly above average students.

Jeanne's teaching reflected a view of mathematics as a coherent collection of interrelated concepts and procedures, and as a subject free of ambiguities and arbitrariness.

This view could be inferred from her marked tendency to stress the meaning of the concepts taught in terms of their relationship to other mathematics concepts (e.g., percents as fractions; division as repeated subtraction), and to emphasize the reasons or logic underlying the mathematical procedures used in class. A view of mathematical activity as some sort of game of symbols played according to rules whose justification is an essential part of the game seemed implicit in the way that she dealt with the content. Although not rigorous, her approach in presenting the content was formal. She typically relied on mathematical symbols in her explanations and frequently referred to the structural properties of mathematics. She seldom appealed to intuition—her's or the students—and did not allude to the practical significance of the topics studied.

Consistently, Jeanne's remarks indicated that she regarded mathematics as the mathematics of the school curriculum. She admitted that she rarely thought about mathematics as a scientific discipline. She clearly held two separate, unrelated views of mathematics that seemed to be the result of two distinct experiences in her study of the subject. One was a positive view that seemed to have been influenced by a favorable experience with precollege mathematics. The other view was related to an unpleasant experience with college mathematics—specifically with calculus and linear algebra. This experience appeared to have caused Jeanne to question her mathematical ability, which she conceded was not very strong.

Jeanne's remarks revealed a view of the content of mathematics as fixed and predetermined, as dictated by the physical world. At no time during either the lessons or the interviews did she allude to the generative processes of mathematics. It seemed apparent that she regarded mathematics as a finished product to be assimilated.

The appeal that mathematics held for Jeanne lay in the logical interrelatedness of its topics and the organization inherent in its underlying structure. Because of these characteristics, mathematics, in her view, was worthy of study for its own sake, independent of its utility. Although she was aware of its practical utility, this, she admitted, was not a characteristic that contributed to her liking mathematics or that she alluded to in teaching. Aside from teaching, mathematics held little relevance in her life. Once while discussing percents smaller than 1%, a student indicated that such percents frequently appeared in interest rates and stock market reports. In response to the student's remark Jeanne indicated: "I don't know very much about that because my husband takes care of those things at home."

Jeanne's conception of mathematics teaching can be characterized in terms of her view of her role in teaching the subject and the students' role in learning it. These were, in gross terms, that she was to disseminate information, and the students were to receive it. Her professed conceptions of mathematics teaching are summarized in the following statements:

- The teacher must establish and maintain an atmosphere of order, respect, and courtesy in the classroom.

- The role of the teacher is to present the content in a clear, logical, and precise manner. To accomplish this she must stress the reasons and logic underlying mathematical rules and procedures and emphasize the logical relations among concepts (to establish their mathematical meaning).

- It is the responsibility of the teacher to direct and control all instructional activities, including the classroom discourse. To this end, she must have a clear plan for the development of the lesson.

- The teacher has a task to accomplish—to present the lesson planned—and must see that it is accomplished without digressions from or inefficient changes in the plan.

- The role of the students is to assimilate the content. "Assimilate" means that the students "see" the relationships between the new topic and those already studied as explained by the teacher.

- Students learn best by attending to the teacher's explanations and responding to her questions.

- Students should not be satisfied with just knowing how to carry out mathematical procedures; they should seek to understand the logic behind the procedures.

On numerous occasions while discussing specific events of the day's lesson, Jeanne's comments revealed a great concern for maintaining control over the development of the lesson and avoiding digressions from a preconceived plan. Not only was her need for control apparent from the discourse and the way that she conducted class, but it seemed to have physical manifestations as well. During her presentations, she usually stood in the front of the room facing the students and holding the textbook in her arms.

Jeanne's discomfort with unanticipated events in the course of a lesson, which was a result of her strong concern for control, appeared to rule out the use of a problem-solving approach in teaching. The unpredictability and uncertainty that characterize such an approach clashed with her need to remain in control and her view of her role as a teacher, specifically with her expressed belief that a good teacher should have a well-delineated plan to which she should adhere in order to ensure clarity.

Jeanne's concern for control seemed to have a strong influence on her instructional decisions, and in several cases it seemed to account for her failure to implement practices that she identified as important or desirable in teaching mathematics. The most striking contrast between her professed views and her teaching was posed by her indication that it is important for the teacher to encourage student participation in class and to be alert to clues from the students to adjust the lesson to their needs.

Although Jeanne conducted class in a question-and-answer fashion, there were no observable signs that she was making an effort to encourage discussion among the students or between them and her. The students' participation typically was limited to responding to her questions, which for the most part were intended to elicit short, simple answers. Her professed belief in the importance of encouraging the students to participate in class seemed to be in sharpest contrast with her tendency to disregard the students' suggestions and not to follow through with their ideas. This behavior seemed motivated by her need to adhere to a mental "script" of the lesson and by her limited confidence in her ability to discuss aspects of a topic for which she was not prepared.

Only once during the 4 weeks of observation did Jeanne give the students an assignment related to problem solving. This consisted of a worksheet with 12 story problems involving percentages. The first 11 problems called for finding the percentage given the base and rate. The last problem gave the percentage and base and asked for the rate. The students worked on this assignment in class, but were allowed to finish at home. Prior to distributing the worksheets, Jeanne worked one similar problem on the board, stressing the setting up of the equation. On the day following the assignment, Jeanne asked the students to correct their own papers while she called out the answers to the problems. Most of the students failed to solve the last problem correctly. A few days later after Jeanne had looked at the students' papers, she commented during the interview that the difficulty caused by the last problem was due to the fact that it was different from the preceding ones. She explained that the reason she included it was to use it as a lead into the next day's topic, which was to find the rate given percentage and base, indicating that because she had not presented the appropriate equation for solving this type of problem, she had not expected the students to solve it.

I noticed that Jeanne had skipped some pages in the textbook containing story problems involving rates and proportions. Because of this, I asked her to go through the topics that were listed in the table of contents for the chapter that she was teaching at the time and to tell me which topics she thought were the most important. She then indicated that the reason for her skipping the pages involving problems was that the students did not enjoy working them and that problems caused them to experience a great deal of frustration with mathematics.

From this and other remarks Jeanne had made earlier, I concluded that her criteria for judging the importance of a topic were related to (1) whether the topic constituted prerequisite knowledge for the study of other topics in the eighth-grade curriculum or for the further study of mathematics in high school; (2) whether the topic dealt with skills that the students had studied in earlier grades, but were still weak in; and (3) whether the topic was emphasized in external examinations.

Kay

Kay had taught mathematics for 5 years and was in charge of the mathematics component of a program for "gifted" students at a suburban middle school in northeast Georgia. Her undergraduate major was in mathematics. Before teaching she had worked as a computer programmer for 2 years. She became dissatisfied with her work and decided to take the necessary courses to obtain a teaching certificate. Since then, she had been teaching mathematics to sixth-, seventh-, and eighth-graders in the gifted program at her middle school. She was observed teaching a seventh-grade general mathematics class.

An enthusiasm for mathematics was apparent in Kay's teaching. Her enjoyment of mathematics was most clearly manifested during the frequent problem-solving sessions that she conducted in her classes. On several occasions she remarked to the students about the excitement and satisfaction to be derived from dealing with a challenging problem and being able to solve it. Whenever the students made insightful comments about the topic at hand or succeeded in making a discovery, Kay shared in their excitement and encouraged them in this type of activity.

Kay's teaching reflected a view of mathematics as a subject that allows for the discovery of properties and relationships through personal inquiry. Her teaching suggested the following conceptions:

- Mathematics is more a subject of ideas and mental processes than a subject of facts.

- Mathematics can be best understood by rediscovering its ideas.

- Discovery and verification are essential processes in mathematics.

- The main objective of the study of mathematics is to develop reasoning skills that are necessary for solving problems.

- Mathematical notational schemes are not verifiable, but are more or less arbitrarily determined and conventionally adopted.

- The nature of mathematical proof is such that conclusions must be derived only from the given or logically (not empirically) substantiated information.

- Mathematics is a useful tool for the study of science.

- Mathematical knowledge is necessary in many professions.

Kay indicated that, in her view, the primary purpose of mathematics is to serve as a tool for the sciences and other fields of human endeavor and that mathematical content originates from two sources: from the needs of the sciences and other practical needs, and from mathematics itself.

Kay expressed a view of mathematics as a challenging, rigorous, and abstract discipline whose study provides the opportunity for a wide spectrum of high-level mental activity. Thus, she explained, "the study of mathematics sharpens one's ability to reason logically." She added that what made mathematics appealing to her was the challenge of its problems and the gratifying experience of succeeding in solving them. Although she acknowledged the practical value of mathematics, her prevailing view of the subject bore little connection to its practical and scientific applications. She conceded that it was not its practical value that made mathematics appealing to her. Rather, its appeal lay in the challenge of its problems, the aesthetic quality of its theory, and the disciplinary effects of its study.

A taste for mental work, specifically for activities that challenge the mind by calling into play one's inventiveness and reasoning skills, was apparent in Kay's remarks. Her enjoyment of mathematics was derived in part from the self-satisfaction ensuing from succeeding in tasks considered difficult by many. More than the content per se, the mental processes called for in mathematical activity appeared to account for her enjoyment of and enthusiasm for the subject.

Kay's professed views of mathematics were consistent with her teaching. Furthermore, they appeared to have a strong influence on the instructional decisions she made. The heuristic approach that she often used in presenting the content and the frequent problem-solving sessions that she conducted in class were consistent with her view of mathematics as a stimulating and challenging subject. She frequently encouraged the students, in a rather persuasive tone, to guess, conjecture, and reason on their own, explaining to them the importance of these processes in the acquisition of mathematical knowledge.

A view of mathematics as a formal discipline was manifested in discussions of geometric proofs involving congruent triangles that Kay held with her class. She insisted on the importance of deriving conclusions only from the stated information and not from what appeared to be true based on the drawing. In other contexts, however, her instructional approach was more empirical and intuitive than formal. She explained that, because of the grade level of the class, she often needed to compromise rigor in favor of intuition in order to make the material more meaningful to the students.

Kay was confident about her knowledge of mathematics and her ability to teach it. This confidence was apparent in her remarks as well as in her instructional behavior. Her confidence seemed to result from her successful experience in studying mathematics, which she attributed in part to a natural inclination toward analytic thinking and logical reasoning.

Several basic aspects of Kay's conceptions of mathematics teaching could be inferred from her characteristic instructional practices. The conception of her role as the teacher that was reflected in her teaching is summarized in the following views:

- The teacher must create and maintain an open and informal classroom atmosphere to ensure the students' freedom to ask questions and express their ideas.

- The teacher must be receptive to the students' suggestions and ideas and should capitalize on them.

- The teacher should encourage the students to guess and conjecture and should allow them to reason things on their own rather than show them how to reach a solution or an answer. The teacher must act in a supporting role.

- The teacher should appeal to the students' intuition and experiences when presenting the material in order to make it meaningful.

- The teacher should probe for potential misconceptions in the students by using carefully chosen examples and counter-examples.

With regard to the preparation and planning of lessons, Kay expressed a belief in the importance of being well prepared in her knowledge of the topic in order to handle the students' questions and suggestions properly; using other references besides the textbook in order to ensure her own knowledge of the topic and to provide variety in her presentations; and analyzing students' difficulties and misconceptions by determining their sources, keeping notes of these to improve future presentations. These were practices that she both advocated and routinely implemented.

The practices that Kay identified as essential in teaching mathematics were using a variety of approaches to stimulate the students' interest and to suit the different topics; asking questions frequently; encouraging students to ask questions, guess, theorize, and not fear being wrong; using appropriate examples and counter-examples; providing a variety of justifications; showing practical or mathematical applications of the topics taught; and using games and puzzles as motivational devices. In addition, Kay expressed a strong belief in the teacher's knowledge of and enthusiasm for mathematics as necessary qualities of a good teacher. She expressed a concern for positive student attitudes toward mathematics and a belief in the importance of the teacher's ability to transmit her enthusiasm for the subject to the students, her ability "to sell" mathematics.

Kay often reflected on methodological issues. Although in theory she favored the use of discovery methods and frequently used them in teaching, she was aware of the potential shortcomings in their implementation. Her comments in this regard revealed a view of teaching as a nonprescriptive task in which the teacher frequently has to make difficult decisions. In her view, there was no single most effective method to teach mathematics. Her judgment was that the appropriateness of a particular method was highly circumstantial and generally unpredictable. She explained that the difficulties experienced at times by some of the students caused her to compromise her views of the benefits of discovery. Despite these remarks, she seemed uncompromising in her view of the importance of allowing the students the opportunity to reason for themselves.

Kay's primary concerns regarding the outcomes of her teaching, as evidenced in her comments during the interviews, were the development of reasoning skills and an attitude of inquiry in the students; the students' understanding and mastery of the content; and the development of positive student attitudes toward mathematics. The questions that Kay asked the students in class, her test items, and some of her interview remarks indicated that in her view mathematical understanding was evidenced in the students' ability to identify the relevant attributes of mathematical concepts; in the meaning and logic of rules, formulas, and procedures; and in their ability to integrate these into more general processes used in the solution of problems.

When discussing the students' difficulties, Kay generally attributed them to difficulties inherent in the content or to an oversight on her part in presenting it. She believed that the most common reasons for insufficient progress by the students were their weak background, a habit to learn the content in a rote fashion, and inattention or lack of motivation. As an aside, Kay expressed a view that in general girls were less motivated than boys in taking up and persevering in challenging mathematical tasks, such as puzzles and problems. On the other hand, she believed that girls tended to be more conscientious about their school work and, consequently, in overall academic performance tended to do better than the boys.

An aspect of Kay's personality that seemed to contribute to the consistency between her professed conceptions and her teaching was a tendency to reflect upon her instructional actions vis-à-vis her students' apparent progress. By reflecting on her own actions and their effect on the students, she had developed her own views about the effectiveness of different instructional approaches and practices. Likewise, she had gained insights into the sources of students' difficulties in learning the content that helped her to anticipate their potential problems and to plan her lessons accordingly.

There was only one inconsistency between Kay's expressed beliefs and her teaching: her view concerning the practical value of mathematics—the instrumental role it plays in the study of science and in other fields of human endeavor—was not reflected in her teaching. Although on several occasions she referred to this in class, she did so in general and not in reference to the applications of a specific topic. With the exception of a unit in statistics, she did not refer to the applications of the topics studied during the observations. That she showed a tendency to disregard the practical applications of the topics may have been the result of her admitted lack of interest in the practical applications of mathematics.

DISCUSSION

The summaries of the case studies show the sharp contrast between Jeanne and Kay in their conceptions of mathematics and its teaching, as well as in their characteristic instructional practices. Although the complexity of the relationship between conceptions and practice defies the simplicity of cause and effect, much of the contrast observed in the teachers' instructional emphases may be explained by differences in their prevailing views of mathematics.

One of the most striking differences observed was in the teachers' practices regarding the role of problem solving in the mathematics curriculum. Although it may not be accurate to say that Jeanne did not regard problem-solving competence as a desirable or important goal of teaching mathematics, this was clearly an aspect of mathematics teaching that she neglected. As mentioned earlier, this neglect could be explained by her pervasive concern with maintaining control over the classroom discourse, combined with her view of her role as transmitter of the content and her limited confidence in her mathematical ability. The combination of these elements kept her from venturing into the kinds of discussions that are essential in teaching problem solving.

The natural question that arises from all of this is whether Jeanne's views and practice with regard to the teaching of mathematical problem solving can be modified. It seems clear that her conceptions of mathematics and its teaching would somehow have to be extended or modified to reflect the generative processes of mathematics. It is unlikely that her conceptions and instructional practice, as firmly established as they appeared to be, could be changed in a brief period of time. One may even question whether they could be modified at all.

There is a need to examine the extent to which teachers' conceptions and practice can be modified, if at all. Traditionally, in-service programs have been designed to develop teachers' skills in the use of instructional methods and strategies that are deemed effective through research and tradition. This approach has been only marginally successful in effecting changes in teachers' performance (Shulman et al., 1975). A skills development approach is unlikely to bring about significant changes in the teachers' views of the subject matter and its teaching. How then can desired changes in both teachers' conceptions and practice be brought about?

I do not have an answer to this question. However, it is clear that we need to design programs that do more than just train teachers to teach mathematics; our programs must educate them in mathematics. We need to provide teachers with experiences that expand their knowledge of and about mathematics. Without this knowledge, how can they be equipped to deal effectively with open-ended discussions with their students or to capitalize on and explore student-initiated ideas?

There is research evidence that teachers' conceptions and practices, particularly those of beginning teachers, are largely influenced by their schooling experience prior to entering methods of teaching courses. Very often, the conceptions of mathematics that have been formed from that experience are not supportive of the teaching practices and approaches that are propitious to the development of problem-solving abilities. We need to explore ways in which to articulate mathematical content courses that teachers are required to take with methods courses, so that the learning experiences and instructional approaches used in the former are consistent with those advocated in the latter.

Since my work with Jeanne and Kay, I have worked with many elementary and secondary school teachers for whom I have taught in-service courses in mathematics education. I have become increasingly aware of the large number of teachers who share Jeanne's views and concerns and who, as a result, either avoid or neglect to teach problem solving. In those courses, I have attempted to engage the teachers in activities that force them to reflect on their views of mathematics and of their role in teaching the subject. We have spent a large portion of the time in these courses discussing the role of problem solving in the mathematics curriculum. As a result, I have become increasingly aware of the need for teachers (1) to experience mathematical problem solving from the perspective of the problem solver *before* they can adequately deal with its teaching; (2) to *reflect* upon the thought processes that they use in solving problems, to gain insights into the nature of the activity; and (3) to become acquainted with the literature on research on problem solving and instruction in problem solving.

In brief, it seems that the first step for many teachers involved in in-service courses on the teaching of problem solving should be to experience problem solving in a manner similar to what we would like their students to experience. One teacher of an in-service course made the following comment:

The changes that I have experienced are more affective than cognitive. The affective changes are releasing the already present cognition. I am much more able to give myself permission not to know everything immediately—it's amazing to me how great it feels and how quickly it came after 50 years of not being able to do it.

Much more remains to be learned about teachers' conceptions and how these affect instructional practice before we begin to understand their role in the teaching of mathematics and accordingly design in-service programs. Each of the case studies presented in this paper was constructed from observations of a single class over 4 weeks. As such, it was not possible to gain insights as to whether the composition of the class or the mathematical content bore any relationship to the teachers' conceptions and their characteristic instructional patterns. One may be inclined to think that Kay's practices and professed views would be quite different if she had a class of low-achieving rather than gifted students. Indeed, it is not uncommon to find teachers who are convinced that problem solving is appropriate only for the more capable students.

There is a need for researchers to investigate the stability of teachers' conceptions, specifically whether or not they are likely to change with changes in grade level, the students' academic aptitude, and the mathematical content taught. Such studies may identify stable patterns of views and beliefs as well as those beliefs that are more susceptible to contextual factors. In order to better understand how teachers' conceptions mediate and interact with contextual factors, there is a need to examine the continuing development of stable patterns of beliefs over time and under different conditions. Only when we reach an understanding of how conceptions are formed and modified will the findings be useful to those attempting to improve the quality of mathematics education in the classroom.

REFERENCES

Bawden, R., Burke, S., & Duffy, G. *Teacher conceptions of reading and their influence on instruction* (Research Series No. 47). East Lansing: Michigan State University, Institute for Research on Teaching, 1979.

Bush, W.S. *Preservice secondary mathematics teachers' knowledge about teaching mathematics and decision-making processes during teacher training.* Unpublished doctoral dissertation, University of Georgia, 1982.

Copes, L. *The Perry development scheme and the teaching of mathematics.* Paper presented at the annual meeting of the International Group for the Psychology of Mathematics Education, Warwick, England, 1979.

Harvey, O., Hunt, D., & Schroder, H. *Conceptual systems and personality organization.* New York: John Wiley & Sons, 1961.

Joyce, B. Toward a theory of information processing in teaching. *Educational Research Quarterly* **3**, 66–67, 1978–79.

Lester, F.K., Jr. Research on mathematical problem solving. In R.J. Shumway (Ed.), *Research in mathematics education.* Reston, VA: National Council of Teachers of Mathematics, 1980.

MacKay, D.A., & Marland, P. *Thought processes of teachers.* Paper presented at the annual meeting of the American Educational Research Association, Toronto, March 1978.

Methany, W. *The influences of grade and pupil ability levels on teachers' conceptions of reading* (Research Series No. 69). East Lansing: Michigan State University, Institute for Research on Teaching, January 1980.

Meyerson, L.N. *Conceptions of knowledge in mathematics: Interactions with and applications to a teaching methods course.* Unpublished doctoral dissertation, State University of New York at Buffalo, 1977.

Conference Board of the Mathematical Sciences. NACOME. *Overview and analysis of school mathematics: Grades K–12.* Washington, DC: Author, 1975.

Neisser, U. *Cognition and reality.* San Francisco: W.H. Freeman & Co., 1976.

Peterson, P., & Clark, C.M. Teachers' reports of their cognitive processes during teaching. *American Educational Research Journal* 15, 555–65, 1978.

Polya, G. *How to solve it* (2nd ed.). New York: Doubleday, 1957.

Polya, G. *Mathematical discovery: On understanding, learning, and teaching problem solving* (Vol. 1). New York: John Wiley & Sons, 1962.

Polya, G. *Mathematical discovery: On understanding, learning, and teaching problem solving* (Vol. 2). New York: John Wiley & Sons, 1965.

Rokeach, M. The organization of belief-disbelief systems. In M. Rokeach (Ed.), *The open and closed mind*. New York: Basic Books, 1960.

Scheffler, I. *Conditions of knowledge: An introduction to epistemology and education*. Chicago: Scott, Foresman, 1965.

Shavelson, R.J., & Stern, P. Research on teachers' pedagogical thoughts, judgments, decision, and behavior. *Review of Educational Research* 51, 455–98, 1981.

Shirk, G.B. *An examination of conceptual frameworks of beginning mathematics teachers.* Unpublished doctoral dissertation, University of Illinois, Urbana-Champaign, 1972.

Shroyer, J.C. *Critical moments in the teaching of mathematics.* Paper presented at the annual meeting of the American Educational Research Association, Toronto, March 1978.

Shulman, L.S., & Elstein, A.S. Studies of problem solving, judgment and decision making. In F.H. Kerlinger (Ed.), *Review of research in education* (Vol. 3). Itasca, IL: F.E. Peacock, 1975.

Shulman, L.S., Good, T., Kilpatrick, J., Lesh, R., Lightfoot, S., Mehan, H., Novak, J., & Budd Rowe, M. *Research on teaching/learning processes.* Panel report to the National Science Foundation Education Directorate, Washington, DC: 1975.

Thompson, A.G. *Teachers' conceptions of mathematics and mathematics teaching: Three case studies.* Unpublished doctoral dissertation, University of Georgia, 1982.

The Teacher and Classroom Instruction: Neglected Themes in Problem-Solving Research

Douglas A. Grouws

University of Missouri

The purpose of this paper is to suggest some areas of problem solving that recent research has examined inadequately or neglected altogether. I will identify themes that deserve increased attention on the basis of logical examination or research in other areas that shows these themes to be relevant and important. I hope this discussion will stimulate additional research on problem solving and result in a better understanding of the process of learning to solve problems and a clearer picture of how this learning can be enhanced in classrooms.

Educators and professional organizations alike readily acknowledge the importance of problem solving. For example, in their position paper on basic skills, the National Council of Supervisors of Mathematics (1977, 1978) states that "learning to solve problems is the principal reason for studying mathematics." Similarly, in its *Agenda for Action*, the National Council of Teachers of Mathematics (1980) argues that problem solving should be the focus of school mathematics in the 1980s. Both of these positions recognize that for many individuals the value of mathematics accrues from being able to use it in problem-solving situations. As the late Ed Begle (1979) said, "The real justification for teaching mathematics is that it is a useful subject and, in particular, that it helps in solving many kinds of problems."

Despite continuing interest in this area, the National Assessment of Educational Progress (NAEP) data from the 1973 and 1978 assessments in mathematics showed that student achievement in problem solving at all grade levels assessed was low, especially in comparison to such areas as whole-number computation (Carpenter et al., 1981). Further, the results of the third NAEP assessment showed no overall improvement in student ability to solve problems (Carpenter et al., 1984). It therefore seems clear that problem solving should be studied intensively from a variety of perspectives in order to improve student performance.

RECENT RESEARCH ON PROBLEM SOLVING

Research on problem solving has been popular for many years, and the number of studies completed is indeed vast. In my view, important research is currently being conducted in the following areas: the use of microcomputers to develop problem-solving ability; how students represent problems mentally; how teachers can promote student understanding of various problem-solving methods; problem-solving strategies that can increase student problem-solving performance; and conceptual work in metacognition.

A careful look at the research literature shows that most problem-solving studies can be grouped according to several themes. A large number of studies carefully examine the heuristics students use in solving problems. That is, they focus on problem solvers and examine not just the products of their work, as most research has, but also the general processes students employ in searching for solutions. Particular attention has been given to how students select and develop a plan of attack, use related problems, and retrospectively reflect on solution methods. Another body of research emphasizes task variables—variables associated with a problem and the related task of solving it. Typical of this research are investigations of how problem characteristics interact with problem-solving performance. Such information is useful in many ways; for example, it assists in the identification, description, and control of pertinent problem variables in problem-solving studies. Goldin and McClintock (1979) present a detailed review of research related to task variables. Still another group of studies is concerned with specific techniques problem solvers use, such as drawing graphs, finding patterns, writing equations, and making tables. Lester (1980) discusses the nature and contribution of these studies of "tool skills." Although these categories are neither exhaustive nor mutually exclusive, they characterize current research endeavors reasonably well.

In spite of their diversity, these studies have important commonalities. First, most of the research took place in laboratory settings rather than in classrooms. Thus the environments were carefully controlled with respect to the problems examined or presented. Instruction, if any, was prescriptive and clearly outlined in advance. These situations are in marked contrast to naturally occurring classroom settings, where students regularly work on problems the teacher has planned, but where problems also frequently arise spontaneously in a variety of lesson contexts. Often, teachers must give consideration to the latter problems in unplanned ways. Sometimes a worthwhile learning experience occurs and sometimes not.

The second common feature is that these studies concentrate on the individual, generally in a one-to-one relationship with a researcher (or teacher). Any verbal interactions examined are between the individual and the researcher, who is a mature problem solver. Even studies based in classrooms focus on teacher-pupil interaction, while interaction between peers, suggestions from fellow students, and similar events are seldom studied.

These generalizations about contemporary problem-solving research are broad enough that a number of exceptions probably exist. Still, it seems clear that programmatic research in mathematical problem solving is heavily inclined toward clinical or laboratory studies as opposed to studies in classroom settings. A major exception to this trend is the preponderance of short-term treatment studies that are generally based on experimenter intuition rather than theory, and usually produce inconsistent results. What is still lacking is theory-based research that systematically examines and later manipulates problem-solving activity in classrooms.

There is also a genuine need to study the acquisition of problem-solving skills in classrooms, in spite of the difficulty of describing and controlling relevant, potentially important variables. Current research has attended almost exclusively to the individual without due regard to groups of learners and their interactions in classrooms. (The Stanford work [Noddings et al., 1983] on small-group problem solving is a notable exception.) In summary, there are two broad areas that need attention in order to increase our understanding of how problem-solving ability is acquired and promoted: current practices of teaching problem solving and the role of the teacher and peers in the acquisition process. Those areas will now be discussed in detail.

NEEDED RESEARCH
Current Teaching Practices

Noticeably absent from the literature are characterizations of current practice in the teaching of problem solving in classrooms. We do not know how teachers conceptualize problem solving, nor how they attempt to teach it. We do not have answers to such questions as the following: How much time is devoted to instruction in problem solving? Are special problems or materials used to supplement basic textbook work? Do teachers stress tool skills? What types of questions do students ask? Do teachers give attention to general heuristics? Are reflection and post hoc analysis of problem situations an integral part of problem-solving instruction? Are alternate solution methods solicited? How long do students persist before giving up on a problem? Do students tend to seek the advice or assistance of their peers? Is that their preferred source of help? What is done to convey the importance of problem solving? Those questions and related ones are important if one wishes to improve the problem-solving ability of students. At present they are unanswered.

Considering the interest in problem solving over the last few years, it seems remarkable that such basic information is not available. Whether one believes that problem-solving ability acquired in schools is adequate, inadequate, or somewhere in between, it would be desirable to know the circumstances associated with the development of such performance levels. Currently, unsatisfactory national test results in problem solving are a disaster looking for a cause. Because of the lack of information concerning classroom practice, the search for causes has quickly become a search for a scapegoat (e.g., modern mathematics, lack of qualified mathematics teachers, severe financial constraints, and so on), and has not focused on the true relationship between classroom events and validly assessed outcomes.

The lack of descriptive information involves more than the practical and political considerations just discussed. Obviously, establishing relationships between classroom events and learning outcomes can contribute to our understanding of how problem-solving ability is currently acquired and to the establishment of a theoretical base for the teaching of problem solving. While a theoretical base for teaching must be consistent with learning theory, past experience suggests that teaching theory does not follow directly or easily from learning theory. The latter, at least in its early stages, seems to be descriptive in nature, whereas teaching theory, of necessity, must become prescriptive rather quickly. Consequently, explicit attention must be given to instruction in order to make progress toward the long-range goal of improving student problem-solving performance.

One wonders whether there is a lack of data concerning classroom instruction in other types of mathematical learning, as well. I suspect that there is, but that we *think* we know more about some other areas, such as the development of computational skills.

And indeed we may know a bit more, primarily because textbooks detail instruction on those topics more comprehensively than on problem solving. Further, teachers tend to follow such recommendations closely—or so we are told.

The need for information concerning what goes on in American classrooms during mathematics has been recognized previously. The National Advisory Committee on Mathematical Education (NACOME) (1975) report pointed out that "one is immediately confronted by the fact that a major gap in existing data occurs here. Appallingly little is known about teaching in any large fraction of U.S. classrooms" (p. 68). The situation has improved slightly since then, with the results of an exploratory survey of 1,220 teachers commissioned by NACOME now available. Survey data gathered by the Research Triangle Institute and case studies compiled by Easley and Stake (see Fey, 1979, for an overview of these NSF-funded projects) are also helpful. These studies have two major shortcomings, however. First, the questions they addressed were very general: How much time is spent on mathematics? How often are manipulative materials used? How is the classroom organized for instruction? Answers to such questions are useful, but of diminished value when considered apart from specific contexts. More precise information is needed: How much time is spent on particular outcomes, such as problem solving? How are materials used, if at all, to develop problem-solving skills? It is also critical that the behaviors described be linked to the focus of the lesson, both as the lesson occurs and as the teacher perceives it to occur.

The second shortcoming of these studies concerns the case study and survey methodology they use. Case studies provide detailed information, but only in a very limited context. Hence, their use in providing accurate global information is questionable. The survey method, used to some extent in each of the studies (teachers were asked to respond to questionnaires about their classrooms), also has a serious validity problem in my view. For whatever reasons (perhaps it is worthy of research), teachers do not always provide accurate information about what takes place in their classrooms through self-report instruments. What is needed are observational studies of problem-solving instruction, supplemented by appropriate questionnaire and self-report data. With these reservations about previous work in mind and the fact that previous work related to problem solving is rare, we now consider some tasks and guideposts worthy of consideration in planning and conducting research on classroom problem-solving practice.

Defining Classroom Problem Solving

Developing a detailed and accurate portrait of similarities and differences across classrooms will require numerous studies by various researchers. In order to combine results from studies and replicate findings, common, valid definitions are essential. Thus, defining what constitutes mathematical problem solving in classrooms is the first major hurdle that researchers must overcome. The definition developed should interpret problem solving broadly (Grouws & Thomas, 1981). Developing an adequate definition involves at least two problems. First, the definition must be clearly stated and make sense, that is, be meaningful to researchers of different persuasions and to teachers. Second, the definition should allow trained observers to reliably code instances and "noninstances" of classroom problem solving.

Although a workable, carefully prepared definition of problem solving in classrooms that would be widely accepted cannot be offered at this time, suggestions can be made for undertaking the task. First, the definitions commonly found in the literature will not suffice, because without exception they deal with an individual. In order to formulate a workable definition of classroom problem solving, however, it will *not* be necessary for the problem situation to be a "true problem" for every member of the class. The difficulties with setting a minimum number of pupils are readily apparent. A procedure must also be developed for deciding whether a situation is a true problem for the various students in a class. Second, a definition must address the fact that students do not solve problems only when the focus of the lesson is problem solving. Rather, problem solving also occurs in small episodes within lessons that emphasize skills and concepts. Finally, a definition must take into account the common descriptions of problem solving found in the literature. To this end, it is advantageous to describe classroom problem solving using categories such as verbal, nonroutine, and application problem solving. Kantowski (1981) and others have elaborated on the differences among these types. Such a scheme would enable readers of research reports to interpret findings in terms of their own conceptualizations of problem solving. To reiterate, the characterization of classroom problem solving must relate to students as a class, be capable of distinguishing problem solving within a variety of instructional focuses, be broad enough to encompass the wide variety of conceptions held by persons interested in the field, and be specific enough so that findings can be interpreted within an individual's own belief system about what constitutes problem solving.

Identifying Descriptive Variables

After a suitable definition has been constructed, researchers can initiate a wide variety of descriptive studies in which observation is used to generate reliable information about important variables. At present, it is not known which variables will contribute substantially to a theory of problem-solving learning in classrooms.

Information about how much time is devoted to problem solving should receive early consideration in naturalistic studies, due to its prominence in the literature and its demonstrated association with achievement gains. On similar grounds, researchers should determine the number and types of problems considered in classes.

Many related questions must also be explored. For example, do individual teachers vary daily or weekly the time allocated to classroom problem solving, and is there variability among teachers? How does time spent on problem solving within other topics compare to time devoted solely to problem-solving instruction? The amount of problem solving done in geometric settings as compared to numeric settings also deserves study.

However, how time devoted to problem solving is used is perhaps the most significant research question. What the teacher and students do with this time is crucial to learning. The qualitative dimension may involve high-inference ratings of such things as clarity (see Smith, 1977, for one objective way of measuring clarity in mathematics instruction), enthusiasm, appropriateness of examples, and attention to individual differences, to name a few possible variables. Some qualitative measures will be low-inference (e.g., student engagement rates, problem counts, number of tool skills considered). These considerations probably suggest others that are related to quality of time. The problem for the researcher who explores problem-solving learning in classrooms is one of setting priorities for initial work and limiting the questions investigated to a manageable number. In making these decisions, the researcher should be mindful of important interactions and relationships among the variables examined. For example, it would be very interesting to study the relationship between clarity and engagement rates or between clarity and number of problems used by the teacher.

There are a few additional variables that merit research attention. The way the classroom is organized for instruction may affect the number, type, and quality of verbal interactions that take place. A continuum with whole-class organization at one end, students working independently at the other end, and small-group instruction somewhere between is one way of effectively conceptualizing classroom organization. Students in large-group settings are more often exposed to teacher-pupil interactions and also have more opportunities to initiate interaction with the teacher than do students in other organizational patterns. Potential characteristics of each organizational framework can be identified and their relationship to the acquisition of problem-solving skills hypothesized. This is a fertile area for investigation.

Descriptive information and answers to questions about problem solving on homework assignments, teacher-made tests, and problems from textbooks and related materials would be welcomed by practitioners and researchers alike. Teachers consider those three areas (textbooks, tests, and homework) to be extremely important, and various research efforts over the years have linked them to student achievement. For example, Good and Grouws (1979) used a specific kind of homework (short, regular, and success-oriented) as part of an instructional program that produced large achievement gains in fourth-grade mathematics classes. Not all aspects of the three variables will be associated with learning gains in problem solving; rather, some specific forms of the variables may have a larger effect on problem-solving achievement than the same variables in alternate forms. For example, the kinds of problems (verbal, nonroutine, applications) assigned may be more important than the number assigned. Or how homework is evaluated (correct answers, correct processes) may outweigh the number of problems assigned.

Proper classroom climate and atmosphere have frequently been mentioned in the expository literature (e.g., Burton, 1984) as important factors in problem-solving instruction. Teachers are often advised to develop "a questioning atmosphere" and a climate that fosters "intelligent guessing." Considering the popularity of that kind of suggestion, data relating such factors to student outcomes are needed to test the value of the recommendations. In the collection of descriptive data, classroom environment must be assessed not just through the eyes of observers but also through the perceptions of the students. What is objectively noted by an observer may be viewed quite differently by pupils. For example, the teacher may call on students in order to promote guessing, but students may view it as a classroom control device or as a disciplinary measure. Similar perceptual mismatches are not difficult to imagine, and they emphasize the importance of considering student perceptions in the evaluation of classroom climate.

Importance of the Student

The student is of obvious importance in all aspects of characterizing classroom problem-solving instruction. Surprisingly, many researchers collect student data only by traditional questionnaire techniques. There are many worthwhile student behaviors that can be observed, behaviors that are difficult to measure using self-report methods. Student interactions with peers and student perseverance in working on difficult problems are two variables that seem to have good explanatory potential. Student perceptions can be assessed by interviews. This area seems particularly ripe for the development of innovative and unobstrusive ways of gathering valid student data. Whether novel means of measuring student behavior and perceptions are rapidly forthcoming or not, we must begin at once to consider multiple student variables in classroom problem-solving research.

THE TEACHER'S ROLE

Most suggestions for teaching problem solving are based on studies of how students solve problems in controlled settings. Although such suggestions are important, most students study problem solving, especially methods and techniques, in large-group classroom situations. Teachers exert substantial control over all aspects of the setting and intervene regularly in the interaction between pupil and problem. The nature and quality of teachers' interventions in the learning process may impact significantly and differentially on student learning. What is needed is careful scientific inquiry on the teacher's role in the acquisition by students of problem-solving ability. While a logical argument has been made for advocating attention to the teacher, the rationale for this position is also supported by research.

Numerous studies have shown that teachers affect student learning (Berliner & Tikunoff, 1976; McDonald & Elias, 1976; Rakow et al., 1978). Good and Grouws (1977) identified 9 effective and 9 less-effective elementary mathematics teachers from a sample of 41 teachers. Over a three-year period effective teachers consistently produced better-than-expected results in mathematics achievement (residualized gain scores on a standardized achievement test), while less effective teachers consistently produced lower-than-predicted gains. Evertson et al. (1980) identified a sample of junior high mathematics teachers who were relatively effective and ineffective, based on the gains of their pupils on general mathematics achievement measures. These studies show that teachers do make a difference and the differences are large enough that teachers of varying impact can be identified and studied.

What is needed, then, is similar intensive study of the teacher's role in problem-solving skill acquisition. Such research could address questions like the following: How much time do teachers devote to problem solving? What methods do teachers use? Are the methods similar to those they employ when teaching for other outcomes, such as skills and concepts? Do these behaviors tend to be consistent from day to day? How much variance is there among teachers in the methods used? When the measurement of learning is restricted to problem-solving achievement, are some teachers more effective than others? Are gains in problem-solving achievement made at the expense of learning in other areas? Do teachers who generate large problem-solving gains achieve them uniformly across student aptitude levels?

There are at least six reasons why it is important for research to examine the role of the teacher in problem-solving instruction. First, the information is needed to develop a theory of problem-solving instruction and to understand the natural acquisition of problem-solving ability. Second, such data are needed to explain variation in teacher performance. Third, such data are required to validly assess the extent of implementation of contemporary advice to teachers. Fourth, survey data will enable experimenters conducting treatment studies to determine the extent to which control-group instruction is representative. Fifth, descriptive data will assist researchers doing experimental studies to explain how treatment teachers must modify their behavior. Finally, such studies will have implications for both preservice and inservice teacher education.

Despite the importance of the teacher in problem-solving instruction, only one study could be found in that area, a dissertation by Stillwell (1967). The study was concerned with geometric problem solving and used a modified form of Flander's instrument to study amounts of teacher and student talk. The main conclusion of interest was that teachers do not spend much time on problem solving.

Teachers may be the most important influence on students' acquisition of problem-solving skills. Both the rate and quality of problem-solving attainment may be affected. Further, teachers probably contribute in a major way to pupils' enjoyment of problem solving and their desire to improve their current status. Research indicates that the teacher affects students' general mathematics achievement (see, for example, Grouws, 1980). It is indeed time that the teacher's role be given the attention it merits in problem-solving research.

Guidelines for Research

The following principles may expedite productive research on the effects of teacher behavior on student-problem solving. First, both qualitative and quantitative data will provide useful information in developing descriptions and searching for relationships. Second, teacher characteristics will never influence student outcomes as strongly as teacher behavior. What the teacher does is more important than what the teacher is. Teacher characteristics may help to explain teacher behavior and may suggest needed changes in behavior, but they will not overshadow the process of teaching. Finally, the ultimate measure of the influence of teacher behavior and characteristics is student outcomes.

Recommending teaching behaviors that affect student acquisition of problem-solving skills is a bit like playing Russian roulette. One can draw upon the general behaviors suggested by previous research, where the criterion for importance is how much a behavior contributes to gains in general mathematics achievement. Alternatively, many teacher behaviors are implied by the literature, although often they are not based on substantive research. Or one can proceed on the basis of intuition, which no doubt is influenced by the two previous alternatives. Since the research suggestions and the teacher recommendations are retrievable from the literature, I will suggest a few aspects of teaching that seem, based on my intuition, to warrant early attention. Some may be important; others will be valuable only in that they add to the descriptive information available.

Modeling Problem Solving

My experience in classrooms suggests that some teachers regularly and proficiently model the problem-solving process and that this is a positive influence on students. Such teachers pause at times to think, think aloud while considering subsequent steps, follow paths that do not lead to a solution, check the reasonableness of answers, and so on. Note that proficiency in modeling a computational algorithm would involve quite different behaviors. The value and critical aspects of modeling are yet to be determined, but they merit attention.

Questioning and Feedback

Teacher questioning and feedback have been studied regularly, but the studies have produced mixed results. The potential contribution to theory development has not been realized because researchers have not studied the two variables in sufficient depth. They must be considered in terms of context, timing, and quality. Computation and problem solving are quite different skills, yet past research on questioning and feedback has often examined the teaching of those topics together, as mathematics. That approach has obscured the contribution each of the variables makes, because quite different questions and feedback may be appropriate from one context to another. Studying them within the context of problem solving is a step in the proper direction.

The second consideration is timing. Most teachers would agree that asking a question or providing feedback *at the right time* is crucial to the value of the question or feedback. The sequencing of questions and feedback is also important. Finally, the quality of such behaviors may very well influence the benefits students derive from them.

Development

A number of studies show that the length of the development portion of a lesson is closely related to student achievement. Good et al. (1983) define development in mathematics instruction as

> ... the process whereby a teacher facilitates the meaningful acquisition of an idea by a learner. Meaningful acquisition means that an idea is related in a logical manner to a learner's previously acquired ideas in ways that are independent of a particular working or special symbol system. Thus, development can be conceptualized as a collection of acts controlled by the teacher that promote a particular kind of learning. (p. 207)

The ability to solve mathematical problems is clearly related to content. However, mastering the prerequisite skills necessary to solve a problem does not necessarily enable one to solve the problem. How new knowledge is stored and related to previously acquired knowledge may determine how students use new knowledge to solve a problem. This suggests a relationship between development and problem solving. The linkage is not clear, but the relationship seems logical, and hence development is well worth studying. I predict that research will show that the quality of development is highly correlated with students' acquisition of problem-solving skills. The first step in assessing quality of development is to identify its essential components. Exploratory work (Grouws, 1982) has described five interrelated components of development.

Metacognition

From information-processing analyses of problem-solving behavior comes the idea of executive processes that monitor and regulate the cognitive processes involved in problem solving. Metacognition refers to those executive processes and involves an individual's awareness of his or her cognitive processes as well as the regulation and synchronization of them. The importance of metacognition seems to be a recent point of agreement among researchers actively studying problem solving (Lester, 1982).

Given the ascribed importance of metacognition, the teacher's role in developing and promoting executive processes in the classroom should be investigated. Descriptive studies of relevant teacher behavior would be useful. For example, one could examine teachers' modeling of the problem-solving process. Another relevant behavior would be teachers' responses to student questions such as, How do I get started on a problem? or How do I decide when to try a new approach to a problem? A third potential approach would involve studying what teachers suggest to pupils on how to take a problem-solving test. The amount of attention given to this variable is small in most classrooms and nonexistent in others. It would be useful to know if particularly effective teachers of problem solving give attention to metacognition, either explicitly or implicitly.

Heuristics, Strategies, Tool Skills

Discussions and descriptions of heuristics (e.g., think of a related problem), strategies (e.g., work backwards), tool skills (e.g., draw a diagram), and suggestions from research (e.g., spend more time on problem solving) are bountiful in the literature and will not be elaborated on here. (For a substantial listing of research recommendations see Suydam, 1980.) It is important, however, that descriptive and correlational studies generate information about the frequency, quality, and implementation of those topics in problem-solving instruction. There is a paucity of descriptive studies in this area.

Teacher Judgment, Plans, and Decisions

Teachers make judgments, plans, and decisions that affect what students learn and how well they learn it (Shavelson, 1983). Some of those decisions have more impact than others. Deciding to wait to teach problem solving until computational skills are mastered is much more consequential than deciding to call on one student instead of another during a class problem-solving episode. That does not diminish the importance of small decisions that teachers make, for many times they are a part of a regular pattern, and as such can have dramatic effects. For example, deciding not to assign any difficult problems on a given day may be inconsequential, but never assigning difficult problems is obviously quite different.

Almost every aspect of classroom instruction in problem solving involves teacher judgments, plans, and decisions. Descriptive data are needed about what they are and how they are related to learning. Information is also needed about what decisions teachers make concerning problem solving and textbooks, grouping of students, classroom organization, homework, testing, and so on. Cooney (1981) suggests that such decisions can be meaningfully categorized into cognitive, affective, and managerial decisions. That is a good beginning, but the scheme does not take into account the fact that some decisions can be pondered over time and others must be made almost instantaneously. For example, decisions about curriculum materials or homework assignments can be made prior to instruction. The decision whether or not to follow up a student-suggested solution path during a problem-solving session, however, cannot be leisurely. It seems reasonable, therefore, to add a temporal dimension to Cooney's classifications.

Research also needs to determine *how* teachers make plans, judgments, and decisions. This would involve questions like the following: Was information about mathematics content used? Did pupil ability enter into the decision-making process? Was classroom control an issue considered? However, the most important aspect of teacher decisions is the consequences of the decisions for students' acquisition of problem-solving skills. For example, do teacher decisions based on low achievement expectations for students contribute to learning problems or the slow development of problem-solving ability? Answers to these and other substantive questions will provide a basis for advice given to teachers.

Other variables—teachers' instructional goals, conceptualization of mathematics, and plans—influence and determine many classroom events associated with problem solving. The extent of impact of each is of interest, as are the relationships among them. Information about such variables is not directly observable in classroom events. Techniques for generating useful data about them are discussed later, but the following questions in this area merit attention: How do teachers conceptualize mathematics? Do they consider it a closed or expanding system? Do they consider it an independent body of knowledge or closely related to other disciplines? What are their thoughts about learners' cognitive and affective characteristics? What broad goals do teachers have for their students? Is problem solving one of them? Do they see problem solving as a topic to be dealt with separately or to be integrated into instruction on other topics? Do teachers view mathematics content as a product or a process? How do they plan for problem solving? Do they plan differently for it than for other topics? How are these variables interrelated? What effect do they have on problem-solving instruction, and more importantly, on student learning? This is but a sampling of pertinent questions.

APPROPRIATE RESEARCH METHODOLOGY

The questions posed in this paper call for descriptive studies, studies that link classroom descriptions and processes with outcomes, and research that delves into teachers' actions and thinking both inside and outside the classroom. Guidelines for conducting descriptive and observational studies are abundant in the literature, and interested readers will not have difficulty locating appropriate sources. Grouws (1981) and Grouws and Good (1980) describe the method, associated problems, and results from process-product studies in mathematics, which link classroom process data with student outcomes. A number of techniques can be employed to study teachers' thinking and decision making, including policy-capturing models, lens-modeling studies, problem tracing, stimulated recall, and case studies. Shavelson (1983) describes each of these methods.

There are, however, many impediments to finding answers to the questions posed in this paper. There are three important obstacles that future research should consider.

Lack of Instruction in Problem Solving

This paper calls for descriptive studies of classroom instruction in problem solving and related student learning. A serious problem in this regard is the amount of time that must be spent in classrooms in order to observe any problem solving. I am convinced that researchers who define classroom problem solving in terms of the nonroutine problems mentioned earlier may never observe problem solving.

What is needed is a study comparing naturally occurring problem-solving instruction in classrooms with instruction (in the same classrooms) that is initiated by the teacher at the researcher's request. If significant differences in teacher and student behavior are not found between the two settings, then researchers can schedule observations to coincide with times when the teacher and researcher agree that problem solving will be taught. It is overly optimistic to think that induced problem-solving instruction will be appropriate for all types of investigations, but the approach may be useful in some studies.

Slow Development of Problem-Solving Ability

It is generally agreed that growth in problem-solving ability is a slow process. There will thus be a need for longitudinal studies that cover more than a single academic year. Because only a small number of longitudinal studies are reported in the literature, this limitation is a serious one.

Multiple Outcome Measures

This paper emphasizes the importance of linking the descriptive measures of classrooms and teachers with student outcomes to generate testable hypotheses and begin the development of a theory of the teaching of problem solving. A major step in doing that well will be to use multiple measures of student outcomes. Researchers must give adequate attention to affective as well as cognitive outcomes. Tests that measure the acquisition of problem-solving processes as well as correct answers must be administered, and retention and transfer effects cannot be ignored.

In conclusion, there are many obstacles to doing research on the acquisition of problem-solving ability in natural classroom settings. However, the need is sufficiently great that research efforts must proceed. Whatever extra effort is required will be well rewarded as student problem-solving ability is better understood and we acquire the means to better assist students in its development.

REFERENCES

Begle, E.G. *Critical variables in mathematics education.* Washington, DC: Mathematics Association of America and the National Council of Teachers of Mathematics, 1979.

Berliner, D., & Tikunoff, W.J. The California Beginning Teacher Evaluation Study: Overview of the ethnographic study. *Journal of Teacher Education* **27**, 24–30, 1976.

Burton, L. Mathematical thinking: The struggle for meaning. *Journal for Research in Mathematics Education* **15**, 35–49, 1984.

Carpenter, T.P., Corbitt, M.K., Kepner, H.A., Jr., Lindquist, M.M., & Reys, R.E. *Results from the Second Mathematics Assessment of the National Assessment of Educational Progress.* Reston, VA: National Council of Teachers of Mathematics, 1981.

Carpenter, T.P., Lindquist, M., Matthews, W., & Silver, E. Achievement in mathematics: Results from National Assessment. *Elementary School Journal* **84**, in press.

Cooney, T. Teachers' decision making. In E. Fennema (Ed.), *Mathematics education research: Implications for the 80's.* National Council of Teachers of Mathematics and Association for Supervision and Curriculum Development. Reston, VA: NCTM, 1981.

Evertson, C., Emmer, E., & Brophy, J. Predictors of effective teaching in junior high mathematics classrooms. *Journal for Research in Mathematics Education* **11**, 167–78, 1980.

Fey, J. Mathematics teaching today: Perspectives from three national surveys. *Mathematics Teacher* **72**, 490–504, 1979.

Goldin, G.A., & McClintock, C.E. (Eds.). *Task variables in mathematical problem solving.* Columbus, OH: ERIC Clearinghouse for Science, Mathematics, and Environmental Education, 1979.

Good, T., & Grouws, D. Teaching effects: Process-product study in fourth-grade mathematics classrooms. *Journal of Teacher Education* **28**, 49–54, 1977.

Good, T., & Grouws, D. The Missouri Mathematics Project: An experimental study of fourth-grade classrooms. *Journal of Educational Psychology* **71**, 355–62, 1979.

Good, T.L., Grouws, D.A., & Ebmeier, H. *Active mathematics teaching.* New York: Longman, 1983.

Grouws, D. The teacher variable in mathematics instruction. In M. Lindquist (Ed.), *Selected issues in mathematics education.* Berkeley, CA: National Society for Studies in Education, 1980.

Grouws, D.A. An approach to improving teacher effectiveness. *Cambridge Journal of Education* **11**, 2–14, 1981.

Grouws, D.A. *Research in mathematics teaching: Implications and considerations.* London: University of London, Chelsea College, Shell Centre for Science Education, 1982.

Grouws, D.A., & Good T.L. Process-product research. In E. Fennema (Ed.), *Mathematics education research: Implications for the 80's.* Reston, VA: National Council of Teachers of Mathematics, 1981.

Grouws, D.A., & Thomas, W.E. Problem solving: A panoramic view. *School Science and Mathematics* **81**, 307–14, 1981.

Kantowski, M.G. Problem solving. In E. Fennema (Ed.), *Mathematics education research: Implications for the 80's.* Reston, VA: National Council of Teachers of Mathematics, 1981.

Lester, F.K. Research on mathematical problem solving. In R.J. Shumway (Ed.), *Research in mathematics education.* (NCTM Professional Reference Series). Reston, VA: National Council of Teachers of Mathematics, 1980.

Lester, F.K. Building bridges between psychological and mathematics education research on problem solving. In F.K. Lester & J. Garofalo (Eds.), *Mathematical problem solving: Issues in research.* Philadelphia: The Franklin Institute Press, 1982.

McDonald, F.J., & Elias, P. *The effects of teacher performance on pupil learning.* (Beginning Teacher Evaluation Study, Phase II, Final Report Vol. 1). Princeton, NJ: Educational Testing Service, 1976.

National Advisory Committee on Mathematical Education. *Overview and analysis of school mathematics, Grades K-12.* Washington, DC: Conference Board of the Mathematical Sciences, 1975.

National Council of Supervisors of Mathematics. Position paper on basic mathematical skills. *Arithmetic Teacher* **25**, 19–22, 1977. *Mathematics Teacher* **71**, 147–152, 1978.

National Council of Teachers of Mathematics. *An agenda for action: Recommendations for school mathematics of the 1980s.* Reston, VA: Author, 1980.

Noddings, N., Gilbert-Macmillan, K., & Leitz, S. *What do individuals gain in small group mathematical problem solving?* Paper presented at the annual meeting of the American Educational Research Association, Montreal, April 1983.

Rakow, E.A., Airasian, P., & Madaus, G.F. Assessing school and program effectiveness: Estimating teacher level effects. *Journal of Educational Measurement* **15**, 15–21, 1978.

Shavelson, R.J. Review of research on teachers' pedagogical judgments, plans, and decisions. *Elementary School Journal* **83**, 392–413, 1983.

Smith, L.R. Aspects of teacher discourse and student achievement in mathematics. *Journal for Research in Mathematics Education* **8**, 195–204, 1977.

Stillwell, M.E. *The development and analysis of a category system for systematic observation of teacher-pupil interaction during geometry problem-solving activity.* Unpublished doctoral dissertation, Cornell University, 1967.

Suydam, M.N. Untangling clues from research on problem solving. In S. Krulik (Ed.), *Problem Solving in School Mathematics*. Reston, VA: National Council of Teachers of Mathematics, 1980.

Conceptual Analyses of Problem-Solving Performance[1]

Richard Lesh

Northwestern University

This conference was organized around themes which were identified as under-represented in research on problem solving (Silver, this volume). My assignment is to describe one of these themes: *conceptual* analyses of problem-solving performance. What is a conceptual analysis? How is it similar to, and different from, other types of analyses? To answer these questions, I will begin by describing three related types of analyses: task analyses, idea analyses, and analyses of students' cognitive characteristics. Distinctions that these descriptions generate will then be used to discuss some possible implications of conceptual analyses for problem-solving research and instruction.

I will claim that (*a*) idea analyses represent a major subset of a more general class, conceptual analyses; (*b*) conceptual analyses require and emphasize the kinds of knowledge that mathematics educators are uniquely able to contribute to research on problem solving; and (*c*) some of the most promising research relevant to mathematical problem solving is moving in the direction of conceptual analyses from an idea analysis, task analysis, or analysis of students' cognitive characteristics perspective.

Among researchers working in the field of mathematical problem solving, there is no general agreement about the "true meaning" of the theoretical and methodological constructs that I will be discussing. My goal is not to formulate definitive descriptions of terms like "conceptual analyses" and "task analyses"; rather, I will attempt to clarify some distinctions that are important for any theoretical perspective (and accompanying construct definitions) an individual researcher chooses to adopt. I apologize in advance to colleagues who may dislike interpretations that I assign to some of their favorite jargon.

1. The Applied Mathematical Problem Solving project and the Rational Number project referred to in this paper were supported in part by the National Science Foundation grants SED-79-20591, SED-80-17771, and SED-81-20591. Any opinions, findings, and conclusions expressed in this paper are those of the author and do not necessarily reflect the views of the National Science Foundation.

IDEA ANALYSES VERSUS ANALYSES OF STUDENTS'
DOMAIN-INDEPENDENT COGNITIVE CHARACTERISTICS

In the past decade, some of the most productive areas of mathematics education research have been those clarifying the nature of students' primitive conceptualizations of a variety of mathematical ideas, such as early number concepts, rational number concepts, and spatial/geometric concepts. Many of these subareas correspond to chapters in books edited by Ginsburg (1983) and by Lesh and Landau (1983). Recently, some of these idea analyses have begun to evolve into studies of problem-solving processes, heuristics, and student characteristics. There are two phases to the evolution:

1. A program of research begins by attempting to describe the development of a given idea. As details about the evolution of the concept are identified, interdependencies between content-understanding and process-use begin to emerge as salient. For example, in research related to our Rational Number Project (e.g., Behr et al., 1983; Lesh et al., 1983) we have found that certain processes such as "modeling" processes and representational processes are important components contributing to the underlying *meaning* and usability of basic mathematical ideas. Carpenter's and Moser's work on the evolution of children's early number concepts has reached similar conclusions (see Carpenter's chapter in this book, or Carpenter & Moser, 1983).

2. Idea analysis techniques (and perspectives used to investigate what it means to "understand" given *ideas*) are applied directly to problem-solving processes, heuristics, and understandings. For example, in our own Applied Mathematical Problem Solving (AMPS) and Rational Number (RN) projects, we assume not only that students' mathematical *concepts* are developing but also that the processes associated with these concepts are developing. We have investigated primitive conceptions of problem-solving processes and heuristics using "idea analysis" techniques similar to those we have used to investigate primitive conceptualizations of rational-number concepts (e.g., Behr, Lesh, Post, & Silver, 1983), spatial/geometric concepts (e.g., Lesh & Mierkiewicz, 1978), or other mathematical ideas.

Conceptual analyses of problem-solving performance may include either, or both, of these two idea analysis approaches. In either case, the validity of instructional implications depends on distinctions between idea analyses and analyses of students' domain-independent *cognitive characteristics*; links between process-use and content-understanding are apparent.

Beginning with "Idea Analyses" of Individual Concepts

One of the first assumptions that an "idea analysis" perspective tends to impart on problem-solving research is that *ideas develop;* they do not go from "not known" to "understood" in a single step. When students use mathematical ideas to solve problems, most of their ideas are at intermediate stages of development. This idea-development assumption has important and far-reaching implications for problem-solving research. For example, in the problem-solving sessions that we observed in our AMPS research, the students' conceptualizations of the underlying ideas (or sets of ideas) were at intermediate stages of evolution and the idea(s) had to be refined and adapted to fit the problem situation. The students' conceptualizations of underlying ideas actually *developed* (locally) during 40-minute problem-solving episodes (Lesh, 1983). Consequently, the problem-solving mechanisms (e.g., processes, skills, and understandings) that were helpful were those that facilitated local idea development. Conversely, many heuristics that perform productive functions in the presence of mature understandings actually tended to be counterproductive in the presence of primitive conceptualizations (Landau, 1983; Lesh & Zawojewski, 1983). Later in this paper, more will be said about these and other implications of an idea-development perspective on problem-solving research and instruction. First, it will be useful to identify several important similarities and differences between idea analyses and analyses of students' cognitive characteristics.

Because human development often is described in terms of conceptual capabilities related to particular logical/mathematical ideas, idea development research frequently appears to be indistinguishable from child development research. The differences may be subtle, but they are important. Human development research, or analyses of students' cognitive characteristics, results in domain-independent generalizations about *students* rather than about students' *ideas* in a particular domain. Idea analyses on the other hand result in generalizations about behaviors that can be expected from a student who has acquired a particular conceptualization of the given idea (or set of ideas) in a specific domain. Human development research tends to focus on very general ideas that develop naturally; idea analyses focus on ideas that are unlikely to evolve outside artificial, instructional settings. Idea analyses assume that behavior varies across content topics, and that performance characteristics can be modified through instruction. Analyses of students' cognitive characteristics tend to generate labels (concrete operational, impulsive, field-dependent, spatial/geometric thinker, etc.) which are associated with a given *student,* assumed to be invariant across tasks and time, and assumed to be difficult or impossible to influence through instruction.

Whereas naturalistic observations can be used to trace the development of ideas that evolve naturally, idea-development research typically must rely on interventionist "teaching experiments" (Kantowski, 1978) or longitudinal development studies in mathematically rich environments. Many mathematical ideas simply do not evolve outside of such artificial environments. Furthermore, to mathematics educators, the interest is less with what students can do "naturally," than with what they can do given certain "cultural amplifiers" (e.g., powerful and economical language systems, symbol systems, or representation systems) or given certain performance-optimizing "managerial systems" (e.g., metacognitive or heuristic suggestions).

Therefore, a major goal of idea development research is to describe the impact of "capability amplifiers" on the acquisition and use of particular ideas. The focus is on *ideas* and the role of powerful and economical amplifiers, not on "natural" development or behavior.

Research on individual differences or cognitive style can be used to illustrate the distinction between idea analyses and analyses of students' cognitive characteristics. "Individual difference" research is founded on the observation that different students respond differently to identical problems or stimuli. The additional assumption usually made is that "significant" characteristics must be invariant across large content domains, and across diverse sets of tasks and situations. The emphasis is on demonstrating and explaining *similarities* in behavior across seemingly unrelated situations; variability across tasks is of less interest. Instructional goals consist largely of finding ways to assign labels to students which will allow them to be sorted into groups, perhaps for the purpose of providing differentiated educational experiences (Gould, 1981). By contrast, idea analyses focus on cognitive processes and capabilities that are linked to specific content understandings; *variability* across content and context is explained in terms of *conceptual* understandings. It is assumed that the students' tendencies can be influenced through instruction and that instruction does more than simply compensate for characteristic ''givens.''

Recently, idea analysis perspectives have begun to lead to new types of individual difference constructs (Akerstrom, 1983; Flavell, 1982; Lawry, Welsh, & Wendell, 1983). The nature of these constructs is illustrated by the observation that many parents can identify a handful of characteristics of each of their children (or of their children's best friends) which distinguish them from many other children and which might lead an observer to misinterpret their behaviors if they were not taken into account. These characteristics, or behaviors associated with them, do not necessarily manifest themselves in all (or even most) tasks. They might be beneficial for achieving some goals in some situations, yet be detrimental in other circumstances; and they might be modifiable by training or instruction. Yet in spite of all of this variability, such characteristics are sufficiently important to play a role in the interpretation of an individual's behavior. In a given situation, even if the characteristics were not apparent in observable actions, they may be important ''background factors'' influencing behavior.

In our AMPS project, rather than interpreting characteristics like reflection-impulsivity as *constants* (i.e., as invariant labels for given students), we have interpreted them as *functions* of other variables (Akerstrom, 1983). Furthermore, we have assumed that it may be possible to consciously monitor and manipulate these variables so that nonproductive cognitive characteristics can be minimized, or so that both impulsive and reflective behaviors can be used to advantage by the student. For some problems, or at certain stages in the solution of some problems, nonreflective behaviors may be beneficial. Brainstorming is one example. In many of our AMPS problem-solving sessions, a student's unwillingness to ''jump in'' or ''postpone critical analyses'' sometimes was an impediment to progress. Impulsive behaviors were not always bad, nor were reflective behaviors necessarily good. Successful problem solvers used ''smart'' behaviors at the ''right'' times. Questions for future research to address include the following: What understandings of cognitive tendencies can students acquire, and what behavioral cues can they use to help them manipulate their own cognitive tendencies? How subject-matter-specific, context-specific, or stage-specific are cognitive tendencies? Can variability-producing factors be monitored and manipulated by students? Finding answers to such questions will require researchers to submit problem-solving processes, heuristics, and characteristics to research techniques similar to those that have been used to investigate the nature and development of concepts within domains.

Applying Idea Analyses to Processes and Heuristics

In the same way that idea analysis research has shown that it is naive to speak of students ''having'' or ''not having'' particular ideas, it seems plausible that problem-solving processes, heuristics, and characteristics should be submitted to developmentally oriented conceptual analyses. What is the nature of students' primitive conceptualizations of particular processes or heuristics, and what factors hinder or facilitate their evolution?

Again, distinctions between idea analyses and analyses of students' cognitive characteristics are related to the validity of instructional implications. For example, when comparisons are made between "gifted" students and "average-ability" students, or between "good problem solvers" and "average problem solvers," the content-independent nature of processes, heuristics, and characteristics tends to be emphasized; an analysis of students' cognitive characteristics perspective implicitly tends to be taken. Idea analyses assume that "giftedness" varies across subject-matter domains, and that a problem solver who is "good" at problems related to one topic may be "not so good" at others. Idea analyses anticipate that most productive heuristics and strategies will be content-*dependent*.

In a number of recent research studies focusing on problems involving the application of substantive content understandings, the utility of all-purpose, content-independent processes has been challenged (Elstein, Shulman, & Sprafka, 1978; Lave, 1984). Research in conceptually rich problem-solving situations (Larkin, McDermott, Simon & Simon, 1980) has suggested that it often is *poor* problem solvers in the relevant content domain who use general-but-weak strategies such as "working backwards," "hill climbing," or other "means-ends analysis" techniques; good problem solvers in the domain tend to use powerful content-*related* processes. Results from our AMPS project yield similar conclusions: students who have substantive ideas to bring to bear on a problem tend to use them, together with powerful content-related processes; students who do not have relevant ideas in a particular domain are, in general, poor problem solvers in that domain, even if they have had extensive training in the use of general, content-independent heuristics and strategies (Lesh, 1983).

Sometimes problem-solving research assumes content-independence in subtle ways. For example, heuristics often are assumed to provide answers to the question, "What should I do when I am stuck?" This question transforms easily into "What should I do when I have no substantive ideas to bring to bear on the problem?" Research relevant to this latter issue can focus on problems in which no substantive ideas (and consequently no content-related processes) are needed. The results, however, may have little relevance for conceptually rich problem-solving situations.

Krutetskii's research (1976) is useful to consider from an "idea analysis" versus "analysis of students" perspective. Krutetskii identified several types of mathematical giftedness (analytic thinkers, geometric thinkers, and harmonic thinkers); he clearly was sensitive to variability in performance across content and tasks. Nonetheless, what was most striking about Krutetskii's subjects was their general (i.e., content- and context-independent) giftedness. Therefore, his generalizations tend to reflect an analysis of students, rather than an idea analysis, perspective. For example, Krutetskii concluded that good problem solvers perceive and remember the structure of problems; he did not conclude that students who understand the structure of a problem (or the idea underlying the problem) perceive and remember it (Lesh, 1983). His generalizations were about *students* more than about students' *ideas*.

It is important to note that Krutetskii's goal was not to use gifted students' abilities as instructional objectives for average-ability students. In fact, Krutetskii emphasized ways that his (relatively domain-independent) "gifted" problem solvers were qualitatively different from average-ability problem solvers; success in problem solving was not portrayed as the result of mastering and using a few isolated skills, heuristics, or strategies. The differences between average students and Krutetskii's gifted students are analogous to differences between Piaget's preoperational and formal-operational children. "Higher order" thinkers not only know *more*, they know *differently*. Behaviors of "gifted" problem solvers cannot be lifted uncritically and used as instructional objectives for average-ability students.

Many others (Bell, 1979; Charles & Lester, 1982; Hatfield, 1978; Kulm, 1979; Noddings, 1983; Sowder, 1981) have discussed instructional fallacies resulting from attempts to teach *(in isolation and without modification)* strategies and heuristics that "good problem solvers" are known to use. Using techniques that have been successful investigating what it means to "understand" primitive versions of various mathematical ideas, recent problem-solving research has made significant progress in clarifying what it means to "understand" a variety of heuristics, strategies, and problem-solving processes. For example, Schoenfeld's metacognitive understandings (1982), managerial functions (1982), and belief systems (1983) are components of heuristic understanding. The research of Landau (1983), Lester (1983), and others has made it clear that "understanding" a given heuristic or process, like "draw a picture," means knowing (*a*) *when* it should be used, (*b*) *how* it is related to other heuristics, (*c*) *which* of a variety of pictures best fit a particular idea, situation, or set of relationships, and (*d*) *that* the heuristic may serve different functions at different stages in a problem's solution (e.g., interpretation stages versus verification stages).

In our AMPS project, because of the nature of the problems and subjects that we investigate, we see virtually no conscious or overt uses of commonly discussed heuristics. We *do,* however, see many instances of behaviors which appear to be based on primitive versions of heuristics and strategies. At this stage of our research, it is by no means clear that these behaviors reflect first steps in the direction of mature strategic or heuristic understandings. Furthermore, even if developmental links can be traced, it is not clear that instruction should parallel development. It does, however, seem sensible that instructional considerations should be informed by developmental knowledge. As a later section of this paper will explain, many heuristics and strategies appear to require significant reconceptualization to prevent them from yielding counterproductive results when they are used by students with unstable conceptual systems.

IDEA ANALYSES VERSUS TASK ANALYSES

Essentially, deciding to use a task analysis, an idea analysis, or an analysis of students' cognitive characteristics means choosing a unit of analysis that will be most useful for the kinds of practical or theoretical decisions one is trying to make; it is a choice of "how far down to crank the microscope" when examining problem-solving performance.

- Analyses of students' cognitive characteristics yield generalizations about *students;* variability across content topics is deemphasized; and malleability of characteristics is seldom considered.

- Idea analyses yield generalizations about various conceptualizations of particular *ideas;* content-*dependent* mechanisms are of prime concern; and it is assumed that the way ideas are taught influences behavior.

- Task analyses go one step further than idea analyses concerning the issue of variability. Compared with idea analyses, little attempt is made to explain similarities in behavior across tasks characterized by the same idea. Compared with analyses of students' characteristics, task analyses assume that variability within an individual across tasks is more important than variability within tasks across individuals (Newell & Simon, 1972). Task variables are of prime interest (Goldin & McClintock, 1979; Hayes, 1981).

Recently, some of the most theoretically interesting types of task analyses have been accompanied by attempts to create information-processing (IP) models, sometimes artificial-intelligence (AI) based, to simulate students' problem-solving performance (Briars, 1982; Heller & Greeno, 1979; Mayer, 1983). Compared with strict task analyses, which are intentionally naive with respect to internal processes, IP task analyses are midway between idea analyses and task analyses. AI-based IP models assume that students' interpretations of a given task are influenced as much by internal "programs" or representations as by external task variables. Still, it is one thing to create a program which behaves similarly to humans on a given task, and quite another to create a program simulating the way students' substantive *ideas* influence behavior on the task. Sufficiency in the former sense is considerably different from sufficiency in the latter (see Kaput, this volume); furthermore, the distinction is particularly important in mathematics education, because teaching a student to perform a task is not at all the same as introducing the student to a concept which can be applied to an unbounded cluster of tasks and which is related in nonarbitrary and substantive ways to other concepts (Ausubel, 1963; Lesh, 1976).

Both idea analyses and AI-based task analyses assume that the organizational/relational systems that mathematicians use to interpret a task may not correspond to the ones used by youngsters. This is why task analyses begin with a set of tasks, and *then* demonstrate task relatedness based on detailed observations of student behaviors; that is, they begin with a set of tasks, and *then* create a model (Note: the model is the researcher's) to explain students' capabilities and understandings by simulating behaviors. In contrast, idea analyses begin with models (i.e., hypotheses about the structures that characterize students' mathematical ideas), and *then* create tasks to test these hypotheses.

In our RN and AMPS projects, theoretical perspectives have been influenced by biases about the nature of mathematics and what it means to *do* mathematics. Our first hypothesis is that in real situations, for students to make judgments involving mathematical ideas, they must "read in" *some* organizational/relational system in order to "read out" mathematics-relevant information. Mathematics isn't *in* things, it is the study of structures that are *imposed on* things; that is, the content of mathematics consists of structures, and to do mathematics is to create and manipulate structures. These structures, whether they are embedded in pictures, spoken language, real objects, or written symbols, are skeletons (Hofstadter, 1979) of the conceptual models that mathematicians and mathematics students use to interpret and solve problems.

A major goal of our RN project has been to describe in detail the nature of students' primitive conceptualizations of a series of central rational-number and/or proportional-reasoning ideas. We also attempt to describe the evolution of the underlying conceptual models associated with these ideas.

Our second hypothesis in the RN and AMPS projects is that many of the most important factors influencing learning and problem-solving capabilities are directly related to the stability (e.g., wholeness or degree of coordination, internal consistency, consistency with the modeled world) of the relevant conceptual models. In particular, this view assumes that one can investigate mechanisms influencing the evolution of conceptual models without necessarily knowing all of the details about the exact structural characteristics of the underlying idea(s). This has been the general approach adopted by our AMPS research.

In both our RN and AMPS projects, we are not simply interested in describing "states" of knowledge, we are interested in the way transitions are made from one state to another. Our goal is to model students' modeling behaviors (Lesh, 1983; Saari, 1982, 1983). Like AI-based IP models of problem solving, we consider the student to be an adaptive organism whose interpretations of problems are influenced by internal models as well as by external stimuli. However, our student is a "modeler" more than a "processor," and mathematics furnishes the conceptual models for interpreting and transforming problem situations.

Until recently, most mathematics-relevant AI-based IP models had only attempted to simulate various *states* of knowledge. Currently, some models are attempting to describe the way transitions are made from one state to another (Klahr & Wallace, 1976; Larkin, 1982; Siegler, 1981). Still, these descriptions tend to treat cognitive growth as incremental and quantitative; that is, as a process of adding and deleting specific productions. This restricted view of cognitive adaptation is not an inherent property of AI systems; rather, it appears to result from the tendency of certain types of AI models to represent mathematical ideas as node-like entities with little or no internal structure—that is, the models are constrained by their representing language (Kaput, this volume).

Production systems are far from theoretically neutral (Newell, 1973); not all theories view learners as symbol manipulators (Beilin, 1983). Other forms of representation (e.g., imagery) are commonplace.

In mathematics learning and problem-solving research, studies that deemphasize the internal complexity and holistic character of conceptual structures tend to hypothesize relatively powerful processes; studies hypothesizing the existence of powerful relational/organizational structures need only relatively weak processes. When research is based on a "weak structure, powerful process" perspective, cognitive growth tends to be described in terms of incremental and cumulative changes; (quantitative) additions and deletions of procedures are emphasized rather than (qualitative) reorganizations of structured wholes. A "powerful structure, weak process" perspective, on the other hand, predisposes researchers to confront and explain insights, intuitions, and other conceptual discontinuities.

In our AMPS and RN research, the development of conceptual models has been characterized by both incremental quantitative growth and discrete qualitative discontinuities (Saari, 1983). Models of cognition that encounter difficulties reconciling continuous changes with discrete jumps often do so because mathematical concept development and problem solving are described using models that do not allow a whole system to be more than the sum of its parts—as though psychological units (analogous to chemical units of hydrogen and oxygen) can never be combined to form something with new properties (water), and as though continuous or incremental quantitative changes imposed on the system can never give rise to qualitative structural changes (analogous to changes in temperature turning water into ice or steam).

Holism versus reductionism has been a perennial issue in educational psychology (Beilin, 1983; Block, 1981; Koestler, 1979; McCorduck, 1979; Simon, 1981; Sloman, 1979; Sober, 1980; Weiss, 1967), and the underlying issues are related to many recurring controversies in educational practice. One example has to do with current conflicting curriculum recommendations from proponents of "basic skills" versus those who want to focus on "problem solving." Recently, one of the most clever treatments of holism/reductionism issues has been given by Hofstadter (1979) and Hofstadter and Dennett (1981), who ask, "Is the soul greater than the *hum* of its parts?" (p. 191). Hofstadter (1979) compares the behavior of an ant colony and the functioning of the brain, viewed as a colony of neurons. The colony has several structural layers — teams,

teams of teams (or "signals"), teams of "signals" (or "symbols"), etc. — which are critical to the understanding of the colony's activities. A given pattern of caste distribution in a colony of ants is compared to a "piece of knowledge," i.e., an idea:

> The caste distribution cannot remain as one single rigid pattern; it must constantly be changing—to keep in line with the present circumstances facing the colony. . . . Colonies survive because their caste distributions have meaning, and that meaning is a holistic aspect, invisible at lower levels. (pp. 171, 173)

The symbols Hofstadter refers to are active subsystems of a complex system and are composed of lower-level active subsystems.

> They are therefore quite different from passive symbols, external to the system, such as letters of the alphabet or musical notes, which sit there immobile waiting for an active system to process them. —When a symbol becomes active, it does not do so in isolation. —Symbols can cause other symbols to be triggered. (p.176)

Hofstadter describes characteristics that an "intelligent" AI system must have. Defining a representation system as "an active, self-updating collection of structures organized to mirror the world as it evolves" (p.193), he believes that such a system should be able to continue even if it is cut off from contact with the reality it is modeling. Its representations, or symbols, "interact among themselves according to their own internal logic—(and) this logic, although it runs without ever consulting the external world, nevertheless creates a faithful enough model of the way the world works" (p. 193).

Hofstadter (1979) considers himself to be in between the extreme views on AI, the one that sees the human mind as basically unprogrammable, and one that "says that you merely need to assemble the appropriate heuristic devices—multiple optimizers, pattern-recognition tricks, planning algebras, recursive administrations procedures, and the like and you will have intelligence" (p. 679). To create intelligent programs, Hofstadter (1979) says that we must build up a series of levels of hardware and software. He believes that as many as several dozen layers exist "between the machine language level and the level where true intelligence will be reached. . . . [with] each new layer building on and extending the flexibilities of the layer below" (p. 300). Hofstadter reminds us of Godel's proof, which suggests that there may be a high level of the mind/brain. "This level might have explanatory power which does not exist, not even in principle, on lower levels" (p. 707). As stated by Hofstadter and Dennett (1981):

> The brain needs this multi-leveled structure because its mechanisms must be extraordinarily flexible. —Rigid programs will go extinct rapidly. —An intelligent system must be able to reconfigure itself. —Such flexibility requires only the most abstract kinds of mechanisms to remain unchanged. (p. 196)

Fundamental to Hofstadter and Dennett's views are the notions that

- Ideas (or symbols) attain meaning from both internal and external structures, as well as from mappings to other systems.

- Knowledge is represented in hierarchical layers.

- There are close relationships between form and content; for example, forms at one level become content at other levels.

• Distinctions between declarative and procedural information are not absolute (Bobrow & Collins, 1975); for example, there are "strange loops" in which rules or structures at one level change themselves or are changed by higher-level rules or structures.

The notions of "active symbols (with internal structure)" and "hierarchical systems of hardware and software" are well known in the AI literature (Pattee, 1973; Simon, 1979, 1981; Winston, 1975). For example, according to Simon (1969) "a symbol is simply a pattern that can be discriminated by an information processing system" (p. 70). However, while Simon's conception of a representation system appears to subsume the kinds of "symbols with complex internal structures" that Hofstadter emphasizes (and that I believe are critical in mathematics learning), Simon's "internal structures" clearly tend to be the type in which the whole is no more than the sum of its parts. Simon (1968) speaks of "decomposable systems," whose parts retain their identities during interaction, and "nearly decomposable" systems with weakly interacting modules, which maintain their own identity even though they are modified through interaction. I claim that mathematics is a domain of knowledge in which form and content not only are interrelated, but, to a large extent, content *is* form. Some ideas are characterized by structures which are virtually *non*-decomposable; that is, the mathematical meaning of the parts is derived *entirely* from the system in which it is an element. I have previously (Lesh, 1976) discussed this phenomenon using the rubric of "structural integration"; Piaget (1966) refers to the phenomenon as "reflective abstraction." Relevant analogies from disciplines other than mathematics are less like hydrogen and oxygen molecules in water (which is perhaps no more than a nearly decomposable system) than like "renormalized particles" or quarks in quantum physics. Inside a proton or neutron, quarks not only cannot be seen as clearly identifiable parts, they cannot even be pulled out. *All* of their "meaning" derives from the systems in which they are "embedded."

If mathematical ideas are characterized by internal structures ("patterns"), it is perhaps not surprising that some of the AI models that appear to be most relevant have to do with visual perception or pattern recognition (Bongard, 1970; Frisby, 1980; Gregory, 1977; Harmon, 1973; Lesh & Mierkiewicz, 1978; Norman, 1979; Savage, 1978; Winston, 1975). Explanations for pattern recognition frequently deal with holistic functioning characteristics like focusing and filtering, or with qualitative shifts in these characteristics. Such AI explanations of *perception* often sound quite similar to the *conceptual* filtering and focusing characteristics that we have observed in our AMPS research. Some explanations for the construction and modification of templates or "frames" (Minsky, 1968) also sound similar to the ways we claim "conceptual models" are constructed in AMPS problem-solving sessions. For example, Newell (1972) identifies four types of functional processes by which IP systems, viewed as functioning wholes, might develop: *induction,* going from no knowledge to knowledge; *assembly,* constructing a program out of component primitive operations; *compilation,* obtaining a program specific to a task from a general one; and *adaptation,* going from an analogical program to a specific program. Newell's functional processes correspond quite closely to the kind of coordinating, generalizing, particularizing, integrating, and differentiating functions that our RN and AMPS publications have used to describe students' adaptive conceptual structures. Unfortunately, in AI-based IP accounts of mathematical learning or problem solving, one will see little evidence of Newell-like functions. Furthermore, after fine philosophical discussions of holism/reductionism, active and structurally complex symbols, hierarchical levels of knowledge, and so forth, concrete AI research models of mathematics learning and problem solving tend to return to business as usual—with n-level systems (with n very small) which are highly mechanistic and reductionistic. Conceptual analyses of mathematical ideas, on the other hand, inevitably seem to lead to the identification of functions and characteristics of structured wholes.

In the next section of this paper, I will describe some key assumptions and conclusions associated with our AMPS research. I hope this will clarify some ways that a conceptual analysis of problem solving may complement (both differ from and fit with) AI-based IP models. I agree with Hofstadter's (1979) conclusion that "people who study the mechanisms of thought must become conversant with ways of translating back and forth between purely reductionistic language and a sort of 'holistic' language in which wholes do indeed exert a visible effect on their parts, do indeed possess 'downward causality'" (p. 196).

Clearly, some of the best IP models are beginning to take into account some important structural properties of mathematical ideas, and some of the best conceptually focused mathematics education research is beginning to achieve a degree of specificity comparable to that which once was attainable only in the context of extremely restricted task domains. As these trends continue, both vague idea analyses and naive task analyses can be expected to move progressively closer toward a form of conceptual analysis.

A decade ago, Newell (1973) stated:

> Our task in psychology is first to discover that structure which is fixed and invariant (underlying a set of tasks) so that we can theoretically infer the method (used to perform the task). . . . Without such a framework within which to work, the generation of new explanations will go on ad nauseam. There will be no discipline for it, as there is none now. (p. 296)

Today current research at the interface of mathematics and psychology is only beginning to address Newell's challenge.

AN EXAMPLE OF CONCEPTUAL ANALYSES OF MATHEMATICAL PROBLEM SOLVING

Our AMPS problem-solving research differs from most research in mathematics education because it evolved out of idea analyses attempting to clarify the nature of youngsters' primitive conceptualizations of rational numbers, spatial/geometric concepts, or early number and measurement concepts. It is *not* the goal of the AMPS project to study problem solving per se; our goal is to enrich what educators mean when they say a student *understands* a mathematical idea. We investigate the processes, skills, and understandings that average-ability students need in order to adapt their mathematical ideas to model everyday situations.

A surprisingly small percentage of the problem-solving research in mathematics education is more than tangentially relevant to questions about using mathematics in realistic settings (Bell, 1979; Lesh, 1981). In fact, strategies and techniques that "good problem solvers" use to attack problems when they are "stuck" (i.e., when they have no substantive ideas to bring to bear on the situation) often are counterproductive to average-ability students—who are attempting to use ideas that they *do have* but which are "unstable" (a construct that I will say more about in this section). Our ultimate instructional objective is to help average-ability students use ideas that they *do have,* not to function better in situations in which they have none (or to function better in puzzle or game situations in which no substantive ideas are relevant).

The problems we investigate are simulations of realistic everyday situations in which elementary mathematics concepts (i.e., basic arithmetic, measurement, and number ideas) are used by students or their families. Characteristics of such problems have been discussed elsewhere (Lesh, 1981; Nesher, 1980). Most of our problems require at least 15–40 minutes to complete; realistic "tools" (e.g., calculators, rulers, graph paper, reference books) are available.

In this section, I will focus on one major point which characterizes most of our problem-solving sessions: Students more often construct solutions by gradually organizing, integrating, and differentiating unstable *conceptual* structures (e.g., conceptual models) than by linking together stable *procedural* systems (e.g., production systems associated with AI-based IP theories). Some key assumptions and conclusions of our project are given in the following subsections.

Critical Non-Answer-Giving Stages

Our "realistic" everyday problems can seldom be characterized as situations in which students need to get from explicit "givens" to well-defined "goals" using clearly specified procedures. In our problems, the definition of problems, givens, goals, and acceptable solution paths all require input from the student. For most of our problems, non-answer-giving stages are critical; acceptable solutions vary in both type and sophistication. The goals are not simply to arrive at mathematical answers; mathematics is a means to an end, not an end in itself (Lesh, 1981; Lesh & Akerstrom, 1981).

Conceptual (Organizational/Relational) Systems Imposed on the Situation

Alternative ways of conceptualizing problems require different organizational/relational systems to be imposed on the situation. These distinct systems result in different ways of filtering, organizing, and interpreting "givens" and "goals." Stages in the development of a given model can be identified depending on the complexity and refinement of the underlying systems (Lesh et al., 1983).

Cognitive Characteristics of Unstable Conceptual Models

Primitive versions of a given model, or conceptualization, typically are based on relatively unstable[2] (poorly coordinated) relational/organizational systems. Students using poorly coordinated systems tend to notice only the most salient relationships and information in the problem situation, filtering out other important but less striking

---

2. In this section, for simplicity, I will describe the evolution of conceptual models using language which suggests that "stable" (well-adapted) models is a term synonymous with "good" (sophisticated, complex) models. In general, in most of our AMPS problem-solving sessions, this simplifying assumption was justified. However, conceptual evolution can lead to models that oversimplify or distort reality in much the same way that biological evolution does not always lead to higher-order organisms (Gould, 1978).

characteristics; and/or neglect to notice model-reality mismatches, thus imposing subjective and unwarranted relationships or interpretations based on a priori assumptions.

Progressively more stable versions of a given model tend to take into account more information (and more different kinds of information), and they impose fewer irrelevant or debilitating restrictions, or subjective false assumptions.[3] For an initial interpretation (i.e., model), the student selects, organizes, and interprets a subset of the available information; this interpreted information then requires certain aspects of the model to be refined or elaborated; and the refined or elaborated model allows new information and relationships to be noticed, thus giving rise to a new modeling cycle (Lesh, 1982, 1983).

Multiple Modeling Cycles Involved in Solutions

The most appropriate characterization of most of our AMPS sessions is that the students moved among two to four distinct interpretations or models of the situation (including goals and givens), with different conceptualizations often recurring in several distinct stages of complexity, refinement, and stability. We have examples of sessions in which students went through as many as ten modeling cycles during a 40-minute session (Lesh, 1982). Differences between model types, or between different forms of a given model type, were based on different data being selected or filtered, different types of relational/organizational systems being imposed on the data, and different ways of simplifying, combining, or synthesizing the data.

During early stages of many of our sessions, several half-formulated (often logically incompatible) conceptualizations operated simultaneously, each suggesting half-formulated solution procedures and/or alternative ways to select, filter, interpret, relate, organize, or synthesize information. Students often moved from one conceptualization to another in the following general way. First, a particular type of relationship was noticed which was associated with a given conceptualization. Then, as attention shifted away from the overall conceptualization, the relationship began to be treated as part of an entirely different conceptualization. The phenomenon resembled a repeating cycle of "losing the forest when looking at the trees" and "losing the trees when looking at the forest." This sort of "mutation" from wholes to parts, to new wholes, to new parts sometimes led to new productive ideas or interpretations; in other cases, it derailed promising solution efforts.[4]

The previous description refers to *relational* subsystems within students' conceptual models. Similar phenomena also occur for *operational* or *procedural* subsystems. For example, unstable procedural systems are characterized by (a) losing cognizance of overall goals (or the subsuming network of procedures) when attention is focused on individual

---

3. All models have *some* properties that the modeled world does not have, and/or they filter out some properties that the modeled world *does* have. If this were not true, the model would not *represent* the modeled world, it would be *indistinguishable* from the modeled world (Bender, 1978; Burghes, Huntley, & McDonald, 1982).

4. In conceptual evolution, a "good" model is one that fits the modeled reality; "better" models tend to account for more information within more complex relational/organizational systems, with less distortion. "Stable" models are internally consistent and "well coordinated" in the sense that the forest and the trees do not lead to conflicting views.

subprocedures, or (*b*) misexecuting "easy" subprocedures when attention is focused on overall goals (or the subsuming network of procedures).

Conceptual Versus Procedural Considerations

If information processing was going on in our sessions, the information was not simply raw data, or even multiple attributes associated with raw data; rather, it was the imposed organizational/relational systems that were being processed and transformed. That is, it was primarily the conceptual models themselves that were being "processed" during solution attempts (Lesh, 1983).

During solution attempts, the most beneficial decisions were seldom procedural ("What shall I *do* next?"). Students and groups who seemed preoccupied with *doing* typically did not *do* well compared with their peers. Beneficial considerations tended to be *conceptual* in nature, focusing on thinking about ways to *think about* the situation (i.e., relationships among "givens," or interpretations of "givens" or "goals," rather than ways to get from "givens" to "goals"). This conceptual versus procedural distinction was especially important during early stages of solution attempts when students' conceptual models were most unstable (Lesh & Zawojewski, 1983).

Relevance of Developmental Theories

Because many of our 40-minute sessions resembled compact versions of phenomena that developmental psychologists have observed over time periods of several years (e.g., concerning the evolution of particular mathematical ideas), we frequently have characterized our sessions as "local conceptual development" episodes. For example, I describe a proportional-reasoning problem-solving session (Lesh 1983) in which the sequence of stages that the students went through were remarkably similar to accounts of the "natural" development of proportional-reasoning capabilities given by Noelting (1979), Karplus, Pulos and Stage (1983), and others. The students moved from conceptualizations dealing with facts, relationships, or information focusing on one at a time and focusing on only the most salient or superficial characteristics, to dealing with *sets* of variables in well-organized systems.

Because of the local conceptual development character of our sessions, a variety of developmental perspectives provide constructs relevant to our work. Our model of students' modeling behaviors borrows key elements from the following perspectives:

- Parallels between mechanisms that influence local conceptual development and mechanisms that facilitate or hinder general (or "natural") cognitive development. For example, Piaget (1971) and Vygotsky (1962) have different explanations for roles that peer-group interactions can play to help students acquire certain problem-solving skills.

- Parallels between the "local" evolution of adaptive conceptual systems and the evolution of biological organisms (e.g., Gould, 1980; Piaget, 1971). For example, under certain circumstances evolution may not lead to higher-order organisms; adaptation may not lead to greater complexity and increasing heterogeneity. The popular picture of evolution as a continuous sequence of ancestors and descendants is misleading.

Biological evolutionists in general see periods of rapid change followed by long periods of tranquility; several lineages frequently coexist, none clearly derived from another. Gould (1980) states:

> The "sudden" appearance of species... is the proper prediction of evolutionary theory as we understand it. Evolution usually proceeds by (local) "speciation"—the splitting of one lineage from a parental stock—not by the slow and steady transformation of the large (central) parental stock. Repeated episodes of speciation produce a bush. Evolutionary "sequences" are not like rungs on a ladder. (p. 61)

• Parallels between "idea development" in the context of particular problem-solving situations and "knowledge development" as it is interpreted in recent "history of science" perspectives (Gould, 1980; Kuhn, 1971; Lakatos, 1970; Suppe, 1977). For example, early developmental stages frequently are characterized by the coexistence of a number of distinct (in retrospect) yet relatively undifferentiated (at that time) world views. Development-by-accumulation often fails to explain important aspects of conceptual evolution; conceptual reorganizations often radically alter perceptions of what is "intuitive" or "obvious."

Minimizing Negative Cognitive Characteristics

If problem solving is characterized as a process of linking together stable *procedural* systems, then the most important heuristics and strategies may appear to be those that help the problem solvers select and sequence their activities. That is, they serve managerial or executive functions governing the use of more powerful, less general, and more content-dependent processes. However, if (as in most of our AMPS sessions) solutions are constructed by gradually refining, integrating, and differentiating unstable *conceptual* systems (i.e., conceptual models), then the most important heuristics and strategies are those dealing with how deficiencies in various models are detected, how the debilitating influences associated with the use of unstable conceptual models are minimized, how successively more complex and refined models are gradually constructed, and how competing interpretations are differentiated, reconciled, and/or integrated. In our sessions, many of the most effective activities facilitating solution attempts functioned not so much to help the problem solver amplify his or her problem-solving abilities as they did to help the problem solver minimize the effect of cognitive characteristics that lead to inappropriate use of conceptual models.

Several years ago, when Piagetians attempted to specify implications for classroom practice, the question "Can cognitive development be accelerated?" was referred to as the "American question." Our AMPS research is showing that Piaget's theory, as well as several other "developmental" perspectives, appear to have new relevance; for example, Vygotsky in psychology, Gould (1980) in biology, and Kuhn (1971), Lakatos (1970), Pepper (1942), and Suppe (1977) in the history and philosophy of science. The new relevance results from the nature of the problems that we address, and because of the local conceptual development character of typical solution attempts. The new "American question" appears to be "How can we minimize cognitive regression (or conceptual difficulties that are naturally associated with unstable problem conceptualizations)?"

In our problem-solving sessions, we frequently found students doing poorly because of things that they had learned in their mathematics classes about the nature of mathematics and mathematical problem solving. Or, activities (heuristics, strategies, processes, etc.) which were beneficial at one stage of problem solving were counterproductive at others. Beneficial activities varied across problems, and across stages in the solution of individual problems.

Content-Dependent Processes

Like others whose current research is focused on problems involving the application of substantive content understandings (Chi, 1978; Elstein et al., 1978), we have found that successful problem solvers tend to use powerful content-dependent processes rather than general (and weaker) content-independent processes. The processes that we have found to be most beneficial to our students not only are the powerful and content-dependent variety, they contribute to both the *meaningfulness* and the *usability* of specific mathematical concepts. They are integral parts of the underlying conceptual models (Lesh, 1983; Lesh et al., 1983; Lesh & Zawojewski, 1983).

Instructional Implications

Because of the nature of our students and problems, we have had to reconceptualize or redefine many popular heuristics and strategies to make them suitable for (*a*) non-answer-giving stages of problem solving, (*b*) processes that are content-dependent, (*c*) solution paths involving multiple modeling cycles, and (*d*) conceptual models based on unstable organizational/relational (as well as procedural) systems.

We have shown that a given heuristic or strategy may have either positive or negative consequences depending on its content-relatedness, its conceptual (relational/organizational) versus procedural focus, the function it is to serve at a particular stage in which it is used, and the stability of the underlying conceptual model. Stage-dependent, content-dependent, conceptually focused techniques tend to be most beneficial when their main function is to help problem solvers minimize the negative influences of unstable conceptual systems more than to maximize the effectiveness of stable procedural systems (Lesh, 1983).

Our research has made us sensitive to the tendency of educators to turn a "means to an end" into an "end in itself." Heuristics should be taught in a way that does not conceal the goals that give rise to them (Noddings, 1983). For example, in problem-solving situations, one does not "look for a similar problem" as an end in itself; the goal usually is to "look for a similar problem in order to better understand the given problem." One does not draw a picture as an end in itself; the picture is drawn for some *purpose*—and the most useful purposes facilitate one or more of the *functions* that are critical to local conceptual development. A major goal of our research is to identify some of the most important of these local conceptual development functions or mechanisms. To identify these functions we treat both substantive mathematical ideas and problem-solving processes (or heuristics) developmentally.

CONCLUSION

Throughout this paper, I have contrasted idea analyses with task analyses and with analyses of students' cognitive characteristics. I have used our RN and AMPS projects as examples of studies which, in general, use conceptual analyses. Because of our assumptions and conclusions about the nature of mathematics, applied mathematics problems, and applied mathematical problem-solving processes, our research has not attempted to compare high-ability (or "gifted") students with average-ability students, nor have we compared "experts" with "novices." Instead, the most relevant comparisons have been between average-ability novices who succeed and average-ability novices who fail on a given problem. Or, because the productivity of a student's activities often vary considerably within a 40-minute session, it is even more accurate to say that our comparisons have been between beneficial versus non-beneficial behaviors of average-ability students as they attempt to use elementary mathematical concepts in everyday situations.

In our AMPS project, a problem is defined as a situation in which a stable conceptual model *is not* available to the student (or group). Problems, according to our restricted definition, cannot be solved simply by linking together stable systems. Content-domain experts, on the other hand, are precisely those people who have acquired stable and accessible conceptual models for interpreting and manipulating information in that problem domain. Therefore, even when these individuals do not have an immediate response to a question, they *do* have well-organized conceptual and procedural systems for producing a response. Thus, the situation is not really a problem at all for these individuals; it is just a (perhaps complex) exercise. Behaviors of experts in a given problem domain therefore can be expected to be qualitatively different from that of novices.

The problem-solving behaviors of gifted students also can be expected to be qualitatively different from those of average-ability students. For example, gifted students "see" connections among problems (or situations, or ideas) that average-ability students do not recognize (Krutetskii, 1976); and "learning disabilities" students frequently fail to recognize connections among problems (or situations, or ideas) that appear obvious to average-ability students (Lesh, 1979). Qualitative differences in problem-solving capabilities are analogous to those that distinguish Piaget's preoperational levels of thought from formal-operational levels.

Identifying heuristics, skills, and strategies that are used by either experts or gifted students, and attempting to teach them (in isolation, and in an unmodified form) to average-ability novices may yield negligible, or even negative, results. It seems plausible that childrens' conceptions of problem-solving processes, strategies, and heuristics must develop in a manner similar to the way other mathematical ideas (e.g., counting, whole-number arithmetics, rational-number concepts) are known to develop. Yet, research has seldom viewed heuristics developmentally. Conceptual analyses of problem-solving performance are based on the notion that, to help students' heuristic/strategic conceptions evolve toward mature understandings, educators must be knowledgeable about the intermediate stages of the development of mathematical ideas and problem-solving mechanisms—stages in which problem-solving understandings, skills, and heuristics are linked to unstable conceptual systems.

REFERENCES

Akerstrom, M. *Individual differences and group problem solving: A study of the cognitive style reflection-impulsivity.* Unpublished doctoral dissertation, Northwestern University, 1983.

Ausubel, D.P. *The psychology of meaningful verbal learning.* New York: Grune & Stratton, 1963.

Behr, M., Lesh, R., Post, T., & Silver, E. Rational number concepts. In R. Lesh & M. Landau (Eds.), *Acquisition of mathematics concepts and processes.* New York: Academic Press, 1983.

Beilin, H. The new functionalism and Piaget's program. In H.W. Schnolvich (Ed.), *New trends in conceptual representations.* Hillsdale, NJ: Lawrence Erlbaum Associates, 1983.

Bell, M.S. Applied problem solving as a school emphasis: An assessment and some recommendations. In R. Lesh, D. Mierkiewicz, & M.G. Kantowski (Eds.), *Applied mathematical problem solving.* Columbus, OH: ERIC Clearinghouse for Science, Mathematics, and Environmental Education, 1979.

Bender, E.A. *An introduction to mathematical modelling.* New York: John Wiley & Sons, 1978.

Block, N. *Readings in philosophy of psychology.* Cambridge, MA: Harvard University Press, 1981.

Bobrow, D., & Collins, A. (Eds.). *Representation and understandings: Studies in cognitive science.* New York: Academic Press, 1975.

Bongard, M. *Pattern recognition.* Rochelle Park, NJ: Spartan Books, 1970.

Briars, D.J. Implications from information-processing psychology for research on mathematics learning and problem solving. In F.K. Lester & J. Garofalo (Eds.), *Mathematical problem solving: Issues in research.* Philadelphia: The Franklin Institute Press, 1982.

Burghes, D.N., Huntley, I., & McDonald, J. *Applying mathematics, a course in mathematical modelling.* New York: John Wiley & Sons, 1982.

Carpenter, T.P., & Moser, J.M. The acquisition of addition and subtraction concepts. In R. Lesh & M. Landau (Eds.), *Acquisition of mathematics concepts and processes.* New York: Academic Press, 1983.

Charles, R.I., & Lester, F.K. *Teaching problem solving: What, why and how.* Palo Alto, CA: Dale Seymour, 1982.

Chi, M.T.H. Knowledge structures and memory development. In R.S. Siegler (Ed.), *Children's thinking: What develops?* Hillsdale, NJ: Lawrence Erlbaum Associates, 1978.

Elstein, A.S., Shulman, L.S., & Sprafka, S.A. *Medical problem solving: An analysis of clinical reasoning.* Cambridge, MA: Harvard University Press, 1978.

Flavell, J.H. On cognitive development. *Child Development* **53**, 1–10, 1982.

Frisby, J.R. *Seeing: Illusion, brain, and mind.* Oxford: Oxford University Press, 1980.

Ginsburg, H.P. (Ed.). *The development of mathematical thinking.* New York: Academic Press, 1983.

Goldin, G.A., & McClintock, C.E. (Eds.). *Task variables in mathematical problem solving.* Columbus, OH: ERIC Clearinghouse for Science, Mathematics, and Environmental Education, 1979.

Gould, J.G. *Ever since Darwin.* New York: W.W. Norton, 1978.

Gould, J.G. *Ontogeny and phylogeny.* New York: W.W. Norton, 1980.

Gould, J.G. *The mismeasure of man.* New York: W.W. Norton, 1981.

Gregory, R.L. *Eye and brain* (3rd ed.). London: Weidenfeld & Nicolson, 1977.

Harmon, L. The recognition of faces. *Scientific American* **229**, 70–82, 1973.

Hatfield, L.L. Heuristical emphases in the instruction of mathematical problem solving: Rationales and research. In L.L. Hatfield & D.A. Bradbard (Eds.), *Mathematical problem solving: Papers from a research workshop.* Columbus, OH: ERIC Clearinghouse for Science, Mathematics, and Environmental Education, 1978.

Hayes, J.R. *The complete problem solver.* Philadelphia: The Franklin Institute Press, 1981.

Hayes, J.R., & Simon, H.A. Psychological differences among problem isomorphs. In N.J. Castellan, D.B. Pisoni, & G.R. Potts (Eds.), *Cognitive theory* (Vol. 2). Hillsdale, NJ: Lawrence Erlbaum Associates, 1977.

Heller, J.I., & Greeno, J.G. Information processing analyses of mathematical problem solving. In R. Lesh, D. Mierkiewicz, & M.G. Kantowski (Eds.), *Applied mathematical problem solving.* Columbus, OH: ERIC Clearinghouse for Science, Mathematics, and Environmental Education, 1979.

Hofstadter, D. *Godel, Escher, Bach: An eternal golden braid.* New York: Basic Books, 1979.

Hofstadter, D., & Dennett, D.C. *The mind's I: Fantasies and reflections on self and soul.* New York: Basic Books, 1981.

Kantowski, M.G. The teaching experiment and Soviet studies of problem solving. In L.L. Hatfield & D.A. Bradbard (Eds.), *Mathematical problem solving: Papers from a research workshop.* Columbus, OH: ERIC Clearinghouse for Science, Mathematics, and Environmental Education, 1978.

Karplus, R., Pulos, S., & Stage, E. Proportional reasoning of early adolescents. In R. Lesh & M. Landau (Eds.), *Acquisition of mathematics concepts and processes.* New York: Academic Press, 1983.

Klahr, D., & Wallace, J.G. *Cognitive development: An information processing view.* Hillsdale, NJ: Lawrence Erlbaum Associates, 1976.

Koestler, A. *Janus: A summing up.* New York: Vintage, 1979.

Krutetskii, V.A. *The psychology of mathematical abilities in school children.* Chicago: University of Chicago Press, 1976.

Kuhn, T.S. *The structure of scientific revolutions* (3rd ed.). Chicago: University of Chicago Press, 1971.

Kulm, G. The classification of problem-solving research variables. In G.A. Goldin & C.E. McClintock (Eds.), *Task variables in mathematical problem solving.* Columbus, OH: ERIC Clearinghouse for Science, Mathematics, and Environmental Education, 1979.

Lakatos, I. Falsification and the methodology of scientific research programmes. In I. Lakatos & A. Musgrave (Eds.), *Criticism and the growth of knowledge.* Cambridge: Cambridge University Press, 1970.

Landau, M.S. *The effects of spatial ability and problem presentation format on mathematical problem solving performance of middle school students.* Unpublished doctoral dissertation, Northwestern University, 1983.

Larkin, J.H. The role of problem representation in physics. In D. Gentner & A.L. Stevens (Eds.), *Mental models.* Hillsdale, NJ: Lawrence Erlbaum Associates, 1982.

Larkin, J.H., McDermott, J., Simon, D.P., & Simon, H.A. Expert and novice performance in solving physics problems. *Science* 208, 1335–42, 1980.

Lave, J. *Paper-and-pencil skills in the real world.* Paper presented at the annual meeting of the American Educational Research Association, New Orleans, April 1984.

Lawry, J., Welsh, C., & Wendall, J. Cognitive tempo and complex problem solving. *Child Development* 54, 912–20, 1983.

Lesh, R. An interpretation of advanced organizers. *Journal for Research in Mathematics Education* 7(2), 69–74, 1976.

Lesh, R. Mathematical learning disabilities: Considerations for identification, diagnosis, and remediation. In R. Lesh, D. Mierkiewicz, & M.G. Kantowski (Eds.), *Applied mathematical problem solving.* Columbus, OH: ERIC Clearinghouse for Science, Mathematics, and Environmental Education, 1979.

Lesh, R. Applied mathematical problem solving. *Educational Studies in Mathematics* 12(2), 235–65, 1981.

Lesh, R. Modeling students' modeling behaviors. In *Proceedings of the International Group for the Psychology of Mathematics Education.* Athens: University of Georgia, 1982.

Lesh, R. *Modeling students' modeling behaviors.* Paper presented at the annual meeting of the American Educational Research Association, Montreal, April 1983.

Lesh, R., & Akerstrom, M. Applied problem solving: A priority focus for mathematics education research. In F.K. Lester & J. Garofalo (Eds.), *Mathematical problem solving: Issues in research.* Philadelphia: The Franklin Institute Press, 1981.

Lesh, R., & Landau, M. (Eds.). *Acquisition of mathematics concepts and processes.* New York: Academic Press, 1983.

Lesh, R., Landau, M., & Hamilton, E. Conceptual models in applied mathematical problem solving. In R. Lesh & M. Landau (Eds.), *Acquisition of mathematics concepts and processes.* New York: Academic Press, 1983.

Lesh, R., & Mierkiewicz, D. Perception, imagery, and conception. In R. Lesh (Ed.), *Recent research concerning the development of spatial and geometric concepts.* Columbus, OH: ERIC Clearinghouse for Science, Mathematics, and Environmental Education, 1978.

Lesh, R., & Zawojewski, J. *The influence of social understandings on individual problem solving strategies and heuristics.* Paper presented at the annual meeting of the American Educational Research Association, Montreal, April 1983.

Lester, F.K. Trends and issues in mathematical problem-solving research. In R. Lesh & M. Landau (Eds.), *Acquisition of mathematics concepts and processes.* New York: Academic Press, 1983.

Mayer, R.E. *Thinking, problem solving, and cognition.* San Francisco: W.H. Freeman & Co., 1983.

McCorduck, P. *Machines who think: A personal inquiry into the history and prospects of artificial intelligence.* San Francisco: W.H. Freeman & Co., 1979.

Minsky, M. (Ed.). *Semantic information processing.* Cambridge, MA: The MIT Press, 1968.

Nesher, P. The stereotyped nature of school word problems. *For the Learning of Mathematics* 1(1), 41–48, 1980.

Newell, A. A note on process-structure distinctions in developmental psychology. In S. Farnham-Diggory (Ed.), *Information processing in children.* New York: Academic Press, 1972.

Newell, A. You can't play 20 questions with nature and win: Projective comments on the papers of the symposium. In W.G. Chase (Ed.), *Visual information processing.* New York: Academic Press, 1973.

Newell, A., & Simon, H.A. *Human problem solving.* Englewood Cliffs, NJ: Prentice-Hall, 1972.

Noddings, N. *What do individuals gain in small group mathematical problem solving?* Paper presented at the annual meeting of the American Educational Research Association, Montreal, April 1983.

Noelting, G. *The development of proportional reasoning in the child and the ratio concept: The orange juice experiment.* Quebec: Université Laval, Ecole de Psychologie, November 1979.

Norman, D.E. (Ed.). *Perspectives on cognitive science.* Norwood, NJ: Ablex, 1979.

Pattee, H.H. (Ed.). *Hierarchy theory.* New York: George Braziller, 1973.

Pepper, S.C. *World hypotheses, a study in evidence.* Berkeley: University of California Press, 1942.

Piaget, J. *Biology and knowledge.* Chicago: University of Chicago Press, 1971.

Piaget, J., & Beth, E.W. *Mathematical epistemology and psychology.* Dordrecht, The Netherlands: D. Reidel, 1966.

Saari, D.G. *Cognitive development and the dynamics of adaptation: Accommodation.* Unpublished manuscript, 1982. (Available from the author, Mathematics Department, Northwestern University)

Saari, D.G. *Cognitive development and the dynamics of adaptation: Assimilation.* Unpublished manuscript, 1983. (Available from the author, Mathematics Department, Northwestern University)

Savage, C.W. (Ed.). *Perception and cognition: Issues in the foundations of psychology.* Minneapolis: University of Minnesota Press, 1978.

Schoenfeld, A.H. Some thoughts on problem solving research and mathematics education. In F.K. Lester & J. Garofalo (Eds.), *Mathematical problem solving: Issues in research.* Philadelphia: The Franklin Institute Press, 1982.

Schoenfeld, A.H. Episodes and executive decisions in mathematical problem-solving. In R. Lesh & M. Landau (Eds.), *Acquisition of mathematics concepts and processes.* New York: Academic Press, 1983.

Siegler, R.S. Development sequences within and between concepts. *Monographs of the Society for Research in Child Development* 46(2, Serial No. 189), 1981.

Simon, H.A. *The architecture of complexity*. 1968.

Simon, H.A. *The sciences of the artificial*. Cambridge, MA: The MIT Press, 1969.

Simon, H.A. The functional equivalence of problem solving skills. In H.A. Simon (Ed.), *Models of thought*. New Haven, CT: Yale University Press, 1979.

Simon, H.A. *The sciences of the artificial* (2nd ed.). Cambridge, MA: The MIT Press, 1981.

Sloman, A. *The computer revolution in philosophy*. Brighton, England: Garvester, 1979.

Sober, E. Holism, individualism, and the units of selection. *Proceedings of Philosophy of Science Association* (Vol. 2), 1980.

Sowder, L. Problem solving/response. In E. Fennema (Ed.), *Mathematics education research: Implications for the 80's*. Reston, VA: National Council of Teachers of Mathematics, 1981.

Suppe, F. *The structure of scientific theories* (2nd ed.). Urbana: University of Illinois Press, 1977.

Weiss, P. One plus one does not equal two. In G.C. Quarton, T. Melnechuk, & F. Schmitt (Eds.), *The neurosciences: A study program*. New York: Rockefeller University Press, 1967.

Winston, P.H. *The psychology of computer vision*. New York: McGraw-Hill, 1975.

Vygotsky, L.S. *Thought and language*. Cambridge, MA: The MIT Press, 1962.

Individual Differences and Mathematical Problem Solving

Judith Threadgill-Sowder

Northern Illinois University

What is the role of individual differences in the study of mathematical problem solving? Researchers in mathematics education have traditionally considered individual differences in problem solving along two distinguishable though somewhat overlapping research lines. Some have concentrated on the problem solvers themselves, distinguishing between "good" and "poor" problem solvers and their characteristic approaches to problem solving. Krutetskii's (1976) monumental work on mathematical abilities is one example of this line of research; Bloom and Broder's (1950) description of successful and unsuccessful problem solvers is another. Recent interest in "expert" and "novice" problem solvers also fits into this category. Other researchers have sought to identify more general aptitudes or individual characteristics, such as spatial ability, which interact or correlate with problem-solving ability.

As educators, a major concern is the manner in which individual differences affect learning. Hunt (1978) claims that the understanding of individual variations in human cognition is dependent upon the understanding of the interplay between three sources of differences. The first of these is knowledge, which although held constant in much psychological research, is recognized as being important when extrapolating from psychological research to school settings. Problem-solving methods of mathematics, acquired through instruction, fall into this category. The second source of individual differences is based on the mechanics of information processing, and includes both automatic and controlled attention-demanding processes. Automatic processes are relatively content-independent and appear as stable individual traits; controlled processes are more content-specific and are less effective predictors of cognitive performance because they are less stable. Hunt speculates that the reason a person's problem-solving ability seems so unstable and dependent on temporary changes of state is because this ability is more dependent on controlled processes than on automatic processes. Although Hunt is not necessarily referring to mathematical problem solving in this context, such an extension seems reasonable. The third source of human variation comes from general information-processing strategies. These are simple strategies which are used as steps in larger problems. Examples would be repeating numbers to be remembered or choosing ways of representing problems. Polya's heuristics would fit under this source. Hunt cites Baron's (1977) proposal that the facility with which we use these general information processes is much the same as what we refer to as general intelligence.

An emphasis on cognitive processes as important sources for individual differences, such as Hunt suggests, is relatively new to mathematics education research. Egan (1979) clarifies this new approach by contrasting it with the traditional approach to the study of abilities. Traditionally, a score on an aptitude test of some sort was taken as a measure of an underlying factor. "The score is unitary and opaque. It places the subject with respect to the rest of the population on a dimension, but gives little insight into what the dimension is, or what kinds of difficulty the subject might be having" (p. 2). On the other hand, if an information-processing model is used, one would have several different scores for a particular kind of task where each score measured performance on an underlying process. This model provides a conceptual grasp of what the tests are indeed measuring, which in turn leads to improved methods of assessing abilities. In the area of problem solving, then, this information could be helpful in adapting instruction to better suit the learner.

The purpose of this paper is to attempt to explore the role of processes for interpreting individual differences both in problem-solving ability itself and in other aptitudes which have been shown to relate to problem-solving ability. The effect of process considerations on aptitude-treatment interaction studies and on adaptive instruction will also be considered. Finally, some new directions for research on individual differences in mathematical problem solving will be discussed.

Problem-solving researchers have often been faulted for not defining what they mean by problem solving. Here is a brief definition of what is meant by problem solving in this paper. The definition needs to be broad, since under its umbrella we should be able to fit many different types of problem-solving research. The definition given here is borrowed and extended from one given by Anderson (1980): Mathematical problem solving is an activity which is goal-directed and which involves a sequence of operations having a significant cognitive component, where the goal can be expressed in terms of mathematical content.

INDIVIDUAL DIFFERENCES AS PROCESSES

In his oft-quoted presidential address to the American Psychological Association, Cronbach (1957) declared that psychological research was being impeded by the separation of experimental psychology from the study of individual differences. He argued that the experimentalists with their concern for treatment variables and the correlationists with their interest in organismic variables needed to unite to form a new discipline with a common theory, common constructs, and common methodologies. The resulting "budding but fitful and hesitant courtship" (Carroll & Maxwell, 1979, p. 604) was greatly influenced by social and scientific advances which forced a conceptual break between past and present ways of viewing and assessing individual differences (Pellegrino & Glaser, 1979, 1980). On the social side, the psychometric tradition of assessing differences through intelligence test scores was being severely criticized as being too gross a method to predict academic achievement. Psychometric assessments were also faulted for lacking a sound theoretical framework for dealing with cognitive processes, while at the same time cognitive psychologists were making theoretical advances which were well suited to the study of individual differences in cognitive processing. Horn (1979) suggested that a catalyst promoting the union of the two psychological disciplines was the "lure of study of intellectual development" (p. 198), considerably aided by shifts in research funding.

Whatever the reasons behind the attempt to unite, individual differences psychology became caught up in the flow of cognitive psychological research with its emphasis on the study of processes. In his general comments on Gagné's 1965 conference on learning and individual differences, Melton (1967) stated that the dominant theme of the conference papers was the necessity "that we frame out hypotheses about individual differences variables in terms of the process constructs of contemporary theories of learning and performance" (p. 239). Underwood (1975) echoed Melton by again pointing out that the critical individual differences variables, in terms of constructing theories powerful enough to deal with fundamental processes of behavior, were process variables.

Although the courtship between the psychometricians and experimentalists may have instigated the characterization of individual differences as processes, the conceptual differences between the two camps prevented the courtship from developing into a marriage. At the present time, there continue to be two distinct approaches to the study of individual differences. Pellegrino and Glaser (1979, 1980) call the first of these approaches the "cognitive correlates" approach. Researchers following this approach use aptitude or intelligence tests "to define subgroups that are compared on laboratory tasks that have relatively well defined cognitive processing characteristics. [They then] seek to specify the elementary information processes that correlate with high and low levels of aptitude" (Pellegrino & Glaser, 1980, p. 179).

Typical of this first approach is the work of Earl Hunt and his colleagues (Hunt, 1976, 1978; Hunt, Lunneborg, & Lewis, 1975; Hunt & MacLeod, 1979; Lansman, Donaldson, Hunt, & Yantis, 1982). These researchers use a basic information-processing model to interpret behavior on conventional test tasks. They are not interested in explaining the tests themselves. Rather, the tests are simply convenient measures useful in obtaining a range of competencies in order to understand how information processing varies over individuals (Hunt, 1980). For example, in the Hunt et al. 1975 study, the active memory capacities of high-verbal and low-verbal college students were examined. The explanation given for the fact that the high-verbal students established an initial advantage was that these students could code information more rapidly. The results of several studies, including this one, led Hunt (1980) to the conclusion that high-verbals have a greater short-term memory capacity. This allows them to devote part of their capacity to problem-solving strategies. These strategies are not available to low-verbals, who need more capacity for actually remembering items. This allows high-verbals to perform better on verbal tasks of the type used in these studies. Could something similar be happening when some people perform better on mathematical problem-solving tasks?

The second research approach identified by Pellegrino and Glaser (1979, 1980), which they call the "cognitive components" approach, is more task analytic and "attempts to identify directly the information-processing components of performance on tasks used to assess aptitude" (1980, p. 179). The goal of psychologists employing this approach is to develop models of task performance which can be used in individual differences analysis. To meet this goal, performance on psychometric test tasks is subjected to theoretical and empirical analyses. There are several examples of this research which are pertinent to those interested in mathematical problem solving.

In the first instance, Carroll (1976) examined a representative sample of tests from the Kit of Reference Tests for Cognitive Factors (French, Ekstrom, & Price, 1963), many of which have been frequently used by mathematical problem-solving researchers. He classified tests based on the type of memory tapped (short-term, intermediate-term, or long-term), the modality or contents of memory, the operations specified or implied in the task instructions, and the strategies individuals might choose to use. For example, the test used to measure flexibility of closure, the Hidden Figures Test, is often used in research as a measure of Witkin's field independence-dependence, or cognitive restructuring. This factor, as analyzed by Carroll, principally involves visual short-term memory. Individuals will vary on image of figure-in-ground, on capacity of short-term memory, and on the length of time it takes to separate the figure from the ground. Carroll concluded that it might be impossible to identify "pure" factors of individual differences, since each kind of memory and control process has several different parameters.

Sternberg, long associated with work in componential analyses, has been involved in formulating a unified theory of human reasoning, which would encompass subtheories of inductive and deductive reasoning. For example, in formulating a process model of analogy solutions, which are a form of rule induction, Sternberg (1977) conducted a series of experiments which varied content domains (verbal, geometric, and picture-like) and task forms (true-false and forced choice). He proposed a theory of component processes necessary for successful performance: encoding individual terms, inferring relationships in the first and second term, mapping the relationships onto the third term, applying results to generate a fourth term, justifying a choice of solution given alternatives, and responding by indicating the choice. Models including some or all of the processes were tested through an additive process. A model of "best-fit" was sought in each instance which would account for maximum variance in response time. The best model included all of the components. Individual subject responses in terms of latency parameters for the different components were analyzed.

Sternberg's work in deductive processes (Sternberg, Guyate, & Turner, 1980) follows in a similar vein, with the purpose of developing "an understanding of the representations and processes subjects use in solving a variety of deduction problems" (p. 244). Of particular interest here perhaps is Sternberg's recognition that the manner in which individuals perform these processes can change over content areas. "How these different types of information are abstracted and further processed and integrated into problem solving strategies may be very different in the various forms of the task and may account for differences in various specific factors of intelligence" (p. 206). Although it is admittedly impossible to do justice to Sternberg's work in this brief summary, it should be clear that his work holds promise of detailing the components of many problem-solving activities that are important in mathematics, and of leading us to better understand individual differences in the processes which, when considered jointly, make up what we now call problem-solving ability.

INDIVIDUAL DIFFERENCES IN MATHEMATICAL PROBLEM SOLVING

Carroll's and Sternberg's works have influenced the thinking of mathematics educators involved in the Mathematical Abilities Project (McKee, 1979). They have reanalyzed hypothesized abilities in terms of process components. For example, what Krutetskii called "perception" is, in their model, a combination of memory, executive, and perception components, while "flexibility of thinking" appears as an executive process. For the most part, however, researchers interested in mathematical problem solving have not concerned themselves with the identification or modification of individual differences in problem-solving ability through analyses of cognitive processes involved in solving problems. Allwood (1976) suggests that such analyses would need to take three factors into account: the type of problem, the individual's knowledge base, and the strategies characteristically used by the individual when interacting with the problem type.

Suppose we consider these three factors in turn. Certainly the type of problem has been of concern to mathematics educators (Goldin & McClintock, 1979). In a gross fashion, problems are categorized by such terminology as "routine," "non-routine," "word problems," "*aha*-type problems," and "applied problems." Most researchers use more refined categories—"algebraic word problems," for example, or "addition and subtraction" word problems. We have recently begun to see finely discriminated categories, such as in a Briars and Larkin (1982) study, where problems are described in such terminology as "action-cued double-role counters, and action-uncued, comparison, single-role counters" (p. 59).

The individual's knowledge base is probably the most critical of the three factors. Even Hunt (1978), who seemingly ignores prior knowledge in most of his "cognitive correlates" work, acknowledges its importance, and reminds psychologists that extrapolation from the laboratory (where knowledge is often controlled) to practical situations, such as school classrooms, must take this factor into account. One example of research in mathematical problem solving related to the effect of knowledge would be the recent work on problem schemata. Silver (1982) has nicely reviewed research studies on the influence and use of problem schemata, including that of Mayer (1982), who concluded that students recognized and used problem categories. Silver's suggestion that we pay more attention to the mechanisms of schema formation is worth serious consideration by researchers interested in individual differences, since the schemata of good and poor problem solvers seem to be formed according to different criteria. He also suggests that careful observation of individual differences in both schema content and schema utilization would be valuable in terms of understanding skill in problem solving. Another example of the role of knowledge in mathematical problem solving can be found in research on learned problem-solving strategies, such as work by Charles and Lester (1984) and Schoenfeld (1980).

Allwood's third area for analyses of individual differences in problem solving involves the processes likely to be used by the problem solver in reaching a solution to a particular problem type, such as attending to relevant information or inferring a relationship between two variables. While the former two areas have been most studied by mathematics educators and most slighted by cognitive psychologists, the reverse now seems true. This contrast defines, to some extent, the differences between the two disciplines. Psychologists are less interested in content areas and applications of theory than educators. Likewise, educational researchers are less inclined to spend their years building such monumental structures as Sternberg's ambitious theory of intelligence. But this focus on processes is a promising area for reaching a better understanding of individual differences in mathematical problem solving. Certainly we mathematics educators can borrow from the work of psychologists such as Hunt and Sternberg. We can begin by attempting to specify, for problem types, the processes used by students. We can begin to categorize these processes along lines that suggest possible instructional adaptations. Which of these processes are controlled and which are automatic? Which are stable and which are transient? Which are content-independent and which are content-specific? Which are modifiable and which are permanent?

APTITUDE BY TREATMENT INTERACTIONS AND ADAPTIVE INSTRUCTION

Some psychologists, in answering Cronbach's call to unite the two disciplines of psychology, attempted to adapt psychometric methodology to experimental purposes, while others tried to adapt experimental methodology to psychometric theory. Still a third group became interested in fusing the two methodologies by seeking aptitude by treatment interactions (ATI's). Most early ATI studies used a very simple design in which an aptitude was measured and subjects were randomly assigned to one of two treatments. Interactions between the aptitude measure and outcome measure were then tested for significance. Cronbach and Snow (1977) found this design to be inadequate for most studies, and urged researchers to consider multitrait, multimethod designs. In their review (Cronbach & Snow, 1977) of ATI studies, they found some promising results, but certainly the findings have not been strong enough to warrant any fundamental changes in instructional policies. Shuell (1980) believes ATI research is still in its infancy, while Glaser (1980) claims that lack of strong ATI findings is due to our ignorance of "the processes that relate the three components of ATI experiments—namely, the tasks measured by aptitude, the instructional activities presented, and the criterion tasks to be learned" (p. 314). Both Glaser (1980) and Snow (1980) exhort researchers to seek out detailed models of the cognitive processes and strategies underlying the aptitude constructs we have been using, such as spatial visualization and memory span.

The goal of ATI research is to find results that presumably can be used to assign individuals to optimal learning environments. Salomon (1972) suggested three models for doing this. If a treatment can be shown to capitalize on student capabilities, then this treatment can be considered "preferential." Presumably, this type of treatment would capitalize on particular styles of processing information. In a somewhat different fashion, measures of general abilities or modes of information processing in a "compensatory" treatment may be found to provide learners with mediators which they cannot provide for themselves, or which neutralize the effects of learner deficiencies. Finally, when measures are more task-specific, "remedial" treatments can sometimes be found which make up for the lack of mastery of certain prerequisites on the part of some students. These models can become somewhat tangled. For example, if a particular cognitive process can be modified by appropriate training, then "is it better to assign instructional treatments to capitalize on potent cognitive processes, or to assign instructional treatments to improve upon impotent cognitive processes?" (Federico, 1980, p. 14). Customarily, ATI studies use a pretreatment measure of the aptitude or ability in question. Federico (1980) has suggested that within-task measures of performance such as number of errors, response latencies, and emotive states could be useful in ATI work. Atkinson (1976) has attempted, through highly individualized computer-assisted instructional programs, to use student responses to make instructional decisions that optimize individual student learning. It is also possible to use both pretask and within-task measures to adapt teaching strategies for individuals.

More basic questions regarding adaptive instruction also need to be addressed (Shuell, 1980). Certainly, it is necessary to clarify exactly what is to be accomplished. If we are trying to achieve equality by attempting to eliminate differences that exist among people, our procedures would be different than if we are trying to allow people to maximize their accomplishments. Carroll (1967) warned that truly effective adaptive instruction might have the effect of accentuating rather than decreasing individual differences.

Any number of aptitude constructs have been shown to be or at least hypothesized to be related to problem solving, particularly facets of general ability and cognitive style.

Since it is not possible, or perhaps even desirable, to consider all of them in this paper, one from each category will be discussed and interpreted in terms of the processing involved in each.

Spatial Visualization

Spatial visualization will be considered in this section; but first, some background is provided on the choice of terminology. In Cattell's (1971) model of abilities, all primary abilities can be categorized as loading under broader factors of fluid intelligence, crystallized intelligence, and visualization, where visualization refers to the ability to imagine movement or spatial displacement. Snow (1980) generally agrees with this distinction, although he suggests that practically speaking, it is difficult always to make clear whether fluid ability or general ability is being measured. (The literature also distinguishes between spatial visualization and spatial orientation [McGee, 1979] whether or not Cattell's model is followed. We shall be concerned here only with visualization.)

Evidence suggesting that spatial ability relates positively to problem-solving performance is frequently noted in research literature (e.g., Fennema & Sherman, 1977; Krutetskii, 1976; Meyer, 1978; Moses, 1978; Wilson & Begle, 1972). Spatial visualization tests will probably continue to play a part in mathematical problem-solving research. Yet researchers complain about the tests now available, expressing doubts about their validity as measures of spatial visualization ability. Validity questions only serve to magnify our basic lack of understanding of what most visualization tests are really measuring. Spatial visualization tests supposedly require the examinee to mentally rotate, fold, or in some other way manipulate visual representations of objects. On a traditional test such as the Paper Folding Test (French et al., 1963), each item contains a drawing, then several alternative drawings of which one shows the first drawing as it should look after the presumed mental manipulation. In information-processing studies, however, only two drawings of an object are usually presented, and the examinee must tell whether the second drawing represents the same or a different object after mentally manipulating the first (Egan, 1979). This type of item allows the experimenter to more easily modify the tasks or break the tasks into components and to collect latency scores, in order to delineate what sequence of mental operations takes place between the time a stimulus item is presented and the time a response is executed.

As an example of this information-processing approach to visual tasks, let us consider the now classic rotation task introduced by Shepard and Metzler (1971). In this study, subjects were asked whether two perspective drawings of three-dimensional objects were the "same" or "different." Some pairs were rotated in the picture plane, some were rotated in depth, and some could not be rotated into congruence. The time subjects took to determine whether two objects were the same in shape increased linearly with the angular difference between the two objects. This led to the hypothesis that subjects performed the task by "mentally rotating" the internal representation until a match or mismatch was found. This linear relationship has been found in several subsequent studies with different populations, other stimulus materials, and other task modifications (e.g., Cooper & Shepard, 1975; Cooper & Podgorny, 1976).

By analyzing eye fixations and response latencies on this task, Just and Carpenter (1976) proposed a three-step model consisting of search, transform, and confirm. In the search process, a subject identifies and encodes features of a figure, then searches the corresponding figure for the same features and encodes them. In the second stage, transformation, the subject compares the two figures and rotates the second figure in an iterative fashion until it is oriented like the first one. In the final stage, the subject determines whether or not the two figures are congruent. The time it takes a subject to complete each stage increases as the angular difference between the two figures increases. Although this same sequence is followed by all subjects, the time it takes to complete each phase of the task varies for subjects. This model suggests, then, that performances on spatial test items can be broken down into a sequence of distinct cognitive processes, and that there is individual variation in the speed and accuracy for completing each phase or process. Could it be that individual component operations are more highly related to some types of problem solving than the task as a whole is? Egan (1979) also pointed out that the different processes affect item difficulty in different ways, and that such information should be useful in future test design. He also discussed the problem of spatial test validity. He has evidence, for example, that intercepts but not slopes from a visualization test will predict aviation training performance, indicating that the search operation may be more important than the transformation operation in this context. This type of information could be useful in devising tests with better predictive validity.

Another approach to studying spatial information processing uses systematic individual differences to assist in the understanding of basic spatial processes. The individual differences of importance here are in patterns of performance on spatial tasks, rather than on quantitative measures (Cooper, 1980). In a series of experiments conducted on spatial comparison processes, Cooper (1980) found two qualitatively distinct but reliable patterns of performance. The Type I subject compared a test shape with a visual memory representation in a holistic, parallel fashion, whereas a Type II subject used a more analytic comparison process. There is also other evidence that different subjects use qualitatively different processing approaches to solving spatial problems (Tapley & Bryden, 1977). Such results lead quite naturally into our next topic.

Cognitive Restructuring

Interest in cognitive style constructs as dimensions suitable for instructional adaptations has been particularly strong within the past decade. Kogan (1980) suggests two reasons for this interest. First, the traditional aptitudes were almost exclusively concerned with accuracy and efficiency, and new constructs were needed to deal with new concerns, such as the form and manner of performance. Second, cognitive-style researchers focused on an area relating cognition to other aspects of the individual, an area that lay someplace between cognition and personality and that had been traditionally ignored by both camps. Glaser's (1972) suggestion that cognitive style constructs might be among the "new" aptitudes relevant to individual differences research highlighted the perceived need for such new research constructs.

Interest in cognitive styles is still prevalent (Messick, 1982), although the idea of what cognitive styles are has undergone some reconceptualization. Messick (1982) now defines cognitive styles in such terms as "information processing regularities that develop in congenial ways around underlying personality trends" (p. 4). Guilford (1980) refers to them as functions as well as traits. Guilford also suggests that if there are executive functions that initiate and control motor activity, then it seems reasonable that there are executive functions that govern intellectual functioning, and that cognitive styles or cognitive controls might fit this conceptualization.

The proliferation of research on field dependence-independence (FDI) in the past 10 years is but one example of the ongoing interest in cognitive style (Linn & Kyllonen, 1981). Among these research studies are several showing FDI and problem solving to be related (e.g., Ehr, 1980; Threadgill-Sowder & Sowder, 1982).

The FDI construct itself has undergone extensive reconceptualizations, which perhaps confuses some of the past research results (although knowledge of instruments used should offer some clarification). First conceived as a method of reconciling conflicting visual and postural experiences (Witkin, Dyk, Faterson, Goodenough, & Karp, 1962), it was later extended to include the ability to perceive items as discrete from an embedding field, and to restructure problem material symbolic in nature. In this broader approach, FDI was viewed as a personal, stable process of functioning which encompasses a wider range of perceptual and intellectual situations (Witkin & Goodenough, 1977). Researchers outside Witkin's laboratory have been less certain about the nature of FDI. Horn (1976) claimed that common FDI measures rarely test flexibility of closure. Cronbach and Snow (1977) claimed that FDI is, in whole or in part, fluid ability.

Responding to such criticism, Witkin (Witkin & Goodenough, 1977, 1981) revised his model in a manner that separated FDI into two related functions: reliance on vestibular or visual field referents, and cognitive restructuring. Linn and Kyllonen (1981) found that FDI tests did indeed cluster into two factors, which they called general fluid visualization and familiar field. They noted that Witkin's cognitive restructuring measures related highly with fluid ability measures and spatial measures, and in fact adopt Witkin's (Witkin & Goodenough, 1977) definition of cognitive restructuring—that is, the ability to dis-embed relevant information in complex situations—as a definition of general fluid visualization. (Most ATI research in mathematics education that used FDI as an aptitude construct employed measures that would fall into the cognitive restructuring category, such as the Embedded Figures Test and the Hidden Figures Test.)

Although the common interpretation of cognitive restructuring ability emphasizes its analytic quality, Guilford (1980) prefers to think of it as a matter of flexibility. He views it as ''a readiness to make changes in information, an ability or an inclination (or both) to effect transformation'' (p. 720). This interpretation gives insight into why people who score high on cognitive restructuring measures tend to like and do well in mathematics.

There is much yet to be done before we can better understand and take advantage of the relationships that we know to exist between constructs such as cognitive restructuring and mathematical endeavors such as problem solving. Perhaps Snow (1980) says it best:

> Process theories of these aptitudes, the distinctions between them, their development through formal and informal learning experiences, and their respective relations to new learning in different instructional situations are a basic need in cognitive and instructional psychology. These theories will need to account not only for individual differences in performance but also for the assembly and control processes that organize and maintain the performance: It may be these aspects of aptitude that account for relations among aptitude tests and their persistent relation to learning outcomes. (p. 59)

FUTURE DIRECTIONS

The suggestion that the study of processes, such as those postulated by the information-processing model, is the most promising direction for future individual differences research in mathematics education might be a bit intimidating to some researchers. However, this is not the first time researchers interested in individual differences research have been told that the road ahead may be a difficult one. When Carroll (1967) responded to Cronbach's suggestions for adapting instruction, he predicted that "the study of instructional methods and individual differences is going to be extremely difficult and frustrating, even if it is 'most interesting' psychologically" (p. 41). Carroll was right. It *has* been difficult. But perhaps the difficulty stems from our unwitting designs of research around factors that have been unpredictive because they ignore the process variables most intimately related to the learning task. Defining and measuring these processes is certainly one of the important tasks that lie ahead. Steps being taken in this direction are promising. For example, Hunt (1982) described a modification of the Minnesota Form Board Test which isolates and stresses component stages of the task. He claims that it is a better measure of spatial ability than the original or even other standard spatial tests. He also suggests that models of arithmetic reasoning such as Brown and Burton's (1978) lend themselves to the construction of tests that test the manner in which the skills are used rather than simply the level of the skill.

The CHIPS (Concrete Human-like Inferential Problem-Solver) model of Briars and Larkin (1982), which categorizes and breaks down simple addition and subtraction word problems into component parts, has already been used to analyze the way children in school do these problems. Important differences between the manner in which more able and less able students attacked the problems led to suggestions on more effective ways to teach word problems. This study could be considered a prototype for future research on using individual differences information to plan optimal instructional methods for teaching word problems. Rose (1980) refers to such developments as "second-generation methodologies—techniques that increase the power of previous methods as well as expand the scope of potential applications" (p. 66).

One of our present-day advantages, probably undreamed of by Carroll 15 years ago, is the widespread availability of microcomputers. These should make designing new psychometric tests a far easier venture. Such tests will require latency measures and selective presentation of information dependent on student responses, design features highly suited to computerized testing. Not only aptitude measures but also the treatments themselves used in ATI studies can be computerized and regulated, with within-task tests defining the treatments.

Although the cognitive psychologists have thus far defined the directions for research on individual differences in processing, much of it has the strong flavor of the laboratory setting. In order to build accommodative instructional environments based on the knowledge gained by such research, educators must lead the way from the laboratory into the instructional setting. Perhaps, rather than concerning ourselves with the union of the experimentalists and the psychometricians, we ought to be directing our energies toward a uniting of cognitive psychology and educational psychology. We end with a promising note from Snow and Yalow (1982), speaking about the usefulness of cognitive psychology to educators: "The theoretical machinery finally appears to be equal to the complexity of educational hypotheses, so there is now hope that such hypotheses can be addressed, unraveled, and understood" (p. 513).

REFERENCES

Allwood, C.M. A review of individual differences among problem solvers and attempts to improve problem solving ability. *Goteborg Psychological Reports* 6, 1–27, 1976.

Anderson, J.R. *Cognitive psychology and its implication.* San Francisco: W.H. Freeman & Co., 1980.

Atkinson, R.C. Adaptive instructional systems: Some attempts to optimize the learning process. In D. Klahr (Ed.), *Cognition and instruction.* Hillsdale, NJ: Lawrence Erlbaum Associates, 1976.

Baron, J. Intelligence and general strategies. In B.J. Underwood (Ed.), *Strategies in information processing.* New York: Academic Press, 1977.

Bloom, B.S., & Broder, L.J. *Problem-solving processes of college students.* Chicago: University of Chicago Press, 1950.

Briars, D.J., & Larkin, J.H. *An integrated model of skill in solving elementary word problems* (Working Paper No. 2). Pittsburgh: Carnegie-Mellon University, 1982.

Brown, J.S., & Burton, R.R. Diagnostic models for procedural bugs in basic mathematical skills. *Cognitive Science* **2**, 155–92, 1978.

Carroll, J.B. Instructional methods and individual differences. In R.M. Gagné (Ed.), *Learning and individual differences.* Columbus, OH: Charles E. Merrill, 1967.

Carroll, J.B. Psychometric tests as cognitive tasks: A new "Structure of Intellect." In L.B. Resnick (Ed.), *The nature of intelligence.* Hillsdale, NJ: Lawrence Erlbaum Associates, 1976.

Carroll, J.B., & Maxwell, S.E. Individual differences in cognitive abilities. *Annual Review of Psychology* **30**, 603–40, 1979.

Cattell, R.B. *Abilities: Their structure, growth, and action.* Boston: Houghton Mifflin, 1971.

Charles, R.I., & Lester, F.K. An evaluation of the process-oriented instructional program in mathematical problem-solving in grades five and seven. *Journal for Research in Mathematics Education* **15**, 15–34, 1984.

Cooper, L.A. Spatial information processing: Strategies for research. In R.E. Snow, P.A. Federico, & W.E. Montague (Eds.), *Aptitude, learning, and instruction: Cognitive process analyses.* Hillsdale, NJ: Lawrence Erlbaum Associates, 1980.

Cooper, L.A., & Podgorny, P. Mental transformations and visual comparison processes: Effects of complexity and similarity. *Journal of Experimental Psychology: Human Perception and Performance* **2**, 503–14, 1976.

Cooper L.A., & Shepard, R.N. Mental transformations in the identification of left and right hands. *Journal of Experimental Psychology: Human Perception and Performance* **104**, 48–56, 1975.

Cronbach, L.J. The two disciplines of scientific psychology. *American Psychologist* **12**, 671–84, 1957.

Cronbach, L.J., & Snow, R.E. *Aptitudes and instructional methods.* New York: Irvington, 1977.

Egan, D.E. Testing based on understanding: Implications from studies of spatial ability. *Intelligence* **3**, 1–15, 1979.

Ehr, C.K. Cognitive style and information selection during the solution of mathematical word problems. *Dissertation Abstracts International* **40**, 5768A, 1980.

Federico, P.A. Adaptive instruction: Trends and issues. In R.E. Snow, P.A. Federico, & W.E. Montague (Eds.), *Aptitude, learning, and instruction: Cognitive process analyses.* Hillsdale, NJ: Lawrence Erlbaum Associates, 1980.

Fennema, E., & Sherman, J. Sex-related differences in mathematics achievement, spatial visualization, and affective factors. *American Educational Research Journal* **14** (1), 51–71, 1977.

French, J.W., Ekstrom, R.B., & Price, L.A. *Kit of reference tests for cognitive factors.* Princeton, NJ: Educational Testing Service, 1963.

Glaser, R. Individuals and learning: The new aptitudes. *Educational Researcher* **1**, 5–13, 1972.

Glaser, R. General discussion: Relationships between aptitude, learning, and instruction. In R.E. Snow, P.A. Federico, & W.E. Montague (Eds.), *Aptitude, learning, and instruction: Cognitive process analyses.* Hillsdale, NJ: Lawrence Erlbaum Associates, 1980.

Goldin, G.A., & McClintock, C.E. (Eds.). *Task variables in mathematical problem solving.*

Columbus, OH: ERIC Clearinghouse for Science, Mathematics, and Environmental Education, 1979.

Guilford, J.B. Cognitive styles: What are they? *Educational and Psychological Measurement* **40**, 715–35, 1980.

Horn, J.L. Human abilities: A review of research and theory in the early 1970's. *Annual Review of Psychology* **27**, 437–85, 1976.

Horn, J.L. Trends in the measurement of intelligence. In R.J. Sternberg & D.K. Detterman (Eds.), *Human intelligence: Perspectives on its theory and measurement.* Norwood, NJ: Ablex, 1979.

Hunt, E. Varieties of cognitive power. In L.B. Resnick (Ed.), *The nature of intelligence.* Hillsdale, NJ: Lawrence Erlbaum Associates, 1976.

Hunt, E. Mechanics of verbal ability. *Psychological Review* **85** (2), 109–30, 1978.

Hunt, E. The foundations of verbal comprehension. In R.E. Snow, P.A. Federico, & W.E. Montague (Eds.), *Aptitude, learning, and instruction: Cognitive process analyses.* Hillsdale, NJ: Lawrence Erlbaum Associates, 1980.

Hunt, E. Towards new ways of assessing intelligence. *Intelligence* **6**, 231–40, 1982.

Hunt, E., Lunneborg, C., & Lewis, J. What does it means to be verbal? *Cognitive Psychology* **7**, 194–227, 1975.

Hunt, E., & MacLeod, C.M. The sentence-verification paradigm: A case study of two conflicting approaches to individual differences. In R.J. Sternberg & D.K. Detterman (Eds.), *Human intelligence: Perspectives on its theory and measurement.* Norwood, NJ: Ablex, 1979.

Just, M.A., & Carpenter, P.A. Eye fixations and cognitive processes. *Cognitive Psychology* **8**, 441–80, 1976.

Kogan, N. A cognitive-style approach to metaphoric thinking. In R.E. Snow, P.A. Federico, & W.E. Montague (Eds.), *Aptitude, learning, and instruction: Cognitive process analyses.* Hillsdale, NJ: Lawrence Erlbaum Associates, 1980.

Krutetskii, V.A. *The Psychology of mathematical abilities in schoolchildren.* (J. Kilpatrick & I. Wirszup, Eds., J. Teller, Trans.) Chicago: University of Chicago Press, 1976.

Lansman, M., Donaldson, G., Hunt, E., & Yantis, S. Ability factors and cognitive processes. *Intelligence* **6**, 347–86, 1982.

Linn, M.C., & Kyllonen, P. The field dependence-independence construct: Some, one, or none. *Journal of Educational Psychology* **73**, 261–73, 1981.

Mayer, R.E. Memory for algebra story problems. *Journal of Educational Psychology* **74**, 199–216, 1982.

McGee, M.G. Human spatial abilities: Psychometric studies and environmental, genetic, hormonal, and neurological influences. *Psychological Bulletin* **86**, 889–918, 1979.

McKee, L. *Information-processing approaches to research on mathematical abilities.* Paper presented at the annual meeting of the National Council of Teachers of Mathematics, Boston, 1979.

Melton, A.W. Individual differences and theoretical process variables: General comments on the conference. In R.M. Gagné (Ed.), *Learning and individual differences.* Columbus, OH: Charles E. Merrill, 1967.

Messick, S. *Cognitive styles in educational practice.* Princeton, NJ: Educational Testing Service, 1982.

Meyer, R.A. Mathematical problem-solving performance and intellectual abilities of fourth-grade children. *Journal for Research in Mathematics Education* **9**, 334–48, 1978.

Moses, B.E. The nature of spatial ability and its relationship to mathematical problem solving. *Dissertation Abstracts International* **38**, 4640A, 1978.

Pellegrino, J.W., & Glaser, R. Cognitive correlates and components in the analysis of individual differences. *Intelligence* **3**, 187–214, 1979.

Pellegrino, J.W., & Glaser, R. Components of inductive reasoning. In R.E. Snow, P.A. Federico,

& W.E. Montague (Eds.), *Aptitude, learning, and instruction: Cognitive process analyses.* Hillsdale, NJ: Lawrence Erlbaum Associates, 1980.

Rose, A.M. Information-processing abilities. In R.E. Snow, P.A. Federico, & W.E. Montague (Eds.), *Aptitude, learning, and instruction: Cognitive process analyses.* Hillsdale, NJ: Lawrence Erlbaum Associates, 1980.

Salomon, G. Heuristic models for the generation of aptitude-treatment hypothesis. *Review of Educational Research* 42, 327–43, 1972.

Schoenfeld, A.H. Teaching problem-solving skills. *American Mathematical Monthly* 87, 794–805, 1980.

Shepard, R.N., & Metzler, J. Mental rotation of three-dimensional objects. *Science* 171, 701–73, 1971.

Shuell, T.J. Learning theory, instructional theory, and adaptation. In R.E. Snow, P.A. Federico, & W.E. Montague (Eds.), *Aptitude, learning, and instruction: Cognitive process analyses.* Hillsdale, NJ: Lawrence Erlbaum Associates, 1980.

Silver, E.A. Problem solving performance and perceptions of problem similarity: Retrospect and prospect. *Journal of Mathematical Behavior* 3, 169–81, 1982.

Snow, R.E. Aptitude processes. In R.E. Snow, P.A. Federico, & W.E. Montague (Eds.), *Aptitude, learning, and instruction: Cognitive process analyses.* Hillsdale, NJ: Lawrence Erlbaum Associates, 1980.

Snow, R.E., Federico, P.A., & Montague, W.E. (Eds.), *Aptitude, learning, and instruction: Cognitive process analyses* (Vols. 1 & 2). Hillsdale, NJ: Lawrence Erlbaum Associates, 1980.

Snow, R.E., & Yalow, E. Education and Intelligence. In R.J. Sternberg (Ed.), *Handbook of human intelligence.* Cambridge: Cambridge University Press, 1982.

Sternberg, R.J. *Intelligence, information processing, and analogical reasoning: The componential analysis of human abilities.* Hillsdale, NJ: Lawrence Erlbaum Associates, 1977.

Sternberg, R.J., Guyote, M.J., & Turner, M.E. Deductive reasoning. In R.E. Snow, P.A. Federico, & W.E. Montague (Eds.), *Aptitude, learning, and instruction: Cognitive process analyses.* Hillsdale, NJ: Lawrence Erlbaum Associates, 1980.

Tapley, S.M., & Bryden, M.P. An investigation of sex differences in spatial ability: Mental rotation of three-dimensional objects. *Canadian Journal of Psychology* 31, 122–30, 1977.

Threadgill-Sowder, J., & Sowder, L. Drawn versus verbal formats for mathematical story problems. *Journal for Research in Mathematics Education* 13, 324–31, 1982.

Underwood, B.J. Individual differences as a crucible in theory construction. *American Psychologist* 30, 128–34, 1975.

Wilson, J.W., & Begle, E.G. *Intercorrelations of mathematical and psychological variables* (NLSMA Reports No. 33). Stanford, CA: School Mathematics Study Group, 1972.

Witkin, H.A., Dyk, R.B., Faterson, H.F., Goodenough, D.R., & Karp, S.A. *Psychological differentiation.* New York: John Wiley & Sons, 1962.

Witkin, H.A., & Goodenough, D.R. *Field dependence revisited* (Research Bulletin RB 77-16). Princeton, NJ: Educational Testing Service, 1977.

Witkin, H.A., & Goodenough, D.R. Cognitive styles: Essence and origins: Field dependence and field independence. *Psychological Issues: Monograph 51,* 1981.

Small Groups as a Setting
For Research on
Mathematical Problem Solving[1]

Nel Noddings

Stanford University

Research on mathematical problem solving has been influenced by both mathematical content and instructional methods on the one hand and by research methods extraneous to the subject field on the other. Many examples come instantly to mind: group theory, attempts to describe mental operations in group-theoretical terms, and subsequent efforts to validate these structures psychologically (Gay & Cole, 1967; Piaget, 1970); the structure of the disciplines movement and attempts to find correlations between structural presentations and achievement (Rudnitsky, 1977; Shavelson, 1972, 1973); increasing interest in graph theory and attempts to describe cognitive structure by way of trees (Shavelson, 1974a, 1974b; Stanton, 1980); growth in computer science and a proliferation of attempts to describe mathematical behavior in terms of information processing (Greeno, 1978; Paige & Simon, 1966). Clearly, we could extend the list and supply pages of references in each category.

Right now, still another "outside" research effort is exerting some influence on problem-solving research. Everyone seems to be interested in small-group processes: sociologists, linguists, psychologists, ... and, of course, mathematics educators and researchers. There is good reason for our interest. The literature on small-group learning supports the claim that positive learning effects are associated with small-group processes. The best documented effects are, so far, in the social-emotional aspects of learning (Cohen, 1980; Johnson & Johnson, 1975; Schmuck & Schmuck, 1979; Sharan, Hertz-Lazarowitz, & Ackerman, 1980; Slavin, 1980). These effects are important in themselves, but we still need to know more about cognitive effects on both individual and group problem-solving processes. Here the results are not altogether clear. Although Johnson and Johnson (1982) concluded from their meta-analysis that concept attainment

---

1. The research reported here was partly sponsored by a seed grant from the Spencer Foundation. I wish to thank Lee Shulman, Kathleen Gilbert-Macmillan, and Steven Leitz for helpful ideas in constructing the framework presented in this paper.

and verbal problem solving improve more in cooperative settings than in competitive or individualistic settings, Webb (1982) has pointed out discrepancies in these studies. Where there is solid evidence of enhanced achievement through small-group processes (Slavin, 1983a), it is not clear that the *procedures* in small groups are responsible for the documented growth. Rather, motivational factors may be paramount (Slavin, 1983b).

What we need, if we wish to document the procedural effectiveness of small groups, is a well-grounded and well-explicated theoretical framework that will suggest what kinds of things we should look for and why we should expect to find them. Such a framework should assist us not only in generating testable hypotheses but also in pinpointing techniques and methods that need refinement. I shall present here an outline of the proposed research program.

A MODEL OF PROBLEM SOLVING
FOR SCHOOL MATHEMATICS

Most current theories of problem solving—even in business, engineering, and philosophy—trace their roots to John Dewey's (1933) basic plan. Interpretations vary, of course, and Dewey's model itself may be described in four, five, or six stages depending on the emphasis one wishes to make. The six possible stages are as follows:

1. Undergoing or feeling a lack—identifying a problematic situation.

2. Defining the problem.

3. Engaging in means-ends analysis; devising a plan.

4. Executing; carrying out the plan.

5. Undergoing or living through the consequences.

6. Evaluating: looking back to assess whether the result satisfies the initial conditions; looking ahead to generalization of both methods and results.

If we consider the first two stages with respect to mathematical problem solving, we see that they have often been collapsed into one stage called "translation." Some mathematics educators have charged that this error is induced at least in part by the artificiality of school word problems (Lesh, 1981; Nesher, 1980). Since the problems are presented in a predefined fashion, there is no real need for the student to struggle with a "problematic situation" and wring from it a problem definition. If we were to act on this complaint, we would put our efforts into changing the form of school word problems. Although I agree that at least some textbook problems should be "real world" in their appearance, I want to suggest two reasons for caution in moving on this recommendation. First, school word problems serve more than one function. They are used not only to teach something called "problem solving" but also to illustrate mathematical concepts and their application. In an important sense, they deepen and broaden the student's understanding of concepts and the ability to manipulate symbols, and they do this in an efficient way. Second, changing the problems themselves is not the only way to encourage a more genuine problem-solving process. Even if the problem is predefined in its surface features, there is still the task of *understanding* the problem. One would think that it is possible to approach even artificial school-bound problems intelligently.

A move in this direction was accomplished by George Polya (1945), who concentrated his attention on mathematical problem solving. His four-stage model is very like Dewey's:

1. Understanding the problem.

2. Devising a plan.

3. Executing the plan.

4. Evaluating or reflecting on the completed process.

Here we have collapsed Dewey's first two stages in a way that is appropriate to school problem solving, but we have also eliminated Dewey's "undergoing the consequences" stage. The elimination may be crucially important. This stage was meant to describe problem solving in natural situations. When we define a problem, devise a plan for its solution, and execute that plan, we *live through* the consequences. We *feel* something as a result of what we have done. This implies that some picture or representation, some set of expectations, guides our thinking. We do not move, like machines, to a simple check on our calculations; rather, we evaluate in the context of all we have thought, done, and felt.

Without the crucial "living through" stage, the artificiality of school problem solving becomes deadly. Even curriculum makers and researchers have supposed that, given Polya's truncated model, "understanding the problem" becomes a direct translation of ordinary language into mathematical expressions and that "evaluating the results" means an algebraic and computational check together with a generalization to "type forms" for problems and their solution.

With the tremendous emphasis on "observables" in psychological research, it was predictable that even the four stages of Polya would be reduced to three by mathematics educators and researchers. "Understanding the problem," while essential for the problem solver, is not observable to either teacher or researcher, but devising a plan—exhibited as a set of mathematical expressions— *is* observable. Hence the typical model of mathematical problem solving became

1. Translating words to mathematical expressions.

2. Executing; that is, calculating.

3. Checking results in initial equations.

Here we have an artificiality not only of *problems* but of problem solving as well. Notice that the end of the process, a formal "check" on the answer, is referred to the mathematical sentence that resulted from the translation process. This represents another weakness of the truncated model. Because the student seizes upon surface features of the problem, he or she is likely to use the mathematical expression as the representation of the problem. Hence, the stage of evaluation deteriorates also. Instead of a real-world check—a check against an original full representation—we see only a check on the solution of the mathematical expression. We might predict, further, that the forward-looking function of evaluation would also be distorted. Instead of generalizing from and to mathematical principles, the student might generalize from surface features to the restricted use of specific heuristics and algorithms.

What we would like to encourage is a deep analysis of the relations among elements of the problematic situation instead of the usual rush to selection of an operation that is encouraged by the translation model. This analysis requires the creation of a representation (Behr, Lesh, & Post, 1981; Hayes & Simon, 1977; Mayer, 1982; Silver, 1982). The problem solver must create a picture of the situation. We know very little about the kinds of pictures people create in problem solving, although we have some information on the effects of creating images (Paivio & Csapo, 1973) and of *presenting* certain kinds of visual pictures (Rohwer, 1970). But even if we know little about the form of representation, we may be able to provide the setting for its creation. One way to do this might be to make inner talk public in open small-group discussion, and I shall argue a bit later that this is one of the great strengths of group problem solving.

If we agree that the "translation, calculation, check" model is demonstrably invalid for true problem solving (even though experienced problem solvers working with stereotypical word problems *do* work effectively this way), we might enthusiastically welcome a model that abandons the faulty translation stage. A newer, and almost certainly truer, model that eliminates translation is accepted by cognitive psychologists working from information-processing models. Indeed, it is not unusual for cognitive psychologists to emphasize just *two* steps in the problem-solving process:

> Representation (understanding the problem)—The problem statement is translated into an internal mental representation that includes the given state, goal state, and allowable operators. The problem space can be built upon the subject's understanding of the problem.

> Solution (searching the problem space)—The problem solver attempts to search for a path through the problem space. The problem solver keeps applying operators to problem states until the goal is achieved. (Mayer, 1982, p. 4)

Of course, translation in this description is very different from translation in the older model. It does not refer to the direct decoding of verbal symbols and encoding into mathematical symbols. It refers, rather, to a process through which the objective problem becomes a problem of thought, a configuration that directs thinking. This "new" way of looking at problem solving was described by John Dewey (1933, p. 15): "The nature of the problem fixes the end of thought, and the end controls the process of thinking."

But, I would argue, while we have gained something at the beginning of the process by adopting a stage of "representation," we have lost something by terminating the description of the process with "solution." Surely, the objective of school problem solving is not simply the solution of the problem at hand but a progressive cognitive reorganization that creates more powerful problem-solving processes. Serious acceptance of this objective entails careful attention to the stages we referred to earlier as undergoing the consequences and evaluating. I shall return to these, but let's concentrate briefly on the gains we have made by deciding to study representation.

Because there are so many possible ways in which to describe the creation of representations, we might do well to refrain from premature attempts to describe the process in detail. When the mind is engaged, when the intuitive capacity is actively looking, all sorts of things happen: associations spring to mind, doing-and-looking are undertaken (Noddings & Shore, 1984), things are tried out against already acquired knowledge, pictures are drawn on paper, schemes are created in the imagination (Peirce, 1956). If we seriously want to recognize the role of intuition in problem solving—and virtually all mathematicians recognize its contribution—then we need to fill out this stage of representation with concrete accounts rather than detailed and prespecified theoretical steps.

Clearly, in this short paper, I cannot undertake an exploration of intuition and its various ramifications, but I can predict a new clash of theories as those who take intuition seriously begin to critique information-processing models. The two groups will be in agreement on opposing the older behavioristic and formalistic descriptions; both will favor "mentalistic" accounts. But the intuitionists will be reluctant to describe the representation stage in specific detail. That does not mean that those of us who lean toward an emphasis on intuition will neglect rich and concrete description; rather, it is the linear prespecification of steps that will be resisted. Perhaps at our best we do think rather like machines (even that is questionable), but while we are learning we do not, and it may even be the case that our best and most lasting learning is very *un*machinelike in its nature.

I suggest, then, that we modify the two-stage information-processing model and retain the crucial undergoing and evaluating stages. We have, as a result, four stages:

1. Creation of a representation.

2. Executing a plan based on the representation.

3. Undergoing the consequences.

4. Evaluating the results.

Adoption of this model presents several problems for researchers: Three of the four stages go on largely in the heads of the problem solvers; only "executing the plan" is immediately accessible to the observer. Nevertheless, if this is a credible model for school problem solving, let's persevere for a bit and see if we can find ways of investigating these stages.

COGNITIVE THEORIES AND SMALL-GROUP PROCESSES

Since I want to build a framework that synthesizes social theories of cognition and models of problem solving, the next thing to do is to look at social theories of cognition. We are, at present, far from having a coherent theory that specifies the roles of culture, cognition, and schooling in attacking mathematical problems (Lancy, 1983). Cross-cultural studies tend to support Piaget's developmental claims up to the stage of operational thought, but after that culture and schooling seem to play increasingly important roles. Early studies by John Gay and Michael Cole (1967) put great emphasis on the role of schooling in mathematical development, but Cole's later studies (1981) attribute differences in competence largely to contextual features. Is cognition, then, context-bound? We face a similar dilemma with respect to literacy. We would expect from the work of Bruner (1966), Olson (1976), and others that symbolic acquisitions in the form of literacy would contribute considerably to cognitive processes, yet Scribner and Cole (1981) found no such result. Are higher cognitive processes, then, language-independent?

For those interested in learning in small groups, possibly the most useful theoretical position is that of Vygotsky (1978). Here we find a middle ground with respect to both context and language questions: language and cognition become more and more thoroughly interrelated as the child grows, and competence is at least partly a function of variety in contexts; some concepts develop "spontaneously" and others only in a scientific or schooled environment. Vygotsky claims, further, that individual mental functions are internalized from relations among children in groups, and that reflection is induced by the need for each child to defend his views against challenges brought by other children. If he is right, we might conclude that mathematics educators should certainly be encouraging more small-group work in mathematics.

But let's move slowly in making recommendations. Do mental functions grow only out of "relations among children"? Or do children who have rich dialogues with adults and older children develop even more rapidly and strongly? Is the small-group setting the best environment for all children to learn problem-solving strategies or only for some? In our problem-solving project (Noddings, 1982; Noddings et al., 1981; Noddings, Gilbert-Macmillan, & Leitz, 1983), my co-workers and I were enormously impressed by the accomplishments of children from a school that ranks near the bottom in state percentiles on mathematics achievement tests. Working in small groups, these children learned together and for themselves how to solve a batch of problems that baffled them in the beginning. Last year, I would have said enthusiastically that "small groups are the way to go." Now, I am not so sure. Our latest results (not yet analyzed), from a community at the opposite end of the achievement spectrum, seem to indicate that thoughtful whole-class instruction can produce as good or even better results than small groups. Caution is indicated here because we have not yet looked at the all-important process variables, but if achievement alone is the criterion, small groups are not yet "The Answer."

It certainly complicates our work both instructionally and in research to consider the possibility that children with different sorts of backgrounds should be taught differently. For researchers, such consideration raises all the nightmares associated with aptitude-treatment-interaction research. For teachers, questions of discrimination and prejudice arise, even though no one suggests that the alleged differences are caused by race or ethnicity. The *association* is enough to raise red flags. But none of this has to impede our work at this early stage. If some children seem to profit less than others from small-group processes, it may be because they are engaging in vital interactions in other settings (e.g., at home or in smaller classes at school). Instead of being discouraged by apparently contradictory results, we should mark these differences for future investigation. By persisting in this way, we may find out what underlies the apparent effectiveness of small-group processes in other settings.

Theoretically, the learning environment of cooperative small groups appears promising for developing effective problem-solving processes. The kind of structural reorganization revealed in the creation of representations is integral to the process of cognitive transformation and, thus, to intellectual growth. Three features of small-group processes seem especially important in structural reorganization. The first is that students encounter challenge and disbelief from their peers. This encounter may lead them to examine their own beliefs and strategies more closely and to discard those that are clearly untenable. Since dialogue brings many of the assumed, implicit processes out into the open, small-group problem solving may be an effective context not only for the introduction of felt dissonance but also for the induction of both reflective and reflexive thought. Students begin to think about their own strategies. In one group that we observed, for example, a youngster suggested that the group should "add, subtract, and multiply these two numbers" and then see which answer "looked" best. Other members of the group were shocked and said, "Donna! We can't do that. We have to figure it out."

Donna tried that strategy only once more and then it disappeared from her public repertoire.

The second important feature of small groups is that the collective supplies background information that individual children may not possess. Many of the Polya heuristics, for example, may be of little use to the novice who lacks sufficient information to employ them. The suggestion to "eliminate irrelevant information" may be of little use if one does not know what is relevant, and sometimes students seem to need to settle "irrelevant" matters before they can proceed. In one of our protocols, the youngsters felt the need to settle the question "What is a papaya?" before they could tackle the arithmetic involved in a problem asking about the price of fruit. Similarly, the suggestion to "look at a similar problem" may not be a useful strategy for the student who cannot understand the problem well enough to identify critical criteria. In such cases, looking at the problem from someone else's point of view might be a better tactic (Lesh, 1981).

Individuals working in small groups help each other in constructing cognitive elaborations. Dialogue and argument serve to build connections between elements of the problem and prior knowledge and help also to build the logical relationships among problem components. As Silver (1982) points out, elaboration tends to make new information more meaningful. Heuristics such as interpreting, restating, clarifying or seeking clarification, and adding concrete details are all part of elaboration.

A third important feature of small groups is that children, in taking charge of their own procedures, may begin to internalize orderly approaches to problematic situations. They begin to assume some responsibility not only for their own learning but also for the learning of their peers (Easley, 1982). We know from past studies that *giving help* is associated with gains in achievement (Webb, 1982). But it may be that procedural participation has benefits beyond the obvious giving and receiving of actual and direct help. It may be that the *relations* and operations developed in the group—orders of operation, standard questions ("Does everyone agree?"), sticking to an agenda, participating in goal construction, turn taking—become internalized as powerful executive procedures in problem solving.

In adapting Vygotsky's theoretical framework to research on mathematical problem solving, what should we include as the essential features of our research framework? What expectations should we posit and investigate? I suggest two areas. First, children should be able to achieve more in a group than they can individually. Gradually, however, what the group does should be internalized and should appear in the mental functions of individual children:

- Useful heuristics should begin to spread through the group; less useful ones should fall away.

- Challenge at the group level should appear as reflection at the individual level.

- Requests for explanation in the group should be reflected in an internalized heuristic, "Why is this?"

- The procedures of the group should reappear as an orderly attack on problems by the individual.

Second, language and thought become inextricably interdependent:

- The exchange of peripheral information in the group should result in vocabulary development in individuals.

- References to other contexts in the group should produce contextual sophistication (less contextual dependence) in the thinking of individuals.

- Conversation in the group should be reflected in a greater volume of problem-oriented inner talk in individuals.

The next question to consider is how to bring these two theoretical frameworks together in a sound program of research on school problem solving in mathematics.

A RESEARCH PROGRAM

In this section we want to keep in mind the things we should expect to find if Vygotsky's ideas (and our interpretation of them) are sound. We have four stages of problem solving to consider. The first involves creation of a representation. What sort of heuristics may be associated with the creation of representations? Over a period of years, mathematics educators have developed an impressive set of heuristics to look at. Most of these, as Goldin (1982) points out, are based on Polya's pioneering work: Kilpatrick (1967), Lucas (1972), Kantowski (1974), Blake (1976), Lucas et al. (1979), and Noddings et al. (1981). Now we need to go through these lists to identify the heuristics that obviously belong to the representation stage; we need also to assess the rational effectiveness of each heuristic; and, then, we need to know something about the empirical frequency and actual effectiveness of each heuristic. Besides identifying and counting heuristics, we should also attempt to "tell stories"; that is, to connect the heuristics with the goals that give rise to them and to the ordinary language in which they are expressed. These are exciting tasks for researchers to undertake.

Among the heuristics we should expect to find at the representation stage are the following:

- Concretizing the problem—identifying aspects of the problem with personal experience. For example, in one of our protocols, children discussed the following problem:

John is 22 years old. John is 8 years younger than Sue. How old is Sue?

Three of four children argued for "14" as the answer, but one, Dan, held out for "30," insisting, "John is younger, *younger.*" Then he said, "'Cause he's younger than his sister." Now, clearly, there is no mention of "sister" in the problem, yet none of the children noticed this. Dan had a picture of reality that guided him and, in that picture, Sue was John's sister. We have noted many cases of this sort.

- Organizing relevant data in lists, charts, or other pictorial representations. The children we have studied have been surprisingly inept at constructing useful pictorial representations. In fraction problems, for example, we found that they could easily illustrate pies and pizzas cut into even numbers of parts, but they had a difficult time cutting pies into five or seven nearly equal pieces.

- Interpreting the vocabulary of the problem. Here we might expect several things to happen. First, an exchange of peripheral information should result in vocabulary development as a positive by-product of attacking problems in small groups. With the right sort of problems, this is easily tested. Second, there should be a gradual realization that the meaning of some words is irrelevant to the construction of an appropriate mathematical representation; that is, we should observe a move toward decontextualization in the group. This, too, is testable and of considerable interest.

- Attempting to construct a domain of relevant dimensions. This heuristic is closely related to "concretizing the problem" and "interpreting the vocabulary" but concentrates on quantities and sizes of elements in the problem. Children in our studies have asked questions about the sizes of various objects even though such quantities are irrelevant to the problem solutions. "How big is the gas tank?" "How large is the pizza?" These are typical questions and, in our protocols, no child has ever answered such a query with "It doesn't matter." This sort of question *does* disappear for particular problem types, but the interesting question for researchers is whether and when it tends to disappear *generally*. If it does not, we would have some evidence to support claims concerning the impermeability of contexts.

In addition to these heuristics, which seem clearly to be involved in the construction of representations, we find others that may be associated either with such construction or with an attempt to perform the translation so often required in school problem solving. In roughly the order of frequency that we have encountered them are these heuristics:

- Rereading the problem.

- Focusing on the questioning.

- Anticipating arithmetical operations—the child mumbles or repeats relevant quantities. This heuristic might be renamed "isolating quantifiers."

- Referring to past problems.

- Rejecting alternatives. This usually takes the form of "You can't divide," "Multiplying would make it too big," or "You can't subtract three numbers."

- Relating means and ends. We have seen this very rarely and never at the early stage of problem solving. It may occur, but we have only heard it at the stage of evaluation where one child is defending his or her answer against challenge.

I am inclined at this stage of our research to consider "rereading the problem" and "focusing on the question" as facilitative in constructing representations, to regard "isolating quantifiers," "referring to past problems," and "rejecting alternatives" as artifacts of stereotypical school problems, and to put aside "means-ends analysis" as a heuristic that remains implicit (at least for fifth- and sixth-grade children) during the initial stage of problem solving.

Besides connecting heuristics and tracing their uses in group processes, we are interested in whether the heuristics become internalized in the strategies of individual children. To find out whether this happens, we need to follow target children through a series of clinical episodes. Historically, retrospection, overt thinking, and introspection have all been used for such purposes (Lester, 1982). Of these, overt thinking seems to minimize the subject's tendency to edit, but the method and its variants are still loaded with difficulties (Ericsson & Simon, 1980; Ginsburg, 1981; Nisbett & Wilson, 1977; Smith & Miller, 1978; Swanson, Schwartz, Ginsburg, & Kossan, 1981; Trivett, 1981;

White, 1980). It seems reasonable to suggest that the method should be used in its "pure" form for these purposes, since any "channeling" directed by the interviewer might replicate the functions of group members in triggering thinking that the child is capable of in a social situation but unlikely to produce working alone.

As we study the protocols of individual children thinking aloud (and, of course, we must study both children involved in group processes and some who are not), we should look for signs of growing reflection. Children involved in group processes where they experience continual challenge and demand for explanations should begin to show signs of reflection in their inner talk—comments such as "What am I doing?" "Why is this?" "Let's see, will this work?" The difficulty is that children rarely talk this way in the presence of an interviewer. We *do* observe this sort of inner talk occasionally in the group process itself. We have recorded chains of "reflexive talk" in which one child ignores others in the group and talks, revealingly, to himself, but we cannot count on the appearance of reflexive talk, and, if we train our groups in small-group procedures, this interesting phenomenon might disappear entirely. Possibly, the solution to this dilemma is to design our clinical interviews in two phases: a first, "pure" phase in which we would hope to record the heuristics characteristic of the creation of representation stage; and a second, channeled phase in which we would test the child's willingness to reflect, to entertain alternatives, and to offer orderly accounts of his or her own procedures. If we know what we are looking for, a split interview of this sort should be useful.

Now, let's go on to a brief discussion of the other stages of problem solving. The stage of execution is for the most part public and straightforward, so we need not comment on it here. But undergoing the consequences and evaluating hold special interest.

In our project, we have given special attention to the stage of undergoing consequences. Agreeing with both Dewey and Vygotsky on this, we believe it is important for youngsters to "live through" what they have planned and executed in order that the final stage of evaluation may be truly reflective. We, therefore, provide a debriefing period at the end of each problem-solving session. After the children have handed in a group answer sheet, we give them a set of correct answers and ask them to discuss their errors in just the way they proceeded in the main problem-solving session. During this time, they try to figure out where they went wrong and how they can get the correct answer. It should be noted that giving a group a set of answers without comment or instruction is very different from doing the same thing with an individual in, say, individually prescribed instruction. An individual, exposed to the restricted dissonance of "wrong" and "right" answers, often develops odd strategies for converting wrong answers to right ones (Erlwanger, 1973). In a group, however, nonmathematical strategies are often challenged; that is, the group tends to maintain dissonance until its members come around to an appropriate way of thinking. A word of caution is needed here. Even in group processes, odd strategies may appear and be accepted. The children we studied used several poor strategies to get the right answer in fraction problems. One such strategy was to convert an incorrect "$7/3$" to the correct "$3/7$"—"because the smaller number has to go on top." Since all of our sessions were either observed or recorded, we were aware of such occurrences and could provide subsequent problems that challenged the faulty heuristic. When teachers use small groups for problem solving, they should be aware that problems have to be designed to augment the challenge that arises naturally in group processes.

In the method I am describing, we have taken very seriously the notion that relations and operations appear first in social intercourse and later in mental operations. Since we want children to develop a form of internal talk that conforms to a model of mathematical problem solving, we do not distract the group from the problems by providing grades or other incentives. We want them to respond to an incorrect answer by asking "What did we do wrong? What shall we try now?" and not by comparing grades, vying with other groups for points and the like (but cf. Slavin, 1983a). Another question to be answered in our research program is whether these procedures are facilitative toward the process goals I have been discussing or whether the widely used methods employing group incentives are just as effective in the long run.

Another problem that we face in this theoretical framework is one of devising appropriate methods to study the discourse of our groups. Just as researchers in the information-processing camp urge mathematics educators to pay attention to the work of cognitive psychologists, we might suggest that attention be given to work in sociolinguistics. We started out using the work of Barnes (1969, 1971) and Barnes and Todd (1977) and instruments developed by Sinclair and Coulthard (1975), Mehan (1979), and Wood et al. (1977). We transcribed and coded every utterance from 24 problem-solving and debriefing sessions. Further, every act was coded in five ways: interactive position (e.g., initiation, response, follow-up); communicative context or domain (problem, feeling, or ritual/procedure); grammatical form (question, command, or statement); specific communicative function (e.g., giving or seeking information, giving or seeking acceptance, challenging); and, for utterances in the problem domain, a mathematical function (e.g., specific heuristic, explanation, algorithm).

It took 2 years to develop a reliable instrument and complete the coding. Looking back, I would say that we made a mistake that should by now be familiar to all of us in mathematics education. We adopted too readily and too completely methods developed for purposes quite different from our own; or perhaps, our purposes changed. We were interested at that time in describing the discourse of groups engaged in solving word problems. Now that our interest is in how group problem-solving processes become internalized in the mental operations of individuals, we shall have to revise our instruments to meet this new purpose. Of particular interest now will be the set of specific communicative functions. A measure of richness in this domain might be expected to correlate reasonably with an increase in measures of individual reflective thinking and decontextualized thinking.

Sociolinguistic methods are useful, again, in studying the stage of evaluation. Here we hope, of course, that children will refer their checks and evaluations to the representations with which they started out, and they do seem to do this. We have been impressed by the differences in small-group evaluation processes and those typical of whole-class operations. Typically, teachers elicit a student response in the form of an operation ("What shall we do?" "Add."), and then evaluate the response ("Good"); this is followed by another cycle of elicitation ("Now what's the answer?"), response ("15"), and evaluation ("Good try, but not quite.") (Griffin & Mehan, 1979).

Groups of children engage in much more extended evaluation episodes, particularly when they are under directions to seek consensus. We have been surprised at how long it takes them to agree on an answer after it has been suggested. Even if no challenge has been offered, children seem to need time to mull things over: they refer to initial conditions—"Yeah, that's about what things cost these days," "Well, if it was a small pizza, I guess she could eat that much," "She's his girlfriend, so she's probably younger!" Listening to them debate the wisdom of a proferred answer suggests that we reconsider the pace at which we move in whole-class instruction. Children need time to think. A plea we hear often in small groups is, "Wait, wait!" We wonder how often children would like to say in class, as the answers keep rolling forth, "Wait, wait, I don't agree yet!"

Children's evaluative episodes differ in another way from teacher-student episodes: they rarely contain praise. Usually a positive evaluation consists of a "cascade" of affirmations. If one child gives an answer "¾," for example, the others may follow up by saying "¾," "Yep, ¾," "I agree, ¾."

Similarly, their negative evaluations are usually more direct and impersonal than the evaluations of their teachers. They say "Uh-uh," "No way," "Can't be, 'cause . . . ," or they directly respond with a competing answer. The lack of an authority, particularly in homogeneous groups, seems to encourage all members to participate, to offer their answers and defend their positions. Negative personal evaluations do appear occasionally in debriefing situations, particularly when the group has settled on a wrong answer after lengthy debate during which the right answer was offered. On such occasions, children are likely to turn on the perceived culprit with "You turkey, that was *your* idea" or "I knew you were wrong on that."

Finally, we have not observed any forward-looking evaluation in our group protocols. Children may generalize for future problem solving but, if they do, we have not caught them at it. Overt generalization is another phenomenon we may be able to prompt by clever channeling in clinical interviews.

SUMMARY

I have tried to do several things in this paper. The main task was to outline a theoretical framework for the study of problem solving in small groups. I have suggested that a four-stage model based on Dewey's and modified by recent work in cognitive psychology be coupled with the social-cognitive theories of Vygotsky to construct a framework especially designed to study school problem solving in small groups. I have suggested, further, that methods from sociolinguistics be refined and adapted for the analysis of problem-solving discourse and that this adaptation be guided by the proposed framework.

In addition to the development of a theoretical framework, I have shared some of our findings, mistakes, nagging questions, and plans for future research. Much hard theoretical work needs to be done before we can hope to get substantial results and guidance from our efforts at empirical research.

REFERENCES

Barnes, D. Language in the secondary classroom. In D. Barnes, J. Britton, & H. Rosen, *Language, the learner and the school.* Middlesex, England: Penguin Books, 1969.

Barnes, D. Language and learning in the classroom. *Journal of Curriculum Studies* 3, 27–38, 1971.

Barnes, D., & Todd, F. *Communication and learning in small groups.* London: Routledge and Kegan Paul, 1977.

Behr, M., Lesh, R., & Post, T. *Rational number ideas and the role of representational systems.* Paper presented at the annual meeting of the American Educational Research Association, Los Angeles, April 1981.

Blake, R.N. *The effect of problem context upon the problem-solving processes used by field dependent and independent students.* Unpublished doctoral dissertation, University of British Columbia, 1976.

Bruner, J.S. On cognitive growth: I and II. In J.S. Bruner, R.R. Olver, & P.M. Greenfield (Eds.), *Studies in cognitive growth.* New York: John Wiley & Sons, 1966.

Cohen, E.G. *Status equalization project: Changing expectations in the integrated classroom.* Unpublished final report, Stanford University, 1980.

Cole, M., & Means, B. *Comparative studies of how people think: An introduction.* Cambridge, MA: Harvard University Press, 1981.

Dewey, J. *How we think.* Chicago: Henry Regnery, 1933.

Easley, J., & Easley, E. *Math can be natural: Kitamaeno priorities introduced to American teachers.* Urbana-Champaign: University of Illinois, Bureau of Educational Research, 1982.

Ericsson, K.A., & Simon, H.A. Verbal reports as data. *Psychological Review* 87(3), 215–51, 1980.

Erlwanger, S.H. Benny's conception of rules and answers in IPI mathematics. *Journal of Children's Mathematical Behavior* 1, 7–26, 1973.

Gay, J., & Cole, M. *The new mathematics and an old culture.* New York: Holt, Rinehart & Winston, 1967.

Ginsburg, H. The clinical interview in psychological research on mathematical thinking: Aims, rationales, techniques. *For the Learning of Mathematics* 1(3), 4–11, 1981.

Goldin, G.A. The measure of problem-solving outcomes. In F.K. Lester, & J. Garofalo (Eds.), *Mathematical problem solving: Issues in research.* Philadelphia: The Franklin Institute Press, 1982.

Greeno, J.G. A study of problem solving. In R. Glaser (Ed.), *Advances in instructional psychology* (Vol. 1). Hillsdale, NJ: Lawrence Erlbaum Associates, 1978.

Griffin, P., & Mehan, H. *Sense and ritual in classroom discourse.* San Diego: University of California, Laboratory of Comparative Human Cognition (D-003), 1979.

Hayes, J.R., & Simon, H.A. Psychological differences among problem isomorphs. In N.J. Castellan, D.B. Pisoni, & G.R. Potts (Eds.), *Cognitive theory* (Vol. 2). Hillsdale, NJ: Lawrence Erlbaum Associates, 1977.

Johnson, D., & Johnson, R. *Learning together and alone.* Englewood Cliffs, NJ: Prentice-Hall, 1975.

Johnson, D., & Johnson, R. *The internal dynamics of cooperative learning groups.* Paper presented at the annual meeting of the American Educational Research Association, New York, March 1982.

Kantowski, E.L. *Processes involved in mathematical problem solving.* Unpublished doctoral dissertation, University of Georgia, 1974.

Kilpatrick, J. *Analyzing the solution of word problems in mathematics: An exploratory study.* Unpublished doctoral dissertation, Stanford University, 1967.

Lancy, D.F. *Cross-cultural studies in cognition and mathematics.* New York: Academic Press, 1983.

Lesh, R. Applied mathematical problem solving. *Educational Studies in Mathematics* 12(2), 235–64, 1981.

Lester, F.K. Building bridges between psychological and mathematics education research on problem solving. In F.K. Lester & J. Garofalo (Eds.), *Mathematical problem solving: Issues in research.* Philadelphia: The Franklin Institute Press, 1982.

Lucas, J.F. *An exploratory study in the diagnostic teaching of elementary calculus.* Unpublished doctoral dissertation, University of Wisconsin, 1972.

Lucas, J.F., Branca, N., Goldberg, D., Kantowski, M.G., Kellogg, H., & Smith, J.P. A process-sequence coding system for behavioral analysis of mathematical problem solving. In G.A. Goldin and C.E. McClintock (Eds.), *Task variables in mathematical problem solving.* Columbus, OH: ERIC Clearinghouse for Science, Mathematics, and Environmental Education, 1979.

Mayer, R. The psychology of mathematical problem solving. In F.K. Lester & J. Garofalo (Eds.), *Mathematical problem solving: Issues in research.* Philadelphia: The Franklin Institute Press, 1982.

Mehan, H. *Learning lessons: Social organization in the classroom.* Cambridge, MA: Harvard University Press, 1979.

Nesher, P. The stereotyped nature of school word problems. *For the Learning of Mathematics* 1(1), 41–48, 1980.

Nisbett, R.E., & Wilson, T.D. Telling more than we can know: Verbal reports on mental processes. *Psychological Review* 84(3), 231–59, 1977.

Noddings, N. *The use of small group protocols in analysis of children's arithmetical problem solving.* Paper presented at the annual meeting of the American Educational Research Association, New York, March 1982.

Noddings, N., Chaffe, P., Enright, D.S., Gilbert, K., Leitz, S., & Noddings, V. *How children approach mathematical word problems.* Paper presented at the annual meeting of the American Educational Research Association, April 1981.

Noddings, N., Gilbert-Macmillan, K., & Leitz, S. *What do individuals gain in small group mathematical problem solving?* Paper presented at the annual meeting of the American Educational Research Association, Montreal, April 1983.

Noddings, N., & Shore, P. *Awakening the inner eye: Intuition in education.* New York: Teachers College Press, 1984.

Olson, D.R. Culture, technology and intellect. In L.B. Resnick (Ed.), *The nature of intelligence.* Hillsdale, NJ: Lawrence Erlbaum Associates, 1976.

Paige, N.M., & Simon, H.A. Cognitive processes in solving algebra word problems. In B. Kleinmuntz (Ed.), *Problem solving.* New York: John Wiley & Sons, 1966.

Paivio, A., & Csapo, K. Picture superiority in free recall: Imagery or dual coding? *Cognitive Psychology* 5, 176–206, 1973.

Peirce, C.S. The essence of mathematics. In J.R. Newman (Ed.), *The world of mathematics.* New York: Simon & Schuster, 1956.

Piaget, J. *Genetic epistemology.* New York: Columbia University Press, 1970.

Polya, G. *How to solve it.* Princeton, NJ: Princeton University Press, 1945.

Rohwer, W.D. Images and pictures in children's learning. *Psychological Bulletin* 73, 393–403, 1970.

Rudnitsky, A.N. *The graphic representation of structure in similarity/dissimilarity matrices: Alternative matrices.* Paper presented at the meeting of the American Educational Research Association, New York, 1977.

Schmuck, R., & Schmuck, P. Group processes in the classroom. Dubuque, IA: Wm. C. Brown Group, 1979.

Scribner, S., & Cole, M. *The psychology of literacy.* Cambridge, MA: Harvard University Press, 1981.

Sharan, S., Hertz-Lazarowitz, R., & Ackerman, F. Academic achievement of elementary school children in small group versus whole-class instruction. *Journal of Experimental Education* 48(2), 125–29, 1980.

Shavelson, R.J. Some aspects of the correspondence between content structure and cognitive structure in physics instruction. *Journal of Educational Psychology* 63(3), 225–34, 1972.

Shavelson, R.J. Learning from physics instruction. *Journal of Research in Science Teaching* 10, 101–11, 1973.

Shavelson, R.J. Methods for examining representations of a subject-matter structure in a student's memory. *Journal of Research in Science Teaching* 11(3), 231–49, 1974(a).

Shavelson, R.J. Some methods for examining content structure and cognitive structure in instruction. *Educational Psychologist* 11, 110–22, 1974(b).

Silver, E.A. Knowledge organization and mathematical problem solving. In F.K. Lester & J.

Garofalo (Eds.), *Mathematical problem solving: Issues in research*. Philadelphia: The Franklin Institute Press, 1982.

Sinclair, J.McH., & Coulthard, R.M. *Towards an analysis of discourse*. London: Oxford University Press, 1975.

Slavin, R. Cooperative learning. *Review of Educational Research* **50**, 315–42, 1980.

Slavin, R. *Cooperative learning*. New York: Longman, 1983(a).

Slavin, R. Personal communication, May 1983(b).

Smith, E.R., & Miller, F.A. Limits on perception of cognitive processes: A reply to Nisbett and Wilson. *Psychological Review* **85**(4), 355–62, 1978.

Stanton, G. *Effects of content structure, algorithms, and generativity on cognitive structure and achievement in mathematics*. Unpublished doctoral dissertation, Stanford University, 1980.

Swanson, D., Schwartz, R., Ginsburg, H., & Kossan, N. The clinical interview: Validity, reliability, and diagnosis. *For the Learning of Mathematics* **2**(2), 31–38, 1981.

Trivett, J. The clinical interview: A comment. *For the Learning of Mathematics* **2**(1), 51, 1981.

Vygotsky, L. *Mind in society*. Cambridge, MA: Harvard University Press, 1978.

Webb, N. Student interaction and learning in small groups. *Review of Educational Research* **52**, 421–45, 1982.

White, P. Limitations of verbal reports of internal events: A refutation of Nisbett and Wilson and of Bem. *Psychological Review* **87**(1), 105–12, 1980.

Wood, B.S., Brown, K., Chiosk, S.N., Ecroyd, D., Hopper, R., Rowland-Morris, P., & Wrather, N. *Development of functional communication competencies pre-K–Grade 6*. Urbana, IL: ERIC Clearinghouse on Reading and Communication Skills, 1977.

Metacognitive and
Epistemological Issues
in Mathematical Understanding

Alan H. Schoenfeld

The University of Rochester

This paper explores aspects of mathematical "understanding" that extend beyond the mastery of routine facts and procedures. It deals with three aspects of such understanding, summarized in the following three assertions:

1. Metacognitive skills and a "mathematical epistemology" are essential components of competent mathematical performance.

2. Most students do not develop very many metacognitive skills or a mathematical epistemology to any degree, largely because mathematical instruction focuses almost exclusively on mastery of facts and procedures rather than "understanding"; these are basic causes of students' mathematical difficulties.

3. It is possible, although difficult, to develop such skills in students.

These statements are not unique to mathematics. In fact, I would like to begin this paper with a discussion of a nonmathematical study that makes some of the same points. Having seen the clear documentation of these issues in another domain, we may be more willing to accept their presence in our own.

Perkins (1982) summarized the results of a 3-year study of "informal" reasoning. In the study, 320 subjects with different levels of educational experience were asked to think about such issues as "Would restoring the military draft significantly increase America's ability to influence world events?" and "Is a controversial modern sculpture, the stack of bricks in the Tate Gallery, London, really a work of art?" Each subject was given 5 minutes to think about an issue, reaching a conclusion if possible. The conclusion was to be explained and justified. In a "postmortem" the investigator probed further, testing the solidity of the argument.

The protocols from the subjects were scored according to a variety of criteria, including rough measures of argument complexity (length and number of different arguments used to reach the conclusion) and coherence (resistance to objection, focus, depth of explanation). Each argument was rated on a 5-point scale for overall quality. The quality ratings are given in Figure 1.

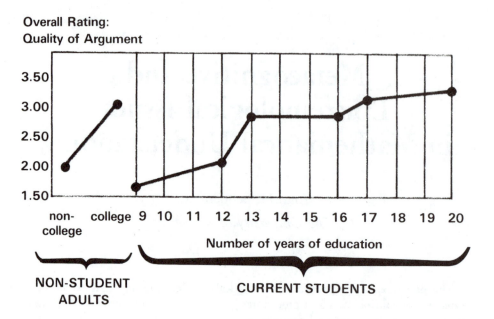

Figure 1. Mean ratings of the quality of arguments on a scale of 1 to 5.

The left-hand side of Figure 1 gives scores for adults who had been out of school for at least 5 years. Those who were college-educated clearly did far better than those whose education stopped at high school. However, a look at the right-hand side of Figure 1 indicates that there is little cause for celebration. The steepest gains occur in the periods between years 12–13 and 16–17. These jumps represent the effects of *selection*: those who make it into college or graduate school are generally those who are good at informal argument (it correlates well with IQ and other selection criteria). Some 55% of the increase from Grades 9 through 20 was attributable to selection, and most of the rest took place in Grades 9 through 12—a time of general intellectual maturation. Increases during the college years (during which one certainly does learn an enormous amount of factual material) were not only not significant, they were neligible: an average gain of .01 per year.

What makes things worse is that the skills that would produce higher ratings can be easily learned, and in fact were often possessed by the subjects in the experiment. Subjects could produce counterexamples to their own arguments when asked; they could rebut their claims, and then defend against the rebuttals; they could fill in gaps, or offer multiple lines of argument as well. Yet they did not, a large part of the time. Perkins states:

> The findings . . . present a paradoxical picture: people learn to reason better quite slowly, yet it seems as though they should learn much faster. For instance, people could surely form cautionary habits like always trying to find counter-examples, and only a few such habits would substantially increase their scores on the measure employed.

> The paradox is interpreted as follows. Sound informal reasoning depends both on general intellectual ability and on know-how about argumentation and its pitfalls. Conventional schooling improves the former but little, as one would expect, and simply does not address the latter. (p. 4)

I have dwelt on the Perkins study at length because it illustrates the major themes I wish to discuss. In spite of the large number of hours that our students spend in the study of mathematics—and that includes time spent studying "problem solving"—they may be seeing, and learning, nearly nothing about thinking mathematically. One major component of mathematical competence consists of being able to use the resources at one's disposal with some degree of efficiency when working somewhat unfamiliar problems. To master certain formal techniques is one thing. To call upon them when appropriate, to abandon ones that are not, to lean but not depend solely on intuitions that correspond to formal procedures, to evaluate the quality of one's argument as one is making it, and to try to make it stronger—these are components of mathematical thinking that correspond closely to components of informal reasoning. They have been called metacognitive, managerial, or executive skills in the literature, and there are strong indications that they are major determinants of success or failure in problem-solving performance. Some of the literature, and some examples, are discussed in the next section.

The second theme is more nebulous. I have referred to it elsewhere (Schoenfeld, 1983a) as a question of "belief systems"; perhaps it would be better to call it an issue of underlying mathematical epistemology. Again, Perkins's study serves to illustrate the issue. Perkins, Allen, and Hafner (1983) attribute some of the differences in the subjects' type and quality of informal arguments to the subjects' possession of differing epistemologies. Skilled (and somewhat idealized) reasoners have a "critical epistemology," which includes a sense of epistemological realism (a sense of concordance between models they build of phenomena about which they argue, and the phenomena themselves), dialectical style and skills, and, last but not least, access to tools of formal reasoning when appropriate. In contrast, naive reasoners are posited to have what might be called a "makes sense" epistemology: "they act as though the test of truth is that a proposition makes intuitive sense, sounds right, rings true. They see no need to criticize or revise accounts that do make sense—the intuitive feel of fit suffices" (p. 10). This notion of naive beliefs, or a naive epistemology, as a "driving force" behind cognition, is not limited to informal reasoning.

METACOGNITION AND "CONTROL"—OR LACK OF IT

Since "metacognition" has been almost as much of a catch phrase in the recent psychological literature as has "problem solving" in mathematics, I had best begin with that. One of the first broad definitions of metacognition was given by Flavell (1976):

> "Metacognition" refers to one's knowledge concerning one's own cognitive processes or anything related to them, e.g., the learning-relevant properties of information or data. For example, I am engaging in metacognition . . . if I notice that I am having more trouble learning A than B; if it strikes me that I should double-check C before accepting it as a fact; if it occurs to me that I had better scrutinize each and every alternative in a multiple choice type task before deciding which is the best one. . . . Metacognition refers, among other things, to the active monitoring and consequent regulation and orchestration of those processes in relation to the cognitive objects or data on which they bear, usually in the service of some concrete goal or objective. (p. 232)

This definition appears almost all-encompassing, and needs to be narrowed in scope before we can make profitable use of it. Yet, I would point out one limitation that appears implicitly but consistently throughout the literature. Metacognitive *acts* are precisely that: active, often intentional, and (at least implicitly) things of which the individual is aware.

Most of the psychological research has focused on metamemory, one's awareness of the storage and retrieval of information. A large part of that work has been developmental, tracing the growth of "meta"-behavior in children. The metamemory literature was surveyed by Flavell and Wellman (1977). Some typical issues in the literature are as follows:

- "[T]he question of how people become aware of their own comprehension failure. It is argued that a partial answer to this question can be derived from recent demonstrations that comprehension involves constructive processing." (Markman, 1977, p. 986)

- "Metamemory, the ability to interrogate the contents of one's permanent memory, may be an important factor in using one's knowledge to cope with the environment. Metamemorial *accuracy* and *efficiency* can be assessed." (Lachman, Lachman, & Thronesbery, 1979, p. 543)

- "A self-monitoring process was suggested to be essential for evaluating one's own level of performance and the effectiveness of various mnemonic strategies." (Ringel & Springer, 1980, p. 322)

Brown's (1978) review makes more direct connections with the literatures of information-processing psychology and artificial intelligence. "The particular problem solving skills selected for review are those attributed to the executive in many theories of human and machine intelligence: predicting, checking, monitoring, reality testing, and coordination and control of deliberate attempts to learn or solve problems. I believe these are the basic characteristics of thinking efficiently in a wide range of learning situations" (p. 78). In a discussion of the requirements for an effective "executive," Brown points out that it must include the ability to

> (1) predict the system's capacity limitations; (2) be aware of its repertoire of heuristic routines and their appropriate domain of utility; (3) identify and characterize the problem at hand; (4) plan and schedule appropriate problem-solving activities; (5) monitor and supervise the effectiveness of those routines it calls into service; and (6) dynamically evaluate these operations in the face of success or failure so that termination of strategic activities can be strategically timed. These forms of executive decision making are perhaps the crux of efficient problem solving because the use of an appropriate piece of knowledge or routine to obtain that knowledge at the right time and in the right place is the essence of knowledge. (p. 82)

Research on metacognition has clear implications for mathematics education: see, for example, discussions by Silver (Silver, 1982; Silver, Branca, & Adams, 1980) and Lester (p. 41). But the work also has some serious limitations. One major "difficulty" with descriptions of competent executives such as the one given by Brown is that they characterize idealized behavior. Little of such behavior is to be seen in students as they work on tasks that are "real" problems to them—problems for which they do not have almost-ready packaged solutions for implementation. Rather, their behavior, and often their failures, can in part be attributed to the absence of productive metacognitions. A second difficulty is that many discussions of executive or "meta"-behavior (my own included) tend to isolate this kind of behavior too much from other levels of cognition. It might be well, here, to couch the issues under discussion in terms of a broad theoretical approach to human cognitive performance.

A great deal of competent human performance (of all types, not just "problem solving") can be attributed to the almost automatic, often unconscious, accessing of what might be called "situational representations and associated sets of responses." This awkward language was chosen to avoid a bias in favor of any of the competing instantiations of such archetypes: scripts, schemata, and frames, for example. All, however, are based on the same premise: The individual (or better, the "adaptive organism," to use Lesh's, 1983b, felicitous phrase that allows us to consider groups as "individuals"), in almost automatic response to certain features of the environment, brings "to mind" a stereotypical representation of that environment, and with that representation brings a set of expectations as to "routine, ordinary, and productive" behaviors.

A classic example of a "script" for understanding stories was described by Shank and Abelson (1977). As soon as a knowledgeable person reads a story about a restaurant, certain expectations are "activated": the person who enters is hungry, will sit at a table or counter, will read a menu, has money to pay for the meal that is eaten, will give a tip for service, and so on. Minsky (1975) developed "frames" as such archetypal representations, with "slots" to be filled with information when it is revealed (e.g., the reader of a gothic romance has a slot for a lover who may be named "X" until his name is revealed). Research on problem "schemata" is based on similar assumptions. For example, Hinsley, Hayes, and Simon (1977) read snippets of algebra word problems to people. After hearing "A river steamer . . ." subjects said things like "It's going to be one of those river things, with upstream, downstream, and still water. You are going to compare times upstream and downstream—or if the time is constant, it will be the distance" (p. 97). Clearly the algebraic formulation for such problems was also close at hand. Hinsley et al. set out to verify the following four assertions:

1. People can categorize problems into types.

2. People can categorize problems without completely formulating them for solution.

3. People have a body of information about each problem type which is potentially useful in formulating problems of that type for solution.

4. People use category identifications to formulate problems in the course of actually solving them. (p. 92)

When things work well, such routine access of useful representations (which I shall now call schema-access) saves time and trouble, and allows the individual to function efficiently. When things do not work well, schema-access unchecked by metacognitive skills can lead to disaster. The following two examples of students working a favorite problem of mine illustrates this:

> Three points are chosen on the circumference of a circle of radius R, and the triangle containing them is drawn. What choice of points results in the triangle with the largest possible area? Justify your answer as best you can.

Example 1. Students D and E took 20 seconds to read the problem, and began to sketch a "reasonable" solution.

D: "Why don't we pick a special case, like an equilateral triangle?"
E: "If we could make . . . you know how we do max-min problems where you have two for-
     mulas and you reduce it to one variable and all that."
D: "We can do it for an equilateral triangle, but will it work for all cases? I guess all he
     wants us to do is find out."
E: "Why don't we try the equilateral first?"

They then spend about 6 minutes deriving the area of the equilateral triangle inscribed in the circle, which (X being the side of the triangle) is $(X^2/4)\sqrt{3}$. Having obtained a formula they "maximize" it by differentiating it and setting it equal to zero. This leads to the conclusion that X must equal 0. After some confusion, they give up.

Example 2. Another attempt to solve the same problem has been described at length in my "Episodes" paper (Schoenfeld, 1983b). Less than a minute into the solution, students K and A conjectured that the equilateral triangle is the largest and decided to compute its area. They embarked on a tortuous series of computations, and were still involved in those calculations when the session ended 20 minutes later. I then asked them what good it would do them to know the area of the equilateral. They could not tell me.

In the first example, students D and E began a calculation that, upon reflection, could be shown to be meaningless: one cannot maximize a "special case." They never recovered from that initial attempt, which could have been forestalled. In the second example, students K and A went off on a wild goose chase and never returned from it. Seven of 12 videotapes made of students solving such problems in a 1979 experiment were of the "read the problem, pick a direction, and then work on it until you run out of time" variety. All seven of the choices were wild goose chases; all seven could have been forestalled or curtailed. But in the absence of certain metacognitive skills, they were not. Other tapes showed students coming up with partial solutions that could have been exploited to yield complete answers; but when the approaches taken did not solve the problem completely, they were abandoned (and the good ideas with them). These, too, are metacognitive failures: a good "executive" asks if there is anything to be salvaged from unsuccessful attempts, before moving on.

In two recent papers, Lesh (1983a, 1983b) has provided many instances of his "adaptive organisms" working at various levels of success to solve rather complex real-world problems. At recent AERA meetings, Lesh described the work produced by a group of students on a problem for which they were to find the number of pieces of baseboard (each 16 feet long) required for a room whose dimensions were 21 × 28. Lesh characterizes the students as passing through a number of "unstable conceptual models" of the situation. Among them were the following:

1. The students quickly drew a diagram, but labeled the corners (!) rather than the sides

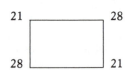

2. The formula for area was almost instantly invoked, and the students began to calculate 21 × 28.

3. Without any apparent reason, "perimeter" was mentioned and (21 + 28) was calculated; this was modified to (21 + 21 + 28 + 28).

In this particular case, the students' attempts generally meandered in the direction of a solution. Why inappropriate schemata (area, for example) were replaced with appropriate ones (perimeter) is a deep and open question. But it is clear that schema-access without executive control, "monitoring," or (best) "understanding" can cause a lot of trouble. Why, for example, did the diagram in (1) have the lengths of the sides at the corners? It is pure conjecture, but might that representation have anything to do with another archetype, such as the following generic representation of quadrilaterals?

Why was area invoked? It probably had something to do with a "recency" phenomenon: area had been studied in the recent past, and accessing the formula ($B \times H$) for a rectangle was an almost automatic response. Why did perimeter replace area? I wish I knew what allowed these students (precipitously, without discussion or evaluation) to abandon an inappropriate approach for a good one, while the students in my protocols doggedly pursued the wrong course. But I do know two things:

1. Had either group possessed rudimentary executive skills, the solutions would not have evolved the way they did. The questions "What good will this approach do you?" or "Is this approach (or representation) justified?" would have forestalled inappropriate approaches in either case; "Am I making enough progress to continue this approach?" might have curtailed a wild goose chase. The students did not think to ask them, however.

2. The students were most unlikely to ask themselves such questions, since such issues are almost never discussed in the classroom. (More about this in the sections on classroom instruction.)

BELIEFS AND EPISTEMOLOGY

Let us briefly return to Perkins's study. A fact of great interest is that many of Perkins's subjects were capable of making far stronger arguments than the ones they actually produced: they could have engaged in dialectical arguments, looked for and produced counterexamples, and so on. One might attribute their failure to do so to "executive failure." Clearly the efficient monitoring and assessing of a line of reasoning as it evolves would improve that line of reasoning. But why were such executive actions not taken, when the individual had the requisite skills? Here an epistemological argument provides a reasonable explanation.

Suppose that one has[1] a "makes-sense epistemology," where the plausibility of an argument, or the fact that it "feels right," is sufficient for the argument to be considered completely acceptable and convincing. Under these circumstances, that individual would not even think to engage in dialectical arguments or to seek counterexamples; there is no need to do so! One's "world view" (or set of beliefs, or epistemology) determines the kind of reasoning (and meta-reasoning) one does.

The most extensive epistemological studies in mathematics education are the investigations of children's arithmetic errors that have come from Xerox PARC. Early studies (Brown & Burton, 1978) provided "epistemological snapshots" of cognitive states revealing that students had well-developed (but incorrect) conceptions of certain procedures. That is, the students had not failed to master the "right" arithmetic procedures; they had, instead, consistently implemented incorrect procedures. This is a critically important observation, for it indicates that students are not tabula rasae waiting to be written upon; they are active processors of information who make the best sense of their environment that they can, in remarkably consistent ways. One cannot simply assume that students have not "gotten it"; one may have to discover what they have "gotten," and "debug" it. Later work in the same area focused on where "buggy" procedures came from: first as "repairs" to partially understood procedures (VanLehn, 1981) and later as the result of student-text interactions in which the individual students construct their knowledge in response to the sequence of examples in their texts (VanLehn, 1983).

Perhaps the most compelling evidence about naive epistemologies comes from the "misconception" literature in physics (perhaps because "naive physics" can so easily lead one astray). Again, it may appear at first blush (as in the arithmetic studies) that students' difficulties come from their having failed to master what is admittedly difficult subject matter. For example, a series of studies by McDermott and her colleagues (e.g., McDermott, 1983; Trowbridge & McDermott, 1980) indicate that students consistently confuse the rate of change of a quantity with measures of the quantity itself. In the Trowbridge and McDermott study, two balls were rolled down parallel tracks of an inclined plane in a way that one ball passed the other on the way down. The students were asked if the two balls had the same speed at any point, and the answer was often yes: the two balls must have had the same speed at the point where they were adjacent. McDermott (1983) gives a number of examples of students' confusion about the relationships among position, velocity, and acceleration (in general, about interpreting changes in a quantity).

Since the topics in McDermott's examples are difficult, there may again be the tendency to excuse student performance on the ground that the students have failed to master the relevant information. There are indications, however, that the source of the misconceptions is deep and that the misconceptions are difficult to change. Part of the reason is that the misconceptions appear to come from perceptions (or misperceptions) of everyday phenomena. For example, Lochhead (1983) reported that students in a college physics class will argue that a projectile thrown upward will have positive velocity for a while, will stop *for a while*, and then will have negative velocity (apparently the particle

---

1. The word "has" is a bit strong; the phrase "behaves as if one has" is probably more appropriate. There is not a presumption here that an individual who "has" a particular epistemology is aware of having it, or would be capable of elucidating it. Nor is there the presumption that one's "world view" is logically consistent.

must "rest" before reversing directions). This misperception continued through physics instruction. Misconceptions about acceleration, whose abstractions are further removed from "reality," occur with great frequency and are remarkably resistant to change: Lochhead reported 80% to 90% error rates. Minstrell (in press), reported on the Aristotelian notions held by modern students of physics. Nickerson (1982) reported Minstrell's results as follows:

> When asked to explain why a cart that has started to roll across a horizontal smooth table top by being given a push eventually slows to a stop, students often suggested that the push is used up as the cart moves across the table and that force is required to keep objects in motion because their natural tendency is to be at rest. (p. 9)

Again, naive interpretations of real-world experience drive one's interpretation of physical phenomena. Janvier (1978) reports similar results.

A series of experiments on projectile motion by McCloskey, Caramazza, and Green (1980); Caramazza, McCloskey, and Green (1981); and McCloskey (1983) provide strong evidence of both the development of naive (and incorrect) epistemologies and their persistence through formal instruction. For example, students were asked to predict the motion of projectiles after they had been blown through tubes as in Figure 2.

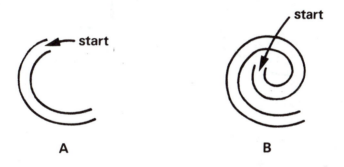

Figure 2. Projectile motion problem.

A large number of these students (49% of those with no formal physics instruction, 34% of those who had successfully completed at least one high school physics course, and 14% of those who completed college physics courses) predicted curved trajectories like those in Figure 3, with a tighter spiral (naturally!) appearing frequently in Figure 3B.

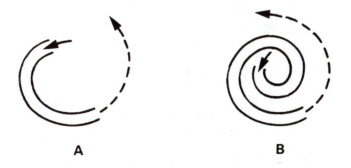

Figure 3. Trajectories predicted by students.

Two other examples of persistent misconceptions are given in Figures 4 and 5 as reported by McCloskey (1983). For the experiment shown in Figure 4, college students were asked to draw the trajectory of a ball whirled at the end of a string after the string breaks. For the experiment shown in Figure 5, college students were asked to push to puck and release it so that it would travel across a segment of a ring painted on a table without touching the curved edges of the painted figure. Figures 4A and 5A present the correct solutions to the problems. There were a large number of incorrect solutions, with the two most frequent ones given below; 30% of the subjects thought that after the string broke the path of the ball would be curved (Figure 4B), and 25% of the subjects believed that they could impart a ''circular impetus'' to the puck (Figure 5B) so that it would continue moving in a circular path. (The correct path is drawn in dotted lines.)

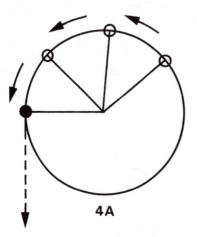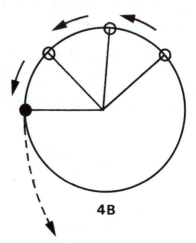

Figure 4. The trajectory problem.

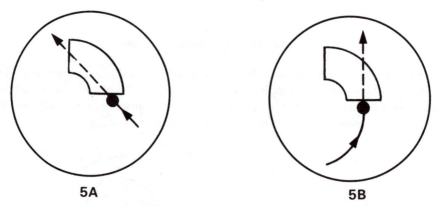

Figure 5. The puck problem.

For a deep attempt at a theory of developmental epistemology of physics misconceptions, see diSessa (1983), whose ''phenomenological primitives'' provide a step toward a theory unifying the preceding collection of examples. Those examples indicate that one's world view (or epistemology, or belief system) is largely shaped by one's empirical experience, including one's (perceptions of) instructional experience. Moreover, one's belief systems serve in large part to determine what one ''sees'' in given phenomena, how one explains them, how one approaches problems, and so on. My own research in mathematical problem solving indicates that misperceptions about the *utility* of mathematics, derived from empirical experience in the classroom, have an equally strong effect in shaping the ways that students solve problems.

A detailed discussion of the issues raised here and an attempt at a theoretical structure for characterizing some key components of mathematical competence are given in another paper (Schoenfeld, 1983a). Here I shall simply summarize two representative problem-solving sessions. The reasoning processes of a dozen pairs of students were recorded, as they worked the following problem:

> You are given two intersecting straight lines and a point *P* on one of them, as in the figure below. Show how to construct, with straightedge and compass, a circle that is tangent to both lines and that has the point *P* as its point of tangency to one of them.

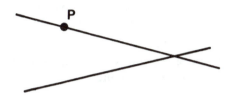

Students S and B, freshmen who had both completed a semester of college calculus and had studied a year of plane geometry in high school, produced a typical protocol. They guessed at a solution within a minute of reading the problem (that the midpoint of the line segment from *P* to the *P′* directly opposite *P* was the center of the desired circle), and spent about 5 minutes with straightedge and compass in hand trying to test the construction. The construction failed to meet their empirical standards, and they made another conjecture. It too failed. A third conjecture "worked." It took the students about 16 minutes to "solve" the problem, and more than 80% of that time was spent with straightedge and compass in hand. When I asked the students to tell me why their solution worked, they could not: "It just does."

Students M and S, also college freshmen who had studied a year of geometry in high school, produced a much more interesting (and less typical) solution. They made a conjecture that was incorrect, and tried the construction suggested by the conjecture. It was rejected. Then a correct conjecture was made. It too was tested by construction, and — their tools being mediocre, the construction sloppy — it too failed! Given this, they tried to "patch" both constructions. After "repair" the two constructions looked equally good. They said "We can prove it two different ways" and offered me both solutions, even though the two solutions were mutually contradictory.

Not one pair of the twelve pairs of students derived a solution to the problem. All twelve pairs proceeded by trial and error, and all were satisfied with their solutions; only one pair tried, after reaching a solution, to justify it via mathematical argumentation. For all the rest, empirical substantiation sufficed, even though the students were capable of the mathematical argumentation. After they finished the problem sessions, I asked them to show that the points of tangency on the circle were equidistant from the vertex, and that the line segment from the center of the circle to the vertex bisected the vertex angle—points that the students had conjectured and relied upon without proof. *All* pairs managed to do so, usually within 5 minutes. Thus, they had the means to solve the problem easily within their reach, but did not call upon them. They did not even *think* to call upon them!

The parallels to Perkins's study are clear. These students' epistemology does not include the notion that mathematical argumentation is useful. A possible explanation rests on the students' empirical experience: when they studied geometry in high school, "proof" was used to confirm either (*a*) what they already believed was obvious for intuititive reasons or (*b*) what the teacher attested to be true, and which they were to *verify*. In either case, mathematical argumentation was never used to discover anything. Thus a part of the students' belief systems may have become,"proof is worthless for discovery. Never use it; rely on intuition for suggestions, construction for verification." Three components of a "nonmathematical epistemology," which I conjecture may be possessed by a large number of our students (recall that an individual may not be consciously aware of having a belief), are listed here, and the implications of these beliefs are pursued in the following sections.

Belief 1: Formal mathematics has little or nothing to do with real thinking or problem solving. Corollary: Ignore it when you need to solve problems.

Belief 2: Mathematics problems are always solved in less than 10 minutes, if they are solved at all. Corollary: Give up after 10 minutes.

Belief 3: Only geniuses are capable of discovering or creating mathematics. First corollary: If you forget something, too bad. After all, you're not a genius and you won't be able to derive it on your own. Second corollary: Accept procedures at face value, and don't try to understand why they work. After all, they are derived knowledge passed on "from above."

PRACTICAL SUGGESTIONS FOR TEACHING "CONTROL"

As indicated above, students' metacognitive skills are remarkably poor. This should come as no great surprise, since virtually all instruction focuses on the mastery of facts and procedures (even heuristic procedures); standard instruction does not deal with metacognition at all. The notion of serving as one's own "manager" or "coach" is alien to my students. Their perception is that their minds are essentially autonomous with regard to problem solving; they just do "what comes to mind." Moreover, the results of executive failures can usually be attributed elsewhere: for example, "I just didn't see what to do." I suggest that one bring such matters out into the open, and provide models of control decisions for students, by engaging in "real" problem solving in the classroom. At a minimum the teacher can elucidate the nature of decision process when presenting solutions to problems in class. ("All right, what are the options here? We might look at A or B, or maybe C. It looks like A might be worth a try for a few minutes, because ...") It is useful to work through problems on this kind of "blow-by-blow" basis, even when they are familiar. Although the teacher knows what to do and why, the student does not: seeing the decision process modeled will, at least, "legitimize" it for the students. Even so, this legitimization is only the first step. I suggest two methods of group problem solving during class sessions (and use each with equal frequency). They are both described extensively, with some sample classroom sessions, in another paper (Schoenfeld, 1983c).

Method A: The Class Works the Problem as a Whole
While the Teacher Acts as "Manager"

I pose a problem for the class to solve, and invite suggestions for its solution. A typical problem is reasonably difficult and may take the class as a whole anywhere from 10 to 50 minutes (or longer) to solve. Often suggestions will come quickly—too quickly, and frequently barely relevant to the problem (the first step of what might well be a wild goose chase). My role is not to judge the suggestions, for the kind of interaction I wish to promote only works well when the students feel free to make suggestions. There is a delicate tension between the wish to critique suggestions and the fear that students, once "scolded," will cease to participate. The way out of this difficulty is for the teacher to stay strictly in the role of "monitor," raising questions about the efficacy of suggested steps (both when they are useful, and not useful). When the suggestions are ill-founded, the students will discover that for themselves. By my questions, however, I can point out the speed with which the students made their suggestions: "Is everyone sure that they understand the problem, before we proceed with the solution?" If the answer is "no," the class takes whatever steps are appropriate to remedy that: examining the conditions of the problem, looking at special cases, drawing a diagram or finding another appropriate representation, and so on.

We then return to the original suggestions, and the class is asked if they seem reasonable. (If one or more of the suggestions now appears unreasonable, this may occasion a "sermon" about making sure you understand before proceeding, and about the dangers of wild goose chases.) We look for new suggestions: "Is there anything else we ought to look at or try?" If there is only one plausible approach, we take it—after making sure that what we are doing is reasonably well defined, and that we have a sense of how we will use it in the solution. If there is more than one (as is often the case when you work "problems" rather than "exercises"), we discuss the relative merits of the approaches and what we might gain from them. The three "generic" questions for this discussion are listed in Method B. Having made our choice, we proceed with the solution. After 5 minutes or so have elapsed, we pause: "All right, we've been doing this for a while. Is it working? Are things going according to plan, or should we reconsider?"

It is important to ask these questions even when things seem to be going well. Otherwise, they become a "cue" from the teacher that directions should be changed. The idea is that these questions should always be in the back of one's mind; they advance to the front when solutions seem to bog down. The class may decide to proceed, to proceed with caution ("we'll give it another 3 minutes, and then reconsider"), or to change directions: "Before we abandon this approach, is there anything in it that should be salvaged? Are there any ideas in it that we might want to return to, or are there related topics suggested by this approach that we might want to explore if our new approach doesn't work out?" The discussion continues in this vein until (with luck) the problem is solved. We may then pursue some of the other suggestions, and solve the problem two or three different ways. We will occasionally stop at an impasse, and continue with the problem another day. On those occasions when, after such an impasse, it still appears that the class is ignorant of some relevant knowledge and is unlikely to derive it, I may then provide them with it.

While the class works on the problem, my contributions are kept to a minimum. If the class decides to pursue a direction that I know leads to a dead end, I will let them—as long as the decision was reasonably made. That happens, after all, in good problem solving; an effective "monitor/assessor" keeps such decisions from being fatal. In general, the role of the "external manager" played by the teacher is to help the students to get the most out of what they know: to ensure that they have fully understood a problem before embarking on its solution, that they have looked for good representations, that they generate and select approaches to the problem with care, that they capitalize on opportunities that arise during the solution, that they employ the resources at their disposal, and that they avoid squandering their energies on responses which are clearly inappropriate. The actions of the external manager do not depend on knowledge of the problem not accessible to the students; everything this manager does could be done (with the same positive effects) by the students themselves. In other words, all of the "control" functions performed in the classroom discussion could be internalized by the students, without additional knowledge.

After the problem has been solved, I step back into the role of teacher to do a postmortem. This includes a discussion of problem representations, of related knowledge that might or should have been called into play, of the students' effective or ineffective use of control strategies (I occasionally let the class go on a wild goose chase, to point out what happens when one fails to exert executive control), and of elements in the students' approach that could, if pursued or exploited differently, have yielded insights into the problem or different solutions of it.

Method B: The Class Breaks Into Small Groups to Work on Problems While The Teacher Acts as Roving "Consultant"

About a third of the time in my problem-solving course is spent with the class divided into groups of four, working on problems that I have just handed out. As the students work on the problems, I circulate through the class as a possible source of help. Again, my role is not simply to provide information or hints, although I will if the situation calls for it. More often than not, my response to a request for a hint will be in the form of a (heuristic) question: Does that problem remind you of anything? Have you done something similar recently? Can you reduce it to something simpler?

In the small groups the emphasis on control decisions remains, but the responsibility for it shifts from the external manager to the students. There is a large poster in the classroom with the following three executive questions:

> What (exactly) are you doing?
> (Can you describe it precisely?)
>
> Why are you doing it?
> (How does it fit into the solution?)
>
> How does it help you?
> (What will you do with the outcome when
> you obtain it?)

Their frequent inability, at the beginning of the course, to answer these questions—coupled with the realization that if they cannot, they have most likely been wasting their time—serves as a strong catalyst for the internalization of these questions. I should point out that these questions are not meant to rule out exploration. "I'm mucking around for a few minutes hoping to find some inspiration" is a perfectly good answer—as long as the student is aware of what is taking place, and doesn't let the solution process degenerate into an extensive and directionless series of random explorations. The purpose of the questions is simply to make sure the student is "in control."

To cast the preceding discussions in one of a number of possible theoretical frameworks, we can see the large-group and small-group discussions as the social mediating factors that help move the student through a "zone of proximal development" (à la Vygotsky, 1978) to the point where the appropriate behaviors are internalized. At a more pragmatic level, the following reasons justify the use of class time for this admittedly time-consuming process:

1. This format affords the teacher the unique opportunity to intervene directly as the students solve problems, rather than being faced with a "finished product." That intervention is much stronger than it could be in any other instructional format. Moreover, group formats bring these ordinarily covert control processes out in the open, where they can be examined.

2. Solving problems with a small number of one's peers provokes discussions of plausible choices. When a student works a problem alone, the first plausible option is often the one taken. When different students have proposed approaches to the problem and they must settle on one, there must be a discussion of the merits of the approaches they have proposed—precisely the kind of discussion that the students should be having internally.

3. Problem solving is not always a solitary endeavor. This opportunity to engage in collaborative efforts does them no harm.

4. Students are remarkably insecure about their abilities, especially in a course of this nature. Working on problems with other students is reassuring: one sees that one's fellow students must also struggle to learn.

PRACTICAL SUGGESTIONS FOR DEALING WITH BELIEFS AND SHAPING PERSPECTIVES

Dealing with beliefs and shaping perspectives is a far more subtle issue than the preceding one, and my suggestions are far more primitive. As with the case of control strategies, students need to become aware of "positive instances." Doing this in a reasonable way is difficult enough. But the real difficulty comes in helping students to remove inappropriate beliefs or ideas: those beliefs must be discovered before they can be removed.

We are most unlikely to see evidence of misconceptions or "misbeliefs" as long as we are presenting material to the students or they are presenting to us what they believe we want to see—for example, formal mathematics or formal physics in an obviously "formal" setting. Misbeliefs are only likely to surface if students are given the opportunity to show us what they "know." In the classroom I have found that the most effective way to find out what lies beneath the surface of students' performance is to repeat in different forms, one simple question: *Why?* I shall give one example here.

The following discussions took place at Rochester, in my "problem-solving" class. I had 18 students, all of whom studied geometry in high school, and most of whom took calculus at the college level (and did well in it). I introduced geometric constructions with the simplest problem I could think of:

Suppose you had line segments of lengths *A, B, C,* respectively. How do you (using straightedge and compass) construct the triangle whose sides have lengths *A, B, C*?

The class, acting as a whole group, solved the problem in less than a minute (mark off a line segment of length *A*; from its endpoints swing arcs of length *B* and *C* respectively; draw the line segments from the endpoint of the first segment to the point of intersection), and agreed unanimously that they had the solution.

"Why does that work?"

Long silence.

"Why do you swing the arcs?"

More silence.

"When you swing the arc of length *B* around this endpoint, what do you get?"

There were some answers to this, and we proceeded from there. The class eventually decided that the point (singular) of intersection had the property that it was simultaneously at distance *B* from one vortex of the desired triangle (whose base had been established as *A*), and distance *C* from the other: this must be the triangle we wanted.

"Are there any others?" In response to the puzzled looks, I pointed out that the construction was not unique. Extended, the arcs (circles) intersected twice; moreover, one might use arcs of lengths *C* and *B*, respectively, instead of *B* and *C*. This construction led to four solutions. Response: "They're all the same."

"Why?"

After a long pause, one student said, "All the triangles you get are congruent. They're the same." The class agreed.

"Are there any different-looking triangles with sides *A*, *B*, and *C*?"

This question left them nonplussed. The sentiment was "no," but there was no coherent argument to support that sentiment.

"Suppose you had two different triangles, each of which had sides *A*, *B*, and *C*. What could you say?"

They're congruent, of course.... Hmm, maybe congruence has something to do with this idea of uniqueness (my language).... Forty minutes had elapsed when we closed this discussion of the problem they had "solved" in less than a minute.

We began the next session of class with the following question: "How do you bisect an angle?" Again, the class produced the construction in short order.

"Why does the construction work?"

I will spare you the details and report the result: It took longer than a half hour for the class to see that the (standard) construction yielded two congruent triangles, and that the line that resulted lay between two equal angles that had been created; thus it was the angle bisector.

In sum, my class spent a week (at the college level) uncovering the reasons for two constructions that they had been able to produce from memory in less than 2 minutes. Was this a waste of time? I believe just the opposite. The discussions not only explained "where the constructions came from"—a minor goal—but also served to legitimize geometric reasoning (notions of proof and congruence) as useful tools in thinking geometrically. In subsequent discussions "proof" and "congruence" were invoked frequently both as reasons that things worked and (*much* more importantly) as ways of finding out what might work. This week of discussions had "unlocked" for use the content of a full year of study that had lain stagnant in long-term memory—not because it could not be accessed, but because it had been deemed worthless. The shame is that these discussions were "remedial" and took place in a collegiate problem-solving course. Proper attention to the context of learning, to making knowledge meaningful, and to making sure that students "understand" should make such remediation unnecessary.

Even though this example is anecdotal, I consider it important; I intend to find "rigorous" documentation in the near future. I hope the following two points have emerged clearly from my discussion:

1. Teaching students to solve problems calls for attention to resources, control, and beliefs.

2. While the task of getting students to focus on "understanding" is far from easy, it can be done (and is rewarding).

DISCUSSION

Research on issues of metacognition and epistemology is fraught with difficulty. One major set of concerns is methodological: how does one investigate such nebulous phenomena? My personal bias is that the techniques of the psychological community for exploring metacognition, while useful, will prove far too limited for the purposes of mathematics education. We will need a variety of techniques for the analysis of problem-solving protocols, for clinical interviews, and for "natural" classroom observations. I think I have made a start on the parsing of protocols (Schoenfeld, 1983b) but it is just a start; much more needs to be done.

Metacognitive issues are fairly well understood in comparison to epistemological ones. As the discussion of misconceptions indicates, many things beyond the immediate environment and current instruction shape what one sees and does in problem situations. Ultimately, we need a theory that explains just that: why one sees what one does in given situations, and how conscious access to "control strategies" can help a person to gain some leverage over his or her perceptions/conceptions. Such detailed explorations into mental mechanisms are a major issue in cognitive science, beyond the present concerns of mathematics education, but they will have to become a concern of mathematics education. Conversely, there are issues that mathematics education can address that are beyond the scope of cognitive science: classroom realities, and ways to shape them so that useful learning and understanding can be promoted. We do not lack for interesting tasks in the foreseeable future.

REFERENCES

Brown, A.L. Knowing when, where, and how to remember: a problem of metacognition. In R. Glaser (Ed.), *Advances in instructional psychology* (Vol. 1). Hillsdale, NJ: Lawrence Erlbaum Associates, 1978.

Brown, J.S., & Burton, R.R. Diagnostic models for procedural bugs in basic mathematical skills. *Cognitive Science* 2, 155–92, 1978.

Caramazza, A., McCloskey, M., & Green, B. Naive beliefs in sophisticated subjects: Misconceptions about trajectories of objects. *Cognition* 9, 117–23, 1981.

diSessa, A. Phenomenology and the evolution of intuitions. In D. Gentner & A. L. Stevens (Eds.), *Mental models*. Hillsdale, NJ: Lawrence Erlbaum Associates, 1983.

Flavell, J. Metacognitive aspects of problem solving. In L.B. Resnick (Ed.), *The nature of intelligence*. Hillsdale, NJ: Lawrence Erlbaum Associates, 1976.

Flavell, J., & Wellman, H. Metamemory. In R.V. Kail and J.W. Hagen (Eds.), *Perspectives on the development of memory and cognition*. Hillsdale, NJ: Lawrence Erlbaum Associates, 1977.

Hinsley, D., Hayes, J., & Simon, H. From words to equations: Meaning and representation in algebra word problems. In P.A. Carpenter & M.A. Just (Eds.), *Cognitive processes in comprehension*. Hillsdale, NJ: Lawrence Erlbaum Associates, 1977.

Janvier, C. *The interpretation of complex Cartesian graphs representing situations — Studies and teaching experiments*. Unpublished doctoral thesis, University of Nottingham, 1978.

Lachman, J., Lachman, R., & Thronesbery, C. Metamemory through the adult life span. *Developmental Psychology* 15(5), 543–51, 1979.

Lesh, R. *Metacognition in Mathematical Problem Solving*. Unfinished manuscript, 1983(a).

Lesh, R. *Modeling middle school students' modeling behaviors in applied mathematical problem solving*. Paper presented at the annual meeting of the American Educational Research Association, Montreal, April 1983(b).

Lochhead, J. *Research on students' scientific misconceptions. Some implications for teaching*. Paper presented at the annual meeting of the American Educational Research Association, Montreal, April 1983.

Markman, E.M. Realizing that you don't understand: A preliminary investigation. *Child Development* 48, 986–92, 1977.

McCloskey, M. Intuitive physics. *Scientific American*, 122–30, April 1983.

McCloskey, M., Caramazza, A., & Green, B. Curvilinear motion in the absence of external forces: Naive beliefs about the motions of objects. *Science* 210, 1139–41, 1980.

McDermott, L. *Identifying and overcoming student conceptual difficulties in physics*. Paper presented at the annual meeting of the American Educational Research Association, Montreal, April 1983.

Minsky, M. A framework for representing knowledge. In P. Winston (Ed.), *The psychology of computer vision*. New York: McGraw-Hill, 1975.

Minstrell, J. Conceptual development research in the natural setting of the classroom. In M.B. Rowe (Ed.), *Science for the 80's*. National Education Association, in press.

Nickerson, R. *Understanding understanding*. Draft manuscript. Cambridge, MA: Bolt, Beranek, and Newman, 1982.

Perkins, D. *Difficulties in everyday reasoning and their change with education*. Final report to the Spencer Foundation, 1982. (Available from author, Graduate School of Education, Harvard University)

Perkins, D.N., Allen, R., & Hafner, J. Difficulties in everyday reasoning. In W. Maxwell (Ed.), *Thinking: The frontier expands*. Philadelphia: The Franklin Institute Press, 1983.

Ringel, B., & Springer C. On knowing how well one is remembering: The persistence of strategy use during transfer. *Journal of Experimental Child Psychology* 29, 322–33, 1980.

Schoenfeld, A.H. Beyond the purely cognitive: Belief systems, social cognitions, and metacognitions as driving forces in intellectual performance. *Cognitive Science* 7, 329–63, 1983(a).

Schoenfeld, A.H. Episodes and executive decisions in mathematical problem solving. In R. Lesh & M. Landau (Eds.), *Acquisition of mathematics concepts and processes*. New York: Academic Press, 1983(b).

Schoenfeld, A.H. *Problem solving in the mathematics curriculum: A report, recommendations, and an annotated bibliography*. Washington, DC: Mathematical Association of America, 1983(c).

Shank, R., & Abelson, R. *Scripts, plans, goals, and understanding*. Hillsdale, NJ: Lawrence Erlbaum Associates, 1977.

Silver, E.A. *Thinking about problem solving: Toward an understanding of metacognitive aspects of mathematical problem solving*. Paper presented at the Conference on Thinking, Suva, Fiji, January 1982.

Silver, E.A., Branca, N., & Adams, V. Metacognition: The missing link in problem solving? In R. Karplus (Ed.), *Proceedings of the Fourth International Conference For the Psychology of*

Mathematics Education. Berkeley: University of California, 1980.

Trowbridge, D.E., & McDermott, L.C. Investigation of student understanding of the concept of velocity in one dimension. *American Journal of Physics* **48**(12), 1020–28, 1980.

VanLehn, K. *Bugs are not enough: Empirical studies of procedural flaws, impasses, and repairs in procedural skills* (Technical Report CIS-11). Palo Alto, CA: Xerox Palo Alto Research Center, 1981.

VanLehn, K. On the representation of procedures in repair theory. In H.P. Ginsburg (Ed.), *The development of mathematical thinking.* New York: Academic Press, 1983.

Vygotsky, L.S. *Mind in society.* Cambridge, MA: Harvard University Press, 1978.

Representation and Problem Solving: Methodological Issues Related to Modeling

James J. Kaput

Southeastern Massachusetts University

A currently active issue in problem-solving research has to do with how students choose and then work with a mental representation when confronted with a problem to solve. Whatever the details, most would agree that *some* idea of representation seems to be at the heart of understanding problem-solving processes. Moreover, our understanding of these processes is increasingly based on the construction of appropriate models—representations—of the mental representations presumed to be involved.

There is another reason to believe that problem-solving research might benefit from a more complete and explicit exegesis of the term "representation." Problem-solving research is at the juncture of three other research areas that use the term in somewhat proprietary ways. Cognitive psychology, artificial intelligence, and mathematics almost define current problem-solving research by their common intersection. A fourth area, epistemology, acts as an umbrella for all the others and provides shelter for a fourth usage, which is the idea of representation as explanation. The analyses offered here do not deal directly with a fifth cluster of areas that is growing in importance, which includes study of social, institutional, and affective factors in problem solving.

I will sort out the different uses of "representation" by first giving a very general definition that any usage should satisfy and which in fact is shared by all the uses examined. Then, I will focus on the particular usages in order to develop a more critical perspective on the role of representation and modeling in the explanation of problem-solving behavior. Some conditions that are required for our models to be *adequate* explanations in the traditional philosophy-of-science sense of explanatory adequacy are discussed. I close with a discussion of the philosophic and practical implications of our criteria for adequate representation-explanations, drawing an analogy between the cultural magnitude of accepting Newton's description of the physical universe and the acceptance of a computational theory of mind.

At the heart of this paper is an outline of several key difficulties associated with the use of computer representations of problem-solving processes:

- The fact that they provide weak and contingent sufficiency arguments, but not necessary connections, between machine and human behaviors and the respective representations on which they are assumed to be based.

- The limitations of the von Neumann architecture on which they are based.

- Their profound linguistic bias.

- The problem of reference and the resulting problems of "impoverishedness."

- The bootlegged meaning associated with the names of the formalisms used in the computer representations.

I offer a set of operational criteria to help counter these weaknesses and which also apply to virtually any use of models, both formal and informal:

- Transparency of the representations and their underlying correspondences.

- Explicit justification on the choice of languages used in the representations.

- Maximization of the level of detail at both the analytic and empirical levels of explanation.

- Incorporation of an ontogenetic or developmental framework into the model so that more than temporal or phenomenological cross sections are modeled.

The general issue of representation in mathematical problem solving and learning also involves (1) how representation operates in mathematics proper, (2) how the common core mathematical curriculum can be viewed as an interlocking collection of representation systems, (3) how the choice of symbol system affects our ability to use mathematical ideas, and (4) how an approach to mathematical education research that deals with representation systems and symbol systems in a focal way can illuminate certain critical areas where student performance difficulty is well known and persistent. Such areas include translation of mathematical ideas across representation systems and the application of mathematical ideas to concrete problems. It is hoped that my current investigations will also shed light on certain well-known and persistent research issues such as the relation and distinction between representations and processes, declarative and procedural knowledge, conceptual and rote learning, and between executive and automatic processes (Sternberg, 1983).

The overarching assumption of this line of inquiry is that more direct attention needs to be paid to the ways we use symbols and combinations of symbols in representation systems. We need a theoretical framework which can support understanding of how we and our students relate cognitively and linguistically to the ubiquitous external representations we all too often take for granted in our discussions of mathematics problem solving and learning. This understanding would take into explicit account, among other facts, that almost all of K–8 school mathematics is not about numbers but about *representations* of numbers (in the base ten placeholder system), and that natural language provides an ambient interpretation system for most mathematical notations at all levels. It would also provide systematic criteria and vocabulary for discussing how the different representation systems vary in their ability to "carry" certain mathematical ideas and what kinds of mental processing are required to translate ideas across representation systems.

THE GENERAL IDEA OF REPRESENTATION

In its broadest sense a representation is something that stands for something else, and so must inherently involve some kind of relationship between symbol and referent, although each may itself be a complex entity. The idea is used with varying degrees of precision all across the intellectual landscape and is very subtle and manifold. In some ways it is what Shapere (1969) would call a "trans-theoretical term." In other ways it functions as a local undefined primitive whose meaning unfolds gradually through usage within a particular domain of inquiry.

Another example of such a term is "concept," which has served an enormous variety of purposes ranging greatly in specificity. As Toulmin (1972) has noted, "concept" has been used by virtually every discipline over the years. Sociologists and historians use it almost exclusively in a collective sense, psychologists use it in a variety of special ways, mathematicians sometimes use it to identify the objects that they study ("the concept of topological space"), philosophers use it in other technical ways, educators use it to identify that which is supposed to pass into or develop within student heads, and even advertisers use it in regular ways ("a new concept in skin care!"). Seldom, even in philosophy or psychology, is the term defined with a great deal of rigor. Nonetheless, it manages to serve reasonably well. Until recently the same could have been said about "representation" even in cognitive psychology and artificial intelligence.

However, there are differences in usage lying in quite close proximity. We are interested in the following five uses of "representation," each of which relates importantly to problem-solving research:

1. mental representation,

2. computer representation,

3. explanatory representation,

4. mathematical representation,

5. symbolic representation—as with external mathematical notation.

A good deal can and eventually will be said about each of these five arenas of meaning and their interrelationships. This paper will concentrate on the first three.

First we should agree on what any systematic use of the idea of representation must satisfy. Following Palmer (1977) and building on our starting point that a representation must involve two related but functionally separate entities, let us agree to call one entity the representing world and the other the represented world. There should then be a correspondence between some aspects of the represented world and some aspects of the representing world. Therefore, a rigorous specification of a representation should include the following entities:

- The represented world.

- The representing world.

- What aspects of the represented world are being represented.

- What aspects of the representing world are doing the representing.

- The correspondence between the two worlds.

This specification is a tall order, especially since in many of the interesting cases one or both of the worlds may be hypothetical entities. Nonetheless, we can use this definition as a measure of any proposed representation's rigor and as a means of getting our many different uses of the term under some kind of functional control.

MENTAL REPRESENTATION

Kant, regarded by some as the first cognitive psychologist, argued that our experience deals with representations (''Vorstellungen'') not with ''things in themselves,'' which are unknowable except indirectly through the formal grammar and structure of the representations. He was trying to lay to rest—actually, to transcend—the empiricist/rationalist debate raging through the eighteenth century. The empiricists (e.g., Locke and Hume) tried to explain ''knowing'' via their contemporary notions of perceptual processing, whereas the rationalists came at the problem via logic, mathematics, and especially deductive geometry, the best formal system in town.

The last decade of cognitive science (which was also its first decade) has produced a consensus shared by the remainder of the related branches of psychology, a consensus that among sentient organisms, humans and perhaps others have some way of representing internally their experience of their environment. On the other hand there is no consensus on the nature of this representing activity or even its functional role in behavior. There is also divergence on the genesis of representation within individuals. Philosophers have further stretched the meaning of representation and have criticized psychological meanings on a variety of grounds. However, one continues to hear echoes of the eighteenth century debate today regarding the nature of these representations and their role in ''knowing.'' For the rationalists, the role of deductive logic and mathematics has been updated to a more general notion of ''computation,'' as seen for example in the writing of Pylyshyn (1973, 1979, 1980) or Fodor (1975, 1980). On the other hand, the empiricists, who are mostly cognitive psychologists, because this is where the relevant empirical work is by definition being done, have fanned out to a range of positions based on one or another theoretical and experimental approaches. Their diversity is seen in the writings of Grossberg (1980), Kohler (1947), Kosslyn (1980), and Gibson (1979). The philosophers continue to fret over what is being represented, the veridicality of the representation, and the epistemic and ontological relationships between the ''software'' and the ''wetware'' of the human cognizing apparatus. The psychologists deal with issues of development, functionality, and character (analog, linguistic, etc.) of the mental representations.

It does not require a great deal of shrewdness to realize that we have not given any kind of a specification of what is meant by a mental representation. To do so successfully would certainly alter the work plans—if not the leisure plans—of a good number of working cognitive psychologists. Nonetheless, Palmer (1977) has shown that careful application of the representation definition given earlier coupled with certain abstractly definable properties of representations, especially regarding the cognitive or perceptual operations that actually define the representation, can uncover surprising information-theoretical properties of the mental representations posited by particular theories. For example, he shows how those that appear to be very different can be informationally equivalent. The details are beyond the scope of this paper.

COMPUTER REPRESENTATION

Much of the recent thinking on mental representations has, of course, been stimulated by work in artificial intelligence, where the issues necessarily get crisp and rigorous explication in specific hardware and software, and as Kosslyn (1978) put it, one "can be general while remaining explicit" (p. 306). The starting point of an understanding of computer representations is Minsky's (1968) classic definition of artificial intelligence: "the science of making machines do things that would require intelligence if done by men" (p. v). There has been no radical change in this definition over the years, but there have been simultaneous tendencies to project "intelligence" onto the machines as the machines get more capable of imitating human *behaviors* and to redefine the terms in which human intelligence is discussed. These tendencies are perhaps best exemplified in the writings of Simon (Langley & Simon, 1981; Simon, 1978) and Douglas Hofstadter (1980). Vigorous criticism of Hofstadter's "strong AI" position has been voiced by Searle (1980). More general critiques have been articulated by Weizenbaum (1976). We shall discuss the interaction between artificial and natural intelligence first in general terms to set the stage for a more specific argument regarding the role of formal computer models in representing mental models.

The impact of artificial intelligence on notions of mental representations comes by way of a round trip between the world of cognitive research and the world of cybernetic modeling: people make hypotheses about the nature of mental representations from observation of specific human behaviors, and they create quasi-formal representations of these hypothetical mental representations. They may then write computer programs which embody *aspects* of these quasi-formally represented hypotheses—for example, in the way they structure, access, and manipulate information—and note whether the machine thus programmed exhibits "behavior" isomorphic (at some level of detail) to the human behavior that gave rise to the original quasi-formal representation of the presumed mental representation. One seldom hears of a case where they don't, not because such are unworthy of publication—after all, negative information is sometimes useful—but rather *because of the almost infinite degree of freedom one has in writing the programs.* Given the match in behaviors, the conclusion is then drawn that the humans have mental representations in some way isomorphic to that of the machine programs, thus completing the round trip between the quasi-formal representation and the computer representation.

It will become clear, especially after the next section, that due to the degrees of freedom exercised on the artificial intelligence side of the itinerary and the level of detail which may not be accounted for, the whole process yields mainly a meta-heuristic. This heuristic assists formation and evaluation of the quasi-formal representation in terms of the nature and (behavioral) functionality of mental representations thereby represented. The only *direct* logical conclusions available from this method concern the relations between the machine programs and the concomitant *machine* behaviors, and, of course, any inferences (about the formalisms) associated with the formal relationships among the program formalisms. The latter can be very useful in elaborating the quasi-formal representation.

The formal machine-behavioral linkages can be applied to mental representations in negative instances (providing a sufficiency condition) if it can be shown that a particular computer behavior does not follow from a particular computer representation, because then a particular human behavior cannot follow from the hypothesized isomorphic mental representation—*Provided one assumes that the hypothesized mental representation bears a causal-like relationship to the human behavior* and *the isomorphism between the machine-behavior link and the human-behavior link preserves causality*. This last condition is crucial to the value of the computer representation in explaining mental representations. Similar contingent conclusions can be drawn based on other parameters such as processing efficiency. The existence of a computer model with certain properties amounts to a "weak sufficiency" condition for the existence of a human system with analogous properties.

The "round trip" discussion omits some important factors. First, a source of metaphors for the quasi-formal representation of mental representations is the architecture, both hard and soft, of the computers of the day. The language of computation has come to be reflected back to the description of mental phenomena. Thus in a sense there is more than a round trip involved. But in fact there may be many round trips because if one looks at the language and concepts used to describe computers and computational processes, one sees the same descriptive apparatus that has previously been used to describe the human mind.

But this is not yet the whole epistemological story either. Given the assumption that our knowledge and understandings are about our mental representation of the world and not about the world in itself, then in fact the whole previous round trip discussion must be lifted one level of representation, because the round trips are between—you guessed it—mental representations of mental representations and mental representations of computer representations. Fortunately, this "lifting" need not be infinite. Figure 1 depicts the situation described so far.

EXPLANATORY REPRESENTATION

There is yet another source of complexity in the interaction between mental and computer representations. This source has to do with the role of representation in explanation generally, a role that is also associated with the words "model" and "analogy," and even to some extent with "metaphor."

Note that this and the previous section would be easier to read if the word "representation" were replaced by appropriately modified alternatives of these terms. However, the adherence to the term "representation" is not founded on a gratuitous penchant for linguistic consistency, but rather is intended to highlight the commonalities of meaning underlying these various usages. This includes functions common to the role of internal mental representations in dealing with experience and the role of explanatory representation (next paragraph) in doing the same thing, but on a more collective, public level. In a later paper I will attempt to show how the interactions among

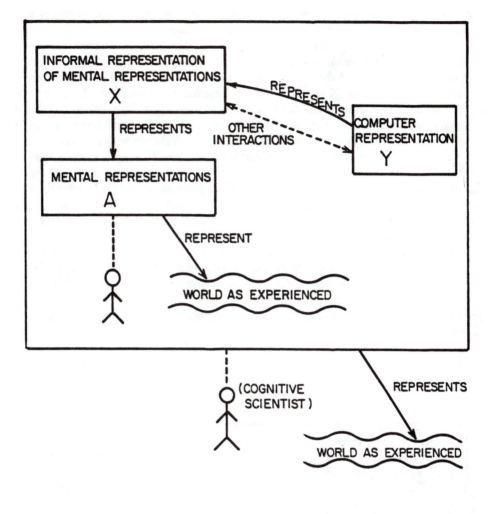

Figure 1.

these individual and collective functions are in part mediated by the choice of symbol systems.

E-Representation

In trying to explain X, one sometimes uses Y, where Y is a "representation" of X. Y embodies some aspects of X which are assumed to be critical to what we are trying to explain or understand about X, but Y embodies these aspects in a way that is simpler, more explicit, or more familiar than the way X does. To the extent that the five criteria of the abstract definition of representation are satisfied, we are thus referring to the same underlying idea of representation as earlier. However, there is more to *explanatory representation* than simply representation in this sense. The added ingredients are best isolated by looking further into the use of computer representations.

First of all, it is important to realize that *computer representations of mental representations act as formalisms in the same way that formalisms have traditionally been used in science*. In terms of the X and Y used above, Y, as a computer representation, is a formalism representing X where X is an informal representation of the mental representations. The added ingredients are the theory, which includes the choice of languages for both X and Y, the meta-language in which all the justification arguments are couched, the choice of observables, and the arguments themselves. We shall say that the *theory* is an "explanation-representation" of mental representations, or E-representation for short. This approach thus parallels a fairly common contemporary distinction between theories and models, whereby a given theory may be exemplified by more than one model. It also emphasizes the role of the informal representation and the ambient theory in order to counter a common confusion which regards the computer representation as a representation of mental representations directly. As seen in Figure 2, Y represents mental representations only indirectly as mediated by the informal representation *and* the theory. Note also a diagrammatic inadequacy in Figure 2 whereby the mental representations box must be both outside and inside the theory box. (This actually is a self-reference problem in using the same token to denote a pretheoretical item in natural language and a theoretical item within the meta-language [Tarski, 1951].)

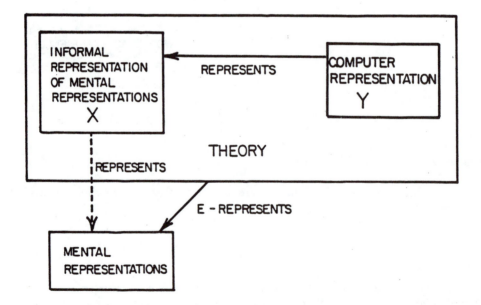

Figure 2.

Having now discussed the various uses and distinctions of the term "representation" where several meanings overlap and are subject to confusion, I will now relax the lexical straitjacket and frequently use the word "model" to refer to the computer and informal representations as described above.

Explanatory Adequacy

The following discussion lays out some strong criteria regarding the application of computer representations in explaining mental processes. Although we concentrate on computer (formal) models, much of what is said can also be applied to the use of informal models, especially the call for detailed, transparent, and well-supported explanations.

Explanatory adequacy has two components: empirical and analytic. Of the two, especially regarding computer models, analytic adequacy is the more critical and difficult to satisfy *despite* their mutual dependence. The major empirical issue is the severity of the computer idealization, the level of detail of the description—how much behavior is being described and how much is being ignored (e.g., social, affective, or linguistic behaviors) and how much of the ontogenetic or developmental processes are included.[1]

Achieving analytic adequacy is a more subtle, delicate, and decisive matter for several reasons, each of which can be recognized as an elaboration of the specifications for a well-defined representation.

The first adequacy issue is the "sufficiency only" limitation mentioned earlier. Machine sufficiency (to produce a given collection of behaviors) does *not* imply cognitive necessity. Or, to bend a phrase from Putnam (1975), designers of computer models have no privileged access to cognitive necessity. (It is, in fact, mathematically impossible to specify the internal state change structure of a standard [Moore] finite state machine from even an exhaustive knowledge of its input-output relations.) In terms of the definition of representation, this amounts to the ultimate inscrutability of the correspondence between the representing and represented worlds, at least until the connection between physiology and mental representations can be made entirely explicit or until we can "see" the mental states.

The second adequacy issue is the assumption that the contemporary architecture of computers is appropriate to represent mental architecture; that is, that our minds are structured the same way that the first computers are (the von Neumann storage/processor model). Distributed processing has not yet changed the nature of the computations and our way of thinking about computers, but one wonders about putting too many explanatory eggs in one basket, especially one which is basically a technological accident and which is likely to be succeeded by others. Even now, with the networking of personal workstations and other larger computers, one can no longer be certain where the

---

1. I became aware of an important discussion of these same methodological issues by VanLehn, 1983, between drafts of this paper. He discusses these issues from a very similar point of view via an extended description of the development of a particular model. I have altered some of the language and expanded this part of the paper to be consistent with and take advantage of his brilliant account.

"computer" is! This is not to say, however, that critical insights may not be gained by examining computer models at the level of fundamental design principles, as has been done by Winograd (1975). This assumption amounts to a choice of the representing world.

The third adequacy issue is the scope of explanation: the wider the coverage and the fewer the independent hypotheses, the more adequate the explanation (Hempel, 1965). This is the decision of how much of the representing and represented worlds will be part of the E-representation.

The fourth adequacy issue is the transparency of the computer model. If the representation is not transparent in terms of expressing what aspects of the informal model are being represented by what aspects of the computer model, and how they are being represented, then all we have is one (hypothetical) black box representing another, which is obviously inadequate as an explanation.

The fifth adequacy issue is that the degrees of freedom that the designer of the computer model exercises at two levels of language choice determine a great many outcomes as well as the economy and transparency of the model. One level of choice is representing language; for example, production systems, semantic nets, and scripts. This amounts to the further specification of the representing world. As with most global hypotheses, this one is the hardest to argue for, yet perhaps the most critical in terms of methodology and the structure of the data that can be represented. Moreover, given the enormous weight of its overhead and all the ramifications of altering it both for the project at hand and often for others, it carries a great deal of methodological momentum. The second level of choice is detailed specifications of the actual relationships among the formalisms of the chosen language, that is, the program. This amounts to the specification of the relations among the elements of the representing world. (The practical impact of language choice is described further in the next section.)

The sixth adequacy issue is that the profound linguistic bias of most computer models is based on (*a*) the propositional character of our observation-language (which is not necessarily due to the use of computer models, but which is reinforced by their use) and (*b*) the propositional character of most representation languages at both the program level and the output level—the programs are almost always given as linguistic lists of relations and actions, as are the machine "behaviors." This happens to be our best-developed mode of formal representation. Note, however, the case in mathematics where there are alternative modes of formal description which in turn embody entirely different kinds of information than do the discursive modes. For example, the propositions of Euclidean geometry amounted to an extended attempt to give geometric information in discursive form. Descartes' invention of geometric representations of algebraic entities and relations is perhaps a better example of how information content is sensitive to the formalisms in which it is couched. Another clear example is the great difference in the respective formalisms of rectangular versus polar coordinates in their ability to represent algebraic information. What is efficiently represented in one system is usually difficult to represent in the other. Other more contemporary examples include the various topologies and algebraic geometries whose *content* is "known" (by the mathematicians who work in those areas) in strictly nondiscursive ways (Hadamard, 1945; Hammond, 1978). The point is that computer formalisms have not yet developed such alternative representation systems, although computer graphics methods may provide the means before too long.

The seventh adequacy issue is the need for models to account for the fact that human competence and performance develop over a period of time as a consequence of specific experiences. Thus only a very limited form of explanatory adequacy is available from models that present temporal or developmental cross sections of phenomena without formal regard for their extended ontogenesis. An ideal model should include structures and procedures within its mechanisms that provide some kind of dynamic/historical account for the information available in the kind of "snapshot" that is given by, for example, a model of an individual solving a particular problem at a particular time.

The adequacy issues listed here have to do mainly with analytic adequacy, but the level-of-detail issue cuts across both empirical and analytic adequacy, and coupled with the choice of language is probably decisive in determining explanatory adequacy. Given the choice of language, adequacy ultimately rests on a sufficiently detailed empirically supported correspondence between the informal and formal models that can compensate for all the other shortcomings and difficulties that were listed. While it may be relatively easy to achieve correspondences between a formalism's "behavioral" concomitants and those of an informal model at a gross level of processing detail, it is much harder at the level of fine structure (Bower, 1978). It is even more difficult if one attempts to explain ontogenetic data in an explicit integral part of the model. However, given a detailed enough, principled, and empirically supported correspondence between model and organism, one has an explanation which is more than adequate—it can be extremely powerful, especially if it successfully *predicts* newly observable behaviors.

For problem-solving researchers concerned with computer models, the adequacy of the explanation entails deciding which aspects of mental representations are critical to understanding problem solving and whether these are adequately E-represented by the computer model and its theoretical framework. Both issues are far from settled.

The Critical Role of Representing Language

Any computer model of "naturally occurring" mental representations that I've seen seems to be a model of a very impoverished, skeletal cross section of a human representation system (and of a modal one at that) which ignores much more than it represents. But, of course, by their very nature and purpose formalisms underrepresent their referent phenomena, often by representing "ideal" phenomena—as with the "modal" subject. This is simultaneously the source of any formalism's explanatory power as well as its weakness. The key is to keep operational the realization that the correspondences between the computer and informal models of mental representations are manipulable hypotheses, and must be supported empirically and by careful argument as must any hypotheses. This is nothing more than the meaning of the word "science" in the phrase "cognitive science."

VanLehn (1983) describes in considerable detail the underlying choices that went into his computer model of student learning and performance in use of the standard subtraction algorithm. In so doing he gives testimony to the practical importance of the choice of representation language:

> *Getting the knowledge representation "right" allows the model to be made simple and to obey strong principles.*...The changes in the representation language were absolutely necessary for bringing the model into conformance with psychologically interesting principles. A typical scenario was to note a particularly ugly part of the model that could be simplified and made more elegant by changing the representation language; after the change was made, reflection on the new elegance of the model uncovered a principle that the model now con-

formed to. Hard on the heels of that insight would often come several more ideas, usually of the form that changing a component process of the model to take advantage of the new construct in the representation language would allow it also to become simpler and to obey a new principle. In short, the evolution of the principles of the theory went hand in hand with the evolution of the representation language. (pp. 249-50)

Language plays another subtle role in the evaluation of the explanatory adequacy of a given computer representation since the formalisms themselves are often given names based on earlier psychological or colloquial uses (e.g., ''schema,'' ''scripts''). The formalisms may thus be loaded with layers of meaning which may serve to disguise the paucity of a given representation's explanatory adequacy. After all, if the formalism is to function in an explanatory way, its effectiveness depends on the *formal* relationships among the formalisms and *not* on the extra meaning, which may have been bootlegged via their associated psychological connotations. This is an argument familiar to those who heard the behaviorism debates of the late sixties.

But there is more than a superficial parallel between behaviorist assumptions and computer simulation assumptions. The behaviorists insisted that one could have an essentially complete description of an organism via a ''neutral'' description of its externally observable behaviors and their regularities. If one argued that there were aspects of human experience that are not describable in this way (e.g., love, daydreams, linguistic competences), then they would counter with the argument that one's description was inadequate—it needs more detail and subtlety. The epistemological position of one who insists that humans are totally describable as information-processing systems (''programmed computer and human problem solver are both species belonging to the genus 'Information Processing System','' Newell & Simon, 1972, p. 870) is parallel—the only thing needed is enough detail. The difference is that now the detail concerns relations between hypothetical internal states and observable behaviors. This difference can be seen neatly by comparing behaviorist stimulus-response pairs with the condition-action pairs (which are a particular kind of production system) of one school of computer modeling (Anderson, 1980).

Stimulus-response pairs suffered from the fatal weaknesses of being highly specific and atomistic decompositions of externally observable phenomena and so were unable to account for (*a*) the general nature of most skills (cognitive and otherwise), (*b*) the contingencies of responses to whole patterns of stimuli rather than to individual stimuli, and, most importantly, (*c*) the fact that much behavior seems to be mediated by internal (not directly observable) sources. These weaknesses are answered directly by condition-action pairs, because these take the form of very general pairs, the first of which can be any kind of condition to be satisfied in order for the second item in the pair (an action) to be executed. The condition-action pair is, in fact, nothing more than an abstract formalism which had its roots in computer science. It was first introduced during the early forties in the area of mathematical combinatorics by Post (1943). However, it is used in computer models of procedural knowledge because the condition of a particular production system can be chosen to represent internal as well as external conditions to be satisfied, and the action can likewise represent either hypothesized internal phenomena or observable behavior. Furthermore, these pairs can be networked and sequenced in virtually any fashion as the modeler sees fit, thereby accounting for any constellation of ''conditions.'' In this way the operational weaknesses of stimulus-response pairs are overcome through the exercise of an enormous amount of freedom in assigning referents to the formalisms. On the other hand, one must face a whole host of difficulties as have already been outlined, ranging from the weak sufficiency problem to the choice of language problem (Why this particular formalism?), to the matter of bootlegged meanings (which require considerable diligence to isolate from the formal relationships among the pairs and the production systems themselves). For a detailed discussion of production systems as a modeling formalism see Davis and King (1977), and for a recent technical criticism see VanLehn (1983), especially p.226.

Of course, behaviorism died not because of the impossibility of gaining enough detail of the right type, but because of its explanatory inadequacy. The methodological value of computer modeling, including production systems, will be determined on the same ultimate grounds, although the level of detail the model is describing, in terms of what internal processes are mediating the observable behaviors, is likely to be critical. Another difference between the behaviorist and computer-modeling approaches concerns the role of formal descriptions in the latter and the resulting potential for prediction rather than the mere classification of behavioral regularities. Therefore, the importance of the choice of representing language is all the more important.

There is, however, another danger with computer formalisms—in our uncritical tendency to reify them and project their existence into the heads of the humans whose hypothetical mental representations are being formally modeled. This tendency is especially likely when much of the content of what is being represented (mentally and cybernetically) is itself a structured collection of formalisms and operations on them, as when mathematical or logical problem solving is being modeled. This encourages confusion regarding what is representing what. It is therefore important to require as much rigor as possible in terms of the definition of representation and the adequacy issues outlined earlier. It is also critical to maintain the ontological distinctions between the different formalisms (Feldman & Toulmin, 1976; Kaput, 1979).

None of this caution, however, prohibits one from hypothesizing that mental representations themselves "work" in computationally formal ways (Fodor, 1975, 1980; Hofstadter & Dennet, 1981—see especially Parts IV–VI for an entertaining view of the consequences of this and similar hypotheses; Pylyshyn, 1980). However, as a result of these assumptions some fairly deep issues arise which have practical as well as philosophic implications to be developed in the next subsection.

The Problem of Reference and Its Implications

We shall now look at a potentially important epistemological distinction between computer and human representation systems, particularly given the common tendency of researchers who use computer models as E-representations to ignore or disacknowledge that theirs are models of quasi-formal models of mental representations. The tendency to shortcut the route between A and Y in Figure 1 is the first step toward the reification/projection trap already mentioned. One of the points of the following discussion is to help keep apparent the differences among these models and the mental representations, all of which are embedded in a theory about mental representations. Maintaining this difference will also assist in outlining the limitations of current application of computer models.

Basically, the epistemological difference is that *the computer representation does not refer to the external world or to experiences of the external world the same way its designer did when writing its program*—if it can be said to refer to anything at all. Suppose the program is designed to output the best center in the National Basketball

Association (NBA) if asked the question, "Who is the best center in the NBA this year?" (Note the slipperiness of language here: we speak of "asking the computer a question" when in fact we send some electrical signals to a device which will change the internal states of the hardware which in turn sends an electrical signal to some other "output" device, which puts it in a form constructed to be readable by us. We likewise speak of the computer representations as "solving problems." Philosophers refer to this as the "slippery slope" problem in language use. See Stolzenberg, 1978, for an account of the "tug of language.") We read "Moses Malone" as the output. Now look again at Figure 1. The only sense in which the computer program refers to Moses Malone is via the composite of the three "represent" arrows leading to "world as experienced," or, if you are a certain kind of realist, via the quadruple composite leading to "world as experienced" (by the cognitive scientist) in the lower right side of the diagram. In either case the referential connection directly involves the cognitive scientist's or the programmer's representational activity. If we substitute ourselves for the cognitive scientist, then *we* supply the referential act. The program can "refer" only to itself or its different embodiments at different levels of language within its implementation.

Fodor (1980) uses Winograd's (1972) blocks-world simulated robot to make this point on the way to arguing a more elaborate view of the relation between mental representations and what they represent. He notes that Winograd's computer was programmed to respond to questions and commands regarding an environment of blocks which, in fact, did not exist because Winograd wanted to factor out the extraneous mechanical difficulties associated with building the required robot. As Fodor puts it, "the device is in precisely the situation that Descartes dreads; it's a mere computer which dreams that it's a robot" (p. 63).

The point is that a computer representation does not refer to anything in the world in the same sense that we do—unless we radically stretch the notion of reference, as some students of artificial intelligence have suggested. The matter of reference is of practical importance because it is commonly thought that the computer representation which "solves" a problem somehow refers to that problem in a way analogous to the way we or students refer to it. But, of course, if that problem refers to our wider world of experience, then the computer representation is impoverished compared to ours. Caveat emptor.

This issue of reference thus has a great deal to do with explanatory adequacy. Mental representations (A in Figure 1) represent the world as experienced by the subject, which even for very young subjects is a complicated world indeed, and its presumed mental representation via imagistic and linguistic representational systems is correspondingly complex and interconnected. (After all, only a fraction of a gram of protein in a honeybee's nervous system is able to encode a startlingly complex set of behaviors.) This complexity is evident if one looks at the history of linguistics or continuing attempts at cybernetic natural language comprehension.

Therefore, the heuristic use of computer representations seems to make current sense only in domains that are relatively self-contained and participate minimally in this "real-world" interconnectedness and complexity. Moreover, competence in such domains should have a relatively simple and independent ontogenesis so that the model can satisfy the ontogenetic criterion. Obvious candidates are areas of school instruction that deal with the learning of formal systems in isolation of wider experience, e.g., numerical or algebraic algorithms, certain types of computer programming, perhaps spelling, or aspects of formal geometry. Nonschool domains such as chess and other games are also sufficiently isolated to be manageable.

It should be clear that I believe that computer representation of much of school word-problem-solving activity is thus probably premature, at least in the sense of providing reliable insights into these activities at a level of detail and generality sufficient to enhance instruction. It seems that the success of the extended work done by the more successful teams using computer models of youngsters solving fairly simple arithmetic word problems, for example, has relatively little to do with the computer modeling and a great deal to do with the perspicacity and hard work of the researchers in building intuitively and empirically informed *informal* models. On the other hand, the Xerox PARC work of Brown, Burton, and VanLehn modeling the relatively isolated cognitive processes involved in learning and using the standard arithmetic subtraction algorithm (Brown & Burton, 1978; Brown & VanLehn, 1980; VanLehn, 1981, 1983) is stunning in its conceptual complexity—of the processes being modeled and the resultant complexity of the models themselves. The difference between this work and most of the other work with which I am familiar is the extent to which they are strict in adhering to the criteria for explanatory adequacy. They insist on a tight and very detailed correspondence among the data, their informal models, and the computer model. As seen in the earlier quote, VanLehn (1983) argues explicitly for the choice of language and formalisms and goes so far as to vary the representation language systematically in order to exhibit its effect. Further, the goal of his model is to embed the data in a coherent ontogenetic framework that accounts for the widest variety of observable phenomena in an optimally simple manner. The conceptual complexity of the supporting theory in such a narrow domain of application is a strong indicator of how impoverished computer models in other less restricted domains actually are. It is also an indicator of the true magnitude of the task of modeling mental representations in such domains.

Of course, there are dangers inherent in confining one's empirical and theoretical work to "nonnatural" learning domains to the exclusion of areas where learning takes place without deliberate instruction and is universally successful (e.g., natural language learning, visual and spatial processing). In fact, the systematic constraints and developmental invariants of one area may be entirely different from the other, as suggested by Keil (1981).

There is a compromise position for task domains intermediate to these extremes and which probably includes most tasks that researchers in mathematical problem solving regard as important. It amounts to the use of computational metaphors in informal models which are in turn closely tied to detailed empirical data of an extremely dense sort, whose density can be obtained currently only by detailed observation of individuals or interaction of small groups, often for extended periods. This position, advocated and exemplified so well by Davis (1980) and Davis, Jockusch, and McKnight (1978) comes closest to my position. However, I also advocate alternating this form of data gathering and model building with systematic studies of populations so as to account for systematic individual differences and developmental phenomena, which often can only be "seen" in aggregate form.

PHILOSOPHIC REFLECTIONS

As we have already noted, the differences between human and nonhuman information-processing systems on the matter of reference do not prohibit a computational theory of mind, nor do parallel problems having to do with consciousness or intentionality and computers (Searle, 1980). Such a computational theory is actually a refinement of the "information processing" view in cognitive psychology to include the hypothesis that not only do humans behave like formal information-processing systems, but also their internal representations of information and the processes that operate on them *do* compute as formal systems. Extremely capable people in psychology, philosophy, and artificial intelligence are devoting considerable interest and energy to the furtherance of such a theory and are gathering credibility and building consensus steadily. Moreover, the enormous difficulty of creating explanatory computer models does not dissuade researchers from the challenge. Why is this the case? They seem to have made a great leap of faith. But what are its foundations?

There is a deep sense in which the leap of faith to a computational theory of mind is analogous to the leap of faith made a few centuries ago in accepting Newton's representation of the physical universe. In several ways Newton's representation made sense: by connecting local and global phenomena (e.g., falling bodies and tides with planetary motion); in accounting for a disparate collection of phenomena; and so on. (One should not forget, however, that many of the implications were developed later over a period of centuries.) Nonetheless, there were nontrivial assumptions involved in the leap: for example, the notion of action at a distance and the idea of mass as a property of all matter. But it was also the case that these ideas fit into and then greatly enhanced a general mechanistic conceptual ecology that operated at all levels, both in and outside of science ("natural philosophy").

I believe that the current move to acceptance of a computational theory of mind is comparable in scope and analogous as a leap of faith to the Newtonian leap. It likewise fits into and greatly enhances an emerging conceptual ecology—which is no longer mechanistic in the old sense, but rather assumes that *information, structure, and process are real, are the primary ingredients of our world,* and *are the means by which we understand it*.

The epistemic gestalt has changed, and our epistemic self-portrait has likewise changed. This is the main reason why computer representations have become so popular as "explainers" at all levels, without strict regard to their true adequacy. It is also the reason why we need to be deliberate in holding these models to high standards of rigor in terms of the definition of representation and in terms of their explanatory adequacy. The models should be transparent and detailed, and their underlying choices, especially regarding representational language, must be fully argued.

That this is not easy and is not often done has already been pointed out. However, it amounts to experiencing at a concrete operational level all the recent observations in the philosophy of science about the interdependence of theory, language, and data; the evaporation of the authority of received knowledge and methodologies; and the multiplicity of the rational processes utilized in the acquisition of the reliable knowledge that we call "science"—or, in the case at hand, "cognitive science."

REFERENCES

Anderson, J.R. *Cognitive psychology and its implications.* San Francisco: W.H. Freeman, 1980.

Bower, G.H. Representing knowledge development. In R.S. Seigler (Ed.), *Children's thinking: What develops?* Hillsdale, NJ: Lawrence Erlbaum Associates, 1978.

Brown, J.S., & Burton, R.B. Diagnostic models for procedural bugs in basic mathematical skills. *Cognitive Science* 2, 155–92, 1978.

Brown, J.S., & VanLehn, K. Repair theory: A generative theory of bugs in procedural skills. *Cognitive Science* 4, 379–426, 1980.

Davis, R., & King, J. An overview of production systems. In E.W. Elcock & D. Michie (Eds.), *Machine intelligence: Machine representations of knowledge* (Vol. 8). New York: John Wiley & Sons, 1977.

Davis, R.B. The postulation of certain specific, explicit commonly held frames. *Journal of Mathematical Behavior* 3, 167–201, 1980.

Davis, R.B., Jockusch, E., & McKnight, C. Cognitive processes in learning algebra. *Journal of Children's Mathematical Behavior* 2, 10–320, 1978.

Feldman, C.F., & Toulmin, S. Logic and the theory of mind. In W.J. Arnold (Ed.), *Proceedings of the 1975 Nebraska Symposium on Motivation*. Lincoln: University of Nebraska Press, 1976.

Fodor, J.A. *The language of thought.* New York: Thomas Y. Crowell, 1975.

Fodor, J.A. Methodological solipsism considered as a research strategy in cognitive psychology. *Behavioral and Brain Sciences* 3, 63–110, 1980.

Gibson, J.J. *The ecological approach to visual perception.* Boston: Houghton Mifflin, 1979.

Grossberg, S. How does a brain build a cognitive code? *Psychological Review* 97, 1–51, 1980.

Hadamard, J. *The psychology of invention in the mathematical field.* Princeton, NJ: Princeton University Press, 1945.

Hammond, A.L. Mathematics—Our invisible culture. In L.A. Steen (Ed.), *Mathematics today: Twelve informal essays.* New York: Springer-Verlag, 1978.

Hempel, C. The theoretician's dilemma. *Aspects of scientific explanation.* New York: Harper & Row, 1965.

Hofstadter, D.R. *Godel, Escher, Bach: An eternal golden braid.* New York: Basic Books, 1980.

Hofstadter, D.R., & Dennet, D.C. *The mind's I: Fantasies and reflections on self and soul.* New York: Basic Books, 1981.

Kaput, J.J. Mathematics and learning: Roots of epistemological status. In J. Lochhead & J. Clement (Eds.), *Cognitive process instruction: Research on teaching thinking skills.* Philadelphia: The Franklin Institute Press, 1979.

Keil, F.C. Constraints on knowledge and cognitive development. *Psychological Review* 88, 197–227, 1981.

Kohler, W. *Gestalt psychology.* New York: Liveright, 1947.

Kosslyn, S.M. Imagery and cognitive development: A teleological approach. In R.S. Siegler (Ed.), *Children's thinking: What develops?* Hillsdale, NJ: Lawrence Erlbaum Associates, 1978.

Kosslyn, S.M. *Image and mind.* Cambridge, MA: Harvard University Press, 1980.

Langley, P., & Simon, H.A. The central role of learning in cognition. In J.R. Anderson (Ed.), *Cognitive skills and their acquisition.* Hillsdale, NJ: Lawrence Erlbaum Associates, 1981.

Minsky, M. (Ed.). *Semantic information processing.* Cambridge, MA: The MIT Press, 1968.

Newell, A., & Simon, H.A. *Human problem solving.* Englewood Cliffs, NJ: Prentice-Hall, 1972.

Palmer, S.E. Fundamental aspects of cognitive representation. In E. Rosch, & B.B. Lloyd (Eds.), *Cognition and categorization.* Hillsdale, NJ: Lawrence Erlbaum Associates, 1977.

Post, E. Formal reductions of the general combinatorial problem. *American Journal of Mathematics* 65, 197–268, 1943.

Putnam, H. The meaning of meaning. *Mind, language, and reality.* Cambridge: Cambridge University Press, 1975.

Pylyshyn, Z.W. What the mind's eye tells the mind's brain: A critique of mental imagery. *Psychological Bulletin* 80, 1–24, 1973.

Pylyshyn, Z.W. Validating computational models: A critique of Anderson's indeterminacy of representation claim. *Psychological Review* 86, 383–94, 1979.

Pylyshyn, Z.W. Computation and cognition: Issues in the foundations of cognitive science. *Behavioral and Brain Sciences* 3, 111–32, 1980.

Searle, J.R. Minds, brains, and programs. *Behavior and Brain Sciences* 3, 417–58, 1980.

Shapere, D. Towards a post-positivistic interpretation of science. In P. Achenstein & S. Barker (Eds.), *The legacy of logical positivism.* Baltimore: Johns Hopkins University Press, 1969.

Simon, H.A. Information-processing theory of human problem solving. In W.K. Estes (Ed.), *Handbook of learning and cognitive processes: Human information processing* (Vol. 5). Hillsdale, NJ: Lawrence Erlbaum Associates, 1978.

Sternberg, R.J. Criteria for intellectual skills training. *Educational Researcher* 12, 6–12, 26, 1983.

Stolzenberg, G. Can an inquiry into the foundations of mathematics tell us anything interesting about mind? In G.A. Miller & E. Lenneberg (Eds.), *Psychology and biology of language and thought.* New York: Academic Press, 1978.

Tarski, A. The concept of truth in formalised languages. In A. Tarski (Ed.), *Logic, semantics and metamathematics.* New York: Basic Books, 1951.

Toulmin, S. *Human understanding* (Vol.1). Princeton, NJ: Princeton University Press, 1972.

VanLehn, K. *Bugs are not enough: Empirical studies of bugs, impasses, and repairs in procedural skills* (Technical Report CIS-11). Palo Alto, CA: Xerox Palo Alto Research Center, 1981.

VanLehn, K. On the representation of procedures in repair theory. In H.P. Ginsburg (Ed.), *The development of mathematical thinking.* New York: Academic Press, 1983.

Weizenbaum, J. *Computer power and human reason.* San Francisco: Freeman Press, 1976.

Winograd, T. *Understanding natural language.* New York: Academic Press, 1972.

Winograd, T. Frame representations and the declarative-procedural controversy. In D.G. Bobrow & A.M. Collins (Eds.), *Representation and understanding: Studies in cognitive science.* New York: Academic Press, 1975.

Problem-Solving Derailers: The Influence of Misconceptions on Problem-Solving Performance

J. Michael Shaughnessy

Oregon State University

Several years ago Shulman and Elstein (1975) wrote a paper that compared models of problem solving, judgment, and decision making. Their purpose at that time was to highlight the importance of various models for research on teaching, where the teacher is considered as an information processor and a decision maker. Included in their literature review was a series of papers by Kahneman and Tversky which dealt with the subject of intuitive probabilistic estimates for the likelihood of events (Kahneman & Tversky, 1972, 1973a, 1973b, 1974; Tversky & Kahneman, 1971). This series of papers has largely been responsible for stimulating a decade of psychological research on people's intuitive use of probability to make judgments or decisions. Recent excellent summaries of the research on decision making are contained in a synthesis of the literature on human inference by Nisbett and Ross (1980) and in an anthology of papers on judgment under uncertainty (Kahneman, Slovic, & Tversky, 1982).

The psychologists in judgment and decision making have primarily been concerned with discovering the mechanisms for people's decision-making behavior in probabilistic situations, and in pointing out the role that these mechanisms can play in risky decisions made by consumers, employers, government officials, and political interest groups (Fischhoff, Slovic, & Lichtenstein, 1981; La Breque, 1980; Slovic, Fischhoff, & Lichtenstein, 1980).

This body of research raises some interesting questions for research on the teaching of problem solving. First, these psychological researchers have expended a great deal of time and effort trying to understand *why people fail* at inferential tasks. Thus they have uncovered some information which may be useful to researchers who are trying to understand why people fail at problem-solving tasks in general. Second, researchers in judgment and decision making have explored one particular area of problem solving in great detail, stochastic problem solving in probability and statistics. This is an area that is not frequently dealt with in this country in mathematics education, although it is of major concern in Europe and Asia (Beyth-Maron & Dekel, 1983; Scholtz, 1981; Shaughnessy, 1982).

399

Among the questions that come to mind are (*1*) What are some of the reasons why people fail at problem-solving tasks, and what can the literature on misconceptions of probability add to our understanding of faulty solution processes? and (*2*) Can research on misconceptions of probability and statistics help to clarify and improve the *teaching* of problem solving in general?

The psychologists have predominantly been concerned with analyzing why people are inept at making probabilistic inferences, and so have not often addressed the second question, the problem of improving people's problem-solving abilities through instruction. On the other hand, mathematics educators often concentrate on what people "do right" when solving problems. A better understanding of what people "do wrong" may shed some light on how teachers can enhance the problem solving of their students. Researchers in the teaching of problem solving need to carefully analyze the reasons for people's failure at problem-solving tasks in order to anticipate and overcome those potential failures when they build problem-solving models or develop instructional materials. Why, then, has a closer look at problem solving in probability and statistics largely been neglected when so many things can "go wrong" in inferential tasks?

In this paper we will first explore some of the reasons for people's failure to solve problems, problem-solving "derailers" so to speak, and investigate the role of probabilistic misconceptions as one possible derailer. Second, we will consider the implications of what can "go wrong" when we solve problems for research on the teaching of problem solving. Since the research in misconceptions is within content-dependent domains, such as physics, statistics and probability, this paper is primarily concerned with the teaching of problem solving to secondary students and college students, although there are implications for younger subjects as well.

PROBLEM-SOLVING DERAILERS

Prior to recent attempts of problem-solving researchers in mathematics education to explore processes and build models, the most common reason given by mathematicians for their students' failures to solve problems was "They just don't know enough." One can still hear this conversation echoing through the halls of most college mathematics departments. However, research in problem solving has helped to unveil and clarify the complexity behind this simple statement. For example, the word "misconceptions" has frequently been used as an umbrella for a myriad of problem-solving illnesses. Perhaps at the end of this section, our colleagues may still be tempted to say, "Yeah, that's what I mean, they just don't know enough! They have all sorts of misconceptions." In spite of that hazard, let us attempt to analyze a bit more carefully some of the reasons why things "go wrong" for our students when they attempt to solve problems. Perhaps the discussion can best be initiated by presenting some problems and typical responses.

Problem 1: Suppose that we have a quadrilateral with both pairs of opposite sides congruent. Are the opposite sides parallel? Why?

The most frequent answers obtained from high school geometry students at the *end* of a geometry course were "Of course they are, because I can't draw them any other way," and "Yes, because if the opposite sides are parallel, then they must be congruent" (Burger, Hoffer, & Shaughnessy, 1984).

Problem 2: You know that the average math SAT score in a large school system is 400. You randomly select five students from this population. The first four students in your sample have scores of 380, 420, 400, and 600. What would you expect the fifth student's score to be?

The correct answer is 400. Many college students solve for the missing score, 200, which will yield 400 as the sample mean (Pollatsek, Lima, & Well, 1981). Silver and I have presented this problem to college senior *mathematics majors* in the middle of a course on probability and statistics, and have obtained the same results as Pollatsek did with nonmajors.

Problem 3: Suppose that a person walks in a straight line past a point light source, say, a street lamp. What is the path traced out by the top of the person's shadow?

Most people, including mathematics graduate students, erroneously believe that the shadow traces out some sort of curve like a parabola or a hyperbola.

Problem 4: About one half of the babies born in the world are boys. Are there more days during the year when at least 60% of the babies born are boys (*A*) in a large hospital, (*B*) in a small hospital, or (*C*) it makes no difference if it's a large hospital or a small hospital?

College students overwhelmingly choose response *C* when asked this question (Kahneman & Tversky, 1972; Shaughnessy, 1977), neglecting the effects of sample size upon the likelihood of the event.

Each of these problems points out a different way in which a solution attempt can go astray. Let's consider some potential problem-solving derailers in more detail, and in doing so take a closer look at the problems above as well as some other problems.

Lack of Appropriate Knowledge Structure or Knowledge Organization

Recent papers by Mayer (1982) and Silver (1982) point out some of the types of knowledge that are necessary conditions for successful problem solving. Mayer singles out four types of knowledge. In order to solve problems, we must not only know something about the content arena of our problem (linguistic and factual), but also have a store of problem types (schematic), an arsenal of computational procedures (algorithmic), and facility for when to apply procedures and how to represent our problems (strategic). Silver reflects on the organization of knowledge base and possible influences upon the organization, such as belief in an underlying structure of mathematics. Perhaps it is a lack of *structural knowledge* that prevents most high school geometry students from even attempting some sort of proof on Problem 1. The students were asked, if opposite sides were parallel, must they be congruent. The responses were either totally visual, "I can't draw it any other way," or they exhibited faulty "converse" reasoning, interchanging the hypothesis and the conclusion. Yet these students had had an entire year of geometry. The visual responses indicate that the students didn't even approach the question as a logico-deductive one, or that they simply reduced their level of thinking about geometric concepts to a visual level. Those students who exhibited "converse" reasoning do not understand logico-structural "ground rules."

This tendency for the students to interchange the role of necessary and sufficient conditions occurs frequently in Burger's (1982) interview procedure. In the activity called What's My Shape?, a series of clues about a quadrilateral are revealed one at a time to the students (see Appendix A). At each clue, the student either asks for another clue, or stops the interviewer when he or she has just enough information to determine the shape for certain. Most students use the clues as *necessary* rather than *sufficient* conditions. They approach the task with a shape in mind, and try to fit the clues to their shape. As long as their shape has the properties revealed so far, it must be correct. Of course, the students are quite surprised when a clue is revealed that torpedoes their hypothesized shape.

Johnson-Laird and Wason (1977) studied people's reasoning processes on deductive tasks and also found that their subjects did not understand the difference between necessary and sufficient conditions. Subjects exhibited the same sort of "converse" reasoning as in Burger's study, interchanging the hypothesis and the conclusion. Johnson-Laird and Wason note that performance on such deductive tasks can be improved dramatically if the task relates closely to a subject's experience.

We might add *logico-structural* knowledge to Mayer's list of types that are necessary for problem solving. At least there are certain kinds of problems, especially in mathematics, for which this type of knowledge would seem crucial. Without it, students may only be able to think about some mathematical concepts at a *preconceptual* stage. For example, logico-structural knowledge is required in order to define the concept of rectangle. At a preconceptual level, a student may only think of a rectangle as a "bundle of properties," a list of necessary conditions. The logico-structural knowledge helps a student to refine the "bundle of properties" into necessary and sufficient conditions for a definition of rectangle.

Algorithmic Bugs

Computational errors are responsible for some problem-solving failures, but more importantly, *systematic* computational errors can provide a barrier to successful problem solving, usually near the end of the process at that. This is quite frustrating for our students. The diagnostic procedures discussed by Brown and Burton (1978) provide a mechanism for analyzing and discovering systematic computational errors, false algorithms.

The idea of diagnosing algorithmic bugs provided some of the motivation for this paper. If we attempt to diagnose *problem-solving bugs*, reasons for failures on problems, perhaps we can better understand which sorts of problem-solving tasks are likely to elicit certain sorts of problem-solving bugs under certain conditions.

Lack of Problem-Solving Strategies

We have all encountered students who when confronted with a problem say, "I just don't know where to begin." Clearly one necessary condition for successful problem solving is an adequate supply of problem-solving strategies, and knowledge of when to apply them (and when *not* to). Schoenfeld (1980), among others, strongly advocates teaching problem-solving strategies like any other part of mathematics, and teaching a *small* number of them. The emphasis should be on *explicit* instruction in the use of particular strategies—say, look for a pattern, try a simpler problem, recall a similar problem—and on using them to develop good approaches to problems. The problems should be selected in order to "trigger" the use of a particular strategy.

While the first three problem-solving derailers discussed above are predominantly cognitive, the remainder of our list contains examples that are either metacognitive or at least possess a metacognitive component. Metacognition has been receiving increased attention over the past several years (Lester & Garofalo, 1982; Silver, Branca, & Adams, 1980) from researchers in mathematics education.

Relinquished Executive Control

Schoenfeld (1981) has reported instances in protocols of college students where the problem solvers made a disastrous decision at the planning stage of a problem, and thereby never got anywhere on the solution. These students were very knowledgeable in the content and were instructed in problem-solving strategies, but they made a "bad" decision. Unless we point out to our students the importance of monitoring their own planning behavior (Is this a reasonable approach? Am I getting too far away from the original question? etc.), they may get their solution process rolling like a freight train and then run out of track. Perhaps explicit instruction on monitoring one's processes while solving problems would help reduce the tendency for students to relinquish executive control.

Belief System

People's confidence in themselves as problem solvers, or their beliefs and feelings about the nature of mathematics—its inherent structure or lack of structure—can exert a strong prohibitive force on their ability to solve or even initially attack problems in a productive way.

Recent attitudinal research reported by Haladyna, Shaughnessy, and Shaughnessy (1983) points out the predominance of "fatalism" in mathematics classrooms that surfaces in junior high school years and persists throughout secondary mathematics classrooms. Many students really feel that they are "not in control" when they work mathematics problems. Something or somebody else pulls all the strings. It is possible that their fatalistic locus of control phenomena is at first a symptom of cognitive deficiency in problem-solving skills. However, after a continual lack of successful experiences in mathematics, our students actually *believe* that they cannot solve problems, and then we are confronted with a formidable affective barrier to problem-solving success. Models of problem solving, which have heretofore been predominantly cognitive models, must also consider the affective attributes of the problem-solving process.

Perhaps the importance of belief systems in problem solving is most evident when students are asked to solve stochastic problems in probability and statistics. Well, Pollatsek, and Konold (1983) report some interesting examples of beliefs which surfaced in protocols of the following problem. This problem, called the Taxi-Cab Problem (for obvious reasons) has been thoroughly studied by psychologists (Ajzen, 1977; Bar-Hillel, 1980; Kahneman & Tversky, 1973; Tversky & Kahneman, 1980).

Problem 5: A cab was involved in a hit-and-run accident at night. Two cab companies, the Green and the Blue, operate in the city. You are given the following data:

1.   85% of the cabs in the city are Green and 15% are Blue.

2. A witness identified the cab as a Blue cab. The court tested his ability to identify cabs under appropriate visibility conditions. When presented with a sample of cabs (half of which were Blue and half of which were Green), the witness made correct identifications in 80% of the cases and erred in 20% of the cases.

Question: What is the probability that the cab involved in the accident was Blue rather than Green?

This problem has been administered to subjects with probability backgrounds ranging from complete naivete through senior-math-major-probability-course credentials. There have been many variations of the problem.

Well et al. (1983) report that a number of students said that the probability that it was a Blue cab was 100%. When asked why, some students said they "just believed it was a Blue cab." Other students said, "Oh, the witness was right. It was a Blue cab." Well and his colleagues have investigated conceptions of probability for several years and have amassed protocol evidence which indicates that many people just don't "believe" in probability. For example, Konold (1983) carried out extensive interviews with 16 college students on three problems, the Weather Problem, the Misfortune Problem, and the Bone Problem (see Appendix B). The study was conducted to explore the students' conceptions of probability. Konold concludes that the students interpret probability questions as requests for *single outcome* predictions. As a result, students predict outcomes from preconceived causes, or from personal beliefs. In the Bone Problem, the subject is shown a six-sided "bone" (irregular polyhedron) and asked to predict which side is most likely to turn up. Konold found subjects who tenaciously held to their own beliefs about which side would most likely occur, even when confronted with frequency data from 1,000 rolls of the bone which contradicted their belief (see Appendix C for an example).

For many students, the only mathematical models are deterministic models, the only types of problems one solves are deterministic problems, and there is no such thing as "maybe" or a confidence interval. Of course, this is not so surprising if we reflect upon the overemphasis on deterministic scientific models in mathematics and science courses in our schools (Fischbein, 1976).

Folklore Paradigms

At times, existing "conventional wisdom" can present a barrier to successful problem solving. In a report on people's internal representations of the physical world, McCloskey, Caramazza, and Green (1980) report that students in physics courses believe "laws" of motion that are at a variance with physical reality. If a ball is passed through a curved tube, many people believe it will exit the other end of the tube and continue on the same curved path indefinitely in the absence of other forces. This particular paradigm of physical motion was popular in the middle ages before the birth of Newtonian physics and prior to Kepler. It implies that when mud flies off a rotating automobile tire it travels in a circle. Another example of a folklore paradigm is what Tversky and Kahneman call belief in the Law of Small Numbers (1971). According to this paradigm, a very small number of trials will yield results that are representative of a large sample or of long-run behavior. Thus even short runs of coin tosses should "appear" random. Even researchers skilled in probability and statistics are susceptible to the Law of Small Numbers when they jeopardize their research hypotheses with studies based on inordinately small samples.

Physical phenomena seem particularly susceptible to the generation of folklore paradigms. We have already noted the motion study of McCloskey et al. Consider, once again, the Light Source Problem (Problem 3) raised earlier in the paper. Most people conjecture that the tip of the shadow must move past the light source in a curved path. This solution is probably triggered by some sort of perceptual illusion acquired by watching our own shadow. If students work in pairs and actually trace the tip of their shadow, they are surprised to find a straight-line solution. Some *still* don't believe it. A different representation of this problem can make the solution apparent. When asked what path is traced by the top of a shadow from a straight-line fence, many students correctly respond "a straight line," and then say "Oh!"

We might call a belief that has been allowed to grow unchallenged and unchecked to the point where it becomes a popularized theory a folklore paradigm. Folklore paradigms provide a stock response, and so may prevent a person from even recognizing that there actually is a problem to be solved at all.

Inadequate Problem Representations and Ill-Chosen Schema

Lester (1982) points out that the way a problem is represented affects the solver's level of understanding, a stage that, according to Lester, is often neglected because of the emphasis upon planning and solving behaviors in our instruction. Representing really means *re*-presenting, and clearly the Light Source Problem (for example) becomes more tractable when it is *re*-presented in terms of the fence.

Representations of problems are sometimes predetermined by the firing (or misfiring) of schema. Let's reconsider another of the problems presented earlier. In the problem of the expected SAT score (Problem 2), Pollatsek et al. (1981) reported that most college students set up an equation and solved for the value of the missing score (200), which together with the four known scores (380, 420, 400, 600) would force the sample average to be the same as the population mean, namely 400. I have presented this same problem to a class of 13 prospective secondary teachers, college mathematics majors, in the middle of their course on probability and statistics, prior to a discussion of the mean. One student correctly said that you could only expect the population mean, 400, for the fifth score. Three students were confused and guessed "less than 400," and the other nine classified the problem with the same algebra schema as Pollatsek's college freshmen. Two weeks later the same class was given two tasks. In task 1, the students were given the standard algebra problem: "You sample 5 scores. You know that the *sample average* is 400. Four of the scores are 380, 420, 600, and 400. What is the fifth score? Explain why." The second task was exactly the same as the question administered 2 weeks earlier, "What would you *expect* for the fifth score?" Would they see any difference between the two tasks? Four of the nine students who used the algebra schema the first week changed their responses on task 2 to 400 and gave correct statistical reasons for their answers. The other five people saw no difference in the two questions, and calculated 200 for *both* problems. The questions were then used as a teaching device in class to explicitly point out the differences in the two problems.

There are several possible explanations for these responses. Students might not understand what "random" means. Or they might not view the problem in a stochastic setting, and so they apply a deterministic model. Another possibility is that the original problem solicits an algebra schema, because it is "so much like problems in algebra we have done before." Schema are in some sense the software of our "similar problem" heuristic. We can go astray in solving problems by *over-generalizing* a similar problem strategy. In such cases, nonroutine problems may appear to be routine because they seem to fit nicely into some familiar schematic mold. Thus, the somewhat nonroutine problem of recognizing the population mean as an estimating parameter is translated as a routine exercise in algebra.

Evidence of the need for *flexible* representations is discussed by Silver (1983). Many students may be hampered in problem solving (and computation as well) that involves rational numbers because they have only one dominant interpretation of rational numbers, as part-of-a-whole. The level of our understanding may depend not only on having at least one representation for a problem, but also on our facility for admitting and analyzing *various* representations. Consider, for example, the following problem:

> *Problem 6*: In how many different ways can three people sit in ten chairs in a straight line at a lunch counter so that no two of them sit in adjacent seats?

Discussions with students and colleagues on this problem have led to a rich variety of problem representations. For example, we could systemtically begin a list and look for a pattern; thus this problem could be represented as a special case of some pattern. Or perhaps one would attempt to count the number of adjacencies and subtract these from all possible seatings (for which there is a "formula"). In this approach, one calls upon a schema that doesn't quite work, and then tries to modify it for the occasion. Another possibility is to first seat the people in three chairs, and then begin to arrange the empty chairs around them. This approach provides a completely different representation.

Improvement of problem representation skills in our students will require explicit discussions of various approaches to problems, and attempts to tie different solutions together. Likewise, we will have to carefully identify for our students those cues in a problem that make the use of schematic knowledge appropriate, and then provide instances where overgeneralization of a schema is inappropriate, as in the SAT Score Problem.

Misconceptions Arising From Reliance Upon Intuitive Heuristics

The research cited at the beginning of this paper has discovered that some of people's misconceptions of probability and statistics are the result of intuitive heuristics used to make inferential estimates (Kahneman & Tversky, 1972, 1973a, 1973b, 1974). Consider, for example, the Hospital Problem (Problem 4). Statistically naive college students choose "It makes no difference if it's a large or small hospital" by a very wide margin over the other two choices. Apparently they feel the percentage of boys should be about the same each day, regardless of the hospital size. Thus, the event is perceived as "representative" of the parent population no matter what the sample size. It is more likely to have 60% boys in the smaller hospital, with fewer babies each day.

I have found that even third- and fourth-year college mathematics majors in a course on probability and statistics tend to neglect the effects of sample size in the hospital problem. "Representativeness" can account for neglect of sample size, failure to attend to base-rate, failure to account for regression, and failure to attend to the quality—even the validity—of evidence when either naive people or "experts" make inferences (Fischhoff et al., 1981; Tversky & Kahneman, 1971).

In addition to this representativeness heuristic, people judge the likelihood of events by how easily they can be recalled from their own experiences, by their "availability." Misuse of this heuristic can lead to strong inferential bias; for example, a person might judge the accident rate or divorce rate for a city to be much higher than it really is if he recently witnessed several accidents or if a number of his acquaintances were divorced.

The existence of such heuristics certainly poses added challenges to instructors of probability and statistics (Shaughnessy, 1981). Attempts have been made to sequence activities in probability and statistics so as to expose intuitive heuristics and point out their limitations to students (Beyth-Maron & Dekel, 1983; Shaughnessy, 1977), and also to analyze the interplay of psychology and mathematics education for teaching probability and statistics (Shaughnessy, 1983).

Misapplication of intuitive heuristics poses another barrier to successful problem solving. These heuristics are another example of the *over-generalization* of the similar problem strategy. People judge likelihoods by how similar they are to other problems or other situations in which they have been before. Certainly, this is an important skill to have and often will lead to good estimates or reasonable inferences. There is, in fact, considerable conceptual and experiential support for the use of such heuristics. If we've been mugged on Lime Street, we're not going to go back there again. If a 3-4 pass rush allows Dan Fouts to complete 80% of his passes, there is a potential inference about the defensive alignment. The challenge to teaching problem solving is to help students recognize when the application of such heuristics is appropriate and when it is misleading, and even dangerous, such as in judging risks (Fischhoff et al., 1981). These intuitive heuristics appear to be highly resistant to change, perhaps because they have a metacognitive as well as a cognitive component. People actually *believe* that the man with glasses and a calculator strapped to his belt is an engineer, not a historian, even when they are told that the sample contains 70% historians and the man was randomly chosen (neglect of base-rate data, Kahneman & Tversky, 1972).

RESEARCH ISSUES

One of the purposes of this paper is to address the question: What implications does the literature on misconceptions of probability and statistics have for research on teaching problem solving? The use of intuitive inferential heuristics has been discussed as one of several possible problem-solving derailers, reasons why people may fail to successfully solve or even attack a problem. However, I would also like to point out several issues for research on the teaching of problem solving that seem particularly prominent when one surveys the research on probabilistic problem solving and on decision making.

Strong Influence of Beliefs

Problem-solving researchers have worried that people's beliefs can affect their problem-solving ability. Problems in probability and statistics provide excellent examples for researchers to examine belief systems more closely (Well et al., 1983). Thus, the influences of beliefs upon inferences can be made *explicit* to students. It is also apparent that part of teaching problem solving involves helping to make students aware of their own metacognitive processes. Problems dealing with probabilistic misconceptions can provide an inroad for investigating and monitoring belief systems in our students.

Need for Flexible Representation

Probabilistic problems may also help students to develop alternative models for representing a problem situation. The overemphasis in our schools upon deterministic models, in which there is a *definite* answer to a problem, may prevent students from recognizing a probabilistic problem situation. Thus, for example, students feel there must be a definitive answer to the Taxi-Cab Problem. Either it was a Blue cab, or it wasn't. Either the witness was correct, or he wasn't. There can be no such thing as a confidence interval for students who only see the world through deterministic eyes.

Overgeneralization Phenomenon

We have noted a strong tendency for people to look for similar problems and to push this strategy too far. This phenomenon appears under many different guises. Schemata are accessed from memory, triggered by cues that are inappropriate for the problem (the SAT Problem). Conventional wisdom sources nourish the creation of folklore paradigms, "stock answer" responses that people make when they overgeneralize the behavior of physical phenomena. Misconceptions of probability and statistics are the result of overgeneralizing intuitive heuristic strategies of inference. Thus it is important, particularly for probabilistic problem solving, that students learn the "boundaries" of the similar problem strategy and learn to critique its appropriateness in a given situation. They must learn to question stock responses and intuitive estimates and examine them for the possible overgeneralization of techniques that do not apply. It is perhaps in this area that concept-learning literature is most applicable to problem solving (Shumway, 1982). To teach a concept, it is necessary to point out nonexamples as well as examples so that students can filter out irrelevant features. In order to teach the limits of a problem-solving strategy, say the similar problem strategy, we have to outline more clearly the boundaries of the strategy, delineating appropriate and inappropriate applications through examples of particular problems.

Need to Make Reasons for Failure Explicit

An underlying message from research on each of the problem-solving derailers mentioned in this paper has been to make the potential reasons for solution failures explicit in our courses. Teach strategies explicitly (Schoenfeld, 1980); help make students aware of their metacognitive processes (Silver et al., 1980); carefully sequence activities to develop structural knowledge and point out preconceptual limitations (Burger et al., 1983); openly confront students' intuitive beliefs and heuristics (Shaughnessy, 1977). Thus, it seems that teaching the things that good problem solvers "do right" is not sufficient to develop good problem-solving ability. We may also have to *explicitly* point out what can go wrong and try to overcome it.

DISCUSSION

Problems from probability and statistics trigger a rich variety of problem-solving derailers. Deterministic schema interfere; people's beliefs readily surface; intuitive heuristics lead one down the garden path; folklore paradigms abound (Law of Small Numbers, the Gambler's Fallacy); inadequate representations of problems lead to false conclusions (Schrage, 1980). Yet problems from probability and statistics have not been used very often by researchers in the teaching of problem solving. This is somewhat understandable with younger subjects, who might not have an adequate mathematics background to tackle such problems. However, studies of problem solving that examine probabilistic tasks have also been conspicuously absent among adolescents and older subjects. Let's consider some possible reasons for this void.

First, these problems may just seem "too messy" for problem-solving research, because they can unearth all sorts of beliefs, values, and intuitions. How does one write a computer program to simulate the messy heuristic strategies and deterministic beliefs that appear in solutions of the Taxi-Cab Problem by humans? Indeed, most of the current models of problem solving are concerned with cognitive processes and do not adequately deal with such unpredictable metacognitive components as may appear in an inference problem.

Second, it is often hard enough just to model the cognitive components of some probabilistic problems. There may be different representations of a problem leading to several reasonable but conflicting solutions (Bar-Hillel & Falk, 1982), only one of which is really "correct." The rules of probabilistic modeling are not as fixed in cement as they are for other types of problems.

Third, psychological research on probabilistic problems has generally posed tasks to subjects so that it seems that there is *an opinion to be rendered* rather than *a problem to be solved*. Thus, the merging of decision and judgment models with problem-solving models (suggested by Shulman & Elstein, 1975) has not yet occurred in research on decision making. The recent work by Well et al. (1983) is an exception which analyzes student verbal protocols on inferential tasks and explores students' problem-solving strategies.

As a result, it is easy for research on the teaching of problem solving to avoid probabilistic problems. It is simpler to consider them as "special weird cases" and to build clear-cut models for problem solving which are satisfactory for deterministic problems. There are several reasons why this state of affairs should not continue.

The first reason is that *probabilistic tasks demand problem formulation*. If people react to probability tasks as opinions to be rendered rather than as problems to be solved, it may be because they have not noticed that there *is* a problem in the first place. Many inferential tasks are couched within a *problem situation* unaccompanied by a clearly stated, well-posed problem (see the Hospital Problem, for example). It is up to the subject to formulate a well-defined problem from this problem situation. This stage of problem formulation is often neglected in research on problem solving. Probabilistic problems can provide a rich variety of problem situations to help develop students' ability to pose problems.

The second reason is that *metacognitive aspects are brought into sharp focus in problems involving probability and statistics*. We have already discussed in detail the kinds of beliefs, intuitions, and heuristics that people bring to bear upon problems from probability and statistics.

The third reason is that *stochastic problems are good examples of applied problems*. Recent concern over the lack of research on applied problem-solving processes (Lesh, 1981) can be addressed through problems in probability and statistics. Data gathering, data organization, and data analysis are crucial steps in the formulation and solution of many applied problems. In fact, the "solution" to many applied problems requires a probability estimate or a best choice based on available data; a judgment, in other words.

The fourth reason is that *lack of experience with inferential problems may deprive solvers of a powerful technique*. Simon speaks of the need to arm our students with a few powerful techniques as well as ways to represent large amounts of knowledge (1980). These techniques play a particularly important role when a person is investigating an area outside of his own expertise. One powerful problem-solving technique that is overlooked is simulation of an experiment. This strategy seldom occurs on anyone's list of top problem-solving strategies that should be taught. Yet it is exactly this strategy that elevates a whole range of inferential tasks from the level of opinion rendering to the level of problem posing and solving, and allows even mathematically inexperienced problem solvers to gather and analyze data. A simulation *is* a *re*-presentation of the problem.

Probabilistic problems provide an excellent source for examining most of the facets of problem solving that are of current concern to researchers, including knowledge representations, beliefs, strategies, intuitive heuristics, applications, and feelings. There is a challenging mixture of cognitive and metacognitive processes that take place in naive, as well as expert, attempts to solve inferential tasks. Many of the causes of people's failure in problem-solving tasks occur *explicitly* during their attempts to attack problems in probability and statistics. For these reasons we believe there is much to be gained from studying the implications of probabilistic problem solving for general problem solving.

APPENDIX A

What's My Shape?
(Shape B)

1. It is a closed figure with 4 straight lines.

2. It has 2 long sides and 2 short sides.

3. It has a right angle.

4. The 2 long sides are parallel.

5. It has 2 right angles.

6. The 2 long sides are not the same length.

7. The 2 short sides are not the same length.

8. The 2 short sides are not parallel.

9. The 2 long sides make right angles with one of the short sides.

10. It has only 2 right angles.

APPENDIX B

Weather Problem. What does it mean when a weather forecaster says that tomorrow there is a 70% chance of rain? What does the number, in this case the 70%, tell you? How do they arrive at a specific number?

Suppose the forecaster said that there was a 70% chance of rain tomorrow and, in fact, it didn't rain. What would you conclude about the statement that there was a 70% chance of rain?

Suppose you wanted to find out how good a particular forecaster's predicting was. You observed what happened on 10 days for which a 70% chance of rain had been reported. On 3 of those 10 days there was no rain. What would you conclude about the accuracy of this forecaster? If he had been perfectly accurate, what would have happened? What should have been predicted on the days it didn't rain? With what percent chance?

Numbers are often assigned to various events like elections, sporting events, and causes of death. For example, you might hear something like "A person's chances of dying before the age of 40 are 25%." What does the 25% tell you? Or you might hear "The Equal Rights Amendment has a 25% chance of being ratified by the June 1982 deadline." What does the 25% in this case tell you?

Misfortune Problem. I know a person to whom all of the following things happened on the same day. First, his son totaled the family car and was seriously injured. Next, he was late for work and nearly got fired. In the afternoon he got food poisoning at a fast-food restaurant. Then in the evening he got word that his father had died. How would you account for all these things happening on the same day? Have you ever had something very unlikely happen to you? To someone you know? How do you make sense of a day when everything seems to go wrong?

Bone Problem. I have here a bone that has six surfaces. I've written the letters A through F, one on each surface. (Subject is handed the bone which is labeled A, B, C, and D on the surfaces around the long axis, and E and F on the two surfaces at the ends of the long axis.) If you were to roll that, which side do you think would most likely land upright? How likely is it that x will land upright? (Subject is asked to roll the bone to see what happens.) What do you conclude about your prediction? What do you conclude having rolled the bone once? Would rolling the bone more times help you conclude which side is most likely to land upright?

(Subject is asked to roll the bone as many times as desired.) What do you conclude having rolled the bone several times? How many times would you want to roll the bone before you were absolutely confident about which side is most likely to land upright?

One day I got ambitious and rolled the bone 1,000 times and recorded the results. This is what I got. (Subject is handed the list which showed A-50, B-279, C-244, D-375, E-52, F-0.) What do you conclude looking at these? Would you be willing to conclude that D is more likely than B? That B is more likely than C? That E is more likely than A? If asked what the chance was of rolling a D, what would you say?

I'm going to ask you to roll the bone ten times, but before you do, predict how many of each side you will get. How did you arrive at those specific values? (Subject rolls the bone and notes the results of each trial on the sheet of paper.) After the eighth trial the subject is asked: How do you feel about your predictions? If you were going to roll the bone ten more times, what would you predict that you would get?

APPENDIX C

The response of Subject 12 to the Bone Problem provides the most extreme example of someone maintaining a belief based on the physical properties of the bone, despite frequency data that runs contrary to her belief.

I: If you were to roll that, which side do you think would land upright?

S12:   I think B would be up ... D looks like it has four fairly flat corners. Then I could be totally wrong.

I: How likely is it that B will come up?

S12:   I'd give it about a 75 % chance. [Rolls a B.] Ha. What do you know.

I: What do you conclude about your prediction?

S12:   I guess my reasoning is somewhere on the ball. I think if you inspect things you can understand them, or if you question things, you can understand them better if you just go ahead and make some free decision about something.

I: What do you conclude from having rolled it once?

S12:   That my prediction was just about on the nose.

I: Would rolling it more help you decide which side was most likely?

S12:   I don't know. I'm pretty sure about my prediction. But just for the fun of it I could do it—you know, just curiosity sake. [Rolls D.] Uh-oh.

I: "Uh-oh" what?

S12:   It landed on the opposite side.

I: So what does that make you think?

S12:   That there's more than one possible answer to something—to this problem. [Rolls D, C.] Oh. Well, I'm getting a little frustrated. 'Cause when you first get something right you're really happy about it ... But then when it turns out another way, well, that's OK too. But it starts to make you a little shaky. Now that this has happened—the third C—well, I'm beginning to think this rock is quite equal all around.

I: So by "equal all around," what do you mean?

S12:   That it could be stable landing on any of the sides. It's just a matter of, sort of, chance, maybe.

I: Any idea of which side is most likely to come up? Or is there one that is more likely than the others?

S12:   Well, I think D, C, or B are more likely than E or F. Then I could be wrong.

I: That's on the basis of—How do you know that?

S12:   Well, E and F have less of a mass around them. [Rolls C, D, B, B.] Yeah. I think I'll go along with that last statement.

I: D, C, or B?

S12:   Yeah.

I: And do you think one of these—D, C, or B—is more likely than the other two?

S12:   Yeah. C.

I: Why?

S12: I don't know. The top part—it looks more stable because it's like a pyramid shape. The bottom is very thick and long . . . It has all that base under it.

I: Would rolling that a lot more times help you, in any way, decide which side was most likely to come up—whether C was most likely?

S12: I don't think so. [Refers to data from 1,000 rolls.] So D you found most likely.

I: Would you feel safe in concluding looking at this that D is, in fact, more likely than B?

S12: I don't know. Not really. I think it could just have something to do with your luck, or your chance. If I did the same number of rolls, I don't know if it would come out the same.

I: What is your belief about which side is most likely to come up if you rolled it?

S12: I have to look at this again. It changed shape in the past few minutes. [Inspects bone.] I still think C.

REFERENCES

Ajzen, I. Intuitive theories of events and the effects of base-rate information on prediction. *Journal of Personality and Social Psychology* 35(5), 303–14, 1977.

Bar-Hillel, M. The base-rate fallacy in probability judgments. *Acta Psychologica* 44, 211–33, 1980.

Bar-Hillel, M., & Falk, R. Some teasers concerning conditional probabilities. *Cognition* 11, 109–22, 1982.

Beyth-Maron, R., & Dekel, S. A curriculum to improve thinking under uncertainty. *Instructional Science* 12, 67–82, 1982.

Brown, J.S., & Burton, R.B. Diagnostic models for procedural bugs in basic mathematics skills. *Cognitive Science* 2, 155–92, 1978.

Burger, W. *Using the Van Hiele model to describe reasoning processes in geometry.* Paper presented at the annual meeting of the American Educational Research Association, New York, March 1982.

Burger, W., Hoffer, A., & Shaughnessy, J.M. *Assessing children's intellectual development in geometry* (Final report of Grant SED 7920568). National Science Foundation, 1984.

Fischbein, E. The intuitive sources of thinking in children and adolescents. In R. Bechauf (Ed.), *Forschung züm Prozess des Mathematiklernens* (Band 2). Bielefeld, West Germany: Institut für Didaktik der Mathematik der Universität Bielefeld, 1976.

Fischhoff, B., Slovic, P., & Lichtenstein, S. Lay foibles and expert fables in judgments about risk. In T. O'Riordan & R.K. Turner (Eds.), *Progress in resource management and environment planning* (Vol. 3). Chichester, England: John Wiley & Sons, 1981.

Haladyna, T., Shaughnessy, J.M., & Shaughnessy, J.M. A causal analysis of attitude toward mathematics. *Journal for Research in Mathematics Education* 14, 19–29, 1983.

Johnson-Laird, P.M., & Wason, P.C. A theoretical analysis of insight into a reasoning task. In P.M. Johnson-Laird & P.C. Wason (Eds.), *Thinking.* Cambridge, England: Cambridge University Press, 1977.

Kahneman, D., Slovic, P., & Tversky, A. *Judgment under uncertainty: Heuristics and Biases.* New York: Cambridge University Press, 1982.

Kahneman, D., & Tversky, A. Subjective probability: A judgment of representativeness. *Cognitive Psychology* 3, 430–54, 1972.

Kahneman, D., & Tversky, A. Availability: A heuristic for judging frequency and probability. *Cognitive Psychology* 5, 207–32, 1973(a).

Kahneman, D., & Tversky, A. On the psychology of prediction. *Psychological Review* 80, 237–51, 1973(b).

Kahneman, D., & Tversky, A. Judgment under uncertainty: Heuristics and biases. *Science* 185, 1124–31, 1974.

Konold, C.E. *Conceptions of probability: Reality between a rock and a hard place.* Unpublished doctoral dissertation, University of Massachusetts, 1983.

La Breque, M. On reaching sounder judgments: Strategies and snares. *Psychology Today* 14, 33–42, 1980.

Lesh, R. Applied mathematical problem solving. *Educational Studies in Mathematics* 12, 235–64, 1981.

Lester, F.K. Building bridges between psychological and mathematics education research on problem solving. In F.K. Lester & J. Garofalo (Eds.), *Mathematical problem solving: Issues in research.* Philadelphia: The Franklin Institute Press, 1982.

Lester, F.K., & Garofalo, J. *Metacognitive aspects of elementary school students' performance on arithmetic tasks.* Paper presented at the annual meeting of the American Educational Research Association, New York, March 1982.

Mayer, R.E. The psychology of mathematical problem solving. In F.K. Lester & J. Garofalo (Eds.), *Mathematical problem solving: Issues in research.* Philadelphia: The Franklin Institute Press, 1982.

McCloskey, M., Caramazza, A., & Green, B. Curvilinear motion in the absence of external forces: Naive beliefs about the motion of objects. *Science* 210, 1139–41, 1980.

Nisbett, R.E., & Ross, L. *Human inference: Strategies and shortcomings of social judgment.* Englewood Cliffs, NJ: Prentice-Hall, 1980.

Pollatsek, A., Lima, S., & Well, A.D. Concept or computation: Students' understanding of the mean. *Educational Studies in Mathematics* 12, 191–204, 1981.

Schoenfeld, A. Teaching mathematical problem solving skills. *American Mathematical Monthly* 87, 794–805, 1980.

Schoenfeld, A. *Episodes and executive decisions in mathematical problem solving.* Paper presented at the annual meeting of the American Educational Research Association, Los Angeles, April 1981.

Scholtz, R. *Stochastic Problemaufgaben-Analysen aus Didaktischer und Psychologischer Perspective* (Materialen und Studien, Baud 23). Bielefeld, West Germany: Institut für Didaktik der Mathematik der Universität Bielefeld, 1981.

Schrage, G. Schwiengkeiten mit stochastischer Modelbildung. Zwei Beispiele aus der Praxis. *Journal für Mathematik Didaktik* 1, 86–101, 1980.

Shaughnessy, J.M. Misconceptions of probability. *Educational Studies in Mathematics* 8, 295–316, 1977.

Shaughnessy, J.M. Misconceptions of probability: From systematic errors to systematic experiments and decisions. In A. Shulte (Ed.), *Teaching statistics and probability.* Reston, VA: National Council of Teachers of Mathematics, 1981.

Shaughnessy, J.M. Misconceptions of probability: Teaching probability and statistics so as to overcome some misconceptions. In L. Rade (Ed.), *Proceedings of the First International Conference on the Teaching of Statistics* 2, 784–801, 1982.

Shaughnessy, J.M. The psychology of inference and the teaching of probability and statistics: Two sides of the same coin? In R. Scholz (Ed.), *Decision making under uncertainty.* Amsterdam: North Holland Publishing, 1983.

Shulman, L.S., & Elstein, A.S. Studies of problem solving, judgment, and decision making: Implications for educational research. In F.N. Keilinger (Ed.), *Review of research in education.* Itasca, IL: F.E. Peacock, 1975.

Shumway, R. Problem-solving research: A concept learning perspective. In F.K. Lester & J.

Garofalo (Eds.), *Mathematical problem solving: Issues in research*. Philadelphia: The Franklin Institute Press, 1982.

Silver, E.A. Knowledge organization and mathematical problem solving. In F.K. Lester & J. Garofalo (Eds.), *Mathematical problem solving: Issues in research*. Philadelphia: The Franklin Institute Press, 1982.

Silver, E.A. Probing young adults' thinking about rational numbers. *Focus on Learning Problems in Mathematics* 5, 105–117, 1983.

Silver, E.A., Branca, N.A., & Adams, V.M. Metacognition: The missing link in problem solving. In R. Karplus (Ed.), *Proceedings of the Fourth International Conference for the Psychology of Mathematics Education*. Berkeley: University of California, 1980.

Simon, H.A. Problem solving and education. In D.T. Tuma & F. Reif (Eds.), *Problem solving and education: Issues in teaching and research*. Hillsdale, NJ: Lawrence Erlbaum Associates, 1980.

Slovic, P., Fischoff, B., & Lichtenstein, S. Risky assumptions. *Psychology Today* 14, 44–48, 1980.

Tversky, A., & Kahneman, D. Belief in the law of small numbers. *Psychological Bulletin* 76, 105–10, 1971.

Tversky, A., & Kahneman, D. Causal schemata in judgment under uncertainty. In M. Fischbein (Ed.), *Progress in social psychology*. Hillsdale, NJ: Lawrence Erlbaum Associates, 1980.

Well, A.D., Pollatsek, A., & Konold, C. *Probability estimation and the use of base-rate information*. Unpublished manuscript, 1983. (Available from A.D. Well, University of Massachusetts, Amherst)

Computers in Research
on Mathematical Problem Solving

Patrick W. Thompson

San Diego State University

The use of computers as tools of trade has become commonplace in many areas. In research on mathematical problem solving, computers have been used mostly for testing performance models. Their use as tools in investigating students' processes and competencies in mathematical problem solving has hardly been explored. The purpose of this paper is to discuss computers as methodological tools in research on mathematical problem solving.

In classifying methodological uses of computers in problem-solving research, it is useful to focus upon the relationship of problems to subject matter. There is problem solving within a mathematical subject matter and problem solving that uses a mathematical subject matter. Proving theorems and forming hypotheses about relationships among concepts are examples of solving problems within a subject matter. Real-world applications involve using a subject matter. Of course, proving theorems and forming hypotheses could involve the use of a subject matter—one could, for example, use linear algebra in proving theorems and forming hypotheses about relationships among classes of continuous functions. Similarly, real-world applications could lead to solving problems within a subject matter, as has happened in regard to computer security systems and number theory. Nevertheless, this classification provides a useful heuristic.

The discussion of the relationship between problems and subject matter lends itself nicely to classifying potential uses of computers in research on mathematical problem solving. As a tool in solving problems within a subject matter, a computer can be programmed with a model of the subject matter itself. The computer, so programmed, then provides an environment within which students may explore problems at whatever level of formality they choose.

As a tool in solving problems that use a subject matter, a computer can be programmed to put a computational resource kit at the students' disposal. The students may then focus upon strategic issues within the problems. The word "computational" is used in its widest sense, which includes having the computer draw inferences, generate examples, or create graphic illustrations.

The computer-as-tool in solving problems within a subject matter gives researchers an entry into students' thought processes at a number of levels. At the lowest level, one may make a detailed qualitative assessment of their understanding of the basic concepts of the subject matter in relation to the problems. At the highest level, one may focus upon students' abilities to abstract structural relationships within and among problems and concepts (Thompson, this volume).

The computer-as-tool in solving problems that use a subject matter provides researchers with a way to focus upon students' representational and strategic processes. If one is assured that a student meets a study's basic performance criteria in the subject matter to be used in the problems, then one may hand him or her an ''expert'' assistant to do any computations the student wishes done. For example, if the problem domain uses calculus, then we might give the students a program that symbolically differentiates and integrates, such as *muMath*.

COMPUTERIZED ENVIRONMENTS FOR
SOLVING PROBLEMS WITHIN A SUBJECT MATTER

This section describes a computer microworld that embodies the additive group of integers, and gives an example of how one might use it to investigate students' problem solving.

Several excellent studies have investigated students' abilities to solve problems involving integers (Fisher, 1979; Marthe, 1979; Vergnaud, 1982). The problems posed in these studies were typically like the following:

> Pierre played two games of marbles. In the first game he won four marbles. In the second game he lost six marbles. What has happened altogether?

As an integer statement, the Pierre problem would be written $4 + -6 = -2$. However, students need not think of adding integers to solve questions like the above. They can just as well think of starting with some number, adding four, subtracting six, and then reporting that there are two fewer than the starting number. They need not think of an integer as a transformation of a quantity nor of a sum of integers as a composite of two transformations (Thompson, this volume).

To determine whether students are thinking of integers as we mean them, and whether they are thinking of adding integers as producing a sum, I use as the criterion whether or not they can predict, for example that $-(4 + -6) = 2$ *because* $(4 + -6) = -2$ and $-(-2) = 2$. In other words, the criterion is that they formally equate $a + b$ (adding two addends) and $(a + b)$ (a sum composed of two addends), in the sense that any operation applied to one may just as well be applied to the other.

To pose a problem that has the structure of $-(4 + -6)$ in a context like Pierre's marble games is a trick, to say the least. One method I have tried is to ask students to think of 17 as $20 - 3$, for example, and then use that fact to solve $40 - 17 = \_\_$. It did not work. They just solved $40 - 17 = \_\_$. Another way is to ask what the games of marbles looked like from the perspective of Pierre's opponent (assuming there was just one). This appears more than a little awkward, and even contrived. Other models of integers (Battista, 1983; Bennett & Nelson, 1979) are equally problematic when trying to construct models of quantified integer expressions.

The Microworld for Integers

The computerized environment that I have developed to investigate problem solving within integers has as its focus a ''turtle'' (a triangular graphics object) that moves back and forth on a number line. The program, called INTEGERS, allows one to command the turtle to move with the structure of the additive group of integers.[1] The commands that allow one to do this are given in Table 1.

Table 1. Rules by which the turtle moves.

Command	Action
<number>	The turtle goes <number> turtle steps in its current direction.
−<number>	The turtle turns around, goes <number> turtle steps, and then turns back around.
GOTO x	Places the turtle at the "street address" named by x. GOTO −50 places the turtle 50 turtle steps to the left of 0. GOTO 50 places the turtle 50 turtle steps to the right of 0. (Note that GOTO does not take an *integer* argument. The arguments to GOTO are nominal numbers.)

When GOTO is entered, the turtle merely appears at its new address. When <number> is entered, the turtle draws a vertical line to show its starting position, slowly moves <number> turtle steps, draws a vertical line to show its ending position, and then draws an arrow between the two positions (Figure 1). Several numbers may be entered at once; each is executed in succession and then a white arrow is drawn to show the net result of each group (Figure 2). If numbers are grouped, then a white arrow is also drawn to show the net result (Figure 3). A list of numbers is also a number, so a list may be negated (Figure 4). Finally, new operations may be defined (Figure 5).

Within the environment supplied by INTEGERS, it is possible to pose questions identical in structure to those in Vergnaud (1982), but with much more attention to the subtleties of the nature of integers and operations upon them. Moreover, it is possible to go beyond Vergnaud's questions by posing questions about quantified integer expressions.

Following is an illustration of what one may do with students within the INTEGERS environment. The excerpts are from an interview held near the end of the school year with a fifth-grade student. The student will be called SI.

SI is a middle-level achiever in school mathematics (according to his mother). He has shown no special aptitude for mathematics, nor has he shown an interest in computers. In fact, he is somewhat skeptical about getting involved with them, as his true interest is art. SI reported that he had seen number lines before, but that he had never seen numbers such as "−50," nor had he heard of negative numbers.

The interview opened with a brief discussion of its purpose. Then questions similar to those used by Vergnaud (1982) were asked of SI to get base-line data on SI's understanding of integers.

SI had no difficulty with questions about children who began with a given number of marbles and then successively won or lost some. Nor did he appear to have any difficulty with questions where the beginning amount was unspecified and two games subsequently played. All questions involved final marble accounts being greater than

---

1. The INTEGERS program is available from Cosine, Inc., Box 2017, N. Lafayette, IN 47906.

beginning ones. It was not clear, however, whether SI was thinking in terms of integers (changes in quantity) or absolute quantities. The following exchanges occurred prior to his being introduced to INTEGERS:

Int: ˙I'm going to tell you two stories. I don't want you to answer with a number this time. Just listen to the stories, okay?

SI: Okay.

Int: Here's the first story: Sally had 6 marbles. She played a game of marbles and won 2. Now here's the second story: Henry played 2 games. In the first he won 6 marbles, and in the second he won 2. Did I tell you the same story both times?

SI: Uh-huh (yes). (Repeats first story.) And she had 8. In the second game, the boy played two games. In the first, he had 6, and then he had 8. There is no difference, cause they both ended up with 8.

Int: So they both ended up with 8. Could you tell me the two stories again?

SI: A girl played a game of marbles. She has six, and she won 2. And, uh, the guy played a game and won 6, and played another game and won 2.

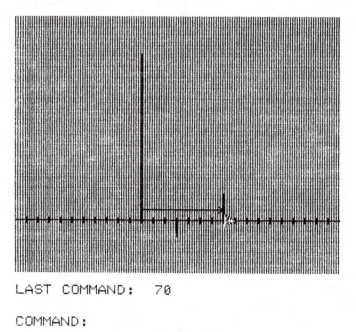

Figure 1. Effect of entering 70. Turtle began at −30. Student entered 70; turtle "walked" 70 turtle steps, marking his beginning and ending positions and drawing an arrow between them.

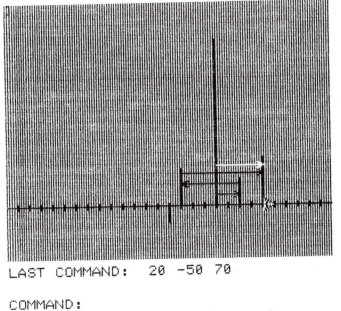

LAST COMMAND: 20 −50 70

COMMAND:

POS: 80

Figure 2. Turtle began at 40; student entered 20 −50 70. Turtle executed each in turn as if entered by itself. White arrow shows net displacement of the turtle from its starting position.

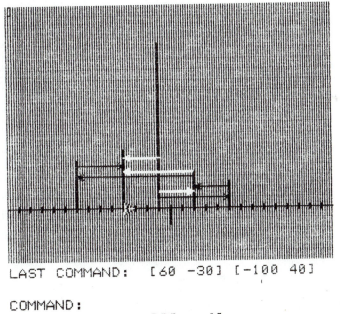

LAST COMMAND: [60 −30] [−100 40]

COMMAND:

POS: −40

Figure 3. Effect of entering [60 −30] [−100 40]. Turtle executed each group as if entered on one line. Lowest white arrow shows net displacement due to [60 −30]. Middle white arrow shows net displacement due to [−100 40]. Uppermost white arrow shows total net displacement.

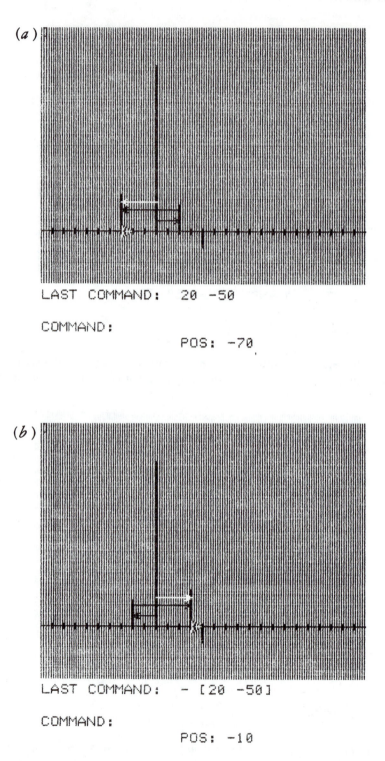

Figure 4. Comparison of effects of (*a*) 20 −50 and (*b*) −[20 −50]. Note that every action in (*b*) is the reverse (opposite) of its corresponding action in (*a*).

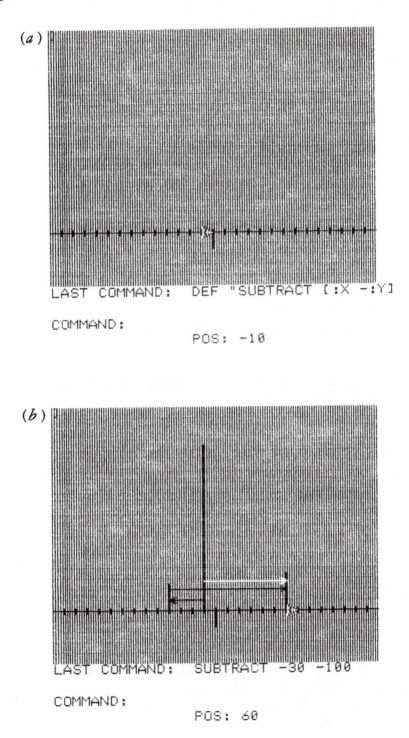

Figure 5. (*a*): Student commanded INTEGERS to define SUBTRACTION as taking two arguments, executing the first and then executing the negative of the second. (*b*): Student commanded the turtle to move by SUBTRACT −30 −100.

It seemed apparent that SI was thinking in terms of absolute quantities (numbers of marbles) and not in terms of changes in numbers of marbles. That this was the case we confirmed in the next few questions.

Int: How many did the guy start off with?

SI: Zero.

Int: Suppose I tell you that he started off with 10?

SI: Then he would have won, uh, 18.

Int: Suppose I tell you that he started off with 4?

SI: He would have won 12.

Int: He would have won 12?

SI: No . . . he would have had 12.

Int: He had 12. How many did he win?

SI: Six. Wait . . . Eight, eight.

Int: Okay. How many games were there in the first story?

SI: One.

Int: Did you know how many Henry started off with in the second story?

SI: Uh-uh (no).

Int: You just figured zero?

SI: Yeah.

Int: Did you know how many Sally started off with?

SI: She started off with six.

Int: And Henry . . .

SI: I just figured he had zero.

It might have been that SI's thinking of the quantities in terms of cardinal numbers was merely convenient, since, in terms of an answer, "had" and "won" were, from his perspective, interchangeable. The next excerpt explores that possibility.

Int: How about this one last story. Henry played two different games. In the first game, he won four, and in the second he lost six. What's happened altogether?

SI: (Pause.) He had . . . uh . . . (unintelligible) . . . okay. He had . . . uh . . . four the first time and he lost six, so he had . . . two left over to, uh, give back. He has two more left to . . . to owe back.

Int: How many did he start off with?

SI: He won four.

Int: How many did he start off with . . . before he started playing?

SI: Zero.

Int: Suppose I tell you he started off with ten?

SI: Uh, four . . . he had . . . two left.

Int: How do you figure that? He won four and then he lost six.

SI: Oh. He had eight left.

Int: Suppose I tell you he started off with 20.

SI: Twenty? Then he had . . . ummmm . . . 18 left.

Int: How did you get 18? You seem pretty sure.

SI: Cause you said he had twenty, and he won four. So he had 24. And six from 24 is 18.

There are two aspects of the above excerpt that deserve comment. First, SI's default value for "number at start" was zero. Apparently, SI was interpreting the stories by an addition schema wherein if it is not explicitly mentioned that the subject began with a number of some objects, then it assumed that he had none. Second, and more significantly, SI appeared not to equate "won four and lost six" with "lost two," as he added four and subtracted six for each of the hypothetical starting values instead of simply subtracting two.

SI was introduced to INTEGERS. We discussed the number line, the conventions of naming numbers on the number line, and the command GOTO. SI had no difficulty placing the turtle at 30, 50, −30, and −90 using GOTO. His initial response to making the turtle go to a negative street address showed a parallel in his thinking to the Pierre-type problems.

Int: How would you put the turtle at −30?

SI: Type GOTO 30 negative.

Int: Go ahead and try it. Here's the key for negative. <Points to the "−" key.>

SI: <Types GOTO 30−>

Int: No. The negative sign goes before the 30.

SI's inclination to say "negative" after a number-name and type "−" after a numeral suggests that "negative" was a qualifier to be tacked onto a number after it was formed. It was not part of the number. This is consistent with his apparent tendency to initially think of the numbers in the Pierre-type problems as being cardinal numbers, and qualifying them only in the face of further probing.

SI quickly picked up from an example that if you enter a (positive) number, the turtle walks that many steps from where it is. When the turtle was placed at 50 and SI was asked what number he needed to enter to make the turtle end up at 80, he quickly responded, "Thirty, 'cause 5 plus 3 is 8 . . . and 30 plus 50 is 80."

When asked what he thought would happen were he to enter −50, SI responded that the turtle would end up at −50 (it was at 50). After he saw that it ended at 0, the turtle was placed at 10. SI predicted that it would end "at 40 . . . on the other side" were

−50 entered again. The nature of SI's comments indicated that he thought ''−'' made the turtle go to its left. The next question investigated that hypothesis.

Int: Does the negative sign always tell the turtle to go to the left?

SI: Uh-huh <yes>.

Int: Can you tell me what the turtle might think when you type in −30?

SI: Means to go this way <left>.

Int: Okay. Type in this <writes − −30>. Don't press return. <SI types − −30.> What do you think he's going to do? <Note: Turtle is at −10.>

SI: <Long pause.> He'll end up there <−40>. He'll turn this way (left) and he's going to end up there <−40>.

Int: He's going to turn around?

SI: Yeah. He's going to turn left and then he's going to go 30 spaces.

Int: Okay. Go ahead and press return. Now watch very carefully, because I want you to tell me exactly what happens.

SI: <Presses RETURN; watches the turtle.> *Oh! Gosh!*

SI was truly surprised that the turtle moved to its right rather than its left. He scratched his head, muttering something to himself about that ''crazy'' turtle. He thought that the turtle only turned once; after entering − −30 once more, he noticed that it turned twice. After a long pause, he offered the hypothesis that since there was only a space next to the first ''−'' the turtle decided there was nothing to do but to turn back around. But then he couldn't explain why the turtle didn't turn around again (to the left) upon encountering the second ''−''. After another long pause SI offered that, perhaps, the negative sign told the turtle just to turn around. So the two negative signs together told the turtle to turn around twice. SI then confirmed his hypothesis by entering − −30 once more. He also predicted that the turtle would turn around three times and end up going 30 spaces to the left for −[− −30].

The discussion changed to the idea of entering a negative number to effect a left displacement of the turtle, for example, to move from 50 to 10. SI had no difficulty with this, so the discussion then turned to entering two numbers at once.

Int: <Clears the screen; turtle is at −90.> What would happen if you type this. One hundred, space, 20? Where will he end up after you type those two numbers?

SI: <Long pause.> At 30 . . . 40.

Int: How do you figure that?

SI: Cause he'll go 120 spaces from 90.

Int: He's at 90?

SI: Yeah.

Int: How do you know he's at 90?

SI: 'Cause it says position 90 . . . he's at −90. To there <10> is 100 and he'll go another 30.

Int: Go ahead.

SI: I mean he'll go to 30. Not another 30.

The purpose for asking SI to enter two numbers at once was to see if he could consider them as constituting a unit—one number. If he thought of 100 20 as one number, then he could predict the turtle's new position by counting the net result, 120.

By asking SI to think of two numbers as composing one, the stage was also set for asking him to predict the net result of the negative of a composite number, which is the test of whether or not he could think formally of integer quantities.

SI successfully predicted the outcome of entering 60 −80. He estimated what the turtle would do by counting six slashes to the turtle's right and eight to its left. After pressing RETURN, SI reported that the turtle went 140 steps, which was a reasonable answer if one was thinking of net result as one would think of the distance a car had traveled. Only after being asked how far it went *from where it started* did SI say that it went ''twenty . . . going back.''

SI's reasoning in the context of INTEGERS reflects the same processing constraints that appeared in his reasoning about the Pierre problems. He did not equate the net result with the process of achieving it. That is, he did not equate (a + b) and a + b. Without the benefit of further data, we would wonder if SI's main difficulty was that he did not understand the rules of the interview—that one should think in terms of net displacement and not in terms of ending position or total number of steps that the turtle has taken. However, the excerpt below shows SI's difficulty in solving −[20 −70] even after having solved 20 −70. That is, we will see that SI's difficulty appeared to come from a source other than a misunderstanding of the interviewer's intent.

Int: This time I'll cover it up. <Clears screen; covers screen with paper.> Now type 20, space, negative 70. <SI types 20 −70.> How much will he end up moving?

SI: <Pause.> Fifty spaces.

Int: Which way?

SI: That way <right>.

Int: How do you figure that?

SI: Cause if he's here and goes 20 spaces to the left and then he'll go 70 more spaces to the right.

Int: What was it you typed in?

SI: 20 −70.

Int: And he will go 20 to the left and 70 to the right?

SI: Uh-uh (no). He will go 20 the right and 70 to the left.

Int: So how much would he end up moving?

SI: Fifty to the left.

Int: Let's see. <SI presses RETURN; Int removes cover.> Sure enough. So putting in
        20 and then −70 makes him go 50 to the left?

SI: Yeah.

Int: Suppose we type in this <Types −[20 −70].> We typed in 20 −70 before.

SI: Right.

Int: And that made him go 50 to the left.

SI: Yeah.

Int: So now I'm going to type in the negative of that.

SI: Yeah.

Int: So what's going to happen?

SI: He'll end up right there <50 to the left.>

Int: Go ahead and press return. <SI presses RETURN.> What happened?

SI: He didn't do it.

Int: He didn't do what you thought.

SI: He was supposed to move 20 this way <right>, cause he's right here, and 70
        that way <left>.

Int: Which way did he do the 20 in?

SI: That way . . . to the left.

Int: And which way did he do the −70?

SI: To the right.

Int: How come? I thought −70 made him go to the left?

SI: <Long pause. Says something quietly to himself.>

Int: Which one are you trying to remember? 20 −70?

SI: When we put −[− −30]. I can't remember what happened. I think he went the
        opposite way.

Int: What does negative tell him to do?

SI: Oh! I see what happened! He went 20 the opposite way because the negative
        . . . the negative would . . . the last one would be uh . . . every other negative
        makes him go the other way. And that makes it go that way and the 70 went in
        the opposite way . . . to the right.

Int: Oh, the first negative told him to turn around.

SI: Yeah.

Int: And then when he did 20, what did he do?

SI: He was facing this way <left> and it said negative and he, uh, he was facing to
        the right, and it said negative so it goes to the left and it went 20 and then it
        said negative so it went 70 to the opposite side.

Int: So negative doesn't say left or right, does it. It . . .

SI: It says opposite.

It seems clear that SI did not think of combining integers on a line as an operation upon them. He never used the fact that 20 −70 has the same effect on the turtle as −50 to estimate the effect of −[20 −70]. Rather, he tried to mentally act out the turtle's actions, treating it as a problem unrelated to predicting the net result of [20 −70].

The last excerpt appears to suggest that SI constructed a mathematically correct meaning for the negative sign—"it says opposite." However, it became clear from SI's responses to succeeding questions that he was not thinking of "−" as an operator upon an integer or an integer expression, but rather as a command to the turtle to turn around. That is, "−" meant "turn around." It did not mean "turn around and do __." When asked to predict what the turtle would do in response to −20 60, SI said that it would go 80 to the left. Further probing revealed that SI was parsing −20 60 as follows

−	20	60
Turn around.	Go 20.	Go 60.

instead of as

−20	60
Turn around and go 20. Done, turn back.	Go 60.

That is, SI interpreted −20 60 just as he would −[20 60]. Negation, as an operator, had no scope to SI. This was reconfirmed when SI went on to predict that −20 −60 would make the turtle move 40 to the right.

To test the resiliency of SI's inability to apply negation with any scope, he was told the rules by which the turtle worked (Table 1). Even then, SI thought that −10 −40 should move the turtle 30 to the right.

The substance of SI's interview can be summed up by saying that he did not, and at that time probably could not, construct an integer as a formal object. We should not be surprised at this when we consider that SI was a fifth-grader, and that the level of formality required to have a full concept of integer is quite high (Thompson, this volume).

We can be surprised by the level of detail at which the INTEGERS microworld allowed us to map the constraints in SI's thinking. SI could not construct an integer as a composite quantity (magnitude in a relative direction) nor could he equate a net result with the process of achieving it. He could, however, correctly simulate an integer expression as long as it did not involve rules of scope for negation.

One might have noticed that SI was not given the rules by which the turtle operates at the outset of the interview. Had the interview been a teaching session, they would have been given to him. Given that the purpose of the interview was to see if SI already possessed a concept of integer, the assumption was that if he did, it would have become apparent in his attempts to predict and explain the behavior of the turtle. If he didn't, then his success in constructing and reconstructing hypotheses that accounted for the turtle's behavior could be taken as a rough measure of his distance from a concept of integer.

The interview with SI was quite long. It lasted two sessions that together spanned over 3 hours. The level of detail of the discussions with SI was made possible by the use of

INTEGERS as a context in which to pose questions. The INTEGERS microworld provided, as Papert (1980) has said, a model in which SI could apply his mental operations—a model to think by.

SI was truly puzzled by the turtle's behavior and wanted to come up with viable explanations of it. I was the one who cut the interview short. In fact, the second interview continued 10 minutes after it officially ended because SI wanted to experiment some more.

Finally, it should be pointed out that the nature of interviews in an environment such as INTEGERS can be more discussion-oriented than otherwise. If done properly they can take on the flavor of "theory testing," in the sense that the interviewer and interviewee do not discuss correct or incorrect answers, but instead discuss hypotheses, their inspiration, and their confirmation or disconfirmation. The key to this feature of what would otherwise be an interview is an environment that provides feedback that is objective from the student's point of view.

The methodology illustrated in SI's interview can be thought of as an extension of the Piagetian clinical interview. The objects and actions about which the interviewer and subject speak "contain" a mathematical structure. The focus of the interview is upon the student's operational structures as he assimilates questions and accommodates to conflicts.

Other Examples

Two studies that used computerized environments similar in principle to INTEGERS for solving problems within a subject matter are reported in Moser and Carpenter (1982) and diSessa (1982). The Moser and Carpenter study focused upon teaching arithmetical problem solving to first-graders. A child could use the computer to mimic a solution to an arithmetic problem with physical objects by creating a display of counters, one counter at a time, to which he or she could add counters or take them away. The child could also create displays by entering a numeral, which commanded the computer to create a display of that many counters; or the child could make the computer create a display and perform appropriate actions upon it by entering an entire number sentence. The role of the computer was to provide an environment wherein children could develop semantics for number sentences. Moser and Carpenter (1982) reported that three of the four children in the pilot study transferred their experiences from within the computerized environment to more traditional problems. The children wrote number sentences as part of their plans of solution.

Carpenter and Moser did not use their computerized environment to study problem solving per se, but rather as a medium for teaching one type of planning strategy—writing a number sentence. However, one could easily imagine their program being used in an interview in much the same way that INTEGERS was used with SI. Their program has enough flexibility to allow the interviewer to adjust the level of formality to whatever seems to best suit the situation.

One addition to their program that might prove interesting would be to limit the children to the use of numerals for which displays have already been defined, and to give them the ability to create new displays from previously defined ones. For example, the program might have supplied displays for multiples of ten, and the digits. An exchange might look like this:

Student: (Enters 27.)

Computer: I don't know 27. How do I make it?

Student: 20 + 9

Computer: I'm counting . . . oops. I count 29, not 27.

Student: 20 + 7 (or 30 − 3, or 10 + 17 if 17 has already been defined.)

Computer: I'm counting . . . Ok. Now I know 27. (creates display)

.

.

.

Student: (Enters 34.)

Computer: I don't know 34. How do I make it?

Student: 24 + 10

Computer: I don't know 24. How do I make it?

Student: 20 + 4

Computer: I'm counting . . . Ok. Now I know 24. I'm counting . . . Ok. Now I know
              34. (creates display)

DiSessa's (1982) study investigated concepts of Newtonian physics, but his study is noteworthy for research on mathematical problem solving. He used a computer microworld, called DYNA (for dynamic turtle), which contained a graphics object (the turtle) that moved according to the first two of Newton's three laws—the laws of inertia and force. The students could act upon the turtle by pressing R(ight), L(eft), or K(ick). Pressing R or L made the turtle turn in place 30 degrees. Pressing K applied a force of constant magnitude in the direction in which the turtle pointed.

The problem that diSessa gave his students was this: The display shows the turtle moving vertically at a constant velocity. A target is to one side of the turtle's path. The student is to make the turtle hit the target with as small a velocity as possible. DiSessa reported that a universal first strategy was to turn the turtle to point towards the target and then kick it at the moment the turtle reached a point in its path where it pointed directly at the target—a strategy founded firmly in Aristotelian physics.

The Common Theme

The example of SI's interview in the context of the INTEGERS microworld and the studies by Carpenter and Moser and diSessa contain a common theme in regard to using a computer as a methodological tool for studying problems within a subject matter. It is that the computer provides an objective environment in which students' directives are disinterestedly carried out.

The environments have a structure built into them; the objects within the microworlds behave with the structure of the subject matter. Students' choices of directives and their predictions of effects reveal underlying conceptual processes and constraints in those processes.

COMPUTERIZED ENVIRONMENTS FOR SOLVING PROBLEMS
THAT USE A SUBJECT MATTER

This section must be more speculative than the previous one. There are few programs of the kind I have in mind, and to my knowledge no published studies of their use in research on mathematical problem solving. Rather, the programs developed so far appear to be aimed at instructional applications. Their use in research on problem solving has yet to be explored.

An obvious example of a computer program that allows students to use a subject matter in solving problems is muMATH, a program that symbolically integrates, differentiates, and simplifies algebraic and trigonometric functions and expressions. Heid (1983) reported the use of muMATH in introductory calculus courses for nonscience majors. Though she gave few details of its actual use by students, she claimed that they were freed of complex calculations and excelled at problem formulation and interpretation. It should be noted that the students Heid spoke of used muMATH as an integrated part of their course, so instruction was not only on the subject matter, but also on how to use muMATH to solve problems. If you have ever used muMATH, then you will appreciate the need for extensive training in its conventions. The program (actually, a set of programs) is not what one would call "user friendly."

That last comment raises a critical concern. If we wish to introduce computers-as-tools into studies of mathematical problem solving in order to allow us to focus on students' strategic and representational processes, then we must ensure that the computer is a neutral agent in the problem-solving process. That is, the use of a computer must not, in itself, pose a problem to the student. The criterion I propose is that a student may use the computer in the same way that he or she might use a human assistant. Were students to use a human assistant, then they would say what they wished done in fairly cryptic natural language: I need to know if there is a theorem that relates triangles to circles. Tell me what you can find. Or, what is the sum of the first 20 square numbers?

For the computer to be as neutral an agent as possible in the problem-solving process is a heavy constraint. In essence, it requires that a natural language interface be built into the program, or that the syntax of the command structure be simple enough to teach in 5 or 10 minutes, yet powerful enough to construct complex commands.

The following is a very elementary example of what I mean by a tool kit that is neutral to the problem-solving process. It is given to students in conjunction with this problem:

A number is *perfect* if it is equal to the sum of its proper divisors (i.e., divisors less than itself). The first three perfect numbers are 6, 28, and 496. What are the next two perfect numbers?

The tool kit allows students to enter commands such as

PRINT THE PROPER DIVISORS OF 496
To which the computer responds: 1 2 4 8 16 31 62 124 248

PERFECT? 496
To which the computer responds: TRUE

WHAT IS THE SUM OF THE FACTORS OF 28
To which the computer responds: 56

PRIME? 378923
To which the computer responds: FALSE

PRINT THE PRIME FACTORIZATION [or P.F] OF 378923
To which the computer responds: 167 × 2269

WHAT IS THE LCM OF THE FACTORS OF 496 AND THE FACTORS OF 28
To which the computer responds: 3472

The program has not been used with students except on an informal basis. (It takes them about 10 minutes to familiarize themselves with the available tools before they turn to solving the problem.) Nevertheless, it serves as an example of the kind of interaction that must be allowed if students are to be able to use a program without first having to take a course on its use.

As mentioned earlier, a natural language interface is not absolutely necessary. However, the program must still provide an environment that is powerful with respect to the problems and yet simple enough to use with minimal instruction. Here is another example. The problem is presented on the computer.

Problem: a. A man is to eat 3 cookies from a package of 20 cookies, 8 of which are bad. If he eats 2 or more bad cookies he will get sick. What is the probability that he gets sick?

                b. Suppose the second cookie he eats is bad. What is the probability that he gets sick?

The students can, if they wish, enter TREE, which commands the computer to draw a tree diagram of the problem. A selection of a good cookie is labeled G; a selection of a bad cookie is labeled B. Or, they can enter DIAGRAM, which signals to the computer that they want to construct their own tree diagram and provide their own labels. To compute an answer to (a), a student might enter

$$PROB\ [[G\ B\ B][B\ G\ B][B\ B\ G][B\ B\ B]],$$

which translates into the sum of the probabilities of the branches containing at least two bad cookies, assuming they labeled their outcomes G and B. To answer question (b), a student might enter

$$GIVEN\ [[G\ B][B\ B]],$$

which tells the computer that any subsequent probabilities are to be computed relative to the assumption that the only possible branches are those that contain the second cookie being bad.

Another example of a program that can be used as a tool in solving problems that use a subject matter is reported by Helzer (1983a). Helzer (1983b) reports a package of routines (functions) in APL that allow one to flexibly and easily perform calculations in linear algebra.

In our package the Gaussian reduction routine is a function called ECHELON. To row reduce a stored matrix A to its echelon form E, one simply uses the expression

$$E = ECHELON(A).$$

To display a stored variable such as E one types its name. To accomplish more complicated tasks, composition of functions is used. For example, suppose that we wish an orthonormal basis of the null space of the stored matrix A. The APL expression A,0 produces A augmented by a column of zeros and the expression

$$BASIS = ORTHO\ (BACKSUB(ECHELON(A,0)))$$

... [where] BACKSUB produces a matrix whose column space is the null space of A and ORTHO(X) produces an orthonormal basis of the column space of the matrix X. (p. 6)

Helzer's package of routines would put tremendous power into the hands of a student solving problems requiring the use of linear algebra. Concomitantly, researchers of problem solving in applied linear algebra could give more interesting and intricate problems than would be possible without such a tool kit. The focus of the study could then be upon how students represent the problems to themselves and upon their strategies of attack.

CONCLUSION

I have discussed two broad categories of uses of computers as methodological tools in research on mathematical problem solving. These are as tools for presenting and solving problems within a subject matter and as tools for solving problems that use a subject matter. I discussed prototypic programs and their uses within each category. In this section I will consider extensions of the prototypes in light of recent developments in artificial intelligence, and possible pitfalls of using computers in the ways so far proposed.

Artificial Intelligence

Research in artifical intelligence has always been concerned with making machines perform tasks that would otherwise be done by intelligent beings—specifically, humans. More recently, a growing area of interest has been in making machines perform tasks that would otherwise require *expert* humans (Barr & Feigenbaum, 1981, 1982; Michie, 1979). Diagnosing blood diseases, locating mineral deposits from geological data, and decoding the molecular structure of an unknown compound are only a few examples of what have become known as *expert systems*.

Bramer (1982) described an expert system as

... a computing system which embodies organized knowledge concerning some specific area of human expertise, sufficient to perform at a skillful and cost-effective level. (p. 3)

The tools we have seen in the previous sections might be thought of as very elementary expert systems, although that would be an unconventional use of the term. They were expert in the restricted domains of creating representations of problems within a subject matter, or in the domain of complex computations that use a subject matter.

What would these tools look like if they were expanded to the level of today's expert systems? An expert system that could be used in solving problems within a subject matter would not only be able to present representations of problems, but would have a map of "facts" and procedures that relate to it. It would also have prototypic examples of concepts and rules for creating analogies and drawing inferences (Rissland, this volume). To envision an expert system that could be used in solving problems that use a subject matter is more problematic. It would probably be much like muMATH, but embedded in something like Helzer's calculator, so that results could be referred to symbolically.

How could bona fide expert systems be used in studies of mathematical problem solving? That is an open question. We do not want to make programs-as-tools so powerful that they exceed the students' competence to use them, nor so powerful that a student could have the computer solve the problem that the student is to solve. At the same time we want the programs to be powerful enough so that students can operate efficiently at their highest levels of competence.

One way to achieve a balance between power and methodological utility might be to incorporate techniques that have been used in developing intelligent tutoring systems that feature the computer's construction of a model of the student-user (Burton & Brown, 1979; O'Shea, 1982). As the student displays his competence, the system would make more powerful features available. The same effect may be achieved by the interviewer controlling the features of the program that are available to students (e.g., by not mentioning a feature till sure that the student can make use of it).

We must ask ourselves how the methodological introduction of computers-as-tools affects the processes students use in solving problems. There is some evidence that students solve problems differently in the presence of an interviewer than when by themselves, and differently still when working together in small groups (Noddings, this volume). We should not think that their introduction to a computerized environment would have any less effect on students' cognitive processes than the presence of an interviewer.

REFERENCES

Barr, A., & Feigenbaum, E.A. *The Handbook of Artificial Intelligence* (Vols. I & II). Los Altos, CA: William Kaufmann, Inc., 1981–82.

Battista, M.T. A complete model for operations on integers. *Arthimetic Teacher* **30**, 26–31, 1983.

Bennett, A.B., & Nelson, L.T. *Mathematics: An informal approach.* Boston: Allyn & Bacon, 1979.

Bramer, M. A survey and critical review of expert systems research. In D. Michie (Ed.), *Introductory readings in expert systems.* New York: Gordon & Breach, 1982.

Burton, R., & Brown, J. An investigation of computer coaching for informal learning activities. *International Journal for Man-Machine Studies* **11**, 5–24, 1979.

diSessa, A. Unlearning Aristotelian physics: A study of knowledge-based learning. *Cognitive Science* **6**, 37–76, 1982.

Fisher, J.P. La perception des problèmes soustractifs aux débuts de l'apprentissage de la soustraction. *Thesis,* Université de Nancy I, IREM de Lorraine, Nancy, France, 1979.

Heid, M. Calculus with muMATH: Implications for curriculum reform. *Computing Teacher* **11**(4), 46–49, 1983.

Helzer, G. *Applied linear algebra with APL.* Waltham, MA: Little, Brown, 1983(a).

Helzer, G. A linear algebra calculator. *CIMSE Newsletter* **3**(1), 5–6, 1983(b).

Marthe, P. Additive problems and directed numbers. In *Proceedings of the Annual Meeting of the International Group for the Psychology of Mathematics Education,* Warwick, England, 1979.

Michie, D. (Ed.). *Expert systems in the micro-electronic age.* Edinburgh: University of Edinburgh Press, 1979.

Moser, J., & Carpenter, T. *Using the microcomputer to teach problem solving skills: Program development and initial pilot study* (Working Paper No. 38). Madison: University of Wisconsin, Wisconsin Center for Education Research, July 1982.

O'Shea, T. Intelligent systems in education. In D. Michie (Ed.), *Introductory readings in expert systems.* New York: Gordon & Breach, 1982.

Papert, S. *Mindstorms: Children, computers, and powerful ideas.* New York: Basic Books, 1980.

Vergnaud, G. A classification of cognitive tasks and operations of thought involved in addition and subtraction problems. In T.P. Carpenter, J.M. Moser, & T.A. Romberg (Eds.), *Addition and subtraction: A cognitive perspective.* Hillsdale, NJ: Lawrence Erlbaum Associates, 1982.

SUMMARY

On Teaching Problem Solving and Solving the Problems of Teaching

Lee S. Shulman

Stanford University

A large number of interesting and provocative ideas were presented in the conference that led to this volume. Surely, there are many schemata or frames through which we, as readers, can interpret the papers. This paper represents my own kind of schematization or thematic summary. Since this volume contains 24 separate offerings, it is not possible for me to comment on each paper individually. Rather, I will deal very generally with five broad topics: (*1*) problem solving, (*2*) methodology, (*3*) curriculum, (*4*) teaching and learning, and (*5*) teaching and teacher education.

PROBLEM SOLVING

One of the topics discussed in a number of the papers was, "What is problem solving?" I have a favorite epigram about what a problem is. I first encountered it in an essay by Jerome Bruner (1961). Bruner cites a British philosopher named Weldon who asserted that three basic things ought to be considered in defining what is a problem: troubles, puzzles, and problems. A *trouble* is a circumstance, a situation, that leaves one upset and at loose ends; one knows that things aren't going very well. It is a source of vague, but persistent discomfort. A *puzzle* has a nice tight form, clear structure, and a neat solution. A *problem,* then, is what you get if you can find a puzzle form to lay on top of a trouble. This conception may serve as a framework for examining several topics discussed at the conference.

In his paper, Mayer's concern is with the translation process as it related to the question of problem types. In fact all of the discussion about types seems to revolve around the kind of cognitive processes and associated pedagogical processes that are involved in finding the appropriate mathematical puzzle forms to lay on troubles to transform them into problems that a learner knows something about. As Sowder pointed out in his reaction, there are some researchers who do not even consider the solution of standard textbook story problems to be problem solving.

In search for the definition of problem solving, Dewey's name has been invoked repeatedly. In their papers, Nel Noddings and Patrick Thompson remind us how much Dewey had contributed to this area. And of course, in this conclave of mathematicians,

439

the most frequently cited source on the subject is Polya. But I am not sure that even these venerable sources help us to make progress on the subject. The message that Kilpatrick tries to give us in his paper, via six types of problem definition, is that it is not profitable to try to answer the question of what problem solving is. Rather, it would be much more useful to try to evolve analytically some sort of typology of problem solving so that in any particular study or instructional program we could identify the kind of problem solving about which we are talking. Kilpatrick's six exemplars constitute one kind of typology. I would like to consider another one that could be useful.

In our chapter "Research on the Teaching of Natural Science," Tamir and I (Shulman and Tamir, 1974) attempt to deal with the question, "To what extent did the science curricula of the 1960's, like PSSC (physics) and BSCS (biology), in fact teach problem solving, or at least provide an opportunity for problem solving in their laboratory exercises?" We tried to develop what we called, borrowing from linguistics, a "distinctive features" approach. Our scheme had been suggested by Schwab. Schwab suggested that there are basically three components to a problem: some statement of the problem itself, ways and means for dealing with the problem, and a solution to the problem (Figure 1).

Level	Form of Instruction	Problems	Ways and Means	Solutions
1	Exposition	Given	Given	Given
2	Guided	Given	Given	Not Given
3	Discovery	Given	Not Given	Not Given
.	.	.	.	.
.	.	.	.	.
.	.	.	.	.
.	.	.	.	.
8	"Pure" Inquiry	Not Given	Not Given	Not Given

Figure 1.

The highest level of guided learning, full exposition, occurs where the problem is given, the ways and means are given, and the solution is given. That is referred to in the discovery learning literature as expository learning or highly guided learning. It was generally frowned upon by discovery learning zealots, but it seemed to do a pretty good job in a number of circumstances. The other extreme was what we called pure inquiry. *Pure inquiry* may occur where the problem is not given, the ways and means are not given, and the solution is not given. Certainly you do find examples of that in the science teaching literature, albeit rarely. For example, David Hawkins (1966) has materials in the Elementary Science Study, in which you simply leave some apparatus such as balance beams sitting on a table in the room and allow the children to "mess around." You don't have to order children to "mess around"; it comes to them quite naturally. They call it playing. Forms of "guided discovery" can be located in the intermediate levels of the scheme.

Pure inquiry might be tried using microworlds such as those suggested by Patrick

Thompson (this volume) but the microworlds would be designed differently from the way that he describes them. I think microworlds would be an extraordinary way to teach a variety of modes of reasoning to children. If you could be very clever about structuring the microworlds so that they were analogs to certain kinds of substantive worlds in the science and mathematics curricula, the instructional possibilities are numerous.

Messing around in such microworlds would be an example of the pure inquiry (Not given—Not given—Not given) mode with which Tamir and I were concerned. The mode we often found in the science labs was Level 3, Given—Not given—Not given, in which you are given a problem, but you are not explicitly told what ways and means to use or what the solution is. Even more often, we found Level 2, Given—Given—Not given, where students were presented with both a problem and a method, needing only to achieve a solution. I don't suggest this as an ideal typology, but rather as an example that could be emulated in doing a distinctive-features analysis appropriate to a particular area or subarea of mathematics. When analyzing problem solving, one could specify some of the details concerning the kind of problem solving under analysis, rather than arguing about whether a particular instance is or is not "real" problem solving.

Such a structural approach remains a limited way of looking at problems. Its limitations are revealed by a question that was asked at the conference: What is the reward for the student in solving the problem, or in completing the task? One of the insights emerging from research in the cognitive psychology of instruction and what I have called the educational ethnography of instruction is a much richer and more differentiated notion of what we mean by a *task* (Shulman, 1983). We typically believe that the problem or task with which a child is dealing is the same one that we gave him or her. One of the important lessons in cognitive psychology has been the inevitable distinction between the *task environment* and the *problem space*. The task environment as presented is not what the student works on; rather, what gets worked on is the task as apprehended or transformed. Cognitive psychologists try to account for the way students deal with tasks in light of the schema-driven transformations that learners use to apprehend and transform the tasks as-given into "problems to solve." Most of those tasks have not merely been encountered by students, but have been assigned either by an experimenter or by a teacher. Thus there is yet a third sense of the task to consider, the task as an assignment, a set of obligations incurred in a school context and in a relationship with an authority figure.

As soon as you think about the task as an assignment, you have to invoke an entirely different set of studies. It is a relatively new body of work; some of it emerges from some older work of Becker et al. (1968), who suggest that the way to look at a classroom is as a marketplace in which students exchange performance for grades. If you want to understand why they do what they do, you have to understand the basis of the barter system. Essentially, you have to ask, What is in it for them?

The way this kind of work is often done is to observe very carefully as students work on assignments and either stop them while they are working or interview them as soon as they are done and ask them what they did and why. As you observe them doing worksheets in mathematics, for example, I think you will find first of all that they *do* talk to one another. But the typical question that is asked is not "How do you do this one?" It isn't even "What answer did you get?" I think the most frequent question is "Which one are you on?" It becomes clear that while the *task* may be to solve a set of addition problems, the *assignment* is to complete the task in respectable time. There is a social psychology of the setting, and given the relationship of exchange between the assigned performance and the grade, the pupil's goal is to complete the work satisfactorily, with or without understanding.

A classic exemplar of this genre of research is the case study of Benny by Stanley Erlwanger (1975). Benny's behavior cannot be understood if you use a cognitive psychology approach. It is not a schema-driven set of transformations that accounts for the incredible inventiveness (and error) of Benny's system of arithmetic. To get the full picture, you must understand the *assignment* as defined by Benny in the context of IPI (Individually Prescribed Instruction) mathematics. When I use Benny as a case study with my teacher-education students, the students see Benny as rather dull. They can't imagine how anyone could be so foolish as to have mutually incompatible rules for a single system called mathematics. I remind them that Benny already has mastered at least one very powerful and effective generative system of rules, which he uses constantly and which he learned long before he learned mathematics. It is the grammar of his native language. It is the most powerful generative system of rules he has, and he learned it as a set of mutually incompatible rules. When he was little and he said, "I goed," somebody said to him "No, I went." That made no sense to him at all. When he kept on saying "I goed," extrapolating and generalizing the rule the way a good axiomatic deducer should, he was repeatedly corrected. Finally, he made the "proper" generalization. It is not his fault that when he applied the principle to the next set of such rules that he was being taught, namely elementary level arithmetic, teachers didn't think it was supposed to work that way. I don't think Benny is foolish at all; Benny is a very smart kid. In any event, to understand Benny and to understand a lot of what is going on in the classroom we have to look at how students respond to school tasks as assignments.

However, even that formulation is inadequate, because the notion of the task as an assignment still preserves an aspect of myth, and that is that children are in school alone. One very interesting kind of research is the work of Michael Cole and his colleagues (e.g., Cole & Traupmann, 1980) on what I have called the task as socially negotiated. Problem solving in a small group is treated by children as a job they work on together.

In Cole and Traupmann's (1980) study, a learning disabled youngster looked as if he had very different levels of aptitude depending on the setting in which they observed him. They first observed him in a cooking club out of school; he was one of the leaders of the cooking club. When they learned that the school considered him learning disabled, they were stunned because they couldn't see evidence of the learning disability in his performance in the cooking club. It was only when they carefully studied what he did in school on tasks where the school organization precluded his collaboration with others, that the deficiencies, which he very cleverly overcame through collaborating with others in the cooking club, became manifest.

Thus, one kind of assignment that makes the task very different occurs when, instead of an individually performed task, you have one that can be socially negotiated, parceled out among members of the group and then worked on collectively. That kind of problem solving will look very different from the kind of problem solving pursued individually.

One very interesting question that Nel Noddings (this volume) and her students are looking at now is, What is the relationship between the kind of learning that occurs in this sort of setting and what eventually becomes part of the capacity of the individual problem solver working alone? I think the reverse question might turn out to be equally fruitful. We rarely look at changes in working groups because we still think of the natural unit of analysis as the individual working alone. I wonder in our present society if that in fact is an appropriate assumption. There are other ways of looking at the task.

At this point, having suggested an array that fits nicely with what James Greeno called the radical constructivism of Patrick Thompson (and about which he was a little concerned), I'd like to remind you that constructivism was not invented by modern cognitive psychologists. It is a much older tradition in the social sciences. If you go back to the literature of sociology of the 1920's and 1930's, to what was called the Chicago School of Sociology, you find a sociologist named W.I. Thomas talking about the "definition of the situation." There was even something called Thomas' theorem, which was: "Situations defined as real, are real in their consequences." In some ways this insight became the basis for Robert Merton's (1948) work on the self-fulfilling prophecy: the manner in which one defines a situation can often lead to behavior and responses consistent with that definition or expectation. But there is a warning, which typically gets ignored, that I call Merton's lemma to Thomas' theorem. Merton reminds us that *real* situations not defined as real remain real in their consequences. In other words, this is not a reversible theorem. It does not say, If you don't take something seriously, it won't have real consequences for you. Try that with a car that you don't want to define as real bearing down on you as you cross a busy street.

There has been some danger, especially among those who work on teacher expectations, of thinking that if you could only change children's motivation, change their conceptions of themselves as mathematics learners, and change both their teachers' and their own expectations for children's ability to learn mathematics, everything else would automatically fall into place. Those preoccupied with the more cognitive instructional aspects of mathematics learning would argue that that is simply not the case. Appropriate expectations must be combined with effective instruction.

That is all I want to say about ways of looking at the problem and at problem solving. As you can see, I moved off the question, "What is a problem?" to what became the subquestion of the volume, "When you are looking at what you think is problem solving, what is really going on there?" I think that is the central question for many of these papers, especially for those people who advocate descriptive studies of problem solving and problem-solving instruction in the classroom.

METHODOLOGY

The next general category is methodology. There is sometimes a troublesome mismatch between the language we use to discuss teaching and learning—a language that we learned from a particular kind of experimental psychology—and the language we use to describe the research methods that are needed in the empirical study of problem-solving instruction. Not only do we find ourselves calling everything a *variable*, we still have trouble talking about thinking: thinking is "cognitive behaviors," and feeling or emotion is still "affective behavior." We don't have situations, we have "context variables." Those terms are not trivial. They carry with them a significant set of beliefs or epistemology. They are just as significant for the way researchers look at what they are studying as are conceptions of mathematics for the teaching and learning of mathematics.

The kind of epistemology that we have all been led to accept is one in which it is assumed that the way to explain what goes on in classrooms or teaching/learning situations is to decompose what is observed into the smallest units of analysis. We call them variables, we measure them, and we aggregate them in a variety of ways. Our answers to questions are phrased in terms of proportions of variance accounted for in regression models or analyses of variance. For certain classes of questions that may be an appropriate language, but that won't work if what you are calling for are some of the kinds of naturalistic and rich "thick descriptions"—to use Clifford Geertz's (1973) term that Frank Lester advocates in his paper.

Again, the important thing to understand is that this is not merely methodological; we are carrying a lot of theoretical baggage along with that methodological language. As an example, if you think that the way to talk about biology is to begin by talking about the properties of cells and then to account for larger and larger aggregates of cells through additive models or through additive and interactive models of the way individual cell behavior cumulates, you end up with a particular kind of biology. If on the other hand, you think the proper starting point is the organism itself as the unit, then you will try to account for the behavior of its parts in terms of the ways they contribute to that whole unit. You will then end up with a very different kind of biology.

That still may not be the kind of biology you want to do. You may be another kind of biologist who doesn't think of the organism as the natural unit of analysis. You may think of the community, or family, as the unit of analysis. If that is the real starting point for you, organisms (much less cells) will have meaning only insofar as they are understood as having relationships among themselves as part of the community.

In a seminar he taught to the research staff of the Institute for Research on Teaching, Joseph Schwab provided an example of the latter principle. It demonstrates to us that not even an attribute as fundamental as *gender* can be argued to be a property of the individual organism. There was a study of sex change in a particular species of coral reef fish that swam in schools off the Great Barrier Reef in Australia. The head fish of a school always had male gender characteristics. All of the rest had female gender characteristics. When the dominant male died, the senior remaining fish became male. Now what defined gender? It was community; it was somehow gender as a role, not gender as fundamental structure.

There is a curricular implication here. The three approaches to biology that I just portrayed were the bases of three versions in which the Biological Science Curriculum Study (BSCS) was written. BSCS went nowhere for the first couple of years of curriculum development because it seemed that the participating biologists had different tacit definitions of biology. They could not agree on how to work out the curriculum until finally somebody came along, as one tale has it, sorted out the fact that there was not "the" structure of biology, but there were at least three structures of biology. He made a suggestion: Wouldn't it be simpler, rather than just voting on which one is best, to develop three alternative curricula? Then teachers, too, could identify what kind of biology they wanted to teach and then teach that kind.

What I am arguing here is that the different kinds of method—the experimental, variable-oriented kind, the more ethnographic, social-interaction/group-configuration kind, and so on—are not merely alternative methods, some of which give you numbers, some of which give you narrative descriptions, and some of which give you computer programs. They are not merely alternative languages; they carry very different ways of conceptualizing the phenomenon that is being studied. I think that has got to be understood and carefully examined.

In the last ten years, the person who probably has been the methodological "guru" in American educational research, Lee Cronbach, has been undergoing a major personal transformation in his view of educational research methodology. He has moved from what he himself would view as a narrow quantitative experimental psychometric view to one that is far more eclectic, muddled, troubling, rich, exciting and vague (Cronbach,

1975; 1982). In essence, what Cronbach is arguing is that no matter what kind of study we do, whether it is an experiment or a survey, whether it is a computer simulation or an interview, whether it concerns a single individual or a thousand, when it has been completed and written up, it is a case, and it becomes in a sense a part of what we treat as case knowledge. This view of what social science evidence means with respect to practice and policy is radically different, I think, from what we have tended, in the past, to view as a social science more nearly like physics.

Cronbach is raising some serious questions about what generalizability means in the social sciences. If you take his argument seriously, there is a need for those of us who serve as gatekeepers—for example, as editors of journals—not to be doctrinaire or dogmatic methodologically about what it is we will accept as disciplined inquiry. We must look at all of our journals because we may be turning away some of the richest sources of information. Cronbach (personal communication) gives several examples of why we need this more eclectic, differentiated, and rich notion of what kinds of research are valuable. One of the examples is the Brownell and Moser (1949) study of subtraction, in which they taught four different kinds of subtraction, some meaningful, some not. What was fascinating was Cronbach's interpretation of the results of that study. The most valuable information was not in the main effects, but in the residuals, in trying to figure out why the effects weren't bigger. There was one meaningful instructional treatment that in general worked a little bit better, but the question was, Why didn't it work better for everybody? As it happened, that question could only be answered when Brownell and Moser looked at the learning histories of the different students within the treatments and concluded that the children who profited from meaningful instruction were those whose previous teachers had taught them in a meaningful fashion. Those who hadn't had meaningful instruction in the past could make very little use of the meaningfulness of the treatment and did as well or better with different forms of rote treatment.

Cronbach points out that such insights are typically obscured because researchers strive to keep the experimental setting insulated from the prior histories of the people participating in the experiment. We accomplish that by random assignment. He gives the example of the famous Manager and the Worker Study by Roethlisberger and Dixon (1939), in which the major finding was the "Hawthorne Effect." The study was originally intended to learn about the relationship between different levels of illumination and productivity among the workers. The fine scholars who did the study were smart enough to anticipate Greeno's (this volume) admonition to observers to carefully write down everything people say to one another and describe behavior as richly as possible. They took the trouble to describe carefully, independent of their hypothesis, everything they saw happening and to bootstrap a different kind of understanding from that. Cronbach also points out that the finding about the Hawthorne effect has become quite controversial again, as some people have reanalyzed the original data and others have replicated aspects of the study. That is precisely what a detailed description is for. If it is rich enough, you can deliberate about it, you can reflect on it, and you can turn it over and look at it from different perspectives. If it is not, if all you have is an F-test, what you see is what you get. Let me simply echo and amplify the call that Frank Lester makes in his paper for increasing the diversity of methods we use, with the added observation that to do more qualitative or naturalistic research does not mean that in some doctrinaire way you stop counting, stop using statistical tests, stop being as precise as you possibly can when precision is possible. What it simply means is that you don't do research with one hand tied behind your back.

CURRICULUM

Let us briefly consider matters of curriculum. I was fascinated by Patrick Thompson's (this volume) description of two curricula. After that statement of fascination, I want to add two caveats. The first is that the microworld exercises constitute, not a curriculum, but a unit of work. The two descriptions do not inform us of what comes before them and what goes after them. We cannot see them in the context of a progressively organized body of subject matter, which is what the descriptor "curriculum" must entail. This is a major question for mathematics curriculum. Many of the problems of mathematical problem-solving instruction lie in the way it is typically discussed—in isolation from the concern for curriculum at large. That is one of the areas where I implore those in mathematics education to do more work. Help us understand the mathematical context, in terms of curriculum, over a longer period of time, within which such marvelous instructional examples as these microworlds should rest.

Having said that, let me issue the second caveat. It is an admonition against "mathocentric" thought. With very few exceptions, the conference discussions of mathematics instruction occurred as if nothing else is taught in schools. Even when we were talking about physics, the question was not, How does the mathematics they learn possibly relate to the physics they might learn? Instead, it was, How can we take what we learn about physics problem solving and apply it to mathematics problem solving? (See Heller and Hungate, this volume.)

Mathematics lessons and curriculum are embedded in a much larger curricular context. It is the full set of things that are taught and learned in school. A number of those subject areas have problems very similar to the problems we have with mathematics, both with regard to the progressive organization of the subject matter and the absence of meaningful, problem-oriented instruction. I suggest that the most effective way of trying to deal with this problem in mathematics may not be to start with mathematics, but to look at the curriculum more broadly and examine the interrelationships among parts of the curriculum. There have been earlier failed attempts, but we have to keep looking for alternatives.

It just may be that computer technology and the current excitement it has generated may be our entrée. Everybody wants to get the computer into the curriculum, but we can't let them do it by adding another course called computer literacy. We have got to learn that such moments of change, when an enormous social force is inserting yet another curricular topic, may be the chance to get people to integrate different areas. I have a sense that we are not going to accomplish meaningful instruction even if we use computers, by just looking at mathematics alone.

TEACHING AND LEARNING

Many of these papers address the definition of problem solving, but say very little about the definition of instruction. Contributors either assumed that they had a shared meaning for this term, or that no consensus was necessary before meaningful discussion could take place. Although there seemed to be no shared meaning for the term "instruction," there was considerable agreement about teachers. I'm always fascinated by the ways in which teaching and learning are discussed by instructional psychologists, cognitive instructional psychologists, and mathematics or science educators. It is difficult to infer from the discussion that teachers and students are members of the same species.

we define learners, we put on our hats as optimistic constructivists. Learners are
d as those who learn, construct, cognize, metacognize, transform, and actively
on their environment. They are truly impressive. It doesn't matter what you teach
they heuristically transform it into something else. Learners are quite formidable.

Unfortunately, when they grow older and become teachers, they either can't, don't
n't learn how to teach. They haven't got a prayer for learning the subject matter.
They act as though a Berlin Wall or a fluoride shield separates the true conception of the
subject matter or problem solving from the students. Even though we don't mention
"teacher-proofing" any more, we still talk that way by simply ignoring the teacher. At
best, we hope teachers will be a friction-free conduit for the instructional ideas to reach
the students. I am reminded of the old saying that a lecture is a way of getting ideas from
the notes of the teacher to the notes of the student without passing through the minds of
either. We mechanistically talk about teaching as a set of relationships between teaching
behavior and pupil responses. For the process-product researcher, teaching is apparently
a way of getting knowledge from the behavior of the teacher to the behavior of the
students without passing through the minds of either.

Fortunately, one of the most encouraging things about contemporary research on
teaching, a topic which was discussed most extensively in papers by Alba Thompson and
Doug Grouws (this volume), is that there is something very exciting going on in mathematics. It is one generation beyond the process-product work, which looks at teacher
behaviors and student behaviors. In this work, we are looking at the teachers' cognitive
processes during teacher planning and decision making, at teacher knowledge and
understanding of the subject, and even more important at this point, at the student
cognitive mediation of instruction. The question researchers ask now is not, "How does
teaching change student behavior?" but rather, "What effect on students' thinking during and immediately after instruction does teaching have?" They are looking at learning,
not as a change of behavior, but as the student making sense of what is happening
around him or her in the classroom. It is a fascinating body of work. It is getting more
and more active. It is going to require careful, meticulous, thick descriptions, not only of
the individual cognitions, but of the settings in which these occur. It will not be sum-
marizable in F-tests, nor for quite a long while in computer simulations. Those kinds of
analyses, in a shared theoretical language for discussing both learning and teaching, will
be very important.

TEACHING AND TEACHER EDUCATION

Finally, what about teaching and teacher education? One of the questions that
recurred as I read the papers in this volume was, What does this say about how you want
to educate teachers? In particular, What do you want teachers to know? and, What do
you want them to know how to do? Here again, I think we have to recognize that learning to teach has got to be at least as difficult as learning physics. We are developing a very
complex notion of what it takes to learn physics and to solve physics problems. Yet we
still tend to operate with a very simple notion of how to train someone to be a teacher.
When you begin to think about it, to be a teacher requires extensive and highly organized bodies of knowledge, not only the knowledge that has to be taught, but also the
knowledge of teaching. Moreover, it also requires various kinds of perceptual schemata
for making sense of what is going on in classrooms, for making sense of what students are
saying and doing.

First, we must develop a representation of teachers' pedagogical knowledge of mathematics that is different from the knowledge of mathematics that a mathematician has. I, at least, want to work on the assumption that they are different. I would like to see designed, at least hypothetically, an examination to screen teachers or teacher candidates. I want that examination to have the following two kinds of discriminatory characteristics. I want it to be able to distinguish between teachers who know enough mathematics to teach it and those who don't. And much more difficult, I want it to be able to discriminate between mathematicians and mathematics teachers in the same way that I think I can write an examination that will distinguish physiologists from physicians or political scientists from politicians.

Second, when you do that kind of exercise, that kind of mental experiment, I think you will also be doing another experiment, which addresses these questions: If we remove the constraints under which we currently work, what would we do in teacher education programs for mathematics teachers that we are not doing now? and, How would we teach mathematics teachers to know what to do? I don't think the answer would be what seems to be coming out of some of the NSF commissions: teach them more mathematics. More, perhaps, but what more and in what sense? Those are very important questions.

The last thing I will mention is that many of the questions that have been suggested with regard to learners have direct parallel with respect to teachers. Frank Lester (this volume) calls for studies in the form of teaching experiments—a kind of ongoing, continually changing experimental instructional treatment with one child or a small group of children in which the researcher describes in detail how mathematics is taught and learned. Let me suggest that we need precisely that form of study with respect to the education of mathematics teachers. Let's take people learning to teach mathematics and carefully document our experimental interaction with them over time, as we try to make them into mathematics teachers. We don't have anything remotely like that in the teacher education literature.

A number of the papers called for more studies of mathematical metacognition. There is a pedagogical kind of metacognition, the kinds of things the teacher has to think about in order to decide what to do and when to do it. There is pedagogical problem solving. When do I tell and when do I not tell? If I tell, what do I tell? How do I know whether the pupils have understood or not? When do I say it again or when do I use a new metaphor or an analogy? When do I draw a picture and when do I explain propositionally? How many nods make a consensus? Observation of pedagogical metacognition is part and parcel of what is needed to conduct studies of learning to teach mathematics.

The most poignant cry of all in many of the papers was for studies of affect in the learning of mathematics. I hope it is not an unanswered call. While we think about it, let's think about teacher affect in the teaching of mathematics, as well. At the conference, we often asked, "What is in it for the student?" My question is, "What is in it for the teacher?" What are the sources of gratification for teachers in the teaching of mathematics? What are they now? What might they be? For example, we ask the teacher in most of our problem-solving recommendations not to give the student the answer. But teachers need some reassurance that they are teaching something, and the safest way to do it is to tell it. At least that way you know that at least somebody got the answer.

To put it another way, most of us have an image of mathematical problem solving as a developed capacity. We have a vivid mental representation of what a person who has that capacity might look like, and a strong faith that by engaging in certain kinds of activities now, and doing them consistently, even though those activities require that we forego immediate pedagogical gratification, we will eventually achieve that goal. That faith carries us through because the long-term image is so vivid and real. It is, I would contend, not unlike the way in which devout believers are able to forego immediate gratification in this world because of a very vivid image of a world to come which they incorporated into their ways of thinking very early in their lives. I don't think that most teachers of mathematics have such an image of what it means to be educated mathematically, an image that could sustain them in the short run when frustrations are high. Therefore, to make it possible for them to forego the immediate gratification of telling someone an answer and getting them to respond in kind, we'd better think through what we are going to do to help them replace it with another source of gratification. The answer is not skill training; the answer is cognitive and affective in the heads of teachers.

CONCLUSION

Jeremy Kilpatrick began with a couple of personal reminiscences about where he was 25 years ago. The story that I will tell is about Benjamin Bloom. Bloom was my teacher in Chicago and I went to him committed to doing a dissertation in the area of problem solving. Bloom discouraged me. He had done some work on problem solving 10 years earlier; no one had paid any attention to it, and he felt that it was a dead end. I was stubborn and did the dissertation anyway. About 15 years later we had another talk and he decided that he had been wrong; the area seemed to have been resuscitated. But I don't think that even Bloom anticipated the kind of vigor that the field would be experiencing 20 years later. And he realized only recently the increased frequency with which we now read and hear references to that original Bloom and Broder (1950) study.

It is one of the earliest studies in which we have "thinking aloud" protocols. The study was done quasi-naturalistically, in the context of the examiner's office in Chicago, with students who exhibited interesting performance patterns on Chicago's comprehensive exams, which were based on Bloom's taxonomy. The students in the study seemed to perform equally well on the knowledge items but not on the problem-solving items. Bloom and Broder make the very strong argument that one of the major distinctions between the successful problem solvers and unsuccessful problem solvers was affective, was belief, was in the feeling that a problem was soluble, even if one didn't immediately see the answer or the ways and means.

At the conference that resulted in this book, Ed Silver asked us to consider the suggestions made over 40 years ago by Brownell (1941) in his review of problem-solving research. He challenged us to examine modern research on problem solving and to improve upon Brownell's suggestions. Many of the participants were somewhat embarrassed to find that Brownell's suggestions were still so vital and difficult to improve upon, although we certainly have available a level of detail that was not present in the research Brownell reviewed. In light of the renewed relevance of the Bloom and Broder research, I conclude by saying let's not feel embarrassed if we find Brownell's 1941 admonitions to be of continued relevance and fruitfulness. I think we are working in a domain in which practical maxims have had to be developed and could not wait for a well refined, empirically defined, research-based technology. Certainly, gamblers in the third century did not have to await probability theory to become very good at their craft, and similarly, navigators did not sail around lost waiting for the appropriate theoretical formulations, which were developed much later than ships began to sail long distances. So I think we ought to look back on those maxims; set our task as refining them, grounding them, and by and large, elaborating on them; and recognize that the way in which our research-based knowledge becomes useful, and will always become useful, is through being combined with the thoughtful and reflective wisdom of practitioners, which many of us are in our spare time.

REFERENCES

Becker, H.S., Geer, B., & Hughes, E. *Making the grade: The academic side of college life.* New York: John Wiley & Sons, 1968.

Bloom, B.S., & Broder, L. Problem solving processes of college students. *Supplementary Education Monograph.* Chicago: University of Chicago Press, 1950.

Brownell, W.A., & Moser, H.E. Meaningful versus mechanical learning: A study in grade III subtraction. *Duke University Research Studies in Education,* No. 8, 1949.

Bruner, J.S. The act of discovery. *Harvard Educational Review* 31, 21–32, 1961.

Cole, M., & Traupmann, K. *Comparative cognitive research: Learning from a learning disabled child.* Paper presented at the Minnesota Symposium on Child Development, St. Paul, 1980.

Cronbach, L.J. Beyond the two disciplines of scientific psychology. *American Psychologist* 30, 116–127, 1975.

Cronbach, L.J. Prudent aspirations for social science. In W. Kruskal (Ed.), *The future of the social sciences.* Chicago: University of Chicago Press, 1982.

Erlwanger, S. Case studies of children's conceptions of mathematics, Part I. *Journal of Children's Mathematical Behavior* 1, 157–283, 1975.

Geertz, C. Thick description. In C. Geertz, *Interpretation of cultures.* New York: Basic Books, 1973.

Hawkins, D. Learning the unteachable. In L.S. Shulman & E. Keislar (Eds.), *Learning by discovery: A critical appraisal.* Chicago: Rand-McNally, 1966.

Merton, R.K. The self-fulfilling prophecy. *Antioch Review,* 193–210, 1948 (Summer).

Roethlisberger, F.J., & Dixon, W.J. *Management and the worker.* New York: John Wiley & Sons, 1939.

Shulman, L.S., & Tamir, P. Research on teaching in the natural sciences. In R.M.W. Travers (Ed.), *Second Handbook of Research on Teaching.* Chicago: Rand-McNally, 1973.

INDEX

Author Index

Subject Index